CODE OF FEDERAL REGULATIONS

Title 19

Customs Duties

Part 200 to End

Revised as of April 1, 2018

Containing a codification of documents
of general applicability and future effect

As of April 1, 2018

Published by the Office of the Federal Register
National Archives and Records Administration
as a Special Edition of the Federal Register

Table of Contents

	Page
Explanation	v

Title 19:

Chapter II—United States International Trade Commission 3

Chapter III—International Trade Administration, Department of Commerce 211

Chapter IV—U.S. Immigration and Customs Enforcement, Department of Homeland Security [Reserved]

Finding Aids:

Table of CFR Titles and Chapters 359

Alphabetical List of Agencies Appearing in the CFR 379

List of CFR Sections Affected 389

Explanation

The Code of Federal Regulations is a codification of the general and permanent rules published in the Federal Register by the Executive departments and agencies of the Federal Government. The Code is divided into 50 titles which represent broad areas subject to Federal regulation. Each title is divided into chapters which usually bear the name of the issuing agency. Each chapter is further subdivided into parts covering specific regulatory areas.

Each volume of the Code is revised at least once each calendar year and issued on a quarterly basis approximately as follows:

Title 1 through Title 16..as of January 1
Title 17 through Title 27 ....as of April 1
Title 28 through Title 41 ....as of July 1
Title 42 through Title 50..as of October 1

The appropriate revision date is printed on the cover of each volume.

LEGAL STATUS

The contents of the Federal Register are required to be judicially noticed (44 U.S.C. 1507). The Code of Federal Regulations is prima facie evidence of the text of the original documents (44 U.S.C. 1510).

HOW TO USE THE CODE OF FEDERAL REGULATIONS

The Code of Federal Regulations is kept up to date by the individual issues of the Federal Register. These two publications must be used together to determine the latest version of any given rule.

To determine whether a Code volume has been amended since its revision date (in this case, April 1, 2018), consult the "List of CFR Sections Affected (LSA)," which is issued monthly, and the "Cumulative List of Parts Affected," which appears in the Reader Aids section of the daily Federal Register. These two lists will identify the Federal Register page number of the latest amendment of any given rule.

EFFECTIVE AND EXPIRATION DATES

Each volume of the Code contains amendments published in the Federal Register since the last revision of that volume of the Code. Source citations for the regulations are referred to by volume number and page number of the Federal Register and date of publication. Publication dates and effective dates are usually not the same and care must be exercised by the user in determining the actual effective date. In instances where the effective date is beyond the cut-off date for the Code a note has been inserted to reflect the future effective date. In those instances where a regulation published in the Federal Register states a date certain for expiration, an appropriate note will be inserted following the text.

OMB CONTROL NUMBERS

The Paperwork Reduction Act of 1980 (Pub. L. 96–511) requires Federal agencies to display an OMB control number with their information collection request.

Many agencies have begun publishing numerous OMB control numbers as amendments to existing regulations in the CFR. These OMB numbers are placed as close as possible to the applicable recordkeeping or reporting requirements.

PAST PROVISIONS OF THE CODE

Provisions of the Code that are no longer in force and effect as of the revision date stated on the cover of each volume are not carried. Code users may find the text of provisions in effect on any given date in the past by using the appropriate List of CFR Sections Affected (LSA). For the convenience of the reader, a "List of CFR Sections Affected" is published at the end of each CFR volume. For changes to the Code prior to the LSA listings at the end of the volume, consult previous annual editions of the LSA. For changes to the Code prior to 2001, consult the List of CFR Sections Affected compilations, published for 1949-1963, 1964-1972, 1973-1985, and 1986-2000.

"[RESERVED]" TERMINOLOGY

The term "[Reserved]" is used as a place holder within the Code of Federal Regulations. An agency may add regulatory information at a "[Reserved]" location at any time. Occasionally "[Reserved]" is used editorially to indicate that a portion of the CFR was left vacant and not accidentally dropped due to a printing or computer error.

INCORPORATION BY REFERENCE

What is incorporation by reference? Incorporation by reference was established by statute and allows Federal agencies to meet the requirement to publish regulations in the Federal Register by referring to materials already published elsewhere. For an incorporation to be valid, the Director of the Federal Register must approve it. The legal effect of incorporation by reference is that the material is treated as if it were published in full in the Federal Register (5 U.S.C. 552(a)). This material, like any other properly issued regulation, has the force of law.

What is a proper incorporation by reference? The Director of the Federal Register will approve an incorporation by reference only when the requirements of 1 CFR part 51 are met. Some of the elements on which approval is based are:

(a) The incorporation will substantially reduce the volume of material published in the Federal Register.

(b) The matter incorporated is in fact available to the extent necessary to afford fairness and uniformity in the administrative process.

(c) The incorporating document is drafted and submitted for publication in accordance with 1 CFR part 51.

What if the material incorporated by reference cannot be found? If you have any problem locating or obtaining a copy of material listed as an approved incorporation by reference, please contact the agency that issued the regulation containing that incorporation. If, after contacting the agency, you find the material is not available, please notify the Director of the Federal Register, National Archives and Records Administration, 8601 Adelphi Road, College Park, MD 20740-6001, or call 202-741-6010.

CFR INDEXES AND TABULAR GUIDES

A subject index to the Code of Federal Regulations is contained in a separate volume, revised annually as of January 1, entitled CFR INDEX AND FINDING AIDS. This volume contains the Parallel Table of Authorities and Rules. A list of CFR titles, chapters, subchapters, and parts and an alphabetical list of agencies publishing in the CFR are also included in this volume.

An index to the text of "Title 3—The President" is carried within that volume.

The Federal Register Index is issued monthly in cumulative form. This index is based on a consolidation of the "Contents" entries in the daily Federal Register.

A List of CFR Sections Affected (LSA) is published monthly, keyed to the revision dates of the 50 CFR titles.

REPUBLICATION OF MATERIAL

There are no restrictions on the republication of material appearing in the Code of Federal Regulations.

INQUIRIES

For a legal interpretation or explanation of any regulation in this volume, contact the issuing agency. The issuing agency's name appears at the top of odd-numbered pages.

For inquiries concerning CFR reference assistance, call 202-741-6000 or write to the Director, Office of the Federal Register, National Archives and Records Administration, 8601 Adelphi Road, College Park, MD 20740-6001 or e-mail *fedreg.info@nara.gov.*

SALES

The Government Publishing Office (GPO) processes all sales and distribution of the CFR. For payment by credit card, call toll-free, 866-512-1800, or DC area, 202-512-1800, M-F 8 a.m. to 4 p.m. e.s.t. or fax your order to 202-512-2104, 24 hours a day. For payment by check, write to: US Government Publishing Office – New Orders, P.O. Box 979050, St. Louis, MO 63197-9000.

ELECTRONIC SERVICES

The full text of the Code of Federal Regulations, the LSA (List of CFR Sections Affected), The United States Government Manual, the Federal Register, Public Laws, Public Papers of the Presidents of the United States, Compilation of Presidential Documents and the Privacy Act Compilation are available in electronic format via *www.ofr.gov.* For more information, contact the GPO Customer Contact Center, U.S. Government Publishing Office. Phone 202-512-1800, or 866-512-1800 (toll-free). E-mail, *ContactCenter@gpo.gov.*

The Office of the Federal Register also offers a free service on the National Archives and Records Administration's (NARA) World Wide Web site for public law numbers, Federal Register finding aids, and related information. Connect to NARA's web site at *www.archives.gov/federal-register.*

The e-CFR is a regularly updated, unofficial editorial compilation of CFR material and Federal Register amendments, produced by the Office of the Federal Register and the Government Publishing Office. It is available at *www.ecfr.gov.*

OLIVER A. POTTS,
Director,
Office of the Federal Register
April 1, 2018

THIS TITLE

Title 19—CUSTOMS DUTIES is composed of three volumes. The first two volumes, parts 0—140 and parts 141—199 contain the regulations in Chapter I—U.S. Customs and Border Protection, Department of Homeland Security; Department of the Treasury. The third volume, part 200 to end, contains the regulations in Chapter II—United States International Trade Commission; Chapter III—International Trade Administration, Department of Commerce; and Chapter IV—U.S. Immigration and Customs Enforcement, Department of Homeland Security. The contents of these volumes represent all current regulations issued under this title of the CFR as of April 1, 2018.

A Subject Index to Chapter I—U.S. Customs and Border Protection, Department of Homeland Security; Department of the Treasury appears in the Finding Aids section of the first two volumes.

For this volume, Robert J. Sheehan, III was Chief Editor. The Code of Federal Regulations publication program is under the direction of John Hyrum Martinez, assisted by Stephen J. Frattini.

Title 19—Customs Duties

(This book contains part 200 to End)

	Part
CHAPTER II—United States International Trade Commission	200
CHAPTER III—International Trade Administration, Department of Commerce	351
CHAPTER IV—U.S. Immigration and Customs Enforcement; Department of Homeland Security [Reserved]	

CHAPTER II—UNITED STATES INTERNATIONAL TRADE COMMISSION

Part		Page
200	Employee responsibilities and conduct	5

SUBCHAPTER A—GENERAL

201	Rules of general application	16

SUBCHAPTER B—NONADJUDICATIVE INVESTIGATIONS

202	Investigations of costs of production	69
204	Investigations of effects of imports on agricultural programs	70
205	Investigations to determine the probable economic effect on the economy of the United States of proposed modifications of duties or of any barrier to (or other distortion of) international trade or of taking retaliatory actions to obtain the elimination of unjustifiable or unreasonable foreign acts or policies which restrict U.S. commerce	71
206	Investigations relating to global and bilateral safeguard actions, market disruption, trade diversion, and review of relief actions	73
207	Investigations of whether injury to domestic industries results from imports sold at less than fair value or from subsidized exports to the United States	97
208	[Reserved]	

SUBCHAPTER C—INVESTIGATIONS OF UNFAIR PRACTICES IN IMPORT TRADE

210	Adjudication and enforcement	132
212	Implementation of the Equal Access to Justice Act	195

SUBCHAPTER D—SPECIAL PROVISIONS

213	Trade remedy assistance	202
214–219	[Reserved]	

Part		Page
220	Process for consideration of petitions for duty suspensions and reductions	204
221–299	[Reserved]	

PART 200—EMPLOYEE RESPONSIBILITIES AND CONDUCT

Subpart A—General Provisions

Sec.
200.735–101 Purpose.
200.735–102 Definitions.
200.735–103 Counseling service.
200.735–104 Disciplinary and other remedial action.

Subpart B—Provisions Governing Ethical and Other Conduct and Responsibilities of Employees

200.735–104a Proscribed actions.
200.735–105 Gifts, entertainment, and favors.
200.735–106 Outside employment and other activities.
200.735–107 Financial interests.
200.735–108 Use of Government property.
200.735–109 Misuse of information.
200.735–110 Indebtedness.
200.735–111 Gambling, betting, and lotteries.
200.735–112 General conduct prejudicial to the Government.
200.735–113 Miscellaneous statutory provisions.

Subpart C—Provisions Governing Statements of Employment and Financial Interests

200.735–114 Employees required to submit statements.
200.735–114a Employees not required to submit statements.
200.735–114b Employee complaints on filing requirements.
200.735–114c Voluntary submission by employees.
200.735–115 Forms—Interests not to be reported.
200.735–116 Time and place for submission of employees' statements.
200.735–117 Supplementary statements.
200.735–118 Interests of employees' relatives.
200.735–119 Information not known by employees.
200.735–120 Information prohibited.
200.735–121 Confidentiality of employees' statements.
200.735–122 Special Government employees.
200.735–123 Effect of employees' and special Government employees' statements on other requirements.

Subpart D—Provisions for Administrative Enforcement of Postemployment Conflict of Interest Restrictions

200.735–124 General.
200.735–125 Exemption from restrictions.
200.735–126 Administrative enforcement proceedings.

AUTHORITY: E.O. 11222, 30 FR 6469, 3 CFR, 1965 Supp.; 5 CFR 735.101 *et seq.*, 5 CFR 2638.101 *et seq.*, unless otherwise noted.

SOURCE: 31 FR 2593, Feb. 10, 1966, unless otherwise noted.

Subpart A—General Provisions

§ 200.735–101 Purpose.

The purpose of the regulations in this part is to maintain the highest standards of honesty, integrity, impartiality, and conduct on the part of all employees of the U.S. International Trade Commission and to maintain public confidence that the business of the Commission is being conducted in accordance with such standards.

[31 FR 2593, Feb. 10, 1966, as amended at 46 FR 17542, Mar. 19, 1981]

§ 200.735–102 Definitions.

In this part:

(a) *Commission* means the U.S. International Trade Commission.

(b) *Commissioner* means a Commissioner of the U.S. International Trade Commission.

(c) *Employee* means a Commissioner, employee, or special Government employee of the Commission.

(d) *Executive order* means Executive Order 11222 of May 8, 1965.

(e) *Person* means an individual, a corporation, a company, an association, a firm, a partnership, a society, a joint stock company, or any other organization or institution.

(f) *Special Government employee* means a "special Government employee" as defined in section 202 of Title 18 of the United States Code who is employed by the Commission.

[31 FR 2593, Feb. 10, 1966, as amended at 44 FR 23823, Apr. 23, 1979; 46 FR 17542, Mar. 19, 1981; 56 FR 36726, Aug. 1, 1991]

§ 200.735–103 Counseling service.

(a) The Chairman shall appoint a Designated Agency Ethics Official (DAEO) who serves as liaison to the Office of Government Ethics and who is responsible for carrying out the Commission's ethics program. The program shall be designed to implement titles II, IV, and V of the Ethics in Government Act of 1978, Executive Order No. 11222, the regulations in this part, and other statutes and regulations applicable to agency ethics matters. The DAEO will be a senior Commission employee with experience demonstrating the ability to review financial disclosure reports and counsel employees with regard to resolving conflicts of interest, review the financial disclosures of Presidential nominees to the Commission prior to confirmation hearings, counsel employees with regard to ethics standards, assist supervisors in implementing the Commission's ethics program, and periodically evaluate the ethics program.

(b) The Chairman shall select an Alternate Agency Ethics Official who will serve as Deputy DAEO to whom any of the DAEO's statutory and regulatory duties may be delegated.

(c) The DAEO shall coordinate and manage the agency's ethics program. The DAEO duties shall consist of:

(1) Liaison with the Office of Government Ethics;

(2) Review of financial disclosure reports, including reports filed by Presidential nominees to the Commission;

(3) Initiation and maintenance of ethics education and training programs;

(4) Monitoring administrative actions and sanctions; and

(5) Implementation of the specific program elements listed in Office of Government Ethics regulations, 5 CFR 738.203(b).

[46 FR 17542, Mar. 19, 1981, as amended at 56 FR 36726, Aug. 1, 1991]

§ 200.735–104 Disciplinary and other remedial action.

(a) An employee who violates any of the regulations in this part may be disciplined. The disciplinary action may be in addition to any other penalty prescribed by law for the violation. In addition to, or in lieu of, disciplinary action, remedial action to end conflicts or appearance of conflicts of interest may include, but is not limited to:

(1) Changes in assigned duties;

(2) Divestment by the employee of his conflicting interest; or

(3) Disqualification for a particular assignment.

(b) Remedial action, whether disciplinary or otherwise, shall be effected in accordance with any applicable laws, Executive orders, and regulations.

Subpart B—Provisions Governing Ethical and Other Conduct and Responsibilities of Employees

§ 200.735–104a Proscribed actions.

An employee shall avoid any action, whether or not specifically prohibited by this subpart, which might result in, or create the appearance of:

(a) Using public office for private gain;

(b) Giving preferential treatment to any person;

(c) Impeding Government efficiency or economy;

(d) Losing complete independence or impartiality;

(e) Making a Government decision outside official channels; or

(f) Affecting adversely the confidence of the public in the integrity of the Government.

[32 FR 16210, Nov. 28, 1967]

§ 200.735–105 Gifts, entertainment, and favors.

(a) Except as provided in paragraph (b) of this section, no employee may solicit or accept, directly or indirectly, any gift, gratuity, favor, entertainment, loan, or any other thing of monetary value from any person who:

(1) Has, or is seeking to obtain, contractual or other business or financial relations with the Commission;

(2) Conducts operations or activities that are being investigated by the Commission; or

(3) Has interests that may be substantially affected by the performance or nonperformance of the employee's official duty.

(b) The prohibitions set forth under paragraph (a) of this section shall not apply to:

(1) Solicitations or acceptances based on obvious family or personal relationships (such as those between parents, children, or spouse of the employee and the employee) when the circumstances make it clear that it is those relationships rather than the business of the persons concerned which are the motivating factors;

(2) The acceptance of food and refreshments of nominal value on infrequent occasions in the ordinary course

of a luncheon or dinner meeting or other meeting or on a field trip, and of ground transportation of nominal value in the course of a field trip, where an employee may properly be in attendance.

(3) The acceptance of loans from banks or other financial institutions on customary terms to finance proper and usual activities of employees, such as home mortgage loans; and

(4) The acceptance of unsolicited advertising or promotional material, such as pens, pencils, note pads, calendars, and other items of nominal value.

(c) An employee shall not solicit a contribution from another employee for a gift to an official superior, make a donation as a gift to an official superior, or accept a gift from an employee receiving less pay than himself (5 U.S.C. 7351). However, this paragraph does not prohibit a voluntary gift of nominal value or donation in a nominal amount made on a special occasion such as marriage, illness, or retirement.

(d) An employee shall not accept a gift, present, decoration, or other thing from a foreign government unless authorized by Congress as provided by the Constitution and in 5 U.S.C. 7342.

(e) Neither this section nor § 200.735–106 precludes an employee from receipt of bona fide reimbursement, unless prohibited by law, for expenses of travel and such other necessary subsistence as is compatible with this part for which no Government payment or reimbursement is made. However, this paragraph does not allow an employee to be reimbursed, or payment to be made on his behalf, for excessive personal living expenses, gifts, entertainment or other personal benefits, nor does it allow an employee to be reimbursed by a person for travel on official business under agency orders when reimbursement is proscribed by Decision B–128527 of the Comptroller General dated March 7, 1967.

[32 FR 16210, Nov. 28, 1967, as amended at 46 FR 41036, Aug. 14, 1981]

§ 200.735–106 Outside employment and other activities.

(a) An employee may engage in outside employment or other outside activity not incompatible with the full and proper discharge of the duties and responsibilities of his Government employment: *Provided*, That no Commissioner shall actively engage in any other business, vocation, or employment than that of serving as a Commissioner (19 U.S.C. 1330(c)). Incompatible activities include but are not limited to:

(1) Acceptance of a fee, compensation, gift, payment of expense, or any other thing of monetary value in circumstances in which acceptance may result in, or create the appearance of, conflicts of interest; or

(2) Outside employment tending to impair the employee's capacity to perform his Government duties and responsibilities in an acceptable manner.

(b) An employee (except a special Government employee) shall not receive any salary or anything of monetary value from a private source as compensation for his services to the Government (18 U.S.C. 209).

(c) Employees are encouraged to engage in teaching, lecturing, and writing that is not prohibited by law, the Executive order, or this part. However, an employee shall not, either for or without compensation, engage in teaching, lecturing, or writing, including teaching, lecturing, or writing for the purpose of the special preparation of a person or class of persons for an examination of the Civil Service Commission or Board of Examiners for the Foreign Service, that is dependent on information obtained as a result of his Government employment, except when that information has been made available to the general public or will be made available on request, or when the Commission gives authorization for the use of nonpublic information (other than information received in confidence) on the basis that the use is in the public interest and would not be in violation of law. In addition, Commissioners shall not receive compensation or anything of monetary value for any consultation, lecture, discussion, writing, or appearance the subject matter of which is devoted substantially to the responsibilities, programs, or operations of the Commission, or which draws substantially on official data or ideas which have not become part of the body of public information.

(d) This section does not preclude an employee from:

(1) Participation in the activities of national or State political parties not proscribed by law.

(2) Participation in the affairs of, or acceptance of, an award for a meritorious public contribution or achievement given by a charitable, religious, professional, social, fraternal, nonprofit educational and recreational, public service, or civic organization.

[33 FR 8447, June 7, 1968]

§ 200.735–107 Financial interests.

(a) An employee shall not:

(1) Have a direct or indirect financial interest that conflicts substantially, or appears to conflict substantially, with his Government duties or responsibilities; or

(2) Engage in, directly or indirectly, a financial transaction as a result of, or primarily relying on, information obtained through his Government employment.

(b) This section does not preclude an employee from having a financial interest or engaging in financial transactions to the same extent as a private citizen not employed by the Government so long as it is not prohibited by law, the Executive order, or this part.

(c) Pursuant to the authority contained in 18 U.S.C. 208(b), the following types of financial interests are considered too remote or inconsequential to affect a Commission employee's integrity or services and do not constitute a conflict of interest under 18 U.S.C. 208(a):

(1) In widely-held, diversified mutual funds or regulated investment companies, regardless of their value; and

(2) In state or local government bonds, or other noncorporate bonds, regardless of their value.

[31 FR 2593, Feb. 10, 1966, as amended at 44 FR 23823, Apr. 23, 1979]

§ 200.735–108 Use of Government property.

An employee shall not directly or indirectly use, or allow the use of, Government property of any kind, including property leased to the Government, for other than officially approved activities. An employee has a positive duty to protect and conserve Government property, including equipment, supplies, and other property issued to him.

§ 200.735–109 Misuse of information.

For the purpose of furthering a private interest, an employee shall not, except as provided in § 200.735–106(c), directly or indirectly use, or allow the use of, official information obtained through or in connection with his Government employment which has not been made available to the general public.

§ 200.735–110 Indebtedness.

An employee shall pay each just financial obligation in a proper and timely manner, especially one imposed by law such as Federal, State or local taxes. For the purpose of this section a *just financial obligation* means one acknowledged by the employee or reduced to judgment by a court, and *in a proper and timely manner* means in a manner which the Commission determines does not, under the circumstances, reflect adversely on the Government as his employer. In the event of a dispute between an employee and an alleged creditor, the Commission shall make no determination of the validity or amount of the disputed debt.

§ 200.735–111 Gambling, betting, and lotteries.

An employee shall not participate, while on Government-owned or leased property or while on duty for the Government, in any gambling activity including the operation of a gambling device, in conducting a lottery or pool, in a game for money or property, or in selling or purchasing a numbers slip or ticket. However, this section does not preclude activities:

(a) Necessitated by an employee's law enforcement duties; or

(b) Under section 3 of Executive Order 10927 and similar Commission-approved activities.

§200.735-112 General conduct prejudicial to the Government.

An employee shall not engage in criminal, infamous, dishonest, immoral, or notoriously disgraceful conduct, or other conduct prejudicial to the Government.

§200.735-113 Miscellaneous statutory provisions.

Each employee shall familiarize himself with each statute that relates to his ethical and other conduct as a Government employee, including the following statutes:

(a) House Concurrent Resolution 175, 85th Congress, 2d Session, 72 Stat. B12, the "Code of Ethics for Government Service."

(b) Chapter 11 of Title 18, United States Code, relating to bribery, graft, and conflicts of interest.

(c) The prohibition against lobbying with appropriated funds (18 U.S.C. 1913).

(d) The prohibitions against disloyalty and striking (5 U.S.C. 7311, 18 U.S.C. 1918).

(e) The prohibition against the employment of a member of a Communist organization (50 U.S.C. 784).

(f) The prohibitions against (1) the disclosure of classified information (18 U.S.C. 798, 50 U.S.C. 783); and (2) the disclosure of confidential information (18 U.S.C. 1905).

(g) The provision relating to the habitual use of intoxicants to excess (5 U.S.C. 7352).

(h) The prohibition against the misuse of a Government vehicle (31 U.S.C. 638a(c)).

(i) The prohibition against the misuse of the franking privilege (18 U.S.C. 1719).

(j) The prohibition against the use of deceit in an examination or personnel action in connection with Government employment (18 U.S.C. 1917).

(k) The prohibition against fraud or false statements in a Government matter (18 U.S.C. 1001).

(l) The prohibition against mutilating or destroying a public record (18 U.S.C. 2071).

(m) The prohibition against counterfeiting and forging transportation requests (18 U.S.C. 508).

(n) The prohibitions against—

(1) Embezzlement of Government money or property (18 U.S.C. 641);

(2) Failing to account for public money (18 U.S.C. 643); and

(3) Embezzlement of the money or property of another person in the possession of an employee by reason of his employment (18 U.S.C. 654).

(o) The prohibition against unauthorized use of documents relating to claims from or by the Government (18 U.S.C. 285).

(p) The prohibitions against political activities in subchapter III of chapter 73 of title 5, United States Code and 18 U.S.C. 602, 603, 607, and 608.

(q) The prohibition against an employee acting as an agent of a foreign principal registered under the Foreign Agents Registration Act (18 U.S.C. 219).

[31 FR 2593, Feb. 10, 1966, as amended at 32 FR 16210, Nov. 28, 1967]

Subpart C—Provisions Governing Statements of Employment and Financial Interests

§200.735-114 Employees required to submit statements.

Except as provided in §200.735-114a, the following employees shall submit confidential statements of employment and financial interests:

(a)(1) Employees in grade GS-13 or above under section 5332 of title 5, United States Code, or in comparable or higher positions not subject to that section, other than those employees who are required to file public financial disclosure reports by title II of the Ethics in Government Act of 1978.

(2) The Director of Personnel shall list all such positions, shall include the listing in the chapter of the Commission's Policy Manual pertaining to the filing of confidential statements of employment and financial interests, and shall furnish copies thereof to the Deputy DAEO and to affected employees.

(3) The Director of Personnel shall update the listing required by paragraph (a)(2) of this section and shall take all other steps required by paragraph (a)(2) as of January 1 and July 1 of each year.

(b)(1) Employees classified below GS-13 under section 5332 of title 5, United States Code, or at a comparable pay level under other authority, other than those employees who are required to file public financial disclosure reports by title II of the Ethics in Government Act of 1978, who are: (i) Responsible for making a decision or taking an action in regard to Commission contracting or procurement, (ii) responsible for conducting investigative and research activities where the decision to be made or action to be taken could have an economic impact on any non-Federal enterprise, or (iii) responsible for exercising the authority of any supervisory or investigative employee in the absence of such employee.

(2) The Director of Personnel, upon obtaining the advice of the General Counsel, shall be responsible for determining which positions below GS–13 meet the criteria of paragraph (b)(1) of this section. The Director of Personnel shall justify his or her determination in writing and shall submit it to the Office of Personnel Management for its approval. Upon obtaining the approval of the Office of Personnel Management, the Director of Personnel shall include the listing of these positions in the chapter of the Commission's Policy Manual pertaining to the filing of confidential statements of employment and financial interests and shall furnish copies thereof to the Deputy DAEO and to affected employees.

(3) The Director of Personnel shall evaluate the determination under paragraph (b)(2) of this section as of January 1 and July 1 of each year. When organizational changes or personnel actions indicate that positions should be either added to or taken from the list of positions which the Director of Personnel has determined meet the criteria of paragraph (b)(1) of this section, the Director of Personnel shall make a new determination under paragraph (b)(2) of this section and shall take all other steps required by paragraph (b)(2) of this section immediately upon the implementation of said organizational changes or personnel actions.

[46 FR 17543, Mar. 19, 1981, as amended at 56 FR 36726, Aug. 1, 1991]

§ 200.735–114a Employees not required to submit statements.

(a) Employees in positions that meet the criteria in paragraphs (b)(1) or (c)(1) of § 200.735–114 of this subpart may be exempted from the reporting requirement of § 200.735–114 if the Director of Personnel, upon obtaining the advice of the General Counsel, determines that:

(1) The duties of a position are such that the likelihood of the incumbent's involvement in a conflict-of-interest situation is remote;

(2) The duties of a position are at such a level of responsibility that the submission of a statement of employment and financial interests is not necessary because of the degree of supervision and review over the incumbent or the inconsequential effect on the integrity of the Government.

(b) All determinations made pursuant to paragraph (a) shall be documented in a writing which shall be annexed to the listings required by paragraphs (b)(2) and (c)(2) of § 200.735–114 of this subpart. The factual bases and reasons for determinations under paragraphs (a)(1) and (a)(2) of this section shall be specified by the Director of Personnel in said writing. Said writing shall refer to the *position* only and shall not include the name, or other identifying particular, of the incumbent occupying the position.

(c) A statement of employment and financial interests from commissioners is not required by this subpart. Such employees are subject to separate reporting requirements under section 401 of Executive Order 11222 (3 CFR 306 (1964–1965 Comp.)).

[42 FR 59958, Nov. 23, 1977]

§ 200.735–114b Employee complaints on filing requirements.

Any employee who believes that his position has been improperly included under the reporting requirements of § 200.735–114 may obtain a review thereof through the Commission's grievance procedures.

[42 FR 59958, Nov. 23, 1977]

§ 200.735–114c Voluntary submission by employees.

Any employee not required to submit a statement of employment and financial interests under the criteria established by § 200.735–114 may submit such a statement to the Deputy Counselor in the manner specified in §200.735–116 if he or she so desires.

[42 FR 59958, Nov. 23, 1977]

§200.735–115 Forms—Interests not to be reported.

(a) Statements required to be submitted by the provisions of this subpart shall be prepared on forms (the format of which is prescribed by the Office of Government Ethics, Office of Personnel Management) available from the Deputy DAEO.

(b) Employees, GS–15 and below, who are required to file a statement of employment and financial interests under §200.735–114 of this part, need not report to the Deputy DAEO those financial interests specified in §200.735–107(c) (1) and (2) of this part. Commissioners and Commission employees, GS–16 and above, are required to report the financial interests specified in §200.735–107(c) (1) and (2) of this part under section 202(a) of the Ethics in Government Act of 1978.

[44 FR 23823, Apr. 23, 1979, as amended at 56 FR 36726, Aug. 1, 1991]

§200.735–116 Time and place for submission of employees' statements.

(a) An employee required to submit such a statement shall submit it not later than:

(1) Ninety days after the effective date of the regulations in this part, if employed on or before that effective date; or

(2) Thirty days after his entrance on duty, but not earlier than ninety days after the effective date, if appointed after the effective date.

(b) Each such statement shall be submitted to the Office of the General Counsel of the Commission and shall be marked "Submitted in Confidence to the Deputy DAEO.": *Provided*, That the statement of the Deputy DAEO shall be submitted directly to the DAEO.

[31 FR 2593, Feb. 10, 1966, as amended at 56 FR 36726, Aug. 1, 1991]

§200.735–117 Supplementary statements.

Changes in, or additions to, the information contained in an employee's statement of employment and financial interests shall be reported in a supplementary statement as of June 30 each year. If no changes or additions occur, a negative report is required. Notwithstanding the filing of the annual report under this section, each employee shall at all times avoid acquiring a financial interest that could result, or taking an action that would result, in a violation of the conflicts of interest provisions of section 208 of title 18, United States Code, or the regulations in this part.

[32 FR 16211, Nov. 28, 1967]

§200.735–118 Interests of employees' relatives.

The interest of a spouse, minor child or other member of an employee's immediate household is considered to be an interest of the employee. For the purpose of this section, *member of an employee's immediate household* means those blood relations who are residents of the employee's household.

§200.735–119 Information not known by employees.

If any information required to be included in a statement of employment and financial interests or supplementary statement, including holdings placed in trust, is not known to the employee but is known to another person, the employee shall request that other person to submit information on his behalf.

§200.735–120 Information prohibited.

An employee is not required to submit in a statement of employment and financial interests or supplementary statement any information relating to the employee's connection with, or interest in, a professional society or a charitable, religious, social, fraternal, recreational, public service, civic, or political organization or similar organization not conducted as a business enterprise. For the purpose of this section, educational and other institutions doing research and development or related work involving grants of money from, or contracts with, the Government are deemed *business enterprises* and are required to be included in an employee's statement of employment and financial interests.

§ 200.735-121 Confidentiality of employees' statements.

Each statement of employment and financial interests, and each supplementary statement, shall be held in confidence. To ensure this confidentiality, the Deputy DAEO is authorized to review and retain the statements. He shall be responsible for maintaining the statements in confidence and shall not allow access to, or allow information to be disclosed from, a statement except to carry out the purpose of this part. The Deputy DAEO may not disclose information from the statement except as the Civil Service Commission or the Chairman of the Tariff Commission may determine for good cause shown.

[32 FR 16211, Nov. 28, 1967, as amended at 56 FR 36726, Aug. 1, 1991]

§ 200.735-122 Special Government employees.

(a) Except as provided in paragraph (b) of this section, each special Government employee shall submit a statement of employment and financial interests which reports:

(1) All of his employment; and

(2) The financial interests of the special Government employee which the Commission determines are relevant in the light of the duties he is to perform.

(b) The Commission may waive the requirement in paragraph (a) of this section for the submission of a statement of employment and financial interests in the case of a special Government employee who is not a consultant or an expert when the Commission finds that the duties of the position held by that special Government employee are of a nature and at such a level of responsibility that the submission of the statement by the incumbent is not necessary to protect the integrity of the Government. For the purpose of this paragraph, *consultant* and *expert* have the meanings given those terms by Chapter 304 of the Federal Personnel Manual.

(c) A statement of employment and financial interests required to be submitted under this section shall be submitted as provided for employees in § 200.735-116. Each special Government employee shall keep his statement current throughout his employment with the Commission by the submission of supplementary statements.

[31 FR 2593, Feb. 10, 1966, as amended at 32 FR 16211, Nov. 28, 1967]

§ 200.735-123 Effect of employees' and special Government employees' statements on other requirements.

The statements of employment and financial interests and supplementary statements required of employees and special Government employees are in addition to, and not in substitution for, or in derogation of, any similar requirement imposed by law, order, or regulation. The submission of a statement or supplementary statement by an employee or special Government employee does not permit him or any other person to participate in a matter which his or the other person's participation in is prohibited by law, order, or regulation.

Subpart D—Provisions for Administrative Enforcement of Postemployment Conflict of Interest Restrictions

AUTHORITY: Ethics in Government Act of 1978, Pub. L. 95-521, 92 Stat. 1864 (18 U.S.C. 207), as amended by Pub. L. 96-28, 93 Stat. 76 (1979); 45 FR 7402, (1979) (5 CFR part 737).

SOURCE: 45 FR 31988, May 15, 1980, unless otherwise noted.

§ 200.735-124 General.

The procedures in this subpart are established pursuant to subsection 207(j) of title 18, United States Code, for the administrative enforcement of the restrictions on postemployment activities in Title V of the Ethics in Government Act of 1978 (18 U.S.C. 207 (a), (b), and (c)) and implementing regulations published by the Office of Government Ethics (5 CFR part 737). Subsections 207 (a), (b), and (c) of Title 18, United States Code, prohibit certain forms of representational activity or communications by former Commission employees.

§ 200.735–125 Exemption from restrictions.

(a) *Scientific and technological information solicited by the Commission.* Communications of a former Commission employee solely for the purpose of furnishing scientific or technological information solicited by the Commission in the course of its statutory investigations are exempted from the restrictions on postemployment practices.

(b) *Exemption for persons with special qualifications in a technical discipline—* (1) *Applicability.* A former Commission employee may be exempted from the restrictions on postemployment practices if the Chairman, in consultation with the Director, Office of Government Ethics (the Director), executes a certification published in the FEDERAL REGISTER that the former Commission employee has outstanding qualifications in a scientific, technological, or other technical discipline; that the former Commission employee is acting with respect to a particular matter which requires such qualifications; and that the national interest would be served by the former Commission employee's participation.

(2) *Certification authority.* Certification shall be by the Chairman, or in the absence thereof, by the acting head of the Commission. Consultation with the Director shall precede any certification. The exemption is effective upon the execution of the certification. The Secretary shall immediately transmit the certification to the FEDERAL REGISTER for publication.

(c) *Testimony and statement under oath are subject to penalty of perjury—*(1) *Applicability.* A former Commission employee may testify before any court, board, commission, or legislative body with respect to matters of fact within the personal knowledge of the former Commission employee. This provision does not, however, allow a former Commission employee, otherwise barred under 18 U.S.C. 207 (a), (b), or (c), to testify on behalf of another as an expert witness except (i) to the extent that the former employee may testify from personal knowledge as to occurrences which are relevant to the issues in the proceeding, including those in which the Commission employee participated, utilizing his or her expertise, or (ii) in any proceeding where it is determined that another expert in the field cannot practically be obtained, that it is impracticable for the facts or opinions on the same subject to be obtained by other means, and that the former Commission employee's testimony is required in the interest of justice.

(2) *Statements under penalty of perjury.* A former Commission employee may make any statements required to be made under penalty of perjury, such as those required in registration statements for securities, tax returns, or security clearances. The exception does not, however, permit a former employee to submit pleadings, applications, or other documents in a representational capacity on behalf of another merely because the attorney or other representative must sign the documents under oath or penalty of perjury.

§ 200.735–126 Administrative enforcement proceedings.

The following are basic guidelines for administrative enforcement of restrictions on postemployment activities:

(a) *Initiation of administrative disciplinary hearing.* (1) On receipt of information regarding a possible violation of 18 U.S.C. 207, and after determining that such information does not appear to be frivolous, the Chairman shall expeditiously provide such information, along with any comments or agency regulations, to the Director and to the Criminal Division, Department of Justice. Any investigation or administrative action will be coordinated with the Department of Justice to avoid prejudicing criminal proceedings, unless the Department of Justice informs the Commission that it does not intend to initiate criminal prosecution.

(2) Whenever the Chairman has determined after appropriate review that there is reasonable cause to believe that a former Commission employee has violated 18 U.S.C. 207 (a), (b), or (c) or implementing regulations of the Office of Government Ethics (5 CFR part 737), he or she shall initiate an administrative disciplinary proceeding by providing the former Commission employee with notice as defined in paragraph (b).

(3) The Chairman shall take all necessary steps to protect the privacy of former employees prior to a determination of sufficient cause to initiate an administrative disciplinary hearing.

(b) *Notice.* (1) The Chairman shall provide the former Commission employee with notice of an administrative disciplinary proceeding and an opportunity for a hearing.

(2) Notice to the former Commission employee must include—

(i) A statement of allegations and the basis thereof in detail sufficient to enable the former Commission employee to prepare an adequate defense;

(ii) Notification of the right to a hearing;

(iii) An explanation of the method by which a hearing may be requested; and

(iv) A copy of this subpart.

(c) *Examiner.* (1) The presiding official at proceedings under this subpart shall be an individual to whom the Chairman has delegated authority to make a recommended determination (hereinafter referred to as examiner).

(2) An examiner shall be an experienced government attorney of high moral character and sound judgment.

(3) An examiner shall be impartial. No individual who has participated in any manner in the decision to initiate the proceedings may serve as an examiner in those proceedings.

(d) *Scheduling of hearing.* In setting a hearing date, the examiner shall give due regard to the former Commission employee's need for—

(1) Adequate time to prepare a defense properly, and

(2) An expeditious resolution of allegations that may be damaging to his or her reputation.

(e) *Hearing rights.* A hearing shall include, at a minimum, the following rights:

(1) To be represented by counsel,

(2) To introduce and examine witnesses and to submit physical evidence,

(3) To confront and cross-examine adverse witnesses,

(4) To present oral argument; and

(5) To obtain a transcript or recording of the proceeding on request.

(f) *Burden of proof.* In any hearing under this subpart the Commission has the burden of proof and must establish a violation by clear and convincing evidence. The case of the Commission shall be presented by the Office of the General Counsel.

(g) *Recommended determination.* (1) The examiner shall make a recommended determination exclusively on matters of record in the proceeding and shall set forth therein all findings of fact and conclusions of law relevant to the matters at issue. The recommended determination shall be delivered to the parties.

(2) Within ten (10) days of the date of receipt of the recommended determination either party may submit to the Chairman exceptions to the recommended determination and alternative findings of fact and conclusions of law.

(h) *Final administrative decision.* (1) Within forty (40) days of the date of the recommended determination, the Chairman shall make a final administrative decision based solely on the record of the proceedings.

(2) In the event that no hearing is requested, the Chairman shall make a final administrative decision within forty (40) days of the date notice is provided to the former employee and the record of the proceedings shall consist of the statement of allegations as defined in paragraph (b)(2)(i) and whatever written response the former employee shall provide.

(3) The Chairman shall specify in the final administrative decision the findings of fact and conclusions of law that differ from the recommended determination of the hearing examiner.

(i) *Administrative sanctions.* The Chairman may take appropriate action in the case of any individual who is found in violation of 18 U.S.C. 207(a), (b), or (c) or implementing regulations of the Office of Government Ethics (5 CFR part 737) after a final administrative decision by—

(1) Prohibiting the individual from making, on behalf of any other person (except the United States), any formal or informal appearance before, or, with the intent to influence, any oral or written communication to, the Commission on any matter of business for a period not to exceed five (5) years. This prohibition may be enforced by directing Commission employees to refuse to

participate in any such appearance or to accept any such communication;

(2) Taking other appropriate disciplinary action.

(j) *Judicial review*. Any person found to have participated in a violation of 18 U.S.C. 207(a), (b), or (c) or these regulations may seek judicial review of the administrative determination. Review shall be before the appropriate United States district court.

SUBCHAPTER A—GENERAL

PART 201—RULES OF GENERAL APPLICATION

Sec.
201.0 Seal.
201.1 Applicability of part.

Subpart A—Miscellaneous

201.2 Definitions.
201.3 Commission offices, mailing address, and hours.
201.3a Missing children information.
201.4 Performance of functions.
201.5 Attendance fees and mileage.
201.6 Confidential business information.

Subpart B—Initiation and Conduct of Investigations

201.7 Investigative authority and initiation of investigations.
201.8 Filing of documents.
201.9 Methods employed in obtaining information.
201.10 Public notices.
201.11 Appearance in an investigation as a party.
201.12 Requests.
201.13 Conduct of nonadjudicative hearings.
201.14 Computation of time, additional hearings, postponements, continuances, and extensions of time.
201.15 Attorneys or agents.
201.16 Service of process and other documents.

Subpart C—Availability of Information to the Public Pursuant to 5 U.S.C. 552

201.17 Procedures for requesting access to records.
201.18 Denial of requests, appeals from denial.
201.19 Notification regarding requests for confidential business information.
201.20 Fees.
201.21 Availability of specific records.

Subpart D—Safeguarding Individual Privacy Pursuant to 5 U.S.C. 552a

201.22 Purpose and scope.
201.23 Definitions.
201.24 Procedures for requests pertaining to individual records in a records system.
201.25 Times, places, and requirements for identification of individuals making requests.
201.26 Disclosure of requested information to individuals.
201.27 Special procedures: Medical records.
201.28 Requests for correction or amendment of records.
201.29 Commission disclosure of individual records, accounting of record disclosures, and requests for accounting of record disclosures.
201.30 Commission review of requests for access to records, for correction or amendment to records, and for accounting of record disclosures.
201.31 Fees and employee conduct.
201.32 Specific exemptions.

Subpart E—Opening Commission Meetings to Public Observation Pursuant to 5 U.S.C. 552b

201.33 Purpose and scope.
201.34 Definitions.
201.35 Notices to the public.
201.36 Closing a portion or portions of a meeting or a series of meetings.
201.37 Changing the time, place, subject matter, or determination to open or close a meeting following a public notice.
201.38 Requests by interested persons that the Commission close a portion of a Commission meeting.
201.39 General Counsel's certification of Commission action in closing a meeting or a series of meetings.
201.40 Records-retention requirements.
201.41 Public inspection and copying of records; applicable fees.

Subpart F—National Security Information

201.42 Purpose and scope.
201.43 Mandatory declassification review.

Subpart G—Enforcement of Nondiscrimination on the Basis of Handicap in Programs or Activities Conducted by the U.S. International Trade Commission

201.101 Purpose.
201.102 Application.
201.103 Definitions.
201.104–201.109 [Reserved]
201.110 Self-evaluation.
201.111 Notice.
201.112–201.129 [Reserved]
201.130 General prohibitions against discrimination.
201.131–201.139 [Reserved]
201.140 Employment.
201.141–201.148 [Reserved]
201.149 Program accessibility: Discrimination prohibited.
201.150 Program accessibility: Existing facilities.
201.151 Program accessibility: New construction and alterations.

201.152–201.159 [Reserved]
201.160 Communications.
201.161–201.169 [Reserved]
201.170 Compliance procedures.
201.171–201.999 [Reserved]

Subpart H—Debt Collection

201.201 Definitions.
201.202 Purpose and scope of salary and administrative offset rules.
201.203 Delegation of authority.
201.204 Salary offset.
201.205 Salary adjustments.
201.206 Administrative offset.
201.207 Administrative offset against amounts payable from Civil Service Retirement and Disability Fund.
201.208 Tax refund offset.

AUTHORITY: 19 U.S.C. 1335; 19 U.S.C. 2482, unless otherwise noted.

SOURCE: 27 FR 12118, Dec. 7, 1962, unless otherwise noted.

§ 201.0 Seal.

(a) Pursuant to section 331(g) of the Tariff Act of 1930, as amended (19 U.S.C. 1331(g)), the United States International Trade Commission has adopted an official seal, the depiction of which follows:

(b) Custody and certification obligations. The Secretary shall have custody of the seal of the United States International Trade Commission and he, or the Acting Secretary, may execute under seal any certification required to authenticate any books, records, papers, or other documents as true copies of official records of the United States International Trade Commission.

(Sec. 331(g), Tariff Act of 1930, as amended (19 U.S.C. 1331(g)))

[40 FR 53384, Nov. 18, 1975; 40 FR 55838, Dec. 2, 1975]

§ 201.1 Applicability of part.

This part relates generally to functions and activities of the Commission under various statutes and other legal authority. Rules having special application appear separately in parts 202 through 207, inclusive, and parts 210, 212 and 213, of this chapter. In case of inconsistency between a rule of general application and a rule of special application, the latter is controlling.

[68 FR 32973, June 3, 2003]

Subpart A—Miscellaneous

§ 201.2 Definitions.

As used in this chapter—

(a) *Commission* means the United States International Trade Commission;

(b) *Inspector General* means the Inspector General of the Commission;

(c) *Tariff Act* means the Tariff Act of 1930, 19 U.S.C. 1202–1677j, 1677m–n;

(d) *Trade Expansion Act* means the Trade Expansion Act of 1962, 19 U.S.C. 1801–1991;

(e) *Trade Act* means the Trade Act of 1974, 19 U.S.C. 2101–2487;

(f) *Trade Agreements Act* means the Trade Agreements Act of 1979, Public Law 96–39, 93 Stat. 144;

(g) *Rule* means a section of the Commission Rules of Practice and Procedure (19 CFR chapter II);

(h) *Secretary* means the Secretary of the Commission.

(i) Except for adjudicative investigations under subchapter C of this chapter, *party* means any person who has filed a complaint or petition on the basis of which an investigation has been instituted, or any person whose entry of appearance has been accepted pursuant to §201.11 (a) or (c). Mere participation in an investigation without an accepted entry of appearance does not confer party status.

(j) *Person* means an individual, partnership, corporation, association, or public or private organization.

[56 FR 11922, Mar. 21, 1991, as amended at 60 FR 37336, July 20, 1995; 68 FR 32973, June 3, 2003]

§ 201.3 Commission offices, mailing address, and hours.

(a) *Offices.* The Commission's offices are located in the United States International Trade Commission Building on 500 E Street SW., Washington, DC.

(b) *Mailing address.* All communications to the Commission should be addressed to the "Secretary, U.S. International Trade Commission, 500 E Street SW., Washington, DC 20436."

(c) *Hours.* The business hours of the Commission are from 8:45 a.m. to 5:15 p.m., eastern standard or daylight savings time, whichever is in effect in Washington, DC. Any document filed with the Secretary of the Commission after 5:15 p.m. will be considered filed the next business day. If filing on that day would be untimely, the filing may not be accepted unless a request is made for acceptance of a late filing for good cause shown pursuant to 201.14(b)(2).

[45 FR 80276, Dec. 4, 1980, as amended at 68 FR 32973, June 3, 2003]

§ 201.3a Missing children information.

(a) Pursuant to 39 U.S.C. 3220, penalty mail sent by the Commission may be used to assist in the location and recovery of missing children. This section establishes procedures for such use and is applicable on a Commission-wide basis. The Commission's Office of Facilities Management, telephone 202–205–2741, shall be the point of contact for matters related to the implementation of this section.

(b) Missing children information shall be inserted in or affixed to such mailings of Commission monthly calendars, notices, press releases, and other documents as the Commission may direct. Such missing children information shall be obtained exclusively from the National Center for Missing and Exploited Children.

(c) The procedure established in subsection (b) above will result in missing childern information being inserted in an estimated 25 percent of the Commission's penalty mail and will cost an estimated $1,500 for the first year of implementation. The Director of Administration shall make such changes in the procedure as he deems appropriate to maximize the use of missing children information in the Commission's mail.

[51 FR 25195, July 11, 1986, as amended at 68 FR 32974, June 3, 2003]

§ 201.4 Performance of functions.

(a) *Conduct of business.* A majority of the members of the Commission constitutes a quorum. The Commission may meet and exercise its powers at any place, and may, by one or more of its members, or by such agents as it may designate, prosecute any inquiry necessary to its duties in any part of the United States or in any foreign country.

(b) *Alteration or waiver of rules.* Rules in this chapter may be amended, waived, suspended, or revoked by the Commission only. A rule may be waived or suspended only when in the judgment of the Commission there is good and sufficient reason therefor, provided the rule is not a matter of procedure required by law.

(c) *Authority to make decisions.* Authority to interpret the Commission's rules and the laws applying to the Commission, and to make findings, determinations, or other decisions not relating to matters of internal management, is retained in the Commission itself and is not delegated.

(d) Presentation of matter that may come within the purview of other laws. Whenever any party or person, including the Commission staff, has reason to believe that (1) a matter under investigation pursuant to section 337 of the Tariff Act of 1930, or (2) a matter under an investigation pursuant to section 202 of the Trade Act of 1974 (19 U.S.C. 2252), which is causing increased imports may come within the purview of another remedial provision of law not the basis of such investigation, including but not limited to the antidumping provisions (19 U.S.C. 1673 *et seq.*) or the countervailing duty provisions (19 U.S.C. 1671 *et seq.*) of the Tariff Act of 1930, then the party or person may file a suggestion of notification with the Commission that the appropriate agency be notified of such matter or circumstances, together with such information as the party or person has available. The Secretary shall promptly thereafter publish notice of the filing of such suggestion and information, and make them available for inspection and copying to the extent permitted by law. Any person may comment on the suggestion within 10 days after the publication of said notice.

Thereafter, the Commission shall determine whether notification is appropriate under the law and, if so, shall notify the appropriate agency of such matters or circumstances. The Commission may at any time make such notification in the absence of a suggestion under this rule when the Commission has reason to believe, on the basis of information before it, that notification is appropriate under law.

[27 FR 12118, Dec. 7, 1962, as amended at 45 FR 80276, Dec. 4, 1980; 68 FR 32974, June 3, 2003]

§201.5 Attendance fees and mileage.

(a) *Deponents and witnesses.* Any person compelled to appear in person to depose or testify in response to a subpoena shall be paid the same fees and mileage as are paid witnesses in the courts of the United States: Provided, that salaried employees of the United States summoned to depose or testify as to matters related to their public employment, irrespective of at whose instance they are summoned, shall be paid in accordance with applicable Government regulations.

(b) *Responsibility.* The fees and mileage referred to in this section shall be paid by the party at whose instance deponents or witnesses appear: Provided, that when it is the Commission, one or more Commissioners, or one of its employees at whose instance deponents or witnesses appear, such fees and mileage shall be paid by the Commission.

[41 FR 17710, Apr. 27, 1976]

§201.6 Confidential business information.

(a) *Definitions*—(1) *Confidential business information* is information which concerns or relates to the trade secrets, processes, operations, style of works, or apparatus, or to the production, sales, shipments, purchases, transfers, identification of customers, inventories, or amount or source of any income, profits, losses, or expenditures of any person, firm, partnership, corporation, or other organization, or other information of commercial value, the disclosure of which is likely to have the effect of either impairing the Commission's ability to obtain such information as is necessary to perform its statutory functions, or causing substantial harm to the competitive position of the person, firm, partnership, corporation, or other organization from which the information was obtained, unless the Commission is required by law to disclose such information. The term "confidential business information" includes "proprietary information" within the meaning of section 777(b) of the Tariff Act of 1930 (19 U.S.C. 1677f(b)). Nonnumerical characterizations of numerical confidential business information (e.g., discussion of trends) will be treated as confidential business information only at the request of the submitter for good cause shown.

(2) *Nondisclosable confidential business information* is privileged information, classified information, or specific information (e.g., trade secrets) of a type for which there is a clear and compelling need to withhold from disclosure. Special rules for the handling of such information are set out in §206.17 and §207.7 of this chapter.

(b) *Procedure for submitting business information in confidence.* (1) A request for confidential treatment of business information shall be addressed to the Secretary, United States International Trade Commission, 500 E Street SW., Washington, DC 20436, and shall indicate clearly on the envelope that it is a request for confidential treatment.

(2) In the absence of good cause shown, any request relating to material to be submitted during the course of a hearing shall be submitted at least three (3) working days prior to the commencement of such hearing.

(3) With each submission of, or offer to submit, business information which a submitter desires to be treated as confidential business information, under paragraph (a) of this section, the submitter shall provide the following, which may be disclosed to the public:

(i) A written description of the nature of the subject information;

(ii) A justification for the request for its confidential treatment;

(iii) A certification in writing under oath that substantially identical information is not available to the public;

(iv) A copy of the document

(A) Clearly marked on its cover as to the pages on which confidential information can be found;

(B) With information for which confidential treatment is requested clearly identified by means of brackets; and

(C) With information for which nondisclosable confidential treatment is requested clearly identified by means of triple brackets (except when submission of such document is withheld in accord with paragraph (b)(4) of this section); and

(v) A nonconfidential copy of the documents as required by § 201.8(d).

(4) The submission of the documents itemized in paragraph (b)(3) of this section will provide the basis for rulings on the confidentiality of submissions, including rulings on the confidentiality of submissions offered to the Commission which have not yet been placed under the possession, control, or custody of the Commission. The submitter has the option of providing the business information for which confidential treatment is sought at the time the documents itemized in paragraph (b)(3) of this section are provided or of withholding them until a ruling on their confidentiality has been issued.

(c) *Identification of business information submitted in confidence.* Business information which a submitter desires to be treated as confidential shall be clearly labeled "confidential business information" when submitted, and shall be segregated from other material being submitted.

(d) *Approval or denial of requests for confidential treatment.* Approval or denial of requests shall be made only by the Secretary or Acting Secretary. An approval or a denial of a request for confidential treatment shall be in writing. A denial shall specify the reason therefor, and shall advise the submitter of the right to appeal to the Commission.

(e) *Appeals from denial of confidential treatment.* (1) For good cause shown, the Commission may grant an appeal from a denial by the Secretary of a request for confidential treatment of a submission. Any appeal filed shall be addressed to the Chairman, United States International Trade Commission, 500 E Street SW., Washington, DC 20436, and shall clearly indicate that it is a con-

fidential submission appeal. An appeal may be made within twenty (20) days of a denial or whenever the approval or denial has not been forthcoming within ten (10) days (excepting Saturdays, Sundays, and Federal legal holidays) of the receipt of a confidential treatment request, unless an extension notice in writing with the reasons therefor has been provided the person requesting confidential treatment.

(2) An appeal will be decided within twenty (20) days of its receipt (excepting Saturdays, Sundays, and Federal legal holidays) unless an extension notice in writing with the reasons therefor, has been provided the person making the appeal.

(3) The justification submitted to the Commission in connection with an appeal shall be limited to that presented to the Secretary with the original or amended request. When the Secretary or Acting Secretary has denied a request on the ground that the submitter failed to provide adequate justification, any such additional justification shall be submitted to the Secretary for consideration as part of an amended request. For purposes of paragraph (e)(1) of this section, the twenty (20) day period for filing an appeal shall be tolled on the filing of an amended request and a new twenty (20) day period shall begin once the Secretary or Acting Secretary has denied the amended request, or the approval or denial has not been forthcoming within ten (10) days of the filing of the amended request. A denial of a request by the Secretary on the ground of inadequate justification shall not obligate a requester to furnish additional justification and shall not preclude a requester from filing an appeal with the Commission based on the justification earlier submitted to the Secretary.

(f) *Appeals from approval of confidential treatment.* (1) For good cause shown, the Commission may grant an appeal from an approval by the Secretary of a request for confidential treatment of a submission. Any appeal filed shall be addressed to the Chairman, United States International Trade Commission, 500 E Street, SW., Washington, DC 20436, shall show that a copy thereof has been served upon the submitter, and shall clearly indicate that it is a confidential submission appeal. An appeal may be made within twenty (20) days of the approval by the Secretary of a request for confidential treatment or whenever the approval or denial has not been forthcoming within ten (10) days (excepting Saturdays, Sundays, and Federal legal holidays) of the receipt of a confidential treatment request, unless an extension notice in writing with the reasons therefor has been provided the person requesting confidential treatment.

(2) An appeal will be decided within twenty (20) days of its receipt (excepting Saturdays, Sundays, and Federal legal holidays) unless an extension notice, in writing with the reasons therefor, has been provided the person making the appeal.

(g) *Granting confidential status to business information.* Any business information submitted in confidence and determined to be entitled to confidential treatment shall be maintained in confidence by the Commission and not disclosed except as required by law. In the event that any business information submitted to the Commission is not entitled to confidential treatment, the submitter will be permitted to withdraw the tender within five days of its denial of confidential treatment unless it is the subject of a request under the Freedom of Information Act or of judicial discovery proceedings. After such five day period, the business information deemed not entitled to confidential treatment, and not withdrawn, will be treated as public information.

(h) *Scope of provisions.* The provisions of §§ 201.6(b) and 201.6 (d) through (g) shall not apply to adjudicative investigations under subchapter C, part 210, of the Commission's rules of practice and procedure.

[41 FR 28951, July 14, 1976, as amended at 49 FR 32571, Aug. 15, 1984; 54 FR 13678, Apr. 5, 1989; 61 FR 37827, July 22, 1996; 68 FR 32974, June 3, 2003]

Subpart B—Initiation and Conduct of Investigations

§ 201.7 Investigative authority and initiation of investigations.

(a) *Investigative authority.* In order to expedite the performance of its functions, the Commission may engage in investigative activities preliminary to and in aid of any authorized investigation, consolidate proceedings before it, and determine the scope and manner of its proceedings;

(b) *Initiation of investigations.* Investigations may be initiated by the Commission on the Commission's own motion, upon request of the President or the United States Trade Representative, upon resolution of the Committee on Ways and Means of the House of Representatives or the Committee of Finance of the Senate, upon resolution of either branch of Congress, or upon application, petition, complaint, or request of private parties, as required or provided for in the pertinent statute, Presidential proclamation, Executive Order, or in this chapter.

[44 FR 76476, Dec. 26, 1979, as amended at 63 FR 29351, May 29, 1998]

§ 201.8 Filing of documents.

(a) *Applicability; where to file; date of filing.* This section applies to all Commission proceedings except, notwithstanding any other section of this chapter, those conducted under 19 U.S.C. 1337, which are covered by requirements set out in part 210 of this chapter. Documents shall be filed at the office of the Secretary of the Commission in Washington, DC. Such documents, if properly filed within the hours of operation specified in § 201.3(c), will be deemed to be filed on the date on which they are actually received in the Commission.

(b) *Conformity with rules.* Each document filed with the Commission for the purpose of initiating any investigation shall be considered properly filed if it conforms with the pertinent rules prescribed in this chapter. Substantial compliance with the pertinent rules may be accepted by the Commission provided good and sufficient reason is stated in the document for inability to comply fully with the pertinent rules.

(c) *Specifications for documents.* Each document filed under this chapter shall be signed, double-spaced, clear and legible, except that a document of two pages or less in length need not be double-spaced. All submissions shall be in letter-sized format (8.5 × 11 inches), except copies of documents prepared for another agency or a court (e.g. pleadings papers), and single sided. The name of the person signing the original shall be typewritten or otherwise reproduced on each copy.

(d) *Filing.* (1) Except as provided in paragraphs (d)(2) through (6) and (f) of this section, all documents filed with the Commission shall be filed electronically. Completion of filing requires the submission of paper copies by 12 noon, Eastern time, on the next business day. A paper copy provided for in this section must be a true copy of the electronic version of the document, *i.e.*, a copy that is identical in all possible respects. All paper copies of electronic submissions exceeding fifty (50) pages in length must have a divider page and an identifying tab preceding each exhibit and/or attachment. The divider page and/or tab must be labeled with a letter or number that corresponds to a more fully descriptive index. All filings shall comply with the procedures set forth in the Commission's Electronic Document Information System Web site at *https:// edis.usitc.gov.* Failure to comply with the requirements of this chapter and the Handbook on Filing Procedures that apply to the filing of a document may result in the rejection of the document as improperly filed.

(2) Briefs, statements, responses, comments, and requests filed pursuant to § 201.12, § 201.14, § 206.8, § 207.15, § 207.23, § 207.25, § 207.28, § 207.30, § 207.61, § 207.62, § 207.65, § 207.67, or § 207.68 of this chapter shall be filed electronically and the requisite number of true paper copies of these documents shall be submitted to the Commission in accordance with the provisions of the applicable section.

(3) Petitions and requests filed under § 206.2 or § 207.10 of this chapter shall be filed in paper form and exhibits, appendices, and attachments to the documents shall be filed in electronic form on CD–ROM, DVD or other portable electronic media approved by the Secretary in accordance with the provisions of the applicable section. Submitted media will be retained by the Commission, except that media may be returned to the submitter if a document is not accepted for filing.

(4) Supplementary material and witness testimony provided for under § 201.13, § 207.15, or § 207.24 of this chapter shall be filed in paper form in accordance with the provisions of the applicable section.

(5) Certain documents filed under § 201.4 of this chapter and applications for administrative protective orders filed under §§ 206.17 and 207.7 of this chapter shall only be filed electronically; no paper copies will be required.

(6) The Secretary may provide for exceptions and modifications to the filing requirements set out in this chapter. A person seeking an exception should consult the Handbook on Filing Procedures.

(7) During any period in which the Commission is closed, deadlines for filing documents electronically and by other means are extended so that documents are due on the first business day after the end of the closure.

(e) *Identification of party filing document.* Each document filed with the Commission for the purpose of initiating any investigation shall show on the first page thereof the name, address, and telephone number of the party or parties by whom or on whose behalf the document is filed and shall be signed by the party filing the document or by a duly authorized officer, attorney, or agent of such party. (Also, any attorney or agent filing the document shall give his address and telephone number.) The signature of the person signing such a document constitutes a certification that he had read the document, that to the best of his knowledge and belief the statements contained therein are true, and that the person signing the document was duly authorized to sign it.

(f) *Nonconfidential copies.* In the event that confidential treatment of a document is requested under § 201.6(b), a nonconfidential version of the document shall be filed, in which the confidential business information shall have been deleted and which shall have been conspicuously marked "nonconfidential" or "public inspection."' The nonconfidential version shall be filed electronically, and two (2) true paper copies shall be submitted on the same business day as this electronic filing, except as provided in § 206.8 or § 207.3 of this chapter. In the event that confidential treatment is not requested for a document under §201.6(b), the document shall be conspicuously marked "No confidential version filed," and the document shall be filed in accordance with paragraph (d) of this section. The name of the person signing the original shall be typewritten or otherwise reproduced on each copy.

(g) *Cover sheet.* When making a paper filing, parties must complete the cover sheet on-line at *http://edis.usitc.gov* and print out the cover sheet for submission to the Office of the Secretary with the paper filing. For documents that are filed electronically, parties must complete the cover sheet for such filing on-line at *http://edis.usitc.gov* at the time of the electronic filing. The party submitting the cover sheet is responsible for the accuracy of all information contained in the cover sheet, including, but not limited to, the security status and the investigation number, and must comply with applicable limitations on disclosure of business proprietary information or confidential information under §201.6 and §§206.8, 206.17, 207.3, and 207.7 of this chapter.

[41 FR 17710, Apr. 27, 1976, as amended at 49 FR 32571, Aug. 15, 1984; 56 FR 11922, Mar. 21, 1991; 67 FR 68037, Nov. 8, 2002; 68 FR 32974, June 3, 2003; 76 FR 61941, Oct. 6, 2011; 79 FR 35924, June 25, 2014]

§201.9 Methods employed in obtaining information.

In obtaining information necessary to carry out its functions and duties, the Commission may employ any means authorized by law. In general, the Commission obtains pertinent information from its own files, from other agencies of the Government, through questionnaires and correspondence, through field work by members of the Commission's staff, and from testimony and other information presented at the hearings.

[27 FR 12118, Dec. 7, 1962, as amended at 44 FR 76476, Dec. 26, 1979]

§201.10 Public notices.

As appropriate, notice of the receipt of documents properly filed, of the institution of investigations, of public hearings, and of other formal actions of the Commission will be given by publication in the FEDERAL REGISTER. In addition to such publication, a copy of each notice will be posted at the Office of the Secretary to the Commission in Washington, DC, and, as appropriate, copies will be sent to press associations, trade and similar organizations of producers and importers, and others known to have an interest in the subject matter.

[63 FR 29347, May 29, 1998]

§201.11 Appearance in an investigation as a party.

(a) *Who may appear as a party.* Any person may apply to appear in an investigation as a party, either in person or by representative, by filing an entry of appearance with the Secretary. Each entry of appearance shall state briefly the nature of the person's reason for participating in the investigation and state the person's intent to file briefs with the Commission regarding the subject matter of the investigation. The Secretary shall promptly determine whether the person submitting the entry of appearance has a proper reason for participating in the investigation. In any investigation conducted under part 207 of this chapter, industrial users, and if the merchandise under investigation is sold at the retail level, representative consumer organizations, will be deemed to have a proper reason for participating in the investigation. If it is found that a person does not have a proper reason for participating in the investigation, that person shall be so notified by the Secretary and shall not be entitled to appear in the investigation as a party. A person found to have a proper reason for participating in the investigation shall be permitted to appear in the investigation as a party, and acceptance of such person's entry of appearance shall be signified by the Secretary's inclusion of such person on the service list established pursuant to paragraph (d) of this section.

(b) *Time for filing.* (1) Except in the case of investigations conducted under part 207 of this chapter, each entry of appearance shall be filed with the Secretary not later than twenty-one (21) days after publication of the Commission's notice of investigation in the FEDERAL REGISTER.

(2) In the case of investigations conducted under subpart B of part 207 of this chapter, each entry of appearance shall be filed with the Secretary not later than seven (7) days after publication of the Commission's notice of investigation in the FEDERAL REGISTER. A party that files a notice of appearance during such time need not file an additional notice of appearance during the portion of the investigation conducted under subpart C of part 207 of this chapter.

(3) Notwithstanding paragraph (b)(2) of this section, a party may file an entry of appearance during the final phase of an investigation conducted under part 207 of this chapter no later than twenty-one (21) days prior to the hearing date listed in the FEDERAL REGISTER notice published pursuant to § 207.24(b) of this chapter.

(4) In the case of reviews conducted under subpart F of part 207 of this chapter, each entry of appearance shall be filed with the Secretary not later than twenty-one (21) days after publication in the FEDERAL REGISTER of the notice of institution described in § 207.60(d) of this chapter.

(5) Notwithstanding paragraph (b)(4) of this section, a party may file an entry of appearance in a review conducted under subpart F of part 207 of this chapter within the period specified in the notice issued under § 207.62(c) of this chapter. This period shall be at least 45 days.

(c) *Late filing.* Any entry of appearance filed with the Secretary after the filing date established in paragraph (b) of this section shall be referred to the Chairman, or other person designated to conduct the investigation, who shall promptly determine whether to accept such entry for good cause shown by the person desiring to file the notice. The Secretary shall promptly notify the submitter of a decision to deny the entry, or if the entry is accepted, include such person on the service list established pursuant to paragraph (d) of this section.

(d) *Service list.* Upon the expiration of the time for filing notices of appearance established in paragraph (b) of this section, the Secretary shall prepare a service list. The service list shall contain the names and addresses of all persons, or their representatives, who are parties to the investigation pursuant to § 201.2(h) and paragraph (a) of this section. Upon the acceptance of a late entry of appearance pursuant to paragraph (c) of this section, the Secretary shall amend the service list to include the name and address of the person whose notice has been accepted and shall promptly forward such notice to all parties to the investigation.

[56 FR 11922, Mar. 21, 1991, as amended at 61 FR 37828, July 22, 1996; 63 FR 30607, June 5, 1998]

§ 201.12 Requests.

Any party to a nonadjudicative investigation may request the Commission to take particular action with respect to that investigation. Such requests shall be made by letter addressed to the Secretary, shall be placed by him in the record, and shall be served on all other parties. Such request shall be filed electronically and two (2) true paper copies shall be submitted on the same business day. The Commission shall take such action or make such response as it deems appropriate.

[76 FR 61941, Oct. 6, 2011]

§ 201.13 Conduct of nonadjudicative hearings.

(a) *In general.* Public hearings are held by the Commission when required by law or, if not required by law, when in the judgment of the Commission there is good and sufficient reason therefor. Public hearings will be held at the time and place specified in notices issued under § 201.10. Public hearings are ordinarily held in the Hearing Room of the International Trade Commission Building, in Washington, DC, but may be held elsewhere at the Commission's discretion.

(b) *Presiding officials*—(1) *Who presides.* Public hearings or conferences in nonadjudicative investigations will be conducted by the Commission or by one or more Commissioners. When the Commission deems it necessary, such hearings will be conducted by one or more designated employees. In all cases the transcript of the testimony at a hearing will be presented for the consideration of the Commission.

(2) *Powers and duties.* The Commission, one or more of the Commissioners, or one or more designated employees shall have all the powers to conduct fair and impartial hearings, to take necessary action to avoid delay in the disposition of proceedings, including the prescription of time allocated to testimony, argument, and questioning, to regulate the course of hearings and the conduct of the parties and their counsel therein, and to maintain order.

(c) *Participation in a hearing*—(1) *Who may participate.* A party may participate in the hearing, either in person or by representative. A nonparty who has testimony or arguments that may aid the Commission's deliberations may also participate, under such conditions as may be established by the presiding officials at the hearing.

(2) *Notices of participation.* Notices of participation in a hearing shall be filed with the Secretary at least three (3) days in advance of the date set for the hearing or two (2) days in advance of the date set in the notice of investigation for a prehearing conference, whichever shall first occur, except that the presiding officials may waive this requirement for good cause. Witnesses on behalf of persons filing notices of participation need not file separate notices.

(d) *Witness list.* Each person who files a notice of participation pursuant to paragraph (c) of this section shall simultaneously file with the Secretary a list of the witnesses he intends to call at the hearing.

(e) *Order of the testimony.* Unless otherwise ordered by the presiding officials, witnesses will give testimony in the order designated by the Secretary to the Commission. Each witness, after being duly sworn, will be permitted to proceed with his or her testimony without interruption except by presiding officials.

(f) *Supplementary material.* A party to the investigation may file with the Secretary supplementary material, other than remarks read into the record, for acceptance into the record. The party shall file any such material with the Secretary at the hearing. Supplementary materials must be marked with the name of the organization sub-mitting it. As used herein, the term *supplementary material* refers to (1) additional graphic material such as charts and diagrams used to illuminate an argument or clarify a position and (2) information not available to a party at the time its prehearing brief was filed.

(g) *Questioning of witnesses.* After completing testimony, a witness may be questioned by any member of the Commission or by its staff. Any participant may, with the permission of the presiding officials, direct questions to the witness, but only for the purpose of assisting the Commission in obtaining relevant and material facts with respect to the subject matter of the investigation.

(h) *Oral argument.* When, in the opinion of the presiding officials, time permits and the nature of the proceedings and the complexity or importance of the questions of fact or law involved warrant, the presiding officials may allow oral argument after conclusion of the testimony in a hearing. The presiding officials will determine in each instance the time to be allowed for argument and the allocation thereof.

(i) *Briefs*—(1) *Parties.* Briefs of the information produced at the hearing and arguments thereon may be presented to the Commission by parties to the investigation. Time to be allowed for submission of briefs will be set after conclusion of testimony and oral argument, if any.

(2) *Nonparties.* Any person who is not a party to an investigation may submit a short statement for the record regarding the subject matter of an investigation.

(j) *Verification of testimony.* Oral or written information submitted at hearings will, upon order of the Commission, be subject to verification from books, papers, and records of the persons submitting the information and from any other available sources.

(k) *Hearing transcripts.* A verbatim transcript of all hearings will be taken. The Commission does not distribute transcripts of the records of such hearings. Any person may inspect the transcript of a hearing at the Commission's office in Washington, DC, or purchase it from the official reporter.

(l) To facilitate the conduct of hearings, parties intending to use easels, audio visual, and similar equipment in the course of hearing presentations should advise the Secretary of their intent to use such equipment at least three (3) working days before the hearing.

(m) *Closed sessions.* (1) Upon a request filed by a party to the investigation no later than seven (7) days prior to the date of the hearing (or three (3) days prior to the date of a conference conducted under § 207.15 of this chapter) that

(i) Identifies the subjects to be discussed;

(ii) Specifies the amount of time requested; and

(iii) Justifies the need for a closed session with respect to each subject to be discussed, the Commission (or the Director, as defined in § 207.2(c) of this chapter, for a conference under § 207.15 of this chapter) may close a portion of a hearing (or conference under § 207.15 of this chapter) held in any investigation in order to allow such party to address confidential business information, as defined in § 201.6, during the course of its presentation.

(2) In addition, during each hearing held in an investigation conducted under section 202 of the Trade Act, as amended, or in an investigation under title VII of the Tariff Act as provided in § 207.24 of this chapter, following the public presentation of the petitioner(s) and that of each panel of respondents, the Commission will, if it deems it appropriate, close the hearing in order to allow Commissioners to question parties and/or their representatives concerning matters involving confidential business information.

[47 FR 6189, Feb. 10, 1982, as amended at 47 FR 33682, Aug. 4, 1982; 54 FR 13678, Apr. 5, 1989; 59 FR 66722, Dec. 28, 1994; 61 FR 37829, July 22, 1996; 68 FR 32975, June 3, 2003]

§ 201.14   Computation of time, additional hearings, postponements, continuances, and extensions of time.

(a) *Computation of time.* Computation of any period of time prescribed or allowed by the rules in this chapter, by order of the Commission, or by order of the presiding officer under part 210 of this chapter shall begin with the first business day following the day on which the act or event initiating such period of time shall have occurred. The last day of the period so computed is to be included, unless it is a Saturday, Sunday, or Federal legal holiday, in which event the period runs until the end of the next business day. When the period of time prescribed or allowed is less than 7 days, intermediate Saturdays, Sundays, and Federal legal holidays shall be excluded from the computation. As used in this rule, a Federal legal holiday refers to any full calendar day designated as a legal holiday by the President or the Congress of the United States. In the event of an early or all-day closing of the Commission on a business day, the Secretary is authorized to accept on the next full business day filings due the day of the early or all-day closing, without requiring the granting of an extension of time by the Chairman of the Commission, or such other person designated to conduct the investigation.

(b) *Additional hearings, postponements, continuances, and extensions of time.* (1) Prior to its final determination in any investigation, the Commission may in its discretion for good cause shown grant additional hearings, postponements, or continuances of hearings.

(2) The Chairman of the Commission or such other person as is designated to conduct the investigation shall determine whether to grant for good cause shown extensions of time for performing any act required by or pursuant to the rules contained in this chapter.

(3) A request that the Commission take any of the actions described in this section shall be filed with the Secretary and served on all parties to the investigation. Such request shall be filed electronically and two (2) true paper copies shall be submitted on the same business day.

[41 FR 17710, Apr. 27, 1976, as amended at 56 FR 11923, Mar. 21, 1991; 68 FR 32975, June 3, 2003; 76 FR 61941, Oct. 6, 2011]

§ 201.15   Attorneys or agents.

(a) *In general.* No register of attorneys or agents who may practice before the Commission is maintained. No application for admission to practice is required. Any person desiring to appear as attorney or agent before the Commission may be required to show to the satisfaction of the Commission his acceptability in that capacity. Any attorney or agent practicing before the Commission, or desiring so to practice, may for good cause shown be suspended or barred from practicing before the Commission, or have imposed on him such lesser sanctions as the Commission deems appropriate, but only after he has been accorded an opportunity to present his views in the matter.

(b) *Former officers or employees.* No former officer or employee of the Commission who personally and substantially participated in a matter which was pending in any manner or form in the Commission during his employment shall be eligible to appear before the Commission as attorney or agent in connection with such matter. No former officer or employee of the Commission shall be eligible to appear as attorney or agent before the Commission in connection with any matter which was pending in any manner or form in the Commission during his employment, unless he first obtains written consent from the Commission.

[27 FR 12118, Dec. 7, 1962, as amended at 56 FR 11923, Mar. 21, 1991]

§201.16 Service of process and other documents.

(a) *By the Commission.* Except when service by another method shall be specifically ordered by the Commission, the service of a process or other document of the Commission shall be served by anyone duly authorized by the Commission and be effected—

(1) By mailing or delivering a copy of the document to the person to be served, to a member of the partnership to be served, to the president, secretary, other executive officer, or member of the board of directors of the corporation, association, or other organization to be served, or, if an attorney represents any of the above before the Commission, by mailing or delivering a copy to such attorney; or

(2) By leaving a copy thereof at the principal office of such person, partnership, corporation, association, or other organization, or, if an attorney represents any of the above before the

Commission, by leaving a copy at the office of such attorney.

(3) By using an express delivery service to send a copy of the document to the principal office of such person, partnership, corporation, association, or other organization, or, if an attorney represents any of the above before the Commission, by serving the attorney by express delivery.

(4) When service is by mail, it is complete upon mailing of the document. When service is by an express service, service is complete upon submitting the document to the express delivery service or depositing it in the appropriate container for pick-up by the express delivery service.

(b) *By a party other than the Commission.* Except when service by another method shall be specifically ordered by the Commission, the service of a document of a party shall be effected:

(1) By mailing or delivering a copy of a nonconfidential version of the document to each party, or, if the party is represented by an attorney before the Commission, by mailing or delivering a nonconfidential version thereof to such attorney; or

(2) By leaving a copy thereof at the principal office of each other party, or, if a party is represented by an attorney before the Commission, by leaving a copy at the office of such attorney.

(3) When service is by mail, it is complete upon mailing of the document.

(4) When service is by mail, it shall be by first class mail, postage prepaid. In the event the addressee is outside the United States, service shall be by first class airmail, postage prepaid.

(c) *Proof of service; certificate.* (1) Each document filed with the Secretary to the Commission by a party in the course of an investigation (as provided in §201.8 of this part) shall be served on each other party to the investigation (as provided in §210.4(i) of this chapter for investigations under 19 U.S.C. 1337).

(2) Each document served by a party shall include a certificate of service, setting forth the manner and date of such service. The certificate of service shall be deemed proof of service of the document. In the event a document is not accompanied by a certificate of service, the Secretary shall not accept

such document for filing and shall promptly notify the submitter.

(d) *Additional time after service by mail.* Whenever a party or Federal agency or department has the right or is required to perform some act or take some action within a prescribed period after the service of a document upon it and the document is served upon it by mail, three (3) calendar days shall be added to the prescribed period, except that when mailing is to a person located in a foreign country, ten (10) calendar days shall be added to the prescribed period.

(e) *Additional time after service by express delivery.* Whenever a party or Federal agency or department has the right or is required to perform some act or take some action within a prescribed period after the service of a document upon it and the document is served by express delivery, one (1) day shall be added to the prescribed period if the service is to a destination in the United States, and five (5) days shall be added to the prescribed period if the service is to a destination outside the United States. "Service by express delivery" refers to a method that would provide delivery by the next business day within the United States and refers to the equivalent express delivery service when the delivery is to a foreign location.

(f) *Electronic service.* Parties may serve documents by electronic means in all matters before the Commission. Parties may effect such service on any party, unless that party has, upon notice to the Secretary and to all parties, stated that it does not consent to electronic service. If electronic service is used, no additional time is added to the prescribed period. However, any dispute that arises among parties regarding electronic service must be resolved by the parties themselves, without the Commission's involvement.

(19 U.S.C. 1335 and the Administrative Procedure Act, 5 U.S.C. 551, *et seq.*)

[41 FR 17711, Apr. 27, 1976, as amended at 47 FR 6190, Feb. 10, 1982; 47 FR 33682, Aug. 4, 1982; 49 FR 32571, Aug. 15, 1984; 67 FR 68037, Nov. 8, 2002; 73 FR 38320, July 7, 2008; 76 FR 61942, Oct. 6, 2011; 78 FR 23840, Apr. 19, 2013]

Subpart C—Availability of Information to the Public Pursuant to 5 U.S.C. 552

AUTHORITY: 19 U.S.C. 1335, 5 U.S.C. 552.

SOURCE: 40 FR 8328, Feb. 27, 1975, unless otherwise noted.

§ 201.17 Procedures for requesting access to records.

(a) *Requests for records.* (1) A request for any information or record shall be addressed to the Secretary, United States International Trade Commission, 500 E Street SW., Washington, DC 20436 and shall indicate clearly in the request, and if the request is in paper form on the envelope, that it is a "Freedom of Information Act Request." A written request may be made either (1) in paper form, or (2) electronically by contacting the Commission at *http://www.usitc.gov/foia.htm.*

(2) Any request shall reasonably describe the requested record to facilitate location of the record. If the request pertains to a record that is part of the Commission's file in an investigation, the request should identify the investigation by number and name. A clear description of the requested record(s) should reduce the time required by the Commission to locate and disclose releasable responsive record(s) and minimize any applicable search and copying charges.

(3) Except as provided in paragraph (b) of this section, requests will be processed in the order in which they are filed.

(4) Requests for transcripts of hearings should be addressed to the official hearing reporter, the name and address of which can be obtained from the Secretary. A copy of such request shall at the same time be forwarded to the Secretary.

(5) Copies of public Commission reports and other publications are available online at *http://www.usitc.gov/publications/by_type.htm,* or can be requested by calling or writing the Office of the Secretary. Certain Commission publications are sold by the Superintendent of Documents, U.S. Government Printing Office, and are available from that agency at the price set by that agency.

(6) A day-to-day, composite record will be kept by the Secretary of each request with the disposition thereof.

(b) *Expedited processing.* (1) Requests for records under paragraph (a)(1) of this section will be taken out of order and given expedited treatment whenever it is determined that they involve:

(i) Circumstances in which the lack of expedited treatment could reasonably be expected to pose an imminent threat to the life or physical safety of an individual;

(ii) An urgency to inform the public about an actual or alleged federal government activity, if made by a person primarily engaged in disseminating information;

(iii) The loss of substantial due process rights; or

(iv) A matter of widespread and exceptional media interest in which there exist possible questions about the government's integrity which affect public confidence.

(2) A request for expedited processing may be made at the time of the initial request for records or at any later time.

(3) A requester who seeks expedited processing must submit a statement, certified to be true and correct to the best of that person's knowledge and belief, explaining in detail the basis for requesting expedited processing. For example, a requester within paragraph (b)(1)(ii) of this section, if not a full-time member of the news media, must establish that he or she is a person whose main professional activity or occupation is information dissemination, though it need not be his or her sole occupation. A requester within paragraph (b)(1)(ii) of this section also must establish a particular urgency to inform the public about the government activity involved in the request, beyond the public's right to know about government activity generally. The formality of certification may be waived as a matter of administrative discretion.

(4) Within ten calendar days of receipt of a request for expedited processing, the Secretary will decide whether to grant it and will notify the requester of the decision. If a request for expedited treatment is granted, the request will be given priority and will be processed as soon as practicable. If a request for expedited processing is denied, any appeal of that decision will be acted on expeditiously.

(c) *Public reading room.* The Commission maintains a public reading room in the Office of the Secretary for access to the records that the FOIA requires to be made regularly available for public inspection and copying. Reading room records created by the Commission on or after November 1, 1996, are available electronically. This includes a current subject-matter index of reading room records, which will indicate which records are available electronically.

(d) *Acknowledgment.* The Secretary will provide to a requester an acknowledgment of the receipt of a request and an individualized tracking number for each request. The requester may obtain information about the status of the request and/or contact the Commission's FOIA Public Liaison by telephone (202–205–2595) or email (*foia.se.se@usitc.gov*). The FOIA Public Liaison is responsible for assisting in reducing delays, increasing transparency and understanding of the status of requests, and assisting in the resolution of disputes.

(e) *First-party requests.* The FOIA applies to third-party requests for documents concerning the general activities of the government and of the Commission in particular. When a U.S. citizen or an alien lawfully admitted for permanent residence requests access to his or her own records, *i.e.*, makes a first-party request, it is considered a Privacy Act request. Although requests are considered either FOIA requests or Privacy Act requests, the Commission processes first-party requests in accordance with both laws, which provides the greatest degree of lawful access while safeguarding an individual's personal privacy.

(f) *Referrals.* If the Secretary refers a request or a portion thereof to another agency, the Secretary will notify the requester of the referral and the part of the request that has been referred. If feasible, the Secretary will provide the requester with a point of contact within the receiving agency regarding the referral.

(g) *Records management.* (1) The Secretary shall preserve all correspondence pertaining to requests received as well as copies of all requested records, until disposition or destruction is authorized by a General Records Schedule of the National Archives and Records Administration (NARA) or other NARA-approved records schedule.

(2) Materials that are identified as responsive to a FOIA request will not be disposed of or destroyed while the request or a related appeal or lawsuit is pending. This is true even if they would otherwise be authorized for disposition under a General Records Schedule or other NARA-approved records schedule.

[63 FR 29347, May 29, 1998, as amended at 68 FR 32975, June 3, 2003; 80 FR 39379, July 9, 2015]

§ 201.18 Denial of requests, appeals from denial.

(a) Written requests for inspection or copying of records shall be denied only by the Secretary or Acting Secretary, or, for records maintained by the Office of Inspector General, the Inspector General. A denial shall be in writing and shall provide information on the exemptions that justify withholding and the amount of information withheld. The denial also shall advise the person requesting of the right to appeal to the Commission.

(b) An appeal from a denial of a request must be received within ninety days of the date of the letter of denial and shall be made to the Commission and addressed to the Chairman, United States International Trade Commission, 500 E Street SW., Washington, DC 20436. Any such appeal shall be in writing, and shall indicate clearly in the appeal, and if the appeal is in paper form on the envelope, that it is a "Freedom of Information Act Appeal." An appeal may be made either in paper form, or electronically by contacting the Commission at *http://www.usitc.gov/foia.htm.*

(c) Except when expedited treatment is requested and granted, appeals will be decided in the order in which they are filed, but in any case within twenty days (excepting Saturdays, Sundays, and legal holidays) unless an extension, noticed in writing with the reasons therefor, has been provided to the person making the request. Notice of the decision on appeal and the reasons therefor will be made promptly after a decision. Requests for expedited treatment should conform with the requirements in § 201.17(c) of this part.

(d) The extensions of time mentioned in paragraph (c) of this section shall be made only for one or more of the following reasons:

(1) The need to search for and collect the requested records from field facilities or other establishments that are separate from the office processing the request;

(2) The need to search for, collect, and appropriately examine a voluminous amount of separate and distinct records which are requested in a single communication; or

(3) The need for consultation, which shall be conducted with all practicable speed, with another agency having a substantial interest in the determination of the request or among two or more components of the agency having a substantial subject-matter interest therein.

(e) The extensions of time mentioned in paragraph (c) of this section shall not exceed ten working days in the aggregate.

(f) A response to an appeal will advise the requester that the Commission's FOIA Public Liaison officer and the Office of Government Information Services both offer mediation services to resolve disputes between FOIA requesters and Federal agencies as a non-exclusive alternative to litigation. The requester may contact the Commission's FOIA Public Liaison officer by telephone (202–205–2595) or email (*foia.se.se@usitc.gov*) or the Office of Government Information Services at National Archives and Records Administration, 8601 Adelphi Road—OGIS, College Park, Maryland 20740–6001.

[40 FR 8328, Feb. 27, 1975, as amended at 54 FR 13678, Apr. 5, 1989; 60 FR 37336, July 20, 1995; 63 FR 29348, May 29, 1998; 68 FR 32975, June 3, 2003; 80 FR 39379, July 9, 2015; 81 FR 86576, Dec. 1, 2016]

§201.19 Notification regarding requests for confidential business information.

(a) *In general.* Business information provided to the Commission by a business submitter which the Commission has designated as "confidential business information" will not be disclosed pursuant to a Freedom of Information Act (FOIA) request except in accordance with this section.

(b) *Definitions.* The following definitions are to be used in reference to this section:

Confidential business information means commercial or financial information that has been designated as confidential business information by the Commission under §201.6 of this part.

Submitter means any person or entity who provides confidential business information, directly or indirectly, to the Commission. The term includes, but is not limited to, corporations, producers, importers, and state and federal governments, as well as others who have an administrative relationship with the Commission such as contractors, bidders and vendors.

(c) *Notice to submitters.* Except as provided for in paragraph (e) of this section, the Commission will, to the extent permitted by law, provide a submitter with prompt written notice of a FOIA request or administrative appeal encompassing its confidential business information whenever required under paragraph (d) of this section, in order to afford the submitter an opportunity to object to disclosure pursuant to paragraph (f) of this section. Such written notice will describe the nature of the confidential business information requested. The requester will also be notified that notice and opportunity to object to are being provided to a submitter.

(d) *When notice is required.* Notice will be given to a submitter in writing at submitter's last known address whenever:

(1) The information the subject of the FOIA request or appeal has been designated by the Commission as confidential business information; and

(2) The Commission has reason to believe that the information may not be protected from disclosure under FOIA Exemptions 3 or 4.

(e) *Exceptions to notice requirment.* The notice requirements of paragraph (c) of this section will not apply if:

(1) The Commission determines that the information should not be disclosed;

(2) The information lawfully has been published or has been officially made available to the public; or

(3) Disclosure of the information is required by law (other than 5 U.S.C. 552).

(f) *Opportunity to object to disclosure.* Through the notice described in paragraph (c) of this section, the Commission will afford a submitter an opportunity, within the period afforded to the Commission to make its decision in response to the FOIA request, to provide the Commission with a detailed written statement of any objection to disclosure. Such statement shall be filed by a deadline set by the Secretary, and it shall specify all grounds for withholding any of the information under any exemption of FOIA. In the case of FOIA Exemptions 3 or 4, it shall demonstrate why the information should continue to be considered confidential business information within the meaning of §201.6 of this part and should not be disclosed. The submitter's claim of continued confidentiality should be supported by a certification by an officer or authorized representative of the submitter. Information provided by a submitter pursuant to this paragraph may itself be subject to disclosure under FOIA.

(g) *Notice of intent to disclose.* The Commission will consider carefully a submitter's objections and specific grounds for nondisclosure prior to determining whether to disclose the information. Whenever the Commission decides to disclose such information over the objection of a submitter, the Commission will forward to the submitter a written notice which will include:

(1) A statement of the reasons for which the submitter's disclosure objections were not sustained;

(2) A description of the information to be disclosed; and

(3) A specified disclosure date.

Such notice of intent to disclose will be forwarded to the submitter a reasonable number of days prior to the specified disclosure date and the requester will be notified likewise.

(h) *Notice of FOIA lawsuit.* Whenever a requester brings suit seeking to compel disclosure of information that the Commission has designated as confidential business information, the Commission will promptly notify the submitter at its last known address. For the purpose of this paragraph, the Secretary may assume such address to be that given on the submission.

[54 FR 13678, Apr. 5, 1989, as amended at 68 FR 32975, June 3, 2003; 80 FR 39379, July 9, 2015]

§ 201.20 Fees.

(a) *In general.* Fees pursuant to 5 U.S.C. 552 shall be assessed according to the schedule contained in paragraph (b) of this section for services rendered by agency personnel in responding to and processing requests for records under this subpart. All fees so assessed shall be charged to the requester, except where the charging of fees is limited under paragraph (c) of this section or where a waiver or reduction of fees is granted under paragraph (d) of this section. The Secretary will collect all applicable fees. Requesters shall pay fees by check or money order made payable to the Treasury of the United States.

(b) *Charges.* In responding to requests under this subpart, the following fees shall be assessed, unless a waiver or reduction of fees has been granted pursuant to paragraph (d) of this section:

(1) *Search.* (i) No search fee shall be assessed with respect to requests by educational institutions, noncommercial scientific institutions, and representatives of the news media as defined in paragraphs (j) (6), (7), and (8) of this section, respectively. Search fees shall be assessed with respect to all other requests, subject to the limitations of paragraph (c) of this section. The secretary may assess fees for time spent searching even if agency personnel fail to locate any respective record or where records located are subsequently determined to be entirely exempt from disclosure.

(ii) For each quarter hour spent by agency personnel in salary grades GS–2 through GS–10 in searching for and retrieving a requested record, the fee shall be $4.00. When the time of agency personnel in salary grades GS–11 and above is required, the fee shall be $6.50 for each quarter hour of search and retrieval time spent by such personnel.

(iii) For computer searches of records, which may be undertaken through the use of existing programming, requester shall be charged the actual direct costs of conducting the search, although certain requesters (as defined in paragraph (c)(2) of this section) shall be entitled to the cost equivalent of two hours of manual search time without charge. These direct costs shall include the cost of operating a central processing unit for that portion of operating time that is directly attributable to searching for records responsive to a request, as well as the costs of operator/programmer salary apportionable to the search (at no more than $6.50 per quarter hour of time so spent).

(2) *Duplication.* Duplication fees shall be assessed with respect to all requesters, subject to the limitations of paragraph (c) of this section. For a paper photocopy of a record (no more than one copy of which need be supplied), the fee shall be $0.10 per page. For copies produced by computer, such as tapes or printouts, the Secretary shall charge the actual direct costs, including operator time, of producing the copy. For other methods of duplication, the Secretary shall charge the actual direct costs of duplicating a record.

(3) *Review.* (i) Review fees shall be assessed with respect to only those requesters who seek records for a commercial use, as defined in paragraph (j)(5) of this section. For each quarter hour spent by agency personnel in reviewing a requested record for possible disclosure, the fee shall be $6.50.

(ii) Review fees shall be assessed only for the initial record review, i.e., all of the review undertaken when a component analyzes the applicability of a particular exemption to a particular record or record portion at the initial request level. No charge shall be assessed for review at the administrative appeal level of an exemption already applied. However, records or record portions withheld pursuant to an exemption that is subsequently determined not to apply may be reviewed again to determine the applicability of other exemptions not previously considered. The costs of such a subsequent review are properly assessable, particularly where that review is made necessary by a change of circumstances.

(c) *Limitations on charging fees.* (1) No search or review fee shall be charged for a quarter-hour period unless more than half of that period is required for search or review.

(2) Except for requesters seeking records for a commercial use (as defined in paragraph (j)(5) of this section), the Secretary shall provide without charge—

(i) The first 100 pages of duplication (or its cost equivalent), and

(ii) The first two hours of search (or its cost equivalent).

(3) Whenever a total fee calculated under paragraph (b) of this section is $25.00 or less, no fee shall be charged.

(4) The provisions of paragraphs (c)(2) and (3) of this section work together. For requesters other than those seeking records for a commercial use, no fee shall be charged unless the cost of search is in excess of two hours plus the cost of duplication in excess of 100 pages exceeds $25.00.

(5) The Commission will not charge fees if it fails to comply with any time limit under the FOIA or these regulations, and if it has not timely notified the requester, in writing, that an unusual circumstance exists. If an unusual circumstance exists, and timely written notice is given to the requester, the Commission will have an additional 10 working days to respond to the request before fees are automatically waived under this paragraph.

(6) If the Commission determines that unusual circumstances apply and that more than 5,000 pages are necessary to respond to a request, it may charge fees if it has provided a timely written notice to the requester and discusses with the requester via mail, Email, or telephone how the requester could effectively limit the scope of the request (or make at least three good faith attempts to do so).

(7) If a court has determined that exceptional circumstances exist, a failure to comply with time limits imposed by these regulations or FOIA shall be excused for the length of time provided by court order.

(d) *Waiver or reduction of fees.* (1) Records responsive to a request under 5 U.S.C. 552 shall be furnished without charge or at a charge reduced below that established under paragraph (b) of this section where the Secretary determines, based upon information provided by a requester in support of a fee waiver request or otherwise made known to the Secretary that disclosure of the requested information is in the public interest, because it is likely to contribute significantly to public understanding of the operations or activities of the Government and is not primarily in the commercial interest of the requester. Requests for a waiver or reduction of fees shall be considered on a case-by-case basis.

(2) In order to determine whether the first fee waiver requirement is met— i.e., that disclosure of the requested information is in the public interest because it is likely to contribute significantly to public understanding of the operations or activities of the government—the Secretary shall consider the following four factors in sequence:

(i) *The subject of the request: Whether the subject of the requested records concerns "the operations or activities of the government."* The subject matter of the requested records, in the context of the request, must specifically concern identifiable operations or activities of the federal government—with a connection that is direct and clear, not remote or attenuated. Furthermore, the records must be sought for their informative value with respect to those government operations or activities; a request for access to records for their intrinsic informational content alone will not satisfy this threshold consideration.

(ii) *The informative value of the information to be disclosed: Whether the disclosure is "likely to contribute" to an understanding of government operations or activities.* The disclosable portions of the requested records must be meaningfully informative on specific government operations or activities in order to hold potential for contributing to increased public understanding of those operations and activities. The disclosure of information that already is in the public domain, in either a duplicative or a substantially identical form, would not be likely to contribute to such understanding, as nothing new would be added to the public record.

(iii) *The contribution of an understanding of the subject by the public likely to result from disclosure: Whether disclosure of the requested information will contribute to "public understanding."* The disclosure must contribute to the understanding of the public at large, as opposed to the individual understanding of the requester or a narrow segment of interested persons. A requester's identity and qualifications—e.g., expertise in the subject area and ability and intention to effectively convey information to the general public—shall be considered. It will be presumed that a representative of the news media (as defined in paragraph (j)(8) of this section) who has access to the means of public dissemination readily will be able to satisfy this consideration. Requests from libraries or other record repositories (or requesters who intend merely to disseminate information to such institutions) shall be analyzed, like those of other requesters, to identify a particular person who represents that he actually will use the requested information in scholarly or other analytic work and then disseminate it to the general public.

(iv) *The significance of the contribution to public understanding: Whether the disclosure is likely to contribute "significantly" to public understanding of government operations or activities.* The public's understanding of the subject matter in question, as compared to the level of public understanding existing prior to the disclosure, must be likely to be enhanced by the disclosure to a significant extent. The Secretary shall not make separate judgments as to whether information, even though it in fact would contribute significantly to public understanding of the operations or activities of the government, is "important" enough to be made public.

(3) In order to determine whether the second fee waiver requirement is met—i.e., that disclosure of the requested information is not primarily in the commercial interest of the requester—the Secretary shall consider the following two factors in sequence:

(i) *The existence and magnitude of a commercial interest: Whether the requester has a commercial interest that would be furthered by the requested disclosure.* The Secretary shall consider all commercial interests of the requester (with reference to the definition of *commercial use* in paragraph (j)(5) of this section), or any person on whose behalf the requester may be acting, but shall consider only those interests which would be furthered by the requested disclosure. In assessing the magnitude of identified commercial interests, consideration shall be given to the role that such FOIA-disclosed information plays with respect to those commercial interests, as well as to the extent to which FOIA disclosures serve those interests overall. Requesters shall be given a reasonable opportunity in the administrative process to provide information bearing upon this consideration.

(ii) *The primary interest in disclosure: Whether the magnitude of the identified commercial interest of the requester is sufficiently large, in comparison with the public interest in disclosure, that disclosure is "primarily in the commercial interest of the requester."* A fee waiver or reduction is warranted only where, once the "public interest" standard set out in paragraph (d)(2) of this section is satisfied, that public interest can fairly be regarded as greater in magnitude than that of the requester's commercial interest in disclosure. The Secretary shall ordinarily presume that, where a news media requester has satisfied the "public interest" standard, that will be the interest primarily served by disclosure to that requester. Disclosure to data brokers or others who compile and market government information for direct economic return shall not be presumed to primarily serve the "public interest."

(4) Where only a portion of the requested records satisfies both of the requirements for a waiver or reduction of fees under this paragraph, a waiver or reduction shall be granted only as to that portion.

(5) Requests for the waiver or reduction of fees shall address each of the factors listed in paragraphs (d) (2) and (3) of this section, as they apply to each record request.

(e) *Notice of anticipated fees in excess of $25.00.* Where the Secretary determines or estimates that the fees to be assessed under this section may amount to more than $25.00, he shall notify the requester as soon as practicable of the actual or estimated amount of the fees, unless the requester has indicated in advance his willingness to pay fees as high as those anticipated. (If only a portion of the fee can be estimated readily, the Secretary shall advise the requester that the estimated fee may be only a portion of the total fee.) In cases where a requester has been notified that actual or estimated fees may amount to more than $25.00, the request will be deemed not to have been received until the requester has agreed to pay the anticipated total fee. A notice of the requester pursuant to this paragraph shall offer him the opportunity to confer with agency personnel in order to reformulate his request to meet his needs at a lower cost.

(f) *Aggregating requests.* Where the Secretary reasonably believes that a requester or a group of requesters acting in concert is attempting to divide a request into a series of requests for the purpose of evading the assessment of fees, the Secretary may aggregate any such requests and charge accordingly. The Secretary may presume that multiple requests of such type made within a 30-day period have been made in order to evade fees. Where requests are separated by a longer period, the Secretary shall aggregate them only where there exists a reasonable basis for determining that said aggregation is warranted, e.g., where the requests involve clearly related matters. Multiple requests involving unrelated matters shall not be aggregated

(g) *Advance payments.* (1) Where the Secretary estimates that a total fee to be assessed under this section is likely to exceed $250.00, the Secretary may require the requester to make an advance payment of an amount up to the entire estimated fee before beginning to process the request, except where the Sec-

retary receives a satisfactory assurance of full payment from a requester with a history of prompt payment.

(2) Where a requester has previously failed to pay a records access fee within 30 days of the date of billing, the Secretary may require the requester to pay the full amount owed, plus any applicable interest (as provided for in paragraph (h) of this section), and to make an advance payment of the full amount of any estimated fee before he begins to process a new request or continues to process a pending request from that requester.

(3) For requests other than those described in paragraphs (g) (1) and (2) of this section, the Secretary shall not require the requester to make an advance payment, i.e., a payment made before work is commenced or continued on a request. Payment owed on work already completed is not an advance payment.

(4) Where the Secretary acts under paragraph (g) (1) or (2) of this section, the administrative time limits described in subsection (a)(6) of the FOIA for the processing of an initial request or an appeal, plus permissible extensions of these time limits, shall be deemed not to begin to run until the Secretary has received payment of the assessed fee.

(h) *Charging interest.* The Secretary may assess interest charges on an unpaid bill starting on the 31st day following the day on which the bill was sent to the requester. Once a fee payment has been received by the Secretary, even if not processed, the accrual of interest shall be stayed. Interest charges shall be assessed at the rate prescribed in section 3717 of title 31 U.S.C. and shall accrue from the date of the billing. The Secretary shall follow the provisions of the Debt Collection Act of 1982, Pub. L. 97–265 (Oct. 25, 1982), and its implementing procedures, including the use of consumer reporting agencies, collection agencies, and offset.

(i) *Other statutes specifically providing for fees.* (1) The fee schedule of this section does not apply with respect to the charging of fees under a statute specifically providing for setting the level of fees for particular types of records—

i.e., any statute that specifically requires a government entity such as the Government Printing Office or the National Technical Information Service, to set and collect fees for particular types of records—in order to:

(i) Serve both the general public and private sector organizations by conveniently making available government information;

(ii) Ensure that groups and individuals pay the cost of publications and other services that are for their special use so that these costs are not borne by the general taxpaying public;

(iii) Operate an information-dissemination activity on a self-sustaining basis to the maximum extent possible; or

(iv) Return revenue to the Treasury for defraying, wholly or in part, appropriate funds used to pay the costs of disseminating government information.

(2) Where records responsive to requests are maintained for distribution by agencies operating statutorily based fee schedule programs, the Secretary shall inform requesters of the steps necessary to obtain records from those sources.

(j) *Definitions.* For the purpose of this section:

(1) The term *direct costs* means those expenditures which the agency actually incurs in searching for and duplicating (and, in the case of commercial use requesters, reviewing) records to respond to a FOIA request. Direct costs include, for example the salary of the employee performing the work (the basic rate of pay for the employee plus 16 percent of that rate to cover benefits) and the cost of operating duplicating machinery. Not included in direct costs are overhead expenses such as costs of space and heating or lighting of the facility in which the records are stored.

(2) The term *search* includes all time spent looking for material that is responsive to a request, including page-by-page or line-by-line identification of material within documents. The Secretary shall ensure, however, that searches are undertaken in the most efficient and least expensive manner reasonably possible; thus, for example, the Secretary shall not engage in line-by-line search where merely duplicating an entire document would be quicker and less expensive.

(3) The term *duplication* refers to the process of making a copy of a record necessary to respond to a FOIA request. Such copies can take the form of paper copy, microform, audio-visual materials, or machine-readable documentation (e.g., magnetic tape or disk), among others. The copy provided shall be in a form that is reasonably usable by requesters.

(4) The term *review* refers to the process of examining a record located in response to a request in order to determine whether any portion of it is permitted to be withheld. It also includes processing any record for disclosure, e.g., doing all that is necessary to excise it and otherwise prepare it for release, although review costs shall be recoverable even where there ultimately is no disclosure of a record. Review time does not include time spent resolving general legal or policy issues regarding the application of exemptions.

(5) The term *commercial use* in the context of a request refers to a request from or on behalf of one who seeks information for a use or purpose that furthers the commercial, trade, or profit interests of the requester or the person on whose behalf the request is made, which can include furthering those interests through litigation. The Secretary shall determine, as well as reasonably possible, the use to which a requester will put the records requested. Where the circumstances of a request suggest that the requester will put the records sought to a commercial use, either because of the nature of the request itself or because the Secretary otherwise has reasonable cause to doubt a requester's stated use, the Secretary shall provide the requester a reasonable opportunity to submit further clarification.

(6) The term *educational institution* refers to a preschool, a public or private elementary or secondary school, an institution of undergraduate higher education, an institution of graduate higher education, an institution of professional education, and an institution of vocational education, which operates a

program or programs of scholarly research. To be eligible for inclusion in this category, a requester must show that the request is being made as authorized by and under the auspices of a qualifying institution and that the records are not sought for a commercial use but are sought in furtherance of scholarly research.

(7) The term *noncommercial scientific institution* refers to an institution that is not operated on a "commercial" basis as that term is referenced in paragraph (j)(5) of this section, and which is operated solely for the purpose of conducting scientific research the results of which are not intended to promote any particular product or industry. To be eligible for inclusion in this category, a requester must show that the request is being made as authorized by and under the auspices of a qualifying institution and that the records are not sought for a commercial use but are sought in furtherance of scientific research.

(8) The term *representative of the news media* refers to any person or entity that gathers information of potential interest to a segment of the public, uses its editorial skills to turn the raw materials into a distinct work, and distributes that work to an audience. The term 'news' means information that is about current events or that would be of current interest to the public. Examples of news-media entities are television or radio stations broadcasting to the public at large and publishers of periodicals (but only if such entities qualify as disseminators of 'news') who make their products available for purchase by or subscription by or free distribution to the general public. These examples are not all-inclusive. Moreover, as methods of news delivery evolve (for example, the adoption of the electronic dissemination of newspapers through telecommunications services), such alternative media shall be considered to be news-media entities. A freelance journalist shall be regarded as working for a news-media entity if the journalist can demonstrate a solid basis for expecting publication through that entity, whether or not the journalist is actually employed by the entity. A publication contract would present a solid basis for such an expectation; the Government may also consider the past publication record of the requester in making such a determination.

(9) The term *requester category* means one of the three categories that requesters are placed in for the purpose of determining whether a requester will be charged fees for search, review and duplication, including commercial requesters; non-commercial scientific or educational institutions or news media requesters, and all other requesters.

(10) The term *fee waiver* means the waiver or reduction of processing fees if a requester can demonstrate that certain statutory standards are satisfied including that the information is in the public interest and is not requested for a commercial interest.

(k) *Charges for other services and materials.* Apart from the other provisions of this section, where the Secretary elects, as a matter of administrative discretion, to comply with a request for a special service or materials, such as certifying that records are true copies or sending them other than by ordinary mail, the actual direct costs of providing the service or materials shall be charged.

[54 FR 13673, Apr. 5, 1989, as amended at 63 FR 29348, May 29, 1998; 80 FR 39379, July 9, 2015; 81 FR 86577, Dec. 1, 2016]

§201.21 Availability of specific records.

(a) *Records available.* The following information, on request to the Secretary of the Commission, is available for public inspection and copying: (1) final opinions, including concurring and dissenting opinions, as well as orders, made in the adjudication of cases; (2) those statements of policy and interpretations which have been adopted by the agency; and (3) administrative staff manuals and instructions to staff that affect a member of the public. Available information includes, but is not limited to: (i) Applications, petitions, and other formal documents filed with the Commission, (ii) notices to the public concerning Commission matters, (iii) transcripts of testimony taken and exhibits submitted at hearings, (iv) reports to the President, to either or both Houses of Congress, or to

Committees of Congress, release of which has been authorized by the President or the legislative body concerned, (v) reports and other documents issued for general distribution. Much of the information described above also is available on the Commission's World Wide Web site. The Commission's home page is at *http:// www.usitc.gov*. The Web site also includes information subject to repeated Freedom of Information Act requests. Persons accessing the Web site can find instructions on how to locate Commission information by following the "Freedom of Information Act" link on the home page.

(b) *Records not available.* Information specifically exempted from disclosure by 5 U.S.C. 552(b), including reports to the President, to either or both Houses of Congress, or to Committees of Congress, the release of which has not been authorized by the President or the legislative body concerned, and confidential business data as defined in 18 U.S.C. 1905 and 19 CFR 201.06 are not available to the public.

(c) *Information requested in cases or matters to which the Commission is not a party.* (1) The procedure specified in this section will apply to all demands directed to Commission employees for the production of documents or for testimony that relates in any way to the employees' official duties. These procedures will also apply to demands directed to former employees if the demands seek nonpublic materials or information acquired during Commission employment. The provisions of paragraph (c)(2) of this section will also apply to demands directed to the agency. For purposes of this section, the term *demand* means any request, order or subpoena for testimony or production of documents; the term *subpoena* means any compulsory process in a case or matter to which the Commission is not a party; the term *nonpublic* includes any material or information which, under § 201.21(b), is exempt from availability for public inspection and copying; the term *employee* means any current or former officer or employee of the Commission; the term *documents* means all records, papers or official files, including without limitation, official letters, telegrams, memoranda,

reports, studies, calendar and diary entries, graphs, notes, charts, tabulations, data analysis, statistical or information accumulations, records of meetings and conversations, film impressions, magnetic tapes, and sound or mechanical reproductions; the term *case or matter* means any civil proceeding before a court of law, administrative board, hearing officer, or other body conducting a legal or administrative proceeding in which the Commission is not a named party.

(2) Prior to or simultaneously with a demand to a Commission employee for the production of documents or for testimony concerning matters relating to official duties, the party seeking such production or testimony must serve upon the General Counsel of the Commission an affidavit, or if that is not feasible, then a statement which sets forth the title of the case, the forum, the party's interest in the case, the reasons for the request, and a showing that the desired testimony or documents are not reasonably available from any other source. Where testimony is sought, the party must also provide a summary of the testimony desired, the intended use of the testimony, and show that Commission records could not be provided and used instead of the requested testimony. A subpoena for testimony from a Commission employee concerning official matters or for the production of documents shall be served in accordance with Rule 45 of the Federal Rules of Civil Procedure and a copy of the subpoena shall be sent to the General Counsel.

(3) Any employee or former employee who is served with a subpoena or other demand shall promptly advise the General Counsel of the service of the subpoena or other demand, the nature of the documents or information sought, and all relevant facts and circumstances.

(4) Absent written authorization from the Chairman of the Commission ("Chairman"), the employee shall respectfully decline to produce the requested documents, to testify, or to otherwise disclose requested information. If a court rules that the demand must be complied with despite the absence of such written authorization,

the employee upon whom the demand is made shall respectfully refuse to comply based upon these regulations and *Touhy* v. *Ragan*, 340 U.S. 462 (1951).

(5) The Chairman will consider and act upon subpoenas under this section with due regard for statutory restrictions, the Commission's rules and the public interest, taking into account such factors as the need to conserve employees' time for conducting official business, the need to prevent the expenditure of the United States government's time and money for private purposes, the need to maintain impartiality between private litigants in cases where no substantial governmental interest is involved, and the relevant legal standards for determining whether justification exists for the disclosure of nonpublic information and documents. If the Chairman determines that the subpoenaed documents or information are protected by a privilege or that the Commission has a duty in law or equity to protect such documents or information from disclosure, the General Counsel shall move the court to quash the subpoena or for other appropriate action.

(6) The General Counsel may consult or negotiate with counsel or the party seeking testimony or documents to refine and limit the demand so that compliance is less burdensome, or obtain information necessary to make the determination described in paragraph (c)(5) of this section. Failure of the counsel or party seeking the testimony or documents to cooperate in good faith to enable the General Counsel to make an informed recommendation to the Chairman under paragraph (c)(5) of this section may serve as the basis for a determination not to comply with the demand.

(7) Permission to testify will, in all cases, be limited to the information set forth in the affidavit as described in paragraph (c)(2) of this section, or to such portions thereof as the Chairman deems proper.

(8) If the Chairman authorizes the testimony of an employee, then the General Counsel shall arrange for the taking of the testimony by methods that are least disruptive of the official duties of the employee. Testimony may, for example, be provided by affidavits, answers to interrogatories, written depositions, or depositions transcribed, recorded, or preserved by any other means allowable by law. Costs of providing testimony, including transcripts, will be borne by the party requesting the testimony. Such costs shall also include reimbursing the Commission for the usual and ordinary expenses attendant upon the employee's absence from his or her official duties in connection with the case or matter, including the employee's salary and applicable overhead charges and any necessary travel expenses.

(9) The Secretary in consultation with the General Counsel is further authorized to charge reasonable fees to parties demanding documents or information. Such fees, calculated to reimburse the government for the expense of responding to such demand, may include the costs of time expended by Commission employees to process and respond to the demand, attorney time for reviewing the demand and for related legal work in connection with the demand, and expenses generated by equipment used to search for, produce and copy the responsive information. In general, such fees will be assessed at the rates and in the manner specified in §201.20 of this part.

(10) This section does not affect the rights and procedures governing the public access to official documents pursuant to the Freedom of Information Act or the Privacy Act.

(11) This section is intended to provide instructions to Commission employees and does not create any right or benefit, substantive or procedural, enforceable by any party against the Commission.

[40 FR 8328, Feb. 27, 1975, as amended at 54 FR 13676, Apr. 5, 1989; 68 FR 32975, June 3, 2003]

Subpart D—Safeguarding Individual Privacy Pursuant to 5 U.S.C. 552a

SOURCE: 63 FR 29348, May 29, 1998, unless otherwise noted.

§ 201.22 Purpose and scope.

This subpart contains the rules that the Commission follows under the Privacy Act of 1974, 5 U.S.C. 552a. The rules in this subpart apply to all records in systems of records maintained by the Commission that are retrieved by an individual's name or other personal identifier. They describe the procedures by which individuals may request access to records about themselves, request amendment or correction of those records, and request an accounting of disclosures of those records by the Commission.

§ 201.23 Definitions.

For the purpose of these regulations:

(a) The term *individual* means a citizen of the United States or an alien lawfully admitted for permanent residence;

(b) The term *maintain* includes maintain, collect, use, or disseminate;

(c) The term *record* means any item, collection, or grouping of information about an individual that is maintained by the Commission, including, but not limited to, his or her education, financial transactions, medical history, and criminal or employment history and that contains his or her name, or the identifying number, symbol, or other identifying particular assigned to the individual;

(d) The term *system of records* means a group of any records under the control of the Commission from which information is retrieved by the name of the individual or by some identifying particular assigned to the individual;

(e) The term *Privacy Act Officer* refers to the Secretary, United States International Trade Commission, 500 E Street SW., Washington, DC 20436, or his or her designee.

[63 FR 29348, May 29, 1998, as amended at 80 FR 39380, July 9, 2015]

§ 201.24 Procedures for requests pertaining to individual records in a records system.

(a) A request by an individual to gain access to his or her record(s) or to any information pertaining to him or her which is contained in a system of records maintained by the Commission shall be addressed to the Privacy Act Officer, United States International Trade Commission, 500 E Street SW., Washington, DC 20436, and shall indicate clearly both on the envelope and in the letter that it is a Privacy Act request.

(b) In order to facilitate location of requested records, whenever possible, the request of the individual shall name the system(s) of records maintained by the Commission which he or she believes contain records pertaining to him or her, shall reasonably describe the requested records, and identify the time period in which the records were compiled.

(c) The Privacy Act Officer shall acknowledge receipt of a request within ten days (excluding Saturdays, Sundays, and legal public holidays), and wherever practicable, indicate whether or not access can be granted. If access is not to be granted, the requestor shall be notified of the reason in writing.

(d) The Privacy Act Officer, or, the Inspector General, if such records are maintained by the Inspector General, shall ascertain whether the systems of records maintained by the Commission contain records pertaining to the individual, and whether access will be granted. Thereupon the Privacy Act Officer shall:

(1) Notify the individual whether or not the requested record is contained in any system of records maintained by the Commission; and

(2) Notify the individual of the procedures as prescribed in Secs. 201.25 and 201.26 of this part by which the individual may gain access to those records maintained by the Commission which pertain to him or her. Access to the records will be provided within 30 days (excluding Saturdays, Sundays, and legal public holidays).

§ 201.25 Times, places, and requirements for identification of individuals making requests.

(a) If an individual wishes to examine his or her records in person, it shall be the responsibility of the individual requester to arrange an appointment with the Privacy Act Officer for the purpose of inspecting individual records. The time of inspection shall be during the regular office hours of the

40

Commission, 8:45 a.m. to 5:15 p.m., Monday through Friday. The time arranged should be mutually convenient to the requester and to the Commission.

(b) The place where an individual may gain access to records maintained by the Commission which pertain to him or her shall be at the United States International Trade Commission Building, 500 E Street SW., Washington, DC 20436. The Privacy Act Officer shall inform the individual requester of the specific room wherein inspection will take place.

(c) An individual may also request the Privacy Act Officer to provide the individual with a copy of his or her records by certified mail.

(d) An individual who requests to gain access to those records maintained by the Commission which pertain to him or her shall not be granted access to those records without first presenting adequate identification to the Privacy Act Officer. Adequate identification may include, but is not limited to, a government identification card, a driver's license, Medicare card, a birth certificate, or a passport. If requesting records by mail, an individual must provide full name, current address, and date and place of birth. The request must be signed and either notarized or submitted under 28 U.S.C. 1746, which permits statements to be made under penalty of perjury as a substitute for notarization. In order to help the identification and location of requested records, a requestor may also, at his or her option, include the individual's social security number.

§ 201.26 Disclosure of requested information to individuals.

(a) Once the Privacy Act Officer has made a determination to grant a request for access to individual records, in whole or in part, the Privacy Act Officer shall inform the requesting individual in writing and permit the individual to review the pertinent records and to have a copy made of all or any portion of them. Where redactions due to exemptions pursuant to § 201.32 would render such records or portions thereof incomprehensible, the Privacy Act Officer shall furnish an abstract in addition to an actual copy.

(b) An individual has the right to have a person of his or her own choosing accompany him or her to review his or her records. The Privacy Act Officer shall permit a person of the individual requester's choosing to accompany the individual during inspection.

(c) When the individual requests the Privacy Act Officer to permit a person of the individual's choosing to accompany him or her during the inspection of his or her records, the Privacy Act Officer shall require the individual requester to furnish a written statement authorizing discussion of the records in the accompanying person's presence.

(d) The Privacy Act Officer shall take all necessary steps to insure that individual privacy is protected while the individual requester is inspecting his or her records or while those records are being discussed. Only the Privacy Act Officer shall accompany the individual as representative of the Commission during the inspection of the individual's records. The Privacy Act Officer shall be authorized to discuss pertinent records with the individual.

§ 201.27 Special procedures: Medical records.

(a) While an individual has an unqualified right of access to the records in systems of records maintained by the Commission which pertain to him or her, medical and psychological records merit special treatment because of the possibility that disclosure will have an adverse physical or psychological effect upon the requesting individual. Accordingly, in those instances where an individual is requesting the medical and/or psychological records which pertain to him or her, he or she shall, in his or her Privacy Act request to the Privacy Act Officer as called for in § 201.24(a) of this part, specify a physician to whom the medical and/or psychological records may be released.

(b) It shall be the responsibility of the individual requesting medical or psychological records to specify a physician to whom the requested records may be released. If an individual refuses to name a physician and insists on inspecting his or her medical or psychological records in the absence of a doctor's discussion and advice, the individual shall so state in his or her Privacy Act request to the Privacy Act Officer as called for in § 201.24(a) of this part and the Privacy Act Officer shall provide access to or transmit such records directly to the individual.

§ 201.28 Requests for correction or amendment of records.

(a) If, upon viewing his or her records, an individual disagrees with a portion thereof or feels sections thereof to be erroneous, the individual may request amendment[s] of the records pertaining to him or her. The individual should request such an amendment in writing and should identify each particular record in question, the system[s] of records wherein the records are located, specify the amendment requested, and specify the reasons why the records are not correct, relevant timely or complete. The individual may submit any documentation that would be helpful. The request for amendment of records shall be addressed to the Privacy Act Officer, United States International Trade Commission, 500 E Street SW., Washington, DC 20436, and shall clearly indicate both on the envelope and in the letter that it is a Privacy Act request for amendment of records.

(b) Not later than 10 days (excluding Saturdays, Sundays and legal public holidays) after the date of receipt of a Privacy Act request for amendment of records, the Privacy Act Officer shall acknowledge such receipt in writing. Such a request for amendment will be granted or denied by the Privacy Act Officer or, for records maintained by the Inspector General. If the request is granted, the Privacy Act Officer, or the Inspector General for records maintained by the Inspector General, shall promptly make any correction of any portion of the record which the individual believes is not accurate, relevant, timely, or complete. If, however, the request is denied, the Privacy Act Officer shall inform the individual of the refusal to amend the record in accordance with the individual's request and give the reason(s) for the refusal. In cases where the Privacy Act Officer or the Inspector General has refused to amend in accordance with an individ-

ual's request, he or she also shall advise the individual of the procedures under § 201.30 of this part for the individual to request a review of that refusal by the full Commission or by an officer designated by the Commission.

§ 201.29 Commission disclosure of individual records, accounting of record disclosures, and requests for accounting of record disclosures.

(a) It is the policy of the Commission not to disclose, except as permitted under 5 U.S.C. 552a(b), any record which is contained in any system of records maintained by the Commission to any person, or to another agency, except pursuant to a written request by, or with the prior written consent of, the individual to whom the record pertains.

(b) Except for disclosures either to officers and employees of the Commission, or to contractor employees who, in the Inspector General's or the Privacy Act Officer's judgment, as appropriate, are acting as federal employees, who have a need for the record in the performance of their duties, and any disclosure required by 5 U.S.C. 552, the Privacy Act Officer shall keep an accurate accounting of:

(1) The date, nature, and purpose of each disclosure of a record to any person or to another agency under paragraph (a) of this section; and

(2) The name or address of the person or agency to whom the disclosure is made.

(c) The Privacy Act Officer shall retain the accounting required by paragraph (b) of this section for at least five years or the life of the record, whichever is longer, after such disclosure.

(d) Except for disclosures made to other agencies for civil or criminal law enforcement purposes pursuant to 5 U.S.C. 552a(b)(7), the Privacy Act Officer shall make any accounting made under paragraph (b) of this section available to the individual named in the record at the individual's request.

(e) An individual requesting an accounting of disclosure of his or her records should make the request in writing to the Privacy Act Officer, United States International Trade

Commission, 500 E Street SW., Washington, DC 20436. The request should identify each particular record in question and, whenever possible, the system[s] of records wherein the requested records are located, and clearly indicate both on the envelope and in the letter that it is a Privacy Act request for an accounting of disclosure of records.

(f) Where the Commission has provided any person or other agency with an individual record and such accounting as required by paragraph (b) of this section has been made, the Privacy Act Officer shall inform all such persons or other agencies of any correction, amendment, or notation of dispute concerning said record.

§201.30 **Commission review of requests for access to records, for correction or amendment to records, and for accounting of record disclosures.**

(a) The individual who disagrees with the refusal of the Privacy Act Officer or the Inspector General for access to a record, to amend a record, or to obtain an accounting of any record disclosure, may request a review of such refusal by the Commission within 60 days of receipt of the denial of his or her request. A request for review of such a refusal should be addressed to the Chairman, United States International Trade Commission, 500 E Street, SW., Washington, DC 20436, and shall clearly indicate both on the envelope and in the letter that it is a Privacy Act review request.

(b) Not later than 30 days (excluding Saturdays, Sundays, and legal public holidays) from the date on which the Commission receives a request for review of the Privacy Act Officer's or the Inspector General's refusal to grant access to a record, to amend a record, or to provide an accounting of a record disclosure, the Commission shall complete such a review and make a final determination thereof unless, for good cause shown, the Commission extends the 30-day period.

(c) After the individual's request has been reviewed by the Commission, if the Commission agrees with the Privacy Act Officer's or the Inspector General's refusal to grant access to a record, to amend a record, or to provide an accounting of a record disclosure, in accordance with the individual's request, the Commission shall:

(1) Notify the individual in writing of the Commission's decision;

(2) For requests to amend or correct records, advise the individual that he or she has the right to file a concise statement of disagreement with the Commission which sets forth his or her reasons for disagreement with the refusal of the Commission to grant the individual's request; and

(3) Notify the individual of his or her legal right, if any, to judicial review of the Commission's final determination.

(d) In any disclosure, containing information about which the individual has filed a statement of disagreement regarding an amendment of an individual's record, the Privacy Act Officer, or, for records maintained by the Inspector General, the Inspector General, shall clearly note any portion of the record which is disputed and shall provide copies of the statement and, if the Commission deems it appropriate, copies of a concise statement of the reasons of the Commission for not making the amendments requested, to persons or other agencies to whom the disputed record has been disclosed.

§201.31 **Fees and employee conduct.**

(a) The Commission shall not charge any fee for the cost of searching for and reviewing an individual's records.

(b) Reproduction, duplication or copying of records by the Commission shall be at the rate of $0.10 per page. There shall be no charge, however, when the total amount does not exceed $25.00.

(c) The Privacy Act Officer shall establish rules of conduct for persons involved in the design, development, operation, or maintenance of any system of records, or in maintaining any record, and periodically instruct each such person with respect to such rules and the requirements of the Privacy Act including the penalties for noncompliance.

[63 FR 29348, May 29, 1998, as amended at 68 FR 32975, June 3, 2003]

§ 201.32 Specific exemptions.

(a) Pursuant to 5 U.S.C. 552a(k)(1), (5) and (6), records contained in the system entitled "Personnel Security Investigative Files" have been exempted from subsections (c)(3), (d), (e)(1), (e)(4)(G) through (I) and (f) of the Privacy Act. Pursuant to section 552a(k)(1) of the Privacy Act, the Commission exempts records that contain properly classified information that pertains to national defense or foreign policy and is obtained from other systems of records or another Federal agency. Application of exemption (k)(1) may be necessary to preclude the data subject's access to and amendment of such classified information under 5 U.S.C. 552a(d). All information about individuals in these records that meets the criteria stated in 5 U.S.C. 552a(k)(5) is also exempted because this system contains investigatory material compiled solely for determining suitability, eligibility, and qualifications for Federal civilian employment, Federal contracts or access to classified information. To the extent that the disclosure of such material would reveal the identity of a source who furnished information to the Government under an express promise that the identity of the source would be held in confidence, or, prior to September 27, 1975, under an implied promise that the identity of the source would be held in confidence, the application of exemption (k)(5) will be required to honor such a promise should an individual request access to the accounting of disclosure, or access to or amendment of the record, that would reveal the identity of a confidential source. All information in these records that meets the criteria stated in 5 U.S.C. 552a(k)(6) is also exempt because portions of a case file record may relate to testing and examining material used solely to determine individual qualifications for appointment or promotion in the Federal service. Access to or amendment of this information by the data subject would compromise the objectivity and fairness of the testing or examining process.

(b) Pursuant to 5 U.S.C. 552a(k)(1) and (k)(2), records contained in the system entitled "Freedom of Information Act and Privacy Act Records" have

been exempted from subsections (c)(3), (d), (e)(1), (e)(4)(G) through (I) and (f) of the Privacy Act. Pursuant to section 552a(k)(1) of the Privacy Act, the Commission exempts records that contain properly classified information pertaining to national defense or foreign policy. Application of exemption (k)(1) may be necessary to preclude individuals' access to or amendment of such classified information under the Privacy Act. Pursuant to section 552a(k)(2) of the Privacy Act, and in order to protect the effectiveness of Inspector General investigations by preventing individuals who may be the subject of an investigation from obtaining access to the records and thus obtaining the opportunity to conceal or destroy evidence or to intimidate witnesses, the Commission exempts records insofar as they include investigatory material compiled for law enforcement purposes. However, if any individual is denied any right, privilege, or benefit to which he is otherwise entitled under Federal law due to the maintenance of this material, such material shall be provided to such individual except to the extent that the disclosure of such material would reveal the identity of a source who furnished information to the Government under an express promise that the identity of the source would be held in confidence.

[63 FR 29348, May 29, 1998, as amended at 82 FR 60865, Dec. 26, 2017]

Subpart E—Opening Commission Meetings to Public Observation Pursuant to 5 U.S.C. 552b

AUTHORITY: 5 U.S.C. 552b; 19 U.S.C. 1335.

SOURCE: 42 FR 11243, Feb. 28, 1977, unless otherwise noted.

§ 201.33 Purpose and scope.

(a) Consistent with the principle that the public is entitled to the fullest practicable information regarding the decisionmaking processes of the Federal Government, it is the purpose of this subpart to open the meetings of the United States International Trade Commission to public observation while protecting the rights of individuals and the ability of the Commission to carry out its statutory functions and responsibilities. These regulations are promulgated pursuant to the directive of section (g) of the Government in the Sunshine Act (5 U.S.C. 552b(g)), and specifically implement sections (b) through (f) of said act (5 U.S.C. 552(b) through (f)).

(b) Public access to documents being considered at Commission meetings may be obtained by access to the public files of the Commission or, where documents are not in said public files, shall be obtained in the manner set forth in subpart C of this part (§§ 201.17 through 201.21).

(c) Unless otherwise provided by the public notices as described in § 201.35 of this subpart, public observation of Commission meetings does not encompass public participation in the deliberations at such meetings.

§ 201.34 **Definitions.**

For the purpose of this subpart:

(a)(1) Except as hereinafter provided, the term *meeting* means the deliberations of at least the number of individual Commissioners required to take action on behalf of the Commission where such deliberations determine or result in the joint conduct or disposition of official Commission business.

(2) The consideration by individual Commissioners of business which is circulated sequentially in writing (circulation by "action jacket") is not considered a meeting under paragraph (a)(1) of this section because circulation by action jacket does not determine or result in the joint conduct or disposition of Commission business until ratification thereof by formal vote of the Commissioners in a meeting as defined by paragraph (a)(1) of this section, although action proposed by action jacket may be taken before or after formal ratification thereof by vote at a Commission meeting.

(3) Conference telephone calls among the Commissioners are considered meetings as defined by paragraph (a)(1) of this section if they involve the number of Commissioners requisite for Commission action, and where the deliberations of the Commissioners determine or result in the joint conduct or

disposition of official Commission business.

(4) Deliberations of a majority of the entire membership of the Commission with the *sole* purpose of determining whether or not to call a meeting at a date earlier than the requisite public notice period as specified in § 201.35 of this subpart are not considered to constitute a meeting or portion of a meeting as defined by paragraph (a)(1) of this section.

(5) Deliberations of a majority of the entire membership of the Commission with the *sole* purpose of determining whether or not to close a portion or portions of a meeting or series of meetings pursuant to § 201.36 of this subpart are not considered to constitute a meeting or portion of a meeting within the meaning of paragraph (a)(1) of this section.

(6) Deliberations of a majority of the entire membership of the Commission with the *sole* purpose of determining whether or not to change the subject matter of a publicly announced meeting, or to change the determination of the Commission to open or close a meeting, or portion thereof, to the public, following a public notice, as permitted under § 201.37(b) of this subpart, are not considered to constitute a meeting or portion of a meeting under paragraph (a)(1) of this section.

(b) The terms *Secretary* and *General Counsel* mean the Secretary and General Counsel of the Commission and their respective designees within their respective offices.

[63 FR 29348, May 29, 1998, as amended at 80 FR 39380, July 9, 2015]

§ 201.35 **Notices to the public.**

(a) At least seven (7) days before each Commission meeting the Commission shall issue a public notice which:

(1) States the time and place of the meeting;

(2) Lists the subjects or agenda items to be discussed at the meeting;

(3) States whether the meeting or portion thereof is to be open or closed to public observation; and

(4) Gives the name and business phone number of the Secretary to the Commission.

(b) When the Commission has voted to close any portion of any meeting in accordance with § 201.36 of this subpart, the notice referred to in paragraph (a) of this section shall also include, or be amended to include, if already issued, (1) A list of the persons reasonably expected to be present at such closed portion or portions of the meeting, (2) A corresponding list of the affiliations of those persons reasonably expected to be present, (3) A written copy of the vote of each Commissioner on whether or not the portion or portions of the meeting or series of meetings should be closed to public observation, (4) A full, written explanation of the Commission's action in closing the portion or portions of the meeting or series of meetings, and (5) A copy of the certification of the General Counsel, called for by § 201.39 of this subpart, that such portion or portions of the meeting or series of meetings were properly closed to the public by the Commission. When a vote to close a portion or portions of a meeting in accordance with § 201.36 of this subpart or a vote to change the subject matter of a meeting or to change a determination to open or close a meeting, or portion thereof, to the public in accordance with § 201.37(b) of this subpart fails for lack of a majority of the entire membership of the Commission, the vote shall also be published as part of the notice required by paragraph (a) of this section.

(c)(1) The 7-day period for public notice provided for in paragraph (a) of this section shall not apply when a majority of the entire membership of the Commission determines by recorded vote that Commission business requires that a particular meeting be called with less than 7 days' notice and that no earlier announcement of such meeting was possible.

(2) When the Commission has voted in conformity with paragraph (c)(1) of this section to shorten the 7-day period for public notice provided for by paragraph (a) of this section with respect to a particular meeting, the Commission shall issue the public notice required by paragraph (a) of this section at the earliest practicable time.

(3) When the Commission not only has voted in conformity with paragraph (c)(1) of this section to shorten the 7-day period for public notice provided for in paragraph (a) of this sec-

tion with respect to a particular meeting, but also has voted to close a portion or portions of such meeting in accordance with § 201.36 of this subpart, the public notice required by paragraph (c)(2) of this section shall also include, or be amended to include, if already issued, those items specified in paragraph (b) of this section.

(d)(1) When the Commission has changed the time or place of a publicly announced meeting by acting under § 201.37(a) of this subpart, the public notice required by paragraph (a) or (c)(2) of this section shall be amended to reflect such changed time or place.

(2) When the Commission has changed the subject matter of a meeting or its determination to open or close a meeting, or portion thereof, to the public following a public notice by acting under § 201.37(b) of this subpart, the public notice required by paragraph (a) or (c)(2) of this section shall be amended to

(i) Include a statement affirming that Commission business required the change in subject matter and that no earlier announcement of such change was possible and

(ii) Indicate the change in subject matter and the vote of each Commissioner upon such change.

(e)(1) The Secretary shall issue the public notices required by this section and such amendments thereto as are appropriate to the specific meeting to which they pertain.

(2) The Secretary

(i) Shall promptly post the public notices referred to in paragraph (e)(1) of this section on bulletin boards outside the Office of the Secretary to the Commission,

(ii) Shall make copies thereof available to interested members of the public, including mailing copies thereof through a mailing list of those persons desiring to receive such notices and distributing copies to the press, whether of specialized or general readership, and

(iii) Shall immediately submit said public notices to the FEDERAL REGISTER for publication.

(3) The Office of the Secretary shall respond to all questions from the public concerning the agendas of Commission meetings. Persons desiring to receive copies of notices of Commission meetings should contact the Office of the Secretary and request to be placed on the mailing list.

[42 FR 11243, Feb. 28, 1977, as amended at 58 FR 64121, Dec. 6, 1993]

§201.36 Closing a portion or portions of a meeting or a series of meetings.

(a) Every meeting of the Commission shall be open to public observation except when the Commission properly determines in the manner specified in paragraph (d) of this section that a portion or portions of a Commission meeting shall be closed to the public for the specific reasons enumerated in paragraph (b) of this section.

(b) The Commission may close a portion or portions of a Commission meeting only when it determines that public disclosure of information to be discussed at such meeting is likely to:

(1) Disclose matters that are (i) Specifically authorized under criteria established by Executive order to be kept secret in the interests of national defense or foreign policy and (ii) in fact properly classified pursuant to such Executive order;

(2) Relate solely to the internal personnel rules and practices of the Commission;

(3) Disclose matters specifically exempted from disclosure by statute (other than the Freedom of Information Act), provided that such statute (i) Requires that the matters be withheld from the public in such a manner as to leave no discretion on the issue, or (ii) Establishes particular criteria for withholding or refers to particular types of matters to be withheld.

(4) Disclose trade secrets and commercial or financial information obtained from a person and privileged or confidential;

(5) Involve accusing any person of a crime, or formally censuring any person;

(6) Disclose information of a personal nature when disclosure would constitute a clearly unwarranted invasion of personal privacy;

(7) Disclose investigatory records compiled for law-enforcement purposes, or information which, if written, would be contained in such records, but only to the extent that the production of such records or information would: (i) Interfere with enforcement proceedings, (ii) deprive a person of a right to a fair trial or to an impartial adjudication, (iii) constitute an unwarranted invasion of personal privacy, or (iv) disclose the identity of a confidential source, and, in the case of a record compiled by a criminal law-enforcement authority in the course of a criminal investigation or by an agency conducting a lawful national-security intelligence investigation, confidential information furnished only by the confidential source;

(8)(i) Disclose information the premature disclosure of which would, in those instances where the Commission regulates commodities, be likely to lead to significant financial speculation in such commodities;

(ii) Disclose information the premature disclosure of which would be likely to significantly frustrate implementation of a proposed Commission action except (A) When the Commission has already disclosed to the public the content or nature of its proposed action or (B) when the Commission is required by law to make such disclosure on its own initiative prior to taking final Commission action on such proposal; or

(9) Specifically concern:

(i) The Commission's issuance of a subpoena,

(ii) The Commission's participation in a civil action or proceeding, or

(iii) The initiation, conduct, or disposition by the Commission of a particular case of formal Commission adjudication under 19 U.S.C. 1337 pursuant to the procedures of 5 U.S.C. 554 or otherwise involving a determination on the record after opportunity for a hearing.

(c)(1) When the Commission has determined that one or more of the specific reasons enumerated in paragraph (b) of this section for closing a portion or portions of a Commission meeting is applicable to the subject matter or matters to be discussed, the Commission shall consider whether or not the public interest requires that such portion or portions of the meeting be open to public observation.

(2) In making the public-interest determination under paragraph (c)(1) of this section, the Commission shall consider whether public disclosure would (i) Interfere with the Commission's carrying out its statutory responsibilities, (ii) Conflict with the individual right of privacy under the Privacy Act of 1974 (5 U.S.C. 552a), or (iii) Place the Commission in violation of any other applicable provision of law, in addition to any other factors which it deems to be relevant to the particular meeting in question.

(d)(1) Action by the Commission to close a portion or portions of a meeting for one or more of the specific reasons enumerated in paragraphs (b) (1) through (9) of this section shall be taken only when a majority of the entire membership of the Commission has voted to take such action.

(2) A single recorded vote of the Commission shall be taken with respect to: (i) Each Commission meeting of which the Commission proposes to close a portion or portions to the public for one or more of the specific reasons enumerated in paragraphs (b) (1) through (9) of this section, or (ii) any information which the Commission proposes to withhold from the public for one or more of the specific reasons enumerated in paragraphs (b) (1) through (9) of this section. No proxy votes are permissible.

(e)(1) Action by the Commission to close a series of meetings of which the Commission proposes to close a portion or portions to the public for one or more of the specific reasons enumerated in paragraphs (b) (1) through (9) of this section may be taken by a single recorded vote of the Commission to close such portion or portions of the series. No proxy votes are permissible.

(2) A series of meetings may be closed pursuant to paragraph (e)(1) of this section so long as each meeting in such series: (i) Involves the same particular matters and (ii) is scheduled to be held no more than 30 days after the initial meeting in such series.

(f) When the Commission (i) Has voted to close a portion or portions of a meeting in accordance with paragraph (d) of this section or (ii) has voted to close a portion or portions of a series of meetings in accordance with paragraph (e) of this section, the public notices referred to in paragraph (a) or (c)(2) of § 201.35 shall be issued or amended in accordance with paragraph (b) or (c)(3) of § 201.35 at the earliest practicable time, but no later than one (1) working day following such vote.

§ 201.37 Changing the time, place, subject matter, or determination to open or close a meeting following a public notice.

(a) The time or place of a Commission meeting may be changed following a public announcement required by § 201.35 only if the Commission publicly announces such change or changes at the earliest practicable time by issuing an appropriate amendment to the public notice as required by § 201.35.

(b) The subject matter or matters of a Commission meeting or the determination of the Commission to open or close a meeting, or portion of a meeting, to the public may be changed following a public announcement required by § 201.35 only if:

(i) A majority of the entire membership of the Commission determines by recorded vote that Commission business so requires and that no earlier announcement of the change was possible and

(ii) The Commission publicly announces such change in subject matter or such change in the determination of the Commission to open or close a meeting, or a portion of a meeting, to the public and the vote of each Commissioner upon such change or changes in a subsequent amendment of the public notice required by § 201.35.

§ 201.38 Requests by interested persons that the Commission close a portion of a Commission meeting.

(a) Whenever any person whose interests may be directly affected by a portion of a Commission meeting requests that the Commission close such portion to the public for any of the specific reasons enumerated in paragraphs (b) (5), (6), or (7) of § 201.36, the Commission, upon the request of any one of the Commissioners, shall take a vote in the manner specified in §201.36 of this subpart on whether or not to close such portion of the meeting.

(b) When the Commission votes on a request to close a portion of a meeting under paragraph (a) of this section in the manner specified in §201.36(d), a public notice as required by paragraphs (a) and (b) of §201.35 shall be issued.

§201.39 General Counsel's certification of Commission action in closing a meeting or a series of meetings.

Before a Commission meeting may be closed for the specific reasons enumerated in paragraphs (b) (1) through (9) of §201.36, the General Counsel (i) Shall, in the related public notice, certify that in his or her opinion the meeting may be closed to the public and (ii) Shall state each applicable exemptive provision of paragraphs (b) (1) through (9) of §201.36.

§201.40 Records-retention requirements.

(a) The Secretary shall maintain a copy of the certification by the General Counsel required by §201.39 for each Commission meeting of which a portion or portions are closed to the public pursuant to a vote under §201.36(d).

(b) The Secretary shall also maintain a copy of a statement from the presiding officer of each Commission meeting or portion thereof which was closed to the public for the specific reasons enumerated in paragraphs (b) (1) through (9) of §201.36(b) setting forth (i) The time and place of the closed meeting, or portion thereof, and (ii) A list of the persons present thereat.

(c) The Secretary shall also maintain a complete transcript or electronic recording of the proceedings of each Commission meeting or portion of a meeting, whether open to public observation or closed to the public. The Secretary shall also maintain a complete transcript or electronic recording of all deliberations conducted under paragraphs (a) (4), (5), and (6) of §201.34 of this subpart.

(d) Where portions of a Commission meeting are closed for the reasons contained in paragraphs (b) (8)(A) or (9) of §201.36, the Commission preserves the option to maintain detailed minutes of such portions. Such detailed minutes shall fully and clearly describe all matters discussed and shall provide a full and accurate summary of any actions taken, and the reasons therefor, including a description of each of the views expressed on any item and the record of any rollcall vote (reflecting the vote of each member on the question). All documents considered in connection with any action shall be identified in such minutes.

(e) The retention period for the records required by paragraphs (a), (b), (c), and (d) of this section shall be for a period of at least two (2) years after the particular Commission meeting, or until one (1) year after the conclusion of any Commission proceeding with respect to which the meeting or portion thereof was held, whichever occurs later.

(f) The requirements of paragraphs (c) and (d) of this section shall not affect or supplant the existing duty of the Secretary to maintain permanent minutes of each Commission meeting. The Secretary shall also maintain permanent minutes of all deliberations conducted under paragraphs (a) (4), (5), and (6) of §201.34 of this subpart.

§201.41 Public inspection and copying of records; applicable fees.

(a) The Secretary shall promptly make available to interested members of the public the transcript or electronic recording of the discussion of any item on the agenda of a Commission meeting or of any item of the testimony of any witness received at the meeting, except for such item or items of such discussion or testimony as the Secretary determines to contain information which may be withheld for reasons specified in paragraphs (b) (1) through (9) of §201.36. The determination of the Secretary shall be in conformity with a prior vote of the Commission under §201.36(d) to close a portion or portions of a meeting.

(b) Public inspection of electronic recordings, transcripts, or minutes of Commission meetings shall take place at the United States International Trade Commission, 500 E Street SW., Washington, DC 20436. A room is designated by the Office of the Secretary and tape recorders with earphones are provided by the Commission for public-inspection purposes when proceedings are recorded on tape.

(c)(1) The Secretary shall provide any person with copies of transcripts, minutes of Commission meetings, or transcriptions of electronic recordings of Commission meetings, which disclose the identity of each speaker, at the actual cost of transcription or duplication.

(2) The Secretary shall not include items of discussion or testimony determined by the Secretary to contain information which may be withheld from the public for the reasons specified in paragraphs (b) (1) through (9) of § 201.36 in the copies furnished to the public in accordance with paragraph (c)(1) of this section. The determination of the Secretary shall be in conformity with a prior vote of the Commission under § 201.36(d) to close a portion or portions of a meeting.

Subpart F—National Security Information

AUTHORITY: 19 U.S.C. 1335; E.O. 13526, 75 FR 707.

SOURCE: 79 FR 46350, Aug. 8, 2014, unless otherwise noted.

§ 201.42 Purpose and scope.

This subpart supplements Executive Order 13526 of December 29, 2009, and its implementing directive (32 CFR part 2001) as it applies to the Commission.

§ 201.43 Mandatory declassification review.

(a) *Requests for mandatory declassification review*—(1) *Definitions.* Mandatory declassification review ("MDR") means the review for declassification of classified information in response to a request for declassification that meets the requirements under section 3.5 of Executive Order 13526.

(2) *Procedures.* Requests for MDR of information in the custody of the Commission that is classified under Executive Order 13526 or predecessor orders shall be directed to the Secretary to the Commission, U.S. International Trade Commission, 500 E Street SW., Washington, DC 20436. MDR requests will be processed in accordance with

Executive Order 13526, its implementing directive, and this section. An MDR request must describe the document or material containing the requested information with sufficient specificity to enable Commission personnel to locate it with a reasonable amount of effort. Requests for broad types of information, entire file series of records, or similar non-specific requests may be denied processing. The Secretary shall notify a requester who has submitted a non-specific request that no further action will be taken on the request unless the requester provides additional description.

(b) *Freedom of Information Act and Privacy Act requests.* (1) Requests for records submitted under the Freedom of Information Act ("FOIA") (5 U.S.C. 552), as amended, or the Privacy Act of 1974 (5 U.S.C. 552a), as amended, which include classified information shall be processed in accordance with the provisions of those acts and applicable Commission regulations (subpart C of this part (FOIA regulations); subpart D of this part (Privacy Act regulations)).

(2) If a requester submits a request under FOIA and also requests MDR, the Secretary shall require the requester to select one process or the other. If the requester fails to select one or the other process, the Secretary will treat the request as a FOIA request unless the requested materials are subject only to MDR.

(c) *Referral of MDR requests.* (1) Because the Commission does not have original classification authority and all U.S. originated classified information in its custody has been originally classified by another Federal agency, the Secretary shall refer all requests for MDR and the pertinent records to the originating agency for review. Following consultations with the originating agency, the Secretary shall notify the requester of the referral unless such association is itself classified under Executive Order 13526 or its predecessor orders. The Secretary shall request that the originating agency, in accordance with 32 CFR 2001.33(a)(2)(ii) and 2001.34(e):

(i) Promptly process the request for declassification,

(ii) Communicate its declassification determination to the Secretary, and

(iii) If the originating agency proposes to withhold any information from public release, notify the Secretary of the specific information at issue and the applicable law that authorizes and warrants withholding such information.

(2) Unless a prior arrangement has been made with the originating agency, the Secretary shall collect the results of that agency's review and inform the requester of any final decision regarding the declassification of the requested information as follows:

(i) If the originating agency denies declassification of the requested information in whole or in part, the Secretary shall ensure that the decision provided to the requester includes notification of the right to file an administrative appeal with the originating agency within 60 days of receipt of the denial and the mailing address for the appellate authority at the originating agency.

(ii) If the originating agency declassifies the requested information in whole or in part, the Secretary shall determine whether the requested declassified information is exempt from disclosure, in whole or in part, under the provisions of a statutory authority, such as the FOIA. The Secretary shall inform the requester that an appeal from a denial of requested declassified information must be received within 60 days of the date of the letter of denial and shall be made to the Commission and addressed to the Chairman, United States International Trade Commission, 500 E Street SW., Washington, DC 20436.

(d) *Foreign Government Information—* (1) *Definitions.* "Foreign government information" ("FGI") means information provided to the United States Government by a foreign government or governments, an international organization of governments, or any element thereof, with the expectation that the information, the source of the information, or both, are to be held in confidence; information produced by the United States Government pursuant to or as a result of a joint arrangement with a foreign government or governments, or an international organization of governments, or any element thereof, requiring that the informa-

tion, the arrangement, or both, are to be held in confidence; or information received and treated as FGI under the terms of a predecessor of Executive Order 13526.

(2) *MDR requests for classified records in Commission custody that contain FGI.* The Commission will handle such MDR requests consistent with the requirements of Executive Order 13526 and 32 CFR part 2001. MDR requests for FGI initially received or classified by another Federal agency shall be referred to such agency following the referral procedures in paragraph (c) of this section.

(e) *Appeals of denials of MDR requests.* MDR appeals are for the denial of classified information only. Appeals of denials are handled in accordance with 32 CFR 2001.33(a)(2)(iii), which provides that the agency appellate authority deciding an administrative appeal of the denial of an MDR request shall notify the requester in writing of the reasons for any denial and inform the requester of his or her final appeal rights to the Interagency Security Classification Appeals Panel.

Subpart G—Enforcement of Nondiscrimination on the Basis of Handicap in Programs or Activities Conducted by the U.S. International Trade Commission

AUTHORITY: 29 U.S.C. 794.

SOURCE: 51 FR 4575, 4579, Feb. 5, 1986, unless otherwise noted.

§201.101 Purpose.

This part effectuates section 119 of the Rehabilitation, Comprehensive Services, and Developmental Disabilities Amendments of 1978, which amended section 504 of the Rehabilitation Act of 1973 to prohibit discrimination on the basis of handicap in programs or activities conducted by Executive agencies or the United States Postal Service.

§201.102 Application.

This part applies to all programs or activities conducted by the agency.

§ 201.103 Definitions.

For purposes of this part, the term—

Assistant Attorney General means the Assistant Attorney General, Civil Rights Division, United States Department of Justice.

Auxiliary aids means services or devices that enable persons with impaired sensory, manual, or speaking skills to have an equal opportunity to participate in, and enjoy the benefits of, programs or activities conducted by the agency. For example, auxiliary aids useful for persons with impaired vision include readers, Brailled materials, audio recordings, telecommunications devices and other similar services and devices. Auxiliary aids useful for persons with impaired hearing include telephone handset amplifiers, telephones compatible with hearing aids, telecommunication devices for deaf persons (TDD's), interpreters, notetakers, written materials, and other similar services and devices.

Complete complaint means a written statement that contains the complainant's name and address and describes the agency's alleged discriminatory action in sufficient detail to inform the agency of the nature and date of the alleged violation of section 504. It shall be signed by the complainant or by someone authorized to do so on his or her behalf. Complaints filed on behalf of classes or third parties shall describe or identify (by name, if possible) the alleged victims of discrimination.

Facility means all or any portion of buildings, structures, equipment, roads, walks, parking lots, rolling stock or other conveyances, or other real or personal property.

Handicapped person means any person who has a physical or mental impairment that substantially limits one or more major life activities, has a record of such an impairment, or is regarded as having such an impairment.

As used in this definition, the phrase:

(1) *Physical or mental impairment* includes—

(i) Any physiological disorder or condition, cosmetic disfigurement, or anatomical loss affecting one or more of the following body systems: Neurological; musculoskeletal; special sense organs; respiratory, including speech organs; cardiovascular; reproductive; digestive; genitourinary; hemic and lymphatic; skin; and endocrine; or

(ii) Any mental or psychological disorder, such as mental retardation, organic brain syndrome, emotional or mental illness, and specific learning disabilities. The term *physical or mental impairment* includes, but is not limited to, such diseases and conditions as orthopedic, visual, speech, and hearing impairments, cerebral palsy, epilepsy, muscular dystrophy, multiple sclerosis, cancer, heart disease, diabetes, mental retardation, emotional illness, and drug addition and alcholism.

(2) *Major life activities* includes functions such as caring for one's self, performing manual tasks, walking, seeing, hearing, speaking, breathing, learning, and working.

(3) *Has a record of such an impairment* means has a history of, or has been misclassified as having, a mental or physical impairment that substantially limits one or more major life activities.

(4) *Is regarded as having an impairment* means—

(i) Has a physical or mental impairment that does not substantially limit major life activities but is treated by the agency as constituting such a limitation;

(ii) Has a physical or mental impairment that substantially limits major life activities only as a result of the attitudes of others toward such impairment; or

(iii) Has none of the impairments defined in subparagraph (1) of this definition but is treated by the agency as having such an impairment.

Qualified handicapped person means—

(1) With respect to any agency program or activity under which a person is required to perform services or to achieve a level of accomplishment, a handicapped person who meets the essential eligibility requirements and who can achieve the purpose of the program or activity without modifications in the program or activity that the agency can demonstrate would result in a fundamental alteration in its nature; or

(2) With respect to any other program or activity, a handicapped person

who meets the essential eligibility requirements for participation in, or receipt of benefits from, that program or activity.

(3) *Qualified handicapped person* is defined for purposes of employment in 29 CFR 1613.702(f), which is made applicable to this part by § 201.140.

Section 504 means section 504 of the Rehabilitation Act of 1973 (Pub. L. 93–112, 87 Stat. 394 (29 U.S.C. 794)), as amended by the Rehabilitation Act Amendments of 1974 (Pub. L. 93–516, 88 Stat. 1617), and the Rehabilitation, Comprehensive Services, and Developmental Disabilities Amendments of 1978 (Pub. L. 95–602, 92 Stat. 2955). As used in this part, section 504 applies only to programs or activities conducted by Executive agencies and not to federally assisted programs.

[51 FR 4575, 4579, Feb. 5, 1986; 51 FR 7543, Mar. 5, 1986]

§§ 201.104–201.109   [Reserved]

§ 201.110   Self-evaluation.

(a) The agency shall, by April 9, 1987, evaluate its current policies and practices, and the effects thereof, that do not or may not meet the requirements of this part, and, to the extent modification of any such policies and practices is required, the agency shall proceed to make the necessary modifications.

(b) The agency shall provide an opportunity to interested persons, including handicapped persons or organizations representing handicapped persons, to participate in the self-evaluation process by submitting comments (both oral and written).

(c) The agency shall, until three years following the completion of the self-evaluation, maintain on file and make available for public inspections:

(1) A description of areas examined and any problems identified, and

(2) A description of any modifications made.

§ 201.111   Notice.

The agency shall make available to employees, applicants, participants, beneficiaries, and other interested persons such information regarding the provisions of this part and its applicability to the programs or activities conducted by the agency, and make such information available to them in such manner as the head of the agency finds necessary to apprise such persons of the protections against discrimination assured them by section 504 and this regulation.

§§ 201.112–201.129   [Reserved]

§ 201.130   General prohibitions against discrimination.

(a) No qualified handicapped person shall, on the basis of handicap, be excluded from participation in, be denied the benefits of, or otherwise be subjected to discrimination under any program or activity conducted by the agency.

(b)(1) The agency, in providing any aid, benefit, or service, may not, directly or through contractual, licensing, or other arrangements, on the basis of handicap—

(i) Deny a qualified handicapped person the opportunity to participate in or benefit from the aid, benefit, or service;

(ii) Afford a qualified handicapped person an opportunity to participate in or benefit from the aid, benefit, or service that is not equal to that afforded others;

(iii) Provide a qualified handicapped person with an aid, benefit, or service that is not as effective in affording equal opportunity to obtain the same result, to gain the same benefit, or to reach the same level of achievement as that provided to others;

(iv) Provide different or separate aid, benefits, or services to handicapped persons or to any class of handicapped persons than is provided to others unless such action is necessary to provide qualified handicapped persons with aid, benefits, or services that are as effective as those provided to others;

(v) Deny a qualified handicapped person the opportunity to participate as a member of planning or advisory boards; or

(vi) Otherwise limit a qualified handicapped person in the enjoyment of any right, privilege, advantage, or opportunity enjoyed by others receiving the aid, benefit, or service.

(2) The agency may not deny a qualified handicapped person the opportunity to participate in programs or activities that are not separate or different, despite the existence of permissibly separate or different programs or activities.

(3) The agency may not, directly or through contractual or other arrangements, utilize criteria or methods of administration the purpose or effect of which would—

(i) Subject qualified handicapped persons to discrimination on the basis of handicap; or

(ii) Defeat or substantially impair accomplishment of the objectives of a program or activity with respect to handicapped persons.

(4) The agency may not, in determining the site or location of a facility, make selections the purpose or effect of which would—

(i) Exclude handicapped persons from, deny them the benefits of, or otherwise subject them to discrimination under any program or activity conducted by the agency; or

(ii) Defeat or substantially impair the accomplishment of the objectives of a program or activity with respect to handicapped persons.

(5) The agency, in the selection of procurement contractors, may not use criteria that subject qualified handicapped persons to discrimination on the basis of handicap.

(c) The exclusion of nonhandicapped persons from the benefits of a program limited by Federal statute or Executive order to handicapped persons or the exclusion of a specific class of handicapped persons from a program limited by Federal statute or Executive order to a different class of handicapped persons is not prohibited by this part.

(d) The agency shall administer programs and activities in the most integrated setting appropriate to the needs of qualified handicapped persons.

§§ 201.131–201.139   [Reserved]

§ 201.140   Employment.

No qualified handicapped person shall, on the basis of handicap, be subjected to discrimination in employment under any program or activity

conducted by the agency. The definitions, requirements, and procedures of section 501 of the Rehabilitation Act of 1973 (29 U.S.C. 791), as established by the Equal Employment Opportunity Commission in 29 CFR part 1613, shall apply to employment in federally conducted programs or activities.

§§ 201.141–201.148   [Reserved]

§ 201.149   Program accessibility: Discrimination prohibited.

Except as otherwise provided in § 201.150, no qualified handicapped person shall, because the agency's facilities are inaccessible to or unusable by handicapped persons, be denied the benefits of, be excluded from participation in, or otherwise be subjected to discrimination under any program or activity conducted by the agency.

§ 201.150   Program accessibility: Existing facilities.

(a) *General.* The agency shall operate each program or activity so that the program or activity, when viewed in its entirety, is readily accessible to and usable by handicapped persons. This paragraph does not—

(1) Necessarily require the agency to make each of its existing facilities accessible to and usable by handicapped persons; or

(2) Require the agency to take any action that it can demonstrate would result in a fundamental alteration in the nature of a program or activity or in undue financial and administrative burdens. In those circumstances where agency personnel believe that the proposed action would fundamentally alter the program or activity or would result in undue financial and administrative burdens, the agency has the burden of proving that compliance with § 201.150(a) would result in such alteration or burdens. The decision that compliance would result in such alteration or burdens must be made by the agency head or his or her designee after considering all agency resources available for use in the funding and operation of the conducted program or activity, and must be accompanied by a written statement of the reasons for reaching that conclusion. If an action would result in such an alteration or

such burdens, the agency shall take any other action that would not result in such an alteration or such burdens but would nevertheless ensure that handicapped persons receive the benefits and services of the program or activity.

(b) *Methods.* The agency may comply with the requirements of this section through such means as redesign of equipment, reassignment of services to accessible buildings, assignment of aides to beneficiaries, home visits, delivery of services at alternate accessible sites, alteration of existing facilities and construction of new facilities, use of accessible rolling stock, or any other methods that result in making its programs or activities readily accessible to and usable by handicapped persons. The agency is not required to make structural changes in existing facilities where other methods are effective in achieving compliance with this section. The agency, in making alterations to existing buildings, shall meet accessibility requirements to the extent compelled by the Architectural Barriers Act of 1968, as amended (42 U.S.C. 4151–4157), and any regulations implementing it. In choosing among available methods for meeting the requirements of this section, the agency shall give priority to those methods that offer programs and activities to qualified handicapped persons in the most integrated setting appropriate.

(c) *Time period for compliance.* The agency shall comply with the obligations established under this section by June 6, 1986, except that where structural changes in facilities are undertaken, such changes shall be made by April 7, 1989, but in any event as expeditiously as possible.

(d) *Transition plan.* In the event that structural changes to facilities will be undertaken to achieve program accessibility, the agency shall develop, by October 7, 1986, a transition plan setting forth the steps necessary to complete such changes. The agency shall provide an opportunity to interested persons, including handicapped persons or organizations representing handicapped persons, to participate in the development of the transition plan by submitting comments (both oral and written). A copy of the transition plan shall be made available for public inspection. The plan shall, at a minimum—

(1) Identify physical obstacles in the agency's facilities that limit the accessibility of its programs or activities to handicapped persons;

(2) Describe in detail the methods that will be used to make the facilities accessible;

(3) Specify the schedule for taking the steps necessary to achieve compliance with this section and, if the time period of the transition plan is longer than one year, identify steps that will be taken during each year of the transition period; and

(4) Indicate the official responsible for implementation of the plan.

[51 FR 4575, 4579, Feb. 5, 1986; 51 FR 7543, Mar. 5, 1986]

§201.151 Program accessibility: New construction and alterations.

Each building or part of a building that is constructed or altered by, on behalf of, or for the use of the agency shall be designed, constructed, or altered so as to be readily accessible to and usable by handicapped persons. The definitions, requirements, and standards of the Architectural Barriers Act (42 U.S.C. 4151–4157), as established in 41 CFR 101–19.600 to 101–19.607, apply to buildings covered by this section.

§§201.152–201.159 [Reserved]

§201.160 Communications.

(a) The agency shall take appropriate steps to ensure effective communication with applicants, participants, personnel of other Federal entities, and members of the public.

(1) The agency shall furnish appropriate auxiliary aids where necessary to afford a handicapped person an equal opportunity to participate in, and enjoy the benefits of, a program or activity conducted by the agency.

(i) In determining what type of auxiliary aid is necessary, the agency shall give primary consideration to the requests of the handicapped person.

(ii) The agency need not provide individually prescribed devices, readers for personal use or study, or other devices of a personal nature.

(2) Where the agency communicates with applicants and beneficiaries by telephone, telecommunication devices for deaf persons (TDD's) or equally effective telecommunication systems shall be used.

(b) The agency shall ensure that interested persons, including persons with impaired vision or hearing, can obtain information as to the existence and location of accessible services, activities, and facilities.

(c) The agency shall provide signage at a primary entrance to each of its inaccessible facilities, directing users to a location at which they can obtain information about accessible facilities. The international symbol for accessibility shall be used at each primary entrance of an accessible facility.

(d) This section does not require the agency to take any action that it can demonstrate would result in a fundamental alteration in the nature of a program or activity or in undue financial and administrative burdens. In those circumstances where agency personnel believe that the proposed action would fundamentally alter the program or activity or would result in undue financial and administrative burdens, the agency has the burden of proving that compliance with § 201.160 would result in such alteration or burdens. The decision that compliance would result in such alteration or burdens must be made by the agency head or his or her designee after considering all agency resources available for use in the funding and operation of the conducted program or activity, and must be accompanied by a written statement of the reasons for reaching that conclusion. If an action required to comply with this section would result in such an alteration or such burdens, the agency shall take any other action that would not result in such an alteration or such burdens but would nevertheless ensure that, to the maximum extent possible, handicapped persons receive the benefits and services of the program or activity.

§§ 201.161–201.169 [Reserved]

§ 201.170 Compliance procedures.

(a) Except as provided in paragraph (b) of this section, this section applies to all allegations of discrimination on the basis of handicap in programs or activities conducted by the agency.

(b) The agency shall process complaints alleging violations of section 504 with respect to employment according to the procedures established by the Equal Employment Opportunity Commission in 29 CFR part 1613 pursuant to section 501 of the Rehabilitation Act of 1973 (29 U.S.C. 791).

(c) The Director, Office of Equal Employment Opportunity, shall be responsible for coordinating implementation of this section. Complaints may be sent to the Director, Office of Equal Employment Opportunity, United States International Trade Commission, 500 E Street SW., Washington, DC 20436.

(d) The agency shall accept and investigate all complete complaints for which it has jurisdiction. All complete complaints must be filed within 180 days of the alleged act of discrimination. The agency may extend this time period for good cause.

(e) If the agency receives a complaint over which it does not have jurisdiction, it shall promptly notify the complainant and shall make reasonable efforts to refer the complaint to the appropriate government entity.

(f) The agency shall notify the Architectural and Transportation Barriers Compliance Board upon receipt of any complaint alleging that a building or facility that is subject to the Architectural Barriers Act of 1968, as amended (42 U.S.C. 4151–4157), or section 502 of the Rehabilitation Act of 1973, as amended (29 U.S.C. 792), is not readily accessible to and usable by handicapped persons.

(g) Within 180 days of the receipt of a complete complaint for which it has jurisdiction, the agency shall notify the complainant of the results of the investigation in a letter containing—

(1) Findings of fact and conclusions of law;

(2) A description of a remedy for each violation found;

(3) A notice of the right to appeal.

(h) Appeals of the findings of fact and conclusions of law or remedies must be filed by the complainant within 90 days of receipt from the agency of the letter required by § 201.170(g). The agency may extend this time for good cause.

(i) Timely appeals shall be accepted and processed by the head of the agency.

(j) The head of the agency shall notify the complainant of the results of the appeal within 60 days of the receipt of the request. If the head of the agency determines that additional information is needed from the complainant, he or she shall have 60 days from the date of receipt of the additional information to make his or her determination on the appeal.

(k) The time limits cited in paragraphs (g) and (j) of this section may be extended with the permission of the Assistant Attorney General.

(l) The agency may delegate its authority for conducting complaint investigations to other Federal agencies, except that the authority for making the final determination may not be delegated to another agency.

[51 FR 4575, 4579, Feb. 5, 1986, as amended at 51 FR 4576, Feb. 5, 1986; 68 FR 32975, June 3, 2003]

§§ 201.171–201.999 [Reserved]

Subpart H—Debt Collection

AUTHORITY: 19 U.S.C. 1335; 5 U.S.C. 5514(b)(1); 31 U.S.C. 3716(b); 31 U.S.C. 3720A(b)(4); 31 CFR chapter IX; 26 CFR 301.6402–6(b).

SOURCE: 62 FR 38019, July 16, 1997, unless otherwise noted.

§ 201.201 Definitions.

Except where the context clearly indicates otherwise or where the term is defined elsewhere in this section, the following definitions shall apply to this subpart.

(a) *Agency* means a department, agency, court, court administrative office, or instrumentality in the executive, judicial, or legislative branch of Government, including government corporations.

(b) *Certification* means a written statement received by a paying agency from a creditor agency that requests the paying agency to offset the salary of an employee and specifies that required procedural protections have been afforded the employee.

(c) *Chairman* means the Chairman of the Commission.

(d) *Compromise* means the settlement or forgiveness of a debt.

(e) *Creditor agency* means an agency of the Federal government to which the debt is owed.

(f) *Director* means the Director, Office of Finance of the Commission or an official designated to act on the Director's behalf.

(g) *Disposable pay* means that part of current basic pay, special pay, incentive pay, retired pay, retainer pay, and, in the case of an employee not entitled to basic pay, other authorized pay, remaining for each pay period after the deduction of any amount required by law to be withheld. The Commission shall allow the following deductions in determining the amount of disposable pay that is subject to salary offset:

(1) Federal employment taxes;

(2) Amounts mandatorily withheld for the United States Soldiers' and Airmen's Home;

(3) Fines and forfeiture ordered by a court-martial or by a commanding officer;

(4) Amounts deducted for Medicare;

(5) Federal, state, or local income taxes to the extent authorized or required by law, but no greater than would be the case if the employee claimed all dependents to which he or she is entitled and such additional amounts for which the employee presents evidence of a tax obligation supporting the additional withholding;

(6) Health insurance premiums;

(7) Normal retirement contributions, including employee contributions to the Thrift Savings Plan;

(8) Normal life insurance premiums (e.g., Serviceman's Group Life Insurance and "Basic Life" Federal Employee's Group Life Insurance premiums), not including amounts deducted for supplementary coverage.

(h) *Employee* means a current employee of the Commission or other agency, including a current member of the Armed Forces or a Reserve of the Armed Forces of the United States.

(i) *Federal Claims Collection Standards (FCCS)* means standards published at 31 CFR chapter IX.

(j) *Hearing official* means an individual responsible for conducting any hearing with respect to the existence or amount of a debt claimed and for rendering a decision on the basis of such hearing. A hearing official may not be under the supervision or control of the Chairman when the Commission is the creditor agency but may be an administrative law judge.

(k) *Notice of Intent to Offset* or *Notice of Intent* means a written notice from a creditor agency to an employee, organization, or entity stating that the debtor is indebted to the creditor agency and apprising the debtor of certain procedural rights.

(l) *Notice of Salary Offset* means a written notice from the paying agency to an employee after a certification has been issued by a creditor agency, informing the employee that salary offset will begin at the next officially established pay interval.

(m) *Office of Finance* means the Office of Finance of the Commission.

(n) *Paying agency* means the agency of the Federal government that employs the individual who owes a debt to an agency of the Federal government. In some cases, the Commission may be both the creditor agency and the paying agency.

[62 FR 38019, July 16, 1997, as amended at 68 FR 32976, June 3, 2003]

§ 201.202 Purpose and scope of salary and administrative offset rules.

(a) *Purpose.* The purpose of sections 201.201 through 201.207 is to implement 5 U.S.C. 5514, 31 U.S.C. 3716, and 31 U.S.C. 3720A which authorize the collection by salary offset, administrative offset, or tax refund offset of debts owed by persons, organizations, or entities to the Federal government. Generally, however, a debt may not be collected by such means if it has been outstanding for more than ten years after the agency's right to collect the debt first accrued. These proposed regulations are consistent with the Office of Personnel Management regulations on salary offset, codified at 5 CFR Part 550, subpart K, and with regulations on administrative offset codified at 31 CFR part 901.

(b) *Scope.* (1) Sections 201.201 through 201.207 establish agency procedures for the collection of certain debts owed the Government.

(2) Sections 201.201 through 201.207 apply to collections by the Commission from:

(i) Federal employees who are indebted to the Commission;

(ii) Employees of the Commission who are indebted to other agencies; and

(iii) Other persons, organizations, or entities that are indebted to the Commission.

(3) Sections 201.201 through 201.207 do not apply:

(i) To debts or claims arising under the Internal Revenue Code of 1986 (26 U.S.C. *et seq.*), the Social Security Act (42 U.S.C. 301 *et seq.*), or the tariff laws of the United States;

(ii) To a situation to which the Contract Disputes Act (41 U.S.C. 601 *et seq.*) applies; or

(iii) In any case where collection of a debt is explicitly provided for or prohibited by another statute (e.g., travel advances in 5 U.S.C. 4108).

(4) Nothing in Sections 201.201 through 201.207 precludes the compromise, suspension, or termination of collection actions where appropriate under the standards implementing the Federal Claims Collection Act (31 U.S.C. 3711 *et seq.*), namely, 31 CFR chapter IX.

[62 FR 38019, July 16, 1997, as amended at 68 FR 32976, June 3, 2003]

§ 201.203 Delegation of authority.

Authority to conduct the following activities is hereby delegated to the Director:

(a) Initiate and effectuate the administrative collection process;

(b) Accept or reject compromise offers and suspend or terminate collection actions where the claim does not exceed $100,000 or such higher amount as the Chairman may from time to time prescribe, exclusive of interest, administrative costs, and penalties as provided herein, as set forth in 31 U.S.C. 3711(a)(2);

(c) Report to consumer reporting agencies certain data pertaining to delinquent debts;

(d) Use offset procedures to effectuate collection; and

(e) Take any other action necessary to facilitate and augment collection in accordance with the policies contained herein and as otherwise provided by law.

§ 201.204 Salary offset.

(a) *Notice requirements before offset where the Commission is the creditor agency.* Deductions under the authority of 5 U.S.C. 5514 will not be made unless the Commission provides the employee with a written Notice of Intent to Offset a minimum of 30 calendar days before salary offset is initiated. The Notice of Intent shall state:

(1) That the Director has reviewed the records relating to the claim and has determined that a debt is owed;

(2) The Director's intention to collect the debt by means of deduction from the employee's current disposable pay account until the debt and all accumulated interest is paid in full;

(3) The amount of the debt and the facts giving rise to the debt;

(4) A repayment schedule that includes the amount, frequency, proposed beginning date, and duration of the intended deductions;

(5) The opportunity for the employee to propose an alternative written schedule for the voluntary repayment of the debt, in lieu of offset, on terms acceptable to the Commission. The employee shall include a justification in the request for the alternative schedule. The schedule shall be agreed to and signed by both the employee and the Director;

(6) An explanation of the Commission's policy concerning interest, penalties, and administrative costs, including a statement that such assessments must be made unless excused in accordance with the Federal Claims Collection Standards;

(7) The employee's right to inspect and copy all records of the Commission not exempt from disclosure pertaining to the debt claimed or to receive copies of such records if the debtor is unable personally to inspect the records, due to geographical or other constraints;

(8) The name, address, and telephone number of the Director to whom requests for access to records relating to the debt must be sent;

(9) The employee's right to a hearing conducted by an impartial hearing official (an administrative law judge or other hearing official not under the supervision or control of the Chairman) with respect to the existence and amount of the debt claimed or the repayment schedule (i.e., the percentage of disposable pay to be deducted each pay period), so long as a request is filed by the employee as prescribed in paragraph (c)(1) of this section;

(10) The name, address, and telephone number of the Director to whom a proposal for voluntary repayment must be sent and who may be contacted concerning procedures for requesting a hearing;

(11) The method and deadline for requesting a hearing;

(12) That the timely filing of a request for a hearing on or before the 15th calendar day following receipt of the Notice of Intent will stay the commencement of collection proceedings;

(13) The name and address of the office to which the request should be sent;

(14) That the Commission will initiate certification procedures to implement a salary offset not less than 30 days from the date of receipt of the Notice of Intent to Offset, unless the employee files a timely request for a hearing;

(15) That a final decision on whether a hearing will be held (if one is requested) will be issued at the earliest practical date;

(16) That any knowingly false or frivolous statements, representations, or evidence may subject the employee to:

(i) Disciplinary procedures appropriate under 5 U.S.C. Chapter 75, 5 CFR part 752, or any other applicable statutes or regulations;

(ii) Penalties under the False Claims Act, 31 U.S.C. 3729–3733, or under any other applicable statutory authority; or

(iii) Criminal penalties under 18 U.S.C. 286, 287, 1001, and 1002 or under any other applicable statutory authority;

(17) Any other rights and remedies available to the employee under statutes or regulations governing the program for which the collection is being made;

(18) That unless there are applicable contractual or statutory provisions to the contrary, amounts paid on or deducted from debts that are later waived

or found not to be owed to the United States will be promptly refunded to the employee; and

(19) That proceedings with respect to such debt are governed by 5 U.S.C. 5514.

(b) *Review of Commission records related to the debt.* (1) An employee who desires to inspect or copy Commission records related to a debt owed to the Commission must send a letter to the Director as designated in the Notice of Intent requesting access to the relevant records. The letter must be received in the office of the Director within 15 calendar days after the employee's receipt of the Notice of Intent.

(2) In response to a timely request submitted by the debtor, the Director will notify the employee of the location and time when the employee may inspect and copy records related to the debt.

(3) If the employee is unable personally to inspect the records, due to geographical or other constraints, the Director shall arrange to send copies of such records to the employee.

(c) *Opportunity for a hearing where the Commission is the creditor agency*—(1) *Request for a hearing.* (i) An employee who requests a hearing on the existence or amount of the debt held by the Commission or on the offset schedule proposed by the Commission must send such request to the Director. The request for a hearing must be received by the Director on or before the 15th calendar day following receipt by the employee of the notice.

(ii) The employee must specify whether an oral hearing is requested. If an oral hearing is desired, the request should explain why the matter cannot be resolved by review of the documentary evidence alone. The request must be signed by the employee and must fully identify and explain with reasonable specificity all the facts, evidence, and witnesses, if any, that the employee believes support his or her position.

(2) *Failure to timely submit.* If the employee files a request for hearing after the expiration of the 15-calendar-day period provided for in paragraph (c)(1) of this section, the Director may accept the request if the employee can show that the delay was the result of circumstances beyond his or her control or that he or she failed to receive actual notice of the filing deadline.

(3) *Obtaining the services of a hearing official.* (i) When the debtor is not a Commission employee and the Commission cannot provide a prompt and appropriate hearing before an administrative law judge or other hearing official, the Commission may request a hearing official from an agent of the paying agency, as designated in 5 CFR part 581, appendix A, or as otherwise designated by the paying agency.

(ii) When the debtor is a Commission employee, the Commission may contact any agent of another agency, as designated in 5 CFR part 581, appendix A, or as otherwise designated by the agency, to request a hearing official.

(4) *Procedure*—(i) *Notice.* After the employee requests a hearing, the hearing official shall notify the employee of the form of the hearing to be provided. If the hearing will be oral, the notice shall set forth the date, time, and location of the hearing, which must occur no more than 30 calendar days after the request is received, unless the employee requests that the hearing be delayed. If the hearing will be conducted by examination of documents, the employee shall be notified within 30 calendar days that he or she should submit evidence and arguments in writing to the hearing official.

(ii) *Oral hearing.* An employee who requests an oral hearing shall be provided an oral hearing if the hearing official determines that the matter cannot be resolved by review of documentary evidence alone (e.g., when an issue of credibility or veracity is involved). The hearing need not be an adversarial adjudication, and rules of evidence need not apply. Witnesses who testify in oral hearings shall do so under oath or affirmation. Oral hearings may take the form of, but are not limited to:

(A) Informal conferences with the hearing official in which the employee and agency representative are given full opportunity to present evidence, witnesses, and argument;

(B) Informal meetings in which the hearing examiner interviews the employee; or

(C) Formal written submissions followed by an opportunity for oral presentation.

(iii) *Documentary hearing.* If the hearing official determines that an oral hearing is not necessary, he or she shall make the determination based upon a review of the written record.

(iv) *Record.* The hearing official shall maintain a summary record of any hearing conducted under this section.

(5) *Date of decision.* The hearing official shall issue a written opinion stating his or her decision, based upon all evidence and information developed at the hearing, as soon as practicable after the hearing, but not later than 60 calendar days after the date on which the request was received by the Commission, unless the hearing was delayed at the request of the employee, in which case the 60 day decision period shall be extended by the number of days by which the hearing was postponed. The decision of the hearing official shall be final.

(6) *Content of decision.* The written decision shall include:

(i) A summary of the facts concerning the origin, nature, and amount of the debt;

(ii) The hearing official's findings, analysis, and conclusions; and

(iii) The terms of any repayment schedules, if applicable.

(7) *Failure to appear.* If, in the absence of good cause shown (e.g., illness), the employee or the representative of the Commission fails to appear, the hearing official shall proceed with the hearing as scheduled, and make his or her determination based upon the oral testimony presented and the documentation submitted by both parties. At the request of both parties, the hearing official may schedule a new hearing date. Both parties shall be given reasonable notice of the time and place of this new hearing.

(d) *Certification where the Commission is the creditor agency.* (1) The Director shall issue a certification in all cases where:

(i) The hearing official determines that a debt exists; or

(ii) The employee admits the existence and amount of the debt, for example, by failing to request a hearing.

(2) The certification must be in writing and must state:

(i) That the employee owes the debt;

(ii) The amount and basis of the debt;

(iii) The date the Government's right to collect the debt first accrued;

(iv) That the Commission's regulations have been approved by OPM pursuant to 5 CFR part 550, subpart K;

(v) If the collection is to be made by lump-sum payment, the amount and date such payment will be collected;

(vi) If the collection is to be made in installments, the number of installments to be collected, the amount of each installment, and the date of the first installment, if a date other than the next officially established pay period; and

(vii) The date the employee was notified of the debt, the action(s) taken pursuant to the Commission's regulations, and the dates such actions were taken.

(e) *Voluntary repayment agreements as alternative to salary offset where the Commission is the creditor agency.* (1) In response to a Notice of Intent, an employee may propose to repay the debt in accordance with scheduled installment payments. Any employee who wishes to repay a debt without salary offset shall submit in writing a proposed agreement to repay the debt. The proposal shall set forth a proposed repayment schedule. Any proposal under paragraph (e) of this section must be received by the Director within 15 calendar days after receipt of the Notice of Intent.

(2) In response to a timely proposal by the debtor, the Director shall notify the employee whether the employee's proposed written agreement for repayment is acceptable. It is within the discretion of the Director to accept, reject, or propose to the debtor a modification of the proposed repayment agreement.

(3) If the Director decides that the proposed repayment agreement is unacceptable, the employee shall have 15 calendar days from the date he or she received notice of the decision in which to file a request for a hearing.

(4) If the Director decides that the proposed repayment agreement is acceptable or the debtor agrees to a modification proposed by the Director, the agreement shall be put in writing and signed by both the employee and the Director.

(f) *Special review where the Commission is the creditor agency.* (1) An employee subject to salary offset or a voluntary repayment agreement may, at any time, request a special review by the Director of the amount of the salary offset or voluntary payment, based on materially changed circumstances, including, but not limited to, catastrophic illness, divorce, death, or disability.

(2) In determining whether, as a result of materially changed circumstances, an offset would prevent the employee from meeting essential subsistence expenses (costs incurred for food, housing, clothing, transportation, and medical care), the employee shall submit to the Director a detailed statement and supporting documents for the employee, his or her spouse, and dependents indicating:

(i) Income from all sources;

(ii) Assets;

(iii) Liabilities;

(iv) Number of dependents;

(v) Expenses for food, housing, clothing, and transportation;

(vi) Medical expenses; and

(vii) Exceptional expenses, if any.

(3) If the employee requests a special review under paragraph (f) of this section, the employee shall file an alternative proposed offset or payment schedule and a statement, with supporting documents, showing why the current salary offset or payments result in extreme financial hardship to the employee.

(4) The Director shall evaluate the statement and supporting documents and determine whether the original offset or repayment schedule imposes extreme financial hardship on the employee. The Director shall notify the employee in writing within 30 calendar days of such determination, including, if appropriate, his or her acceptance of a revised offset or payment schedule.

(5) If the special review results in a revised offset or repayment schedule, the Director shall provide a new certification to the paying agency.

(g) *Notice of salary offset where the Commission is the paying agency.* (1) Upon issuance of a proper certification by the Director (for debts owed to the Commission) or upon receipt of a proper certification from another creditor agency, the Office of Finance shall send the employee a written notice of salary offset. Such notice shall advise the employee:

(i) Of the certification that has been issued by the Director or received from another creditor agency;

(ii) Of the amount of the debt and of the deductions to be made; and

(iii) Of the initiation of salary offset at the next officially established pay interval or as otherwise provided for in the certification.

(2) The Office of Finance shall provide a copy of the notice to the creditor agency and advise such agency of the dollar amount to be offset and the pay period when the offset will begin.

(h) *Procedures for salary offset where the Commission is the paying agency*—(1) *Generally.* (i) The Director shall coordinate salary deductions under this section.

(ii) The Director shall determine the amount of an employee's disposable pay and the amount of the salary offset subject to the requirements in this paragraph.

(iii) Deductions shall begin the pay period following the issuance of the certification by the Director or the receipt by the Office of Finance of the certification from another agency or as soon thereafter as possible.

(2) *Types of collection*—(i) *Lump-sum payment.* If the amount of the debt is equal to or less than 15 percent of the employee's disposable pay, such debt ordinarily will be collected in one lump-sum payment.

(ii) *Installment deductions.* Installment deductions will be made over a period not greater than the anticipated period of employment. The size and frequency of installment deductions will bear a reasonable relation to the size of the debt and the employee's ability to pay. However, the amount deducted for any pay period will not exceed 15 percent of the disposable pay from which the deduction is made unless the employee has agreed in writing to the deduction of a greater amount. The installment payment should normally be sufficient in size and frequency to liquidate the debt in no more than three years. Installment payments of less than $50 should be accepted only in the most unusual circumstances.

(iii) *Lump-sum deductions from final check.* In order to liquidate a debt, a lump-sum deduction exceeding 15 percent of disposable pay may be made pursuant to 31 U.S.C. 3716 and 5 U.S.C. 5514(a)(1) from any final salary payment due a former employee, whether the former employee was separated voluntarily or involuntarily.

(iv) *Lump-sum deductions from other sources.* Whenever an employee subject to salary offset is separated from the Commission, and the balance of the debt cannot be liquidated by offset of the final salary check, the Commission, pursuant to 31 U.S.C. 3716, may offset any later payments of any kind to the former employee to collect the balance of the debt.

(3) *Multiple debts.* Where two or more creditor agencies are seeking salary offset, or where two or more debts are owed to a single creditor agency, the Office of Finance may, at its discretion, determine whether one or more debts should be offset simultaneously within the 15 percent limitation.

(4) *Order of precedence for recovery of debts owed the Government.* (i) For Commission employees, subject to paragraph (h)(3) of this section and (paragraph (h)(4)(ii) of this section, offsets to recover debts owed the United States Government shall be made from disposable pay in the following order of precedence:

(A) Indebtedness due the Commission;

(B) Indebtedness due other agencies.

(ii) In the event that a debt to the Commission is certified while an employee is subject to salary offset to repay another agency, the Office of Finance may, at its discretion, determine whether the debt to the Commission should be repaid before the debt to the other agency, repaid simultaneously, or repaid after the debt to the other agency.

(iii) A levy pursuant to the Internal Revenue Code of 1986 shall take precedence over other deductions under this section, as provided in 5 U.S.C. 5514(d).

(i) *Coordinating salary offset with other agencies*—(1) *Responsibility of the Commission as the creditor agency.* (i) The Director shall be responsible for:

(A) Arranging for a hearing upon proper request by a Federal employee;

(B) Preparing the Notice of Intent to Offset consistent with the requirements of paragraph (a) of this section;

(C) Obtaining hearing officials from other agencies pursuant to paragraph (c)(3) of this section; and

(D) Ensuring that each certification of debt is sent to a paying agency pursuant to paragraph (d)(2) of this section.

(ii) Upon completion of the procedures established in paragraphs (a) through (f) of this section, the Director shall submit a certified debt claim and an installment agreement or other instruction on the payment schedule, if applicable, to the employee's paying agency.

(iii) If the employee is in the process of separating from Government employment, the Commission shall submit its debt claim to the employee's paying agency for collection by lump-sum deduction from the employee's final check. The paying agency shall certify the total amount of its collection and furnish a copy of the certification to the Commission and to the employee.

(iv) If the employee is already separated and all payments due from his or her former paying agency have been paid, the Commission may, unless otherwise prohibited, request that money due and payable to the employee from the Federal Government be administratively offset to collect the debt.

(v) When an employee transfers to another paying agency, the Commission shall not repeat the procedures described in paragraphs (a) through (f) of this section in order to resume collecting the debt. Instead, the Commission shall review the debt upon receiving the former paying agency's notice of the employee's transfer and shall ensure that collection is resumed by the new paying agency.

(2) *Responsibility of the Commission as the paying agency*—(i) *Complete claim.* When the Commission receives a certified claim from a creditor agency, the employee shall be given written notice of the certification, the date salary offset will begin, and the amount of the periodic deductions. Deductions shall be scheduled to begin at the next officially established pay interval or as

otherwise provided for in the certification.

(ii) *Incomplete claim.* When the Commission receives an incomplete certification of debt from a creditor agency, the Commission shall return the debt claim with notice that procedures under 5 U.S.C. 5514 and 5 CFR 550.1104 must be followed and that a properly certified debt claim must be received before action will be taken to collect from the employee's current pay account.

(iii) *Review.* The Commission is not authorized to review the merits of the creditor agency's determination with respect to the amount or validity of the debt certified by the creditor agency.

(iv) *Employees who transfer from one paying agency to another agency.* If, after the creditor agency has submitted the debt claim to the Commission, the employee transfers to an agency outside the Commission before the debt is collected in full, the Commission must certify the total amount collected on the debt. One copy of the certification shall be furnished to the employee and one copy shall be sent to the creditor agency along with notice of the employee's transfer. If the Commission is aware that the employee is entitled to payments from the Civil Service Retirement and Disability Fund, or other similar payments, it must provide written notification to the agency responsible for making such payments that the debtor owes a debt (including the amount) and that the requirements set forth herein and in the Office of Personnel Management's regulation (5 CFR part 550) have been fully met.

(j) Interest, Penalties, and Administrative Costs. Where the Commission is the creditor agency, it shall assess interest, penalties, and administrative costs pursuant to 31 U.S.C. 3717 and 31 CFR 901.9.

(k) *Refunds.* (1) Where the Commission is the creditor agency, it shall promptly refund any amount deducted under the authority of 5 U.S.C. 5514 when:

(i) The debt is compromised or otherwise found not to be owing to the United States; or

(ii) An administrative or judicial order directs the Commission to make a refund.

(2) Unless required by law or contract, refunds under this paragraph (k) shall not bear interest.

(l) *Request from a creditor agency for the services of a hearing official.* (1) The Commission may provide a hearing official upon request of the creditor agency when the debtor is employed by the Commission and the creditor agency cannot provide a prompt and appropriate hearing before a hearing official furnished pursuant to another lawful arrangement.

(2) The Commission may provide a hearing official upon request of a creditor agency when the debtor works for the creditor agency and that agency cannot arrange for a hearing official.

(3) The Director shall arrange for qualified personnel to serve as hearing officials.

(4) Services rendered under this paragraph (l) shall be provided on a fully reimbursable basis pursuant to 31 U.S.C. 1535.

(m) *Non-waiver of rights by payments.* A debtor's payment, whether voluntary or involuntary, of all or any portion of a debt being collected pursuant to this section shall not be construed as a waiver of any rights that the debtor may have under any statute, regulation, or contract except as otherwise provided by law or contract.

(n) Exception to due process procedures. The procedures set forth in this section shall not apply to adjustments described in 5 U.S.C. 5514(a)(3) and 5 CFR 550.1104(c).

[62 FR 38019, July 16, 1997, as amended at 68 FR 32976, June 3, 2003]

§ 201.205 Salary adjustments.

Any negative adjustment to pay arising out of an employee's election of coverage, or a change in coverage, under a Federal benefits program requiring periodic deductions from pay shall not be considered collection of a "debt" for the purposes of this section if the amount to be recovered was accumulated over four pay periods or less. In such cases, the Commission need not comply with § 201.204, but it will provide a clear and concise statement in the employee's earnings statement advising the employee of the previous overpayment at the time the adjustment is made.

§ 201.206 Administrative offset.

(a) *Collection.* The Director may collect a claim pursuant to 31 U.S.C. 3716 from a person, organization, or entity other than an agency of the United States Government by administrative offset of monies payable by the Government. Collection by administrative offset shall be undertaken where the claim is certain in amount, where offset is feasible and desirable and not otherwise prohibited, where the applicable statute of limitations has not expired, and where the offset is in the best interest of the United States.

(b) *Offset prior to completion of procedures.* Prior to the completion of the procedures described in paragraph (c) of this section, the Commission may effect offset if:

(1) Failure to offset would substantially prejudice the Commission's ability to collect the debt; and

(2) The time before the payment is to be made does not reasonably permit completion of the procedures described in paragraph (c) of this section. Such prior offsetting shall be followed promptly by the completion of the procedures described in paragraph (c) of this section.

(c) *Debtor's rights.* (1) Unless the procedures described in paragraph (b) of this section are used, prior to collecting any claim by administrative offset or referring such claim to another agency for collection through administrative offset, the Director shall provide the debtor with the following:

(i) Written notification of the nature and amount of the claim, the intention of the Director to collect the claim through administrative offset, and a statement of the rights of the debtor under this paragraph;

(ii) An opportunity to inspect and copy the records of the Commission not exempt from disclosure with respect to the claim;

(iii) An opportunity to have the Commission's determination of indebtedness reviewed by the Director. Any request for review by the debtor shall be in writing and be submitted to the Commission within 30 calendar days of the date of the notice of the offset. The Director may waive the time limit for requesting review for good cause shown by the debtor. The Commission shall provide the debtor with a reasonable opportunity for an oral hearing when:

(A) An applicable statute authorizes or requires the Commission to consider waiver of the indebtedness involved, the debtor requests waiver of the indebtedness, and the waiver determination turns on an issue of credibility or veracity; or

(B) The debtor requests reconsideration of the debt and the Commission determines that the question of the indebtedness cannot be resolved by review of the documentary evidence, for example, when the validity of the debt turns on an issue of credibility or veracity. Unless otherwise required by law, an oral hearing under this section is not required to be a formal evidentiary hearing, although the Commission shall document all significant matters discussed at the hearing. In those cases where an oral hearing is not required by this section, the Commission shall nevertheless accord the debtor a "paper hearing," (i.e., the Commission will make its determination on the request for waiver or reconsideration based upon a review of the written record); and

(iv) An opportunity to enter into a written agreement for the repayment of the amount of the claim at the discretion of the Commission.

(2) If the procedures described in paragraph (b) of this section are employed, the procedures described in this paragraph shall be effected after offset.

(d) *Interest.* Pursuant to 31 U.S.C. 3717 and 31 CFR 901.9, the Commission shall assess interest, penalties and administrative costs on debts owed to the United States. The Commission is authorized to assess interest and related charges on debts that are not subject to 31 U.S.C. 3717 to the extent authorized under the common law or other applicable statutory authority.

(e) *Refunds.* Amounts recovered by offset but later found not to be owed to the Government shall be promptly refunded.

(f) *Requests for offset to other Federal agencies.* The Director may request that a debt owed to the Commission be administratively offset against funds due and payable to a debtor by another Federal agency. In requesting administrative offset, the Commission, as creditor, will certify in writing to the Federal agency holding funds of the debtor:

(1) That the debtor owes the debt;

(2) The amount and basis of the debt; and

(3) That the Commission has complied with the requirements of its own administrative offset regulations and the applicable provisions of 31 CFR part 901 with respect to providing the debtor with due process.

(g) *Requests for offset from other Federal agencies.* Any Federal agency may request that funds due and payable to its debtor by the Commission be administratively offset in order to collect a debt owed to such Federal agency by the debtor. The Commission shall initiate the requested offset only upon:

(1) Receipt of written certification from the creditor agency:

(i) That the debtor owes the debt;

(ii) The amount and basis of the debt;

(iii) That the agency has prescribed regulations for the exercise of administrative offset; and

(iv) That the agency has complied with its own administrative offset regulations and with the applicable provisions of 31 CFR part 901, including providing any required hearing or review.

(2) A determination by the Commission that collection by offset against funds payable by the Commission would be in the best interest of the United States as determined by the facts and circumstances of the particular case and that such offset would not otherwise be contrary to law.

[62 FR 38019, July 16, 1997, as amended at 68 FR 32976, June 3, 2003]

§ 201.207 Administrative offset against amounts payable from Civil Service Retirement and Disability Fund

(a) Unless otherwise prohibited by law, the Commission may request that moneys which are due and payable to a debtor from the Civil Service Retirement and Disability Fund be administratively offset in reasonable amounts in order to collect in one full payment or a minimal number of payments debt owed to the Commission by the debtor. Such requests shall be made to the appropriate officials of the Office of Personnel Management in accordance with such regulations as may be prescribed by the Director of that Office.

(b) When making a request for administrative offset under paragraph (a) of this section, the Commission shall include a written certification that:

(1) The debtor owes the Commission a debt, including the amount of the debt;

(2) The Commission has complied with the applicable statutes, regulations, and procedures of the Office of Personnel Management; and

(3) The Commission has complied with the requirements of 31 CFR 901.3, including any required hearing or review.

(c) Once the Commission decides to request administrative offset under paragraph (a) of this section, it shall make the request as soon as practical after completion of the applicable procedures. This will satisfy any requirement that offset be initiated prior to expiration of the applicable statute of limitations. At such time as the debtor makes a claim for payments from the Fund, if at least a year has elapsed since the offset request was originally made, the debtor shall be permitted to offer a satisfactory repayment plan in lieu of offset upon establishing that changed financial circumstances would render the offset unjust.

(d) If the Commission collects part or all of the debt by other means before deductions are made or completed pursuant to paragraph (a) of this section, the Commission shall act promptly to modify or terminate its request for offset under paragraph (a) of this section.

[62 FR 38019, July 16, 1997, as amended at 68 FR 32976, June 3, 2003]

§ 201.208 Tax refund offset.

(a) *Scope.* The provisions of 26 U.S.C. 6402(d) and 31 U.S.C. 3720A authorize the Secretary of the Treasury to offset a delinquent debt owed to the United States Government from the tax refund due a taxpayer when other collection efforts have failed to recover the amount due.

(b) *Definitions*—(1) *Debt.* Debt means money owed by an individual, organization or entity from sources which include loans insured or guaranteed by the United States and all other amounts due the United States from fees, leases, services, overpayments, civil and criminal penalties, damages, interest, fines, administrative costs, and all other similar sources. A debt becomes eligible for tax refund offset procedures if:

(i) It cannot currently be collected pursuant to the salary offset procedures of 5 U.S.C. 5514(a)(1);

(ii) The debt is ineligible for administrative offset under 31 U.S.C. 3716(a) by reason of 31 U.S.C. 3716(c)(2) or cannot currently be collected by administrative offset under 31 U.S.C. 3716(a); and

(iii) The requirements of this section are otherwise satisfied.

(2) *Dispute.* A dispute is a written statement supported by documentation or other evidence that all or part of an alleged debt is not past due or legally enforceable, that the amount is not the amount currently owed, that the outstanding debt has been satisfied, or, in the case of a debt reduced to judgment, that the judgment has been satisfied or stayed.

(3) *Notice.* Notice means the information sent to the debtor pursuant to §201.208(d). The date of the notice is the date shown on the notice letter as its date of issuance.

(4) *Past due.* All judgment debts are past due for purposes of this section. Such debts remain past due until paid in full.

(c) The Commission may refer any past due, legally enforceable non-judgment debt of an individual, organization or entity to Treasury for offset if the Commission's or the referring agency's rights of action accrued more than three months but less than ten years before the offset is made. Debts reduced to judgment may be referred at any time. Debts in amounts lower than $25.00 are not subject to referral.

(d) The Commission will provide the debtor with written notice of its intent to offset before initiating the offset. Notice will be mailed to the debtor at the current address of the debtor, as determined from information obtained from the IRS pursuant to 26 U.S.C.

6103(m)(2), (4), (5) or from information regarding the debt maintained by the Commission. The notice sent to the debtor will state the amount of the debt and inform the debtor that:

(1) The debt is past due;

(2) The Commission intends to refer the debt to Treasury for offset from tax refunds that may be due to the taxpayer;

(3) The Commission intends to provide information concerning the delinquent debt exceeding $100 to a consumer reporting bureau unless such debt has already been disclosed; and

(4) The debtor has 65 calendar days from the date of notice in which to present evidence that all or part of the debt is not past due, that the amount is not the amount currently owed, that the outstanding debt has been satisfied, or, if a judgment debt, that the debt has been satisfied, or stayed, before the debt is reported to a consumer reporting agency, if applicable, and referred to Treasury for offset from tax refunds.

(e) If the debtor neither pays the amount due nor presents evidence that the amount is not past due or is satisfied or stayed, the Commission will report the debt to a consumer reporting agency at the end of the notice period, if applicable, and refer the debt to Treasury for offset from the taxpayer's federal tax refund. The Commission shall certify to Treasury that reasonable efforts have been made by the Commission to obtain payment of such debt.

(f) A debtor may request a review by the Commission if the debtor believes that all or part of the debt is not past due or is not legally enforceable, or, in the case of a judgment debt, that the debt has been stayed or the amount satisfied, as follows:

(1) The debtor must send a written request for review to the Director at the address provided in the notice.

(2) The request must state the amount disputed and the reasons why the debtor believes that the debt is not past due, is not legally enforceable, has been satisfied, or, if a judgment debt, has been satisfied or stayed.

(3) The request must include any documents that the debtor wishes to be

considered or state that additional information will be submitted within the time permitted.

(4) If the debtor wishes to inspect records establishing the nature and amount of the debt, the debtor must make a written request to the Director for an opportunity for such an inspection. The office holding the relevant records not exempt from disclosure shall make them available for inspection during normal business hours within one week from the date of receipt of the request.

(5) The request for review and any additional information submitted pursuant to the request must be received by the Director at the address stated in the notice within 65 calendar days of the date of issuance of the notice.

(6) The Commission will review disputes and shall consider its records and any documentation and arguments submitted by the debtor. The Commission's decision to refer to Treasury any disputed portion of the debt shall be made by the Chairman. The Commission shall send a written notice of its decision to the debtor. There is no administrative appeal of this decision.

(7) If the evidence presented by the debtor is considered by a non-Commission agent or other entities or persons acting on the Commission's behalf, the debtor will be accorded at least 30 calendar days from the date the agent or other entity or person determines that all or part of the debt is past-due and legally enforceable to request review by an officer or employee of the Commission of any unresolved dispute.

(8) Any debt that previously has been reviewed pursuant to this section or any other section of this subpart, or that has been reduced to a judgment, may not be disputed except on the grounds of payments made or events occurring subsequent to the previous review or judgment.

(g) The Commission will notify Treasury of any change in the amount due promptly after receipt of payments or notice of other reductions.

(h) In the event that more than one debt is owed, the tax refund offset procedure will be applied in the order in which the debts became past due.

SUBCHAPTER B—NONADJUDICATIVE INVESTIGATIONS

PART 202—INVESTIGATIONS OF COSTS OF PRODUCTION

Sec.
202.1 Applicability of part.
202.2 Applications.
202.3 Preliminary inquiry.
202.4 Public hearing.
202.5 Type of information to be developed at hearing.
202.6 Reports.

AUTHORITY: Sec. 335, 72 Stat. 680; 19 U.S.C. 1335.

SOURCE: 27 FR 12120, Dec. 7, 1962, unless otherwise noted.

§ 202.1 Applicability of part.

This part 202 applies specifically to investigations under section 366 of the Tariff Act (19 U.S.C. 1336).[1] For other applicable rules see part 201 of this chapter.

§ 202.2 Applications.

(a) *Who may file.* Applications for an investigation to which this part 202 relates may be filed by any firm, association of firms, or corporation engaged in the production of a domestic article, or by any duly authorized representative of the foregoing.

(b) *Requirements for applications.* In addition to conforming with the requirements of § 201.8 of this chapter, applications under this part 202 shall include the following:

(1) A clear statement that they are requests for investigations for the purposes of section 336;

---

[1] Section 336(a) of the Tariff Act provides in part that "(1) upon request of the President, or (2) upon resolution of either or both Houses of Congress, or (3) upon its own motion, or (4) when in the judgment of the Commission there is good and sufficient reason therefor, upon application of any interested party, [the commission] shall investigate the differences in the costs of production of any domestic article and of any like or similar foreign article". (19 U.S.C. 1336.) The provisions of section 336 of the Tariff Act may not be applied to any article with respect to the importation of which into the United States a foreign trade agreement has been concluded under the Trade Agreements Act of 1934, as amended, or the Trade Expansion Act. (19 U.S.C. 1352(a)).

(2) The name or description of the article concerning which an investigation is sought;

(3) A reference to the tariff provision or provisions applicable to such article; and

(4) A statement indicating whether an increase or a decrease in the rate of duty is sought.

(c) *Supporting information.* The applicant must file with his application such supporting information as may be in his possession. As far as practicable, information of the following character should be furnished:

(1) Comparability of the domestic and foreign articles and the degree of competition between them.

(2) Trend in recent years of (i) domestic production, (ii) domestic sales, (iii) imports, (iv) costs of production, and (v) prices.

(3) Evidence of difference between domestic and foreign costs of production of the articles involved.

(4) Areas of greatest competition between the imported and domestic products and the principal market or markets in the United States.

(5) Other relevant factors that constitute, in the opinion of the applicant, an advantage or disadvantage in competition, and any other information which the applicant believes the Commission should consider.

§ 202.3 Preliminary inquiry.

Upon the receipt of an application properly filed, the Commission will make a preliminary inquiry for the purpose of determining whether there is good and sufficient reason for a full investigation. If such determination is in the affirmative, a full investigation will be instituted.

§ 202.4 Public hearing.

A public hearing will be held in connection with each full investigation to which this part 202 relates.

§ 202.5 Type of information to be developed at hearing.

Without excluding other factors, but with a view to assisting parties interested to present information necessary for the formulation of findings required by the statute, the Commission will expect attention in the hearing to be concentrated upon facts relating to:

(a) The degree of competition between the foreign and domestic articles in the markets of the United States.

(b) The degree of likeness or similarity between grades, classes, and price groups of the American product and the imported article.

(c) Costs of production and importation. Statements of average cost of production, domestic and, so far as known, foreign, may be submitted subject to verification and review in the Commission's investigation. Such statements should include not only the direct costs for materials and labor, commonly termed prime cost, but also indirect costs such as indirect labor, overhead factory expenses, fixed charges, the portion of general and administrative expense chargeable to manufacture, imputed interest on investment equity, and transportation to markets. For the foreign product the expenses (other than duties) incident to importation are also important. Any information which may be available bearing on the general levels of domestic and foreign costs of production, the differentials between particular elements of domestic and foreign costs, and the extent to which invoice or wholesale prices are reliable evidence of foreign costs, will be pertinent.

(d) Other significant advantages or disadvantages in competition.

§ 202.6 Reports.

After the completion of its investigation, the Commission will incorporate its findings in a report, and the report will be transmitted to the President.

PART 204—INVESTIGATIONS OF EFFECTS OF IMPORTS ON AGRICULTURAL PROGRAMS

Sec.
204.1 Applicability of part.
204.2 Investigations.
204.3 Public hearings.
204.4 Supplemental investigations.
204.5 Reports.

AUTHORITY: 19 U.S.C. 1335.

SOURCE: 27 FR 12121, Dec. 7, 1962, unless otherwise noted.

§ 204.1 Applicability of part.

This part 204 applies specifically to investigations under section 22 of the Agricultural Adjustment Act, as amended (7 U.S.C. 624).[1] For other applicable rules see part 201 of this chapter.

[27 FR 12121, Dec. 7, 1962, as amended at 68 FR 32977, June 3, 2003]

§ 204.2 Investigations.

The Commission will make an investigation for the purposes of section 22(a) of the Agricultural Adjustment

[1] Section 22 provides in part as follows:

"(a) Whenever the Secretary of Agriculture has reason to believe that any article or articles are being or are practically certain to be imported into the United States under such conditions and in such quantities as to render or tend to render ineffective, or materially interfere with * * * any loan, purchase, or other program or operation undertaken by the Department of Agriculture, or any agency operating under its direction, with respect to any agricultural commodity or product thereof, or to reduce substantially the amount of any product processed in the United States from any agricultural commodity or product thereof with respect to which any such program or operation is being undertaken he shall so advise the President, and, if the President agrees that there is reason for such belief, the President shall cause an immediate investigation to be made by the United States Tariff Commission, which shall give precedence to investigations under this section to determine such facts. Such investigation shall be made after due notice and opportunity for hearing to interested parties, and shall be conducted subject to such regulations as the President shall specify.

*   *   *   *   *

"(d) After investigation, report, finding and declaration in the manner provided in the case of a proclamation issued pursuant to subsection (b) of this section, any proclamation or provision of such proclamation may be suspended or terminated by the President whenever he finds and proclaims that the circumstances requiring the proclamation or provision thereof no longer exist or may be modified by the President whenever he finds and proclaims that changed circumstances require such modification to carry out the purposes of this section." (7 U.S.C. 624.)

Regulations of the President are set forth in Executive Order 7233 of November 23, 1935.

Act, as amended, only upon request of the President. [2]

[27 FR 12121, Dec. 7, 1962, as amended at 68 FR 32977, June 3, 2003]

§ 204.3 Public hearings.

A public hearing will be held in connection with each investigation to which this part 204 relates. The Foreign Agricultural Service of the U.S. Department of Agriculture may have a representative or representatives at each hearing who shall have the privilege of examining witnesses.

§ 204.4 Supplemental investigations.

An investigation for the purposes of section 22(d) of the Agricultural Adjustment Act, as amended, will be made upon request of the President, or upon the Commission's own motion when in its judgment there is good and sufficient reason therefor. A public hearing will be held in connection with each such supplemental investigation.

§ 204.5 Reports.

After completion of its investigation, the Commission will transmit to the President a report of the results thereof, including its findings and recommendations based thereon, and a statement of the steps taken in the investigation, together with a transcript of the evidence submitted at the hearing. A copy of such report will be transmitted to the Secretary of Agriculture.

[49 FR 32571, Aug. 15, 1984]

---

[2] Applications for investigations for the purposes of section 22 of this Agricultural Adjustment Act, as amended, must be filed with the Secretary of Agriculture (Executive Order 7233).

PART 205—INVESTIGATIONS TO DETERMINE THE PROBABLE ECONOMIC EFFECT ON THE ECONOMY OF THE UNITED STATES OF PROPOSED MODIFICATIONS OF DUTIES OR OF ANY BARRIER TO (OR OTHER DISTORTION OF) INTERNATIONAL TRADE OR OF TAKING RETALIATORY ACTIONS TO OBTAIN THE ELIMINATION OF UNJUSTIFIABLE OR UNREASONABLE FOREIGN ACTS OR POLICIES WHICH RESTRICT U.S. COMMERCE

Sec.
205.1 Applicability of part.

Subpart A—Investigations To Determine the Probable Economic Effect of Modifications of United States Duties or of Any Barrier to (or Other Distortion of) International Trade on Domestic Industries and on Consumers

205.2 Applicability of subpart.
205.3 Investigations under sections 131 and 503 of the Trade Act of 1974.
205.4 [Reserved]

Subpart B—Investigations Concerning the Probable Impact on the Economy of the United States of the President's Taking Retaliatory Action To Obtain the Elimination of Unjustifiable or Unreasonable Foreign Acts or Policies Which Restrict U.S. Commerce

205.5 Applicability of subpart.
205.6 Investigations under section 301(e)(3) of the Trade Act of 1974.

AUTHORITY: Sec. 335, Tariff Act of 1930 (72 Stat. 680; 19 U.S.C. 1335); sec. 603, Trade Act of 1974 (88 Stat. 2073); (19 U.S.C. 2482).

SOURCE: 42 FR 40426, Aug. 10, 1977, unless otherwise noted.

§ 205.1 Applicability of part.

This part 205 applies to functions and duties of the Commission under sections 131, 301(e)(3), and 503(a) of the Trade Act of 1974. For other applicable rules, see part 201 of this chapter.

Subpart A—Investigations To Determine the Probable Economic Effect of Modifications of United States Duties or of Any Barrier to (or Other Distortion of) International Trade on Domestic Industries and on Consumers

§ 205.2 Applicability of subpart.

This subpart A of part 205 applies to investigations for the purposes of section 131(a)–(b), 131(c), and 503 of the Trade Act of 1974. For other applicable rules, see part 201 of this chapter.

§ 205.3 Investigations under sections 131 and 503 of the Trade Act of 1974.

(a) *Purpose of investigations*—(1) *Sections 131(a)–(b) and 503(a).* Upon the receipt of a list of articles from the President or from the United States Trade Representative as provided in section 131(a) or 503(a), and in Executive Order No. 11846, as amended, which may be considered for modification of United States duties, or as eligible articles for duty-free treatment under the generalized system of preferences, respectively, the Commission shall initiate an investigation to obtain information pertinent to the fomulation of its advice to the President under section 131(b) with respect to such articles to assist him in making an informed judgment as to the impact which might be caused by such duty modifications or duty-free treatment on U.S. manufacturing, agriculture, mining, fishing, labor, and consumers, including whether any reductions in rates of duty should take place over a period longer than the minimum periods provided by section 109(a) of the Trade Act of 1974 (88 Stat. 1985; 19 U.S.C. 2119).

(2) *Section 131(c).* Upon the receipt of a request from the President or from the United States Trade Representative as provided in section 131(c) and in Executive Order No. 11846, as amended, to assist him in his determination of whether to enter into any trade agreement under section 102, the Commission shall institute an investigation to obtain information pertinent to the formulation of its views with respect to the probable economic effects of modifications of any barrier to (or other distortion of) international trade on domestic industries and purchasers and on prices and quantities of articles in the United States.

(b) *Institution and notice of investigation.* An investigation to which this subpart A relates will be instituted promptly after the receipt from the President or the United States Trade Representative of (1) a list of articles which may be considered for duty modifications or duty-free treatment, or (2) a request for an investigation and report concerning the probable economic effects of modifications of any barrier to (or other distortion of) international trade.

(c) *Hearings.* Public hearings will be held in connection with every investigation to which this subpart A relates. For other applicable rules, see § 201.11 of this chapter.

(d) *Report to the President.* After the completion of its investigation, the Commission will incorporate its advice or views in a report which together with hearing transcripts, briefs and other information will be transmitted to the President through the United States Trade Representative.

[42 FR 40426, Aug. 10, 1977, as amended at 63 FR 29351, May 29, 1998]

§ 205.4 [Reserved]

Subpart B—Investigations Concerning the Probable Impact on the Economy of the United States of the President's Taking Retaliatory Action To Obtain the Elimination of Unjustifiable or Unreasonable Foreign Acts or Policies Which Restrict U.S. Commerce

§ 205.5 Applicability of subpart.

This subpart B of part 205 applies to investigations for the purpose of section 301(e)(3) of the Trade Act of 1974. For other applicable rules, see part 201 of this chapter.

§ 205.6 Investigations under section 301(e)(3) of the Trade Act of 1974.

(a) *Purpose of investigation.* The purpose of an investigation by the Commission is to provide the President with its views pursuant to section 301(e)(3) as to the probable impact on the economy of the United States of imposing retaliatory restrictions on imports into the United States from countries or foreign instrumentalities which maintain restrictions against U.S. exports.

(b) *Institution and notice of investigation.* An investigation to which this subpart B relates will be instituted promptly after the receipt from the President of a request for the views of the Commission with regard to the matters indicated in paragraph (a) of this section.

(c) *Public hearings.* If, in the judgment of the Commission, there is good and sufficient reason therefor, the Commission, in the course of its investigation, will hold a public hearing and afford interested parties opportunity to appear and be heard at such hearing. If no notice of public hearing issues concurrently with a notice of investigation, any interested party who believes that a public hearing should be held may, within thirty (30) days after the date of publication in the FEDERAL REGISTER of the notice of investigation, submit a request in writing to the Secretary of the Commission that a public hearing be held, stating the reasons for such request.

(d) *Written statements.* Any interested party may submit to the Commission a written statement of information pertinent to the subject matter of such investigation not later than thirty (30) days after a notice of investigation under paragraph (b) of this section is published in the FEDERAL REGISTER. If a public hearing is held in the investigation, a statement may be received in lieu of or in addition to appearance at the hearing. Statements shall conform with the requirements for documents set forth in §§ 201.6 and 201.8 of this chapter.

(e) *Report to the President.* After the completion of its investigation, the Commission will incorporate its views in a report which will be transmitted promptly to the President.

PART 206—INVESTIGATIONS RELATING TO GLOBAL AND BILATERAL SAFEGUARD ACTIONS, MARKET DISRUPTION, TRADE DIVERSION, AND REVIEW OF RELIEF ACTIONS

Sec.
206.1 Applicability of part.

Subpart A—General

206.2 Identification of type of petition or request.
206.3 Institution of investigations; publication of notice; and availability for public inspection.
206.4 Notification of other agencies.
206.5 Public hearing.
206.6 Report to the President.
206.7 Confidential business information; furnishing of nonconfidential summaries thereof.
206.8 Service, filing, and certification of documents.

Subpart B—Investigations Relating to Global Safeguard Actions

206.11 Applicability of subpart.
206.12 Definitions applicable to subpart B of this part.
206.13 Who may file a petition.
206.14 Contents of petition.
206.15 Institution of investigation.
206.16 Industry adjustment plan and commitments.
206.17 Limited disclosure of certain confidential business information under administrative protective order.
206.18 Time for determinations, reporting.
206.19 Public report.

Subpart C—Investigations Relating to a Surge in Imports From a NAFTA Country

206.21 Applicability of subpart.
206.22 Definition applicable to subpart C.
206.23 Who may file a request.
206.24 Contents of request.
206.25 Time for reporting.
206.26 Public report.

Subpart D—Investigations Relating to Bilateral Safeguard Actions

206.31 Applicability of subpart.
206.32 Definitions applicable to subpart D.
206.33 Who may file a petition.
206.34 Contents of petition.
206.35 Time for determinations, reporting.
206.36 Public report.
206.37 Limited disclosure of certain confidential business information under administrative protective order.

Subpart E—Investigations for Relief From Market Disruption

206.41 Applicability of subpart.
206.42 Who may file a petition.
206.43 Contents of a petition under section 406(a) of the Trade Act.
206.44 Contents of a petition under section 421(b) or (o) of the Trade Act.
206.44a Special rules for conducting investigations under section 421(b) of the Trade Act.
206.45 Time for reporting.
206.46 Public report.
206.47 Limited disclosure of certain confidential business information under administrative protective order.

Subpart F—Monitoring; Advice As to Effect of Extension, Reduction, Modification, or Termination of Relief Action

206.51 Applicability of subpart.
206.52 Monitoring.
206.53 Investigations to advise the President as to the probable economic effect of reduction, modification, or termination of action.
206.54 Investigations with respect to extension of action.
206.55 Investigations to evaluate the effectiveness of relief.

Subpart G—Investigations For Action in Response to Trade Diversion; Reviews of Action Taken

206.61 Applicability of subpart.
206.62 Who may file a petition.
206.63 Contents of petition.
206.64 Institution of investigation or review; publication of notice; and availability for public inspection.
206.65 Public hearing.
206.66 Limited disclosure of certain confidential business information under administrative protective order.
206.67 Time for determination and report.
206.68 Public report.

AUTHORITY: 19 U.S.C. 1335, 2112 note, 2251–2254, 2436, 2451–2451a, 3351–3382, 3805 note, 4051–4065, and 4101.

SOURCE: 59 FR 5091, Feb. 3, 1994, unless otherwise noted.

§ 206.1 Applicability of part.

Part 206 applies to proceedings of the Commission under sections 201–202, 204, 406, and 421–422 of the Trade Act of 1974, as amended (2251–2252, 2254, 2436, 2451–2451a), sections 301–317 of the North American Free Trade Agreement Implementation Act (19 U.S.C. 3351–3382) (hereinafter NAFTA Implementation Act), and the statutory provisions listed in § 206.31 of this part 206 that implement bilateral safeguard provisions in other free trade agreements into which the United States has entered.

[77 FR 37805, June 25, 2012]

Subpart A—General

SOURCE: 60 FR 10, Jan. 3, 1995, unless otherwise noted.

§ 206.2 Identification of type of petition or request.

An investigation under this part may be commenced on the basis of a petition, request, resolution, or motion as provided for in the statutory provisions listed in §§ 206.1 and 206.31. Each petition or request, as the case maybe, filed by an entity representative of a domestic industry under this part shall state clearly on the first page thereof "This is a [petition or request] under section [citing the statutory provision] and Subpart [B, C, D, E, F, or G] of part 206 of the rules of practice and procedure of the United States International Trade Commission." A paper original and eight (8) true paper copies of a petition, request, resolution, or motion shall be filed. One copy of any exhibits, appendices, and attachments to the document shall be filed in electronic form on CD–ROM, DVD, or other portable electronic format approved by the Secretary.

[80 FR 39380, July 9, 2015]

§ 206.3 Institution of investigations; publication of notice; and availability for public inspection.

(a) *Institution of investigation and publication of notice.* Except as provided in § 206.15(b), the Commission, after receipt of a petition or request under part 206, properly filed, will promptly institute an appropriate investigation and publish notice thereof in the FEDERAL REGISTER. The Commission also will institute an investigation and publish a notice following receipt of a resolution or on the Commission's own motion under part 206.

(b) *Contents of notice.* The notice will identify the petitioner or other requestor, the imported article that is the subject of the investigation and its tariff subheading, the nature and timing of the determination to be made, the time and place of any public hearing, dates of deadlines for filing briefs, statements, and other documents, limits on page lengths for posthearing briefs, the place at which the petition or request and any other documents filed in the course of the investigation may be inspected, and the name, address, and telephone number of the office that may be contacted for more information. The Commission will provide the same sort of information in its notice when the investigation was instituted following receipt of a resolution or on the Commission's own motion.

(c) *Availability for public inspection.* The Commission will promptly make each petition, request, resolution, or Commission motion available for public inspection (with the exception of confidential business information).

[60 FR 10, Jan. 3, 1995, as amended at 67 FR 8190, Feb. 22, 2002; 68 FR 32977, June 3, 2003]

§206.4 Notification of other agencies.

For each investigation subject to provisions of part 206, the Commission will transmit copies of the petition, request, resolution, or Commission motion as required by the relevant statute, along with a copy of the notice of investigation.

[67 FR 8190, Feb. 22, 2002]

§206.5 Public hearing.

(a) *Investigations under subpart B of this part.* A public hearing on the question of injury and a second public hearing on remedy (if necessary) will be held in connection with each investigation instituted under subpart B of this part after reasonable notice thereof has been caused to be published in the FEDERAL REGISTER. A hearing on remedy is not necessary if the Commission has made a negative determination on the question of injury.

(b) *Investigations under subpart C, D, E, or G of this part.* A public hearing on the subject of injury and remedy will be held in connection with each investigation instituted under subpart C or D of this part or section 406(a) of the Trade Act and subpart E of this part, after reasonable notice thereof has

been published in the FEDERAL REGISTER. The Commission also will conduct a public hearing in each investigation instituted under section 421(b) or (o) of the Trade Act and subpart E of this part or section 422(b) of the Act and subpart G. The FEDERAL REGISTER notice announcing the institution of such an investigation will list the date, time, and location of the hearing, the subjects to be addressed, and the procedures to be followed.

(c) *Investigations under subpart F of this part.* A public hearing on the subject of whether an action taken under section 203 of the Trade Act of 1974 should be extended will be held in connection with each investigation instituted under subpart F of this part after reasonable notice thereof has been published in the FEDERAL REGISTER.

(d) *Opportunity to appear and to cross-question.* All interested parties and consumers, including any association representing the interests of consumers, will be afforded an opportunity to be present, to present evidence, to comment on the adjustment plan, if any, submitted in the case of an investigation under section 202(b) of the Trade Act of 1974, and to be heard at such hearings. All interested parties and consumers, including any association representing the interests of consumers, will be afforded an opportunity to cross-question interested parties making presentations at the hearing.

[60 FR 10, Jan. 3, 1995, as amended at 67 FR 8190, Feb. 22, 2002]

§206.6 Report to the President.

(a) *In general.* The Commission will include in its report to the President the following:

(1) The determination made and an explanation of the basis for the determination;

(2) If the determination is affirmative or if the Commission is equally divided in its determination, such remedy recommendation or proposal as may be appropriate under the statute and an explanation of the basis for each recommendation or proposal.

(3) Any dissenting or separate views by members of the Commission regarding the determination and any recommendations;

(b) *Additional findings and information.* (1) In the case of a determination made under section 202(b) of the Trade Act, the Commission will also include in its report the following:

(i) The findings with respect to the results of an examination of the factors other than imports which may be a cause of serious injury or threat thereof to the domestic industry;

(ii) A copy of the adjustment plan, if any, submitted by the petitioner;

(iii) Commitments submitted and information obtained by the Commission regarding steps that firms and workers in the domestic industry are taking, or plan to take, to facilitate positive adjustment to import competition;

(iv) A description of the short- and long-term effects that implementation of the action recommended is likely to have on the petitioning domestic industry, other domestic industries, and consumers; and

(v) A description of the short- and long-term effects of not taking the recommended action on the petitioning domestic industry, its workers and communities where production facilities of such industry are located, and other domestic industries.

(2) In the case of a determination made under section 302(b) of the NAFTA Implementation Act, the Commission will also include in its report the findings with respect to the results of an examination of the factors other than imports which may be a cause of serious injury or threat thereof to the domestic industry.

(3) In the case of a determination made under section 421(b) or 422(b) of the Trade Act, the Commission will also include in its report a description of—

(i) The short- and long-term effects that implementation of the action recommended is likely to have on the petitioning domestic industry, on other domestic industries, and on consumers; and

(ii) The short- and long-term effects of not taking the recommended action on the petitioning domestic industry, its workers, and the communities where production facilities of such industry are located, and on other domestic industries.

[60 FR 10, Jan. 3, 1995, as amended at 67 FR 8190, Feb. 22, 2002; 77 FR 3925, Jan. 26, 2012]

§ 206.7 **Confidential business information; furnishing of nonconfidential summaries thereof.**

(a) *Nonrelease of information.* Except as provided for in § 206.17, in the case of an investigation under subpart B, C, D, F, or G of this part or an investigation under section 422 of the Trade Act and subpart E of this part, the Commission will not release information which the Commission considers to be confidential business information within the meaning of § 201.6 of this chapter unless the party submitting the confidential business information had notice, at the time of submission, that such information would be released by the Commission, or such party subsequently consents to the release of the information. When appropriate, the Commission will include confidential business information in reports transmitted to the President and the Trade Representative; such reports will be marked as containing confidential business information, and a nonconfidential version of such report will be made available to the public.

(b) *Nonconfidential summaries.* Except as the Commission may otherwise provide, a party submitting confidential business information shall also submit to the Commission, at the time it submits such information, a nonconfidential summary of the information. If a party indicates that the confidential business information cannot be summarized, it shall state in writing the reasons why a summary cannot be provided. If the Commission finds that a request for confidentiality is not warranted and if the party concerned is either unwilling to make the information public or to authorize its disclosure in generalized or summarized form, the Commission may disregard the submission.

[60 FR 10, Jan. 3, 1995, as amended at 67 FR 8190, Feb. 22, 2002]

§ 206.8 **Service, filing, and certification of documents.**

(a) *Certification.* Any person submitting factual information on behalf of the petitioner or any other interested party for the consideration of the Commission in the course of an investigation to which this part pertains, and any person submitting a response to a Commission questionnaire issued in connection with an investigation to which this part pertains, must certify that such information is accurate and complete to the best of the submitter's knowledge.

(b) *Service.* Any party submitting a document for the consideration of the Commission in the course of an investigation to which this part pertains shall, in addition to complying with §201.8 of this chapter, serve a copy of the public version of such document on all other parties to the investigation in the manner prescribed in §201.16 of this chapter, and, when appropriate, serve a copy of the confidential version of such document in the manner provided for in §206.17(f). The Secretary shall promptly notify a petitioner when, before the establishment of a service list under §206.17(a)(4), an application under §206.17(a) is approved. When practicable, this notification shall be made by facsimile transmission. A copy of the petition including all confidential business information shall then be served by petitioner on those approved applicants in accordance with this section within two (2) calendar days of the time notification is made by the Secretary. If a document is filed before the Secretary's issuance of the service list provided for in §201.11 of this chapter or the administrative protective order list provided for in §206.17, the document need not be accompanied by a certificate of service, but the document shall be served on all appropriate parties within two (2) days of the issuance of the service list or the administrative protective order list and a certificate of service shall then be filed. Notwithstanding §201.16 of this chapter, petitions, briefs, and testimony filed by parties shall be served by hand or, if served by mail, by overnight mail or its equivalent. Failure to comply with the requirements of this rule may result in removal from status as a party to the investigation. The Commission shall make available, upon request, to all parties to the investigation a copy of each document, except

transcripts of hearings, confidential business information, privileged information, and information required to be served under this section, placed in the docket file of the investigation by the Commission.

(c) *Filing.* Documents to be filed with the Commission must comply with applicable rules, including §201.8 of this chapter. If the Commission establishes a deadline for the filing of a document, and the submitter includes confidential business information in the document, the submitter is to file and, if the submitter is a party, serve the confidential version of the document on the deadline and may file and serve the nonconfidential version of the document no later than one business day after the deadline for filing the document. The confidential version shall enclose all confidential business information in brackets and have the following warning marked on every page: "Bracketing of CBI not final for one business day after date of filing." The bracketing becomes final one business day after the date of filing of the document, *i.e.*, at the same time as the nonconfidential version of the document is due to be filed. Until the bracketing becomes final, recipients of the document may not divulge any part of the contents of the document to anyone not subject to the administrative protective order issued in the investigation. If the submitter discovers it has failed to bracket correctly, the submitter may file a corrected version or portion of the confidential document at the same time as the nonconfidential version is filed. No changes to the document other than bracketing and deletion of confidential business information are permitted after the deadline. Failure to comply with this paragraph may result in the striking of all or a portion of a submitter's document.

(d) *Briefs.* All briefs filed in proceedings subject to this part shall be filed electronically, and eight (8) true paper copies shall be filed on the same business day.

[59 FR 5091, Feb. 3, 1994, as amended at 68 FR 32977, June 3, 2003; 76 FR 61942, Oct. 6, 2011]

Subpart B—Investigations Relating to Global Safeguard Actions

SOURCE: 60 FR 12, Jan. 3, 1995, unless otherwise noted.

§ 206.11 Applicability of subpart.

This subpart B applies specifically to investigations under section 202(b) of the Trade Act. For other applicable rules, see subpart A of this part and part 201 of this chapter.

§ 206.12 Definitions applicable to subpart B of this part.

For the purposes of this subpart, the following terms have the meanings hereby assigned to them:

(a) *Adjustment plan* means a plan to facilitate positive adjustment to import competition submitted by a petitioner to the Commission and USTR either with the petition or at any time within 120 days after the date of filing of the petition.

(b) *Commitment* means commitments that a firm in the domestic industry, a certified or recognized union or group of workers in the domestic industry, a local community, a trade association representing the domestic industry, or any other person or group of persons submits to the Commission regarding actions such persons and entities intend to take to facilitate positive adjustment to import competition.

§ 206.13 Who may file a petition.

A petition under this subpart B may be filed by an entity, including a trade association, firm, certified or recognized union, or group of workers, that is representative of a domestic industry producing an article like or directly competitive with a foreign article that is allegedly being imported into the United States in such increased quantities as to be a substantial cause of serious injury, or the threat thereof, to such domestic industry.

§ 206.14 Contents of petition.

A petition under this subpart B shall include specific information in support of the claim that an article is being imported into the United States in such increased quantities as to be a substantial cause of serious injury, or the threat thereof, to the domestic industry producing an article like or directly competitive with the imported article. Such petition shall state whether provisional relief is sought because *critical circumstances* exist or because the imported article is a *perishable agricultural product*. In addition, such petition shall include the following information, to the extent that such information is available from governmental or other sources, or best estimates and the basis therefor if such information is not available:

(a) *Product description.* The name and description of the imported article concerned, specifying the United States tariff provision under which such article is classified and the current tariff treatment thereof, and the name and description of the like or directly competitive domestic article concerned;

(b) *Representativeness.* (1) The names and addresses of the firms represented in the petition and/or the firms employing or previously employing the workers represented in the petition and the locations of their establishments in which the domestic article is produced;

(2) The percentage of domestic production of the like or directly competitive domestic article that such represented firms and/or workers account for and the basis for claiming that such firms and/or workers are representative of an industry; and

(3) The names and locations of all other producers of the domestic article known to the petitioner;

(c) *Import data.* Import data for at least each of the most recent 5 full years which form the basis of the claim that the article concerned is being imported in increased quantities, either actual or relative to domestic production;

(d) *Domestic production data.* Data on total U.S. production of the domestic article for each full year for which data are provided pursuant to paragraph (c) of this section;

(e) *Data showing injury.* Quantitative data indicating the nature and extent of injury to the domestic industry concerned:

(1) With respect to serious injury, data indicating:

78

(i) A significant idling of production facilities in the industry, including data indicating plant closings or the underutilization of production capacity;

(ii) The inability of a significant number of firms to carry out domestic production operations at a reasonable level of profit; and

(iii) Significant unemployment or underemployment within the industry; and/or

(2) With respect to the threat of serious injury, data relating to:

(i) A decline in sales or market share, a higher and growing inventory (whether maintained by domestic producers, importers, wholesalers, or retailers), and a downward trend in production, profits, wages, productivity, or employment (or increasing underemployment);

(ii) The extent to which firms in the industry are unable to generate adequate capital to finance the modernization of their domestic plants and equipment, or are unable to maintain existing levels of expenditures for research and development;

(iii) The extent to which the U.S. market is the focal point for the diversion of exports of the article concerned by reason of restraints on exports of such article to, or on imports of such article into, third country markets; and

(3) Changes in the level of prices, production, and productivity.

(f) *Cause of injury.* An enumeration and description of the causes believed to be resulting in the injury, or threat thereof, described under paragraph (e) of this section, and a statement regarding the extent to which increased imports, either actual or relative to domestic production, of the imported article are believed to be such a cause, supported by pertinent data;

(g) *Relief sought and purpose thereof.* A statement describing the import relief sought, including the type, amount, and duration, and the specific purposes therefor, which may include facilitating the orderly transfer of resources to more productive pursuits, enhancing competitiveness, or other means of adjustment to new conditions of competition;

(h) *Efforts to compete.* A statement on the efforts being taken, or planned to be taken, or both, by firms and workers in the industry to make a positive adjustment to import competition.

(i) *Imports from NAFTA countries.* Quantitative data indicating the share of imports accounted for by imports from each NAFTA country (Canada and Mexico), and petitioner's view on the extent to which imports from such NAFTA country or countries are contributing importantly to the serious injury, or threat thereof, caused by total imports of such article.

(j) *Critical circumstances.* If the petition alleges the existence of critical circumstances, a statement setting forth the basis for the belief that there is clear evidence that increased imports (either actual or relative to domestic production) of the article are a substantial cause of serious injury, or the threat thereof, to the domestic industry, and that delay in taking action would cause damage to that industry that would be difficult to repair, and a statement concerning the provisional relief requested and the basis therefor.

§206.15 Institution of investigation.

(a) *In general.* Except as provided in paragraph (b) of this section, the Commission, after receipt of a petition under this subpart B, properly filed, will promptly institute an appropriate investigation and will cause a notice thereof to be published in the FEDERAL REGISTER.

(b) *Exceptions*—(1) *Reinvestigation within one (1) year.* Except for good cause determined by the Commission to exist, no new investigation will be made under section 202 of the Trade Act with respect to the same subject matter as a previous investigation under section 202 unless one (1) year has elapsed since the Commission made its report to the President of the results of such previous investigation.

(2) *Articles subject to prior action.* No new investigation will be made under section 202 of the Trade Act with respect to an article that is or has been the subject of an action under section 203(a) (3)(A), (B), (C), or (E) of the Trade Act if the last day on which the

President could take action under section 203 of the Trade Act in the new investigation is a date earlier than that permitted under section 203(e)(7) of the Trade Act.

(3) *Articles subject to the Textiles Agreement.* No investigation will be made under section 202 of the Trade Act with respect to an article that is the subject of the WTO Agreement on Textiles and Clothing unless the United States has integrated the article into GATT 1994 and the Secretary of Commerce has published notice to such effect in the FEDERAL REGISTER.

(4) *Perishable agricultural product.* An entity of the type described in § 206.13 that represents a domestic industry producing a perishable agricultural product may petition for provisional relief with respect to such product only if such product has been subject to monitoring by the Commission for not less than 90 days as of the date the allegation of injury is included in the petition.

§ 206.16 Industry adjustment plan and commitments.

(a) *Adjustment plan.* A petitioner may submit to the Commission, either with the petition or at any time within 120 days after the date of filing of the petition, a plan to facilitate positive adjustment to import competition.

(b) *Commitments.* If the Commission makes an affirmative injury determination, any firm in the domestic industry, certified or recognized union or group of workers in the domestic industry, local community, trade association representing the domestic industry, or any other person or group of persons may, individually, submit to the Commission commitments regarding actions such persons and entities intend to take to facilitate positive adjustment to import competition.

§ 206.17 Limited disclosure of certain confidential business information under administrative protective order.

(a)(1) *Disclosure.* Upon receipt of a timely application filed by an authorized applicant, as defined in paragraph (a)(3) of this section, which describes in general terms the information requested, and sets forth the reasons for the request (*e.g.,* all confidential business information properly disclosed pursuant to this section for the purpose of representing an interested party in investigations pending before the Commission), the Secretary shall make available all confidential business information contained in Commission memoranda and reports and in written submissions filed with the Commission at any time during the investigation (except privileged information, classified information, and specific information of a type which there is a clear and compelling need to withhold from disclosure, *e.g.,* trade secrets) to the authorized applicant under an administrative protective order described in paragraph (b) of this section. The term "confidential business information" is defined in § 201.6 of this chapter.

(2) *Application.* An application under paragraph (a)(1) of this section must be made by an authorized applicant on a form adopted by the Secretary or a photocopy thereof. A signed application shall be filed electronically. An application on behalf of an authorized applicant must be made no later than the time that entries of appearance are due pursuant to § 201.11 of this chapter. In the event that two or more authorized applicants represent one interested party who is a party to the investigation, the authorized applicants must select one of their number to be lead authorized applicant. The lead authorized applicant's application must be filed no later than the time that entries of appearance are due. Provided that the application is accepted, the lead authorized applicant shall be served with confidential business information pursuant to paragraph (f) of this section. The other authorized applicants representing the same party may file their applications after the deadline for entries of appearance but at least five days before the deadline for filing posthearing briefs in the investigation, and shall not be served with confidential business information.

(3) *Authorized applicant.* (i) Only an authorized applicant may file an application under this subsection. An authorized applicant is:

(A) An attorney for an interested party which is a party to the investigation;

(B) A consultant or expert under the direction and control of a person under paragraph (a)(3)(i)(A) of this section;

(C) A consultant or expert who appears regularly before the Commission and who represents an interested party which is a party to the investigation; or

(D) A representative of an interested party which is a party to the investigation, if such interested party is not represented by counsel.

(ii) In addition, an authorized applicant must not be involved in competitive decisionmaking for an interested party which is a party to the investigation. Involvement in "competitive decisionmaking" includes past, present, or likely future activities, associations, and relationships with an interested party which is a party to the investigation that involve the prospective authorized applicant's advice or participation in any of such party's decisions made in light of similar or corresponding information about a competitor (pricing, product design, etc.).

(iii) For purposes of this §206.17, the term *interested party* means:

(A) A foreign manufacturer, producer, or exporter, or the United States importer, of an article which is the subject of an investigation under this section or a trade or business association a majority of the members of which are producers, exporters, or importers of such article;

(B) The government of a country in which such article is produced or manufactured;

(C) A manufacturer, producer, or wholesaler in the United States of a like or directly competitive article;

(D) A certified union or recognized union or group of workers which is representative of an industry engaged in the manufacture, production, or wholesale of a like or directly competitive article in the United States;

(E) A trade or business association a majority of whose members manufacture, produce, or wholesale a like or directly competitive article in the United States; and

(F) An association, a majority of whose members is composed of interested parties described in paragraphs (a)(3)(iii) (C), (D), or (E) of this section with respect to a like or directly competitive article.

(4) *Forms and determinations.* (i) The Secretary may adopt, from time to time, forms for submitting requests for disclosure pursuant to an administrative protective order incorporating the terms of this rule. The Secretary shall determine whether the requirements for release of information under this rule have been satisfied. This determination shall be made concerning specific confidential business information as expeditiously as possible but in no event later than fourteen (14) days from the filing of the information, except if the submitter of the information objects to its release or the information is unusually voluminous or complex, in which case the determination shall be made within thirty (30) days from the filing of the information. The Secretary shall establish a list of parties whose applications have been granted. The Secretary's determination shall be final.

(ii) Should the Secretary determine pursuant to this section that materials sought to be protected from public disclosure by a person do not constitute confidential business information or were not required to be served under paragraph (f) of this section, then the Secretary shall, upon request, issue an order on behalf of the Commission requiring the return of all copies of such materials served in accordance with paragraph (f) of this section.

(iii) The Secretary shall release confidential business information only to an authorized applicant whose application has been accepted and who presents the application along with adequate personal identification; or a person described in paragraph (b)(1)(iv) of this section who presents a copy of the statement referred to in that paragraph along with adequate personal identification.

(b) *Administrative protective order.* The administrative protective order under which information is made available to the authorized applicant shall require the applicant to submit to the Secretary a personal sworn statement that, in addition to such other conditions as the Secretary may require, the applicant shall:

(1) Not divulge any of the confidential business information obtained under the administrative protective order and not otherwise available to the applicant, to any person other than

(i) Personnel of the Commission concerned with the investigation,

(ii) The person or agency from whom the confidential business information was obtained,

(iii) A person whose application for access to confidential business information under the administrative protective order has been granted by the Secretary, and

(iv) Other persons, such as paralegals and clerical staff, who are employed or supervised by an authorized applicant; who have a need thereof in connection with the investigation; who are not involved in competitive decisionmaking on behalf of an interested party which is a party to the investigation; and who have signed a statement in a form approved by the Secretary that they agree to be bound by the administrative protective order (the authorized applicant shall be responsible for retention and accuracy of such forms and shall be deemed responsible for such persons' compliance with the administrative protective order);

(2) Use such confidential business information solely for the purposes of representing an interested party in the Commission investigation then in progress;

(3) Not consult with any person not described in paragraph (b)(1) of this section concerning such confidential business information without first having received the written consent of the Secretary and the party or the attorney of the party from whom such confidential business information was obtained;

(4) Whenever materials (*e.g.*, documents, computer disks, etc.) containing such confidential business information are not being used, store such material in a locked file cabinet, vault, safe, or other suitable container;

(5) Serve all materials containing confidential business information as directed by the Secretary and pursuant to paragraph (f) of this section;

(6) Transmit all materials containing confidential business information with a cover sheet identifying the materials as containing confidential business information;

(7) Comply with the provisions of this section;

(8) Make true and accurate representations in the authorized applicant's application and promptly notify the Secretary of any changes that occur after the submission of the application and that affect the representations made in the application (*e.g.*, change in personnel assigned to the investigation);

(9) Report promptly and confirm in writing to the Secretary any breach of the administrative protective order; and

(10) Acknowledge that breach of the administrative protective order may subject the authorized applicant to such sanctions or other actions as the Commission deems appropriate.

(c) *Final disposition of material released under administrative protective order.* At such date as the Secretary may determine appropriate for particular data, each authorized applicant shall return or destroy all copies of materials released to authorized applicants pursuant to this section and all other materials containing confidential business information, such as charts or notes based on any such information received under administrative protective order, and file with the Secretary a certificate attesting to his personal, good faith belief that all copies of such material have been returned or destroyed and no copies of such material have been made available to any person to whom disclosure was not specifically authorized.

(d) *Commission responses to a breach of administrative protective order.* A breach of an administrative protective order may subject an offender to:

(1) Disbarment from practice in any capacity before the Commission along with such person's partners, associates, employer, and employees, for up to seven years following publication of a determination that the order has been breached;

(2) Referral to the United States Attorney;

82

(3) In the case of an attorney, accountant, or other professional, referral to the ethics panel of the appropriate professional association;

(4) Such other administrative sanctions as the Commission determines to be appropriate, including public release of or striking from the record any information or briefs submitted by, or on behalf of, the offender or the party represented by the offender, denial of further access to confidential business information in the current or any future investigations before the Commission, and issuance of a public or private letter of reprimand; and

(5) Such other actions, including but not limited to, a warning letter, as the Commission determines to be appropriate.

(e) *Breach investigation procedure.* (1) The Commission shall determine whether any person has violated an administrative protective order, and may impose sanctions or other actions in accordance with paragraph (d) of this section. At any time within sixty (60) days of the later of

(i) The date on which the alleged violation occurred or, as determined by the Commission, could have been discovered through the exercise of reasonable and ordinary care; or

(ii) The completion of an investigation conducted under this subpart, the Commission may commence an investigation of any breach of an administrative protective order alleged to have occurred at any time during the pendency of the investigation, including all appeals, remands, and subsequent appeals. Whenever the Commission has reason to believe that a person may have breached an administrative protective order issued pursuant to this section, the Secretary shall issue a letter informing such person that the Commission has reason to believe a breach has occurred and that the person has a reasonable opportunity to present his views on whether a breach has occurred. If subsequently the Commission determines that a breach has occurred and that further investigation is warranted, then the Secretary shall issue a letter informing such person of that determination and that the person has a reasonable opportunity to present his views on whether miti-

gating circumstances exist and on the appropriate sanction to be imposed, but no longer on whether a breach has occurred. Once such person has been afforded a reasonable opportunity to present his views, the Commission shall determine what sanction if any to impose.

(2) Where the sanction imposed is a private letter of reprimand, the Secretary shall expunge the sanction from the recipient's record two (2) years from the date of issuance of the sanction, provided that

(i) The recipient has not received another unexpunged sanction pursuant to this section at any time prior to the end of the two year period, and

(ii) The recipient is not the subject of an investigation for possible breach of administrative protective order under this section at the end of the two year period. Upon the completion of such a pending breach investigation without the issuance of a sanction, the original sanction shall be expunged. The Secretary shall notify a sanction recipient in the event that the sanction is expunged.

(f) *Service.* (1) Any party filing written submissions which include confidential business information to the Commission during an investigation shall at the same time serve complete copies of such submissions upon all authorized applicants specified on the list established by the Secretary pursuant to paragraph (a)(4) of this section, and, except as provided in § 206.8(c), a non-confidential version on all other parties. All such submissions must be accompanied by a certificate attesting that complete copies of the submission have been properly served. In the event that a submission is filed before the Secretary's list is established, the document need not be accompanied by a certificate of service, but the submission shall be served within two (2) days of the establishment of the list and a certificate of service shall then be filed.

(2) A party may seek an exemption from the service requirement of paragraph (f)(1) of this section for particular confidential business information by filing a request for exemption from disclosure in accordance with

paragraph (g) of this section. The Secretary shall promptly respond to the request. If a request is granted, the Secretary shall accept the information. The party shall file three versions of the submission containing the information in accordance with paragraph (g) of this section, and serve the submission in accordance with the requirements of § 206.8(b) and paragraph (f)(1) of this section, with the specific information as to which exemption from disclosure under administrative protective order has been granted redacted from the copies served. If a request is denied, the copy of the information lodged with the Secretary shall promptly be returned to the requester.

(3) The Secretary shall not accept for filing into the record of an investigation submissions filed without a proper certificate of service. Failure to comply with paragraph (f) of this section may result in denial of party status and such sanctions as the Commission deems appropriate. Confidential business information in submissions must be clearly marked as such when submitted, and must be segregated from other material being submitted.

(g) *Exemption from disclosure*—(1) *In general.* Any person may request exemption from the disclosure of confidential business information under administrative protective order, whether the person desires to include such information in a petition filed under this subpart B, or any other submission to the Commission during the course of an investigation. Such a request shall only be granted if the Secretary finds that such information is nondisclosable confidential business information. As defined in § 201.6(a)(2) of this chapter, nondisclosable confidential business information is privileged information, classified information, or specific information (*e.g.,* trade secrets) of a type for which there is a clear and compelling need to withhold from disclosure.

(2) *Request for exemption.* A request for exemption from disclosure must be filed with the Secretary in writing with the reasons therefor. At the same time as the request is filed, one copy of the confidential business information in question must be lodged with the Secretary solely for the purpose of obtaining a determination as to the request. The confidential business information for which exemption from disclosure is sought shall remain the property of the requester, and shall not become or be incorporated into any agency record until such time as the request is granted. A request should, when possible, be filed two business days prior to the deadline, if any, for filing the document in which the information for which exemption from disclosure is sought is proposed to be included. The Secretary shall promptly notify the requester as to whether the request has been approved or denied.

(3) *Procedure if request is approved.* If the request is approved, the person shall file three versions of the submission containing the nondisclosable confidential business information in question. One version shall contain all confidential business information, bracketed in accordance with § 201.6 of this chapter and § 206.8(c), with the specific information as to which exemption from disclosure was granted enclosed in triple brackets. This version shall have the following warning marked on every page: "CBI exempted from disclosure under APO enclosed in triple brackets." The other two versions shall conform to and be filed in accordance with the requirements of § 201.6 of this chapter and § 206.8(c), except that the specific information as to which exemption from disclosure was granted shall be redacted from those versions of the submission.

(4) *Procedure if request is denied.* If the request is denied, the copy of the information lodged with the Secretary shall promptly be returned to the requester.

[60 FR 12, Jan. 3, 1995, as amended at 68 FR 32977, June 3, 2003; 70 FR 8511, Feb. 22, 2005; 76 FR 61942, Oct. 6, 2011]

§ 206.18 **Time for determinations, reporting.**

(a) *In general.* The Commission will make its determination with respect to injury within 120 days after the date on which the petition is filed, the request or resolution is received, or the motion is adopted, as the case may be, except that—

(1) If the Commission determines before the 100th day that the investigation is extraordinarily complicated,

the Commission will make its determination within 150 days; or

(2) If critical circumstances are alleged, the Commission will make its determination within 120 days after completion of its investigation with respect to critical circumstances. The Commission will make its report to the President at the earliest practicable time, but not later than 180 days (240 days if critical circumstances are alleged) after the date on which the petition is filed, the request or resolution is received, or the motion is adopted, as the case may be.

(b) *Perishable agricultural product.* In the case of a request in a petition for provisional relief with respect to a perishable agricultural product that has been the subject of monitoring by the Commission, the Commission will report its determination and any finding to the President not later than 21 days after the date on which the request for provisional relief is received.

(c) *Critical circumstances.* If petitioner alleges the existence of critical circumstances in the petition, the Commission will report its determination regarding such allegation and any finding on or before the 60th day after such filing date.

§ 206.19   Public report.

Upon making a report to the President of the results of an investigation to which this subpart B relates, the Commission will make such report public (with the exception of information which the Commission determines to be confidential) and cause a summary thereof to be published in the FEDERAL REGISTER.

Subpart C—Investigations Relating to a Surge in Imports From a NAFTA Country

§ 206.21   Applicability of subpart.

This subpart C applies specifically to investigations under section 312(c) of the NAFTA Implementation Act. For other applicable rules, see subpart A of this part and part 201 of this chapter.

§ 206.22   Definition applicable to subpart C.

For the purposes of this subpart, the term *surge* means a significant increase in imports over the trend for a recent representative base period.

§ 206.23   Who may file a request.

If the President, under section 312(b) of the NAFTA Implementation Act, has excluded imports from a NAFTA country or countries from an action under chapter 1 of title II of the Trade Act of 1974, any entity that is representative of an industry for which such action is being taken may request the Commission to conduct an investigation to determine whether a surge in such imports undermines the effectiveness of the action.

§ 206.24   Contents of request.

The request for an investigation shall include the following information:

(a) The identity of the entity submitting the request; a description of the relief action the effectiveness of which is allegedly being undermined; and a description of the imported article, identifying the United States tariff provision under which it is classified, and the name of the country or countries from which the surge in imports is alleged to be coming;

(b) The information required in § 206.14(b) of this subpart concerning representativeness of the entity filing the request;

(c) Data concerning imports from the NAFTA country or countries that form the basis of requestor's claim that a surge in imports has occurred;

(d) Information supporting the claim that such surge in imports undermines the effectiveness of the relief action.

§ 206.25   Time for reporting.

The Commission will submit the findings of its investigation to the President no later than 30 days after the request is received.

§ 206.26   Public report.

Upon making a report to the President of the results of an investigation to which this subpart C relates, the Commission will make such report public (with the exception of any confidential business information) and cause a summary thereof to be published in the FEDERAL REGISTER.

Subpart D—Investigations Relating to Bilateral Safeguard Actions

§ 206.31 Applicability of subpart.

This subpart D applies specifically to investigations under section 311(b) of the United States-Australia Free Trade Agreement Implementation Act (19 U.S.C. 3805 note), section 311(b) of the United States-Bahrain Free Trade Agreement Implementation Act (19 U.S.C. 3805 note), section 311(b) of the United States-Chile Free Trade Agreement Implementation Act (19 U.S.C. 3805 note), section 311(b) of the United States-Colombia Trade Promotion Agreement Implementation Act (19 U.S.C. 3805 note), section 311(b) of the Dominican Republic-Central America-United States Free Trade Agreement Implementation Act (19 U.S.C. 4061(b)), section 211(b) of the United States-Jordan Free Trade Area Implementation Act (19 U.S.C. 2112 note), section 311(b) of the United States-Korea Free Trade Agreement Implementation Act (19 U.S.C. 3805 note), section 311(b) of the United States-Morocco Free Trade Agreement Implementation Act (19 U.S.C. 3805 note), section 302(b) of the NAFTA Implementation Act (19 U.S.C. 3352(b)), section 311(b) of the United States-Oman Free Trade Agreement Implementation Act (19 U.S.C. 3805 note), section 311(b) of the United States-Panama Trade Promotion Agreement Implementation Act (19 U.S.C. 3805 note), section 311(b) of the United States-Peru Trade Promotion Agreement Implementation Act (19 U.S.C. 3805 note), and section 311(b) of the United States-Singapore Free Trade Agreement Implementation Act (19 U.S.C. 3805 note). For other applicable rules, see subpart A of this part and part 201 of this chapter.

[77 FR 3926, Jan. 26, 2012]

§ 206.32 Definitions applicable to subpart D.

For the purposes of this subpart, the following terms have the meanings hereby assigned to them:

(a) The term *substantial cause* has the same meaning as in section 202(b)(1)(B) of the Trade Act.

(b) The terms *domestic industry*, *serious injury*, and *threat of serious injury*
have the same meanings as in section 202(c)(6) of the Trade Act.

(c) *Critical circumstances* mean such circumstances as are described in section 202(d) of the Trade Act;

(d) *Perishable agricultural product* means any agricultural product or citrus product, including livestock, which is the subject of monitoring pursuant to section 202(d) of the Trade Act.

(e) *Korean motor vehicle article* means a good provided for in heading 8703 or 8704 of the U.S. Harmonized Tariff Schedule that qualifies as an originating good under section 202(b) of the United States-Korea Free Trade Agreement Implementation Act.

[77 FR 3926, Jan. 26, 2012, as amended at 77 FR 37805, June 25, 2012]

§ 206.33 Who may file a petition.

(a) *In general.* A petition under this subpart D may be filed by an entity, including a trade association, firm, certified or recognized union, or group of workers, that is representative of a domestic industry producing an article that is like or directly competitive with an article that is allegedly, as a result of the reduction or elimination of a duty provided for under a free trade agreement listed in paragraph (b) of this section, being imported into the United States in such increased quantities, in absolute terms or relative to domestic production, and under such conditions that imports of the article constitute a substantial cause of serious injury, or (except in the case of a Canadian article) threat thereof, to such domestic industry. Unless the implementation statute provides otherwise, a petition may be filed only during the transition period of the particular free trade agreement.

(b) *List of free trade agreements.* The free trade agreements referred to in paragraph (a) of this section include the United States-Australia Free Trade Agreement, the United States-Bahrain Free Trade Agreement, the United States-Chile Free Trade Agreement, the United States-Colombia Trade Promotion Agreement, the Dominican Republic-Central America-United States Free Trade Agreement, the United States-Jordan Free Trade Area Agreement, the United States-Korea Free Trade Agreement, the United States-

Morocco Free Trade Agreement, the North American Free Trade Agreement (NAFTA), the United States-Oman Free Trade Agreement, the United States-Panama Trade Promotion Agreement, the United States-Peru Trade Promotion Agreement, and the United States-Singapore Free Trade Agreement, to the extent that such agreements have entered into force.

(c) *Critical circumstances.* An entity of the type described in paragraph (a) of this section that represents a domestic industry may allege that critical circumstances exist and petition for provisional relief with respect to imports if such product is from Australia, Canada, Jordan, Korea, Mexico, Morocco, or Singapore.

(d) *Perishable agricultural product.* An entity of the type described in paragraph (a) of this section that represents a domestic industry producing a perishable agricultural product may petition for provisional relief with respect to imports of such product from Australia, Canada, Jordan, Korea, Mexico, Morocco, or Singapore, but only if such product has been subject to monitoring by the Commission for not less than 90 days as of the date the allegation of injury is included in the petition.

(e) *Korean motor vehicle article.* An entity of the type described in paragraph (a) of this section that is filing a petition with respect to a product from Korea shall state whether it represents a domestic industry producing an article that is like or directly competitive with a Korean motor vehicle article.

[77 FR 3926, Jan. 26, 2012]

§206.34 Contents of petition.

A petition under this subpart D shall include specific information in support of the claim that, as a result of the reduction or elimination of a duty provided for under a free trade agreement listed in §206.33(b), an article is being imported into the United States in such increased quantities, in absolute terms or relative to domestic production, and under such conditions that imports of the article constitute a substantial cause of serious injury, or (except in the case of a Canadian article) threat thereof, to the domestic industry producing an article that is like or directly competitive with the imported article. If provisional relief is requested in a petition concerning an article from Australia, Canada, Jordan, Korea, Mexico, Morocco, or Singapore, the petition shall state whether provisional relief is sought because *critical circumstances* exist or because the imported article is a *perishable agricultural product.* In addition, a petition filed under this subpart D shall include the following information, to the extent that such information is publicly available from governmental or other sources, or best estimates and the basis therefor if such information is not available:

(a) *Product description.* The name and description of the imported article concerned, specifying the United States tariff provision under which such article is classified and the current tariff treatment thereof, and the name and description of the like or directly competitive domestic article concerned;

(b) *Representativeness.* (1) The names and addresses of the firms represented in the petition and/or the firms employing or previously employing the workers represented in the petition and the locations of their establishments in which the domestic article is produced;

(2) The percentage of domestic production of the like or directly competitive domestic article that such represented firms and/or workers account for and the basis for claiming that such firms and/or workers are representative of an industry; and

(3) The names and locations of all other producers of the domestic article known to the petitioner;

(c) *Import data.* Import data for at least each of the most recent 5 full years that form the basis of the claim that the article concerned is being imported in increased quantities in absolute terms;

(d) *Domestic production data.* Data on total U.S. production of the domestic article for each full year for which data are provided pursuant to paragraph (c) of this section;

(e) *Data showing injury.* Quantitative data for each of the most recent 5 full years indicating the nature and extent of injury to the domestic industry concerned:

(1) With respect to serious injury, data indicating:

(i) A significant idling of production facilities in the industry, including data indicating plant closings or the underutilization of production capacity;

(ii) The inability of a significant number of firms to carry out domestic production operations at a reasonable level of profit; and

(iii) Significant unemployment or underemployment within the industry; and/or

(2) With respect to the threat of serious injury, data relating to:

(i) A decline in sales or market share, a higher and growing inventory (whether maintained by domestic producers, importers, wholesalers, or retailers), and a downward trend in production, profits, wages, productivity, or employment (or increasing underemployment);

(ii) The extent to which firms in the industry are unable to generate adequate capital to finance the modernization of their domestic plants and equipment, or are unable to maintain existing levels of expenditures for research and development;

(iii) The extent to which the U.S. market is the focal point for the diversion of exports of the article concerned by reason of restraints on exports of such article to, or on imports of such article into, third country markets; and

(3) Changes in the level of prices, production, and productivity.

(f) *Cause of injury.* An enumeration and description of the causes believed to be resulting in the injury, or threat thereof, described under paragraph (e) of this section, and a statement regarding the extent to which increased imports of the subject article are believed to be such a cause, supported by pertinent data;

(g) *Relief sought and purpose thereof.* A statement describing the import relief sought, including the type, amount, and duration, and the specific purposes therefor, which may include facilitating the orderly transfer of resources to more productive pursuits, enhancing competitiveness, or other means of adjustment to new conditions of competition;

(h) *Efforts to compete.* A statement on the efforts being taken, or planned to be taken, or both, by firms and workers in the industry to make a positive adjustment to import competition.

(i) *Critical circumstances.* If the petition alleges the existence of critical circumstances, a statement setting forth the basis for the belief that there is clear evidence that increased imports (either actual or relative to domestic production) of the article are a substantial cause of serious injury, or the threat thereof, to the domestic industry, and that delay in taking action would cause damage to that industry that would be difficult to repair, and a statement concerning the provisional relief requested and the basis therefor.

[77 FR 3926, Jan. 26, 2012]

§ 206.35 Time for determinations, reporting.

(a) *In general.* The Commission will make its determination with respect to injury within 120 days (180 days if critical circumstances are alleged) after the date on which the investigation is initiated. The Commission will make its report to the President no later than 30 days after the date on which its determination is made.

(b) *Perishable agricultural product.* In the case of a request in a petition for provisional relief with respect to a perishable agricultural product that has been the subject of monitoring by the Commission, the Commission will report its determination and any finding to the President not later than 21 days after the date on which the request for provisional relief is received.

(c) *Critical circumstances.* If petitioner alleges the existence of critical circumstances in the petition, the Commission will report its determination regarding such allegation and any finding on or before the 60th day after such filing date.

[77 FR 3927, Jan. 26, 2012]

§ 206.36 Public report.

Upon making a report to the President of the results of an investigation to which this subpart D relates, the Commission will make such report public (with the exception of information which the Commission determines to be confidential) and cause a summary thereof to be published in the FEDERAL REGISTER.

§206.37 Limited disclosure of certain confidential business information under administrative protective order.

Except in the case of an investigation under the United States-Jordan Free Trade Area Implementation Act or the NAFTA, the Secretary shall make available to authorized applicants, in accordance with the provisions of §206.17, confidential business information obtained in an investigation under this subpart.

[77 FR 3927, Jan. 26, 2012]

Subpart E—Investigations for Relief From Market Disruption

§206.41 Applicability of subpart.

This subpart E applies specifically to investigations under section 406(a) or 421(b) or (o) of the Trade Act. For other applicable rules, see subpart A of this part and part 201 of this chapter.

[59 FR 5091, Feb. 3, 1994, as amended at 67 FR 8190, Feb. 22, 2002]

§206.42 Who may file a petition.

(a) A petition under section 406(a) of the Trade Act may be filed by an entity, including a trade association, firm, certified or recognized union, or group of workers, that is representative of a domestic industry producing an article with respect to which there are imports of a like or directly competitive article which is the product of a Communist country, which imports, allegedly, are increasing rapidly, either absolutely or relative to domestic production, so as to be a significant cause of material injury, or the threat thereof, to such domestic industry.

(b) A petition under section 421(b) or (o) of the Trade Act may be filed by an entity, including a trade association, firm, certified or recognized union, or group of workers, which is representative of an industry.

[67 FR 8191, Feb. 22, 2002]

§206.43 Contents of a petition under section 406(a) of the Trade Act.

A petition for relief under section 406(a) of the Trade Act shall include specific information in support of the claim that imports of an article that are the product of a Communist country which are like or directly competitive with an article produced by a domestic industry, are increasing rapidly, either absolutely or relative to domestic production, so as to be a significant cause of material injury, or the threat thereof, to such domestic industry. In addition, such petition shall, to the extent practicable, include the following information:

(a) *Product description.* The name and description of the imported article concerned, specifying the United States tariff provision under which such article is classified and the current tariff treatment thereof, and the name and description of the like or directly competitive domestic article concerned;

(b) *Representativeness.* (1) The names and addresses of the firms represented in the petition and/or the firms employing or previously employing the workers represented in the petition and the locations of their establishments in which the domestic article is produced; (2) the percentage of domestic production of the like or directly competitive domestic article that such represented firms and/or workers account for and the basis for asserting that petitioner is representative of an industry; and (3) the names and locations of all other producers of the domestic article known to the petitioner;

(c) *Import data.* Import data for at least each of the most recent 5 full years which form the basis of the claim that imports from a Communist country of an article like or directly competitive with the article produced by the domestic industry concerned are increasing rapidly, either absolutely or relative to domestic production;

(d) *Domestic production data.* Data on total U.S. production of the domestic article for each full year for which data are provided pursuant to paragraph (c) of this section;

(e) *Data showing injury.* Quantitative data indicating the nature and extent of injury to the domestic industry concerned:

(1) With respect to material injury, data indicating:

(i) An idling of production facilities in the industry, including data indicating plant closings or the underutilization of production capacity;

(ii) The inability of a number of firms to carry out domestic production operations at a reasonable level of profit; and

(iii) Unemployment or underemployment within the industry; and/or

(2) With respect to the threat of material injury, data relating to:

(i) A decline in sales or market share, a higher and growing inventory (whether maintained by domestic producers, importers, wholesalers, or retailers), and a downward trend in production, profits, wages, or employment (or increasing underemployment);

(ii) The extent to which firms in the industry are unable to generate adequate capital to finance the modernization of their domestic plants and equipment, or are unable to maintain existing levels of expenditures for research and development; and

(iii) The extent to which the U.S. market is the focal point for the diversion of exports of the article concerned by reason of restraints on exports of such article to, or on imports of such article into, third country markets;

(f) *Cause of injury.* An enumeration and description of the causes believed to be resulting in the material injury, or threat thereof, described in paragraph (e) of this section; information relating to the effect of imports of the subject merchandise on prices in the United States for like or directly competitive articles; evidence of disruptive pricing practices, or other efforts to unfairly manage trade patterns; and a statement regarding the extent to which increased imports, either actual or relative to domestic production, of the imported article are believed to be such a cause, supported by pertinent data;

(g) *Relief sought and purpose thereof.* A statement describing the import relief sought.

[59 FR 5091, Feb. 3, 1994, as amended at 67 FR 8191, Feb. 22, 2002]

§ 206.44 **Contents of a petition under section 421(b) or (o) of the Trade Act.**

(a) *Petitions under section 421(b).* (1) A petition for relief under section 421(b) of the Trade Act shall provide specific information in support of the claim that products of the People's Republic of China are being imported into the United States in such increased quantities or under such conditions as to cause or threaten to cause market disruption to the domestic producers of like or directly competitive products. In addition, such petition shall include the information described in paragraphs (b) through (j) of this section. The petition shall provide the information required by this paragraph and paragraphs (b) through (j) of this section to the extent that such information is reasonably available to the petitioner with due diligence.

(2) If the petition fails to provide any item of information specified in paragraphs (b) through (j) of this section, the petition shall include a certification that such information was not reasonably available to the petitioner.

(b) *Product description.* Each petition shall include the name and description of the imported product concerned, specifying the United States tariff provision under which such product is classified and the current tariff treatment thereof, and the name and description of the like or directly competitive domestic product concerned.

(c) *Representativeness.* Each petition shall include:

(1) The names and street addresses of the firms represented in the petition and/or the firms employing or previously employing the workers represented in the petition, the locations of the establishments in which each such firm produces the domestic product, and the telephone number and contact person(s) for each such firm;

(2) The percentage of domestic production of the like or directly competitive domestic product that such represented firms and/or workers account for and the basis for asserting that petitioner is representative of an industry; and

(3) The names and street addresses of all other producers of the domestic product known to the petitioner, and

the telephone number and contact person(s) for each such producer.

(d) *Import data.* Each petition shall include import data for at least each of the most recent 5 full years which form the basis of the claim that imports from the People's Republic of China of a product like or directly competitive with the product produced by the domestic industry concerned are increasing rapidly, either absolutely or relatively.

(e) *Domestic production data.* Each petition shall include data on total U.S. production of the domestic product for each full year for which data are provided pursuant to paragraph (d) of this section.

(f) *Data showing injury and/or threat of injury.* Each petition shall include the following quantitative data indicating the nature and extent of injury to the domestic industry concerned:

(1) With respect to material injury, information, including data on production, capacity, capacity utilization, shipments, net sales, profits, employment, productivity, inventories, and expenditures on capital and research and development, indicating:

(i) An idling of production facilities in the industry, including data indicating plant closings or the underutilization of production capacity;

(ii) The inability of a number of firms to carry out domestic production operations at a reasonable level of profit; and

(iii) Unemployment or underemployment within the industry; and/or

(2) With respect to the threat of material injury, data relating to:

(i) Declines in sales or market share, increases in inventory (whether maintained by domestic producers, importers, wholesalers, retailers, or producers or exporters in the People's Republic of China), and/or a downward trend in production, profits, wages, or employment (or increasing underemployment);

(ii) The extent to which firms in the industry are unable to generate adequate capital to finance the modernization of their domestic plants and equipment, or are unable to maintain existing levels of expenditures for research and development;

(iii) The extent to which the U.S. market is the focal point for the diversion of exports of the article concerned by reason of restraints on exports of such article to, or on imports of such article into, third country markets; and

(iv) Data regarding productive capacity in the People's Republic of China, any unused productive capacity, and any potential for product shifting in the People's Republic of China.

(g) *Cause of injury.* Each petition shall enumerate and describe the causes believed to be resulting in the material injury, or threat thereof, described in paragraph (f) of this section. The petition shall provide information relating to the effect of imports of the subject merchandise on prices in the United States for like or directly competitive articles. The petition shall also include a statement regarding the extent to which increased imports, either actual or relative, of the imported product are believed to be such a cause, supported by pertinent data.

(h) *Critical circumstances.* If the petition alleges that critical circumstances exist within the meaning of section 421(i)(1) of the Trade Act, the petition shall provide detailed information supporting that claim as well as detailed information demonstrating that delay in taking action under section 421 of the Act would cause damage to the relevant domestic industry that would be difficult to repair.

(i) *Relief sought and purpose thereof.* The petition shall include a statement describing the import relief sought under section 421(i)(4) and/or section 421(a) of the Trade Act and the purpose thereof.

(j) *Additional information.* The petition shall include:

(1) The names of all U.S. importers and all producers in China of the subject merchandise known to petitioner, and the street address, telephone and fax number, and primary contact person(s) for each such importer and producer in China;

(2) A detailed description of each product for which the petitioner requests the Commission to seek pricing information in its questionnaires, and an explanation of why the petitioner believes the Commission should collect

pricing information for each such product;

(3) For each domestic producer represented by petitioner, the company names of its 10 largest purchasers, and the street address, telephone number, and primary contact person(s) for each such purchaser;

(4) For each allegation of lost sales and/or lost revenues, supporting information with regard to each such alleged loss, including the name of the company represented by petitioner that lost the sale or revenue, the name of the company that captured the sale or whose competition resulted in lost revenue (including company street address, company contact person, and telephone and fax numbers for each contact person), the date and total value of the lost sale or lost revenue, and the total quantity of product involved (by weight or number of units).

(k) *Petitions under section 421(o).* A petition under section 421(o) of the Trade Act shall include evidence of representativeness, as described in paragraph (b) of this section, as well as specific information in support of the claim that action under section 421 of the Act continues to be necessary to prevent or remedy market disruption. The information provided in support of that claim should take into account factors such as those specified in paragraphs (c) through (g) of this section. To comply with this paragraph, the petition should contain all relevant information that is reasonably available to the petitioner with due diligence.

[67 FR 8191, Feb. 22, 2002, as amended at 68 FR 65167, Nov. 19, 2003]

§ 206.44a Special rules for conducting investigations under section 421(b) of the Trade Act.

(a) *Service of the petition.* (1)(i) The Secretary shall promptly notify a petitioner when, before the establishment of a service list under § 206.17(a)(4) of this part, he or she approves an application under § 206.17(a)(2) of this part pursuant to § 206.47. When practicable, this notification shall be made by facsimile transmission. The petitioner shall then serve a copy of the petition, including all confidential business information, on the approved lead authorized applicants in accord with

§ 206.17(f) within 2 calendar days of the time notification is made by the Secretary.

(ii) Upon establishment and issuance of the service list, the petitioner shall serve the lead authorized applicants enumerated on the list established by the Secretary pursuant to § 206.17(a)(4) that have not been served pursuant to paragraph (a)(1)(i) of this section within 2 calendar days of the establishment and issuance of the Secretary's list.

(2) As the Secretary adds new authorized applicants to the service list described in paragraph (a)(1) of this section, the Secretary shall notify the petitioner and issue an amended list, and the petitioner shall serve new lead authorized applicants with a copy of the petition in the same manner as under paragraph (a)(1)(i) of this section.

(3) The petitioner shall serve a copy of the non-confidential version of the petition on those persons enumerated on the list established by the Secretary pursuant to § 201.11(d) of this chapter within 2 calendar days of the establishment and issuance of the Secretary's list, and on any additional persons within 2 calendar days of receiving notification from the Secretary of an amended list.

(4) The petitioner shall attest service of the petition by filing a certificate of service with the Commission.

(b) *Comment on information.* The parties shall have an opportunity to file comments on any information disclosed to them after they have filed their posthearing brief. Comments shall concern only such information, and shall not exceed 15 pages of textual material, double-spaced and on single-sided stationery measuring 8½ × 11 inches. A comment may address the accuracy, reliability, or probative value of such information by reference to information elsewhere in the record, in which case the comment shall identify where in the record such information is found. New factual information and arguments based on that information shall be disregarded. The date on which such comments must be filed will be specified by the Commission when it specifies the time that information will be disclosed. The record shall close on the date such comments are due, except with respect to changes in bracketing of confidential business information permitted by § 206.8(c) of this part.

[68 FR 65168, Nov. 19, 2003]

§ 206.45 Time for reporting.

(a) In an investigation under section 406(a) of the Trade Act, the Commission will make its report to the President at the earliest practical time, but not later than 3 months after the date on which the petition is filed, the request or resolution is received, or the motion is adopted, as the case may be.

(b) In an investigation under section 421(b) of the Trade Act, the Commission will transmit to the President and the United States Trade Representative its determination at the earliest practicable time, but in no case later than 60 days (or 90 days in the case of a petition requesting provisional relief under section 421(i) of the Act) after the date on which the petition is filed, the request or resolution is received, or the motion is adopted. The Commission will transmit its report to the President and the Trade Representative no later than 20 days after the transmittal of the determination.

(c) In an investigation under section 421(b) of the Trade Act in which the petition requests provisional relief under section 421(i) of the Act, the Commission will transmit to the President and the Trade Representative its determination and report with respect to section 421(i) of the Act no later than 45 days after the petition is filed.

(d) In an investigation under section 421(o) of the Trade Act, the Commission shall transmit to the President a report on its investigation and determination not later than 60 days before the action under section 421(m) of the Trade Act is to terminate.

(e) *Date of filing.* Any petition under this subpart E that is filed after 12:00 noon shall be deemed to be filed on the next business day.

[67 FR 8192, Feb. 22, 2002, as amended at 70 FR 8511, Feb. 22, 2005]

§ 206.46 Public report.

Upon making a report to the President of the results of an investigation to which this subpart E relates, the Commission will make such report public (with the exception of information which the Commission determines to be confidential) and cause a summary thereof to be published in the FEDERAL REGISTER.

[59 FR 5091, Feb. 3, 1994. Redesignated at 67 FR 8191, Feb. 22, 2002]

§ 206.47 Limited disclosure of certain confidential business information under administrative protective order.

In an investigation under section 421(b) or (o) of the Trade Act, the Secretary shall make confidential business information available to authorized applicants, subject to the provisions of § 206.17.

[67 FR 8192, Feb. 22, 2002]

Subpart F—Monitoring; Advice As to Effect of Extension, Reduction, Modification, or Termination of Relief Action

SOURCE: 60 FR 10, Jan. 3, 1995, unless otherwise noted.

§ 206.51 Applicability of subpart.

This subpart F applies specifically to investigations under section 204 of the Trade Act. For other applicable rules, see subpart A of this part and part 201 of this chapter.

§ 206.52 Monitoring.

(a) *In general.* As long as any import relief imposed by the President pursuant to section 203 of the Trade Act remains in effect, the Commission will monitor developments with respect to the domestic industry, including the progress and specific efforts made by workers and firms in the industry to make a positive adjustment to import competition.

(b) *Reports.* Whenever the initial period of import relief, or any extension thereof, exceeds three (3) years, the Commission will submit a report on the results of such monitoring to the President and the Congress. Such report will be submitted not later than the date which is the mid-point of the initial period of import relief, or any extension thereof. In the course of preparing each such report, the Commission will hold a hearing at which interested persons will be given a reasonable opportunity to be present, to produce evidence, and to be heard.

(c) Limited disclosure of certain confidential business information under administrative protective order. Upon receipt of a timely application filed by an authorized applicant, the Secretary shall make available to an authorized applicant under administrative protective order all confidential business information contained in Commission memoranda and reports and in written submissions filed with the Commission at any time during an investigation under this section with respect to an article that was the subject of an affirmative Commission determination under section 202 of the Trade Act (except privileged information, classified information, and specific information of a type which there is a clear and compelling need to withhold from disclosure). Such disclosure shall be made in the manner provided for and in accordance with the procedures set forth in § 206.17. The provisions in paragraphs (d) and (e) of § 206.17 relating to Commission responses to a breach of an administrative protective order and breach procedure shall apply with respect to orders issued under this paragraph.

[60 FR 10, Jan. 3, 1995, as amended at 66 FR 32218, June 14, 2001]

§ 206.53 Investigations to advise the President as to the probable economic effect of reduction, modification, or termination of action.

Upon the request of the President, the Commission will conduct an investigation for the purpose of gathering information in order that it might advise the President of its judgment as to the probable economic effect on the industry concerned of any reduction, modification, or termination of the action taken under section 203 of the Trade Act which is under consideration.

§ 206.54 Investigations with respect to extension of action.

(a) *Institution of investigations.* Upon the request of the President, or upon petition on behalf of the industry concerned, the Commission will investigate to determine whether an action taken under section 203 of the Trade Act continues to be necessary to prevent or remedy serious injury and whether there is evidence that the industry is making a positive adjustment to import competition.

(b) *Who may file a petition.* A petition under this § 206.54 may be filed by an entity, including a trade association, firm, certified or recognized union, or group of workers, which is representative of the industry producing the domestic article concerned in the investigation of the Commission which resulted in the imposition by the President of the import relief action.

(c) *Time for filing.* Any petition filed on behalf of an industry for a determination under this § 206.54 must be filed with the Commission not earlier than the date which is 9 months, and not later than the date which is 6 months, before the date any action taken under section 203 of the Trade Act is to terminate.

(d) *Contents of petition.* A petition under this § 206.54 shall include the following information, to the extent that such information is publicly available from governmental or other sources, or best estimates and the basis therefor if such information is not available:

(1) *Identification of relief action.* An identification of the action under section 203, or portion of such action, for which a determination under this § 206.54 is sought;

(2) *Representativeness.* (i) The names and addresses of the firms represented in the petition and/or the firms employing or previously employing the workers represented in the petition and the locations of their establishments in which the domestic article is produced;

(ii) The percentage of domestic production of the like or directly competitive domestic article that such represented firms and/or workers account for and the basis for claiming that such firms and/or workers are representative of an industry; and

(iii) The names and locations of all other producers of the domestic article known to the petitioner;

(3) *Import data.* Import data on the foreign article concerned for each full

year since action was taken under section 203 of the Trade Act, starting with the year in which action was taken;

(4) *Domestic production data.* Data on total U.S. production of the domestic article concerned for each year for which data are provided pursuant to paragraph (d)(3) of this section;

(5) *Efforts to adjust.* Specific information in support of the claim that action under section 203 of the Trade Act continues to be necessary to prevent or remedy serious injury and that there is evidence that the industry is making a positive adjustment to import competition.

(e) *Limited disclosure of certain confidential business information under administrative protective order.* Upon receipt of a timely application filed by an authorized applicant, the Secretary shall make available to an authorized applicant under administrative protective order all confidential business information contained in Commission memoranda and reports and in written submissions filed with the Commission at any time during an investigation under this section with respect to an article that was the subject of an affirmative Commission determination under section 202 of the Trade Act (except privileged information, classified information, and specific information of a type which there is a clear and compelling need to withhold from disclosure). Such disclosure shall be made in the manner provided for and in accordance with the procedures set forth in §206.17. The provisions in paragraphs (d) and (e) of §206.17 relating to Commission responses to a breach of an administrative protective order and breach procedure shall apply with respect to orders issued under this paragraph.

(f) *Time for reporting.* The Commission will make its report to the President at the earliest practical time, but not later than 60 days before the action under section 203 of the Trade Act is to terminate, unless the President specifies a different date.

(g) *Public report.* Upon making a report to the President of the results of an investigation to which this §206.54 relates, the Commission will make such report public (with the exception of information which the Commission determines to be confidential) and cause a summary thereof to be published in the FEDERAL REGISTER.

§206.55 Investigations to evaluate the effectiveness of relief.

(a) *Investigation.* After any action taken under section 203 has terminated, the Commission will conduct an investigation for the purpose of evaluating the effectiveness of the relief action in facilitating positive adjustment by the domestic industry to import competition, consistent with the reasons set out by the President in the report submitted to the Congress under section 203(b) of the Trade Act.

(b) *Hearing.* In the course of such investigation, the Commission will hold a hearing at which interested persons will be given an opportunity to be present, to produce evidence, and to be heard.

(c) *Time for reporting.* The Commission will submit its report to the President and to the Congress by no later than the 180th day after the day on which the action terminated.

Subpart G—Investigations For Action in Response to Trade Diversion; Reviews of Action Taken

SOURCE: 67 FR 8192, Feb. 22, 2002, unless otherwise noted.

§206.61 Applicability of subpart.

The provisions of this subpart G apply to investigations under section 422(b) and/or reviews under section 422(j) of the Trade Act. For other applicable rules, see subpart A of this part and part 201 of this chapter.

§206.62 Who may file a petition.

A petition for an investigation under section 422(b) of the Trade Act may be filed by an entity, including a trade association, firm, certified or recognized union, or group of workers, which is representative of an industry.

§206.63 Contents of petition.

A petition under section 422(b) of the Trade Act shall include specific information in support of the claim that an action described in section 422(c) of the

Trade Act has caused, or threatens to cause, a significant diversion of trade into the domestic market of the United States. To comply with that requirement and the requirements in paragraphs (a) through (f) of this section, the petition shall include all relevant information that is reasonably available to the petitioner with due diligence. The petition shall include the following information:

(a) *Product description.* The name and description of the imported product concerned, specifying the United States tariff provision under which such article is classified and the current tariff treatment thereof, and the name and description of the domestic product concerned;

(b) *Representativeness.* (1) The names and addresses of the firms represented in the petition and/or the firms employing or previously employing the workers represented in the petition and the locations of their establishments in which the domestic product is produced;

(2) The percentage of domestic production of the domestic product that such represented firms and/or workers account for and the basis for asserting that petitioner is representative of an industry; and

(3) The names and locations of all other producers of the domestic product known to the petitioner;

(c) *Description of the action.* A description of the action or actions, as defined in section 422(c) of the Trade Act, that allegedly has caused or threatens to cause a significant diversion of trade into the domestic market of the United States;

(d) *Trade diversion data.* (1) The actual or imminent increase in United States market share held by such imports from the People's Republic of China;

(2) The actual or imminent increase in volume of such imports into the United States;

(3) The nature and extent of the action taken or proposed by the WTO member concerned;

(4) The extent of exports from the People's Republic of China to that WTO member and to the United States;

(5) The actual or imminent changes in exports to that WTO member due to the action taken or proposed;

(6) The actual or imminent diversion of exports from the People's Republic of China to countries other than the United States;

(7) Cyclical or seasonal trends in import volumes into the United States of the products at issue; and

(8) Conditions of demand and supply in the United States market for the products at issue;

(e) *Import data.* Any import data available to the petitioner that will aid the Commission in examining, pursuant to section 422(d)(2) of the Trade Act, the changes in imports into the United States from the People's Republic of China since the time that the WTO member commenced the investigation that led to a request for consultations described in section 422(a) of the Act; and

(f) *Relief sought and purpose thereof.* A statement describing the import relief sought under section 422(h) of the Trade Act and the purpose thereof.

§ 206.64 **Institution of investigation or review; publication of notice; and availability for public inspection.**

(a) Paragraphs (a) and (b) in § 206.3 govern the institution of an investigation under section 422(b) of the Act and the publication of a FEDERAL REGISTER notice concerning the investigation. Following receipt of notification that the WTO member or members involved have notified the Committee on Safeguards of the WTO of a modification in the action taken by them against the People's Republic of China pursuant to consultation referred to in section 422(a) of the Act, the Commission will promptly conduct a review under section 422(j) of the Act regarding the continued need for action taken under section 422(h) of the Act. The Commission also will publish notice of the review in the FEDERAL REGISTER.

(b) The Commission will make available for public inspection the notification document that prompted a review under paragraph (a) of this section, excluding any confidential business information in the document. Paragraph (c) in § 206.3 governs the availability for public inspection of a petition, request, resolution, or motion that prompted the Commission to institute an investigation under section 422(b) of the Act.

§ 206.65 Public hearing.

Public hearings in investigations under section 422(b) of the Act are provided for in § 206.5(b).

§ 206.66 Limited disclosure of certain confidential business information under administrative protective order.

In an investigation under section 422(b) of the Trade Act, the Secretary shall make confidential business information available to authorized applicants, subject to the provisions of § 206.17.

§ 206.67 Time for determination and report.

(a) In an investigation under section 422(b) of the Trade Act, the Commission will transmit its determination under that section of the Act to the President and the Trade Representative at the earliest practical time, but not later than 45 days after the date on which the petition is filed, the request or resolution is received, or the motion is adopted, as the case may be. The Commission shall issue and transmit its report on the determination not later than 10 days after the determination is issued.

(b) In a review under section 422(j) of the Trade Act, the Commission will report its determination to the President not later than 60 days after the notification described in that section of the Act.

§ 206.68 Public report.

Upon making a report to the President of the results of an investigation under section 422(b) or a review under section 422(j) of the Trade Act, the Commission will make such report public (with the exception of information which the Commission determines to be confidential) and cause a summary thereof to be published in the FEDERAL REGISTER.

PART 207—INVESTIGATIONS OF WHETHER INJURY TO DOMESTIC INDUSTRIES RESULTS FROM IMPORTS SOLD AT LESS THAN FAIR VALUE OR FROM SUBSIDIZED EXPORTS TO THE UNITED STATES

Sec.
207.1 Applicability of part.

Subpart A—General Provisions

207.2 Definitions applicable to part 207.
207.3 Service, filing, and certification of documents.
207.4 The record.
207.5 Ex parte meetings.
207.6 [Reserved]
207.7 Limited disclosure of certain business proprietary information under administrative protective order.
207.8 Questionnaires to have the force of subpoenas; subpoena enforcement.

Subpart B—Preliminary Determinations

207.10 Filing of petition with the Commission.
207.11 Contents of petition.
207.12 Notice of preliminary phase of investigation.
207.13 Cooperation with administering authority; preliminary phase of investigation.
207.14 Negative petition determination.
207.15 Written briefs and conference.
207.16 [Reserved]
207.17 Staff report.
207.18 Notice of preliminary determination.

Subpart C—Final Determinations, Short Life Cycle Products

207.20 Investigative activity following preliminary determination.
207.21 Final phase notice of scheduling.
207.22 Prehearing and final staff reports.
207.23 Prehearing brief.
207.24 Hearing.
207.25 Posthearing briefs.
207.26 Statements by nonparties.
207.27 Short life cycle products.
207.28 Anticircumvention.
207.29 Publication of notice of determination.
207.30 Comment on information.

Subpart D—Terminated, Suspended, and Continued Investigations, Investigations to Review Negotiated Agreements, and Investigations To Review Outstanding Determinations

207.40 Termination and suspension of investigation.

207.41 Commission review of agreements to eliminate the injurious effect of subsidized imports or imports sold at less than fair value.
207.42 Investigation continued upon request.
207.43 [Reserved]
207.44 Consolidation of investigations.
207.45 Investigation to review outstanding determination.
207.46 Investigations concerning certain countervailing duty orders.

Subpart E—Judicial Review

207.50 Judicial review.
207.51 Judicial review of denial of application for disclosure of certain business proprietary information under administrative protective order.

Subpart F—Five-Year Reviews

207.60 Definitions.
207.61 Responses to notice of institution.
207.62 Rulings on adequacy and nature of Commission review.
207.63 Circulation of draft questionnaires.
207.64 Staff reports.
207.65 Prehearing briefs.
207.66 Hearing.
207.67 Posthearing briefs and statements.
207.68 Final comments on information.
207.69 Publication of determinations.

Subpart G—Implementing Regulations for the North American Free Trade Agreement

207.90 Scope.
207.91 Definitions.
207.92 Procedures for commencing review of final determinations.
207.93 Protection of proprietary information during panel and committee proceedings.
207.94 Protection of privileged information during panel and committee proceedings.

PROCEDURES FOR IMPOSING SANCTIONS FOR VIOLATION OF THE PROVISIONS OF A PROTECTIVE ORDER ISSUED DURING PANEL AND COMMITTEE PROCEEDINGS

207.100 Sanctions.
207.101 Reporting of prohibited act and commencement of investigation.
207.102 Initiation of proceedings.
207.103 Charging letter.
207.104 Response to charging letter.
207.105 Confidentiality.
207.106 Interim measures.
207.107 Motions.
207.108 Preliminary conference.
207.109 Discovery.
207.110 Subpoenas.
207.111 Prehearing conference.
207.112 Hearings.
207.113 The record.
207.114 Initial determination.
207.115 Petition for review.
207.116 Commission review on its own motion.
207.117 Review by Commission.
207.118 Role of the General Counsel in advising the Commission.
207.119 Reconsideration.
207.120 Public notice of sanctions.

AUTHORITY: 19 U.S.C. 1336, 1671–1677n, 2482, 3513.

SOURCE: 44 FR 76468, Dec. 26, 1979, unless otherwise noted.

§ 207.1 Applicability of part.

Part 207 applies to proceedings of the Commission under section 516A and title VII of the Tariff Act of 1930 (19 U.S.C. 1303, 1516A and 1671–1677n) (the Act), other than investigations under section 783 (19 U.S.C. 1677n), which will be conducted pursuant to procedures specified by the Office of the United States Trade Representative.

[61 FR 37829, July 22, 1996]

Subpart A—General Provisions

SOURCE: 56 FR 11923, Mar. 21, 1991, unless otherwise noted.

§ 207.2 Definitions applicable to part 207.

For the purposes of this part, the following terms have the meanings hereby assigned to them:

(a) The term *the Act* means: The Tariff Act of 1930, as amended.

(b) The term *administering authority* means: The Secretary of Commerce, or any other officer of the United States to whom the responsibility for carrying out the duties of the administering authority under section 303 or title VII of the Act is transferred by law.

(c) The term *Director* means: The incumbent Commission Director or Acting Director, Office of Operations, or, in the absence of either, a person designated by the Director.

(d) The term *ex parte meeting* means: Any communication between

(1) Any interested party or other person providing factual information in connection with an investigation, and

(2) Any Commissioner, or member of a Commissioner's staff, in which less than all parties participate, and which is not a hearing or conference for which an opportunity to participate is given to the parties.

(e) The term *injury* means: Material injury or threat of material injury to an industry in the United States, or material retardation of the establishment of an industry in the United States, by reason of imports into the United States of subject merchandise which is found by the administering authority to be subsidized, or sold, or likely to be sold, at less than its fair value.

(f) The term *record* means:

(1) All information presented to or obtained by the Commission during the course of an investigation, including completed questionnaires, any information obtained from the administering authority, written communications from any person filed with the Secretary, staff reports, all governmental memoranda pertaining to the case, and the record of ex parte meetings required to be kept pursuant to section 777(a)(3) of the Act; and

(2) A copy of all Commission orders and determinations, all transcripts or records of conferences or hearings, and all notices published in the FEDERAL REGISTER concerning the investigation.

(g) The term *coalition or trade association* as used in an investigation referred to in section 771(9)(G) of the Act means a coalition or trade association which is representative of domestic processors, domestic processors and producers, or domestic processors and growers.

[44 FR 76468, Dec. 26, 1979, as amended at 60 FR 21, Jan. 3, 1995]

§ 207.3 Service, filing, and certification of documents.

(a) *Certification.* Any person submitting factual information on behalf of the petitioner or any other interested party for inclusion in the record, and any person submitting a response to a Commission questionnaire, must certify that such information is accurate and complete to the best of the submitter's knowledge.

(b) *Service.* Any party submitting a document for inclusion in the record of the investigation shall, in addition to complying with § 201.8 of this chapter, serve a copy of each such document on all other parties to the investigation in the manner prescribed in § 201.16 of this chapter. If a document is filed before the Secretary's issuance of the service list provided for in § 201.11 of this chapter or the administrative protective order list provided for in § 207.7, the document need not be accompanied by a certificate of service, but the document shall be served on all appropriate parties within two (2) days of the issuance of the service list or the administrative protective order list and a certificate of service shall then be filed. Notwithstanding § 201.16 of this chapter, petitions, briefs, requests to close a portion of the hearing, comments on requests to close a portion of the hearing, and testimony filed by parties pursuant to §§ 207.10, 207.15, 207.23, 207.24, 207.25, 207.65, 207.66, and 207.67, shall be served by hand or, if served by mail, by overnight mail or its equivalent. Failure to comply with the requirements of this rule may result in removal from status as a party to the investigation. The Commission shall make available to all parties to the investigation a copy of each document, except transcripts of conferences and hearings, business proprietary information, privileged information, and information required to be served under this section, placed in the record of the investigation by the Commission.

(c) *Filing.* Documents to be filed with the Commission must comply with applicable rules, including § 201.8 of this chapter. If the Commission establishes a deadline for the filing of a document, and the submitter includes business proprietary information in the document, the submitter is to file and, if the submitter is a party, serve the business proprietary version of the document on the deadline and may file and serve the nonbusiness proprietary version of the document no later than one business day after the deadline for filing the document. The business proprietary version shall enclose all business proprietary information in brackets and have the following warning marked on every page: "Bracketing of BPI not final for one business day after date of filing." The bracketing becomes final one business day after the date of filing of the document, *i.e.*, at the same time as the nonbusiness proprietary version of the document is due

99

to be filed. Until the bracketing becomes final, recipients of the document may not divulge any part of the contents of the document to anyone not subject to the administrative protective order issued in the investigation. If the submitter discovers it has failed to bracket correctly, the submitter may file a corrected version or portion of the business proprietary document at the same time as the nonbusiness proprietary version is filed. No changes, including typographical changes, to the document other than bracketing and deletion of business proprietary information are permitted after the deadline unless an extension of time is granted to file an amended document pursuant to § 201.14(b)(2) of this chapter. Failure to comply with this paragraph may result in the striking from the record of all or a portion of a submitter's document.

[44 FR 76468, Dec. 26, 1979, as amended at 61 FR 37829, July 22, 1996; 63 FR 30607, June 5, 1998; 70 FR 8511, Feb. 22, 2005]

§ 207.4   The record.

(a) *Maintenance of the record.* The Secretary shall maintain the record of each investigation conducted by the Commission pursuant to title VII of the Act. The record shall be maintained contemporaneously with each actual filing in the record. It shall be divided into public and nonpublic sections. The Secretary shall also maintain a contemporaneous index of all materials filed in the record. All material properly filed with the Secretary shall be placed in the record. The Commission need not consider in its determinations or include in the record any material that is not filed with the Secretary. All material which is placed in the record shall be maintained in the public record, with the exception of material which is privileged, or which is business proprietary information submitted in accordance with § 201.6 of this chapter. Privileged and business proprietary material shall be maintained in the nonpublic record.

(b) *Audits.* The Commission may in its discretion verify information received in the course of an investigation. To the extent a verification results in new or different information, the Commission shall place such information on the record.

(c) *Materials provided by the administering authority.* Materials received by the Commission from the administering authority shall be placed on the Commission's record and shall be designated by the Commission as public or nonpublic in conformity with the applicable designation of the administering authority. Any requests to the Commission either to permit access to such materials or to release such materials shall be referred to the administering authority for its advice.

[44 FR 76468, Dec. 26, 1979, as amended at 61 FR 37829, July 22, 1996]

§ 207.5   Ex parte meetings.

There shall be included in the record of each investigation a record of ex parte meetings as required by section 777(a)(3) of the Act. The record of each ex parte meeting shall include the identity of the persons present at the meeting, the date, time, and place of the meeting, and a summary of the matters discussed or submitted.

§ 207.6   [Reserved]

§ 207.7   Limited disclosure of certain business proprietary information under administrative protective order.

(a)(1) *Disclosure.* Upon receipt of a timely application filed by an authorized applicant, as defined in paragraph (a)(3) of this section, which describes in general terms the information requested, and sets forth the reasons for the request (*e.g.,* all business proprietary information properly disclosed pursuant to this section for the purpose of representing an interested party in investigations pending before the Commission), the Secretary shall make available all business proprietary information contained in Commission memoranda and reports and in written submissions filed with the Commission at any time during the investigation (except nondisclosable confidential business information) to the authorized applicant under an administrative protective order described in paragraph (b) of this section. The term "business proprietary information" has the same meaning as the term "confidential business information" as defined in §201.6 of this chapter.

(2) *Application.* An application under paragraph (a)(1) of this section must be made by an authorized applicant on a form adopted by the Secretary or a photocopy thereof. A signed application shall be filed electronically. An application on behalf of a petitioner, a respondent, or another party must be made no later than the time that entries of appearance are due pursuant to §201.11 of this chapter. In the event that two or more authorized applicants represent one interested party who is a party to the investigation, the authorized applicants must select one of their number to be lead authorized applicant. The lead authorized applicant's application must be filed no later than the time that entries of appearance are due. Provided that the application is accepted, the lead authorized applicant shall be served with business proprietary information pursuant to paragraph (f) of this section. The other authorized applicants representing the same party may file their applications after the deadline for entries of appearance but at least five days before the deadline for filing posthearing briefs in the investigation, or the deadline for filing briefs in the preliminary phase of an investigation, or the deadline for filing submissions in a remanded investigation, and shall not be served with business proprietary information.

(3) *Authorized applicant.* (i) Only an authorized applicant may file an application under this subsection. An authorized applicant is:

(A) An attorney for an interested party which is a party to the investigation;

(B) A consultant or expert under the direction and control of a person under paragraph (a)(3)(i)(A) of this section;

(C) A consultant or expert who appears regularly before the Commission and who represents an interested party which is a party to the investigation; or

(D) A representative of an interested party which is a party to the investigation, if such interested party is not represented by counsel.

(ii) In addition, an authorized applicant must not be involved in competitive decisionmaking for an interested party which is a party to the investigation. Involvement in "competitive decisionmaking" includes past, present, or likely future activities, associations, and relationships with an interested party which is a party to the investigation that involve the prospective authorized applicant's advice or participation in any of such party's decisions made in light of similar or corresponding information about a competitor (pricing, product design, etc.).

(4) *Forms and determinations.* (i) The Secretary may adopt, from time to time, forms for submitting requests for disclosure pursuant to an administrative protective order incorporating the terms of this rule. The Secretary shall determine whether the requirements for release of information under this rule have been satisfied. This determination shall be made concerning specific business proprietary information as expeditiously as possible but in no event later than fourteen (14) days from the filing of the information, or seven (7) days in the preliminary phase of an investigation, except if the submitter of the information objects to its release or the information is unusually voluminous or complex, in which case the determination shall be made within thirty (30) days from the filing of the information, or ten (10) days in the preliminary phase of an investigation. The Secretary shall establish a list of parties whose applications have been granted. The Secretary's determination shall be final for purposes of review by the U.S. Court of International Trade under section 777(c)(2) of the Act.

(ii) Should the Secretary determine pursuant to this section that materials sought to be protected from public disclosure by a person do not constitute business proprietary information or were not required to be served under paragraph (f) of this section, then the Secretary shall, upon request, issue an order on behalf of the Commission requiring the return of all copies of such materials served in accordance with paragraph (f) of this section.

(iii) The Secretary shall release business proprietary information only to an authorized applicant whose application has been accepted and who presents the application along with adequate personal identification; or a person described in paragraph (b)(1)(iv) of this section who presents a copy of the statement referred to in that paragraph along with adequate personal identification.

(iv) An authorized applicant granted access to business proprietary information in the preliminary phase of an investigation may, subject to paragraph (c) of this section, retain such business proprietary information during any final phase of that investigation, provided that the authorized applicant has not lost his authorized applicant status (*e.g.*, by terminating his representation of an interested party who is a party). When retaining business proprietary information pursuant to this paragraph, the authorized applicant need not file a new application in the final phase of the investigation.

(b) *Administrative protective order.* The administrative protective order under which information is made available to the authorized applicant shall require the applicant to submit to the Secretary a personal sworn statement that, in addition to such other conditions as the Secretary may require, the applicant shall:

(1) Not divulge any of the business proprietary information obtained under the administrative protective order and not otherwise available to the applicant, to any person other than

(i) Personnel of the Commission concerned with the investigation,

(ii) The person or agency from whom the business proprietary information was obtained,

(iii) A person whose application for access to business proprietary information under the administrative protective order has been granted by the Secretary, and

(iv) Other persons, such as paralegals and clerical staff, who are employed or supervised by the authorized applicant; who have a need thereof in connection with the investigation; who are not involved in competitive decision making for an interested party which is a party to the investigation; and who have signed a statement in a form approved by the Secretary that they agree to be bound by the administrative protective order (the authorized applicant shall be responsible for retention and accuracy of such forms and shall be deemed responsible for such persons' compliance with the administrative protective order);

(2) Use such business proprietary information solely for the purposes of representing an interested party in the Commission investigation then in progress or during judicial or other review of such Commission investigation;

(3) Not consult with any person not described in paragraph (b)(1) of this section concerning such business proprietary information without first having received the written consent of the Secretary and the party or the attorney of the party from whom such business proprietary information was obtained;

(4) Whenever materials (*e.g.*, documents, computer disks, etc.) containing such business proprietary information are not being used, store such material in a locked file cabinet, vault, safe, or other suitable container;

(5) Serve all materials containing business proprietary information as directed by the Secretary and pursuant to paragraph (f) of this section;

(6) Transmit all materials containing business proprietary information with a cover sheet identifying the materials as containing business proprietary information;

(7) Comply with the provisions of this section;

(8) Make true and accurate representations in the authorized applicant's application and promptly notify the Secretary of any changes that occur after the submission of the application and that affect the representations made in the application (*e.g.*, change in personnel assigned to the investigation);

(9) Report promptly and confirm in writing to the Secretary any breach of the administrative protective order; and

(10) Acknowledge that breach of the administrative protective order may subject the authorized applicant to such sanctions or other actions as the Commission deems appropriate.

(c) *Final disposition of material released under administrative protective order.* At such date as the Secretary may determine appropriate for particular data, each authorized applicant shall return or destroy all copies of materials released to authorized applicants pursuant to this section and all other materials containing business proprietary information, such as charts or notes based on any such information received under administrative protective order, and file with the Secretary a certificate attesting to his personal, good faith belief that all copies of such material have been returned or destroyed and no copies of such material have been made available to any person to whom disclosure was not specifically authorized.

(d) *Commission responses to a breach of administrative protective order.* A breach of an administrative protective order may subject an offender to:

(1) Disbarment from practice in any capacity before the Commission along with such person's partners, associates, employer, and employees, for up to seven years following publication of a determination that the order has been breached;

(2) Referral to the United States Attorney;

(3) In the case of an attorney, accountant, or other professional, referral to the ethics panel of the appropriate professional association;

(4) Such other administrative sanctions as the Commission determines to be appropriate, including public release of or striking from the record any information or briefs submitted by, or on behalf of, the offender or the party represented by the offender, denial of further access to business proprietary information in the current or any future investigations before the Commission, and issuance of a public or private letter of reprimand; and

(5) Such other actions, including but not limited to, a warning letter, as the Commission determines to be appropriate.

(e) *Breach investigation procedure.* (1) The Commission shall determine whether any person has violated an administrative protective order, and may impose sanctions or other actions in accordance with paragraph (d) of this section. At any time within sixty (60) days of the later of the date on which the alleged violation occurred or, as determined by the Commission, could have been discovered through the exercise of reasonable and ordinary care, or the completion of an investigation conducted under subpart B or C of this part, the Commission may commence an investigation of any breach of an administrative protective order alleged to have occurred at any time during the pendency of the investigation, including all appeals, remands, and subsequent appeals. Whenever the Commission has reason to believe that a person may have breached an administrative protective order issued pursuant to this section, the Secretary shall issue a letter informing such person that the Commission has reason to believe a breach has occurred and that the person has a reasonable opportunity to present his views on whether a breach has occurred. If subsequently the Commission determines that a breach has occurred and that further investigation is warranted, the Secretary shall issue a letter informing such person of that determination and that the person has a reasonable opportunity to present his views on whether mitigating circumstances exist and on the appropriate sanction to be imposed, but no longer on whether a breach has occurred. Once such person has been afforded a reasonable opportunity to present his views, the Commission shall determine what sanction if any to impose.

(2) Where the sanction imposed is a private letter of reprimand, the Secretary shall expunge the sanction from the recipient's record two (2) years from the date of issuance of the sanction, provided that

(i) The recipient has not received another unexpunged sanction pursuant to this section at any time prior to the end of the two year period, and

(ii) The recipient is not the subject of an investigation for possible breach of administrative protective order under this section at the end of the two year period. Upon the completion of such a pending breach investigation without the issuance of a sanction, the original sanction shall be expunged. The Secretary shall notify a sanction recipient in the event that the sanction is expunged.

(f) *Service.* (1) Any party filing written submissions which include business proprietary information to the Commission during an investigation shall at the same time serve complete copies of such submissions upon all authorized applicants specified on the list established by the Secretary pursuant to paragraph (a)(4) of this section, and, except as provided in § 207.3, a nonbusiness proprietary version on all other parties. All such submissions must be accompanied by a certificate attesting that complete copies of the submission have been properly served. In the event that a submission is filed before the Secretary's list is established, the document need not be accompanied by a certificate of service, but the submission shall be served within two (2) days of the establishment of the list and a certificate of service shall then be filed.

(2) If a party's request under paragraph (g) of this section is granted, the Secretary shall accept the nondisclosable confidential business information into the record. The party shall serve the submission containing such information in accordance with the requirements of § 207.3(b) and paragraph (f)(1) of this section, with the information redacted from the copies served.

(3) The Secretary shall not accept for filing into the record of an investigation submissions filed without a proper certificate of service. Failure to comply with paragraph (f) of this section may result in denial of party status and such sanctions as the Commission deems appropriate. Business proprietary information in submissions must be dealt with as required by § 207.3(c).

(g) *Exemption from disclosure*—(1) *In general.* Any person may request exemption from the disclosure of business proprietary information under administrative protective order, whether the person desires to include such information in a petition filed under § 207.10, or any other submission to the Commission during the course of an investigation. Such a request shall only be granted if the Secretary finds that such information is nondisclosable confidential business information. As defined in § 201.6(a)(2) of this chapter, nondisclosable confidential business information is privileged information, classified information, or specific information (*e.g.*, trade secrets) of a type for which there is a clear and compelling need to withhold from disclosure. The request will be granted or denied not later than thirty (30) days (ten (10) days in a preliminary phase investigation) after the date on which the request is filed.

(2) *Request for exemption.* A request for exemption from disclosure must be filed with the Secretary in writing with the reasons therefor. At the same time as the request is filed, one copy of the business proprietary information in question must be lodged with the Secretary solely for the purpose of obtaining a determination as to the request. The business proprietary information for which exemption from disclosure is sought shall remain the property of the requester, and shall not become or be incorporated into any agency record until such time as the request is granted. A request should, when possible, be filed two business days prior to the deadline, if any, for filing the document in which the information for which exemption from disclosure is sought is proposed to be included. If the request is denied, the copy of the information lodged with the Secretary shall promptly be returned to the requester. Such a request shall only be granted if the Secretary finds that such information is privileged information, classified information, or specific information of a type for which there is a clear and compelling need to withhold from disclosure. The Secretary shall promptly notify the requester as to whether the request has been approved or denied.

(3) *Procedure if request is approved.* If the request is approved, the person shall file three versions of the submission containing the nondisclosable confidential business information in question. One version shall contain all business proprietary information, bracketed in accordance with § 201.6 of this chapter and § 207.3. The other two versions shall conform to and be filed in accordance with the requirements of § 201.6 of this chapter and § 207.3, except that the specific information as to which exemption from disclosure was

granted shall be redacted from the submission.

(4) *Procedure if request is denied.* If the request is denied, the copy of the information lodged with the Secretary shall promptly be returned to the requester. The requester may file the submission in question without that information, in accordance with the requirements of §207.3.

[44 FR 76468, Dec. 26, 1979, as amended at 59 FR 66723, Dec. 28, 1994; 61 FR 37829, July 22, 1996; 68 FR 32978, June 3, 2003; 70 FR 8512, Feb. 22, 2005; 76 FR 61942, Oct. 6, 2011]

§207.8 Questionnaires to have the force of subpoenas; subpoena enforcement.

Any questionnaire issued by the Commission in connection with any investigation under title VII of the Act may be issued as a subpoena and subscribed by a Commissioner, after which it shall have the force and effect of a subpoena authorized by the Commission. Whenever any party or any other person fails to respond adequately to such a subpoena or whenever a party or any other person refuses or is unable to produce information requested in a timely manner and in the form required, or otherwise significantly impedes an investigation, the Commission may:

(a) Use the facts otherwise available in making its determination;

(b) Seek judicial enforcement of the subpoena pursuant to 19 U.S.C. 1333;

(c) Make inferences adverse to such person's position, if such person is an interested party that has failed to cooperate by not acting to the best of its ability to comply with a request for information; and

(d) Take such other actions as necessary to obtain needed information.

[61 FR 37831, July 22, 1996]

Subpart B—Preliminary Determinations

SOURCE: 56 FR 11927, Mar. 21, 1991, unless otherwise noted.

§207.10 Filing of petition with the Commission.

(a) *Filing of the petition.* Any interested party who files a petition with the administering authority pursuant to section 702(b) or section 732(b) of the Act in a case in which a Commission determination under title VII of the Act is required, shall file copies of the petition and all exhibits, appendices, and attachments thereto, pursuant to §201.8 of this chapter, with the Secretary on the same day the petition is filed with the administering authority. A paper original and eight (8) true paper copies of a petition shall be filed. One copy of all exhibits, appendices, and attachments to the petition shall be filed in electronic form on CD–ROM, DVD, or other portable electronic format approved by the Secretary. Petitioners also must file one unbound copy of the petition (the unbound copy of the petition may be stapled or held together by means of a clip). If the petition complies with the provisions of §207.11, it shall be deemed to be properly filed on the date on which the requisite number of copies of the petition is received by the Secretary, provided that, if the petition is filed with the Secretary after 12:00 noon, eastern time, the petition shall be deemed filed on the next business day. Notwithstanding §207.11 of this chapter, a petitioner need not file an entry of appearance in the investigation instituted upon the filing of its petition, which shall be deemed an entry of appearance.

(b) *Service of the petition.* (1)(i) The Secretary shall promptly notify a petitioner when, before the establishment of a service list under §207.7(a)(4), he or she approves an application under §207.7(a). When practicable, this notification shall be made by facsimile transmission. A copy of the petition including all business proprietary information shall then be served by petitioner on those approved applicants in accord with §207.3(b) within two (2) calendar days of the time notification is made by the Secretary.

(ii) The petitioner shall serve persons enumerated on the list established by the Secretary pursuant to §207.7(a)(4) that have not been served pursuant to paragraph (b)(1)(i) of this section within two (2) calendar days of the establishment of the Secretary's list.

(2) A copy of the petition omitting business proprietary information shall

be served by petitioner on those persons enumerated on the list established by the Secretary pursuant to § 201.11(d) of this chapter within two (2) calendar days of the establishment of the Secretary's list.

(3) Service of the petition shall be attested by filing a certificate of service with the Commission.

(c) *Amendments and withdrawals; critical circumstances.* (1) Any amendment or withdrawal of a petition shall be filed on the same day with both the Secretary and the administering authority, without regard to whether the requester seeks action only by one agency.

(2) When not made in the petition, any allegations of critical circumstances under section 703 or section 733 of the Act shall be made in an amendment to the petition and shall be filed as early as possible. Critical circumstances allegations, whether made in the petition or in an amendment thereto, shall contain information reasonably available to petitioner concerning the factors enumerated in sections 705(b)(4)(A) and 735(b)(4)(A) of the Act.

[61 FR 37831, July 22, 1996, as amended at 70 FR 8512, Feb. 22, 2005; 76 FR 61942, Oct. 6, 2011; 79 FR 35924, June 25, 2014]

§ 207.11   Contents of petition.

(a) The petition shall be signed by the petitioner or its duly authorized officer, attorney, or agent, and shall set forth the name, address, and telephone number of the petitioner and any such officer, attorney, or agent, and the names of all representatives of petitioner who will appear in the investigation.

(b)(1) The petition shall allege the elements necessary for the imposition of a duty under section 701(a) or section 731(a) of the Act and contain information reasonably available to the petitioner supporting the allegations.

(2) The petition shall also include the following specific information, to the extent reasonably available to the petitioner:

(i) Identification of the domestic like product(s) proposed by petitioner;

(ii) A listing of all U.S. producers of the proposed domestic like product(s), including a street address, phone number, and contact person(s) with email address(es) for each producer;

(iii) A listing of all U.S. importers of the subject merchandise, including street addresses, email addresses, and phone numbers for each importer.

(iv) Identification of each product on which the petitioner requests the Commission to seek pricing information in its questionnaires; and

(v) A listing of the main purchasers from which each petitioning firm experienced lost sales or lost revenue by reason of the subject merchandise during a period covering the three most recently completed calendar years and that portion of the current calendar year for which information is reasonably available. For each named purchaser, petitioners must provide the email address of the specific contact person, 5-digit zip code, and the information identified in the template spreadsheet specified in the Commission's Handbook on Filing Procedures. Petitioners must certify that all lost sales or lost revenue allegations identified in the petition will also be submitted electronically in the manner specified in the Commission's Handbook on Filing Procedures.

(3) The petition shall contain a certification that each item of information specified in paragraph (b)(2) of this section that the petition does not include was not reasonably available to the petitioner.

(4) Petitioners are also advised to refer to the administering authority's regulations concerning the contents of petitions.

[61 FR 37831, July 22, 1996, as amended at 79 FR 35924, June 25, 2014; 80 FR 52618, Sept. 1, 2015]

§ 207.12   Notice of preliminary phase of investigation.

Upon receipt by the Commission of a petition under § 207.10 or receipt of notice that the administering authority has commenced an investigation under section 702(a) or section 732(a) of the Act, the Director shall, as soon as practicable after consultation with the administering authority, institute an investigation and commence the preliminary phase of the investigation under section 703(a) or section 733(a) of the

Act and shall publish a notice to that effect in the FEDERAL REGISTER.

[61 FR 37832, July 22, 1996]

§ 207.13 Cooperation with administering authority; preliminary phase of investigation.

Subsequent to institution of an investigation pursuant to section 207.12, the Director shall conduct such investigation as the Director deems appropriate. Information adduced in the investigation shall be placed on the record. The Director shall cooperate with the administering authority in its determination of the sufficiency of a petition and in its decision whether to permit any proposed amendment to a petition. Notwithstanding §§ 201.11(c) and 201.14(b) of this chapter, late filings in the preliminary phase of an investigation shall be referred to the Director, who shall determine whether to accept such filing for good cause shown by the person making the filing.

[61 FR 37832, July 22, 1996]

§ 207.14 Negative petition determination.

Upon receipt by the Commission of notice from the administering authority under section 702(d) or section 732(d) of the Act that the administering authority has made a negative petition determination under section 702(c)(3) or section 732(c)(3) of the Act, the investigation begun pursuant to § 207.12 shall terminate. All persons who have received requests for information from the Director shall be notified of the termination.

[61 FR 37832, July 22, 1996]

§ 207.15 Written briefs and conference.

Each party may submit to the Commission on or before a date specified in the notice of investigation issued pursuant to 207.12 a written brief containing information and arguments pertinent to the subject matter of the investigation. Briefs shall be signed, shall include a table of contents, and shall contain no more than fifty (50) double-spaced and single-sided pages of textual material, and shall be filed electronically, and nine (9) true paper copies shall be submitted on the same business day (on paper measuring 8.5 × 11 inches, double-spaced and single-sided). Any person not a party may submit a brief written statement of information pertinent to the investigation within the time specified and the same manner specified for the filing of briefs. In addition, the presiding official may permit persons to file within a specified time answers to questions or requests made by the Commission's staff. If he deems it appropriate, the Director shall hold a conference. The conference, if any, shall be held in accordance with the procedures in § 201.13 of this chapter, except that in connection with its presentation a party may provide written witness testimony at the conference; if written testimony is provided, nine (9) true paper copies shall be submitted. The Director may request the appearance of witnesses, take testimony, and administer oaths.

[79 FR 35924, June 25, 2014]

§ 207.16 [Reserved]

§ 207.17 Staff report.

Prior to the Commission's preliminary determination, the Director shall submit to the Commission a staff report. A public version of the staff report shall be made available to the public after the Commission's preliminary determination and a business proprietary version shall also be made available to persons authorized to receive business proprietary information under § 207.7.

§ 207.18 Notice of preliminary determination.

Whenever the Commission makes a preliminary determination, the Secretary shall serve copies of the determination and a public version of the staff report on the petitioner, other parties to the investigation, and the administering authority. The Secretary shall publish a notice of such determination in the FEDERAL REGISTER. If the Commission's determination is negative, or that imports are negligible, the investigation shall be terminated. If the Commission's determination is affirmative, the notice shall announce commencement of the final phase of the investigation.

[61 FR 37832, July 22, 1996]

Subpart C—Final Determinations, Short Life Cycle Products

SOURCE: 56 FR 11928, Mar. 21, 1991, unless otherwise noted.

§ 207.20 Investigative activity following preliminary determination.

(a) If the Commission's preliminary determination is affirmative, the Director shall continue investigative activities pending notice by the administering authority of its preliminary determination under section 703(b) or section 733(b) of the Act.

(b) The Director shall circulate draft questionnaires for the final phase of an investigation to parties to the investigation for comment. Any party desiring to comment on draft questionnaires shall submit such comments in writing to the Commission within a time specified by the Director. All requests for collecting new information shall be presented at this time. The Commission will disregard subsequent requests for collection of new information absent a showing that there is a compelling need for the information and that the information could not have been requested in the comments on the draft questionnaires.

[61 FR 37832, July 22, 1996, as amended at 79 FR 35925, June 25, 2014]

§ 207.21 Final phase notice of scheduling.

(a) Notice from the administering authority of an affirmative preliminary determination under section 703(b) or section 733(b) of the Act and notice from the administering authority of an affirmative final determination under section 705(a) or section 735(a) of the Act shall be deemed to occur on the date on which the transmittal letter of such determination is received by the Secretary from the administering authority or the date on which notice of such determination is published in the FEDERAL REGISTER, whichever shall first occur.

(b) Upon receipt of notice from the administering authority of an affirmative preliminary determination under section 703(b) or section 733(b) of the Act or, if the administering authority's preliminary determination is negative, notice of an affirmative final determination under section 705(a) or section 735(a) of the Act, the Commission shall publish in the FEDERAL REGISTER a Final Phase Notice of Scheduling.

(c) If the administering authority's preliminary determination is negative, the Director shall continue such investigative activities as the Director deems appropriate pending a final determination by the administering authority under section 705(a) or section 735(a) of the Act.

(d) Upon receipt by the Commission of notice from the administering authority of its final negative determination under section 705(a) or section 735(a) of the Act, the corresponding Commission investigation shall be terminated.

[61 FR 37832, July 22, 1996]

§ 207.22 Prehearing and final staff reports.

(a) *Prehearing staff report.* The Director shall prepare and place in the record, prior to the hearing, a prehearing staff report containing information concerning the subject matter of the investigation. A version of the staff report containing business proprietary information shall be placed in the nonpublic record and made available to persons authorized to receive business proprietary information under § 207.7, and a nonbusiness proprietary version of the staff report shall be placed in the public record.

(b) *Final staff report.* After the hearing, the Director shall revise the prehearing staff report and submit to the Commission, prior to the Commission's final determination, a final version of the staff report. The final staff report is intended to supplement and correct the information contained in the prehearing staff report. A public version of the final staff report shall be made available to the public and a business proprietary version shall also be made available to persons authorized to receive business proprietary information under section 207.7.

[56 FR 11927, Mar. 21, 1991, as amended at 60 FR 22, Jan. 3, 1995. Redesignated at 61 FR 37832, July 22, 1996]

§207.23 Prehearing brief.

Each party who is an interested party shall submit to the Commission, no later than five (5) business days prior to the date of the hearing specified in the notice of scheduling, a prehearing brief. Prehearing briefs shall be signed and shall include a table of contents and shall be filed electronically, and nine (9) true paper copies shall be submitted on the same business day. The prehearing brief should present a party's case concisely and shall, to the extent possible, refer to the record and include information and arguments which the party believes relevant to the subject matter of the Commission's determination under section 705(b) or section 735(b) of the Act. Any person not an interested party may submit a brief written statement of information pertinent to the investigation within the time specified and the same manner specified for filing of prehearing briefs.

[79 FR 35925, June 25, 2014]

§207.24 Hearing.

(a) *In general.* The Commission shall hold a hearing concerning an investigation before making a final determination under section 705(b) or section 735(b) of the Act.

(b) *Procedures.* Any hearing shall be conducted after notice published in the FEDERAL REGISTER. The hearing shall not be subject to the provisions of 5 U.S.C. subchapter II, chapter 5, or to 5 U.S.C. 702. Each party shall limit its presentation at the hearing to a summary of the information and arguments contained in its prehearing brief, an analysis of the information and arguments contained in the prehearing briefs described in §207.23, and information not available at the time its prehearing brief was filed. Unless a portion of the hearing is closed, presentations at the hearing shall not include business proprietary information. Notwithstanding §201.13(f) of this chapter, in connection with its presentation, a party may provide written witness testimony at the hearing; if written testimony is provided, eight (8) true paper copies shall be submitted. In the case of testimony to be presented at a closed session held in response to a re-

quest under §207.24(d), confidential and non-confidential versions shall be filed in accordance with §207.3. Any person not a party may make a brief oral statement of information pertinent to the investigation.

(c) *Hearing transcripts—(1) In general.* A verbatim transcript shall be made of all hearings or conferences held in connection with Commission investigations conducted under this part.

(2) *Revision of transcripts.* Within ten (10) days of the completion of a hearing, but in any event at least one (1) day prior to the date for disclosure of information set pursuant to §207.30(a), any person who testified at the hearing may submit proposed revisions to the transcript of his or her testimony to the Secretary. No substantive revisions shall be permitted. If in the judgment of the Secretary a proposed revision does not alter the substance of the testimony in question, the Secretary shall incorporate the revision into a revised transcript.

(d) *Closed sessions.* Upon a request filed by a party to the investigation no later than seven (7) business days prior to the date of the hearing that identifies the subjects to be discussed, specifies the amount of time requested, and justifies the need for a closed session with respect to each subject to be discussed, the Commission may close a portion of a hearing to persons not authorized under §207.7 to have access to business proprietary information in order to allow such party to address business proprietary information during the course of its presentation. If any party wishes to comment on the request to close a portion of the hearing, such comments must be filed within two (2) business days after the filing of the request. In addition, during each hearing held in an investigation conducted under section 705(b) or section 735(b) of the Act, following the public presentation of the petitioner(s) and that of each panel of respondents, the Commission will, if it deems it appropriate, close the hearing to persons not authorized under §207.7 to have access to business proprietary information in order to allow Commissioners to question parties and/ or their representatives concerning matters involving business proprietary information.

[61 FR 37832, July 22, 1996, as amended at 70 FR 8512, Feb. 22, 2005; 76 FR 61943, Oct. 6, 2011]

§ 207.25 Posthearing briefs.

Any party may file a posthearing brief concerning the information adduced at or after the hearing with the Secretary within a time specified in the notice of scheduling or by the presiding official at the hearing. A posthearing brief shall be filed electronically, and nine (9) true paper copies shall be submitted on the same business day. No such posthearing brief shall exceed fifteen (15) pages of textual material, double-spaced and single-sided, when printed out on paper measuring 8.5 × 11 inches. In addition, the presiding official may permit persons to file answers to questions or requests made by the Commission at the hearing within a specified time. The Secretary shall not accept for filing posthearing briefs or answers which do not comply with this section.

[79 FR 35925, June 25, 2014]

§ 207.26 Statements by nonparties.

Any person other than a party may submit a brief written statement of information pertinent to the investigation within the time specified for the filing of posthearing briefs.

[56 FR 11928, Mar. 21, 1991. Redesignated at 61 FR 37832, July 22, 1996]

§ 207.27 Short life cycle products.

(a) An eligible domestic entity may file a petition to establish a product category for short life cycle merchandise which has been the subject of two or more affirmative dumping determinations. The Commission shall within thirty (30) days of the filing of the petition determine its sufficiency. If the petition is found to be sufficient, the Commission shall institute a proceeding to establish a product category and publish a notice of institution in the FEDERAL REGISTER. Upon request of an interested person filed within fifteen (15) days after publication of the notice of institution, the Commission

shall conduct a hearing which shall be transcribed. The Commission's determination concerning the scope of the product category into which to classify the short life cycle merchandise identified by the petition shall be issued no later than ninety (90) days after the filing of the petition.

(b) The Commission may on its own initiative and at any time modify the scope of a product category established in a proceeding pursuant to paragraph (a) of this section. Ninety (90) days prior to such modification, the Commission shall publish a notice of proposed modification in the FEDERAL REGISTER. Upon request of an interested party filed within fifteen (15) days after publication of the notice of proposed modification, the Commission shall conduct a hearing which shall be transcribed. Written submissions concerning the proposed modification shall be accepted if filed no later than sixty (60) days after publication of the notice of proposed modification.

[56 FR 11928, Mar. 21, 1991. Redesignated at 61 FR 37832, July 22, 1996]

§ 207.28 Anticircumvention.

Prior to providing advice to the administering authority pursuant to section 781(e)(3) of the Act, the Commission shall publish in the FEDERAL REGISTER a notice that such advice is contemplated. Any person may file one written submission concerning the matter described in the notice no later than fourteen (14) days after publication of the notice. Such a statement shall be filed electronically, and nine (9) true paper copies shall be submitted on the same business day. The statement shall contain no more than fifty (50) double-spaced and single-sided pages of textual material, when printed out on paper measuring 8.5 × 11 inches. The Commission shall by notice provide for additional statements as it deems necessary.

[79 FR 35925, June 25, 2014]

§ 207.29 Publication of notice of determination.

Whenever the Commission makes a final determination, the Secretary shall serve copies of the determination and the nonbusiness proprietary version of the final staff report on the petitioner, other parties to the investigation, and the administering authority. The Secretary shall publish notice of such determination in the FEDERAL REGISTER.

[61 FR 37833, July 22, 1996]

§ 207.30 Comment on information.

(a) In any final phase of an investigation under section 705 or section 735 of the Act, the Commission shall specify a date on which it will disclose to all parties to the investigation all information it has obtained on which the parties have not previously had an opportunity to comment. Any such information that is business proprietary information will be released to persons authorized to obtain such information pursuant to § 207.7. The date on which disclosure is made will occur after the filing of posthearing briefs pursuant to § 207.25.

(b) The parties shall have an opportunity to file comments on any information disclosed to them after they have filed their posthearing brief pursuant to § 207.25. A comment shall be filed electronically, and nine (9) true paper copies shall be submitted on the same business day. Comments shall only concern such information, and shall not exceed 15 pages of textual material, double-spaced and single-sided, when printed out on paper measuring 8.5 × 11 inches. A comment may address the accuracy, reliability, or probative value of such information by reference to information elsewhere in the record, in which case the comment shall identify where in the record such information is found. Comments containing new factual information shall be disregarded. The date on which such comments must be filed will be specified by the Commission when it specifies the time that information will be disclosed pursuant to paragraph (a) of this section. The record shall close on the date such comments are due, except with respect to investigations subject to the provisions of section 771(7)(G)(iii) of the Act, and with respect to changes in bracketing of business proprietary information in the comments permitted by § 207.3(c).

[61 FR 37833, July 22, 1996, as amended at 76 FR 61943, Oct. 6, 2011; 79 FR 35925, June 25, 2014]

Subpart D—Terminated, Suspended, and Continued Investigations, Investigations to Review Negotiated Agreements, and Investigations To Review Outstanding Determinations

SOURCE: 56 FR 11929, Mar. 21, 1991, unless otherwise noted.

§ 207.40 Termination and suspension of investigation.

(a) An investigation under title VII may be terminated by the Commission by giving notice in the FEDERAL REGISTER to all parties to the investigation, upon withdrawal of the petition by the petitioner, or upon issuance of a final negative determination or termination of its investigation by the administering authority under section 303, 705 or 735 of the Act. The Commission may not terminate an investigation upon withdrawal of the petition by the petitioner, however, before a determination is made by the administering authority under section 702(c), 703(b), 732(c) or 733(b) of the Act.

(b) Upon receipt of notice of suspension of an investigation by the administering authority under section 704 (b) or (c) or 734(b), (c), or (1), of the Act, the Secretary shall issue a notice of suspension of the Commission investigation. Such suspension shall not prevent the Director from conducting such other investigative activities as he deems appropriate with respect to the subject matter of the suspended investigation.

(c) *Resumption of suspended investigation*—(1) *Purpose.* If the administering authority determines pursuant to section 704(i) or 734(i) of the Act to resume a suspended investigation and so notifies the Commission of its determination, and in the event that the suspended investigation was not terminated, the Commission shall resume the investigation.

111

(2) *Procedures.* The procedures set forth in subpart C shall apply to all investigations instituted under this section.

[56 FR 11927, Mar. 21, 1991, as amended at 60 FR 22, Jan. 3, 1995]

§ 207.41 Commission review of agreements to eliminate the injurious effect of subsidized imports or imports sold at less than fair value.

If the administering authority determines to suspend an investigation upon acceptance of an agreement to eliminate the injurious effect of subsidized imports or imports sold at less than fair value, the Commission shall, upon petition, initiate an investigation to determine whether the injurious effect of imports of the merchandise which was the subject of the suspended investigation is eliminated completely by the agreement. Petitions may be filed by a party to the investigation which is an interested party described in paragraph (C), (D), (E), (F), or (G) of section 771(9) of the Act. Investigations under this section shall be completed within seventy five (75) days of their initiation.

§ 207.42 Investigation continued upon request.

Upon receipt of advice from the administering authority that it has received a request for the continuation of a suspended investigation pursuant to section 704(g) or 734(g) of the Act, the Commission shall continue the investigation. The procedures set forth in subparts B and C of this part, including applicable time limitations, shall apply to all continued investigations within this rule.

§ 207.43 [Reserved]

§ 207.44 Consolidation of investigations.

The Commission may, when appropriate, consolidate continued investigations under section 704(g) or section 734(g) of the Act with investigations to review agreements for the elimination of injury under section 704(h) or section 734(h) of the Act.

§ 207.45 Investigation to review outstanding determination.

(a) *Request for review.* Any person may file with the Commission a request for the institution of a review investigation under section 751(b) of the Act. The person making the request shall also promptly serve copies of the request on the parties to the original investigation upon which the review is to be based. All requests shall set forth a description of changed circumstances sufficient to warrant the institution of a review investigation by the Commission.

(b) *Notice of receipt of a request.* Upon the receipt of a properly filed and sufficient request for a review investigation, the Secretary shall publish a notice of having received such a request in the FEDERAL REGISTER inviting public comment on the question of whether the Commission should institute a review investigation. Persons shall have at least thirty (30) days from the date of publication in the FEDERAL REGISTER within which to submit comments to the Commission.

(c) *Institution of an investigation.* Within forty-five (45) days after the close of the period for public comments following publication of the receipt of a request, the Commission shall determine whether the request shows changed circumstances sufficient to warrant a review and, if so, shall institute a review investigation. The Commission may also institute a review investigation on its own initiative. The review investigation shall be instituted by notice published in the FEDERAL REGISTER and shall be completed within one hundred eighty (180) days of the date of such publication. If the Commission determines that a request does not show changed circumstances sufficient to warrant a review, the request shall be dismissed and a notice of the dismissal published in the FEDERAL REGISTER stating the reasons therefor.

(d) *Conduct of review investigation.* The procedures set forth in subpart C of part 207 shall apply to all investigations instituted under this section.

[56 FR 11929, Mar. 21, 1991, as amended at 63 FR 30607, June 5, 1998; 79 FR 35925, June 25, 2014]

§207.46 Investigations concerning certain countervailing duty orders.

(a) *Definitions.* For purposes of this section:

(1) *Requesting party* means an interested party described in section 771(9) (C), (D), (E), (F), or (G) of the Act.

(2) *Order* means a countervailing duty order issued under section 303 of the Act as to which the requirement of an affirmative determination of material injury under section 303(a)(2) of the Act was not applicable at the time such order was issued.

(3) *WTO Agreement* means the Agreement Establishing the World Trade Organization entered into on April 15, 1994.

(b) *Request for review.* A requesting party may file with the Commission a request for an investigation under section 753 of the Act within the time period established by section 753(a)(3) of the Act. The request should contain the following information:

(1) A description and identification of the relevant domestic like product, the industry in the United States producing that product that is likely to be materially injured by reason of imports of the subject merchandise if the Order is revoked, and each individual member of that industry.

(2) Information reasonably available to the requesting party concerning the names and addresses of all known enterprises believed to be manufacturing, producing, exporting, or importing the subject merchandise;

(3) Information reasonably available to the requesting party documenting that the industry described in paragraph (b)(1) of this section is likely to be materially injured by reason of subject imports if the Order is revoked, including:

(i) Information concerning the capacity, production, sales, market share, inventories, employment, wages, productivity, profits, ability to raise capital, and development and production efforts of the industry described in paragraph (b)(1) of this section.

(ii) Information concerning current and projected production capacity in the exporting country of the subject merchandise, inventories of the subject merchandise, and the existence of barriers to the importation of such merchandise into countries other than the United States.

(4) Information concerning any scope and anticircumvention rulings issued by the administering authority with respect to the Order.

(c) *Initiation of Investigation.* (1) Upon the receipt of a timely filed request for a section 753 investigation satisfying the requirements of paragraph (b) of this section, the Secretary shall publish a notice of initiation of such investigation in the FEDERAL REGISTER.

(2) Subject to paragraph (c)(3) of this section, a section 753 investigation shall be completed within one year of the date of publication of the notice of initiation of such investigation in the FEDERAL REGISTER.

(3) The Commission may take more than one year to complete section 753 investigations for which requests for investigations are received within one year after the date on which the WTO Agreement enters into force with respect to the United States. All such investigations must be completed within four years of that date, however. In determining whether to extend the completion date for a section 753 investigation, the Commission shall consult with the administering authority. Grounds for extending completion include, but are not limited to, the desire to conduct investigations involving the same or similar domestic industries and domestic like products on a simultaneous basis, and the desire to efficiently manage the Commission's caseload.

(d) *Conduct of Investigations.* The procedures set forth in subparts A and C of this part shall apply to all investigations initiated under this section.

(e) *When No Request for Review Is Filed.* When there has been no properly filed and sufficient request for a section 753 investigation of an Order, the Commission shall notify the administering authority that a negative determination has been made under section 753(a) of the Act with respect to that Order.

(f) *Pending and Suspended Section 303 Investigations.* If, on the data on which a country becomes a signatory to the Agreement on Subsidies and Countervailing Measures referred to in section

101(d)(12) of the Uruguay Round Agreements Act, there is a section 303 countervailing duty investigation in progress or suspended with respect to that country's merchandise for which the requirement of a material injury determination under section 303(a)(2) of the Act was not applicable at the time the investigation was initiated, the Commission shall commence an investigation pursuant to the provisions of section 753(c) of the Act with respect to pending investigations and suspended investigations to which section 704(i)(1)(B) of the Act applies.

(g) *Request for simultaneous section 751(c) review.* (1) A requesting party who requests a section 753 review may at the same time request from the Commission and the administering authority a review under section 751(c) of the Act of a countervailing or antidumping duty order involving the same or comparable subject merchandise.

(2) Should the administering authority, after consulting with the Commission, determine to initiate a section 751(c) review, the Commission shall conduct a consolidated review under sections 751(c) and 753 of the Act of the orders involving the same or comparable subject merchandise. Any such consolidated review shall be conducted under the applicable procedures set forth in subparts A and F of this part.

(3) Should the administering authority, after consulting with the Commission, determine not to initiate a section 751(c) review, the Commission will consider the request for a section 753 review pursuant to the procedures established in this section.

[60 FR 23, Jan. 3, 1995, as amended at 63 FR 30607, June 5, 1998]

Subpart E—Judicial Review

SOURCE: 56 FR 11930, Mar. 21, 1991, unless otherwise noted.

§ 207.50   Judicial review.

(a) *In general.* Persons entitled to judicial review under section 516A of the Act may seek review in the U.S. Court of International Trade.

(b) *Transmittal of record.* In the event a Commission determination is appealed to the U.S. Court of International Trade under section 516A, a copy of the record in the investigation before the Commission, as such record is defined in § 207.2(f), or a certified list of all items therein, shall be transmitted to the court by the Secretary in accordance with the rules of the court.

(c) *Service of process.* The Commission's General Counsel shall be the Commission's agent for service of process in cases arising under section 516A of the Act.

§ 207.51   Judicial review of denial of application for disclosure of certain business proprietary information under administrative protective order.

(a) *In general.* Persons entitled to judicial review under section 777(c)(2) of the Commission determination not to disclose business proprietary information may apply to the U.S. Court of International Trade for an order directing the Commission to make the information involved available.

(b) *Transmittal of record.* In the event a court order is sought under section 777(c)(2) requiring the Commission to disclose business proprietary information, the Secretary shall within 20 days after service of a summons and complaint upon the Commission transmit to the court under seal the business proprietary information involved along with pertinent parts of the record.

(c) *Pertinent parts of the record.* The pertinent parts of the record shall consist of:

(1) The application for Commission disclosure together with any documents filed in support thereof or in opposition thereto.

(2) Any Government memoranda relating to the Commission's determination, and

(3) The Commission's action on the application.

(d) *Service of process.* The Commission's General Counsel shall be the Commission's agent for service of process in cases under section 777(c)(2) of the Act.

Subpart F—Five-Year Reviews

SOURCE: 63 FR 30608, June 5, 1998, unless otherwise noted.

§207.60 Definitions.

For purposes of this subpart:

(a) The term *five-year review* means a five-year review conducted pursuant to section 751(c) of the Act. The provisions of part 201 of this chapter and subpart A of this part pertaining to "investigations" are generally applicable to five-year reviews, unless superseded by a provision in this subpart of more specific application.

(b) The term *expedited review* means a five-year review conducted by the Commission pursuant to section 751(c)(3)(B) of the Act.

(c) The term *full review* means a five-year review that has not been expedited by the Commission or terminated pursuant to section 751(c)(3) of the Act.

(d) The term *notice of institution* shall refer to the notice of institution of five-year review that the Commission shall publish in the FEDERAL REGISTER requesting that interested parties provide information to the Commission upon initiation of a five-year review.

§207.61 Responses to notice of institution.

(a) *When information must be filed.* Responses to the notice of institution shall be submitted to the Commission no later than 30 days after its publication in the FEDERAL REGISTER.

(b) *Information to be filed with the Secretary.* The notice of institution shall direct each interested party to make a filing pursuant to §§201.6, 201.8 and 207.3 of this chapter containing the following:

(1) A statement expressing its willingness to participate in the review by providing information requested by the Commission;

(2) A statement regarding the likely effects of revocation of the order(s) or termination of the suspended investigation(s) under review;

(3) Such information or industry data as the Commission may specify in the notice of institution.

(c) *When requested information cannot be supplied.* Any interested party that cannot furnish the information requested by the notice of institution in the requested form and manner shall, promptly after issuance of the notice, notify the Commission, provide a full explanation of why it cannot furnish the requested information, and indicate alternative forms in which it can provide equivalent information. The Commission may modify its requests to the extent necessary to avoid posing an unreasonable burden on that party.

(d) *Submissions by persons other than interested parties.* Any person who is not an interested party may submit to the Commission, in a filing satisfying the requirements of §201.8 of this chapter, information relevant to the Commission's review no later than 50 days after publication of the notice of institution in the FEDERAL REGISTER.

(e) A document filed under this section shall be filed electronically, and nine (9) true paper copies shall be submitted on the same business day.

[44 FR 76468, Dec. 26, 1979, as amended at 74 FR 2849, Jan. 16, 2009; 76 FR 61944, Oct. 6, 2011; 79 FR 35925, June 25, 2014]

§207.62 Rulings on adequacy and nature of Commission review.

(a) *Basis for rulings on adequacy.* The Commission will assess the adequacy of aggregate interested party responses to the notice of institution with respect to each order or suspension agreement under review and, where the underlying affirmative Commission determination found multiple domestic like products, on the basis of each domestic like product.

(b) *Comments to the Commission.* (1) Comments to the Commission concerning whether the Commission should conduct an expedited review may be submitted by:

(i) Any interested party that is a party to the five-year review and that has responded to the notice of institution; and

(ii) Any party, other than an interested party, that is a party to the five-year review.

(2) Comments shall be submitted within the time specified in the notice of institution. In a grouped review, only one set of comments shall be filed per party. Comments shall be filed electronically, and nine (9) true paper copies shall be submitted on the same business day. Comments shall not exceed fifteen (15) pages of textual material, double spaced and single sided, when printed out on paper measuring 8.5 × 11 inches. Comments containing

new factual information shall be disregarded.

(c) *Notice of scheduling of full review.* If the Commission concludes that interested parties' responses to the notice of institution are adequate, or otherwise determines that a full review should proceed, investigative activities pertaining to that review will continue. The Commission will publish in the FEDERAL REGISTER a notice of scheduling pertaining to subsequent procedures in the review.

(d) *Procedures for expedited reviews.* (1) If the Commission concludes that interested parties' responses to the notice of institution are inadequate, it may decide to conduct an expedited review. In that event, the Commission shall direct the Secretary to issue a notice stating that the Commission has decided to conduct an expedited review and inviting those parties to the review described in paragraph (d)(2) of this section to file written comments with the Secretary on what determination the Commission should reach in the review. The date on which such comments must be filed will be specified in the notice to be issued by the Secretary. Comments containing new factual information shall be disregarded.

(2) The following parties may file the comments described in paragraph (d)(1) of this section:

(i) Any interested party that is a party to the five-year review and that has filed an adequate response to the notice of institution; and

(ii) Any party, other than an interested party, that is a party to the five-year review.

(3) Any person that is neither a party to the five-year review nor an interested party may submit a brief written statement (which shall not contain any new factual information) pertinent to the review within the time specified for the filing of written comments.

(4) The Director shall prepare and place in the record, prior to the date on which the comments described in paragraph (d)(1) of this section must be filed, a staff report containing information concerning the subject matter of the review. A version of the staff report containing business proprietary information shall be placed in the nonpublic record and made available to persons authorized to receive business proprietary information under § 207.7, and a nonbusiness proprietary version of the staff report shall be placed in the public record.

(e) *Use of facts available.* The Commission's determination in an expedited review will be based on the facts available, in accordance with section 776 of the Act.

[63 FR 30608, June 5, 1998, as amended at 68 FR 32978, June 3, 2003; 76 FR 61944, Oct. 6, 2011; 79 FR 35925, June 25, 2014]

§ 207.63   Circulation of draft questionnaires.

(a) The Director shall circulate draft questionnaires to the parties for comment in each full review.

(b) Any party desiring to comment on the draft questionnaires shall submit such comments in writing to the Commission within a time specified by the Director. All requests for collecting new information should be presented at this time. The Commission will disregard subsequent requests for collection of new information absent a showing that there is a compelling need for the information and that the information could not have been requested in the comments on the draft questionnaires.

§ 207.64   Staff reports.

(a) *Prehearing staff report.* The Director shall prepare and place in the record, prior to the hearing, a prehearing staff report containing information concerning the subject matter of the five-year review. A version of the staff report containing business proprietary information shall be placed in the nonpublic record and made available to persons authorized to receive business proprietary information under § 207.7, and a nonbusiness proprietary version of the staff report shall be placed in the public record.

(b) *Final staff report.* After the hearing, the Director shall revise the prehearing staff report and submit to the Commission, prior to the Commission's determination, a final version of the staff report. The final staff report is intended to supplement and correct the information contained in the prehearing staff report. The Director shall place the final staff report in the record. A public version of the final staff report shall be made available to the public and a business proprietary version shall also be made available to persons authorized to receive business proprietary information under § 207.7.

[63 FR 30608, June 5, 1998, as amended at 68 FR 32978, June 3, 2003]

§ 207.65 Prehearing briefs.

Each party to a five-year review may submit a prehearing brief to the Commission on the date specified in the scheduling notice. A prehearing brief shall be signed and shall include a table of contents. A prehearing brief shall be filed electronically, and nine (9) true paper copies shall be submitted (on paper measuring 8.5 × 11 inches and single-sided) on the same business day. The prehearing brief should present a party's case concisely and shall, to the extent possible, refer to the record and include information and arguments which the party believes relevant to the subject matter of the Commission's determination.

[79 FR 35925, June 25, 2014]

§ 207.66 Hearing.

(a) *In general.* The Commission shall hold a hearing in each full review. The date of the hearing shall be specified in the scheduling notice.

(b) *Procedures.* Hearing procedures in five-year reviews will conform to those for final phase antidumping and countervailing duty investigations set forth in § 207.24.

§ 207.67 Posthearing briefs and statements.

(a) *Briefs from parties.* Any party to a five-year review may file with the Secretary a posthearing brief concerning the information adduced at or after the hearing within a time specified in the scheduling notice or by the presiding official at the hearing. A posthearing brief shall be filed electronically, and nine (9) true paper copies shall be submitted on the same business day. No such posthearing brief shall exceed fifteen (15) pages of textual material, double spaced and single sided, when printed out on paper measuring 8.5 × 11 inches and single-sided. In addition, the presiding official may permit per-

sons to file answers to questions or requests made by the Commission at the hearing within a specified time. The Secretary shall not accept for filing posthearing briefs or answers which do not comply with this section.

(b) *Statements from nonparties.* Any person other than a party may submit a brief written statement of information pertinent to the review within the time specified for the filing of posthearing briefs.

[63 FR 30608, June 5, 1998, as amended at 76 FR 61944, Oct. 6, 2011; 79 FR 35926, June 25, 2014]

§ 207.68 Final comments on information.

(a) The Commission shall specify a date after the filing of posthearing briefs on which it will disclose to all parties to the five-year review all information it has obtained on which the parties have not previously had an opportunity to comment. Any such information that is business proprietary information will be released to persons authorized to obtain such information pursuant to § 207.7.

(b) The parties shall have an opportunity to file comments on any information disclosed to them after they have filed their posthearing brief pursuant to § 207.67. Comments shall be filed electronically, and nine (9) true paper copies shall be submitted on the same business day. Comments shall only concern such information, and shall not exceed 15 pages of textual material, double spaced and single-sided, when printed out on paper measuring 8.5 × 11 inches and single-sided. A comment may address the accuracy, reliability, or probative value of such information by reference to information elsewhere in the record, in which case the comment shall identify where in the record such information is found. Comments containing new factual information shall be disregarded. The date on which such comments must be filed will be specified by the Commission when it specifies the time that information will be disclosed pursuant to paragraph (a) of this section. The record shall close on the date such comments are due, except with respect to changes in bracketing of business proprietary information in the comments permitted by § 207.3(c).

[63 FR 30608, June 5, 1998, as amended at 76 FR 61944, Oct. 6, 2011; 79 FR 35926, June 25, 2014]

§ 207.69 Publication of determinations.

Whenever the Commission makes a determination concluding a five-year review, the Secretary shall serve copies of the determination and, when applicable, the nonbusiness proprietary version of the final staff report on all parties to the review, and on the administering authority. The Secretary shall publish notice of such determination in the FEDERAL REGISTER.

Subpart G—Implementing Regulations for the North American Free Trade Agreement

AUTHORITY: Sec. 777(d) of the Tariff Act of 1930 (19 U.S.C. 1677f (d); secs. 402(g), 405 of the North American Free Trade Agreement Implementation Act (107 Stat. 2057, Pub. L. 103–182, Dec. 8, 1993).

SOURCE: 59 FR 5097, Feb. 3, 1994, unless otherwise noted.

§ 207.90 Scope.

This subpart sets forth the procedures and regulations for implementation of Article 1904 of the North American Free Trade Agreement under the Tariff Act of 1930, as amended by title IV of the North American Free Trade Agreement Implementation Act (19 U.S.C. 1516a and 1677f). These regulations are authorized by section 402(g) of the North American Free Trade Agreement Implementation Act and 19 U.S.C. 1335.

§ 207.91 Definitions.

As used in this subpart—

Administrative Law Judge means the United States Government employee appointed under section 310(f) of title 5 of the United States Code to conduct proceedings under this part in accordance with section 554 of title 5 of the United States Code;

Agreement means the North American Free Trade Agreement entered into among Canada, the United States of America and the United Mexican States ("Mexico"); or, with respect to

binational panel proceedings between Canada and the United States underway as of the date of enactment of the Agreement, or any binational panel proceedings that may proceed between the United States and Canada following any withdrawal from the Agreement by the United States or Canada, the United States-Canada Free Trade Agreement entered into between the Government of Canada and the Government of the United States of America, effective as of January 1, 1989;

Article 1904 Rules means the Rules of Procedure for Article 1904 Binational Panel Reviews adopted by the United States of America, Canada and Mexico pursuant to the Agreement, or where applicable under the Agreement, the Rules of Procedure for Article 1904 Binational Panel Reviews adopted by the United States of America and Canada pursuant to the United States-Canada Free Trade Agreement, as amended;

Canadian Secretary means the Secretary of the Canadian section of the Secretariat and includes any person authorized to act on the Secretary's behalf;

Charged party means a person who is charged by the Commission with committing a prohibited act under 19 U.S.C. 1677f(f)(3);

Clerical person means a person such as a paralegal, secretary, or law clerk who is employed or retained by and under the direction and control of an authorized applicant;

Commission means the United States International Trade Commission;

Commission Secretary means the Secretary to the Commission;

Complaint means the complaint referred to in the Article 1904 Rules;

Counsel means persons described in the definition of *counsel of record* in Rule 3 of the Article 1904 Rules or the ECC Rules, and counsel for an interested person who plans to file a timely complaint or notice of appearance in the panel review.

Date of Service means the day a document is deposited in the mail or delivered in person;

Days means calendar days, but if a deadline falls on a weekend or United States federal holiday, it shall be extended to the next working day;

Extraordinary challenge committee means the committee established pursuant to Annex 1904.13 of the Agreement to review decisions of a panel or conduct of a panelist;

ECC Rules means the Rules of Procedure for Article 1904 Extraordinary Challenge Committees adopted by the United States of America, Canada and Mexico, or where applicable, the Rules of Procedure for Article 1904 Extraordinary Challenge Committees adopted by the United States of America and Canada pursuant to the United States-Canada Free Trade Agreement, as amended;

Final determination, means "final determination" under Article 1911 of the Agreement;

Free Trade Area Country means the "free trade area country" as defined in 19 U.S.C. 1516a(f)(10);

Investigative attorney means an attorney designated by the Office of Unfair Import Investigations to engage in inquiries and proceedings under 19 CFR 207.100 *et seq.*

Mexican Secretary means the Secretary of the Mexican section of the Secretariat and includes any persons authorized to act on the Secretary's behalf;

NAFTA Act means the North American Free Trade Agreement Implementation Act, Pub. L. 103–182 (December 8, 1993);

Notice of Appearance means the notice of appearance provided for by Article 1904 Rules or by the ECC Rules;

Panel review means review of a final determination pursuant to chapter 19 of the Agreement, including review by an extraordinary challenge committee;

Party means, for the purposes of 19 CFR 207.100 through 207.120, either the investigative attorney(ies) or the charged party(ies);

Person means, for the purposes of 19 CFR 207.100 through 207.120, an individual, partnership, corporation, association, organization, or other entity;

Privileged information means all information covered by the provisions of the second sentence of 19 U.S.C. 1677f(f)(1)(A);

Professional means an accountant, economist, engineer, or other non-legal specialist who is employed by, or under the direction and control, of a counsel;

Prohibited act means the violation of a protective order, the inducement of a violation of a protective order, or the knowing receipt of information the receipt of which constitutes a violation of a protective order;

Proprietary information means confidential business information as defined in 19 CFR 201.6(a);

Protective Order means an administrative protective order issued by the Commission;

Relevant FTA Secretary means the Secretary referred to in Article 1908 of the Agreement;

Secretariat means the Secretariat established pursuant to Article 2002 of the Agreement and includes the Secretariat sections located in Canada, the United States, and Mexico;

Service address means the facsimile number, if any, and address of the counsel of record for a person or, where a person is not represented by counsel, the facsimile number, if any, and address set out by a person in a Request for Panel Review, Complaint or Notice of Appearance as the address at which the person may be served or, where a Change of Service Address has been filed by a person, the facsimile number, if any, and address set out as the service address in that form;

Service list means the list maintained by the Commission Secretary under 19 CFR 201.11(d) of persons in the administrative proceeding leading to the final determination under panel review;

United States Secretary means the Secretary of the United States section of the Secretariat and includes any person authorized to act on the Secretary's behalf;

Except as otherwise provided in this subpart, the definitions set forth in the Article 1904 Rules and the ECC Rules are applicable to this subpart and to any protective orders issued pursuant to this subpart.

§207.92 Procedures for commencing review of final determinations.

(a) *Notice of Intent to Commence Judicial Review.* A Notice of Intent to Commence Judicial Review shall contain such information, and be in such form, manner, and style, including service requirements, as prescribed by the Department of Commerce in its regulations at 19 CFR part 356.

(b) *Request for Panel Review.* A Request for Panel Review shall contain such information, and be in such form, manner, and style, including service requirements, as prescribed by the Department of Commerce in its regulations at 19 CFR part 356.

§ 207.93 Protection of proprietary information during panel and committee proceedings.

(a) *Requests for protective orders.* A request for access to proprietary information pursuant to 19 U.S.C. 1677f(f)(1) shall be made to the Secretary of the Commission.

(b) *Persons authorized to receive proprietary information under protective order.* The following persons may be authorized by the Commission to receive access to proprietary information if they comply with these regulations and such other conditions imposed upon them by the Commission:

(1) The members of a binational panel or an extraordinary challenge committee, any assistant to a member, court reporters and translators;

(2) Counsel and professionals, provided that the counsel or professional does not participate in competitive decision-making, as defined in *US Steel Corp.* v. *United States*, 730 F.2d 1465 (Fed. Cir. 1984), for the person represented or for any person that would gain a competitive advantage through knowledge of the proprietary information sought;

(3) Clerical persons who are employed or retained by and under the direction and control of a person described in paragraph (b) (1), (2), (5) or (6) of this section who has been issued a protective order, if such clerical persons:

(i) Are not involved in the competitive decision-making, or the support functions for the competitive decision-making, of a participant to the proceeding or of any person that would gain a competitive advantage through knowledge of the proprietary information sought, and

(ii) Have agreed to be bound by the terms set forth in the application for protective order of the person who retains or employs him or her;

(4) The Secretaries of the United States, Canadian and Mexican sections of the Secretariat and members of their staffs;

(5) Any officer or employee of the United States Government who the United States Trade Representative informs the Commission Secretary needs access to proprietary information to make recommendations regarding the convening of extraordinary challenge committees; and

(6) Any officer or employee of the Government of Canada or the Government of Mexico who the Canadian Minister of Trade or the Mexican Secretary of Economia, as the case may be, informs the Commission Secretary needs access to proprietary information to make recommendations regarding the convening of extraordinary challenge committees; and

(7) Counsel representing, and other staff providing support to, the investigating authority, the Commission.

(c) *Procedures for obtaining access to proprietary information under protective order*—(1) *Persons who must file an application for release under protective order.* To be permitted access to proprietary information in the administrative record of a determination under panel review, all persons described in paragraphs (b)(1), (2), (4), (5), (6), or (c)(5)(i) of this section shall file an application for a protective order.

(2) *Contents of applications for release under protective order.* (i) The Commission Secretary shall adopt from time to time forms for submitting requests for release pursuant to protective order that incorporate the terms of this rule. The Commission Secretary shall supply the United States Secretary with copies of the forms for persons described in paragraphs (b) (1), (4), (5) and (6) of this section. Other applicants may obtain the forms at the Commission Secretary's office at 500 E Street SW., Washington, DC 20436.

(ii) Such forms shall require the applicant to submit a personal sworn statement that, in addition to such other conditions as the Commission Secretary may require, the applicant will:

(A) Not disclose any proprietary information obtained under protective order and not otherwise available to any person other than:

(1) Personnel of the Commission involved in the particular panel review in which the proprietary information is part of the administrative record,

(2) The person from whom the information was obtained,

(3) A person who is authorized to have access to the same proprietary information pursuant to a Commission protective order, and

(4) A clerical person retained or employed by and under the direction and control of a person described in paragraph (b)(1), (2), (5), or (6) of this section who has been issued a protective order, if such clerical person has signed and dated an agreement, provided to the Commission Secretary upon request, to be bound by the terms set forth in the application for a protective order of the person who retains or employs him or her (the authorized applicant shall be responsible for retention and accuracy of such forms and shall be deemed responsible for such persons' compliance with the administrative protective order);

(B) Not use any of the proprietary information released under protective order and not otherwise available for purposes other than the particular proceedings under Article 1904 of the Agreement;

(C) Upon completion of panel review, or at such other date as may be determined by the Commission Secretary, return to the Commission, or certify to the Commission Secretary the destruction of, all documents released under the protective order and all other material (such as briefs, notes, or charts), containing the proprietary information released under the protective order, except that those described in paragraph (b)(1) of this section may return such documents and other materials to the United States Secretary. The United States Secretary may retain a single file copy of each document for the official file.

(D) Update information in the application for protective order as required by the protective order; and

(E) Acknowledge that the person becomes subject to the provisions of 19 U.S.C. 1677f(f) and to this subpart, as well as corresponding provisions of Canadian and Mexican law on disclosure undertakings concerning proprietary information.

(3) *Timing of applications.* An application for any person described in paragraph (b)(1) or (b)(2) of this section may be filed after a notice of request for panel review has been filed with the Secretariat. A person described in paragraph (b)(4) of this section shall file an application immediately upon assuming official responsibilities in the United States, Canadian or Mexican Secretariat. An application for any person described in paragraph (b)(5) or (b)(6) of this section may be filed at any time after the United States Trade Representative, the Canadian Minister of Trade, or the Mexican Secretary of Economia, as the case may be, has notified the Commission Secretary that such person requires access.

(4) *Filing and service of applications—* (i) *Applications of persons described in paragraph (b)(1) of this section.* A person described in paragraph (b)(1) of this section shall submit the completed original of the form to the United States Secretary, NAFTA Secretariat, room 2061, U.S. Department of Commerce, Pennsylvania Avenue and 14th Street, NW., Washington, DC 20230. The United States Secretary, in turn, shall file the original plus three (3) copies of the application with the Commission Secretary.

(ii) *Applications of persons described in paragraph (b)(2) of this section—*(A) *Filing.* A person described in paragraph (b)(2) of this section, concurrent with the filing of a complaint or notice of appearance in the panel review on behalf of the participant represented by such person, shall file the completed original of the form (NAFTA APO Form C) and three (3) copies with the Commission Secretary, and four (4) copies with the United States Secretary.

(B) *Service.* If an applicant files before the deadline for filing notices of appearance for the panel review, the applicant shall concurrently serve each person on the service list with a copy of the application. If the applicant files after the deadline for filing notices of appearance for the panel review, the applicant shall serve each participant in the panel review in accordance with the applicable Article 1904 Rules and ECC Rules. Service on a person may be effected by delivering a copy to the person's service address; by sending a copy to the person's service address by facsimile transmission, expedited courier service, expedited mail service; or by personal service.

(iii) *Applications of persons described in paragraph (b)(4) of this section.* A person described in paragraph (b)(4) of this section shall file the original and three (3) copies of the protective order application with the Commission Secretary.

(iv) *Applications of persons described in paragraph (b)(5) of this section.* A person described in paragraph (b)(5) of this section shall file the original and three (3) copies with the Commission Secretary and four (4) copies with the United States Secretary.

(v) *Applications of persons described in paragraph (b)(6) of this section.* A person described in paragraph (b)(6) of this section shall submit the completed original of the protective order application to the relevant FTA Secretary. The relevant FTA Secretary in turn, shall file the original and three (3) copies with the Commission Secretary.

(5) *Persons who retain access to proprietary information under a protective order issued during the administrative proceedings.* (i) If counsel or a professional has been granted access in an administrative proceeding to proprietary information under a protective order that contains a provision governing continued access to that information during panel review, and that counsel or professional retains the proprietary information more than fifteen (15) days after a First Request for Panel Review is filed with the Secretariat, that counsel or professional, and such clerical persons with access on or after that date, become immediately subject to the terms and conditions of NAFTA APO Form C maintained by the Commission Secretary on that date including provisions regarding sanctions for violations thereof.

(ii) Any person described in paragraph (c)(5)(i) of this section, concurrent with the filing of a complaint or notice of appearance in the panel review on behalf of the participant represented by such person, shall:

(A) File the completed original of the form (NAFTA APO Form C) and three (3) copies with the Commission Secretary; and

(B) File four (4) copies of the completed NAFTA APO Form C with the United States Secretary.

(iii) Any person described in paragraph (c)(5)(i) of this section must submit a new application for a protective order at the commencement of a panel review.

(d) *Issuance of protective orders*—(1) *Applicants described in paragraphs (b)(1), (4), (5) and (6) of this section.* Upon approval of an application of persons described in paragraphs (b)(1), (4), (5), or (6) of this section, the Commission Secretary shall issue a protective order permitting release of proprietary information. Any member of a binational panel proceeding initiated under the United States-Canada Free Trade Agreement to whom the Commission Secretary issues a protective order must countersign it and return one copy of the countersigned order to the United States Secretary. Any other applicant under paragraph (b)(1) of this section must file a copy of the order with the United States Secretary.

(2) *Applicants described in paragraph (b)(2) of this section.* (i) The Commission shall not rule on an application filed by a person described in paragraph (b)(2) until ten (10) days after the request is filed unless there is a compelling need to rule more expeditiously. Any person may file an objection to the application within seven (7) days of the application's filing date, stating the specific reasons why the Commission should not grant the application. One (1) copy of the objection shall be served on the applicant and on all persons who were served with the application. Any reply to an objection will be considered if it is filed and served before the Commission Secretary renders a decision. Service of objections and replies shall be made in accordance with paragraph (c)(4)(ii)(B) of this section.

(ii) *Denial of application.* The Commission's Secretary may deny an application by serving a letter notifying the applicant of the decision and the reasons therefor within fourteen (14) days of the receipt of the application. The letter shall advise the applicant of the right to appeal to the Commission. Any appeal must be made within five (5) days of the service of the Commission Secretary's letter.

(iii) *Appeal from denial of an application.* An appeal from a denial of a request must be addressed to the Chairman, United States International Trade Commission, 500 E Street, SW., Washington, DC 20436. Such appeal must be served in accordance with paragraph (c)(4)(ii)(B) of this section. The Commission shall make a final decision granting or denying the appeal within thirty (30) days from the day on which the application was filed with the Commission Secretary.

(iv) *Approval of the application.* If the Commission Secretary does not deny an application pursuant to paragraph (d)(2)(ii) of this section, the Commission shall, by the fifteenth day following the receipt of the application, issue a protective order permitting the release of proprietary information to the applicant.

(v) *Filing of protective orders.* If a protective order is issued to a person described in paragraph (b)(2) of this section, the person shall immediately file one (1) copy of the protective order with the United States Secretary.

(e) *Retention of protective orders; service list.* The Commission Secretary shall retain, in a public file, copies of applications granted, including any updates thereto, and protective orders issued under this section, including protective orders filed in accordance with paragraph (b)(6)(ii) of this section. The Secretary shall establish a list of persons authorized to receive proprietary information in a review, including parties whose applications have been granted.

(f) *Filing of amendments to granted applications.* Any person who has been issued a protective order under this section shall:

(1) If a person described in paragraph (b)(1) of this section, submit any amendments to the application for a protective order to the United States Secretary, who shall file the original and three (3) copies with the Commission Secretary;

(2) If a person described in paragraph (b)(2) of this section, file the original and three (3) copies of any amendments to the application with the Commission Secretary and four (4) copies with the United States Secretary; or

(3) If any other person, file the original and three (3) copies of any amendments to the application with the Commission Secretary.

(g) *Modification or revocation of protective orders.* (1) Any person may file with the Commission Secretary a request that a protective order issued under this section be modified or revoked because of changed conditions of fact or law, or on grounds of the public interest. The request shall state the changes desired and include any supporting materials and arguments. The person filing the request shall serve a copy of the request upon the person to whom the protective order was issued.

(2) Any person may file a response to the request within twenty (20) days after it is filed, unless the Commission issues a notice indicating otherwise. After consideration of the request and any responses thereto, the Commission shall take such action as it deems appropriate.

(3) If a request filed under this paragraph alleges that a person is violating the terms of a protective order, the Commission may treat the request as a report of violation under §207.101 of this subpart.

(4) The Commission may also modify or revoke a protective order on its own initiative.

(5) If the Commission revokes, amends or modifies a person's protective order, it shall provide to the person, the United States Secretary and all participants a copy of the Notice of Revocation, amendment or modification.

[59 FR 5097, Feb. 3, 1994, as amended at 70 FR 8512, Feb. 22, 2005]

§207.94 Protection of privileged information during panel and committee proceedings.

When and if a panel or extraordinary challenge committee decides that the Commission is required, pursuant to the United States law, to grant access pursuant to protective order to information for which the Commission has claimed a privilege, any individual to whom a panel or extraordinary challenge committee has directed the Commission release information and who is otherwise within the category of individuals eligible to receive proprietary information pursuant to 19 CFR 207.93(b), may file an application for a protective order with the Commission. Upon receipt of such application, the Commission Secretary shall certify to the Commission that a panel or extraordinary challenge committee has required the Commission to release such information to specified persons, pursuant to 19 U.S.C. 1677f(f)(1). Twenty-four hours following such certification, the Commission Secretary shall issue a protective order releasing such information to any authorized applicant subject to terms and conditions equivalent to those described in 19 CFR 207.93(c)(2).

PROCEDURES FOR IMPOSING SANCTIONS FOR VIOLATION OF THE PROVISIONS OF A PROTECTIVE ORDER ISSUED DURING PANEL AND COMMITTEE PROCEEDINGS

§ 207.100 Sanctions.

(a) A person, other than a person exempted from this regulation by the provisions of 19 U.S.C. 1677f(f)(4), who is determined under this subpart to have committed a prohibited act, may be subject to one or more of the following sanctions:

(1) A civil penalty not to exceed $100,000 for each violation, each day of a continuing violation constituting a separate violation;

(2) Debarment from practice in any capacity before the Commission, which disbarment may, in appropriate circumstances, include such person's partners, associates, employers and employees, for a designated time period following publication of a determination that the protective order has been breached;

(3) Denial of further access to proprietary or privileged information covered by the breached protective order or to proprietary information in future Commission proceedings;

(4) An official reprimand by the Commission;

(5) In the case of an attorney, accountant, or other professional, referral of the facts underlying the prohibited act to the ethics panel or other disciplinary body of the appropriate professional association or licensing authority;

(6) When appropriate, referral of the facts underlying the violation to the United States Trade Representative or his or her designees, or to another government agency; and

(7) Any other administrative sanctions as the Commission determines to be appropriate.

(b) Each partner, associate, employer, and employee described in paragraph (a)(2) of this section is entitled to all the administrative rights set forth in this subpart.

(c) For the purposes of this subpart, the knowing receipt of information the receipt of which constitutes a violation of a protective order includes, but is not limited to, the reading or unauthorized dissemination of the information covered by a protective order by a person who knows or should reasonably believe that he or she is not authorized to read or disseminate such information.

§ 207.101 Reporting of prohibited act and commencement of investigation.

(a) Any person who has information indicating that a prohibited act has been committed shall immediately report all pertinent facts relating thereto to the Commission Secretary.

(b) Upon receipt, the Commission Secretary shall record the information, assign an investigation number, and forward all information he or she received to the Office of Unfair Import Investigations.

(c) As expeditiously as possible, the Office of Unfair Import Investigations shall conduct an inquiry to determine whether there is reasonable cause to believe that a person or persons have committed a prohibited act. At any time, the Office of Unfair Import Investigations may request that the Commission assign an administrative law judge to oversee the inquiry.

(d) At the conclusion of the inquiry, the Office of Unfair Import Investigations shall assess whether the available information is sufficient to provide reasonable cause to believe that a person or persons have committed a prohibited act.

§207.102 Initiation of proceedings.

(a) Upon completion of the inquiry,

(1) If the Office of Unfair Import Investigations concludes that there is not reasonable cause to believe that a person or persons have committed a prohibited act, the Office of Unfair Import Investigations shall:

(i) Submit a report to the Commission; and

(ii) Unless the Commission directs otherwise, the file shall be closed and returned to the Commission Secretary.

(2) If the Office of Unfair Import Investigations concludes that there is reasonable cause to believe that a person or persons have committed a prohibited act, the Office of Unfair Import Investigations shall:

(i) Make a recommendation to the Commission regarding whether and to what extent it is appropriate to notify the person whose proprietary information may have been compromised; and

(ii) Submit a report and recommendation to the Commission regarding whether to initiate sanctions proceedings or to take other appropriate action.

(b) The Commission may make any appropriate determination regarding the initiation of sanctions proceedings, including rejecting, approving, or approving and amending any recommendation made by the Office of Unfair Import Investigations.

(c) If the Commission determines that it is appropriate to issue a charging letter, the Commission shall appoint an administrative law judge to oversee the proceeding and the Commission Secretary shall initiate a proceeding under this subpart by issuing a charging letter as set forth in 19 CFR 207.103.

(d) If the Commission determines that it is appropriate to initiate proceedings, but that the party to be charged is beyond the jurisdiction of the Commission and within the jurisdiction of another Free Trade Area country, or that for other reasons an authorized agency of another Free Trade Area country would be the more appropriate forum for initiation of a proceeding, the Commission shall take the necessary steps for issuance of a letter requesting the authorized agency of another Free Trade Area country to initiate proceedings under applicable law on the basis of an alleged prohibited act.

(e) The Commission may make any determination regarding notification about the alleged prohibited act and the relevant underlying facts to the persons who submitted the proprietary information that allegedly has been disclosed. A determination by the Commission on this subject does not foreclose the administrative law judge from redetermining at any time during the hearing whether notification to the compromised party is appropriate.

(f) If the Commission determines that it is not appropriate to issue a charging letter or to refer the facts to the authorized agency of another Free Trade Area country, the file shall be closed and returned to the Commission Secretary, unless the Commission directs otherwise.

(g) All aspects of the inquiry shall remain confidential, except as deemed reasonably necessary to the Office of Unfair Import Investigations to gather relevant information and to protect the interests of the person who submitted the proprietary information, or except as otherwise ordered by the Commission. Except as the Commission may otherwise order, the Commission Secretary shall maintain all closed investigatory files in confidence to the extent permitted by law, and shall destroy any documentary evidence containing allegations of a prohibited act for which no proceeding is initiated one year after the file is closed.

§207.103 Charging letter.

(a) *Contents of charging letter*. Each charged party shall be served by the Commission with a copy of a charging letter and any accompanying motion for interim measures, as provided for in 19 CFR 207.106. The charging letter shall include:

(1) Allegations concerning a prohibited act;

(2) A citation to §207.100 of this subpart, for a listing of sanctions that may be imposed for a prohibited act;

(3) A statement that a proceeding has been initiated and that an APA hearing will be held before an administrative law judge;

(4) A statement that the charged party or his or her attorney may request the issuance of an appropriate administrative protective order to obtain access to the information upon which the charge is based;

(5) A statement that the charged party has a right to retain an attorney at the charged party's own expense for purposes of representation; and

(6) A statement that the charged party has the right to request in the response described in § 207.104 of this subpart that the proceedings remain confidential to the extent practicable.

(b) *Service of charging letter.* (1) The charging letter shall be served in a double envelope. The inner envelope shall indicate that it is to be opened only by the addressee. Service of a charging letter shall be made by one of the following methods:

(i) Mailing a copy by registered or certified mail addressed to the charged party at the party's last known permanent address; or

(ii) Personal service; or

(iii) Any other method acceptable under Rule 4 of the Federal Rules of Civil Procedure.

(2) Service shall be evidenced by a certificate of service signed by the person making such service.

(c) *Confidentiality of charging letter.* Prior to entry of an order by the administrative law judge under § 207.105 of this subpart, the charging letter will be confidential and disclosed only to necessary Commission staff and the charged parties.

(d) *Amendment of charging letter.* (1) At any time after proceedings have been initiated, the investigative attorney may move for leave to amend or withdraw the charging letter.

(2) If the administrative law judge determines that the charging letter should be amended to include additional parties, the judge shall issue a recommended determination to that effect. The Commission shall review the recommended determination, and issue a determination granting or denying the motion to amend the charging letter to include additional parties.

(3) Upon motion, the administrative law judge may grant leave to amend the charging letter for good cause shown upon such conditions as are necessary to avoid prejudicing the public interest and the rights of the parties already charged.

(4) Any amended charging letter shall be served upon all charged parties in the form and manner set forth in paragraphs (a) and (b) of this section.

§ 207.104 Response to charging letter.

(a) *Time for filing.* A charged party shall have twenty (20) days from the date of service of the charging letter within which to file a written response to the allegations made in the charging letter unless otherwise ordered by the administrative law judge.

(b) *Form and content.* Each response shall be under oath and signed by the charged party or its duly authorized officer, attorney, or agent, with the name, address, and telephone number of the same. Each charged party shall respond to each allegation in the charging letter, and may set forth a concise statement of the facts constituting each ground of defense. There shall be a specific admission or denial of each fact alleged in the charging letter, or if the charged party is without knowledge of any such fact, a statement to that effect.

(c) *Request for confidentiality.* The response shall contain a statement as to whether the charged party seeks an order to maintain the confidentiality of all or part of the proceedings to the extent practicable, pursuant to § 207.105 of this subpart.

§ 207.105 Confidentiality.

(a) *Protection of proprietary and privileged information.* As the administrative law judge deems reasonably necessary for the preparation of the defense of a charged party, the attorney for the charged party may be granted access in these proceedings to proprietary information or to the privileged information, the disclosure of which is the subject of the proceedings. Any such access shall be under protective order consistent with the provisions of this subpart.

(b) *Confidentiality of proceedings.* Upon the request of any charged party pursuant to § 207.106 of this subpart, the administrative law judge will issue an appropriate confidentiality order. This order will provide for the confidentiality, to the extent practicable and permitted by law, of information relating to allegations concerning the commitment of a prohibited act, consistent with public policy considerations and the needs of the parties in conducting the sanctions proceedings. The order will provide that all proceedings under this provision shall be kept confidential within the terms of the order, except to the extent that a discussion of such proceedings is incorporated into a published final decision of the Commission. Any confidential information not disclosed in such decision will remain protected.

§ 207.106 Interim measures.

(a) At any time after proceedings are initiated, the administrative law judge, upon motion, or on his or her own initiative, may issue a recommended determination to revoke the allegedly-violated protective order, to disclose information about the proceedings that would otherwise be kept confidential, or to take other appropriate interim measures.

(b) Before issuing a determination recommending interim sanctions, the administrative law judge shall afford a party against whom such measures are proposed the opportunity to oppose them. The administrative law judge shall ordinarily decide any motion under this section no more than twenty (20) days after it is filed.

(c) The Commission shall review any recommended determination regarding the imposition of interim measures within twenty (20) days from its issuance or such other time as it may order. The Commission may impose any appropriate interim sanctions.

(d) The administrative law judge may recommend to the Commission that interim measures be modified or revoked. The Commission shall rule on such recommendation within ten (10) days after its issuance or such other time as it may order.

(e) The Commission Secretary shall immediately notify the Secretariat of any interim measures that revoke or modify an outstanding protective order in an ongoing panel review. The Commission Secretary shall also immediately notify the Secretariat of any revocation or modification of an interim measure.

§ 207.107 Motions.

(a) *Presentation and disposition.* (1) After issuance of the charging letter and while part of the proceeding is pending before the administrative law judge, all motions relating to that part of the proceeding shall be addressed to the administrative law judge.

(2) While part of a proceeding is pending before the Commission, all motions relating to that part of the proceeding shall be addressed to the Chairman of the Commission. All written motions shall be filed with the Commission Secretary and served upon all parties.

(b) *Content.* All written motions shall state the particular order, ruling, or action desired and the grounds therefor.

(c) *Responses.* Any response to a motion shall be filed within ten (10) days after service of the motions, or within such longer or shorter time as may be designated by the administrative law judge or the Commission. The moving party shall have no right to reply, except as permitted by the administrative law judge or the Commission.

(d) *Service.* All motions, responses, replies, briefs, petitions, and other documents filed in sanctions proceedings under this subpart shall be served by the party filing the document upon each other party. Service shall be made upon the attorney for the party unless the administrative law judge or the Commission orders otherwise.

§ 207.108 Preliminary conference.

As soon as practicable after the response to the charging letter is filed, the administrative law judge shall direct counsel or other representatives for the parties to meet with him or her at a preliminary conference, unless the administrative law judge determines that such a conference is not necessary. At the conference, the administrative law judge shall consider the issuance of such orders as the administrative law judge deems necessary for the conduct of the proceedings. Such orders may include, as appropriate under these regulations, the establishment of a discovery schedule or the issuance of an order, if requested, to provide for maintaining the confidentiality of the proceedings pursuant to § 207.105(b) of this subpart.

§ 207.109 Discovery.

(a) *Discovery methods.* All parties may obtain discovery under such terms and limitations as the administrative law judge may order. Discovery may be by one or more of the following methods:

(1) Depositions upon oral examination or written questions;

(2) Written interrogatories;

(3) Production of documents or things for inspection and other purposes; and

(4) Requests for admissions.

(b) *Sanctions.* If a party or an officer or agent of a party fails to comply with a discovery order, the administrative law judge may take such action as he deems reasonable and appropriate, including the issuance of evidentiary sanctions or deeming the respondent to be in default.

(c) *Depositions of nonparty officers or employees of the United States or another Free Trade Area country government—*(1) *Depositions of Commission officers or employees.* A party desiring to take the deposition of an officer or employee of the Commission (other than a member of the Office of Unfair Import Investigations or of the Office of the Administrative Law Judges), or to obtain nonprivileged documents or other physical exhibits in the custody, control, and possession of such officer or employee, shall file a written motion requesting the administrative law judge to recommend that the Commission direct that officer or employee to testify or produce the requested materials.

(2) *Depositions of officers or employees of other United States agencies, or of the government of another Free Trade Area country.* A party desiring to take the deposition of an officer or employee of another agency, or of the government of another Free Trade Area country, or to obtain nonprivileged documents or other physical exhibits in the custody, control, and possession of such officer or employee, shall file a written motion requesting the administrative law judge to recommend that the Commission seek the testimony or production of requested material from the officer or employee.

§ 207.110 Subpoenas.

(a) *Application for issuance of a subpoena.* Except as provided in § 207.109(c) of this subpart, an application for issuance of a subpoena requiring a person to appear and depose or testify at the taking of a deposition or at a hearing shall be made to the administrative law judge. The application shall be made in writing, and shall specify the material to be produced as precisely as possible, showing the relevancy of the material and the reasonableness of the scope of the subpoena. The application shall be ruled upon by the administrative law judge.

(b) *Enforcement of a subpoena.* A motion for enforcement of a subpoena shall be made to the administrative law judge. Upon consideration of the motion and any response thereto, the administrative law judge shall recommend to the Commission in favor of or against enforcement. The administrative law judge's recommendation shall provide the basis therefor, and shall address each of the criteria necessary for enforcement of an administrative subpoena. After consideration of the administrative law judge's recommendation, the Commission shall determine whether initiation of enforcement proceedings is appropriate.

(c) *Application for subpoena grounded upon the Freedom of Information Act.* No application for a subpoena for production of documents grounded upon the Freedom of Information Act (5 U.S.C. 552) shall be entertained by the administrative law judge or the Commission.

§ 207.111 Prehearing conference.

The administrative law judge may direct the attorney or other representatives for the parties to meet with him or her to consider any or all of the following:

(a) Simplification and clarification of the issues;

(b) Scope of the hearing;

(c) Stipulations and admissions of either fact or the content and authenticity of documents;

(d) Disclosure of the names of witnesses and the exchange of documents or other physical evidence that will be introduced in the course of the hearing; and

(e) Such other matters as may aid in the orderly and expeditious disposition of the proceedings.

§207.112 Hearings.

(a) *Purpose of and scheduling of hearings.* An opportunity for a hearing before an administrative law judge shall be provided for each action initiated under §207.102 of this subpart. The purpose of such hearing shall be to receive evidence and hear argument in order to determine whether a charged party has committed a prohibited act and if so, what sanctions are appropriate. Hearings shall proceed with all reasonable expedition, and, insofar as practicable, shall be held at one place, continuing until completed, unless otherwise ordered by the administrative law judge.

(b) *Joinder or consolidation.* The administrative law judge may order such joinder or consolidation of proceedings initiated under §207.102 of this subpart at the administrative law judge's discretion.

(c) *Compliance with Administrative Procedure Act.* The administrative law judge shall conduct a hearing that complies with the requirements of section 554 of title 5 of the United States Code.

§207.113 The record.

(a) *Definition of the record.* The record shall consist of—

(1) The charging letter and response, motions and responses, and other documents and exhibits properly filed with the Commission Secretary;

(2) All orders, notices, and the recommended or initial determinations of the administrative law judge;

(3) Orders, notices, and any final determination of the Commission;

(4) Hearing transcripts, and evidence admitted at the hearing; and

(5) Any other items certified into the record by the administrative law judge.

(b) *Certification of the record.* The record shall be certified to the Commission by the administrative law judge upon his or her filing of the initial determination.

§207.114 Initial determination.

(a) *Time for filing of initial determination.* (1) Except as may otherwise be ordered by the Commission, within ninety (90) days of the date of issuance of the charging letter, the administrative law judge shall certify the record to the Commission and shall file with the Commission an initial determination as to whether each charged party has committed a prohibited act, and as to appropriate sanctions.

(2) The administrative law judge may request the Commission to extend the time period for issuance of the initial determination for good cause shown.

(b) *Contents of the initial determination.* The initial determination shall include the following:

(1) An opinion making all necessary findings of fact and conclusions of law and the reasons therefor, and

(2) A statement that the initial determination shall become the determination of the Commission unless a party files a petition for review of the determination pursuant to §207.115 or the Commission pursuant to §207.116 of this subpart, orders on its own motion a review of the initial determination or certain issues therein.

(c) *Burden of proof.* A finding that a charged party committed a prohibited act shall be supported by clear and convincing evidence.

(d) *Effect of initial determination.* The initial determination shall become the determination of the Commission forty-five (45) days after the date of service of the initial determination, unless the Commission within such time orders review of the initial determination or certain issues therein pursuant to §207.115 or §207.116 of this subpart or by order shall have changed the effective date of the initial determination. In the event an initial determination becomes the determination of the Commission, the parties shall be notified thereof by the Commission Secretary.

§207.115 Petition for review.

(a) *The petition and responses.* (1) Any party may request a review by the

Commission of the initial determination by filing with the Commission Secretary a petition for review, except that a party who has defaulted may not petition for review of any issue regarding which the party is in default.

(2) Any person who wishes to obtain judicial review pursuant to 19 U.S.C. 1677f(f)(5) must first seek review by the Commission in accordance with the procedures set forth in this regulation governing petitions for review.

(3) Any petition for review must be filed within fourteen (14) days after service of the initial determination on the charged party. The petition shall:

(i) Identify the party seeking review;

(ii) Specify the issues upon which review is sought, including a statement as to whether review is sought of the initial determination regarding the commitment of a prohibited act, or of the initial determination regarding sanctions;

(iii) Set forth a concise statement of the relevant law or material facts necessary for consideration of the stated issues; and

(iv) Present a concise argument setting forth the reasons why review is necessary or appropriate.

(4) Any issue not raised in the petition for review filed under this section will be deemed to have been abandoned and may be disregarded by the Commission.

(5) Any party may file a response to the petition within seven (7) days after service of the petition, except that a party who has defaulted may not file a response to any issue regarding which the party is in default.

(b) *Grant or denial of review.* (1) The Commission shall decide whether to grant a petition for review, in whole or in part, within forty-five (45) days of the service of the initial determination on the parties, or by such other time as the Commission may order.

(2) The Commission shall base its decision whether to grant a petition for review upon the petition and response thereto, without oral argument or further written submissions, unless the Commission shall order otherwise.

(3) The Commission shall grant a petition for review of an initial determination or certain issues therein when at least one of the participating Commissioners votes for ordering review. In its notice, the Commission shall establish the scope of the review and the issues that will be considered and make provisions for the filing of briefs and oral argument if deemed appropriate by the Commission. The notice that the Commission has granted the petition shall be served by the Commission Secretary on all parties.

§ 207.116   Commission review on its own motion.

Within forty-five (45) days of the date of service of the initial determination, the Commission on its own initiative shall order review of an initial determination or certain issues therein upon request of any Commissioner.

§ 207.117   Review by Commission.

On review, the parties may not present argument on any issue that is not set forth in the notice of review; and the Commission may affirm, reverse, modify, set aside or remand for further proceedings, in whole or in part, the initial determination of the administrative law judge. The Commission may make any findings or conclusions that in its judgment are proper based on the record in the proceeding.

§ 207.118   Role of the General Counsel in advising the Commission.

The Assistant General Counsel for Section 337 Investigations shall serve as Acting General Counsel for the purpose of advising the Commission on proceedings brought under this subpart if the prohibited act described in the charging letter involves a protective order issued in connection with a panel review that was pending when the letter was issued, and the General Counsel participated in the panel review. No other Commission attorney shall advise the Commission on proceedings under this subpart concerning a protective order issued during a panel review in which the attorney participated.

§ 207.119   Reconsideration.

(a) *Motion for reconsideration.* Within fourteen (14) days after service of a Commission determination, any party may file with the Commission a motion for reconsideration, setting forth the relief desired and the grounds in support thereof. Any motion filed under this section must be confined to new questions raised by the determination or action ordered to be taken thereunder and upon which the moving party had no opportunity to submit arguments.

(b) *Disposition of motion for reconsideration.* The Commission shall grant or deny the motion for reconsideration. No response to a motion for reconsideration will be received unless requested by the Commission, but a motion for reconsideration will not be granted in the absence of such a request. If the motion to reconsider is granted, the Commission may affirm, set aside, or modify its determination, including any action ordered by it to be taken thereunder. When appropriate, the Commission may order the administrative law judge to take additional evidence.

§207.120   **Public notice of sanctions.**

If the final Commission decision is that there has been a prohibited act, and that public sanctions are to be imposed, notice of the decision will be published in the FEDERAL REGISTER and forwarded to the Secretariat. Such publication will occur no sooner than fourteen (14) days after issuance of a final decision or after any motion for reconsideration has been denied. The Commission Secretary shall also serve notice of the Commission decision upon such departments and agencies of the United States, Canadian and Mexican governments as the Commission deems appropriate.

PART 208 [RESERVED]

SUBCHAPTER C—INVESTIGATIONS OF UNFAIR PRACTICES IN IMPORT TRADE

PART 210—ADJUDICATION AND ENFORCEMENT

Subpart A—Rules of General Applicability

Sec.
210.1 Applicability of part.
210.2 General policy.
210.3 Definitions.
210.4 Written submissions; representations; sanctions.
210.5 Confidential business information.
210.6 Computation of time, additional hearings, postponements, continuances, and extensions of time.
210.7 Service of process and other documents; publication of notices.

Subpart B—Commencement of Preinstitution Proceedings and Investigations

210.8 Commencement of preinstitution proceedings.
210.9 Action of Commission upon receipt of complaint.
210.10 Institution of investigation.
210.11 Service of complaint and notice of investigation.

Subpart C—Pleadings

210.12 The complaint.
210.13 The response.
210.14 Amendments to pleadings and notice; supplemental submissions; counterclaims; consolidation of investigations.

Subpart D—Motions

210.15 Motions.
210.16 Default.
210.17 Other failure to act and default.
210.18 Summary determinations.
210.19 Intervention.
210.20 Declassification of confidential information.
210.21 Termination of investigations.
210.22 [Reserved]
210.23 Suspension of investigation.
210.24 Interlocutory appeals.
210.25 Sanctions.
210.26 Other motions.

Subpart E—Discovery and Compulsory Process

210.27 General provisions governing discovery.
210.28 Depositions.
210.29 Interrogatories.
210.30 Requests for production of documents and things and entry upon land.
210.31 Requests for admission.
210.32 Subpoenas.
210.33 Failure to make or cooperate in discovery; sanctions.
210.34 Protective orders; reporting requirement; sanctions and other actions.

Subpart F—Prehearing Conferences and Hearings

210.35 Prehearing conferences.
210.36 General provisions for hearings.
210.37 Evidence.
210.38 Record.
210.39 In camera treatment of confidential information.
210.40 Proposed findings and conclusions and briefs.

Subpart G—Determinations and Actions Taken

210.41 Termination of investigation.
210.42 Initial determinations.
210.43 Petitions for review of initial determinations on matters other than temporary relief.
210.44 Commission review on its own motion of initial determinations on matters other than temporary relief.
210.45 Review of initial determinations on matters other than temporary relief.
210.46 Petitions for and sua sponte review of initial determinations on violation of section 337 or temporary relief.
210.47 Petitions for reconsideration.
210.48 Disposition of petitions for reconsideration.
210.49 Implementation of Commission action.
210.50 Commission action, the public interest, and bonding by respondents.
210.51 Period for concluding investigation.

Subpart H—Temporary Relief

210.52 Motions for temporary relief.
210.53 Motion filed after complaint.
210.54 Service of motion by the complainant.
210.55 Content of service copies.
210.56 Notice accompanying service copies.
210.57 Amendment of the motion.
210.58 Provisional acceptance of the motion.
210.59 Responses to the motion and the complaint.
210.60 Designating the temporary relief phase of an investigation more complicated for the purpose of adjudicating a motion for temporary relief.

132

210.61 Discovery and compulsory process.
210.62 Evidentiary hearing.
210.63 Proposed findings and conclusions and briefs.
210.64 Interlocutory appeals.
210.65 Certification of the record.
210.66 Initial determination concerning temporary relief; Commission action thereon.
210.67 Remedy, the public interest, and bonding.
210.68 Complainant's temporary relief bond.
210.69 Approval of complainant's temporary relief bond.
210.70 Forfeiture or return of complainant's temporary relief bond.

Subpart I—Enforcement Procedures and Advisory Opinions

210.71 Information gathering.
210.72 Confidentiality of information.
210.73 Review of reports.
210.74 Modification of reporting requirements.
210.75 Proceedings to enforce exclusion orders, cease and desist orders, consent orders, and other Commission orders.
210.76 Modification or rescission of exclusion orders, cease and desist orders, and consent orders.
210.77 Temporary emergency action.
210.78 Notice of enforcement action to Government agencies.
210.79 Advisory opinions.
APPENDIX A TO PART 210—ADJUDICATION AND ENFORCEMENT
APPENDIX B TO PART 210—ADJUDICATION AND ENFORCEMENT

AUTHORITY: 19 U.S.C. 1333, 1335, and 1337.

SOURCE: 59 FR 39039, Aug. 1, 1994, unless otherwise noted.

Subpart A—Rules of General Applicability

§210.1 Applicability of part.

The rules in this part apply to investigations under section 337 of the Tariff Act of 1930 and related proceedings. These rules are authorized by sections 333, 335, or 337 of the Tariff Act of 1930 (19 U.S.C. §§1333, 1335, and 1337) and sections 2 and 1342(d)(1)(B) of the Omnibus Trade and Competitiveness Act of 1988, Pub. L. No. 100–418, 102 Stat. 1107 (1988).

§210.2 General policy.

It is the policy of the Commission that, to the extent practicable and consistent with requirements of law, all investigations and related proceedings under this part shall be conducted expeditiously. The parties, their attorneys or other representatives, and the presiding administrative law judge shall make every effort at each stage of the investigation or related proceeding to avoid delay.

§210.3 Definitions.

As used in this part—

Administrative law judge means the person appointed under section 3105 of title 5 of the United States Code who presides over the taking of evidence in an investigation under this part. If the Commission so orders or a section of this part so provides, an administrative law judge also may preside over stages of a related proceeding under this part.

Ancillary proceeding has the same meaning as *related proceeding*.

Commission investigative attorney means a Commission attorney designated to engage in investigatory activities in an investigation or a related proceeding under this part.

Complainant means a person who has filed a complaint with the Commission under this part, alleging a violation of section 337 of the Tariff Act of 1930.

Intervenor means a person who has been granted leave by the Commission to intervene as a party to an investigation or a related proceeding under this part.

Investigation means a formal Commission inquiry instituted to determine whether there is a violation of section 337 of the Tariff Act of 1930. An investigation is instituted upon publication of a notice in the FEDERAL REGISTER. The investigation entails postinstitution adjudication of the complaint. An investigation can also involve the processing of one or more of the following: A motion to amend the complaint and notice of investigation; a motion for temporary relief; a motion to designate "more complicated" the temporary relief stage of the investigation; an interlocutory appeal of an administrative law judge's decision on a particular matter; a motion for sanctions for abuse of process, abuse of discovery, or failure to make or cooperate in discovery, which if granted, would have an impact on the adjudication of the merits of the complaint; a petition for reconsideration of a final Commission determination; a motion for termination of the investigation in whole or part; and procedures undertaken in response to a judgment or judicial order issued in an appeal of a Commission determination or remedial order issued under section 337 of the Tariff Act of 1930.

Party means each complainant, respondent, intervenor, or the Office of Unfair Import Investigations.

Proposed intervenor means any person who has filed a motion to intervene in an investigation or a related proceeding under this part.

Proposed respondent means any person named in a complaint filed under this part as allegedly violating section 337 of the Tariff Act of 1930.

Related proceeding means preinstitution proceedings, sanction proceedings (for the possible issuance of sanctions that would not have a bearing on the adjudication of the merits of a complaint or a motion under this part), bond forfeiture proceedings, proceedings to enforce, modify, or revoke a remedial or consent order, or advisory opinion proceedings.

Respondent means any person named in a notice of investigation issued under this part as allegedly violating section 337 of the Tariff Act of 1930.

U.S. Customs Service means U.S. Customs and Border Protection.

[59 FR 39039, Aug. 1, 1994, as amended at 59 FR 67626, Dec. 30, 1994; 73 FR 38320, July 7, 2008; 76 FR 24363, May 2, 2011; 78 FR 23840, Apr. 19, 2013]

§ 210.4 Written submissions; representations; sanctions.

(a) *Caption; names of parties.* The front page of every written submission filed by a party or a proposed party to an investigation or a related proceeding under this part shall contain a caption setting forth the name of the Commission, the title of the investigation or related proceeding, the docket number or investigation number, if any, assigned to the investigation or related proceeding, and in the case of a complaint, the names of the complainant and all proposed respondents.

(b) *Signature.* Every pleading, written motion, and other paper of a party or proposed party who is represented by an attorney in an investigation or a related proceeding under this part shall

be signed by at least one attorney of record in the attorney's individual name. A party or proposed party who is not represented by an attorney shall sign, or his duly authorized officer or agent shall sign, the pleading, written motion, or other paper. Each paper shall state the signer's address and telephone number, if any. Pleadings, written motions, and other papers need not be under oath or accompanied by an affidavit, except as provided in § 210.12(a)(1), § 210.13(b), § 210.18, § 210.52(d), § 210.59(b), or another section of this part or by order of the administrative law judge or the Commission. If a pleading, motion, or other paper is not signed, it shall be stricken unless it is signed promptly after omission of the signature is called to the attention of the submitter.

(c) *Representations.* By presenting to the presiding administrative law judge or the Commission (whether by signing, filing, submitting, or later advocating) a pleading, written motion, or other paper, an attorney or unrepresented party or proposed party is certifying that to the best of the person's knowledge, information, and belief, formed after an inquiry reasonable under the circumstances—

(1) It is not being presented for any improper purpose, such as to harass or to cause unnecessary delay or needless increase in the cost of the investigation or related proceeding;

(2) The claims, defenses, and other legal contentions therein are warranted by existing law or by a nonfrivolous argument for the extension, modification, or reversal of existing law or the establishment of new law;

(3) The allegations and other factual contentions have evidentiary support or, if specifically so identified, are likely to have evidentiary support after a reasonable opportunity for further investigation or discovery; and

(4) The denials of factual contentions are warranted on the evidence or, if specifically so identified, are reasonably based on a lack of information or belief.

(d) *Sanctions.* If, after notice and a reasonable opportunity to respond (see paragraphs (d)(1) (i) and (ii) of this section and § 210.25), the presiding administrative law judge or the Commission determines that paragraph (c) of this section has been violated, the administrative law judge or the Commission may, subject to the conditions stated below and in §210.25, impose an appropriate sanction upon the attorneys, law firms, or parties that have violated paragraph (c) or are responsible for the violation. A representation need not be frivolous in its entirety in order for the administrative law judge or the Commission to determine that paragraph (c) has been violated. If any portion of a representation is found to be false, frivolous, misleading, or otherwise in violation of paragraph (c), a sanction may be imposed. In determining whether paragraph (c) has been violated, the administrative law judge or the Commission will consider whether the representation or disputed portion thereof was objectively reasonable under the circumstances.

(1) *How initiated*—(i) *By motion.* A motion for sanctions under this section shall be made separately from other motions or requests and shall describe the specific conduct alleged to violate paragraph (c). It shall be served as provided in paragraph (g) of this section, but shall not be filed with or presented to the presiding administrative law judge or the Commission unless, within seven days after service of the motion (or such other period as the administrative law judge or the Commission may prescribe), the challenged paper, claim, defense, contention, allegation, or denial is not withdrawn or appropriately corrected. See also §210.25 (a) through (c). If warranted, the administrative law judge or the Commission may award to the party or proposed party prevailing on the motion the reasonable expenses and attorney's fees incurred in presenting or opposing the motion. Absent exceptional circumstances, a law firm shall be held jointly responsible for violations committed by its partners, associates, and employees.

(ii) *On the administrative law judge's or the Commission's initiative.* The administrative law judge or the Commission may enter an order sua sponte describing the specific conduct that appears to violate paragraph (c) of this section and directing an attorney, law firm, party, or proposed party to show cause

why it has not violated paragraph (c) with respect thereto.

(2) *Nature of sanctions; limitations.* A sanction imposed for violation of paragraph (c) of this section shall be limited to what is sufficient to deter repetition of such conduct or comparable conduct by others similarly situated. Subject to the limitations in paragraphs (d)(2) (i) through (iv) of this section, the sanction may consist of, or include, directives of a nonmonetary nature, an order to pay a penalty, or, if imposed on motion and warranted for effective deterrence, an order directing payment to the movant of some or all of the reasonable attorney's fees and other expenses incurred as a direct result of the violation.

(i) Monetary sanctions shall not be imposed under this section against the United States, the Commission, or a Commission investigative attorney.

(ii) Monetary sanctions may not be awarded against a represented party or proposed party for a violation of paragraph (c)(2) of this section.

(iii) Monetary sanctions may not be imposed on the administrative law judge's or the Commission's initiative unless—

(A) The Commission or the administrative law judge issues an order to show cause before the investigation or related proceeding is terminated, in whole or in relevant part, as to the party or proposed party which is, or whose attorneys are, to be sanctioned; and

(B) Such termination is the result of—

(1) A motion to withdraw the complaint, motion, or petition that was the basis for the investigation or related proceeding;

(2) A settlement agreement;

(3) A consent order agreement; or

(4) An arbitration agreement.

(iv) Monetary sanctions imposed to compensate the Commission for expenses incurred by a Commission investigative attorney or the Commission's Office of Unfair Import Investigations will include reimbursement for some or all costs reasonably incurred as a direct result of the violation, but will not include attorney's fees.

(3) *Order.* When imposing sanctions, the administrative law judge or the

Commission shall describe the conduct determined to constitute a violation of this rule and explain the basis for the sanction imposed. See also § 210.25(d)–(f).

(e) *Inapplicability to discovery.* Paragraphs (c) and (d) of this section do not apply to discovery requests, responses, objections, and motions that are subject to provisions of §§ 210.27 through 210.34.

(f) *Filing of documents.* (1) Written submissions that are addressed to the Commission during an investigation or a related proceeding shall comply with the Commission's Handbook on Filing Procedures, which is issued by and available from the Secretary and posted on the Commission's Electronic Document Information System Web site at *https://edis.usitc.gov.* Failure to comply with the requirements of this chapter and the Handbook on Filing Procedures in the filing of a document may result in the rejection of the document as improperly filed.

(2) A complaint, petition, or request, and supplements and amendments thereto, filed under § 210.8, § 210.75, § 210.76, or § 210.79 shall be filed in paper form. An original and eight (8) true paper copies shall filed. All exhibits, appendices, and attachments to the document shall be filed in electronic form on one CD–ROM, DVD, or other portable electronic media approved by the Secretary. Sections 210.8 and 210.12 set out additional requirements for a complaint filed under § 210.8. Additional requirements for a petition or request filed under § 210.75, § 210.76, or § 210.79 are set forth in those sections. Submitted media will be retained by the Commission, except that media may be returned to the submitter if a document is not accepted for filing.

(3) Responses to a complaint, briefs, comments and responses thereto, compliance reports, motions and responses or replies thereto, petitions and replies thereto, prehearing statements, and proposed findings of fact and conclusions of law and responses thereto provided for under §§ 210.4(d), 210.13, 210.8, 210.14, 210.15, 210.16, 210.17, 210.18, 210.19, 210.20, 210.21, 210.23, 210.24, 210.25, 210.26, 210.33, 210.34, 210.35, 210.36, 210.38, 210.40, 210.43, 210.45, 210.46, 210.47, 210.50, 210.52, 210.53, 210.57, 210.59, 210.66, 210.70, or

210.71; and submissions filed with the Secretary pursuant to an order of the presiding administrative law judge shall be filed electronically, and true paper copies of such submissions shall be filed by 12 noon, eastern time, on the next business day.

(4) Except for the documents listed in paragraphs (f)(2) and (f)(3) of this section, all other documents shall be filed electronically, and no paper copies will be required.

(5) If paper copies are required under this section, the required number of paper copies shall be governed by paragraph (f)(6) of this section. A paper copy provided for in this section must be a true copy of the electronic version of the document, *i.e.*, a copy that is identical in all possible respects.

(6) Unless the Commission or this part specifically states otherwise:

(i) Two (2) true paper copies of each submission shall be filed if the investigation or related proceeding is before an administrative law judge; and

(ii) Eight (8) true paper copies of each submission shall be filed if the investigation or related proceeding is before the Commission.

(7)(i) If a complaint, a supplement or amendment to a complaint, a motion for temporary relief, or the documentation supporting a motion for temporary relief contains confidential business information as defined in § 201.6(a) of this chapter, the complainant shall file nonconfidential copies of the complaint, the supplement or amendment to the complaint, the motion for temporary relief, or the documentation supporting the motion for temporary relief concurrently with the requisite confidential copies, as provided in § 210.8(a). A nonconfidential copy of all exhibits, appendices, and attachments to the document shall be filed in electronic form on one CD–ROM, DVD, or other portable electronic media approved by the Secretary, separate from the media used for the confidential version.

(ii)(A) Persons who file the following submissions that contain confidential business information covered by an administrative protective order, or that are the subject of a request for confidential treatment, must file nonconfidential copies and serve them on the other parties to the investigation or related proceeding within 10 calendar days after filing the confidential version with the Commission:

(1) A response to a complaint and all supplements and exhibits thereto;

(2) All submissions relating to a motion to amend the complaint or notice of investigation; and

(3) All submissions addressed to the Commission.

(B) Other sections of this part may require, or the Commission or the administrative law judge may order, the filing and service of nonconfidential copies of other kinds of confidential submissions. If the submitter's ability to prepare a nonconfidential copy is dependent upon receipt of the nonconfidential version of an initial determination, or a Commission order or opinion, or a ruling by the administrative law judge or the Commission as to whether some or all of the information at issue is entitled to confidential treatment, the nonconfidential copies of the submission must be filed within 10 calendar days after service of the Commission or administrative law judge document in question. The time periods for filing specified in this paragraph apply unless the Commission, the administrative law judge, or another section of this part specifically provides otherwise.

(8) The Secretary may provide for exceptions and modifications to the filing requirements set out in this chapter. A person seeking an exception should consult the Handbook on Filing Procedures.

(9) *Where to file; date of filing.* Documents shall be filed at the Office of the Secretary of the Commission in Washington, DC. Such documents, if properly filed within the hours of operation specified in § 201.3(c), will be deemed to be filed on the date on which they are actually received in the Commission.

(10) *Conformity with rules.* Each document filed with the Commission for the purpose of initiating any investigation shall be considered properly filed if it conforms with the pertinent rules prescribed in this chapter. Substantial compliance with the pertinent rules may be accepted by the Commission provided good and sufficient reason is stated in the document for inability to comply fully with the pertinent rules.

(11) During any period in which the Commission is closed, deadlines for filing documents electronically and by other means are extended so that documents are due on the first business day after the end of the closure.

(g) *Cover Sheet.* When making a paper filing, parties must complete the cover sheet online at *http://edis.usitc.gov* and print out the cover sheet for submission to the Office of the Secretary with the paper filing. The party submitting the cover sheet is responsible for the accuracy of all information contained in the cover sheet, including, but not limited to, the security status and the investigation number, and must comply with applicable limitations on disclosure of confidential information under § 210.5.

(h) *Specifications.* (1) Each document filed under this chapter shall be double-spaced, clear and legible, except that a document of two pages or less in length need not be double-spaced. All submissions shall be in letter-sized format (8.5 × 11 inches), except copies of documents prepared for another agency or a court (e.g., patent file wrappers or pleadings papers), and single sided. Typed matter shall not exceed 6.5 × 9.5 inches using 11-point or larger type and shall be double-spaced between each line of text using the standard of 6 lines of type per inch. Text and footnotes shall be in the same size type. Quotations more than two lines long in the text or footnotes may be indented and single-spaced. Headings and footnotes may be single-spaced.

(2) The administrative law judge may impose any specifications he deems appropriate for submissions that are addressed to the administrative law judge.

(i) *Service.* Unless the Commission, the administrative law judge, or another section of this part specifically provides otherwise, every written submission filed by a party or proposed party shall be served on all other parties in the manner specified in § 201.16(b) of this chapter.

[59 FR 39039, Aug. 1, 1994; 59 FR 64286, Dec. 14, 1994, as amended at 59 FR 67626, Dec. 30, 1994; 60 FR 32443, June 22, 1995; 68 FR 32978, June 3, 2003; 73 FR 38320, July 7, 2008; 76 FR 61944, Oct. 6, 2011; 78 FR 23840, Apr. 19, 2013]

§ 210.5 Confidential business information.

(a) *Definition and submission.* Confidential business information shall be defined and identified in accordance with § 201.6 (a) and (c) of this chapter. Unless the Commission, the administrative law judge, or another section of this part states otherwise, confidential business information shall be submitted in accordance with § 201.6(b) of this chapter. In the case of a complaint, any supplement to the complaint, and a motion for temporary relief filed under this part, the number of nonconfidential copies shall be prescribed by § 210.8(a) of this part.

(b) *Restrictions on disclosure.* Information submitted to the Commission or exchanged among the parties in connection with an investigation or a related proceeding under this part, which is properly designated confidential under paragraph (a) of this section and § 201.6(a) of this chapter, may not be disclosed to anyone other than the following persons without the consent of the submitter:

(1) Persons who are granted access to confidential information under § 210.39(a) or a protective order issued pursuant to § 210.34(a);

(2) An officer or employee of the Commission who is directly concerned with—

(i) Carrying out or maintaining the records of the investigation or related proceeding for which the information was submitted;

(ii) The administration of a bond posted pursuant to subsection (e), (f), or (j) of section 337 of the Tariff Act of 1930;

(iii) The administration or enforcement of an exclusion order issued pursuant to subsection (d), (e), or (g), a cease and desist order issued pursuant to subsection (f), or a consent order issued pursuant to subsection (c) of section 337 of the Tariff Act of 1930; or

(iv) Proceedings for the modification or rescission of a temporary or permanent order issued under subsection (d), (e), (f), (g), or (i) of section 337 of the Tariff Act of 1930, or a consent order issued under section 337 of the Tariff Act of 1930;

(3) An officer or employee of the United States Government who is directly involved in a review conducted pursuant to section 337(j) of the Tariff Act of 1930; or

(4) An officer or employee of the United States Customs Service who is directly involved in administering an exclusion from entry under section 337 (d), (e), or (g) of the Tariff Act of 1930 resulting from the investigation or related proceeding in connection with which the information was submitted.

(c) *Transmission of certain records to district court.* Notwithstanding paragraph (b) of this section, confidential business information may be transmitted to a district court and be admissible in a civil action, subject to such protective order as the district court determines necessary, pursuant to 28 U.S.C. 1659.

(d) *Confidentiality determinations in preinstitution proceedings.* After a complaint is filed under section 337 of the Tariff Act of 1930 and before an investigation is instituted by the Commission, confidential business information designated confidential by the supplier shall be submitted in accordance with § 201.6(b) of this chapter. The Secretary shall decide, in accordance with § 201.6(d) of this chapter, whether the information is entitled to confidential treatment. Appeals from the ruling of the Secretary shall be made to the Commission as set forth in § 201.6(e) and (f) of this chapter.

(e) *Confidentiality determinations in investigations and other related proceedings.* (1) If an investigation is instituted or if a related proceeding is assigned to an administrative law judge, the administrative law judge shall set the ground rules for the designation, submission, and handling of information designated confidential by the submitter. When requested to do so, the administrative law judge shall decide whether information in a document addressed to the administrative law judge, or to be exchanged among

138

the parties while the administrative law judge is presiding, is entitled to confidential treatment. The administrative law judge shall also decide, with respect to all orders, initial determinations, or other documents issued by the administrative law judge, whether information designated confidential by the supplier is entitled to confidential treatment. The supplier of the information or the person seeking the information may, with leave of the administrative law judge, request an appeal to the Commission of the administrative law judge's unfavorable ruling on this issue, under §210.24(b)(2).

(2) The Commission may continue protective orders issued by the administrative law judge, amend or revoke those orders, or issue new ones. All submissions addressed to the Commission that contain information covered by an existing protective order will be given confidential treatment. (See also §210.72.) New information that is submitted to the Commission, designated confidential by the supplier, and not covered by an existing protective order must be submitted to the Secretary with a request for confidential treatment in accordance with §201.6(b) and (c) of this chapter. The Secretary shall decide, in accordance with §201.6(d) of this chapter, whether the information is entitled to confidential treatment. Appeals from the ruling of the Secretary shall be made to the Commission as provided in §201.6(e) and (f) of this chapter. The Commission shall decide, with respect to all orders, notices, opinions, and other documents issued by or on behalf of the Commission, whether information designated confidential by the supplier is entitled to confidential treatment.

(f) When the Commission or the administrative law judge issues a confidential version of an order, initial determination, opinion, or other document, the Commission, or the presiding administrative law judge if the administrative law judge has issued the confidential version, shall issue any public version of the document within 30 days, unless good cause exists to extend the deadline. An administrative law judge or the Commission may extend this time by order. Upon request by the Commission, or the administrative law judge if the administrative law judge has issued the confidential version, parties must provide support in the record for their claim of confidentiality, pursuant §201.6 of this chapter and §210.4 of this subpart for any proposed redactions that parties may submit to the Commission or the administrative law judge for the preparation of any public version.

[59 FR 39039, Aug. 1, 1994, as amended at 59 FR 67626, Dec. 30, 1994; 60 FR 32444, June 22, 1995; 78 FR 23840, Apr. 19, 2013]

§210.6 Computation of time, additional hearings, postponements, continuances, and extensions of time.

(a) Unless the Commission, the administrative law judge, or this or another section of this part specifically provides otherwise, the computation of time and the granting of additional hearings, postponements, continuances, and extensions of time shall be in accordance with §§201.14 and 201.16(d) and (e) of this chapter.

(b) Whenever a party has the right or is required to perform some act or to take some action within a prescribed period after service of a document upon it, and the document was served by mail, the deadline shall be computed by adding to the end of the prescribed period the additional time allotted under §201.16(d), unless the Commission, the administrative law judge, or another section of this part specifically provides otherwise.

(c) Whenever a party has the right or is required to perform some act or to take some action within a prescribed period after service of a Commission document upon it, and the document was served by express delivery, the deadline shall be computed by adding to the end of the prescribed period the additional time allotted under §201.16(e), unless the Commission, the administrative law judge, or another section of this part specifically provides otherwise.

[78 FR 23840, Apr. 19, 2013]

§210.7 Service of process and other documents; publication of notices.

(a) *Manner of service.* (1) The service of process and all documents issued by or on behalf of the Commission or the administrative law judge—and the service of all documents issued by parties under §§ 210.27 through 210.34 of this part—shall be in accordance with § 201.16 of this chapter, unless the Commission, the administrative law judge, or this or another section of this part specifically provides otherwise.

(2) The service of all initial determinations as defined in § 210.42, all cease and desist orders as set forth in § 210.50(a)(1), and all documents containing confidential business information as defined in § 201.6(a), issued by or on behalf of the Commission or the administrative law judge on a private party, shall be effected by serving a copy of the document by express delivery, as defined in § 201.16(e), on the person to be served, on a member of the partnership to be served, on the president, secretary, other executive officer, or member of the board of directors of the corporation, association, or other organization to be served, or, if an attorney represents any of the above in connection with an investigation under this subtitle, by serving a copy by express delivery on such attorney.

(3) Whenever the Commission effects service of documents issued by or on behalf of the Commission or the administrative law judge upon the private parties by overnight delivery, service upon the Office of Unfair Import Investigations shall also be deemed to have occurred by overnight delivery.

(b) *Designation of a single attorney or representative for service of process.* The service list prepared by the Secretary for each investigation will contain the name and address of no more than one attorney or other representative for each party to the investigation. In the event that two or more attorneys or other persons represent one party to the investigation, the party must select one of their number to be the lead attorney or representative for service of process. The lead attorney or representative for service of process shall state, at the time of the filing of its entry of appearance with the Secretary, that it has been so designated by the party it represents. (Only those persons authorized to receive confidential business information under a protective order issued pursuant to § 210.34(a) are eligible to be included on

the service list for documents containing confidential business information.)

(c) *Publication of notices.* (1) Notice of action by the Commission or an administrative law judge will be published in the FEDERAL REGISTER only as specifically provided in § 201.10, paragraph (c)(2) of this section, by another section in this chapter, or by order of an administrative law judge or the Commission.

(2) When an administrative law judge or the Commission determines to amend or supplement a notice published in accordance with paragraph (c)(1) of this section, notice of the amendment will be published in the FEDERAL REGISTER.

[60 FR 53119, Oct. 12, 1995, as amended at 72 FR 13960, Mar. 23, 2007; 73 FR 38320, July 7, 2008; 78 FR 23840, Apr. 19, 2013]

Subpart B—Commencement of Preinstitution Proceedings and Investigations

§ 210.8 Commencement of preinstitution proceedings.

A preinstitution proceeding is commenced by filing with the Secretary a signed original complaint and the requisite number of true copies.

(a)(1) A complaint filed under this section shall be filed in paper form with the Secretary as follows.

(i) An original and eight (8) true paper copies of the nonconfidential version of the complaint shall be filed. All exhibits, appendices, and attachments to this version of the complaint shall be filed in electronic form on CD–ROM, DVD, or other portable electronic media approved by the Secretary.

(ii) An original and eight (8) true paper copies of the confidential version of the complaint shall be filed. All exhibits, appendices, and attachments to this version of the complaint shall be filed in electronic form on CD–ROM, DVD, or other portable electronic media approved by the Secretary.

(iii) For each proposed respondent, one true copy of the nonconfidential version of the complaint and one true copy of the confidential version of the complaint, if any, along with one true copy of the nonconfidential exhibits and one true copy of the confidential exhibits shall be filed, and

(iv) For the government of the foreign country in which each proposed respondent is located as indicated in the complaint, one true copy of the nonconfidential version of the complaint shall be filed.

NOTE TO PARAGRAPH (a)(1): The same requirements apply for the filing of a supplement or amendment to the complaint.

(2) If the complainant is seeking temporary relief, the complainant must also file:

(i) An original and eight (8) true paper copies of the nonconfidential version of the motion for temporary relief. All exhibits, appendices, and attachments to this version of the motion shall be filed in electronic form on CD–ROM, DVD, or other portable electronic media approved by the Secretary.

(ii) An original and eight (8) true paper copies of the confidential version of the motion for temporary relief. All exhibits, appendices, and attachments to this version of the motion shall be filed in electronic form on CD–ROM, DVD, or other portable electronic media approved by the Secretary; and

(iii) For each proposed respondent, one true copy of the nonconfidential version of the motion and one true copy of the confidential version of the motion along with one true copy of the nonconfidential exhibits and one true copy of the confidential exhibits filed with the motion.

NOTE TO PARAGRAPH (a)(2): The same requirements apply for the filing of a supplement or amendment to the complaint or a supplement to the motion for temporary relief.

(b) *Provide specific information regarding the public interest.* Complainant must file, concurrently with the complaint, a separate statement of public interest, not to exceed five pages, inclusive of attachments, addressing how issuance of the requested relief, i.e., a general exclusion order, a limited exclusion order, and/or a cease and desist order, in this investigation could affect the public health and welfare in the United States, competitive conditions in the United States economy, the production of like or directly competitive articles in the United States, or United

States consumers. If the complainant files a confidential version of its submission on public interest, it shall file a public version of the submission no later than one business day after the deadline for filing the submission. In particular, the submission should:

(1) Explain how the articles potentially subject to the requested remedial orders are used in the United States;

(2) Identify any public health, safety, or welfare concerns relating to the requested remedial orders;

(3) Identify like or directly competitive articles that complainant, its licensees, or third parties make which could replace the subject articles if they were to be excluded;

(4) Indicate whether the complainant, its licensees, and/or third parties have the capacity to replace the volume of articles subject to the requested remedial orders in a commercially reasonable time in the United States; and

(5) State how the requested remedial orders would impact consumers.

(c) *Publication of notice of filing.* (1) When a complaint is filed, the Secretary to the Commission will publish a notice in the FEDERAL REGISTER inviting comments from the public and proposed respondents on any public interest issues arising from the complaint and potential exclusion and/or cease and desist orders. In response to the notice, members of the public and proposed respondents may provide specific information regarding the public interest in a written submission not to exceed five pages, inclusive of attachments, to the Secretary to the Commission within eight (8) calendar days of publication of notice of the filing of a complaint. Comments that substantively address allegations made in the complaint will not be considered. Members of the public and proposed respondents may address how issuance of the requested exclusion order and/or a cease and desist order in this investigation could affect the public health and welfare in the United States, competitive conditions in the United States economy, the production of like or directly competitive articles in the United States, or United States consumers. If a member of the public or proposed respondent files a confidential version of its submission, it shall file a public version of the submission no later than one business day after the deadline for filing the submission. Submissions should:

(i) Explain how the articles potentially subject to the requested remedial orders are used in the United States;

(ii) Identify any public health, safety, or welfare concerns relating to the requested remedial orders;

(iii) Identify like or directly competitive articles that complainant, its licensees, or third parties make which could replace the subject articles if they were to be excluded;

(iv) Indicate whether the complainant, its licensees, and/or third parties have the capacity to replace the volume of articles subject to the requested remedial orders in a commercially reasonable time in the United States; and

(v) State how the requested remedial orders would impact consumers.

(2) Complainant may file a reply to any submissions received under paragraph (c)(1) of this section not to exceed five pages, inclusive of attachments, to the Secretary to the Commission within three (3) calendar days following the filing of the submissions. If the complainant files a confidential version of its submission, it shall file a public version of the submission no later than one business day after the deadline for filing the submission.

(d) *Upon the initiative of the Commission.* The Commission may upon its initiative commence a preinstitution proceeding based upon any alleged violation of section 337 of the Tariff Act of 1930.

[59 FR 39039, Aug. 1, 1994, as amended at 60 FR 32444, June 22, 1995; 68 FR 32978, June 3, 2003; 73 FR 38320, July 7, 2008; 76 FR 61945, Oct. 6, 2011; 76 FR 64808, Oct. 19, 2011; 78 FR 23841, Apr. 19, 2013]

§ 210.9 Action of Commission upon receipt of complaint.

Upon receipt of a complaint alleging violation of section 337 of the Tariff Act of 1930, the Commission shall take the following actions:

(a) *Examination of complaint.* The Commission shall examine the complaint for sufficiency and compliance with the applicable sections of this chapter.

(b) *Informal investigatory activity.* The Commission shall identify sources of relevant information, assure itself of the availability thereof, and, if deemed necessary, prepare subpoenas therefore, and give attention to other preliminary matters.

§ 210.10 Institution of investigation.

(a)(1) The Commission shall determine whether the complaint is properly filed and whether an investigation should be instituted on the basis of the complaint. That determination shall be made within 30 days after the complaint is filed, unless—

(i) Exceptional circumstances preclude adherence to a 30-day deadline;

(ii) Additional time is allotted under other sections of this part in connection with the preinstitution processing of a motion by the complainant for temporary relief;

(iii) The complainant requests that the Commission postpone the determination on whether to institute an investigation; or

(iv) The complainant withdraws the complaint.

(2) If exceptional circumstances preclude Commission adherence to the 30-day deadline for determining whether to institute an investigation on the basis of the complaint, the determination will be made as soon after that deadline as possible.

(3) If additional time is allotted in connection with the preinstitution processing of a motion by the complainant for temporary relief, the Commission will determine whether to institute an investigation and provisionally accept the motion within 35 days after the filing of the complaint or by a subsequent deadline computed in accordance with § 210.53(a), § 210.54, § 210.55(b), § 210.57, or § 210.58 as applicable.

(4) If the complainant desires to have the Commission postpone making a determination on whether to institute an investigation in response to the complaint, the complainant must file a written request with the Secretary. If the request is granted, the determination will be rescheduled for whatever date is appropriate in light of the facts.

(5)(i) The complainant may withdraw the complaint as a matter of right at any time before the Commission votes on whether to institute an investigation. To effect such withdrawal, the complainant must file a written notice with the Commission.

(ii) If a motion for temporary relief was filed in addition to the complaint, the motion must be withdrawn along with the complaint, and the complainant must serve copies of the notice of withdrawal on all proposed respondents and on the embassies that were served with copies of the complaint and motion pursuant to §210.54.

(b) An investigation shall be instituted by the publication of a notice in the FEDERAL REGISTER. The notice will define the scope of the investigation and may be amended as provided in §210.14(b) and (c). The Commission may order the administrative law judge to take evidence and to issue a recommended determination on the public interest based generally on the submissions of the parties and the public under §210.8(b) and (c). If the Commission orders the administrative law judge to take evidence with respect to the public interest, the administrative law judge will limit public interest discovery appropriately, with particular consideration for third parties, and will ensure that such discovery will not delay the investigation or be used improperly. Public interest issues will not be within the scope of discovery unless the administrative law judge is specifically ordered by the Commission to take evidence on these issues.

(c) If the Commission determines not to institute an investigation on the basis of the complaint, the complaint shall be dismissed, and the complainant and all proposed respondents will receive written notice of the Commission's action and the reason(s) therefor.

[59 FR 39039, Aug. 1, 1994, as amended at 73 FR 38321, July 7, 2008; 76 FR 64809, Oct. 19, 2011; 76 FR 71248, Nov. 17, 2011]

§210.11 Service of complaint and notice of investigation.

(a)(1) Unless the Commission institutes temporary relief proceedings, upon institution of an investigation, the Commission shall serve:

(i) Copies of the nonconfidential version of the complaint, the nonconfidential exhibits, and the notice of investigation upon each respondent; and

(ii) Copies of the nonconfidential version of the complaint and the notice of investigation upon the embassy in Washington, DC of the country in which each proposed respondent is located as indicated in the Complaint.

(2) If the Commission institutes temporary relief proceedings, upon institution of an investigation, the Commission shall serve:

(i) Copies of the nonconfidential version of the complaint and the notice of investigation upon each respondent; and

(ii) A copy of the notice of investigation upon the embassy in Washington, DC of the country in which each proposed respondent is located as indicated in the Complaint.

(3) All respondents named after an investigation has been instituted and the governments of the foreign countries in which they are located as indicated in the complaint shall be served as soon as possible after the respondents are named.

(4) The Commission shall serve copies of the notice of investigation upon the U.S. Department of Health and Human Services, the U.S. Department of Justice, the Federal Trade Commission, the U.S. Customs Service, and such other agencies and departments as the Commission considers appropriate.

(b) With leave from the presiding administrative law judge, a complainant may attempt to effect personal service of the complaint and notice of investigation upon a respondent, if the Secretary's efforts to serve the respondent have been unsuccessful. If the complainant succeeds in serving the respondent by personal service, the complainant must notify the administrative law judge and file proof of such service with the Secretary.

[73 FR 38321, July 7, 2008]

Subpart C—Pleadings

§ 210.12   The complaint.

(a) *Contents of the complaint.* In addition to conforming with the requirements of §§ 210.4 and 210.5 of this part, the complaint shall—

(1) Be under oath and signed by the complainant or his duly authorized officer, attorney, or agent, with the name, address, and telephone number of the complainant and any such officer, attorney, or agent given on the first page of the complaint, and include a statement attesting to the representations in § 210.4(c)(1) through (3);

(2) Include a statement of the facts constituting the alleged unfair methods of competition and unfair acts;

(3) Describe specific instances of alleged unlawful importations or sales, and shall provide the Tariff Schedules of the United States item number(s) for importations occurring prior to January 1, 1989, and the Harmonized Tariff Schedule of the United States item number(s) for importations occurring on or after January 1, 1989;

(4) State the name, address, and nature of the business (when such nature is known) of each person alleged to be violating section 337 of the Tariff Act of 1930;

(5) Include a statement as to whether the alleged unfair methods of competition and unfair acts, or the subject matter thereof, are or have been the subject of any court or agency litigation, and, if so, include a brief summary of such litigation;

(6)(i) If the complaint alleges a violation of section 337 based on infringement of a U.S. patent, or a federally registered copyright, trademark, mask work, or vessel hull design, under section 337(a)(1) (B), (C), (D), or (E) of the Tariff Act of 1930, include a statement as to whether an alleged domestic industry exists or is in the process of being established as defined in section 337(a)(2), and include a detailed description of the relevant domestic industry as defined in section 337(a)(3) that allegedly exists or is in the process of being established (*i.e.*, for the former, facts showing significant/substantial investment and employment, and for the latter, facts showing complainant is actively engaged in the steps leading to the exploitation of its intellectual property rights, and that there is a significant likelihood that an industry will be established in the future), and including the relevant operations of any licensees. Relevant information includes but is not limited to:

(A) Significant investment in plant and equipment;

(B) Significant employment of labor or capital; or

(C) Substantial investment in the exploitation of the subject patent, copyright, trademark, mask work, or vessel hull design, including engineering, research and development, or licensing; or

(ii) If the complaint alleges a violation of section 337 of the Tariff Act of 1930 based on unfair methods of competition and unfair acts in the importation or sale of articles in the United States that have the threat or effect of destroying or substantially injuring an industry in the United States or preventing the establishment of such an industry under section 337(a)(1)(A)(i) or (ii), include a detailed statement as to whether an alleged domestic industry exists or is in the process of being established (*i.e.*, for the latter, facts showing that there is a significant likelihood that an industry will be established in the future), and include a detailed description of the domestic industry affected, including the relevant operations of any licensees; or

(iii) If the complaint alleges a violation of section 337 of the Tariff Act of 1930 based on unfair methods of competition or unfair acts that have the threat or effect of restraining or monopolizing trade and commerce in the United States under section 337(a)(1)(A)(iii), include a description of the trade and commerce affected.

(7) Include a description of the complainant's business and its interests in the relevant domestic industry or the relevant trade and commerce. For every intellectual property based complaint (regardless of the type of intellectual property right involved), include a showing that at least one complainant is the owner or exclusive licensee of the subject intellectual property; and

(8) If the alleged violation involves an unfair method of competition or an

unfair act other than those listed in paragraph (a)(6)(i) of this section, state a specific theory and provide corroborating data to support the allegation(s) in the complaint concerning the existence of a threat or effect to destroy or substantially injure a domestic industry, to prevent the establishment of a domestic industry, or to restrain or monopolize trade and commerce in the United States. The information that should ordinarily be provided includes the volume and trend of production, sales, and inventories of the involved domestic article; a description of the facilities and number and type of workers employed in the production of the involved domestic article; profit-and-loss information covering overall operations and operations concerning the involved domestic article; pricing information with respect to the involved domestic article; when available, volume and sales of imports; and other pertinent data.

(9) Include, when a complaint is based upon the infringement of a valid and enforceable U.S. patent—

(i) The identification of each U.S. patent and a certified copy thereof (a legible copy of each such patent will suffice for each required copy of the complaint);

(ii) The identification of the ownership of each involved U.S. patent and a certified copy of each assignment of each such patent (a legible copy thereof will suffice for each required copy of the complaint);

(iii) The identification of each licensee under each involved U.S. patent;

(iv) A copy of each license agreement (if any) for each involved U.S. patent that complainant relies upon to establish its standing to bring the complaint or to support its contention that a domestic industry as defined in section 337(a)(3) exists or is in the process of being established as a result of the domestic activities of one or more licensees;

(v) When known, a list of each foreign patent, each foreign patent application (not already issued as a patent) and each foreign patent application that has been denied, abandoned or withdrawn corresponding to each involved U.S. patent, with an indication of the prosecution status of each such patent application;

(vi) A nontechnical description of the invention of each involved U.S. patent;

(vii) A reference to the specific claims in each involved U.S. patent that allegedly cover the article imported or sold by each person named as violating section 337 of the Tariff Act of 1930, or the process under which such article was produced;

(viii) A showing that each person named as violating section 337 of the Tariff Act of 1930 is importing or selling the article covered by, or produced under the involved process covered by, the above specific claims of each involved U.S. patent. The complainant shall make such showing by appropriate allegations, and when practicable, by a chart that applies each asserted independent claim of each involved U.S. patent to a representative involved article of each person named as violating section 337 of the Tariff Act or to the process under which such article was produced;

(ix) A showing that an industry in the United States, relating to the articles protected by the patent exists or is in the process of being established. The complainant shall make such showing by appropriate allegations, and when practicable, by a chart that applies an exemplary claim of each involved U.S. patent to a representative involved domestic article or to the process under which such article was produced; and

(x) Drawings, photographs, or other visual representations of both the involved domestic article or process and the involved article of each person named as violating section 337 of the Tariff Act of 1930, or of the process utilized in producing the imported article, and, when a chart is furnished under paragraphs (a)(9)(viii) and (a)(9)(ix) of this section, the parts of such drawings, photographs, or other visual representations should be labeled so that they can be read in conjunction with such chart; and

(10) Include, when a complaint is based upon the infringement of a federally registered copyright, trademark, mask work, or vessel hull design—

(i) The identification of each licensee under each involved copyright, trademark, mask work, and vessel hull design;

(ii) A copy of each license agreement (if any) that complainant relies upon to establish its standing to bring the complaint or to support its contention that a domestic industry as defined in section 337(a)(3) exists or is in the process of being established as a result of the domestic activities of one or more licensees.

(11) Contain a request for relief, including a statement as to whether a limited exclusion order, general exclusion order, and/or cease and desist orders are being requested, and if temporary relief is requested under section 337(e) and/or (f) of the Tariff Act of 1930, a motion for such relief shall accompany the complaint as provided in § 210.52(a) or may follow the complaint as provided in § 210.53(a).

(12) Contain a clear statement in plain English of the category of products accused. For example, the caption of the investigation might refer to "certain electronic devices," but the complaint would provide a further statement to identify the type of products involved in plain English such as mobile devices, tablets, or computers.

(b) *Submissions of articles as exhibits.* At the time the complaint is filed, if practicable, the complainant shall submit both the domestic article and all imported articles that are the subject of the complaint.

(c) *Additional material to accompany each patent-based complaint.* There shall accompany the submission of the original of each complaint based upon the alleged unauthorized importation or sale of an article covered by, or produced under a process covered by, the claims of a valid U.S. patent the following:

(1) One certified copy of the U.S. Patent and Trademark Office prosecution history for each involved U.S. patent, plus three additional copies thereof; and

(2) Four copies of each patent and applicable pages of each technical reference mentioned in the prosecution history of each involved U.S. patent.

(d) *Additional material to accompany each registered trademark-based com-* *plaint.* There shall accompany the submission of the original of each complaint based upon the alleged unauthorized importation or sale of an article covered by a federally registered trademark, one certified copy of the Federal registration and three additional copies, and one certified copy of the prosecution history for each federally registered trademark.

(e) *Additional material to accompany each complaint based on a non-Federally registered trademark.* There shall accompany the submission of the original of each complaint based upon the alleged unauthorized importation or sale of an article covered by a non-Federally registered trademark the following:

(1) A detailed and specific description of the alleged trademark;

(2) Information concerning prior attempts to register the alleged trademark; and

(3) Information on the status of current attempts to register the alleged trademark.

(f) *Additional material to accompany each copyright-based complaint.* There shall accompany the submission of the original of each complaint based upon the alleged unauthorized importation or sale of an article covered by a copyright one certified copy of the Federal registration and three additional copies;

(g) *Additional material to accompany each registered mask work-based complaint.* There shall accompany the submission of the original of each complaint based upon the alleged unauthorized importation or sale of a semiconductor chip in a manner that constitutes infringement of a Federally registered mask work, one certified copy of the Federal registration and three additional copies;

(h) *Additional material to accompany each vessel hull design-based complaint.* There shall accompany the submission of the original of each complaint based upon the alleged unauthorized importation or sale of an article covered by a vessel hull design, one certified copy of the Federal registration (including all deposited drawings, photographs, or other pictorial representations of the design), and three additional copies;

(i) *Initial disclosures.* Complainant shall serve on each respondent represented by counsel who has agreed to be bound by the terms of the protective order one copy of each document submitted with the complaint pursuant to §210.12(c) through (h) within five days of service of a notice of appearance and agreement to be bound by the terms of the protective order; and

(j) *Duty to supplement complaint.* Complainant shall supplement the complaint prior to institution of an investigation if complainant obtains information upon the basis of which he knows or reasonably should know that a material legal or factual assertion in the complaint is false or misleading.

[59 FR 39039, Aug. 1, 1994; 59 FR 64286, Dec. 14, 1994, as amended at 73 FR 38321, July 7, 2008; 78 FR 23841, Apr. 19, 2013]

§210.13 The response.

(a) *Time for response.* Except as provided in §210.59(a) and unless otherwise ordered in the notice of investigation or by the administrative law judge, respondents shall have 20 days from the date of service of the complaint and notice of investigation, by the Commission under §210.11(a) or by a party under §210.11(b), within which to file a written response to the complaint and the notice of investigation. When the investigation involves a motion for temporary relief and has not been declared "more complicated," the response to the complaint and notice of investigation must be filed along with the response to the motion for temporary relief—i.e., within 10 days after service of the complaint, notice of investigation, and the motion for temporary relief by the Commission under §210.11(a) or by a party under §210.11(b). (See §210.59.)

(b) *Content of the response.* In addition to conforming to the requirements of §§210.4 and 210.5 of this part, each response shall be under oath and signed by respondent or his duly authorized officer, attorney, or agent with the name, address, and telephone number of the respondent and any such officer, attorney, or agent given on the first page of the response. Each respondent shall respond to each allegation in the complaint and in the notice of investigation, and shall set forth a concise statement of the facts constituting each ground of defense. There shall be a specific admission, denial, or explanation of each fact alleged in the complaint and notice, or if the respondent is without knowledge of any such fact, a statement to that effect. Allegations of a complaint and notice not thus answered may be deemed to have been admitted. Each response shall include, when available, statistical data on the quantity and value of imports of the involved article. Respondents who are importers must also provide the Harmonized Tariff Schedule item number(s) for importations of the accused imports occurring on or after January 1, 1989, and the Tariff Schedules of the United States item number(s) for importations occurring before January 1, 1989. Each response shall also include a statement concerning the respondent's capacity to produce the subject article and the relative significance of the United States market to its operations. Respondents who are not manufacturing their accused imports shall state the name and address of the supplier(s) of those imports. Affirmative defenses shall be pleaded with as much specificity as possible in the response. When the alleged unfair methods of competition and unfair acts are based upon the claims of a valid U.S. patent, the respondent is encouraged to make the following showing when appropriate:

(1) If it is asserted in defense that the article imported or sold by respondents is not covered by, or produced under a process covered by, the claims of each involved U.S. patent, a showing of such noncoverage for each involved claim in each U.S. patent in question shall be made, which showing may be made by appropriate allegations and, when practicable, by a chart that applies the involved claims of each U.S. patent in question to a representative involved imported article of the respondent or to the process under which such article was produced;

(2) Drawings, photographs, or other visual representations of the involved imported article of respondent or the process utilized in producing such article, and, when a chart is furnished under paragraph (b)(1) of this section,

the parts of such drawings, photographs, or other visual representations, should be labeled so that they can be read in conjunction with such chart; and

(3) If the claims of any involved U.S. patent are asserted to be invalid or unenforceable, the basis for such assertion, including, when prior art is relied on, a showing of how the prior art renders each claim invalid or unenforceable and a copy of such prior art. For good cause, the presiding administrative law judge may waive any of the substantive requirements imposed under this paragraph or may impose additional requirements.

(c) *Submission of article as exhibit.* At the time the response is filed, if practicable, the respondent shall submit the accused article imported or sold by that respondent, unless the article has already been submitted by the complainant.

[59 FR 39039, Aug. 1, 1994, as amended at 73 FR 38322, July 7, 2008; 78 FR 23841, Apr. 19, 2013]

§ 210.14 **Amendments to pleadings and notice; supplemental submissions; counterclaims; consolidation of investigations.**

(a) *Preinstitution amendments.* The complaint may be amended at any time prior to the institution of the investigation. If, prior to institution, the complainant seeks to amend a complaint to add a respondent or to assert an additional unfair act not in the original complaint, including asserting a new patent or patent claim, then the complaint shall be treated as if it had been filed on the date the amendment is filed for purposes of §§ 210.8(b) and (c), 210.9, and 210.10(a).

(b) *Postinstitution amendments generally.* (1) After an investigation has been instituted, the complaint or notice of investigation may be amended only by leave of the Commission for good cause shown and upon such conditions as are necessary to avoid prejudicing the public interest and the rights of the parties to the investigation. A motion for amendment must be made to the presiding administrative law judge. A motion to amend the complaint and notice of investigation to name an additional respondent after

institution shall be served on the proposed respondent. If the proposed amendment of the complaint would require amending the notice of investigation, the presiding administrative law judge may grant the motion only by filing with the Commission an initial determination. All other dispositions of such motions shall be by order.

(2) If disposition of the issues in an investigation on the merits will be facilitated, or for other good cause shown, the presiding administrative law judge may allow appropriate amendments to pleadings other than complaints upon such conditions as are necessary to avoid prejudicing the public interest and the rights of the parties to the investigation.

(c) *Postinstitution amendments to conform to evidence.* When issues not raised by the pleadings or notice of investigation, but reasonably within the scope of the pleadings and notice, are considered during the taking of evidence by express or implied consent of the parties, they shall be treated in all respects as if they had been raised in the pleadings and notice. Such amendments of the pleadings and notice as may be necessary to make them conform to the evidence and to raise such issues shall be allowed at any time, and shall be effective with respect to all parties who have expressly or impliedly consented.

(d) *Supplemental submissions.* The administrative law judge may, upon reasonable notice and on such terms as are just, permit service of a supplemental submission setting forth transactions, occurrences, or events that have taken place since the date of the submission sought to be supplemented and that are relevant to any of the issues involved.

(e) *Counterclaims.* At any time after institution of the investigation, but not later than ten business days before the commencement of the evidentiary hearing, a respondent may file a counterclaim at the Commission in accordance with section 337(c) of the Tariff Act of 1930. Counterclaims shall be filed in a separate document. A respondent who files such a counterclaim shall immediately file a notice of removal with a United States district court in which venue for any of the counterclaims raised by the respondent would exist under 28 U.S.C. 1391.

(f) *Respondent submissions on the public interest.* When the Commission has ordered the administrative law judge to take evidence with respect to the public interest under §210.50(b)(1), respondents must submit a statement concerning the public interest, including any response to the issues raised by the complainant pursuant to §210.8(b) and (c)(2), at the same time that their response to the complaint is due. This submission must be no longer than five pages, inclusive of attachments.

(g) *Consolidation of investigations.* The Commission may consolidate two or more investigations. If the investigations are currently before the same presiding administrative law judge, he or she may consolidate the investigations. The investigation number in the caption of the consolidated investigation will include the investigation numbers of the investigations being consolidated. The investigation number in which the matter will be proceeding (the lead investigation) will be the first investigation number named in the consolidated caption.

[59 FR 39039, Aug. 1, 1994, as amended at 59 FR 67627, Dec. 30, 1994; 76 FR 64809, Oct. 19, 2011; 78 FR 23841, Apr. 19, 2013]

Subpart D—Motions

§210.15 Motions.

(a) *Presentation and disposition.* (1) During the period between the institution of an investigation and the assignment of the investigation to a presiding administrative law judge, all motions shall be addressed to the chief administrative law judge. During the time that an investigation or related proceeding is before an administrative law judge, all motions therein shall be addressed to the administrative law judge.

(2) When an investigation or related proceeding is before the Commission, all motions shall be addressed to the Chairman of the Commission. All motions shall be filed with the Secretary and shall be served upon each party.

(b) *Content.* All written motions shall state the particular order, ruling, or action desired and the grounds therefor.

(c) *Responses to motions.* Within 10 days after service of any written motions, or within such longer or shorter time as may be designated by the administrative law judge or the Commission, a nonmoving party, or in the instance of a motion to amend the complaint or notice of investigation to name an additional respondent after institution, the proposed respondent, shall respond or he may be deemed to have consented to the granting of the relief asked for in the motion. The moving party shall have no right to reply, except as permitted by the administrative law judge or the Commission.

(d) *Motions for extensions.* As a matter of discretion, the administrative law judge or the Commission may waive the requirements of this section as to motions for extension of time, and may rule upon such motions ex parte.

[59 FR 39039, Aug. 1, 1994, as amended at 78 FR 23842, Apr. 19, 2013

§210.16 Default.

(a) *Definition of default.* (1) A party shall be found in default if it fails to respond to the complaint and notice of investigation in the manner prescribed in §210.13 or §210.59(c), or otherwise fails to answer the complaint and notice, and fails to show cause why it should not be found in default.

(2) A party may be found in default as a sanction for abuse of process, under §210.4(c), or failure to make or cooperate in discovery, under §210.33(b).

(b) *Procedure for determining default.* (1)(i) If a respondent has failed to respond or appear in the manner described in paragraph (a)(1) of this section, a party may file a motion for, or the administrative law judge may issue upon his own initiative, an order directing respondent to show cause why it should not be found in default.

(ii) If the respondent fails to make the necessary showing pursuant to paragraph (b)(1)(i) of this section, the administrative law judge shall issue an initial determination finding the respondent in default. An administrative law judge's decision denying a motion for a finding of default under paragraph (a)(1) of this section shall be in the form of an order.

(2) Any party may file a motion for issuance of, or the administrative law judge may issue on his own initiative, an initial determination finding a party in default for abuse of process under § 210.4(c) or failure to make or cooperate in discovery. A motion for a finding of default as a sanction for abuse of process or failure to make or cooperate in discovery shall be granted by initial determination or denied by order.

(3) If a proposed respondent has not filed a response to the complaint and notice of investigation pursuant to § 210.13 or § 210.59(c) of this chapter, the proposed respondent may file a notice of intent to default under this section. The filing of a notice of intent to default does not require the administrative law judge to issue the show-cause order of paragraph (b)(1) of this section. The administrative law judge shall issue an initial determination finding the proposed respondent in default upon the filing of a notice of intent to default. Such default will be treated in the same manner as any default under this section.

(4) A party found in default shall be deemed to have waived its right to appear, to be served with documents, and to contest the allegations at issue in the investigation.

(c) *Relief against a respondent in default*—(1) *Types of relief available.* After a respondent has been found in default by the Commission, the complainant may file with the Commission a declaration that it is seeking immediate entry of relief against the respondent in default. The facts alleged in the complaint will be presumed to be true with respect to the defaulting respondent. The Commission may issue an exclusion order, a cease and desist order, or both, affecting the defaulting respondent only after considering the effect of such order(s) upon the public health and welfare, competitive conditions in the U.S. economy, the production of like or directly competitive articles in the United States, and U.S. consumers, and concluding that the order(s) should still be issued in light of the aforementioned public interest factors.

(2) *General exclusion orders.* In any motion requesting the entry of default or the termination of the investigation with respect to the last remaining respondent in the investigation, the complainant shall declare whether it is seeking a general exclusion order. The Commission may issue a general exclusion order pursuant to section 337(g)(2) of the Tariff Act of 1930, regardless of the source or importer of the articles concerned, provided that a violation of section 337 of the Tariff Act of 1930 is established by substantial, reliable, and probative evidence and that the other requirements of 19 U.S.C. 1337(d)(2) are satisfied, and only after considering the aforementioned public interest factors and the requirements of § 210.50(c).

[59 FR 39039, Aug. 1, 1994, as amended at 59 FR 67627, Dec. 30, 1994; 78 FR 23482, Apr. 19, 2013]

§ 210.17 Other failure to act and default.

Failures to act other than the defaults listed in § 210.16 may provide a basis for the presiding administrative law judge or the Commission to draw adverse inferences and to issue findings of fact, conclusions of law, determinations (including a determination on violation of section 337 of the Tariff Act of 1930), and orders that are adverse to the party who fails to act. Such failures include, but are not limited to:

(a) Failure to respond to a motion that materially alters the scope of the investigation or a related proceeding;

(b) Failure to respond to a motion for temporary relief pursuant to § 210.59;

(c) Failure to respond to a motion for summary determination under § 210.18;

(d) Failure to appear at a hearing before the administrative law judge after filing a written response to the complaint or motion for temporary relief, or failure to appear at a hearing before the Commission;

(e) Failure to file a brief or other written submission requested by the administrative law judge or the Commission during an investigation or a related proceeding;

(f) Failure to respond to a petition for review of an initial determination, a petition for reconsideration of an initial determination, or an application for interlocutory review of an administrative law judge's order; and

(g) Failure to participate in temporary relief bond forfeiture proceedings under § 210.70.

(h) *Default by notice.* If a respondent has filed a response to the complaint or notice of investigation under § 210.13 of this chapter, the respondent may still file a notice of intent to default with the presiding administrative law judge at any time before the filing of the final initial determination. The administrative law judge shall issue an initial determination finding the respondent in default upon the filing of a notice of intent to default. Such default will be treated in the same manner as any other failure to act under this section. The filing of a notice of intent to default does not require the administrative law judge to issue an order to show cause as to why the respondent should not be found in default.

The presiding administrative law judge or the Commission may take action under this rule sua sponte or in response to the motion of a party.

[59 FR 39039, Aug. 1, 1994, as amended at 78 FR 23842, Apr. 19, 2013]

§210.18 Summary determinations.

(a) *Motions for summary determinations.* Any party may move with any necessary supporting affidavits for a summary determination in its favor upon all or any part of the issues to be determined in the investigation. Counsel or other representatives in support of the complaint may so move at any time after 20 days following the date of service of the complaint and notice instituting the investigation. Any other party or a respondent may so move at any time after the date of publication of the notice of investigation in the FEDERAL REGISTER. Any such motion by any party in connection with the issue of permanent relief, however, must be filed at least 60 days before the date fixed for any hearing provided for in § 210.36(a)(1). Notwithstanding any other rule, the deadline for filing summary determinations shall be computed by counting backward at least 60 days including the first calendar day prior to the date the hearing is scheduled to commence. If the end of the 60 day period falls on a weekend or holi-

day, the period extends until the end of the next business day. Under exceptional circumstances and upon motion, the presiding administrative law judge may determine that good cause exists to permit a summary determination motion to be filed out of time.

(b) *Opposing affidavits; oral argument; time and basis for determination.* Any nonmoving party may file opposing affidavits within 10 days after service of the motion for summary determination. The administrative law judge may, in his discretion or at the request of any party, set the matter for oral argument and call for the submission of briefs or memoranda. The determination sought by the moving party shall be rendered if pleadings and any depositions, answers to interrogatories, and admissions on file, together with the affidavits, if any, show that there is no genuine issue as to any material fact and that the moving party is entitled to a summary determination as a matter of law.

(c) *Affidavits.* Supporting and opposing affidavits shall be made on personal knowledge, shall set forth such facts as would be admissible in evidence, and shall show affirmatively that the affiant is competent to testify to the matters stated therein. Sworn or certified copies of all papers or parts thereof referred to in an affidavit shall be attached thereto or served therewith. The administrative law judge may permit affidavits to be supplemented or opposed by depositions, answers to interrogatories, or further affidavits. When a motion for summary determination is made and supported as provided in this section, a party opposing the motion may not rest upon the mere allegations or denials of the opposing party's pleading, but the opposing party's response, by affidavits, answers to interrogatories, or as otherwise provided in this section, must set forth specific facts showing that there is a genuine issue of fact for the evidentiary hearing under § 210.36(a)(1) or (2). If the opposing party does not so respond, a summary determination, if appropriate, shall be rendered against the opposing party.

(d) *Refusal of application for summary determination; continuances and other orders.* Should it appear from the affidavits of a party opposing the motion that the party cannot, for reasons stated, present by affidavit facts essential to justify the party's opposition, the administrative law judge may refuse the application for summary determination, or may order a continuance to permit affidavits to be obtained or depositions to be taken or discovery to be had or may make such other order as is appropriate, and a ruling to that effect shall be made a matter of record.

(e) *Order establishing facts.* If on motion under this section a summary determination is not rendered upon the whole case or for all the relief asked and a hearing is necessary, the administrative law judge, by examining the pleadings and the evidence and by interrogating counsel if necessary, shall if practicable ascertain what material facts exist without substantial controversy and what material facts are actually and in good faith controverted. The administrative law judge shall thereupon make an order specifying the facts that appear without substantial controversy and directing such further proceedings in the investigation as are warranted. The facts so specified shall be deemed established.

(f) *Order of summary determination.* An order of summary determination shall constitute an initial determination of the administrative law judge.

[59 FR 39039, Aug. 1, 1994, as amended at 73 FR 38322, July 7, 2008]

§ 210.19 Intervention.

Any person desiring to intervene in an investigation or a related proceeding under this part shall make a written motion. The motion shall have attached to it a certificate showing that the motion has been served upon each party to the investigation or related proceeding in the manner described in § 201.16(b) of this chapter. Any party may file a response to the motion in accordance with § 210.15(c) of this part, provided that the response is accompanied by a certificate confirming that the response was served on the proposed intervenor and all other parties. The Commission, or the administrative law judge by initial determination, may grant the motion to the extent and upon such terms as may be proper under the circumstances.

§ 210.20 Declassification of confidential information.

(a) Any party may move to declassify documents (or portions thereof) that have been designated confidential by the submitter but that do not satisfy the confidentiality criteria set forth in § 201.6(a) of this chapter. All such motions, whether brought at any time during the investigation or after conclusion of the investigation shall be addressed to and ruled upon by the presiding administrative law judge, or if the investigation is not before a presiding administrative law judge, by the chief administrative law judge or such administrative law judge as he may designate.

(b) Following issuance of a public version of the initial determination on whether there is a violation of section 337 of the Tariff Act of 1930 or an initial determination that would otherwise terminate the investigation (if adopted by the Commission), the granting of a motion, in whole or part, to declassify information designated confidential shall constitute an initial determination, except as to that information for which no submissions in opposition to declassification have been filed.

§ 210.21 Termination of investigations.

(a) *Motions for termination.* (1) Any party may move at any time prior to the issuance of an initial determination on violation of section 337 of the Tariff Act of 1930 to terminate an investigation in whole or in part as to any or all respondents, on the basis of withdrawal of the complaint or certain allegations contained therein, or for good cause other than the grounds listed in paragraph (a)(2) of this section. A motion for termination of an investigation based on withdrawal of the complaint, or for good cause, shall contain a statement that there are no agreements, written or oral, express or implied between the parties concerning the subject matter of the investigation, or if there are any agreements concerning the subject matter of the investigation, all such agreements shall be identified, and if written, a copy shall be filed with the Commission along with the motion. If the agreement contains confidential business information within the meaning of §201.6(a) of this chapter, at least one copy of the agreement with such information deleted shall accompany the motion, in addition to a copy of the confidential version. On motion for good cause shown, the administrative law judge may limit service of the agreements to the settling parties and the Commission investigative attorney. The presiding administrative law judge may grant the motion in an initial determination upon such terms and conditions as he deems proper.

(2) Any party may move at any time to terminate an investigation in whole or in part as to any or all respondents on the basis of a settlement, a licensing or other agreement, including an agreement to present the matter for arbitration, or a consent order, as provided in paragraphs (b), (c) and (d) of this section.

(b) *Termination by settlement.* (1) An investigation before the Commission may be terminated as to one or more respondents pursuant to section 337(c) of the Tariff Act of 1930 on the basis of a licensing or other settlement agreement. The motion for termination by settlement shall contain copies of the licensing or other settlement agreements, any supplemental agreements, any documents referenced in the motion or attached agreements, and a statement that there are no other agreements, written or oral, express or implied between the parties concerning the subject matter of the investigation. If the licensing or other settlement agreement contains confidential business information within the meaning of §201.6(a) of this chapter, a copy of the agreement with such information deleted shall accompany the motion. On motion for good cause shown, the administrative law judge may limit the service of the agreements to the settling parties and the Commission investigative attorney.

(2) The motion and agreement(s) shall be certified by the administrative law judge to the Commission with an initial determination if the motion for termination is granted. If the licensing

or other agreement or the initial determination contains confidential business information, copies of the agreement and initial determination with confidential business information deleted shall be certified to the Commission simultaneously with the confidential versions of such documents. Notice of the initial determination and the agreement shall be provided to the U.S. Department of Health and Human Services, the U.S. Department of Justice, the Federal Trade Commission, the U.S. Customs Service, and such other departments and agencies as the Commission deems appropriate. If the Commission's final disposition of the initial determination results in termination of the investigation in its entirety, a notice will be published in the FEDERAL REGISTER. Termination by settlement need not constitute a determination as to violation of section 337 of the Tariff Act of 1930.

(c) *Termination by entry of consent order.* An investigation before the Commission may be terminated pursuant to section 337(c) of the Tariff Act of 1930 on the basis of a consent order. Termination by consent order need not constitute a determination as to violation of section 337. A motion for termination by consent order shall contain copies of any licensing or other settlement agreement, any supplemental agreements, and a statement that there are no other agreements, written or oral, express or implied between the parties concerning the subject matter of the investigation. If the licensing or other settlement agreement contains confidential business information within the meaning of §201.6(a) of this chapter, a copy of the agreement with such information deleted shall accompany the motion. On motion for good cause shown, the administrative law judge may limit service of the agreements to the settling parties and the Commission investigative attorney. If there are no additional agreements, the moving parties shall certify that there are no additional agreements.

(1) *Opportunity to submit proposed consent order—*(i) *Prior to institution of an investigation.* Where time, the nature of the proceeding, and the public interest permit, any person being investigated pursuant to section 603 of the Trade

Act of 1974 (19 U.S.C. § 2482) shall be afforded the opportunity to submit to the Commission a proposal for disposition of the matter under investigation in the form of a consent order stipulation that incorporates a proposed consent order executed by or on behalf of such person and that complies with the requirements of paragraph (c)(3) of this section.

(ii) *Subsequent to institution of an investigation.* In investigations under section 337 of the Tariff Act of 1930, a proposal to terminate by consent order shall be submitted as a motion to the administrative law judge with a stipulation that incorporates a proposed consent order. If the stipulation contains confidential business information within the meaning of § 201.6(a) of this chapter, a copy of the stipulation with such information deleted shall accompany the motion. The stipulation shall comply with the requirements of paragraph (c)(3) of this section. At any time prior to commencement of the hearing, the motion may be filed by one or more respondents, and may be filed jointly with other parties to the investigation. Upon request and for good cause shown, the administrative law judge may consider such a motion during or after a hearing. The filing of the motion shall not stay proceedings before the administrative law judge unless the administrative law judge so orders. The administrative law judge shall promptly file with the Commission an initial determination regarding the motion for termination if the motion is granted. If the initial determination contains confidential business information, a copy of the initial determination with such information deleted shall be filed with the Commission simultaneously with the filing of the confidential version of the initial determination. Pending disposition by the Commission of a consent order stipulation, a party may not, absent good cause shown, withdraw from the stipulation once it has been submitted pursuant to this section.

(2) *Commission disposition of consent order.* (i) If an initial determination granting the motion for termination based on a consent order stipulation is filed with the Commission, notice of the initial determination and the consent order stipulation shall be provided to the U.S. Department of Health and Human Services, the U.S. Department of Justice, the Federal Trade Commission, the U.S. Customs Service, and such other departments and agencies as the Commission deems appropriate.

(ii) The Commission, after considering the effect of the settlement by consent order upon the public health and welfare, competitive conditions in the U.S. economy, the production of like or directly competitive articles in the United States, and U.S. consumers, shall dispose of the initial determination according to the procedures of §§ 210.42 through 210.45. If the Commission's final disposition of the initial determination results in termination of the investigation in its entirety, a notice will be published in the FEDERAL REGISTER. Termination by consent order need not constitute a determination as to violation of section 337. Should the Commission reverse the initial determination, the parties are in no way bound by their proposal in later actions before the Commission.

(3) *Contents of consent order stipulation.* (i) Every consent order stipulation shall contain, in addition to the proposed consent order, the following:

(A) An admission of all jurisdictional facts;

(B) A statement identifying the asserted patent claims, copyright, trademark, mask work, boat hull design, or unfair trade practice, and whether the stipulation calls for cessation of importation, distribution, sale, or other transfers (other than exportation) of subject articles in the United States and/or specific terms relating to the disposition of existing U.S. inventories of subject articles.

(C) An express waiver of all rights to seek judicial review or otherwise challenge or contest the validity of the consent order;

(D) A statement that the signatories to the consent order stipulation will cooperate with and will not seek to impede by litigation or other means the Commission's efforts to gather information under subpart I of this part;

(E) A statement that the enforcement, modification, and revocation of the consent order will be carried out pursuant to subpart I of this part, incorporating by reference the Commission's Rules of Practice and Procedure;

(F) A statement that the signing thereof is for settlement purposes only and does not constitute admission by any respondent that an unfair act has been committed, if applicable; and

(G) A statement that the consent order shall have the same force and effect and may be enforced, modified, or revoked in the same manner as is provided in section 337 of the Tariff Act of 1930 and this part for other Commission actions, and the Commission may require periodic compliance reports pursuant to subpart I of this part to be submitted by the person entering into the consent order stipulation.

(ii) In the case of an intellectual property-based investigation, the consent order stipulation shall also contain—

(A) A statement that the consent order shall not apply with respect to any claim of any intellectual property right that has expired or been found or adjudicated invalid or unenforceable by the Commission or a court or agency of competent jurisdiction, provided that such finding or judgment has become final and nonreviewable;

(B) A statement that each signatory to the stipulation who was a respondent in the investigation will not seek to challenge the validity of the intellectual property right(s), in any administrative or judicial proceeding to enforce the consent order

(4) *Contents of consent order.* The Commission will not issue consent orders with terms beyond those provided for in this section, and will not issue consent orders that are inconsistent with this section. The consent order shall contain:

(i) A statement of the identity of complainant, the respondent, and the subject articles, and a statement of any allegation in the complaint that the respondents sell for importation, import, or sell after importation the subject articles in violation of section 337 by reason of asserted patent claims, copyright, trademark, mask work, boat hull design, or unfair trade practice;

(ii) A statement that the respondents have executed a consent order stipulation (but the consent order shall not contain the terms of the stipulation);

(iii) A statement that the respondent shall not sell for importation, import, or sell after importation the subject articles, directly or indirectly, and shall not aid, abet, encourage, participate in, or induce the sale for importation, the importation, or the sale after importation except under consent, license from the complainant, or to the extent permitted by the settlement agreement between complainant and respondent;

(iv) A statement, if applicable, regarding the disposition of existing U.S. inventories of the subject articles.

(v) A statement, if applicable, whether the respondent would be ordered to cease and desist from importing and distributing articles covered by the asserted patent claims, copyright, trademark, mask work, boat hull design, or unfair trade practice;

(vi) A statement that respondent shall be precluded from seeking judicial review or otherwise challenging or contesting the validity of the Consent Order;

(vii) A statement that respondent shall cooperate with and shall not seek to impede by litigation or other means the Commission's efforts to gather information under subpart I of the Commission's Rules of Practice and Procedure, 19 CFR part 210;

(viii) A statement that Respondent and its officers, directors, employees, agents, and any entity or individual acting on its behalf and with its authority shall not seek to challenge the validity or enforceability of the claims of the asserted patent claims, copyright, trademark, mask work, boat hull design, or unfair trade practice in any administrative or judicial proceeding to enforce the Consent Order;

(ix) A statement that when the patent, copyright, trademark, mask work, boat hull design, or unfair trade practice expires the Consent Order shall become null and void as to such;

(x) A statement that if any claim of the patent, copyright, trademark, mask work, boat hull design, or other unfair trade practice is held invalid or unenforceable by a court or agency of competent jurisdiction or as to any articles that has been found or adjudicated not to infringe the asserted right in a final decision, no longer subject to appeal, this Consent Order shall become null and void as to such invalid or unenforceable claim; and

(xi) A statement that the investigation is hereby terminated with respect to the respondent; provided, however, that enforcement, modification, or revocation of the Consent Order shall be carried out pursuant to Subpart I of the Commission's Rules of Practice and Procedure, 19 CFR part 210.

(5) *Effect, interpretation, and reporting.* The consent order shall have the same force and effect and may be enforced, modified, or revoked in the same manner as is provided in section 337 of the Tariff Act of 1930 and this part for other Commission actions. The Commission will not enforce consent order terms beyond those provided for in this section. The Commission may require periodic compliance reports pursuant to subpart I of this part to be submitted by the person entering into the consent order stipulation.

(d) *Termination based upon arbitration agreement.* Upon filing of a motion for termination with the administrative law judge or the Commission, a section 337 investigation may be terminated as to one or more respondents pursuant to section 337(c) of the Tariff Act of 1930 on the basis of an agreement between complainant and one or more of the respondents to present the matter for arbitration. The motion and a copy of the arbitration agreement shall be certified by the administrative law judge to the Commission with an initial determination if the motion for termination is granted. If the agreement or the initial determination contains confidential business information, copies of the agreement and initial determination with confidential business information deleted shall be certified to the Commission with the confidential versions of such documents. A notice will be published in the FEDERAL REGISTER if the Commission's final disposition of the initial determination results in termination of the investigation in its entirety. Termination based on an arbitration agreement does not constitute a determination as to violation of section 337 of the Tariff Act of 1930.

(e) *Effect of termination.* Termination issued by the administrative law judge shall constitute an initial determination.

[59 FR 39039, Aug. 1, 1994, as amended at 59 FR 67627, Dec. 30, 1994; 60 FR 53120, Oct. 12, 1995; 73 FR 38322, July 7, 2008; 78 FR 23482, Apr. 19, 2013]

§ 210.22 [Reserved]

§ 210.23 Suspension of investigation.

Any party may move to suspend an investigation under this part, because of the pendency of proceedings before the Secretary of Commerce or the administering authority pursuant to section 337(b)(3) of the Tariff Act of 1930. The administrative law judge or the Commission also may raise the issue sua sponte. An administrative law judge's decision granting a motion for suspension shall be in the form of an initial determination.

[59 FR 39039, Aug. 1, 1994, as amended at 59 FR 67627, Dec. 30, 1994]

§ 210.24 Interlocutory appeals.

Rulings by the administrative law judge on motions may not be appealed to the Commission prior to the administrative law judge's issuance of an initial determination, except in the following circumstances:

(a) *Appeals without leave of the administrative law judge.* The Commission may in its discretion entertain interlocutory appeals, except as provided in § 210.64, when a ruling of the administrative law judge:

(1) Requires the disclosure of Commission records or requires the appearance of Government officials pursuant to § 210.32(c)(2); or

(2) Denies an application for intervention under § 210.19. Appeals from such rulings may be sought by filing an application for review, not to exceed 15 pages, with the Commission within five days after service of the administrative law judge's ruling. An answer to the application for review may be filed within five days after service of the application. The application for review should specify the person or party taking the appeal, designate the ruling or part thereof from which appeal is being taken, and specify the reasons and present arguments as to why review is

being sought. The Commission may, upon its own motion, enter an order staying the return date of an order issued by the administrative law judge pursuant to § 210.32(c)(2) or may enter an order placing the matter on the Commission's docket for review. Any order placing the matter on the Commission's docket for review will set forth the scope of the review and the issues that will be considered and will make provision for the filing of briefs if deemed appropriate by the Commission.

(b) *Appeals with leave of the administrative law judge.* (1) Except as otherwise provided in paragraph (a) of this section, § 210.64, and paragraph (b)(2) of this section, applications for review of a ruling by an administrative law judge may be allowed only upon request made to the administrative law judge and upon determination by the administrative law judge in writing, with justification in support thereof, that the ruling involves a controlling question of law or policy as to which there is substantial ground for difference of opinion, and that either an immediate appeal from the ruling may materially advance the ultimate completion of the investigation or subsequent review will be an inadequate remedy.

(2) Applications for review of a ruling by an administrative law judge under § 210.5(e)(1) as to whether information designated confidential by the supplier is entitled to confidential treatment under § 210.5(b) may be allowed only upon request made to the administrative law judge and upon determination by the administrative law judge in writing, with justification in support thereof.

(3) A written application for review under paragraph (b)(1) or (b)(2) of this section shall not exceed 15 pages and may be filed within five days after service of the administrative law judge's determination. An answer to the application for review may be filed within five days after service of the application for review. Thereupon, the Commission may, in its discretion, permit an appeal. Unless otherwise ordered by the Commission, Commission review, if permitted, shall be confined to the application for review and an-

swer thereto, without oral argument or further briefs.

(c) *Investigation not stayed.* Application for review under this section shall not stay the investigation before the administrative law judge unless the administrative law judge or the Commission shall so order.

[59 FR 39039, Aug. 1, 1994, as amended at 59 FR 67627, Dec. 30, 1994]

§ 210.25 Sanctions.

(a)(1) Any party may file a motion for sanctions for abuse of process under § 210.4(d)(1), abuse of discovery under § 210.27(d)(3), failure to make or cooperate in discovery under § 210.33 (b) or (c), or violation of a protective order under § 210.34(c). A motion alleging abuse of process should be filed promptly after the requirements of § 210.4(d)(1)(i) have been satisfied. A motion alleging abuse of discovery, failure to make or cooperate in discovery, or violation of a protective order should be filed promptly after the allegedly sanctionable conduct is discovered.

(2) The administrative law judge (when the investigation or related proceeding is before him) or the Commission (when the investigation or related proceeding is before it) also may raise the sanction issue sua sponte. (See also §§ 210.4(d)(1)(ii), 210.27(d)(3), 210.33(c), and 210.34(c).)

(b) A motion for sanctions shall be addressed to the presiding administrative law judge, if the allegedly sanctionable conduct occurred and is discovered while the administrative law judge is presiding in an investigation or in a related proceeding. During an investigation, the administrative law judge's ruling on the motion shall be in the form of an order, if it is issued before or concurrently with the initial determination concerning violation of section 337 of the Tariff Act of 1930 or termination of the investigation. In a related proceeding, the administrative law judge's ruling shall be in the form of an order, regardless of the point in time at which the order is issued.

(c) A motion for sanctions shall be addressed to the Commission, if the allegedly sanctionable conduct occurred while the Commission is presiding or is filed after the subject investigation or related proceeding is terminated. The Commission may assign the motion to an administrative law judge for issuance of a recommended determination. The deadlines and procedures that will be followed in processing the recommended determination will be set forth in the Commission order assigning the motion to an administrative law judge.

(d) If an administrative law judge's order concerning sanctions is issued before the initial determination concerning violation of section 337 of the Tariff Act of 1930 or termination of the investigation, it may be appealed under § 210.24(b)(1) with leave from the administrative law judge, if the requirements of that section are satisfied. If the order is issued concurrently with the initial determination, the order may be appealed by filing a petition meeting the requirements of § 210.43(b). The periods for filing such petitions and responding to the petitions will be specified in the Commission notice issued pursuant to § 210.42(i), if the initial determination has granted a motion for termination of the investigation, or in the Commission notice issued pursuant to § 210.46(a), if the initial determination concerns violation of section 337. The Commission will determine whether to adopt the order after disposition of the initial determination concerning violation of section 337 or termination of the investigation.

(e) If the administrative law judge's ruling on the motion for sanctions is in the form of a recommended determination pursuant to paragraph (c) of this section, the deadlines and procedures for parties to contest the recommended determination will be set forth in the Commission order assigning the motion to an administrative law judge.

(f) If a motion for sanctions is filed with the administrative law judge during an investigation, he may defer his adjudication of the motion until after he has issued a final initial determination concerning violation of section 337 of the Tariff Act of 1930 or termination of investigation. If the administrative law judge defers his adjudication in such a manner, his ruling on the motion for sanctions must be in the form of a recommended determination and shall be issued no later than 30 days

after issuance of the Commission's final determination on violation of section 337 or termination of the investigation. To aid the Commission in determining whether to adopt a recommended determination, any party may file written comments with the Commission 14 days after service of the recommended determination. Replies to such comments may be filed within seven days after service of the comments. The Commission will determine whether to adopt the recommended determination after reviewing the parties' arguments and taking any other steps the Commission deems appropriate.

[59 FR 39039, Aug. 1, 1994, as amended at 73 FR 38323, July 7, 2008]

§ 210.26 Other motions.

Motions pertaining to discovery shall be filed in accordance with § 210.15 and the pertinent provisions of subpart E of this part (§§ 210.27 through 210.34). Motions pertaining to evidentiary hearings and prehearing conferences shall be filed in accordance with § 210.15 and the pertinent provisions of subpart F of this part (§§ 210.35 through 210.40). Motions for temporary relief shall be filed as provided in subpart H of this part (see §§ 210.52 through 210.57).

Subpart E—Discovery and Compulsory Process

§ 210.27 General provisions governing discovery.

(a) *Discovery methods.* The parties to an investigation may obtain discovery by one or more of the following methods: depositions upon oral examination or written questions; written interrogatories; production of documents or things or permission to enter upon land or other property for inspection or other purposes; and requests for admissions.

(b) *Scope of discovery.* Regarding the scope of discovery for the temporary relief phase of an investigation, see § 210.61. For the permanent relief phase of an investigation, unless otherwise ordered by the administrative law judge, a party may obtain discovery regarding any matter, not privileged, that is relevant to the following:

(1) The claim or defense of the party seeking discovery or to the claim or defense of any other party, including the existence, description, nature, custody, condition, and location of any books, documents, or other tangible things;

(2) The identity and location of persons having knowledge of any discoverable matter;

(3) The appropriate remedy for a violation of section 337 of the Tariff Act of 1930 (see § 210.42(a)(1)(ii)(A)); or

(4) The appropriate bond for the respondents, under section 337(j)(3) of the Tariff Act of 1930, during Presidential review of the remedial order (if any) issued by the Commission (see § 210.42(a)(1)(ii)(B)).

It is not grounds for objection that the information sought will be inadmissible at the hearing if the information sought appears reasonably calculated to lead to the discovery of admissible evidence. All discovery is subject to the limitations of paragraph (d) of this section.

(c) *Specific limitations on electronically stored information.* A person need not provide discovery of electronically stored information from sources that the person identifies as not reasonably accessible because of undue burden or cost. The party seeking the discovery may file a motion to compel discovery pursuant to § 210.33(a). In response to the motion to compel discovery, or in a motion for a protective order filed pursuant to § 210.34, the person from whom discovery is sought must show that the information is not reasonably accessible because of undue burden or cost. If that showing is made, the administrative law judge may order discovery from such sources if the requesting party shows good cause, considering the limitations found in paragraph (d) of this section. The administrative law judge may specify conditions for the discovery.

(d) *General limitations on discovery.* In response to a motion made pursuant to §§ 210.33(a) or 210.34 or *sua sponte*, the administrative law judge must limit by order the frequency or extent of discovery otherwise allowed in this subpart if the administrative law judge determines that:

(1) The discovery sought is unreasonably cumulative or duplicative, or can be obtained from some other source that is more convenient, less burdensome, or less expensive;

(2) The party seeking discovery has had ample opportunity to obtain the information by discovery in the investigation;

(3) The responding person has waived the legal position that justified the discovery or has stipulated to the particular facts pertaining to a disputed issue to which the discovery is directed; or

(4) The burden or expense of the proposed discovery outweighs its likely benefit, considering the needs of the investigation, the importance of the discovery in resolving the issues to be decided by the Commission, and matters of public concern.

(e) *Claiming privilege or work product protection.* (1) When, in response to a discovery request made under this subpart, a person withholds information otherwise discoverable by claiming that the information is privileged or subject to protection as attorney work product, the person must:

(i) Expressly make the claim when responding to a relevant question or request; and

(ii) Within 10 days of making the claim produce to the requester a privilege log that describes the nature of the information not produced or disclosed, in a manner that will enable the requester to assess the claim without revealing the information at issue. The privilege log must separately identify each withheld document, communication, or item, and to the extent possible must specify the following for each entry:

(A) The date the information was created or communicated;

(B) The author(s) or speaker(s);

(C) All recipients;

(D) The employer and position for each author, speaker, or recipient, including whether that person is an attorney or patent agent;

(E) The general subject matter of the information; and

(F) The type of privilege or protection claimed.

(2) If a document produced in discovery is subject to a claim of privilege

or of protection as attorney work product, the person making the claim may notify any person that received the document of the claim and the basis for it.

(i) The notice shall identify the information in the document subject to the claim, preferably using a privilege log as defined under paragraph (e)(1) of this section. After being notified, a person that received the document must do the following:

(A) Within 7 days of service of the notice return, sequester, or destroy the specified document and any copies it has;

(B) Not use or disclose the document until the claim is resolved; and

(C) Within 7 days of service of the notice take reasonable steps to retrieve the document if the person disclosed it to others before being notified.

(ii) Within 7 days of service of the notice, the claimant and the parties shall meet and confer in good faith to resolve the claim of privilege or protection. Within 5 days after the conference, a party may file a motion to compel the production of the document and may, in the motion to compel, use a description of the document from the notice produced under this paragraph. In connection with the motion to compel, the party may submit the document *in camera* for consideration by the administrative law judge. The person that produced the document must preserve the document until the claim of privilege or protection is resolved.

(3) Parties may enter into a written agreement to waive compliance with paragraph (e)(1) of this section for documents, communications, and items created or communicated within a time period specified in the agreement. The administrative law judge may decline to entertain any motion based on information claimed to be subject to the agreement. If information claimed to be subject to the agreement is produced in discovery then the administrative law judge may determine that the produced information is not entitled to privilege or protection.

(4) For good cause, the administrative law judge may order a different period of time for compliance with any requirement of this section. Parties may enter into a written agreement to set a different period of time for compliance with any requirement of this section without approval by the administrative law judge unless the administrative law judge has ordered a different period of time for compliance, in which case the parties' agreement must be approved by the administrative law judge.

(f) *Supplementation of responses.* (1) A party who has responded to a request for discovery with a response is under a duty to supplement or correct the response to include information thereafter acquired if ordered by the administrative law judge or the Commission or in the following circumstances: A party is under a duty seasonably to amend a prior response to an interrogatory, request for production, or request for admission if the party learns that the response is in some material respect incomplete or incorrect and if the additional or corrective information has not otherwise been made known to the other parties during the discovery process or in writing.

(2) A duty to supplement responses also may be imposed by agreement of the parties, or at any time prior to a hearing through new requests for supplementation of prior responses.

(g) *Signing of discovery requests, responses, and objections.* (1) The front page of every request for discovery or response or objection thereto shall contain a caption setting forth the name of the Commission, the title of the investigation or related proceeding, and the docket number or investigation number, if any, assigned to the investigation or related proceeding.

(2) Every request for discovery or response or objection thereto made by a party represented by an attorney shall be signed by at least one attorney of record in the attorney's individual name, whose address shall be stated. A party who is not represented by an attorney shall sign the request, response, or objection and shall state the party's address. The signature of the attorney or party constitutes a certification that to the best of the signer's knowledge, information, and belief formed after a reasonable inquiry, the request, objection, or response is:

(i) Consistent with § 210.5(a) (if applicable) and other relevant provisions of this chapter, and warranted by existing law or a good faith argument for the extension, modification, or reversal of existing law;

(ii) Not interposed for any improper purpose, such as to harass or to cause unnecessary delay or needless increase in the cost of litigation; and

(iii) Not unreasonable or unduly burdensome or expensive, given the needs of the case, the discovery already had in the case, and the importance of the issues at stake in the litigation.

If a request, response, or objection is not signed, it shall be stricken unless it is signed promptly after the omission is called to the attention of the party making the request, response, or objection, and a party shall not be obligated to take any action with respect to it until it is signed.

(3) If without substantial justification a request, response, or objection is certified in violation of paragraph (d)(2) of this section, the administrative law judge or the Commission, upon motion or sua sponte under §210.25 of this part, may impose an appropriate sanction upon the person who made the certification, the party on whose behalf the request, response, or objection was made, or both.

(4) An appropriate sanction may include an order to pay to the other parties the amount of reasonable expenses incurred because of the violation, including a reasonable attorney's fee, to the extent authorized by Rule 26(g) of the Federal Rules of Civil Procedure. Monetary sanctions shall not be imposed under this section against the United States, the Commission, or a Commission investigative attorney.

(5) Monetary sanctions may be imposed under this section to reimburse the Commission for expenses incurred by a Commission investigative attorney or the Commission's Office of Unfair Import Investigations. Monetary sanctions will not be imposed under this section to reimburse the Commission for attorney's fees.

[59 FR 39039, Aug. 1, 1994, as amended at 78 FR 29623, May 21, 2013]

§210.28 Depositions.

(a) *When depositions may be taken.* Following publication in the FEDERAL REGISTER of a Commission notice instituting the investigation, any party may take the testimony of any person, including a party, by deposition upon oral examination or written questions. The presiding administrative law judge will determine the permissible dates or deadlines for taking such depositions. Without stipulation of the parties, the complainants as a group may take a maximum of five fact depositions per respondent or no more than 20 fact depositions whichever is greater, the respondents as a group may take a maximum of 20 fact depositions total, and if the Commission investigative attorney is a party, he or she may take a maximum of 10 fact depositions and is permitted to participate in all depositions taken by any parties in the investigation. Each notice for a corporation to designate deponents only counts as one deposition and includes all corporate representatives so designated to respond, and related respondents are treated as one respondent for purposes of determining the number of depositions. The presiding administrative law judge may increase the number of depositions on written motion for good cause shown.

(b) *Persons before whom depositions may be taken.* Depositions may be taken before a person having power to administer oaths by the laws of the United States or of the place where the examination is held.

(c) *Notice of examination.* A party desiring to take the deposition of a person shall give notice in writing to every other party to the investigation. The administrative law judge shall determine the appropriate period for providing such notice. A party upon whom a notice of deposition is served may make objections to a notice of deposition and state the reasons therefor within ten days of service of the notice of deposition. The notice shall state the time and place for taking the deposition and the name and address of each person to be examined, if known, and, if the name is not known, a general description sufficient to identify him or the particular class or group to which he belongs. A notice may provide for the taking of testimony by telephone, but the administrative law judge may, on motion of any party, require that the deposition be taken in the presence of the deponent. The parties may stipulate in writing, or the administrative law judge may upon motion order, that the testimony at a deposition be recorded by other than stenographic means. If a subpoena duces tecum is to be served on the person to be examined, the designation of the materials to be produced as set forth in the subpoena shall be attached to or included in the notice.

(d) *Taking of deposition.* Each deponent shall be duly sworn, and any adverse party shall have the right to cross-examine. Objections to questions or documents shall be in short form, stating the grounds of objections relied upon. Evidence objected to shall be taken subject to the objections, except that privileged communications and subject matter need not be disclosed. The questions propounded and the answers thereto, together with all objections made, shall be reduced to writing, after which the deposition shall be subscribed by the deponent (unless the parties by stipulation waive signing or the deponent is ill or cannot be found or refuses to sign) and certified by the person before whom the deposition was taken. If the deposition is not subscribed by the deponent, the person administering the oath shall state on the record such fact and the reason therefor. When a deposition is recorded by stenographic means, the stenographer shall certify on the transcript that the witness was sworn in the stenographer's presence and that the transcript is a true record of the testimony of the witness. When a deposition is recorded by other than stenographic means and is thereafter transcribed, the person transcribing it shall certify that the person heard the witness sworn on the recording and that the transcript is a correct writing of the recording. Thereafter, upon payment of reasonable charges therefor, that person shall furnish a copy of the transcript or other recording of the deposition to any party or to the deponent. See paragraph (i) of this section concerning the effect of errors and irregularities in depositions.

(e) *Depositions of nonparty officers or employees of the Commission or of other Government agencies.* A party desiring to take the deposition of an officer or employee of the Commission other than the Commission investigative attorney, or of an officer or employee of another Government agency, or to obtain documents or other physical exhibits in the custody, control, and possession of such officer or employee, shall proceed by written motion to the administrative law judge for leave to apply for a subpoena under § 210.32(c). Such a motion shall be granted only upon a showing that the information expected to be obtained thereby is within the scope of discovery permitted by § 210.27(b) or § 210.61 and cannot be obtained without undue hardship by alternative means.

(f) *Service of deposition transcripts on the Commission staff.* The party taking the deposition shall promptly serve one copy of the deposition transcript on the Commission investigative attorney.

(g) *Admissibility of depositions.* The fact that a deposition is taken and served upon the Commission investigative attorney as provided in this section does not constitute a determination that it is admissible in evidence or that it may be used in the investigation. Only such part of a deposition as is received in evidence at a hearing shall constitute a part of the record in such investigation upon which a determination may be based. Objections may be made at the hearing to receiving in evidence any deposition or part thereof for any reason that would require exclusion of the evidence if the witness were then present and testifying.

(h) *Use of depositions.* A deposition may be used as evidence against any party who was present or represented at the taking of the deposition or who had reasonable notice thereof, in accordance with any of the following provisions:

(1) Any deposition may be used by any party for the purpose of contradicting or impeaching the testimony of a deponent as a witness;

(2) The deposition of a party may be used by an adverse party for any purpose;

(3) The deposition of a witness, whether or not a party, may be used by

any party for any purposes if the administrative law judge finds—

(i) That the witness is dead; or

(ii) That the witness is out of the United States, unless it appears that the absence of the witness was procured by the party offering the deposition; or

(iii) That the witness is unable to attend or testify because of age, illness, infirmity, or imprisonment; or

(iv) That the party offering the deposition has been unable to procure the attendance of the witness by subpoena; or

(v) Upon application and notice, that such exceptional circumstances exist as to make it desirable in the interest of justice and with due regard to the importance of presenting the oral testimony of witnesses at a hearing, to allow the deposition to be used.

(4) If only part of a deposition is offered in evidence by a party, an adverse party may require him to introduce any other part that ought in fairness to be considered with the part introduced, and any party may introduce any other parts.

(i) *Effect of errors and irregularities in depositions*—(1) *As to notice.* All errors and irregularities in the notice for taking a deposition are waived unless written objection is promptly served upon the party giving notice.

(2) *As to disqualification of person before whom the deposition is to be taken.* Objection to taking a deposition because of disqualification of the person before whom it is to be taken is waived unless made before the taking of the deposition begins or as soon thereafter as the disqualification becomes known or could be discovered with reasonable diligence.

(3) *As to taking of depositions.* (i) Objections to the competency of a witness or the competency, relevancy, or materiality of testimony are not waived by failure to make them before or during the deposition, unless the ground of the objection is one which might have been obviated or removed if presented at that time.

(ii) Errors and irregularities occurring at the oral examination in the manner of taking the deposition, in the form of the questions or answers, in the oath or affirmation, or in the conduct of parties, and errors of any kind which might be obviated, removed, or cured if promptly presented, are waived unless seasonable objection thereto is made at the taking of the deposition.

(iii) Objections to the form of written questions submitted under this section are waived unless served in writing upon the party propounding them. The presiding administrative law judge shall set the deadline for service of such objections.

(4) *As to completion and return of deposition.* Errors and irregularities in the manner in which the testimony is transcribed or the deposition is prepared, signed, certified, sealed, indorsed, transmitted, served, or otherwise dealt with by the person before whom it is taken are waived unless a motion to suppress the deposition or some part thereof is made with reasonable promptness after such defect is, or with due diligence might have been, ascertained.

[59 FR 39039, Aug. 1, 1994, as amended at 73 FR 38323, July 7, 2008; 78 FR 23483, Apr. 19, 2013]

§210.29 Interrogatories.

(a) *Scope; use at hearing.* Any party may serve upon any other party written interrogatories to be answered by the party served. Interrogatories may relate to any matters that can be inquired into under §210.27(b) or §210.61, and the answers may be used to the extent permitted by the rules of evidence. Absent stipulation of the parties, any party may serve upon any other party written interrogatories not exceeding 175 in number including all discrete subparts. Related respondents are treated as one entity. The presiding administrative law judge may increase the number of interrogatories on written motion for good cause shown.

(b) *Procedure.* (1) Interrogatories may be served upon any party after the date of publication in the FEDERAL REGISTER of the notice of investigation.

(2) Parties answering interrogatories shall repeat the interrogatories being answered immediately preceding the answers. Each interrogatory shall be answered separately and fully in writing under oath, unless it is objected to,

in which event the reasons for objection shall be stated in lieu of an answer. The answers are to be signed by the person making them, and the objections are to be signed by the attorney making them. The party upon whom the interrogatories have been served shall serve a copy of the answers and objections, if any, within ten days of service of the interrogatories or within the time specified by the administrative law judge. The party submitting the interrogatories may move for an order under § 210.33(a) with respect to any objection to or other failure to answer an interrogatory.

(3) An interrogatory otherwise proper is not necessarily objectionable merely because an answer to the interrogatory involves an opinion or contention that relates to fact or the application of law to fact, but the administrative law judge may order that such an interrogatory need not be answered until after designated discovery has been completed or until a prehearing conference or a later time.

(c) *Option to produce records.* When the answer to an interrogatory may be derived or ascertained from the records of the party upon whom the interrogatory has been served or from an examination, audit, or inspection of such records, or from a compilation, abstract, or summary based thereon, and the burden of deriving or ascertaining the answer is substantially the same for the party serving the interrogatory as for the party served, it is a sufficient answer to such interrogatory to specify the records from which the answer may be derived or ascertained and to afford to the party serving the interrogatory reasonable opportunity to examine, audit, or inspect such records and to make copies, compilations, abstracts, or summaries. The specifications provided shall include sufficient detail to permit the interrogating party to locate and to identify, as readily as can the party served, the documents from which the answer may be ascertained.

[59 FR 39039, Aug. 1, 1994, as amended at 73 FR 38323, July 7, 2008; 78 FR 23484, Apr. 19, 2013]

§ 210.30 **Requests for production of documents and things and entry upon land.**

(a) *Scope.* Any party may serve on any other party a request:

(1) To produce and permit the party making the request, or someone acting on his behalf, to inspect and copy any designated documents (including writings, drawings, graphs, charts, photographs, and other data compilations from which information can be obtained), or to inspect and copy, test, or sample any tangible things that are in the possession, custody, or control of the party upon whom the request is served; or

(2) To permit entry upon designated land or other property in the possession or control of the party upon whom the request is served for the purpose of inspecting and measuring, surveying, photographing, testing, or sampling the property or any designated object or operation thereon, within the scope of § 210.27(b).

(b) *Procedure.* (1) The request may be served upon any party after the date of publication in the FEDERAL REGISTER of the notice of investigation. The request shall set forth the items to be inspected, either by individual item or by category, and describe each item and category with reasonable particularity. The request shall specify a reasonable time, place, and manner of making the inspection and performing the related acts.

(2) The party upon whom the request is served shall serve a written response within 10 days or the time specified by the administrative law judge. The response shall state, with respect to each item or category, that inspection and related activities will be permitted as requested, unless the request is objected to, in which event the reasons for objection shall be stated. If objection is made to part of any item or category, the part shall be specified. The party submitting the request may move for an order under § 210.33(a) with respect to any objection to or other failure to respond to the request or any part thereof, or any failure to permit inspection as requested. A party who produces documents for inspection shall produce them as they are kept in

the usual course of business or shall organize and label them to correspond to the categories in the request.

(c) *Persons not parties.* This section does not preclude issuance of an order against a person not a party to permit entry upon land.

[59 FR 39039, Aug. 1, 1994, as amended at 73 FR 38323, July 7, 2008]

§ 210.31 Requests for admission.

(a) *Form, content, and service of request for admission.* Any party may serve on any other party a written request for admission of the truth of any matters relevant to the investigation and set forth in the request that relate to statements or opinions of fact or of the application of law to fact, including the genuineness of any documents described in the request. Copies of documents shall be served with the request unless they have been otherwise furnished or are known to be, and in the request are stated as being, in the possession of the other party. Each matter as to which an admission is requested shall be separately set forth. The request may be served upon a party whose complaint is the basis for the investigation after the date of publication in the FEDERAL REGISTER of the notice of investigation. The administrative law judge will determine the period within which a party may serve a request upon other parties.

(b) *Answers and objections to requests for admissions.* A party answering a request for admission shall repeat the request for admission immediately preceding his answer. The matter may be deemed admitted unless, within 10 days or the period specified by the administrative law judge, the party to whom the request is directed serves upon the party requesting the admission a sworn written answer or objection addressed to the matter. If objection is made, the reason therefor shall be stated. The answer shall specifically deny the matter or set forth in detail the reasons why the answering party cannot truthfully admit or deny the matter. A denial shall fairly meet the substance of the requested admission, and when good faith requires that a party qualify his answer or deny only a part of the matter as to which an admission is requested, he shall specify so much of it

as is true and qualify or deny the remainder. An answering party may not give lack of information or knowledge as a reason for failure to admit or deny unless he states that he has made reasonable inquiry and that the information known to or readily obtainable by him is insufficient to enable him to admit or deny. A party who considers that a matter as to which an admission has been requested presents a genuine issue for a hearing may not object to the request on that ground alone; he may deny the matter or set forth reasons why he cannot admit or deny it.

(c) *Sufficiency of answers.* The party who has requested the admissions may move to determine the sufficiency of the answers or objections. Unless the objecting party sustains his burden of showing that the objection is justified, the administrative law judge shall order that an answer be served. If the administrative law judge determines that an answer does not comply with the requirements of this section, he may order either that the matter is admitted or that an amended answer be served. The administrative law judge may, in lieu of these orders, determine that final disposition of the request be made at a prehearing conference or at a designated time prior to a hearing under this part.

(d) *Effect of admissions; withdrawal or amendment of admission.* Any matter admitted under this section may be conclusively established unless the administrative law judge on motion permits withdrawal or amendment of the admission. The administrative law judge may permit withdrawal or amendment when the presentation of the issues of the investigation will be subserved thereby and the party who obtained the admission fails to satisfy the administrative law judge that withdrawal or amendment will prejudice him in maintaining his position on the issue of the investigation. Any admission made by a party under this section is for the purpose of the pending investigation and any related proceeding as defined in § 210.3 of this chapter.

[59 FR 39039, Aug. 1, 1994, as amended at 73 FR 38323, July 7, 2008]

§ 210.32 Subpoenas.

(a) *Application for issuance of a subpoena*—(1) *Subpoena ad testificandum.* An application for issuance of a subpoena requiring a person to appear and depose or testify at the taking of a deposition or at a hearing shall be made to the administrative law judge.

(2) *Subpoena duces tecum.* An application for issuance of a subpoena requiring a person to appear and depose or testify and to produce specified documents, papers, books, or other physical exhibits at the taking of a deposition, at a prehearing conference, at a hearing, or under any other circumstances, shall be made in writing to the administrative law judge and shall specify the material to be produced as precisely as possible, showing the general relevancy of the material and the reasonableness of the scope of the subpoena.

(3) The administrative law judge shall rule on all applications filed under paragraph (a)(1) or (a)(2) of this section and may issue subpoenas when warranted.

(b) *Use of subpoena for discovery.* Subpoenas may be used by any party for purposes of discovery or for obtaining documents, papers, books or other physical exhibits for use in evidence, or for both purposes. When used for discovery purposes, a subpoena may require a person to produce and permit the inspection and copying of nonprivileged documents, papers, books, or other physical exhibits that constitute or contain evidence relevant to the subject matter involved and that are in the possession, custody, or control of such person.

(c) *Application for subpoenas for nonparty Commission records or personnel or for records and personnel of other Government agencies*—(1) *Procedure.* An application for issuance of a subpoena requiring the production of nonparty documents, papers, books, physical exhibits, or other material in the records of the Commission, or requiring the production of records or personnel of other Government agencies shall specify as precisely as possible the material to be produced, the nature of the information to be disclosed, or the expected testimony of the official or employee, and shall contain a statement showing the general relevancy of the material, information, or testimony and the reasonableness of the scope of the application, together with a showing that such material, information, or testimony or their substantial equivalent could not be obtained without undue hardship or by alternative means.

(2) *Ruling.* Such applications shall be ruled upon by the administrative law judge, and he may issue such subpoenas when warranted. To the extent that the motion is granted, the administrative law judge shall provide such terms and conditions for the production of the material, the disclosure of the information, or the appearance of the official or employee as may appear necessary and appropriate for the protection of the public interest.

(3) *Application for subpoena grounded upon the Freedom of Information Act.* No application for a subpoena for production of documents grounded upon the Freedom of Information Act (5 U.S.C. § 552) shall be entertained by the administrative law judge.

(d) *Motion to limit or quash.* Any motion to limit or quash a subpoena shall be filed within such time as the administrative law judge may allow.

(e) *Ex parte rulings on applications for subpoenas.* Applications for the issuance of the subpoenas pursuant to the provisions of this section may be made ex parte and, if so made, such applications and rulings thereon shall remain ex parte unless otherwise ordered by the administrative law judge.

(f) *Witness Fees*—(1) *Deponents and witnesses.* Any person compelled to appear in person to depose or testify in response to a subpoena shall be paid the same mileage as are paid witnesses with respect to proceedings in the courts of the United States; provided, that salaried employees of the United States summoned to depose or testify as to matters related to their public employment, irrespective of the party at whose instance they are summoned, shall be paid in accordance with the applicable Federal regulations.

(2) *Responsibility.* The fees and mileage referred to in paragraph (f)(1) of this section shall be paid by the party at whose instance deponents or witnesses appear. Fees due under this paragraph shall be tendered no later

than the date for compliance with the subpoena issued under this section. Failure to timely tender fees under this paragraph shall not invalidate any subpoena issued under this section.

(g) *Obtaining judicial enforcement.* In order to obtain judicial enforcement of a subpoena issued under paragraphs (a)(3) or (c)(2) of this section, the administrative law judge shall certify to the Commission, on motion or sua sponte, a request for such enforcement. The request shall be accompanied by copies of relevant papers and a written report from the administrative law judge concerning the purpose, relevance, and reasonableness of the subpoena. If the request, relevant papers, or written report contain confidential business information, the administrative law judge shall certify nonconfidential copies along with the confidential versions. The Commission will subsequently issue a notice stating whether it has granted the request and authorized its Office of the General Counsel to seek such enforcement.

[59 FR 39039, Aug. 1, 1994, as amended at 73 FR 38233, July 7, 2008]

§210.33 Failure to make or cooperate in discovery; sanctions.

(a) *Motion for order compelling discovery.* A party may apply to the administrative law judge for an order compelling discovery upon reasonable notice to other parties and all persons affected thereby.

(b) *Non-monetary sanctions for failure to comply with an order compelling discovery.* If a party or an officer or agent of a party fails to comply with an order including, but not limited to, an order for the taking of a deposition or the production of documents, an order to answer interrogatories, an order issued pursuant to a request for admissions, or an order to comply with a subpoena, the administrative law judge, for the purpose of permitting resolution of relevant issues and disposition of the investigation without unnecessary delay despite the failure to comply, may take such action in regard thereto as is just, including, but not limited to the following:

(1) Infer that the admission, testimony, documents, or other evidence would have been adverse to the party;

(2) Rule that for the purposes of the investigation the matter or matters concerning the order or subpoena issued be taken as established adversely to the party;

(3) Rule that the party may not introduce into evidence or otherwise rely upon testimony by the party, officer, or agent, or documents, or other material in support of his position in the investigation;

(4) Rule that the party may not be heard to object to introduction and use of secondary evidence to show what the withheld admission, testimony, documents, or other evidence would have shown;

(5) Rule that a motion or other submission by the party concerning the order or subpoena issued be stricken or rule by initial determination that a determination in the investigation be rendered against the party, or both; or

(6) Order any other non-monetary sanction available under Rule 37(b) of the Federal Rules of Civil Procedure. Any such action may be taken by written or oral order issued in the course of the investigation or by inclusion in the initial determination of the administrative law judge. It shall be the duty of the parties to seek, and that of the administrative law judge to grant, such of the foregoing means of relief or other appropriate relief as may be sufficient to compensate for the lack of withheld testimony, documents, or other evidence. If, in the administrative law judge's opinion such relief would not be sufficient, the administrative law judge shall certify to the Commission a request that court enforcement of the subpoena or other discovery order be sought.

(c) *Monetary sanctions for failure to make or cooperate in discovery.* (1) If a party or an officer, director, or managing agent of the party or person designated to testify on behalf of a party fails to obey an order to provide or permit discovery, the administrative law judge or the Commission may make such orders in regard to the failure as are just. In lieu of or in addition to taking action listed in paragraph (b) of this section and to the extent provided in Rule 37(b)(2) of the Federal Rules of Civil Procedure, the administrative law judge or the Commission, upon motion or sua sponte under § 210.25, may require the party failing to obey the order or the attorney advising that party or both to pay reasonable expenses, including attorney's fees, caused by the failure, unless the administrative law judge or the Commission finds that the failure was substantially justified or that other circumstances make an award of expenses unjust. Monetary sanctions shall not be imposed under this section against the United States, the Commission, or a Commission investigative attorney.

(2) Monetary sanctions may be imposed under this section to reimburse the Commission for expenses incurred by a Commission investigative attorney or the Commission's Office of Unfair Import Investigations. Monetary sanctions will not be imposed under this section to reimburse the Commission for attorney's fees.

§ 210.34 Protective orders; reporting requirement; sanctions and other actions.

(a) *Issuance of protective order.* Upon motion by a party or by the person from whom discovery is sought or by the administrative law judge on his own initiative, and for good cause shown, the administrative law judge may make any order that may appear necessary and appropriate for the protection of the public interest or that justice requires to protect a party or person from annoyance, embarrassment, oppression, or undue burden or expense, including one or more of the following:

(1) That discovery not be had;

(2) That the discovery may be had only on specified terms and conditions, including a designation of the time or place;

(3) That discovery may be had only by a method of discovery other than that selected by the party seeking discovery;

(4) That certain matters not be inquired into, or that the scope of discovery be limited to certain matters;

(5) That discovery be conducted with no one present except persons designated by the administrative law judge;

(6) That a deposition, after being sealed, be opened only by order of the Commission or the administrative law judge;

(7) That a trade secret or other confidential research, development, or commercial information not be disclosed or be disclosed only in a designated way; and

(8) That the parties simultaneously file specified documents or information enclosed in sealed envelopes to be opened as directed by the Commission or the administrative law judge. If the motion for a protective order is denied, in whole or in part, the Commission or the administrative law judge may, on such terms and conditions as are just, order that any party or person provide or permit discovery. The Commission also may, upon motion or sua sponte, issue protective orders or may continue or amend a protective order issued by the administrative law judge.

(b) *Unauthorized disclosure, loss, or theft of information.* If confidential business information submitted in accordance with the terms of a protective order is disclosed to any person other than in a manner authorized by the protective order, lost, or stolen, the party responsible for the disclosure, or subject to the loss or theft, must immediately bring all pertinent facts relating to such incident to the attention of the submitter of the information and the administrative law judge or the Commission, and, without prejudice to other rights and remedies of the submitter of the information, make every effort to prevent further mishandling of such information by the party or the recipient of such information.

(c) *Violation of protective order.* (1) The issue of whether sanctions should be imposed may be raised on a motion by a party, the administrative law judge's own motion, or the Commission's own initiative in accordance with § 210.25(a)(2). Parties, including the party that identifies an alleged breach or makes a motion for sanctions, and the Commission shall treat the identity of the alleged breacher as confidential business information unless the Commission issues a public sanction. The identity of the alleged breacher means the name of any individual against whom allegations are made. The Commission or administrative law judge shall allow the parties to make written submissions and, if warranted, to present oral argument bearing on the issues of violation of a protective order and sanctions therefor.

(2) If the breach occurs while the investigation is before an administrative law judge, any determination on sanctions of the type enumerated in paragraphs (c)(3)(i) through (iv) of this section shall be in the form of a recommended determination. The Commission may then consider both the recommended determination and any related orders in making a determination on sanctions. When the motion is addressed to the administrative law judge for sanctions of the type enumerated in paragraph (c)(3)(v) of this section, he shall grant or deny a motion by issuing an order.

(3) Any individual who has agreed to be bound by the terms of a protective order issued pursuant to paragraph (a) of this section, and who is determined to have violated the terms of the protective order, may be subject to one or more of the following:

(i) An official reprimand by the Commission;

(ii) Disqualification from or limitation of further participation in a pending investigation;

(iii) Temporary or permanent disqualification from practicing in any capacity before the Commission pursuant to § 201.15(a) of this chapter;

(iv) Referral of the facts underlying the violation to the appropriate licensing authority in the jurisdiction in which the individual is licensed to practice;

(v) Sanctions of the sort enumerated in § 210.33(b), or such other action as may be appropriate.

(d) *Reporting requirement.* Each person who is subject to a protective order issued pursuant to paragraph (a) of this section shall report in writing to the Commission immediately upon learning that confidential business information disclosed to him or her pursuant to the protective order is the subject of:

(1) A subpoena;

(2) A court or an administrative order (other than an order of a court reviewing a Commission decision);

(3) A discovery request;

(4) An agreement; or

(5) Any other written request, if the request or order seeks disclosure, by him or any other person, of the subject confidential business information to a person who is not, or may not be, permitted access to that information pursuant to either a Commission protective order or § 210.5(b).

NOTE TO PARAGRAPH (d): This reporting requirement applies only to requests and orders for disclosure made for use of confidential business information in non-Commission proceedings.

(e) *Sanctions and other actions.* After providing notice and an opportunity to comment, the Commission may impose a sanction upon any person who willfully fails to comply with paragraph (d) of this section, or it may take other action.

[59 FR 39039, Aug. 1, 1994, as amended at 73 FR 38323, July 7, 2008; 78 FR 23484, Apr. 19, 2013]

Subpart F—Prehearing Conferences and Hearings

§ 210.35 Prehearing conferences.

(a) *When appropriate.* The administrative law judge in any investigation may direct counsel or other representatives for all parties to meet with him for one or more conferences to consider any or all of the following:

(1) Simplification and clarification of the issues;

(2) Negotiation, compromise, or settlement of the case, in whole or in part;

(3) Scope of the hearing;

(4) Necessity or desirability of amendments to pleadings subject, however, to the provisions of § 210.14 (b) and (c);

(5) Stipulations and admissions of either fact or the content and authenticity of documents;

(6) Expedition in the discovery and presentation of evidence including, but not limited to, restriction of the number of expert, economic, or technical witnesses; and

(7) Such other matters as may aid in the orderly and expeditious disposition of the investigation including disclosure of the names of witnesses and the exchange of documents or other physical exhibits that will be introduced in evidence in the course of the hearing.

(b) *Subpoenas.* Prehearing conferences may be convened for the purpose of accepting returns on subpoenas duces tecum issued pursuant to § 210.32(a)(3).

(c) *Reporting.* In the discretion of the administrative law judge, prehearing conferences may or may not be stenographically reported and may or may not be public.

(d) *Order.* The administrative law judge may enter in the record an order that recites the results of the conference. Such order shall include the administrative law judge's rulings upon matters considered at the conference, together with appropriate direction to the parties. The administrative law judge's order shall control the subsequent course of the hearing, unless the administrative law judge modifies the order.

[59 FR 39039, Aug. 1, 1994, as amended at 73 FR 38324, July 7, 2008]

§ 210.36 General provisions for hearings.

(a) *Purpose of hearings.* (1) An opportunity for a hearing shall be provided in each investigation under this part, in accordance with the Administrative Procedure Act. At the hearing, the presiding administrative law judge will take evidence and hear argument for the purpose of determining whether there is a violation of section 337 of the Tariff Act of 1930, and for the purpose of making findings and recommendations, as described in § 210.42(a)(1)(ii), concerning the appropriate remedy and the amount of the bond to be posted by respondents during Presidential review of the Commission's action, under section 337(j) of the Tariff Act.

(2) An opportunity for a hearing in accordance with the Administrative Procedure Act shall also be provided in connection with every motion for temporary relief filed under this part.

(b) *Public hearings.* All hearings in investigations under this part shall be public unless otherwise ordered by the administrative law judge.

(c) *Expedition.* Hearings shall proceed with all reasonable expedition, and, insofar as practicable, shall be held at one place, continuing until completed unless otherwise ordered by the administrative law judge.

(d) *Rights of the parties.* Every hearing under this section shall be conducted in accordance with the Administrative Procedure Act (i.e., 5 U.S.C. §§ 554 through 556). Hence, every party shall have the right of adequate notice, cross-examination, presentation of evidence, objection, motion, argument, and all other rights essential to a fair hearing.

(e) *Presiding official.* An administrative law judge shall preside over each hearing unless the Commission shall otherwise order.

§ 210.37 Evidence.

(a) *Burden of proof.* The proponent of any factual proposition shall be required to sustain the burden of proof with respect thereto.

(b) *Admissibility.* Relevant, material, and reliable evidence shall be admitted. Irrelevant, immaterial, unreliable, or unduly repetitious evidence shall be excluded. Immaterial or irrelevant parts of an admissible document shall be segregated and excluded as far as practicable.

(c) *Information obtained in investigations.* Any documents, papers, books, physical exhibits, or other materials or information obtained by the Commission under any of its powers may be disclosed by the Commission investigative attorney when necessary in connection with investigations and may be offered in evidence by the Commission investigative attorney.

(d) *Official notice.* When any decision of the administrative law judge rests, in whole or in part, upon the taking of official notice of a material fact not appearing in evidence of record, opportunity to disprove such noticed fact shall be granted any party making timely motion therefor.

(e) *Objections.* Objections to evidence shall be made in timely fashion and shall briefly state the grounds relied upon. Rulings on all objections shall appear on the record.

(f) *Exceptions.* Formal exception to an adverse ruling is not required.

(g) *Excluded evidence.* When an objection to a question propounded to a witness is sustained, the examining party may make a specific offer of what he expects to prove by the answer of the witness, or the administrative law judge may in his discretion receive and report the evidence in full. Rejected exhibits, adequately marked for identification, shall be retained with the record so as to be available for consideration by any reviewing authority.

§210.38 Record.

(a) *Definition of the record.* The record shall consist of all pleadings, the notice of investigation, motions and responses, all briefs and written statements, and other documents and things properly filed with the Secretary, in addition to all orders, notices, and initial determinations of the administrative law judge, orders and notices of the Commission, hearing and conference transcripts, evidence admitted into the record (including physical exhibits), and any other items certified into the record by the administrative law judge or the Commission.

(b) *Reporting and transcription.* Hearings shall be reported and transcribed by the official reporter of the Commission under the supervision of the administrative law judge, and the transcript shall be a part of the record.

(c) *Corrections.* Changes in the official transcript may be made only when they involve errors affecting substance. A motion to correct a transcript shall be addressed to the administrative law judge, who may order that the transcript be changed to reflect such corrections as are warranted, after consideration of any objections that may be made. Such corrections shall be made by the official reporter by furnishing substitute typed pages, under the usual certificate of the reporter, for insertion in the transcript. The original uncorrected pages shall be retained in the files of the Commission.

(d) *Certification of record.* The record, including all physical exhibits entered into evidence or such photographic reproductions thereof as the administrative law judge approves, shall be certified to the Commission by the administrative law judge upon his filing of an initial determination or at such earlier time as the Commission may order.

[59 FR 39039, Aug. 1, 1994, as amended at 73 FR 38324, July 7, 2008]

§210.39 In camera treatment of confidential information.

(a) *Definition.* Except as hereinafter provided and consistent with §§ 210.5 and 210.34, confidential documents and testimony made subject to protective orders or orders granting in camera treatment are not made part of the public record and are kept confidential in an in camera record. Only the persons identified in a protective order, persons identified in § 210.5(b), and court personnel concerned with judicial review shall have access to confidential information in the in camera record. The right of the administrative law judge and the Commission to disclose confidential data under a protective order (pursuant to § 210.34) to the extent necessary for the proper disposition of each proceeding is specifically reserved.

(b) *Transmission of certain Commission records to district court.* (1) In a civil action involving parties that are also parties to a proceeding before the Commission under section 337 of the Tariff Act of 1930, at the request of a party to a civil action that is also a respondent in the proceeding before the Commission, the district court may stay, until the determination of the Commission becomes final, proceedings in the civil action with respect to any claim that involves the same issues involved in the proceeding before the Commission under certain conditions. If such a stay is ordered by the district court, after the determination of the Commission becomes final and the stay is dissolved, the Commission shall certify to the district court such portions of the record of its proceeding as the district court may request. Notwithstanding paragraph (a) of this section, the in camera record may be transmitted to a district court and be admissible in a civil action, subject to such protective order as the district court determines necessary, pursuant to 28 U.S.C. 1659.

(2) To facilitate timely compliance with any court order requiring the Commission to transmit all or part of

the record of its section 337 proceedings to the court, as described in paragraph (b)(1) of this section, a party that requests the court to issue an order staying the civil action or an order dissolving the stay and directing the Commission to transmit all or part of the record to the court must file written notice of the issuance or dissolution of a stay with the Commission Secretary within 10 days of the issuance or dissolution of a stay by the district court.

(c) *In camera treatment of documents and testimony.* The administrative law judge shall have authority to order documents or oral testimony offered in evidence, whether admitted or rejected, to be placed in camera.

(d) *Part of confidential record.* In camera documents and testimony shall constitute a part of the confidential record of the Commission.

(e) *References to in camera information.* In submitting proposed findings, briefs, or other papers, counsel for all parties shall make an attempt in good faith to refrain from disclosing the specific details of in camera documents and testimony. This shall not preclude references in such proposed findings, briefs, or other papers to such documents or testimony including generalized statements based on their contents. To the extent that counsel consider it necessary to include specific details of in camera data in their presentations, such data shall be incorporated in separate proposed findings, briefs, or other papers marked "Business Confidential," which shall be placed in camera and become a part of the confidential record.

[59 FR 39039, Aug. 1, 1994, as amended at 59 FR 67627, Dec. 30, 1994; 73 FR 38324, July 7, 2008]

§ 210.40 **Proposed findings and conclusions and briefs.**

At the time a motion for summary determination under § 210.18(a) or a motion for termination under § 210.21(a) is made, or when it is found that a party is in default under § 210.16, or at the close of the reception of evidence in any hearing held pursuant to this part (except as provided in § 210.63), or within a reasonable time thereafter fixed by the administrative law judge, any party may file proposed findings of fact and conclusions of law, together with reasons therefor. When appropriate, briefs in support of the proposed findings of fact and conclusions of law may be filed with the administrative law judge for his consideration. Such proposals and briefs shall be in writing, shall be served upon all parties in accordance with § 210.4(g), and shall contain adequate references to the record and the authorities on which the submitter is relying.

Subpart G—Determinations and Actions Taken

§ 210.41 **Termination of investigation.**

Except as provided in § 210.21 (b)(2), (c), and (d), an order of termination issued by the Commission shall constitute a determination of the Commission under § 210.45(c). The Commission shall publish in the FEDERAL REGISTER notice of each Commission order that terminates an investigation in its entirety.

[60 FR 53120, Oct. 12, 1995]

§ 210.42 **Initial determinations.**

(a)(1)(i) *On issues concerning violation of section 337.* Unless otherwise ordered by the Commission, the administrative law judge shall certify the record to the Commission and shall file an initial determination on whether there is a violation of section 337 of the Tariff Act of 1930 in an original investigation no later than 4 months before the target date set pursuant to § 210.51(a)(1).

(ii) *Recommended determination on issues concerning permanent relief, bonding, and the public interest.* Unless the Commission orders otherwise, within 14 days after issuance of the initial determination on violation of section 337 of the Tariff Act of 1930, the administrative law judge shall issue a recommended determination containing findings of fact and recommendations concerning—

(A) The appropriate remedy in the event that the Commission finds a violation of section 337, and

(B) The amount of the bond to be posted by the respondents during Presidential review of Commission action under section 337(j) of the Tariff Act.

(C) The public interest under sections 337(d)(1) and (f)(1) in investigations where the Commission has ordered the administrative law judge under §210.50(b)(1) to take evidence with respect to the public interest.

(2) *On certain motions to declassify information*. The decision of the administrative law judge granting a motion to declassify information, in whole or in part, shall be in the form of an initial determination as provided in §210.20(b).

(b) *On issues concerning temporary relief or forfeiture of temporary relief bonds*. Certification of the record and the disposition of an initial determination concerning a motion for temporary relief are governed by §§210.65 and 210.66. The disposition of an initial determination concerning possible forfeiture or return of a complainant's temporary relief bond, in whole or in part, is governed by §210.70.

(c) *On other matters*. (1) The administrative law judge shall grant the following types of motions by issuing an initial determination or shall deny them by issuing an order: a motion to amend the complaint or notice of investigation pursuant to §210.14(b); a motion for a finding of default pursuant to §§210.16 and 210.17; a motion for summary determination pursuant to §210.18; a motion for intervention pursuant to §210.19; a motion for termination pursuant to §210.21; a motion to suspend an investigation pursuant to §210.23; or a motion to set a target date for an original investigation exceeding 16 months pursuant to §210.51(a)(1); or a motion to set a target date for a formal enforcement proceeding exceeding 12 months pursuant to §210.51(a)(2).

(2) The administrative law judge shall grant or deny the following types of motions by issuing an initial determination: a motion for forfeiture or return of respondents' bonds pursuant to §210.50(d) or a motion for forfeiture or return of a complainant's temporary relief bond pursuant to §210.70.

(d) *Contents*. The initial determination shall include: an opinion stating findings (with specific page references to principal supporting items of evidence in the record) and conclusions and the reasons or bases therefor necessary for the disposition of all material issues of fact, law, or discretion presented in the record; and a statement that, pursuant to §210.42(h), the initial determination shall become the determination of the Commission unless a party files a petition for review of the initial determination pursuant to §210.43(a) or the Commission, pursuant to §210.44, orders on its own motion a review of the initial determination or certain issues therein.

(e) *Notice to and advice from other departments and agencies*. Notice of each initial determination granting a motion for termination of an investigation in whole or part on the basis of a consent order or a settlement, licensing, or other agreement pursuant to §210.21 of this part, and notice of such other initial determinations as the Commission may order, shall be provided to the U.S. Department of Health and Human Services, the U.S. Department of Justice, the Federal Trade Commission, the U.S. Customs Service, and such other departments and agencies as the Commission deems appropriate. The Commission shall consider comments, limited to issues raised by the record, the initial determination, and the petitions for review, received from such agencies when deciding whether to initiate review or the scope of review. The Commission shall allow such agencies 10 days after the service of an initial determination to submit their comments.

(f) *Initial determination made by the administrative law judge*. An initial determination under this section shall be made and filed by the administrative law judge who presided over the investigation, except when that person is unavailable to the Commission and except as provided in §210.20(a).

(g) *Reopening of proceedings by the administrative law judge*. At any time prior to the filing of the initial determination, the administrative law judge may reopen the proceedings for the reception of additional evidence.

(h) *Effect*. (1) An initial determination filed pursuant to §210.42(a)(2) shall become the determination of the Commission 45 days after the date of service of the initial determination, unless the Commission has ordered review of the initial determination or certain issues therein, or by order has changed the effective date of the initial determination.

(2) An initial determination under § 210.42(a)(1)(i) shall become the determination of the Commission 60 days after the date of service of the initial determination, unless the Commission within 60 days after the date of such service shall have ordered review of the initial determination or certain issues therein or by order has changed the effective date of the initial determination. The findings and recommendations made by the administrative law judge in the recommended determination issued pursuant to § 210.42(a)(1)(ii) will be considered by the Commission in reaching determinations on remedy and bonding by the respondents pursuant to § 210.50(a).

(3) An initial determination filed pursuant to § 210.42(c) shall become the determination of the Commission 30 days after the date of service of the initial determination, except as provided for in paragraph (h)(5) and paragraph (h)(6) of this section, § 210.50(d)(3), and § 210.70(c), unless the Commission, within 30 days after the date of such service shall have ordered review of the initial determination or certain issues therein or by order has changed the effective date of the initial determination.

(4) The disposition of an initial determination granting or denying a motion for temporary relief is governed by § 210.66.

(5) The disposition of an initial determination concerning possible forfeiture of a complainant's temporary relief bond is governed by § 210.70(c).

(6) The disposition of an initial determination filed pursuant to § 210.42(c) which grants a motion for summary determination that would terminate the investigation in its entirety if it were to become the Commission's final determination, shall become the final determination of the Commission 45 days after the date of service of the initial determination, unless the Commission has ordered review of the initial determination or certain issues therein, or by order has changed the effective date of the initial determination.

(i) *Notice of determination.* A notice stating that the Commission's decision on whether to review an initial determination will be issued by the Secretary and served on the parties. Notice of the Commission's decision will be published in the FEDERAL REGISTER if the decision results in termination of the investigation in its entirety, if the Commission deems publication of the notice to be appropriate under § 201.10 of subpart B of this part, or if publication of the notice is required under § 210.49(b) of this subpart or § 210.66(f) of subpart H of this part.

[59 FR 39039, Aug. 1, 1994, as amended at 59 FR 67628, Dec. 30, 1994; 60 FR 53120, Oct. 12, 1995; 73 FR 38324, July 7, 2008; 76 FR 64809, Oct. 19, 2011; 78 FR 23484, Apr. 19, 2013]

§ 210.43 **Petitions for review of initial determinations on matters other than temporary relief.**

(a) *Filing of the petition.* (1) Except as provided in paragraph (a)(2) of this section, any party to an investigation may request Commission review of an initial determination issued under § 210.42(a)(1) or (c), § 210.50(d)(3), § 210.70(c), or § 210.75(b)(3) by filing a petition with the Secretary. A petition for review of an initial determination issued under § 210.42(a)(1) must be filed within 12 days after service of the initial determination. A petition for review of an initial determination issued under § 210.42(c) that terminates the investigation in its entirety on summary determination, or an initial determination issued under § 210.50(d)(3), § 210.70(c) or § 210.75(b)(3), must be filed within 10 days after service of the initial determination. Petitions for review of all other initial determinations under § 210.42(c) must be filed within five (5) business days after service of the initial determination. A petition for review of an initial determination issued under § 210.50(d)(3) or § 210.70(c) must be filed within 10 days after service of the initial determination.

(2) A party may not petition for review of any issue as to which the party has been found to be in default. Similarly, a party or proposed respondent who did not file a response to the motion addressed in the initial determination may be deemed to have consented to the relief requested and may not petition for review of the issues raised in the motion.

(b) *Content of the petition.* (1) A petition for review filed under this section shall identify the party seeking review and shall specify the issues upon which review of the initial determination is sought, and shall, with respect to each such issue, specify one or more of the following grounds upon which review is sought:

(i) That a finding or conclusion of material fact is clearly erroneous;

(ii) That a legal conclusion is erroneous, without governing precedent, rule or law, or constitutes an abuse of discretion; or

(iii) That the determination is one affecting Commission policy.

(2) The petition for review must set forth a concise statement of the facts material to the consideration of the stated issues, and must present a concise argument providing the reasons that review by the Commission is necessary or appropriate to resolve an important issue of fact, law, or policy. If a petition filed under this paragraph exceeds 50 pages in length, it must be accompanied by a summary of the petition not to exceed ten pages. Petitions for review may not exceed 100 pages in length, exclusive of the summary and any exhibits. Petitions for review may not incorporate statements, issues, or arguments by reference. Any issue not raised in a petition for review will be deemed to have been abandoned by the petitioning party and may be disregarded by the Commission in reviewing the initial determination (unless the Commission chooses to review the issue on its own initiative under § 210.44), and any argument not relied on in a petition for review will be deemed to have been abandoned and may be disregarded by the Commission.

(3) Any petition designated by the petitioner as a "contingent" petition for review shall be deemed to be a petition under paragraph (a)(1) of this section and shall be processed accordingly. In order to preserve an issue for review by the Commission or the U.S. Court of Appeals for the Federal Circuit that was decided adversely to a party, the issue must be raised in a petition for review, whether or not the Commission's determination on the ultimate issue, such as a violation of section 337, was decided adversely to the party.

(4) A party's failure to file a petition for review of an initial determination shall constitute abandonment of all issues decided adversely to that party in the initial determination.

(5) *Service of petition.* All petitions for review of an initial determination shall be served on the other parties by messenger, overnight delivery, or equivalent means.

(c) *Responses to the petition.* Any party may file a response within eight (8) days after service of a petition of a final initial determination under § 210.42(a)(1), and within five (5) business days after service of all other types of petitions, except that a party who has been found to be in default may not file a response to any issue as to which the party has defaulted. If a response to a petition for review filed under this paragraph exceeds 50 pages in length, it must be accompanied by a summary of the response not to exceed ten pages. Responses to petitions for review may not exceed 100 pages in length, exclusive of the summary and any exhibits. Responses to petitions for review may not incorporate statements, issues, or arguments by reference. Any argument not relied on in a response will be deemed to have been abandoned and may be disregarded by the Commission.

(d) *Grant or denial of review.* (1) The Commission shall decide whether to grant, in whole or in part, a petition for review of an initial determination filed pursuant to § 210.42(a)(1) within 60 days of the service of the initial determination on the parties, or by such other time as the Commission may order. The Commission shall decide whether to grant, in whole or in part, a petition for review of an initial determination filed pursuant to § 210.42(a)(2) or § 210.42(c), which grants a motion for summary determination that would terminate the investigation in its entirety if it becomes the final determination of the Commission, § 210.50(d)(3), or § 210.70(c) within 45 days after the service of the initial determination on the parties, or by such other time as the Commission may order. The Commission shall decide whether to grant, in whole or in part, a petition for review of an initial determination filed pursuant to § 210.42(c), except as noted above, within 30 days after the service of the initial determination on the parties, or by such other time as the Commission may order.

(2) The Commission shall decide whether to grant a petition for review, based upon the petition and response thereto, without oral argument or further written submissions unless the Commission shall order otherwise. A petition will be granted and review will be ordered if it appears that an error or abuse of the type described in paragraph (b)(1) of this section is present or if the petition raises a policy matter connected with the initial determination, which the Commission thinks it necessary or appropriate to address.

(3) The Commission shall grant a petition for review and order review of an initial determination or certain issues therein when at least one of the participating Commissioners votes for ordering review. In its notice, the Commission shall establish the scope of the review and the issues that will be considered and make provisions for filing of briefs and oral argument if deemed appropriate by the Commission. If the notice solicits written submissions from interested persons on the issues of remedy, the public interest, and bonding in addition to announcing the Commission's decision to grant a petition for review of the initial determination, the notice shall be served by the Secretary on all parties, the U.S. Department of Health and Human Services, the U.S. Department of Justice, the Federal Trade Commission, the U.S. Customs Service, and such other departments and agencies as the Commission deems appropriate.

[59 FR 39039, Aug. 1, 1994, as amended at 59 FR 67628, Dec. 30, 1994; 60 FR 53120, Oct. 12, 1995; 73 FR 38325, July 7, 2008; 78 FR 23484, Apr. 19, 2013]

§ 210.44 Commission review on its own motion of initial determinations on matters other than temporary relief.

Within the time provided in § 210.43(d)(1), the Commission on its own initiative may order review of an initial determination, or certain issues in the initial determination, when at least one of the participating Commis-

sioners votes for ordering review. A self-initiated Commission review of an initial determination will be ordered if it appears that an error or abuse of the kind described in § 210.43(b)(1) is present or the initial determination raises a policy matter which the Commission thinks is necessary or appropriate to address.

§ 210.45 Review of initial determinations on matters other than temporary relief.

(a) *Briefs and oral argument.* In the event the Commission orders review of an initial determination pertaining to issues other than temporary relief, the parties may be requested to file briefs on the issues under review at a time and of a size and nature specified in the notice of review. The parties, within the time provided for filing the review briefs, may submit a written request for a hearing to present oral argument before the Commission, which the Commission in its discretion may grant or deny. The Commission shall grant the request when at least one of the participating Commissioners votes in favor of granting the request.

(b) *Scope of review.* Only the issues set forth in the notice of review, and all subsidiary issues therein, will be considered by the Commission.

(c) *Determination on review.* On review, the Commission may affirm, reverse, modify, set aside or remand for further proceedings, in whole or in part, the initial determination of the administrative law judge. In addition, the Commission may take no position on specific issues or portions of the initial determination of the administrative law judge. The Commission also may make any findings or conclusions that in its judgment are proper based on the record in the proceeding. If the Commission's determination on review terminates the investigation in its entirety, a notice will be published in the FEDERAL REGISTER.

[59 FR 39039, Aug. 1, 1994, as amended at 60 FR 53120, Oct. 12, 1995; 73 FR 38235, July 7, 2008]

§ 210.46 Petitions for and sua sponte review of initial determinations on violation of section 337 or temporary relief.

(a) *Violation of section 337.* An initial determination issued under § 210.42(a)(1)(i) on whether respondents have violated section 337 of the Tariff Act of 1930 will be processed as provided in § 210.42(e), (h)(2), and (i) and §§ 210.43 through 210.45. The Commission will issue a notice setting deadlines for written submissions from the parties, other Federal agencies, and interested members of the public on the issues of remedy, the public interest, and bonding by the respondents. In those submissions, the parties may assert their arguments concerning the recommended determination issued by the administrative law judge pursuant to § 210.42(a)(ii) on the issues of remedy and bonding by respondents.

(b) *Temporary relief.* Commission action on an initial determination concerning temporary relief is governed by § 210.66.

§ 210.47 Petitions for reconsideration.

Within 14 days after service of a Commission determination, any party may file with the Commission a petition for reconsideration of such determination or any action ordered to be taken thereunder, setting forth the relief desired and the grounds in support thereof. Any petition filed under this section must be confined to new questions raised by the determination or action ordered to be taken thereunder and upon which the petitioner had no opportunity to submit arguments. Any party desiring to oppose such a petition shall file an answer thereto within five days after service of the petition upon such party. The filing of a petition for reconsideration shall not stay the effective date of the determination or action ordered to be taken thereunder or toll the running of any statutory time period affecting such determination or action ordered to be taken thereunder unless specifically so ordered by the Commission.

§ 210.48 Disposition of petitions for reconsideration.

The Commission may affirm, set aside, or modify its determination, including any action ordered by it to be taken thereunder. When appropriate, the Commission may order the administrative law judge to take additional evidence.

§ 210.49 Implementation of Commission action.

(a) *Service of Commission determination upon the parties.* A Commission determination pursuant to § 210.45(c) or a termination on the basis of a licensing or other agreement, a consent order or an arbitration agreement pursuant to § 210.21(b), (c) or (d), respectively, shall be served upon each party to the investigation.

(b) *Publication and transmittal to the President.* A Commission determination that there is a violation of section 337 of the Tariff Act of 1930 or that there is reason to believe that there is a violation, together with the action taken relative to such determination under § 210.50(a) or § 210.50(d) of this part, or the modification or rescission in whole or in part of an action taken under § 210.50(a), shall promptly be published in the FEDERAL REGISTER. It shall also be promptly transmitted to the President or an officer assigned the functions of the President under 19 U.S.C. 1337(j)(1)(B), 1337(j)(2), and 1337(j)(4), together with the record upon which the determination and the action are based.

(c) *Enforceability of Commission action.* Unless otherwise specified, any Commission action other than an exclusion order or an order directing seizure and forfeiture of articles imported in violation of an outstanding exclusion order shall be enforceable upon receipt by the affected party of notice of such action. Exclusion orders and seizure and forfeiture orders shall be enforceable upon receipt of notice thereof by the Secretary of the Treasury.

(d) *Finality of affirmative Commission action.* If the President does not disapprove the Commission's action within a 60-day period beginning the day after a copy of the Commission's action is delivered to the President, or if the President notifies the Commission before the close of the 60-day period that he approves the Commission's action, such action shall become final the day after the close of the 60-day period or the day the President notifies the Commission of his approval, as the case may be.

(e) *Duration.* Final Commission action shall remain in effect as provided in subpart I of this part.

[59 FR 39039, Aug. 1, 1994, as amended at 59 FR 67628, Dec. 30, 1994; 73 FR 38325, July 7, 2008]

§ 210.50 Commission action, the public interest, and bonding by respondents.

(a) During the course of each investigation under this part, the Commission shall—

(1) Consider what action (general or limited exclusion of articles from entry or a cease and desist order, or exclusion of articles from entry under bond or a temporary cease and desist order), if any, it should take, and, when appropriate, take such action;

(2) Consult with and seek advice and information from the U.S. Department of Health and Human Services, the U.S. Department of Justice, the Federal Trade Commission, the U.S. Customs Service, and such other departments and agencies as it considers appropriate, concerning the subject matter of the complaint and the effect its actions (general or limited exclusion of articles from entry or a cease and desist order, or exclusion of articles from entry under bond or a temporary cease and desist order) under section 337 of the Tariff Act of 1930 shall have upon the public health and welfare, competitive conditions in the U.S. economy, the production of like or directly competitive articles in the United States, and U.S. consumers;

(3) Determine the amount of the bond to be posted by a respondent pursuant to section 337(j)(3) of the Tariff Act of 1930 following the issuance of temporary or permanent relief under section 337(d), (e), (f), or (g) of the Tariff Act of 1930, taking into account the requirement of section 337(e) and (j)(3) that the amount of the bond be sufficient to protect the complainant from any injury.

(4) Receive submissions from the parties, interested persons, and other Government agencies and departments with respect to the subject matter of paragraphs (a)(1), (a)(2), and (a)(3) of this section. After a recommended determination on remedy is issued by the presiding administrative law judge, the parties are requested to submit to the Commission, within 30 days from service of the recommended determination, any information relating to the public interest, including any updates to the information requested by §§ 210.8(b) and (c) and 210.14(f). Submissions by the parties under this paragraph in response to the recommended determination are limited to 5 pages, inclusive of attachments.

(i) When the matter under consideration pursuant to paragraph (a)(1) of this section is whether to grant some form of permanent relief, the submissions described in paragraph (a)(4) of this section shall be filed by the deadlines specified in the Commission notice issued pursuant to § 210.46(a).

(ii) When the matter under consideration is whether to grant some form of temporary relief, such submissions shall be filed by the deadlines specified in § 210.67(b), unless the Commission orders otherwise.

(iii) Any submission from a party shall be served upon the other parties in accordance with § 210.4(g). The parties' submissions, as well as any filed by interested persons or other agencies shall be available for public inspection in the Office of the Secretary. If a party, interested person, or agency files a confidential version of its submission, it shall file a public version of the submission no later than one business day after the deadline for filing the submission.

(iv) The Commission will consider motions for oral argument or, when necessary, a hearing with respect to the subject matter of this section, except that no hearing or oral argument will be permitted in connection with a motion for temporary relief.

(b)(1) With respect to an administrative law judge's authorization to take evidence or other information and to hear arguments from the parties and other interested persons on the issues of appropriate Commission action, the public interest, and bonding by the respondents for purposes of an initial determination on temporary relief, see

§§ 210.61, 210.62, and 210.66(a). For purposes of the recommended determination required by § 210.42(a)(1)(ii), an administrative law judge shall take evidence or other information and hear arguments from the parties and other interested persons on the issues of appropriate Commission action and bonding by the respondents upon order of the Commission. Unless the Commission orders otherwise, and except as provided for in paragraph (b)(2) of this section, an administrative law judge shall not take evidence on the issue of the public interest for purposes of the recommended determination under § 210.42(a)(1)(ii).

(2) Regarding terminations by settlement agreement, consent order, or arbitration agreement under § 210.21 (b), (c) or (d), the parties may file statements regarding the impact of the proposed termination on the public interest, and the administrative law judge may hear argument, although no discovery may be compelled with respect to issues relating solely to the public interest. Thereafter, the administrative law judge shall consider and make appropriate findings in the initial determination regarding the effect of the proposed settlement on the public health and welfare, competitive conditions in the U.S. economy, the production of like or directly competitive articles in the United States, and U.S. consumers.

(c) No general exclusion from entry of articles shall be ordered under paragraph (a)(1) of this section unless the Commission determines that—

(1) Such exclusion is necessary to prevent circumvention of an exclusion order limited to products of named persons; or

(2) There is a pattern of violation of section 337 of the Tariff Act of 1930 and it is difficult to identify the source of infringing products.

(d) *Forfeiture or return of respondents' bonds.* (1)(i) If one or more respondents posts a bond pursuant to 19 U.S.C. 1337(e)(1) or 1337(j)(3), proceedings to determine whether a respondent's bond should be forfeited to a complainant in whole or part may be initiated upon the filing of a motion, addressed to the administrative law judge who last presided over the investigation, by a complainant within 90 days after the expiration of the period of Presidential review under 19 U.S.C. 1337(j), or if an appeal is taken from the determination of the Commission, within 30 days after the resolution of the appeal. If that administrative law judge is no longer employed by the Commission, the motion shall be addressed to the chief administrative law judge.

(ii) A respondent may file a motion addressed to the administrative law judge who last presided over the investigation for the return of its bond within 90 days after the expiration of the Presidential review period under 19 U.S.C. 1337(j), or if an appeal is taken from the determination of the Commission, within 30 days after the resolution of the appeal. If that administrative law judge is no longer employed by the Commission, the motion shall be addressed to the chief administrative law judge.

(2) Any nonmoving party may file a response to a motion filed under paragraph (d)(1) of this section within 15 days after filing of the motion, unless otherwise ordered by the administrative law judge.

(3) A motion for forfeiture or return of a respondent's bond in whole or part will be adjudicated by the administrative law judge in an initial determination with a 45-day effective date, which shall be subject to review under the provisions of §§ 210.42 through 210.45. In determining whether to grant the motion, the administrative law judge and the Commission will be guided by practice under Rule 65 of the Federal Rules of Civil Procedure (taking into account that the roles of the parties are reversed in this instance).

(4) If the Commission determines that a respondent's bond should be forfeited to a complainant, and if the bond is being held by the Secretary of the Treasury, the Commission Secretary shall promptly notify the Secretary of the Treasury of the Commission's determination.

[59 FR 39039, Aug. 1, 1994, as amended at 59 FR 67628, Dec. 30, 1994; 73 FR 38326, July 7, 2008; 76 FR 64809, Oct. 19, 2011; 78 FR 23485, Apr. 19, 2013]

§ 210.51 Period for concluding investigation.

(a) *Permanent relief.* Within 45 days after institution of an original investigation on whether there is a violation of section 337, or an investigation which is a formal enforcement proceeding, the administrative law judge shall issue an order setting a target date for completion of the investigation. After the target date has been set, it can be modified by the administrative law judge for good cause shown before the investigation is certified to the Commission or by the Commission after the investigation is certified to the Commission.

(1) *Original investigations.* If the target date does not exceed 16 months from the date of institution of an original investigation, the order of the administrative law judge shall be final and not subject to interlocutory review. If the target date exceeds 16 months, the order of the administrative law judge shall constitute an initial determination. Any extension of the target date beyond 16 months, before the investigation is certified to the Commission, shall be by initial determination.

(2) *Formal enforcement proceedings.* If the target date does not exceed 12 months from the date of institution of the formal enforcement proceeding, the order of the administrative law judge shall be final and not subject to interlocutory review. If the target date exceeds 12 months, the order of the administrative law judge shall constitute an initial determination. Any extension of the target date beyond 12 months, before the formal enforcement proceeding is certified to the Commission, shall be by initial determination.

(b) *Temporary relief.* The temporary relief phase of an investigation shall be concluded and a final order issued no later than 90 days after publication of the notice of investigation in the FEDERAL REGISTER, unless the temporary relief phase of the investigation has been designated "more complicated" by the Commission or the presiding administrative law judge pursuant to § 210.22(c) and § 210.60. If that designation has been made, the temporary relief phase of the investigation shall be concluded and a final order issued no later than 150 days after publication of the notice of investigation in the FEDERAL REGISTER.

(c) *Computation of time.* In computing the deadlines imposed in paragraph (b) of this section, there shall be excluded any period during which the investigation is suspended pursuant to § 210.23.

[59 FR 39039, Aug. 1, 1994, as amended at 59 FR 67629, Dec. 30, 1994; 61 FR 43432, Aug. 23, 1996; 73 FR 38326, July 7, 2008; 78 FR 23485, Apr. 19, 2013]

Subpart H—Temporary Relief

§ 210.52 Motions for temporary relief.

Requests for temporary relief under section 337 (e) or (f) of the Tariff Act of 1930 shall be made through a motion filed in accordance with the following provisions:

(a) A complaint requesting temporary relief shall be accompanied by a motion setting forth the complainant's request for such relief. In determining whether to grant temporary relief, the Commission will apply the standards the U.S. Court of Appeals for the Federal Circuit uses in determining whether to affirm lower court decisions granting preliminary injunctions. The motion for temporary relief accordingly must contain a detailed statement of specific facts bearing on the factors the Federal Circuit has stated that a U.S. District Court must consider in granting a preliminary injunction.

(b) The motion must also contain a detailed statement of facts bearing on:

(1) Whether the complainant should be required to post a bond as a prerequisite to the issuance of temporary relief; and

(2) The appropriate amount of the bond, if the Commission determines that a bond will be required.

(c) In determining whether to require a bond as a prerequisite to the issuance of temporary relief, the Commission will be guided by practice under Rule 65 of the Federal Rules of Civil Procedure.

(d) The following documents and information also shall be filed along with the motion for temporary relief:

(1) A memorandum of points and authorities in support of the motion;

(2) Affidavits executed by persons with knowledge of the facts asserted in the motion; and

(3) All documents, information, and other evidence in complainant's possession that complainant intends to submit in support of the motion.

(e) If the complaint, the motion for temporary relief, or the documentation supporting the motion for temporary relief contains confidential business information as defined in §201.6(a) of this chapter, the complainant must follow the procedure outlined in §§210.4(a), 210.5(a), 201.6 (a) and (c), 210.8(a), and 210.55 of this part.

[59 FR 39039, Aug. 1, 1994, as amended at 59 FR 67629, Dec. 30, 1994; 60 FR 32444, June 22, 1995]

§210.53 Motion filed after complaint.

(a) A motion for temporary relief may be filed after the complaint, but must be filed prior to the Commission determination under §210.10 on whether to institute an investigation. A motion filed after the complaint shall contain the information, documents, and evidence described in §210.52 and must also make a showing that extraordinary circumstances exist that warrant temporary relief and that the moving party was not aware, and with due diligence could not have been aware, of those circumstances at the time the complaint was filed. When a motion for temporary relief is filed after the complaint but before the Commission has determined whether to institute an investigation based on the complaint, the 35-day period allotted under §210.58 for review of the complaint and informal investigatory activity will begin to run anew from the date on which the motion was filed.

(b) A motion for temporary relief may not be filed after an investigation has been instituted.

§210.54 Service of motion by the complainant.

Notwithstanding the provisions of §210.11 regarding service of the complaint by the Commission upon institution of an investigation, on the day the complainant files a complaint and motion for temporary relief, if any, with the Commission (see §210.8(a)(1) and (a)(2) of subpart B of this part), the complainant must serve non-confidential copies of both documents (as well as non-confidential copies of all materials or documents attached thereto) on all proposed respondents and on the embassy in Washington, DC of the country in which each proposed respondent is located as indicated in the Complaint. If a complainant files any supplemental information with the Commission prior to institution, non-confidential copies of that supplemental information must be served on all proposed respondents and on the embassy in Washington, DC of the country in which each proposed respondent is located as indicated in the complaint. The complaint, motion, and supplemental information, if any, shall be served by messenger, overnight delivery, or equivalent means. A signed certificate of service must accompany the complaint and motion for temporary relief. If the certificate does not accompany the complaint and the motion, the Secretary shall not accept complaint or the motion and shall promptly notify the submitter. Actual proof of service on each respondent and embassy (e.g., certified mail return receipts, messenger, or overnight delivery receipts, or other proof of delivery)—or proof of a serious but unsuccessful effort to make such service—must be filed within 10 days after the filing of the complaint and motion. If the requirements of this section are not satisfied, the Commission may extend its 35-day deadline under §210.58 for determining whether to provisionally accept the motion for temporary relief and institute an investigation on the basis of the complaint.

[73 FR 38326, July 7, 2008, as amended at 78 FR 23485, Apr. 19, 2013]

§210.55 Content of service copies.

(a) Any purported confidential business information that is deleted from the nonconfidential service copies of the complaint and motion for temporary relief must satisfy the requirements of §201.6(a) of this chapter (which defines confidential information for purposes of Commission proceedings). For attachments to the complaint or motion that are confidential in their entirety, the complainant must provide a nonconfidential summary of what each attachment contains. Despite the redaction of confidential material from the complaint and motion for temporary relief, the nonconfidential service copies must contain enough factual information about each element of the violation alleged in the complaint and the motion to enable each proposed respondent to comprehend the allegations against it.

(b) If the Commission determines that the complaint, motion for temporary relief, or any exhibits or attachments thereto contain excessive designations of confidentiality that are not warranted under § 201.6(a) of this chapter, the Commission may require the complainant to file and serve new non-confidential versions of the aforesaid submissions in accordance with § 210.54 and may determine that the 35-day period under § 210.58 for deciding whether to institute an investigation and to provisionally accept the motion for temporary relief for further processing shall begin to run anew from the date the new non-confidential versions are filed with the Commission and served on the proposed respondents in accordance with § 210.54.

[59 FR 39039, Aug. 1, 1994, as amended at 73 FR 38326, July 7, 2008]

§ 210.56 Notice accompanying service copies.

(a) Each service copy of the complaint and motion for temporary relief shall be accompanied by a notice containing the following text:

Notice is hereby given that the attached complaint and motion for temporary relief will be filed with the U.S. International Trade Commission in Washington, DC on _____, 20__. The filing of the complaint and motion will not institute an investigation on that date, however, nor will it begin the period for filing responses to the complaint and motion pursuant to 19 CFR 210.13 and 210.59.

Upon receipt of the complaint, the Commission will examine the complaint for sufficiency and compliance with 19 CFR 210.4, 210.5, 210.8, and 210.12. The Commission's Office of Unfair Import Investigations will conduct informal investigatory activity pursuant to 19 CFR 210.9 to identify sources of relevant information and to assure itself of the availability thereof. The motion for temporary relief will be examined for sufficiency and compliance with 19 CFR 201.8, 210.4, 210.5, 210.52, 210.53(a) (if applicable), 210.54, 210.55, and 210.56, and will be subject to the same type of preliminary investigative activity as the complaint.

The Commission generally will determine whether to institute an investigation on the basis of the complaint and whether to provisionally accept the motion for temporary relief within 35 days after the complaint and motion are filed or, if the motion is filed after the complaint, within 35 days after the motion is filed—unless the 35-day deadline is extended pursuant to 19 CFR 210.53, 210.54, 210.55(b), 210.57, or 210.58. If the Commission determines to institute an investigation and provisionally accept the motion, the motion will be assigned to a Commission administrative law judge for issuance of an initial determination in accordance with 19 CFR 210.66. See 19 CFR 210.10 and 210.58.

If the Commission determines to conduct an investigation of the complaint and motion for temporary relief, the investigation will be formally instituted on the date the Commission publishes a notice of investigation in the FEDERAL REGISTER pursuant to 19 CFR 210.10(b). If an investigation is instituted, copies of the complaint, the notice of investigation, and the Commission's Rules of Practice and Procedure (19 CFR Part 210) will be served on each respondent by the Commission pursuant to 19 CFR 210.11(a). Responses to the complaint, the notice of investigation, and the motion for temporary relief must be filed within 10 days after Commission service thereof, and must comply with 19 CFR 201.8, 210.4, 210.5, 210.13, and 210.59. See also 19 CFR 201.14 and 210.6 regarding computation of the 10-day response period.

If, after reviewing the complaint and motion for temporary relief, the Commission determines not to institute an investigation, the complaint and motion will be dismissed and the Commission will provide written notice of that decision and the reasons therefor to the complainant and all proposed respondents pursuant to 19 CFR 210.10.

For information concerning the filing and processing of the complaint and its treatment, and to ask general questions concerning section 337 practice and procedure, contact the Office of Unfair Import Investigations, U.S. International Trade Commission, 500 E Street SW., Room 401, Washington, DC 20436, telephone 202–205–2560. Such inquiries will be referred to the Commission investigative attorney assigned to the complaint. (See also the Commissions's Rules of Practice and Procedure set forth in 19 CFR Part 210.)

To learn the date that the Commission will vote on whether to institute an investigation and the publication date of the notice of investigation (if the Commission decides to institute an investigation), contact the Office of the Secretary, U.S. International Trade Commission, 500 E Street SW., room 112, Washington, DC 20436, telephone 202–205–2000.

This notice is being provided pursuant to 19 CFR 210.56.

(b) In the event that the complaint and motion for temporary relief are filed after the date specified in the above notice, the complainant must serve a supplementary notice to all proposed respondents and embassies stating the correct filing date. The supplementary notice shall be served by messenger, overnight delivery, or equivalent means. The complainant shall file a certificate of service and a copy of the supplementary notice with the Commission.

[59 FR 39039, Aug. 1, 1994, as amended at 73 FR 38326, July 7, 2008; 78 FR 23485, Apr. 19, 2013]

§ 210.57 Amendment of the motion.

A motion for temporary relief may be amended at any time prior to the institution of an investigation. All material filed to amend the motion (or the complaint) must be served on all proposed respondents and on the embassies in Washington, DC, of the foreign governments that they represent, in accordance with § 210.54. If the amendment expands the scope of the motion or changes the complainant's assertions on the issue of whether a bond is to be required as a prerequisite to the issuance of temporary relief or the appropriate amount of the bond, the 35-day period under § 210.58 for determining whether to institute an investigation and provisionally accept the motion for temporary relief shall begin to run anew from the date the amendment is filed with the Commission. A motion for temporary relief may not be amended to expand the scope of the temporary relief inquiry after an investigation is instituted.

§ 210.58 Provisional acceptance of the motion.

The Commission shall determine whether to accept a motion for temporary relief at the same time it determines whether to institute an investigation on the basis of the complaint. That determination shall be made within 35 days after the complaint and motion for temporary relief are filed, unless the 35-day period is restarted pursuant to § 210.53(a), § 210.54, § 210.55, or § 210.57, or exceptional cir-

cumstances exist which preclude adherence to the prescribed deadline. (See § 210.10(a)(1).) Before the Commission determines whether to provisionally accept a motion for temporary relief, the motion will be examined for sufficiency and compliance with §§ 210.52, 210.53(a) (if applicable), 210.54 through 210.56, as well as §§ 210.4 and 210.5. The motion will be subject to the same type of preliminary investigatory activity as the complaint. (See § 210.9(b).) Acceptance of a motion pursuant to this paragraph constitutes provisional acceptance for referral of the motion to the chief administrative law judge, who will assign the motion to a presiding administrative law judge for issuance of an initial determination under § 210.66(a). Commission rejection of an insufficient or improperly filed complaint will preclude acceptance of a motion for temporary relief. Commission rejection of a motion for temporary relief will not preclude institution of an investigation of the complaint.

[59 FR 39039, Aug. 1, 1994, as amended at 78 FR 23846, Apr. 19, 2013]

§ 210.59 Responses to the motion and the complaint.

(a) Any party may file a response to a motion for temporary relief. Unless otherwise ordered by the administrative law judge, a response to a motion for temporary relief in an ordinary investigation must be filed not later than 10 days after service of the motion by the Commission. In a "more complicated" investigation, the response shall be due within 20 days after such service, unless otherwise ordered by the presiding administrative law judge.

(b) The response must comply with the requirements of §§ 210.4 and 210.5 of this part, and shall contain the following information:

(1) A statement that sets forth with particularity any objection to the motion for temporary relief;

(2) A statement of specific facts concerning the factors the U.S. Court of Appeals for the Federal Circuit would consider in determining whether to affirm lower court decisions granting or denying preliminary injunctions;

(3) A memorandum of points and authorities in support of the respondent's response to the motion;

(4) Affidavits, where possible, executed by persons with knowledge of the facts specified in the response. Each response to the motion must address, to the extent possible, the complainant's assertions regarding whether a bond should be required and the appropriate amount of the bond. Responses to the motion for temporary relief also may contain counter-proposals concerning the amount of the bond or the manner in which the bond amount should be calculated.

(c) Each response to the motion for temporary relief must also be accompanied by a response to the complaint and notice of investigation. Responses to the complaint and notice of investigation must comply with §§ 210.4 and 210.5 of this part, and any protective order issued by the administrative law judge under § 210.34 of this part.

[59 FR 39039, Aug. 1, 1994, as amended at 78 FR 23846, Apr. 19, 2013

§ 210.60 Designating the temporary relief phase of an investigation more complicated for the purpose of adjudicating a motion for temporary relief.

(a) At the time the Commission determines to institute an investigation and provisionally accepts a motion for temporary relief pursuant to § 210.58, or at any time thereafter, the Commission may designate the temporary relief phase of an investigation "more complicated" pursuant to § 210.60(b) for the purpose of obtaining up to 60 additional days to adjudicate the motion for temporary relief. In the alternative, after the motion for temporary relief is referred to the administrative law judge for an initial determination under § 210.66(a), the administrative law judge may issue an order, sua sponte or on motion, designating the temporary relief phase of the investigation "more complicated" for the purpose of obtaining additional time to adjudicate the motion for temporary relief. Such order shall constitute a final determination of the Commission, and notice of the order shall be published in the FEDERAL REGISTER. As required by section 337(e)(2) of the Tariff Act of

1930, the notice shall state the reasons that the temporary relief phase of the investigation was designated "more complicated." The "more complicated" designation may be conferred by the Commission or the presiding administrative law judge pursuant to this paragraph on the basis of the complexity of the issues raised in the motion for temporary relief or the responses thereto, or for other good cause shown.

(b) A temporary relief phase is designated more complicated owing to the subject matter, difficulty in obtaining information, the large number of parties involved, or other significant factors.

[59 FR 39039, Aug. 1, 1994, as amended at 78 FR 23846, Apr. 19, 2013

§ 210.61 Discovery and compulsory process.

The presiding administrative law judge shall set all discovery deadlines. The administrative law judge's authority to compel discovery includes discovery relating to the following issues:

(a) Any matter relevant to the motion for temporary relief and the responses thereto, including the issues of bonding by the complainant; and

(b) The issues the Commission considers pursuant to sections 337 (e)(1), (f)(1), and (j)(3) of the Tariff Act of 1930, viz.,

(1) The appropriate form of relief (notwithstanding the form requested in the motion for temporary relief),

(2) Whether the public interest precludes that form of relief, and

(3) The amount of the bond to be posted by the respondents to secure importations or sales of the subject imported merchandise while the temporary relief order is in effect. The administrative law judge may, but is not required to, make findings on the issues specified in sections 337 (e)(1), (f)(1), or (j)(3) of the Tariff Act of 1930. Evidence and information obtained through discovery on those issues will be used by the parties and considered by the Commission in the context of the parties' written submissions on remedy, the public interest, and bonding by respondents, which are filed with the Commission pursuant to § 210.67(b).

§210.62 Evidentiary hearing.

An opportunity for a hearing in accordance with the Administrative Procedure Act and §210.36 of this part will be provided in connection with every motion for temporary relief. If a hearing is conducted, the presiding administrative law judge may, but is not required to, take evidence concerning the issues of remedy, the public interest, and bonding by respondents under section 337 (e)(1), (f)(1), and (j)(3) of the Tariff Act of 1930.

§210.63 Proposed findings and conclusions and briefs.

The administrative law judge shall determine whether and, if so, to what extent the parties shall be permitted to file proposed findings of fact, proposed conclusions of law, or briefs under §210.40 concerning the issues involved in adjudication of the motion for temporary relief.

§210.64 Interlocutory appeals.

There will be no interlocutory appeals to the Commission under §210.24 on any matter connected with a motion for temporary relief that is decided by an administrative law judge prior to the issuance of the initial determination on the motion for temporary relief.

§210.65 Certification of the record.

When the administrative law judge issues an initial determination concerning temporary relief pursuant to §210.66(a), he shall also certify to the Commission the record upon which the initial determination is based.

§210.66 Initial determination concerning temporary relief; Commission action thereon.

(a) On or before the 70th day after publication of the notice of investigation in an ordinary investigation, or on or before the 120th day after such publication in a "more complicated" investigation, the administrative law judge will issue an initial determination concerning the issues listed in §§210.52 and 210.59. If the 70th day or the 120th day is a Saturday, Sunday, or Federal holiday, the initial determination must be received in the Office of the Secretary no later than 12:00 noon on the first business day after the 70-day or 120-day deadline. The initial determination may, but is not required to, address the issues of remedy, the public interest, and bonding by the respondents pursuant under sections 337 (e)(1), (f)(1), and (j)(3) of the Tariff Act of 1930.

(b) If the initial determination on temporary relief is issued on the 70-day or 120-day deadline imposed in paragraph (a) of this section, the initial determination will become the Commission's determination 20 calendar days after issuance thereof in an ordinary case, and 30 calendar days after issuance in a "more complicated" investigation, unless the Commission modifies, reverses, or sets aside the initial determination in whole or part within that period. If the initial determination on temporary relief is issued before the 70-day or 120-day deadline imposed in paragraph (a) of this section, the Commission will add the extra time to the 20-day or 30-day deadline to which it would otherwise have been held. In computing the deadlines imposed by this paragraph, intermediary Saturdays, Sundays, and Federal holidays shall be included. If the last day of the period is a Saturday, Sunday, or Federal holiday as defined in §201.14(a) of this chapter, the effective date of the initial determination shall be extended to the next business day.

(c) The Commission will not modify, reverse, or set aside an initial determination concerning temporary relief unless the Commission finds that a finding of material fact is clearly erroneous, that the initial determination contains an error of law, or that there is a policy matter warranting discussion by the Commission. All parties may file written comments concerning any clear error of material fact, error of law, or policy matter warranting such action by the Commission. Such comments must be limited to 35 pages in an ordinary investigation and 45 pages in a "more complicated" investigation. The comments must be filed no later than seven calendar days after issuance of the initial determination in an ordinary case and 10 calendar days after issuance of the initial determination in a "more complicated" investigation. In computing the aforesaid 7-day and 10-day deadlines, intermediary Saturdays, Sundays, and Federal holidays shall be included. If the initial determination is issued on a Friday, however, the filing deadline for comments shall be measured from the first business day after issuance. If the last day of the filing period is a Saturday, Sunday, or Federal holiday as defined in § 201.14(a) of this chapter, the filing deadline shall be extended to the next business day. The parties shall serve their comments on other parties by messenger, overnight delivery, or equivalent means.

(d) Notice of the initial determination shall be served on the other agencies listed in § 210.50(a)(2). Those agencies will be given 10 calendar days from the date of service of the notice to file comments on the initial determination.

(e)(1) Each party may file a response to each set of comments filed by another party. All such reply comments must be filed within 10 calendar days after issuance of the initial determination in an ordinary case and within 14 calendar days after issuance of an initial determination in a "more complicated" investigation. The deadlines for filing reply comments shall be computed in the manner described in paragraph (c) of this section, except that in no case shall a party have fewer than two calendar days to file reply comments.

(2) Each set of reply comments will be limited to 20 pages in an ordinary investigation and 30 pages in a "more complicated" case.

(f) If the Commission determines to modify, reverse, or set aside the initial determination, the Commission will issue a notice and, if appropriate, a Commission opinion. If the Commission does not modify, reverse, or set aside the administrative law judge's initial determination within the time provided under paragraph (b) of this section, the initial determination will automatically become the determination of the Commission. Notice of the Commission's determination concerning the initial determination will be issued on the statutory deadline for

determining whether to grant temporary relief, or as soon as possible thereafter, and will be served on the parties. Notice of the determination will be published in the FEDERAL REGISTER if the Commission's disposition of the initial determination has resulted in a determination that there is reason to believe that section 337 has been violated and a temporary remedial order is to be issued. If the Commission determines (either by reversing or modifying the administrative law judge's initial determination, or by adopting the initial determination) that the complainant must post a bond as a prerequisite to the issuance of temporary relief, the Commission may issue a supplemental notice setting forth conditions for the bond if any (in addition to those outlined in the initial determination) and the deadline for filing the bond with the Commission.

[59 FR 39039, Aug. 1, 1994, as amended at 60 FR 53121, Oct. 12, 1995; 73 FR 38326, July 7, 2008]

§ 210.67 Remedy, the public interest, and bonding.

The procedure for arriving at the Commission's determination of the issues of the appropriate form of temporary relief, whether the public interest factors enumerated in the statute preclude such relief, and the amount of the bond under which respondents' merchandise will be permitted to enter the United States during the pendency of any temporary relief order issued by the Commission, is as follows:

(a) While the motion for temporary relief is before the administrative law judge, he may compel discovery on matters relating to remedy, the public interest and bonding (as provided in § 210.61). The administrative law judge also is authorized to make findings pertaining to the public interest, as provided in § 210.66(a). Such findings may be superseded, however, by Commission findings on that issue as provided in paragraph (c) of this section.

(b) On the 65th day after institution in an ordinary case or on the 110th day after institution in a "more complicated" investigation, all parties shall file written submissions with the Commission addressing those issues.

The submissions shall refer to information and evidence already on the record, but additional information and evidence germane to the issues of appropriate relief, the statutory public interest factors, and bonding by respondents may be provided along with the parties' submissions. Pursuant to §210.50(a)(4), interested persons may also file written comments, on the aforesaid dates, concerning the issues of remedy, the public interest, and bonding by the respondents.

(c) On or before the 90-day or 150-day statutory deadline for determining whether to order temporary relief under section 337 (e)(1) and/or (f)(1) of the Tariff Act of 1930, the Commission will determine what relief is appropriate in light of any violation that appears to exist, whether the public interest factors enumerated in the statute preclude the issuance of such relief, and the amount of the bond under which the respondents' merchandise will be permitted to enter the United States during the pendency of any temporary relief order issued by the Commission. In the event that Commission's findings on the public interest pursuant to this paragraph are inconsistent with findings made by the administrative law judge in the initial determination pursuant to §210.66(a), the Commission's findings are controlling.

[59 FR 39039, Aug. 1, 1994, as amended at 73 FR 38326, July 7, 2008]

§210.68 Complainant's temporary relief bond.

(a) In every investigation under this part involving a motion for temporary relief, the question of whether the complainant shall be required to post a bond as a prerequisite to the issuance of such relief shall be addressed by the parties, the presiding administrative law judge, and the Commission in the manner described in §§210.52, 210.59, 210.61, 210.62, and 210.66. If the Commission determines that a bond should be required, the bond may consist of one or more of the following:

(1) The surety bond of a surety or guarantee corporation that is licensed to do business with the United States in accordance with 31 U.S.C. 9304–9306 and 31 CFR parts 223 and 224;

(2) The surety bond of an individual, a trust, an estate, or a partnership, or a corporation, whose solvency and financial responsibility will be investigated and verified by the Commission; or

(3) A certified check, a bank draft, a post office money order, cash, a United States bond, a Treasury note, or other Government obligation within the meaning of 31 U.S.C. 9301 and 31 CFR part 225, which is owned by the complainant and tendered in lieu of a surety bond, pursuant to 31 U.S.C. 9303(c) and 31 CFR part 225.

The same restrictions and requirements applicable to individual and corporate sureties on Customs bonds, which are set forth in 19 CFR part 113, shall apply with respect to sureties on bonds filed with the Commission by complainants as a prerequisite to a temporary relief under section 337 of the Tariff Act of 1930. If the surety is an individual, the individual must file an affidavit of the type shown in appendix A to §210.68. Unless otherwise ordered by the Commission, while the bond of the individual surety is in effect, an updated affidavit must be filed every four months (computed from the date on which the bond was approved by the Secretary or the Commission).

(b) The bond and accompanying documentation must be submitted to the Commission within the time specified in the Commission notice, order, determination, or opinion requiring the posting of a bond, or within such other time as the Commission may order. If the bond is not submitted within the specified period (and an extension of time has not been granted), temporary relief will not be issued.

(c) The corporate or individual surety on a bond or the person posting a certified check, a bank draft, a post office money order, cash, a United States bond, a Treasury note, or other Government obligation in lieu of a surety bond must provide the following information on the face of the bond or in the instrument authorizing the Government to collect or sell the bond, certified check, bank draft, post office money order, cash, United States bond, Treasury note, or other Government obligation in response to a Commission order requiring forfeiture of the bond pursuant to § 210.70:

(1) The investigation caption and docket number;

(2) The names, addresses, and seals (if appropriate) of the principal, the surety, the obligee, as well as the "attorney in fact" and the registered process agent (if applicable) (see Customs Service regulations in 19 CFR part 113 and Treasury Department regulations in 31 CFR parts 223, 224, and 225);

(3) The terms and conditions of the bond obligation, including the reason the bond is being posted, the amount of the bond, the effective date and duration of the bond (as prescribed by the Commission order, notice, determination, or opinion requiring the complainant to post a bond); and

(4) A section at the bottom of the bond or other instrument for the date and authorized signature of the Secretary to reflect Commission approval of the bond.

(d) Complainants who wish to post a certified check, a bank draft, a post office money order, cash, a United States bond, a Treasury note, or other Government obligation in lieu of a surety bond must notify the Commission in writing immediately upon receipt of the Commission document requiring the posting of a bond, and must contact the Secretary to make arrangements for Commission receipt, handling, management, and deposit of the certified check, bank draft, post office money order, cash, United States bond, Treasury note, or other Government obligation tendered in lieu of a surety bond, in accordance with 31 U.S.C. § 9303, 31 CFR parts 202, 206, and 225 and other governing Treasury regulations and circular(s). If required by the governing Treasury regulations and circular, a certified check, a bank draft, a post office money order, cash, a United States bond, a Treasury note, or other government obligation tendered in lieu of a surety bond may have to be collateralized. See, e.g., 31 CFR 202.6 and the appropriate Treasury Circular.

APPENDIX A TO § 210.68—AFFIDAVIT BY INDIVIDUAL SURETY

United States International Trade Commission Affidavit by Individual Surety 19 CFR 210.68

State of _____

County _____
SS: _____

I, the undersigned, being duly sworn, depose and say that I am a citizen of the United States, and of full age and legally competent; that I am not a partner in any business of the principal on the bond or bonds on which I appear as surety; and that the information herein below furnished is true and complete to the best of my knowledge. This affidavit is made to induce the United States International Trade Commission to accept me as surety on the bond(s) filed or to be filed with the United States International Trade Commission pursuant to 19 CFR 210.68. I agree to notify the Commission of any transfer or change in any of the assets herein enumerated.

1. Name (First, Middle, Last) _____

2. Home Address _____

3. Type & Duration of Occupation _____

4. Name of Employer (If Self-Employed) _____

5. Business Address _____

6. Telephone No.

Home _____

Business _____

7. The following is a true representation of my assets, liabilities, and net worth and does not include any financial interest I have in the assets of the principal on the bond(s) on which I appear as surety.

a. Fair value of solely owned real estate *.

b. All mortgages or other encumbrances on the real estate included in Line a ....

c. Real estate equity (subtract Line b from Line a) ....

d. Fair value of all solely owned property other than real estate ....

e. Total of the amounts on Lines c and d ....

f. All other liabilities owing or incurred not included in Line b ....

g. Net worth (subtract Line f from Line e) ....

*Do not include property exempt from execution and sale for any reason. Surety's interest in community property may be included if not so exempt.

8. LOCATION AND DESCRIPTION OF REAL ESTATE OF WHICH I AM SOLE OWNER, THE VALUE OF WHICH IS IN LINE a, ITEM 7 ABOVE [1]

Amount of assessed value of above real estate for taxation purposes:

9. DESCRIPTION OF PROPERTY INCLUDED IN LINE d, ITEM 7 ABOVE (List the value of each category of property separately)[2]

10. ALL OTHER BONDS ON WHICH I AM SURETY (State character and amount of each bond; if none, so state)[3]

11. SIGNATURE

12. BOND AND COMMISSION INVESTIGATION TO WHICH THIS AFFIDAVIT RELATES
SUBSCRIBED AND SWORN TO BEFORE ME AS FOLLOWS:
DATE OATH ADMINISTERED
MONTH   DAY   YEAR
CITY
STATE (Or Other Jurisdiction) _____

NAME & TITLE OF OFFICIAL
ADMINISTERING OATH   _____
SIGNATURE   _____
MY COMMISSION EXPIRES   _____

INSTRUCTIONS

1. Here describe the property by giving the number of the lot and square or block, and addition or subdivision, if in a city, and, if in the country, after showing state, county, and township, locate the property by metes and bounds, or by part of section, township, and range, so that it may be identified.
2. Here describe the property by name so that it can be identified—for example "Fifteen shares of the stock of the "National Metropolitan Bank, New York City," or "Am. T. & T. s. f.5's 60.''
3. Here state what other bonds the affiant has already signed as surety, giving the name and address of the principal, the date, and the amount and character of the bond.

[59 FR 39039, Aug. 1, 1994; 59 FR 64286, Dec. 14, 1994]

§210.69 Approval of complainant's temporary relief bond.

(a) In accordance with 31 U.S.C. §9304(b), all bonds posted by complainants must be approved by the Commission before the temporary relief sought by the complainant will be issued. See also 31 U.S.C. §9303(a) and 31 CFR 225.1 and 225.20. The Commission's bond approval officer for purposes of those provisions shall be the Secretary.

(b) The bond approval process may entail investigation by the Secretary or the Commission's Office of Investigations to determine the veracity of all factual information set forth in the bond and the accompanying documentation (e.g., powers of attorney), as well as any additional verification required by 31 CFR parts 223, 224, or 225. The Secretary may reject a bond on one or more of the following grounds:

(1) Failure to comply with the instructions in the Commission determination, order, or notice directing the complainant to post a bond;

(2) Failure of the surety or the bond to provide information or supporting documentation required by the Commission, the Secretary, §210.68 of this part, 31 CFR parts 223 or 224, or other governing statutes, regulations, or Treasury circulars, or because of a limitation prescribed in a governing statute, regulation, or circular;

(3) Failure of an individual surety to execute and file with the bond, an affidavit of the type shown in appendix A to §210.68, which sets forth information about the surety's assets, liabilities, net worth, real estate and other property of which the initial surety is the sole owner, other bonds on which the individual surety is a surety (and which must be updated at 4-month intervals while the bond is in effect, measured from the date on which the bond is approved by the Secretary on behalf of the Commission or by the Commission);

(4) Any question about the solvency or financial responsibility of the surety, or any question of fraud, misrepresentation, or perjury which comes to light as a result of the verification inquiry during the bond approval process; and

(5) Any other reason deemed appropriate by the Secretary.

(c) If the complainant believes that the Secretary's rejection of the bond was erroneous as a matter of law, the complainant may appeal the Secretary's rejection of the bond by filing a petition with the Commission in the form of a letter to the Chairman, within 10 days after service of the rejection letter.

(d) After the bond is approved and temporary relief is issued, if any question concerning the continued solvency of the individual or the legality or enforceability of the bond or undertaking develops, the Commission may take the following action(s), sua sponte or on motion;

(1) Revoke the Commission approval of the bond and require complainant to post a new bond; or

(2) Revoke or vacate the temporary remedial order for public interest reasons or changed conditions of law or fact (criteria that are the basis for modification or rescission of final Commission action pursuant to § 210.76(a)(1) and (b)); or

(3) Notify the Treasury Department if the problem involves a corporate surety licensed to do business with the United States under 31 U.S.C. §§ 9303–9306 and 31 CFR parts 223 and 224; or

(4) Refer the matter to the U.S. Department of Justice if there is a suggestion of fraud, perjury, or related conduct.

§ 210.70 Forfeiture or return of complainant's temporary relief bond.

(a)(1) If the Commission determines that one or more of the respondents whose merchandise was covered by the temporary relief order has not violated section 337 of the Tariff Act of 1930 to the extent alleged in the motion for temporary relief and provided for in the temporary relief order, proceedings to determine whether the complainant's bond should be forfeited to one or more respondents in whole or part may be initiated upon the filing of a motion by a respondent within 30 days after filing of the aforesaid Commission determination on violation.

(2) A complainant may file a motion for the return of its bond.

(b) Any nonmoving party may file a response to a motion filed under paragraph (a) of this section within 15 days after filing of the motion, unless otherwise ordered by the administrative law judge.

(c) A motion for forfeiture or return of a complainant's temporary relief bond in whole or part will be adjudicated by the administrative law judge in an initial determination with a 45-day effective date, which shall be subject to review under the provisions of §§ 210.42 through 210.45. In determining whether to grant the motion, the administrative law judge and the Commission will be guided by practice under Rule 65 of the Federal Rules of Civil Procedure.

[59 FR 67629, Dec. 30, 1994]

Subpart I—Enforcement Procedures and Advisory Opinions

§ 210.71 Information gathering.

(a) *Power to require information.* (1) Whenever the Commission issues an exclusion order, the Commission may require any person to report facts available to that person that will help the Commission assist the U.S. Customs Service in determining whether and to what extent there is compliance with the order. Similarly, whenever the Commission issues a cease and desist order or a consent order, it may require any person to report facts available to that person that will aid the Commission in determining whether and to what extent there is compliance with the order or whether and to what extent the conditions that led to the order are changed.

(2) The Commission may also include provisions that exercise any other information-gathering power available to the Commission by law, regardless of whether the order at issue is an exclusion order, a cease and desist order, or a consent order. The Commission may at any time request the cooperation of any person or agency in supplying it with information that will aid the Commission or the U.S. Customs Service in making the determinations described in paragraph (a)(1) of this section.

(b) *Form and detail of reports.* Reports under paragraph (a) of this section are to be in writing, under oath, and in such detail and in such form as the Commission prescribes.

(c) *Power to enforce informational requirements.* Terms and conditions of exclusion orders, cease and desist orders, and consent orders for reporting and information gathering shall be enforceable by the Commission by a civil action under 19 U.S.C. 1333, or, at the Commission's discretion, in the same manner as any other provision of the exclusion order, cease and desist order, or consent order is enforced.

(d) *Term of reporting requirement.* An exclusion order, cease and desist order, or consent order may provide for the frequency of reporting or information gathering and the date on which these activities are to terminate. If no date for termination is provided, reporting and information gathering shall terminate when the exclusion order, cease and desist order, or consent order or any amendment to it expires by its own terms or is terminated.

[59 FR 39039, Aug. 1, 1994, as amended at 73 FR 38327, July 7, 2008]

§210.72 Confidentiality of information.

Confidential information (as defined in §201.6(a) of this chapter) that is provided to the Commission pursuant to exclusion order, cease and desist order, or consent order will be received by the Commission in confidence. Requests for confidential treatment shall comply with §201.6 of this chapter. The restrictions on disclosure and the procedures for handling such information (which are set out in §§210.5 and 210.39) shall apply and, in a proceeding under §210.75 or §210.76, the Commission or the presiding administrative law judge may, upon motion or sua sponte, issue or continue appropriate protective orders.

§210.73 Review of reports.

(a) *Review to insure compliance.* The Commission, through the Office of Unfair Import Investigations, will review reports submitted pursuant to any exclusion order, cease and desist order, or consent order and conduct such further investigation as it deems necessary to insure compliance with its orders.

(b) *Extension of time.* The Director of the Office of Unfair Import Investigations may, for good cause shown, extend the time in which reports required by exclusion orders, cease and desist orders, and consent orders may be filed. An extension of time within which a report may be filed, or the filing of a report that does not evidence full compliance with the order, does not in any circumstances suspend or relieve a respondent from its obligation under the law with respect to compliance with such order.

§210.74 Modification of reporting requirements.

(a) *Exclusion and cease and desist orders.* The Commission may modify reporting requirements of exclusion and cease and desist orders as necessary:

(1) To help the Commission assist the U.S. Customs Service in ascertaining that there has been compliance with an outstanding exclusion order;

(2) To help the Commission ascertain that there has been compliance with a cease and desist order;

(3) To take account of changed circumstances; or

(4) To minimize the burden of reporting or informational access.

An order to modify reporting requirements shall identify the reports involved and state the reason or reasons for modification. No reporting requirement will be suspended during the pendency of such a modification unless the Commission so orders. The Commission may, if the public interest warrants, announce that a modification of reporting is under consideration and ask for comment, but it may also modify any reporting requirement at any time without notice, consistent with the standards of this section.

(b) *Consent orders.* Consistent with the standards set forth in paragraph (a) of this section, the Commission may modify reporting requirements of consent orders. The Commission shall serve notice of any proposed change, together with the reporting requirements to be modified and the reasons therefor, on each party subject to the consent order. Such parties shall be given the opportunity to submit briefs to the Commission, and the Commission may hold a hearing on the matter. Notice of any proposed change in the reporting requirements will be published in the FEDERAL REGISTER if Commission determines to solicit public comment on the proposed change.

[59 FR 39039, Aug. 1, 1994, as amended at 60 FR 53121, Oct. 12, 1995]

§210.75 Proceedings to enforce exclusion orders, cease and desist orders, consent orders, and other Commission orders.

(a) *Informal enforcement proceedings.* Informal enforcement proceedings may be conducted by the Commission, through the Office of Unfair Import Investigations, with respect to any act or omission by any person in possible violation of any provision of an exclusion order, cease and desist order, or consent order. Such matters may be handled by the Commission through correspondence or conference or in any

191

other way that the Commission deems appropriate. The Commission may issue such orders as it deems appropriate to implement and insure compliance with the terms of an exclusion order, cease and desist order, or consent order, or any part thereof. Any matter not disposed of informally may be made the subject of a formal proceeding pursuant to this subpart.

(b) *Formal enforcement proceedings.* (1) The Commission may institute an enforcement proceeding at the Commission level upon the filing by the complainant in the original investigation or his successor in interest, by the Office of Unfair Import Investigations, or by the Commission of a complaint setting forth alleged violations of any exclusion order, cease and desist order, or consent order. If a proceeding is instituted, the complaint shall be served upon the alleged violator and a notice of institution published in the FEDERAL REGISTER. Within 15 days after the date of service of such a complaint, the named respondent shall file a response to it. Responses shall fully advise the Commission as to the nature of any defense and shall admit or deny each allegation of the complaint specifically and in detail unless the respondent is without knowledge, in which case its answer shall so state and the statement shall operate as a denial. Allegations of fact not denied or controverted may be deemed admitted. Matters alleged as affirmative defenses shall be separately stated and numbered. These proceedings are authorized under section 337(b) as investigations on whether there is a violation of section 337 in the same manner as original investigations, and are conducted in accordance with the laws for original investigations as set forth in section 1337 of title 19 and sections 554, 555, 556, 557, and 702 of title 5 of the United States Code and the rules of this part.

(2) Upon the failure of a respondent to file and serve a response within the time and in the manner prescribed herein the Commission, in its discretion, may find the facts alleged in the complaint to be true and take such action as may be appropriate without notice or hearing, or, in its discretion, proceed without notice to take evidence on the allegations set forth in the complaint, provided that the Commission (or administrative law judge, if one is appointed) may permit late filings of an answer for good cause shown.

(3) The Commission, in the course of a formal enforcement proceeding under this section, may hold a public hearing and afford the parties to the enforcement proceeding the opportunity to appear and be heard. The Commission may delegate the hearing to the chief administrative law judge for designation of a presiding administrative law judge, who shall certify an initial determination to the Commission. A presiding administrative law judge shall certify the record and issue the enforcement initial determination to the Commission no later than three months before the target date for completion of a formal enforcement proceeding. Parties may file petitions for review, and responses thereto, in accordance with § 210.43 of this part. The enforcement initial determination shall become the determination of the Commission 45 days after the date of service of the enforcement initial determination, unless the Commission, within 45 days after the date of such service, shall have ordered review of the enforcement initial determination on certain issues therein, or by order shall have changed the effective date of the enforcement initial determination.

(4) Upon conclusion of a formal enforcement proceeding under this section, the Commission may:

(i) Modify a cease and desist order, consent order, and/or exclusion order in any manner necessary to prevent the unfair practices that were originally the basis for issuing such order;

(ii) Bring civil actions in a United States district court pursuant to paragraph (c) of this section (and section 337(f)(2) of the Tariff Act of 1930) to recover for the United States the civil penalty accruing to the United States under that section for the breach of a cease and desist order or a consent order, and to obtain a mandatory injunction incorporating the relief the Commission deems appropriate for enforcement of the cease and desist order or consent order; or

(iii) Revoke the cease and desist order or consent order and direct that the articles concerned be excluded from entry into the United States.

(5) Prior to effecting any modification, revocation, or exclusion under this section, the Commission shall consider the effect of such action upon the public health and welfare, competitive conditions in the U.S. economy, the production of like or directly competitive articles in the United States, and U.S. consumers.

(6) In lieu of or in addition to taking the action provided for in paragraph (b)(1) of this section, the Commission may issue, pursuant to section 337(i) of the Tariff Act of 1930, an order providing that any article imported in violation of the provisions of section 337 of the Tariff Act of 1930 and an outstanding final exclusion order issued pursuant to section 337(d) of the Tariff Act of 1930 be seized and forfeited to the United States, if the following conditions are satisfied:

(i) The owner, importer, or consignee of the article (or the agent of such person) previously attempted to import the article into the United States;

(ii) The article previously was denied entry into the United States by reason of a final exclusion order; and

(iii) Upon such previous denial of entry, the Secretary of the Treasury provided the owner, importer, or consignee of the article (or the agent of such person) with written notice of the aforesaid exclusion order and the fact that seizure and forfeiture would result from any further attempt to import the article into the United States.

(c) *Court enforcement.* To obtain judicial enforcement of an exclusion order, a cease and desist order, a consent order, or a sanctions order, the Commission may initiate a civil action in the U.S. district court. In a civil action under section 337(f)(2) of the Tariff Act of 1930, the Commission may seek to recover for the United States the civil penalty accruing to the United States under that section for the breach of a cease and desist order or a consent order, and may ask the court to issue a mandatory injunction incorporating the relief the Commission deems appropriate for enforcement of the cease and desist order or consent order. The Commission may initiate a proceeding to obtain judicial enforcement without any other type of proceeding otherwise available under section 337 or this subpart or without prior notice to any person, except as required by the court in which the civil action is initiated.

[59 FR 39039, Aug. 1, 1994, as amended at 73 FR 38327, July 7, 2008; 78 FR 23486, Apr. 19, 2013]

§ 210.76 Modification or rescission of exclusion orders, cease and desist orders, and consent orders.

(a) *Petitions for modification or rescission of exclusion orders, cease and desist orders, and consent orders.* (1) Whenever any person believes that changed conditions of fact or law, or the public interest, require that an exclusion order, cease and desist order, or consent order be modified or set aside, in whole or in part, such person may file with the Commission a petition requesting such relief. The Commission may also on its own initiative consider such action. The petition shall state the changes desired and the changed circumstances warranting such action, shall include materials and argument in support thereof, and shall be served on all parties to the investigation in which the exclusion order, cease and desist order, or consent order was issued. Any person may file an opposition to the petition within 10 days of service of the petition.

(2) If the petitioner previously has been found by the Commission to be in violation of section 337 of the Tariff Act of 1930 and if its petition requests a Commission determination that the petitioner is no longer in violation of that section or requests modification or rescission of an order issued pursuant to section 337 (d), (e), (f), (g), or (i) of the Tariff Act of 1930, the burden of proof in any proceeding initiated in response to the petition pursuant to paragraph (b) of this section shall be on the petitioner. In accordance with section 337(k)(2) of the Tariff Act, relief may be granted by the Commission with respect to such petition on the basis of new evidence or evidence that could not have been presented at the prior proceeding or on grounds that would permit relief from a judgment or order under the Federal Rules of Civil Procedure.

(b) *Commission action upon receipt of petition.* The Commission may thereafter institute a proceeding to modify or rescind the exclusion order, cease and desist order, or consent order by issuing a notice. The Commission may hold a public hearing and afford interested persons the opportunity to appear and be heard. After consideration of the petition, any responses thereto, and any information placed on the record at a public hearing or otherwise, the Commission shall take such action as it deems appropriate. The Commission may delegate any hearing under this section to the chief administrative law judge for designation of a presiding administrative law judge, who shall certify a recommended determination to the Commission.

(c) *Comments.* Parties may submit comments on the recommended determination within 10 days from the service of the recommended determination. Parties may submit responses thereto within 5 business days from service of any comments.

[59 FR 39039, Aug. 1, 1994, as amended at 61 FR 43433, Aug. 23, 1996; 78 FR 23486, Apr. 19, 2013]

§ 210.77 Temporary emergency action.

(a) Whenever the Commission determines, pending a formal enforcement proceeding under § 210.75(b), that without immediate action a violation of an exclusion order, cease and desist order, or consent order will occur and that subsequent action by the Commission would not adequately repair substantial harm caused by such violation, the Commission may immediately and without hearing or notice modify or revoke such order and, if it is revoked, replace the order with an appropriate exclusion order.

(b) Prior to taking any action under this section, the Commission shall consider the effect of such action upon the public health and welfare, competitive conditions in the U.S. economy, the production of like or directly competitive articles in the United States, and U.S. consumers. The Commission shall, if it has not already done so, institute a formal enforcement proceeding under § 210.75(b) at the time of taking action under this section or as soon as possible thereafter, in order to give the alleged violator and other interested parties a full opportunity to present information and views regarding the continuation, modification, or revocation of Commission action taken under this section.

§ 210.78 Notice of enforcement action to Government agencies.

(a) *Consultation.* The Commission may consult with or seek information from any Government agency when taking any action under this subpart.

(b) *Notification of Treasury.* The Commission shall notify the Secretary of the Treasury of any action under this subpart that results in a permanent or temporary exclusion of articles from entry, or the revocation of an order to such effect, or the issuance of an order compelling seizure and forfeiture of imported articles.

§ 210.79 Advisory opinions.

(a) *Advisory opinions.* Upon request of any person, the Commission may, upon such investigation as it deems necessary, issue an advisory opinion as to whether any person's proposed course of action or conduct would violate a Commission exclusion order, cease and desist order, or consent order. The Commission will consider whether issuance of such an advisory opinion would facilitate the enforcement of section 337 of the Tariff Act of 1930, would be in the public interest, and would benefit consumers and competitive conditions in the United States, and whether the person has a compelling business need for the advice and has framed his request as fully and accurately as possible. Advisory opinion proceedings are not subject to sections 554, 555, 556, 557, and 702 of title 5 of the United States Code.

(b) *Revocation.* The Commission may at any time reconsider any advice given under this section and, where the public interest requires, revoke its prior advice. In such event the person will be given notice of the Commission's intent to revoke as well as an opportunity to submit its views to the Commission. The Commission will not proceed against a person for violation of an exclusion order, cease and desist order, or consent order with respect to any action that was taken in good faith reliance upon the Commission's advice under this section, if all relevant facts were accurately presented to the Commission and such action was promptly discontinued upon notification of revocation of the Commission's advice.

[59 FR 39039, Aug. 1, 1994, as amended at 73 FR 38327, July 7, 2008]

APPENDIX A TO PART 210—ADJUDICATION AND ENFORCEMENT

Initial determination concerning:	Petitions for review due:	Response to petitions due:	Commission deadline for determining whether to review the initial determination:
1. Violation § 210.42(a)(1)	12 days from service of the initial determination.	8 days from service of any petition.	60 days from service of the initial determination (on private parties).
2. Summary initial determination that would terminate the investigation if it became the Commission's final determination § 210.42(c).	10 days from service of the initial determination.	5 business days from service of any petition.	45 days from service of the initial determination (on private parties).
3. Other matters § 210.42(c) ...	5 business days from service of the initial determination.	5 business days from service of any petition.	30 days from service of the initial determination (on private parties).
4. Forfeiture or return of respondents' bond § 210.50(d)(3).	10 days from service of the initial determination.	5 business days from service of any petition.	45 days from service of the initial determination (on private parties).
5. Forfeiture or return of complainant's temporary relief bond § 210.70(c).	10 days from service of the initial determination.	5 business days from service of any petition.	45 days from service of the initial determination (on private parties).
6. Formal enforcement proceedings § 210.75(b).	10 days from service of the enforcement initial determination.	5 business days from service of any petition.	45 days from service of the enforcement initial determination (on private parties).

[78 FR 23486, Apr. 19, 2013]

APPENDIX B TO PART 210—ADJUDICATION AND ENFORCEMENT

Recommended determination concerning:	Comments due:	Response to comments due:
Modification or Rescission § 210.76(a)(1)	10 days from service of the recommended determination.	5 business days from service of any comments.

[78 FR 23487, Apr. 19, 2013]

PART 212—IMPLEMENTATION OF THE EQUAL ACCESS TO JUSTICE ACT

Subpart A—General Provisions

Sec.
212.01   Purpose.
212.02   When the Act applies.
212.03   Proceedings covered.
212.04   Eligibility of applicants.
212.05   Standards for awards.
212.06   Allowable fees and expenses.
212.07   Rulemaking on maximum rates for attorney fees.

Subpart B—Information Required From Applicants

212.10   Contents of application.
212.11   Net worth exhibit.

212.12   Documentation of fees and expenses.
212.13   When an application may be filed.

Subpart C—Procedures for Considering Applications

212.20   Filing and service of documents.
212.21   Answer to application.
212.22   Reply.
212.23   Comments by other parties.
212.24   Settlement.
212.25   Further proceedings.
212.26   Determination.
212.27   Agency review.
212.28   Judicial review.
212.29   Payment of award.

AUTHORITY: Sec. 203(a)(1), Pub. L. 96–481, 94 Stat. 2325 (5 U.S.C. 504(c)(1)).

SOURCE: 47 FR 9391, Mar. 5, 1982, unless otherwise noted.

195

Subpart A—General Provisions

§ 212.01 Purpose.

(a) The Equal Access to Justice Act, 5 U.S.C. 504 (called "the Act" in this part), provides for the award of attorney fees and other expenses to eligible individuals and entities who are parties to certain administrative proceedings (called "adversary adjudications") before an agency. Under the Act an eligible party may receive an award when it prevails over an agency, unless the agency's position in the proceeding was substantially justified or special circumstances make an award unjust. The rules in this part describe the parties eligible for awards and the Commission proceedings that are covered. They also explain how to apply for awards, and the procedures and standards that the Commission will use to make them.

§ 212.02 When the Act applies.

The Act applies to any adversary adjudication pending before the Commission at any time between October 1, 1981 and September 30, 1984. This includes proceedings begun before October 1, 1981 if final Commission action has not been taken before that date, and proceedings pending on September 30, 1984, regardless of when they were initiated or when final Commission action occurs.

§ 212.03 Proceedings covered.

(a) The Act applies to adversary adjudications conducted by the Commission. These are adjudications under 5 U.S.C. 554 in which the position of the Commission is presented by an attorney or other representative who enters an appearance and participates in the proceeding. The Commission proceedings covered are those conducted under section 337 of the Tariff Act of 1930, 19 U.S.C. 1337. No award shall be made, however, for fees and expenses related to those portions of the proceedings conducted for the consideration of relief, the public interest, and bonding pursuant to subsections 337 (d), (e), and (f) of the Tariff Act of 1930 and 19 CFR 210.14.

(b) An award may be made against the Commission only in connection with a proceeding brought by the Commission upon its own complaint.

(c) If a proceeding includes both matters covered by the Act and matters specifically excluded from coverage, any award made will include only fees and expenses related to covered issues.

§ 212.04 Eligibility of applicants.

(a) To be eligible for an award of attorney fees and other expenses under the Act, the applicant must be a party to the adversary adjudication for which it seeks an award. The term *party* is defined in 5 U.S.C. 551(3) and 19 CFR 210.04. The applicant must show that it meets all conditions of eligibility set out in this subpart and in subpart B.

(b) The types of eligible applicants are as follows:

(1) An individual with a net worth of not more than $1 million;

(2) The sole owner of an unincorporated business who has a net worth of not more than $5 million, including both personal and business interests, and not more than 500 employees;

(3) A charitable or other tax-exempt organization described in section 501(c)(3) of the Internal Revenue Code (26 U.S.C. 501(c)(3)) with not more than 500 employees;

(4) A cooperative association as defined in section 15(a) of the Agricultural Marketing Act (12 U.S.C. 1144j(a)) with not more than 500 employees; and

(5) Any other partnership, corporation, association, or public or private organization with a net worth of not more than $5 million and not more than 500 employees.

(c) For the purpose of eligibility, the net worth and number of employees of an applicant shall be determined as of the date the adversary adjudication was initiated.

(d) An applicant who owns an unincorporated business will be considered to be an "individual" rather than a "sole owner of an unincorporated business" if the issues on which the applicant prevails are related primarily to personal interests rather than to business interests.

(e) The employees of an applicant include all persons who regularly perform services for remuneration for the applicant under the applicant's direction and control. Part-time employees shall be included on a proportional basis.

(f) The net worth and number of employees of the applicant and all of its affiliates shall be aggregated to determine eligibility. Any individual, corporation or other entity that directly or indirectly controls or owns a majority of the voting shares or other interest of the applicant, or any corporation or other entity of which the applicant directly or indirectly owns or controls a majority of the voting shares or other interest, will be considered an affiliate for purposes of this part, unless the presiding officer determines that such treatment would be unjust and contrary to the purposes of the Act in light of the actual relationship between the affiliated entities. In addition, the presiding officer may determine that financial relationships of the applicant other than those described in this paragraph constitute special circumstances that would make an award unjust.

(g) An applicant that participates in a proceeding primarily on behalf of one or more other persons or entities that would be ineligible is not itself eligible for an award.

§ 212.05 Standards for awards.

(a) The determination whether an applicant is a prevailing party shall be made on a case-by-case basis.

(b) A prevailing applicant may receive an award for fees and expenses incurred in connection with an adversary adjudication, or in a significant and discrete substantive portion of the adversary adjudication, unless the position of the Commission investigative attorney was substantially justified. The burden of proof that an award should not be made to an eligible prevailing applicant is on the Commission investigative attorney. An award may be avoided by showing that the position of the Commission was reasonable in law and fact.

(c) An award will be reduced or denied if the applicant has unduly or unreasonably protracted the adversary adjudication or if special circumstances make the award sought unjust. The burden of proof that an award should be reduced or denied for either of these reasons is on the Commission investigative attorney.

§ 212.06 Allowable fees and expenses.

(a) Awards will be based on rates customarily charged by persons engaged in the business of acting as attorneys, agents and expert witnesses, even if the services were made available without charge or at a reduced rate to the applicant.

(b) No award for the fee of an attorney or agent under these rules may exceed $75.00 per hour. No award to compensate an expert witness may exceed the highest rate at which the Commission pays expert witnesses. However, an award may include the reasonable expenses of the attorney, agent, or expert witness as a separate item if the attorney, agent or expert witness ordinarily charges clients separately for such expenses.

(c) In determining the reasonableness of the fee sought for an attorney, agent or expert witness, the presiding officer shall consider the following:

(1) If the attorney, agent or expert witness is in private practice, his or her customary fee for similar services, or, if an employee of the applicant, the fully allocated cost of the service;

(2) The prevailing rate for similar services in the community in which the attorney, agent or expert witness ordinarily performs services;

(3) The time actually spent in the representation of the applicant;

(4) The time reasonably spent in light of the difficulty or complexity of the issues in the adversary adjudication; and

(5) Such other factors as may bear on the value of the services provided.

(d) The reasonable cost of any study, analysis, engineering report, test, project or similar matter prepared on behalf of a party may be awarded to the extent that the charge for the service does not exceed the prevailing rate for similar services and the study or other matter was necessary for preparation of the applicant's case.

§ 212.07 Rulemaking   on   maximum rates for attorney fees.

(a) If warranted by an increase in the cost of living or by special circumstances (such as limited availability of attorneys qualified to handle certain types of proceedings), the Commission may adopt regulations providing that attorney fees may be awarded at a rate higher than $75 per hour in the proceedings covered by this part. The Commission will conduct any rulemaking proceedings for this purpose under the informal rulemaking procedures of the Administrative Procedure Act.

(b) Any person may file with the Commission a petition for rulemaking to increase the maximum rate for attorney fees. The petition should identify the rate the petitioner believes the Commission should establish. It should also explain fully the reasons why the higher rate is warranted. The Commission will respond to the petition within 60 days after it is filed by initiating a rulemaking proceeding, denying the petition, or taking other appropriate action.

Subpart B—Information Required From Applicants

§ 212.10   Contents of application.

(a) An application for an award of fees and expenses under the Act shall identify the applicant and the adversary adjudication for which an award is sought. The application shall show that the applicant has prevailed and identify the position of the Commission investigative attorney that the applicant alleges was not substantially justified. Unless the applicant is an individual, the application shall also state the number of employees of the applicant and describe briefly the type and purpose of its organization or business.

(b) The application shall also include a statement that the applicant's net worth does not exceed $1 million (if an individual) or $5 million (for all other applicants, including their affiliates). However, an applicant may omit this statement if:

(1) It attaches a copy of a ruling by the Internal Revenue Service that it qualifies as an organization described in section 501(c)(3) of the Internal Revenue Code (26 U.S.C. 501(c)(3)) or, in the case of a tax-exempt organization not required to obtain a ruling from the Internal Revenue Service on its exempt status, a statement that describes the basis for the applicant's belief that it qualifies under such section; or

(2) It states that it is a cooperative association as defined in section 15(a) of the Agricultural Marketing Act (12 U.S.C. 1141j(a)).

(c) The application shall state the amount of fees and expenses for which an award is sought.

(d) The application may also include any other matters that the applicant wishes the Commission to consider in determining whether and in what amount an award should be made.

(e) The application shall be signed by the applicant or an authorized officer or attorney of the applicant. It shall also contain or be accompanied by a written verification under oath or under penalty of perjury that the information provided in the application is true and correct.

§ 212.11   Net worth exhibit.

(a) Each applicant except a qualified tax-exempt organization or cooperative association must provide with its application a detailed exhibit showing the net worth of the applicant and any affiliates (as defined in § 212.04(f) of this part) when the proceeding was initiated. The exhibit may be in any form convenient to the applicant that provides full disclosure of the applicant's and its affiliates' assets and liabilities and is sufficient to determine whether the applicant qualifies under the standards in this part. The presiding officer may require an applicant to file additional information to determine its eligibility for an award.

(b) Ordinarily, the net worth exhibit will be included in the public record of the proceeding. However, an applicant that objects to public disclosure of information in any portion of the exhibit and believes there are legal grounds for withholding it from disclosure may submit that portion of the exhibit directly to the presiding officer in a sealed envelope labeled "Confidential Financial Information," accompanied by a motion to withhold the information from public disclosure. The motion shall describe the information sought to be withheld and explain in detail why it falls within one or more of the specific exemptions from mandatory disclosure under the Freedom of

Information Act, 5 U.S.C. 552(b)(1)–(9), why public disclosure of the information would adversely affect the applicant, and why disclosure is not required in the public interest. The material in question shall be served on the Commission investigative attorney or counsel representing another agency against which the applicant seeks an award, but need not be served on any other party to the proceeding. If the presiding officer finds that the information should not be withheld from disclosure, it shall be placed in the public record of the proceeding. Otherwise, any request to inspect or copy the exhibit shall be disposed of in accordance with the Commission's established procedures under the Freedom of Information Act, 19 CFR 201.17–201.21.

§212.12 Documentation of fees and expenses.

The application shall be accompanied by full documentation of the fees and expenses, including the cost of any study, analysis, engineering report, test, project or similar matter, for which an award is sought. A separate itemized statement shall be submitted for each professional firm or individual whose services are covered by the application, showing the hours spent in connection with the proceeding by each individual, a description of the specific services performed, the rate at which each fee has been computed, any expenses for which reimbursement is sought, the total amount claimed, and the total amount paid or payable by the applicant or by any other person or entity for the services provided. The presiding officer may require the applicant to provide vouchers, receipts, or other substantiation for any expenses claimed.

§212.13 When an application may be filed.

(a) An application may be filed whenever the applicant has prevailed in the adversary adjudication or in a significant and discrete substantive portion of the adversary adjudication, but in no case later than 30 days after the Commission's final disposition of the adversary adjudication.

(b) If review or reconsideration is sought or taken of a determination as to which an applicant believes it has prevailed, proceedings for the award of fees shall be stayed pending final disposition of the underlying controversy.

Subpart C—Procedures for Considering Applications

§212.20 Filing and service of documents.

Any application for an award or other pleading or document related to an application shall be filed and served on all parties to the adversary adjudication in the same manner as other pleadings in the adversary adjudication, except as provided in §212.11(b) for confidential financial information.

§212.21 Answer to application.

(a) Within 30 days after service of an application, the Commission investigative attorney shall file an answer to the application.

(b) If the applicant and the Commission investigative attorney believe that the issues in the fee application can be settled, they may jointly file a statement of their intent to negotiate a settlement. The filing of this statement shall extend the time for filing an answer for an additional 30 days, and further extensions may be granted by the presiding officer upon request by the applicant and the Commission investigative attorney.

(c) The answer shall explain in detail any objections to the award requested and identify the facts relied on in support of the position of the Commission. If the answer is based on any alleged facts not already in the record of the adversary adjudication, the Commission investigative attorney shall include with the answer supporting affidavits or a request for further proceedings under §212.25.

§212.22 Reply.

Within 15 days after service of an answer, the applicant may file a reply. If the reply is based on any alleged facts not already in the record of the adversary adjudication, the applicant shall include with the reply either supporting affidavits or a request for further proceedings under §212.25.

§ 212.23   Comments by other parties.

Any party to the adversary adjudication other than the applicant and the Commission investigative attorney may file comments on an application within 30 days after it is served or on an answer within 15 days after it is served. A commenting party may not participate further in proceedings on the application unless the presiding officer determines that the public interest requires such participation in order to permit full exploration of matters raised in the comments.

§ 212.24   Settlement.

The applicant and the Commission may agree on a proposed settlement of the award before final action on the application, either in connection with a settlement of the underlying adversary adjudication, or after the underlying adversary adjudication has been concluded. If a prevailing party and the Commission investigative attorney agree on a proposed settlement of an award before an application has been filed, the application shall be filed with the proposed settlement.

§ 212.25   Further proceedings.

(a) Ordinarily, the determination of an award will be made on the basis of the written record. However, on request of either the applicant or the Commission investigative attorney, or on his or her own initiative, the presiding officer may in his or her discretion order further proceedings, such as an informal conference, oral argument, additional written submissions or an evidentiary hearing. Such further proceedings shall be held only when necessary for full and fair resolution of the issues arising from the application, and shall be conducted as promptly as possible.

(b) A request that the presiding officer order further proceedings under this section shall specifically identify the information sought or the disputed issues and shall explain why the additional proceedings are necessary to resolve the issues.

§ 212.26   Determination.

The presiding officer shall issue a recommended determination on the application within 90 days after completion of proceedings on the application. The determination shall include written findings and conclusions on the applicant's eligibility and status as prevailing party, and an explanation of the reasons for any difference between the amount requested and the amount awarded. The determination shall also include, if at issue, findings on whether the position of the Commission investigative attorney was substantially justified, whether the applicant unduly protracted the proceedings, or whether special circumstances make an award unjust.

§ 212.27   Agency review.

Except as otherwise authorized by the presiding officer, the parties shall be allowed ten (10) days from the date of service of the recommended determination to file exceptions to the recommended determination and alternative findings of fact and conclusions of law with the Commission. Upon receipt of the recommended determination, the Commission shall review the same and issue a final determination on the application or remand the application to the presiding officer for further proceedings.

§ 212.28   Judicial review.

Judicial review of final Commission determinations on awards may be sought as provided in 5 U.S.C. 504(c)(2).

§ 212.29   Payment of award.

An applicant seeking payment of an award shall submit to the Office of Finance of the Commission a copy of the Commission's final determination granting the award, accompanied by a statement that the applicant will not seek review of the decision in the United States courts. The address for submission to the Commission is: United States International Trade Commission, Office of Finance, 500 E Street SW., Washington, DC 20436. The Commission will pay the amount to the applicant within 60 days, unless judicial review of the award or of the underlying determination of the adversary adjudication has been sought by the applicant or any other party to the proceeding.

[68 FR 32979, June 3, 2003]

SUBCHAPTER D—SPECIAL PROVISIONS

PART 213—TRADE REMEDY ASSISTANCE

Sec.
213.1 Purpose and applicability of part.
213.2 Definitions.
213.3 Determination of small business eligibility.
213.4 Disclosure of receipt of technical assistance.
213.5 Access to Commission resources.
213.6 Information concerning assistance.

AUTHORITY: 19 U.S.C. 1335, 1339.

SOURCE: 54 FR 33883, Aug. 17, 1989, unless otherwise noted.

§ 213.1 Purpose and applicability of part.

(a) Section 339 of the Tariff Act of 1930, as amended, establishes in the Commission an office known as the Trade Remedy Assistance Office and directs the Commission to provide general information to the public, upon request, and, to the extent feasible, assistance and advice to interested parties concerning the remedies and benefits available under the trade laws identified in § 213.2(b) and the procedures to be followed and appropriate filing dates in investigations under the trade laws. In coordination with other agencies administering the trade laws, the Trade Remedy Assistance Office also shall provide technical assistance, as defined in § 213.2(d), to eligible small businesses seeking to obtain the remedies and benefits available under the trade laws.

(b) The rules in this part govern the establishment of the Trade Remedy Assistance Office, its function, small business eligibility for technical assistance and procedures for obtaining such assistance. Members of the public seeking general information from the Trade Remedy Assistance Office are not subject to the application procedures set forth in this part.

§ 213.2 Definitions.

(a) *Office*. The Trade Remedy Assistance Office (hereinafter *Office*) provides general information to the public, upon request, and, to the extent feasible, assistance and advice to interested par-

ties concerning the remedies and benefits available under the trade laws identified in § 213.2(b) and the procedures to be followed and appropriate filing dates in investigations under those trade laws. In coordination with other agencies responsible for administering the trade laws listed in § 213.2(b), the Office also provides technical assistance, as defined in § 213.2(d) to eligible small businesses that seek to obtain remedies and benefits under the trade laws. The Office's address is Trade Remedy Assistance Office, U.S. International Trade Commission, 500 E Street SW., Washington, DC 20436.

(b) *Trade laws.* The trade laws (with respect to which general information and technical assistance are available) are defined as:

(1) Chapter 1 of title II of the Trade Act of 1974 (19 U.S.C. 2251 *et seq.*, relating to injury caused by import competition);

(2) Chapters 2 and 3 of such title II (relating to adjustment assistance for workers and firms);

(3) Chapter 1 of title III of the Trade Act of 1974 (19 U.S.C. 2411 *et seq.*, relating to relief from foreign import restrictions and export subsidies);

(4) Title VII of the Tariff Act of 1930 (19 U.S.C. 1671 *et seq.*, relating to the imposition of countervailing duties and antidumping duties);

(5) Section 232 of the Trade Expansion Act of 1962 (19 U.S.C. 1862, relating to the safeguarding of national security);

(6) Section 337 of the Tariff Act of 1930 (19 U.S.C. 1337, relating to unfair practices in import trade); and

(7) Section 406 of the Trade Act of 1974 (19 U.S.C. 2436, relating to market disruption).

(c) *Administering agencies.* Administering agency refers to the agency or agencies responsible for administering a particular trade law. The trade laws relating to injury caused by import competition, unfair practices in import trade and market disruption are administered by the Commission. The trade laws relating to countervailing and antidumping duties are jointly administered by the Commission and the

Department of Commerce. The trade laws relating to adjustment assistance for firms and safeguarding national security are administered by the Department of Commerce. The trade law relating to adjustment assistance for workers is administered by the Department of Labor. The trade law relating to relief from foreign import restrictions and export subsidies is administered by the United States Trade Representative.

(d) *Technical assistance.* Technical assistance is informal advice and assistance, including informal legal advice, provided under 19 U.S.C. 1339(b) and intended to enable eligible small businesses to determine the appropriateness of pursuing particular trade remedies, to prepare petitions and complaints and to seek to obtain the remedies and benefits available under the trade laws identified in § 213.2(b). Technical assistance is available to eligible small businesses at any time until the completion of administrative review or of an appeal to the administering agency regarding proceedings under the trade laws listed in § 213.2(b). Technical assistance does not include legal representation of an eligible small business or advocacy on its behalf and receipt of technical assistance does not ensure that the recipient will prevail in any trade remedy proceeding. The Office provides such technical assistance independently of other Commission staff but may consult with other staff as appropriate.

(e) *Applicant.* An applicant is an individual, partnership, corporation, joint venture, trade or other association, cooperative, group of workers, or certified or recognized union, or other entity that applies for technical assistance under this part.

(f) *Eligible small business.* An eligible small business is an applicant that the Office has determined to be entitled to technical assistance under 19 U.S.C. 1339(b) in accordance with the SBA size standards and the procedures set forth in this part.

(g) *SBA size standards.* The Office has adopted for its use SBA size standards, which are the small business size standards of the Small Business Ad-

ministration set forth in 13 CFR part 121.

[54 FR 33883, Aug. 17, 1989, as amended at 80 FR 39380, July 9, 2015

§ 213.3 Determination of small business eligibility.

(a) *Application for technical assistance from small businesses.* An applicant for technical assistance under 19 U.S.C. 1339(b) must certify that it qualifies as a small business under the appropriate size standard(s) and that it is an independently owned and operated company. An application for technical assistance is available from the Office and on the Commission's Web site. The application must be signed under oath by an officer or principal of the applicant. The completed application should be submitted to the Office at the address set forth in § 213.2(a).

(b) *Application for technical assistance from joint applicants, trade associations and unions.* If several businesses jointly or simultaneously from the same industry apply for technical assistance, each business must meet the appropriate SBA size standard(s) and so certify. If a trade association applies for technical assistance, an officer of the trade association must certify that eighty (80) percent of the trade association's members are companies that meet the appropriate size standard(s) and provide a listing of members of the association. If a union applies for technical assistance, an officer of the union must certify that the union has less than ten thousand (10,000) members within the industry for which trade relief is being sought. Applications for trade associations or for unions to request technical assistance are available from the Office. Applications must be signed under oath by an officer of the association or union and completed applications should be submitted to the Office as set forth in § 213.2(a).

(c) *Determination of eligibility and notification of determination.* The Office shall determine whether the applicant is eligible for technical assistance and notify the applicant of the determination within ten (10) days of receipt of a properly completed application. Pursuant to 19 U.S.C. 1339(c)(1), the Office's determination of eligibility is not reviewable by any other agency or by any court.

(d) *Notification to administering agencies.* When an applicant seeks technical assistance on matters involving the trade laws, and the Office determines that the applicant is eligible for technical assistance, the Office shall:

(1) Promptly notify the appropriate administering agency or agencies of the Office's determination that the applicant is eligible to receive technical assistance; and

(2) Consult with the administering agency or agencies as to the provision of technical assistance to that applicant.

[54 FR 33883, Aug. 17, 1989, as amended at 80 FR 39380, July 9, 2015

§ 213.4 Disclosure of receipt of technical assistance.

An eligible small business that has received technical assistance from the Office must state that it has received technical assistance from the Trade Remedy Assistance Office in any resulting petition, complaint or application which is filed with the Commission or any other agency which administers the trade law under which remedies or benefits are sought.

§ 213.5 Access to Commission resources.

Commission resources, in addition to the Office's resources, are available to an eligible small business to the same extent as those resources are available to members of the general public. No special rights of access to Commission resources shall be accorded to an eligible small business.

§ 213.6 Information concerning assistance.

Any person may contact the Office with questions regarding eligibility for technical assistance. Summaries of the trade laws and the SBA size standards can be obtained by writing to the Trade Remedy Assistance Office, U.S. International Trade Commission, 500 E Street SW., Washington, DC 20436. Information is also provided on the Commission's Web site at *http://www.usitc.gov.*

[80 FR 39380, July 9, 2015]

PARTS 214–219 [RESERVED]

PART 220—PROCESS FOR CONSIDERATION OF PETITIONS FOR DUTY SUSPENSIONS AND REDUCTIONS

Sec.
220.1 Applicability of part.
220.2 Definitions applicable to this part.
220.3 Who may file a petition, format for filing.
220.4 Time for filing.
220.5 Contents of petition.
220.6 Article description.
220.7 Properly filed petition.
220.8 Consolidation of petitions.
220.9 Withdrawal of petitions, amendments to petitions.
220.10 Commission review of petitions and disclosure forms.
220.11 Commission preliminary report.
220.12 Commission final report.
220.13 Confidential business information.
220.14 Application of other Commission rules.

AUTHORITY: 19 U.S.C. 1335; Public Law 114–159, 130 Stat. 396 (19 U.S.C. 1332 note).

SOURCE: 81 FR 67149, Sept. 30, 2016, unless otherwise noted.

§ 220.1 Applicability of part.

This part applies to proceedings of the Commission under the American Manufacturing Competitiveness Act of 2016, Public Law 114–159, 130 Stat. 396 (19 U.S.C. 1332 note).

§ 220.2 Definitions applicable to this part.

For the purposes of this part, the following terms have the meanings hereby assigned to them:

(a) *Act* means the American Manufacturing Competitiveness Act of 2016.

(b) *HTS* means Harmonized Tariff Schedule of the United States.

(c) *Committees* means the House Committee on Ways and Means and Senate Committee on Finance.

(d) *Commission disclosure form* means the information submitted to the Commission by a petitioner as part of a petition for a duty suspension or reduction that contains the following:

(1) The contact information for any known importers of the article to

which the proposed duty suspension or reduction would apply.

(2) A certification by the petitioner that the proposed duty suspension or reduction is available to any person importing the article to which the proposed duty suspension or reduction would apply.

(3) A certification that the petitioner is a likely beneficiary of the proposed duty suspension or reduction.

(e) *Duty suspension or reduction* refers to an amendment to the HTS for a period not to exceed 3 years that—

(1) Extends an existing temporary duty suspension or reduction on an article under chapter 99 of the HTS; or

(2) Provides for a new temporary duty suspension or reduction on an article under that chapter.

(f) *Likely beneficiary* means an individual or entity likely to utilize, or benefit directly from the utilization of, an article that is the subject of a petition for a duty suspension or reduction.

(g) *Domestic producer* means a person that demonstrates production, or imminent production, in the United States of an article that is identical to, or like or directly competitive with, an article to which a petition for a duty suspension or reduction would apply.

(h) *Domestic production* means the production of an article that is identical to, or like or directly competitive with, an article to which a petition for a duty suspension or reduction would apply, for which a domestic producer has demonstrated production, or imminent production, in the United States.

(1) "Identical" article means a domestic article that has the same inherent or intrinsic characteristics and is classified in the same HTS rate line as the article that is the subject of a petition for duty suspension or reduction;

(2) "Like" article means a domestic article that is substantially identical in inherent or intrinsic characteristics (*i.e.*, materials from which made, appearance, quality, texture, etc.) as the article that is the subject of a petition for duty suspension or reduction; and

(3) "Directly competitive" article means a domestic article which, although not substantially identical in its inherent or intrinsic characteristics, is substantially equivalent for commercial purposes, that is, adapted to the same uses and essentially interchangeable therefor as the article that is the subject of a petition for duty suspension or reduction.

(i) *Imminent production* normally means production planned to begin within 3 years of the date on which the petition is filed.

§220.3 **Who may file a petition, format for filing.**

(a) *Who may file.* A petition under this part may be filed by members of the public who can demonstrate that they are likely beneficiaries of duty suspensions or reductions. A member of the public for these purposes would generally be a firm, importer of record, a manufacturer that uses the imported article, or a government entity at the U.S. Federal, state, or local level.

(b) *Format for filing.* Each such petition shall be submitted via the secure Commission web portal designated by the Commission and in the format designated by the Commission. The Commission will not accept petitions submitted in paper or in any other form or format. Petitions, including any attachments thereto, shall otherwise comply with the Commission's Handbook on MTB Filing Procedures as posted on the Commission's Web site.

§220.4 **Time for filing.**

Petitions for duty suspensions and reductions and Commission disclosure forms must be filed not later than 60 days after the Commission publishes in the FEDERAL REGISTER and on its Web site a notice requesting members of the public to submit this information. The Commission will publish notice requesting such petitions and disclosure forms not later than October 15, 2016, and October 15, 2019.

§220.5 **Contents of petition.**

The petition shall include the following information:

(a) The name, telephone number, and postal and email address of the petitioner, and if appropriate, its representative in the matter;

(b) A statement as to whether the petitioner is requesting an extension of an existing duty suspension or reduction or a new duty suspension or reduction; and if a duty reduction, the amount of the reduction;

(c) A certification that the petitioner is a likely beneficiary of the proposed duty suspension or reduction;

(d) An article description that meets the requirements of § 220.6 for the proposed duty suspension or reduction and identifies the permanent classification of the article in chapters 1–97 of the HTS and the Chemical Abstracts Service registry number (if applicable);

(e) To the extent available—

(1) A classification ruling of U.S. Customs and Border Protection (CBP) with respect to the article; and

(2) A copy of CBP documentation indicating where the article is classified in the HTS.

(f) A brief and general description of the article and its uses, and the names of the principal countries from which it is imported.

(g) A brief description of the industry in the United States that uses the article.

(h) For each HTS number included in the article description, an estimate of the total value (in United States dollars) of imports of the article for the calendar year preceding the year in which the petition is filed, for the calendar year in which the petition is filed, and for each of the 5 calendar years after the calendar year in which the petition is filed, including an estimate of the total value of such imports for each HTS article, by the person who submits the petition and by any other importers, if available.

(i) The name of each person that imports the article, if available.

(j) A description of any domestic production of the article, if available.

(k) A Commission disclosure form as defined in § 220.2(d).

(l) The names of any likely beneficiaries, and their contact information.

(m) A certification that the petitioner has not separately filed, and has not withdrawn, a petition for duty suspension or reduction during the current filing cycle:

(1) For an article that is identical to that in the current petition;

(2) For an article whose article description includes the article covered by the current petition; or

(3) For an article that is included in the scope of the current petition.

(n) Such other information as the Commission may require.

§ 220.6   Article description.

(a) *In general.* The article description in the petition shall be provided in a format appropriate to be included in the amendment to chapter 99 of the HTS and shall include language that:

(1) Describes a specific class or kind of imported merchandise and provides any other information needed to distinguish the covered products from other goods;

(2) Is suitable for incorporation in the HTS in the column entitled "Article Description" for each tariff heading in HTS chapter 99 that affords a temporary duty suspension or reduction;

(3) Describes covered products in their condition as imported, based primarily upon the goods' discernible physical characteristics at the time of importation;

(4) Is sufficiently clear as to be administrable by CBP; and

(5) Is otherwise required by this part or accomplishes the purposes of the Act.

(b) *Article descriptions that are not recommended.* The Commission will generally consider proposed article descriptions containing the following kinds of information or criteria as preventing the relevant petition from being recommended for inclusion in a miscellaneous tariff bill, unless input received from the U.S. Department of Commerce (Commerce) or CBP provides a basis for the Commission's analysis under the Act:

(1) "Actual use" or "chief use" criteria;

(2) Trade-marked or similarly protected terms or names, brand names, proprietary names, part numbers, or other company-specific names;

(3) Language—

(i) Describing goods that are illegal to import, where the petitioner is not a government entity;

(ii) Describing goods that are covered by tariff-rate quota provisions; or

(iii) Seeking to alter the tariff treatment provided in subchapter III or IV of chapter 99 of the HTS; or

(4) An HTS subheading number(s) that would alter or attempt to alter the classification of the product in chapters 1 through 97 of the HTS.

§ 220.7 Properly filed petition.

(a) *In general.* A petition will not be considered to be properly filed unless the petition and the Commission disclosure form are filed in accordance with and contain the information required by §§ 220.3 through 220.5

(b) *Identical and overlapping petitions.* (1) A petition will not be considered to be properly filed if the petitioner has previously filed, and has not withdrawn, a petition for duty suspension or reduction during the current filing cycle:

(i) For an article that is identical to that in the current petition;

(ii) For an article whose article description includes the article covered by the current petition; or

(iii) For an article that is included in the scope of the current petition.

(2) Should the Commission find that a petitioner has filed one or more identical or overlapping petitions and that such earlier filed petitions have not been withdrawn, the Commission will generally consider the earliest filed pending petition to be the petition of the petitioner.

§ 220.8 Consolidation of petitions.

Should the Commission receive petitions for duty suspensions or reductions from multiple petitioners for identical or overlapping articles classified in the same HTS subheading or subheadings, the Commission may consolidate the petitions and publish a single recommendation so that a single proposed HTS chapter 99 provision for the articles is presented in the Commission's preliminary and final reports.

§ 220.9 Withdrawal of petitions, amendments to petitions.

(a) *Withdrawal of petitions.* A petitioner may withdraw a petition for duty suspension or reduction filed under this part at any time prior to the date on which the Commission submits its final report. It shall do so by notifying the Commission through the Commission's designated secure web portal of its withdrawal and the notification shall include the name of the petitioner, the Commission identification number for the petition, and the HTS number for the article concerned.

(b) *Submission of new petition.* A petitioner who withdraws a petition for duty suspension or reduction that was timely filed under § 220.4 may submit a new petition, but only during the 60-day period described in § 220.4.

(c) *Amendments to petitions.* A petitioner may not amend or otherwise change a petition once it is submitted. If a petitioner wishes to amend or otherwise change a petition, such as to correct an error, the petitioner must withdraw the petition and file a new petition containing the changes in accordance with paragraphs (a) and (b) of this section.

§ 220.10 Commission review of petitions and disclosure forms.

(a) *Commission publication and public availability.* Not later than 30 days after expiration of the 60-day period for filing petitions for duty suspensions and reductions, the Commission will publish on its Web site the petitions for duty suspensions and reductions submitted under § 220.3 that were timely filed and contain the information required under § 220.5. When circumstances allow, the Commission may post such petitions on its Web site earlier than 30 days after expiration of the 60-day period for filing petitions.

(b) *Public comment.* Not later than 30 days after expiration of the 60-day period for filing petitions, the Commission will also publish in the FEDERAL REGISTER and on its Web site a notice requesting members of the public to submit comments on the petitions for duty suspensions and reductions. To be considered, such comments must be filed through the Commission's secure web portal during the 45-day period following publication of the Commission's notice requesting comments from members of the public. Comments, including any attachments thereto, must otherwise comply with the Commission's Handbook on MTB Filing Procedures as posted on the Commission's

Web site. For purposes of this section, all petitions posted by the Commission on its Web site, whether or not posted early, shall be deemed to be officially published by the Commission on its Web site on the date of publication of the notice seeking written comments from members of the public on the petitions.

§ 220.11 Commission preliminary report.

(a) Not later than 150 days after the Commission publishes the petitions and Commission disclosure forms submitted, the Commission will submit a preliminary report on the petitions filed to the Committees. The report will include the following information for each petition filed—

(1) The HTS heading or subheading in which each article that is the subject of a petition is classified, as identified by documentation supplied to the Commission and any supporting information obtained by the Commission.

(2) A determination of whether or not domestic production of the article that is the subject of the petition exists, taking into account the report of the Secretary of Commerce under section 3(c)(1) of the Act, and, if such production exists, whether or not a domestic producer of the article objects to the duty suspension or reduction.

(3) Any technical changes to the description of the article that is the subject of the petition for the duty suspension or reduction that are necessary for purposes of administration when the article is presented for importation, taking into account the report of the Secretary of Commerce under section 3(c)(2) of the Act.

(4) An estimate of the amount of loss in revenue to the United States that would no longer be collected if the duty suspension or reduction takes effect.

(5) A determination of whether or not the duty suspension or reduction is available to any person that imports the article that is the subject of the duty suspension or reduction.

(6) The likely beneficiaries of each duty suspension or reduction, including whether the petitioner is a likely beneficiary.

(b) The preliminary report will also include the following information:

(1) A list of petitions for duty suspensions and reductions that meet the requirements of the Act without modifications.

(2) A list of petitions for duty suspensions and reductions for which the Commission recommends technical corrections (*i.e.*, corrections to the article description that do not otherwise substantially alter the scope or HTS classification of the articles covered by the petition) in order to meet the requirements of the Act, with the correction specified.

(3) A list of petitions for duty suspensions and reductions for which the Commission recommends modifications to the amount of the duty suspension or reduction that is the subject of the petition to comply with the requirements of the Act, with the modification specified.

(4) A list of petitions for duty suspensions and reductions for which the Commission recommends modifications to the scope of the articles that are the subject of the petitions in order to address objections by domestic producers to such petitions, with the modifications specified.

(5) A list of the following:

(i) Petitions for duty suspensions and reductions that the Commission has determined do not contain the information required under section 3(b)(2) of the Act.

(ii) Petitions for duty suspensions and reductions with respect to which the Commission has determined the petitioner is not a likely beneficiary.

(6) A list of petitions for duty suspensions and reductions that the Commission does not recommend for inclusion in a miscellaneous tariff bill, other than petitions specified in section 3(b)(3)(C)(ii)(V) of the Act.

(c) The Commission will forward to the Committees any additional information submitted to the Commission by the Secretary of Commerce after the Commission transmits its preliminary report.

§ 220.12 Commission final report.

(a) The Commission will submit its final report on each petition for a duty suspension or reduction specified in the preliminary report to the Committees not later than 60 days after the Commission submits its preliminary report. The final report will contain the following information—

(1) The information required to be included in a preliminary report under section 3(b)(3)(C)(i)–(ii) of the Act and updated as appropriate after considering any information submitted by the Committees under section 3(b)(3)(D) of the Act.

(2) A determination of the Commission whether—

(i) The duty suspension or reduction can likely be administered by U.S. Customs and Border Protection;

(ii) The estimated loss in revenue to the United States from the duty suspension or reduction does not exceed $500,000 in a calendar year during which the duty suspension or reduction would be in effect; and

(iii) The duty suspension or reduction is available to any person importing the articles that is the subject of the duty suspension or reduction.

(b) [Reserved]

§ 220.13 Confidential business information.

(a) *In general.* The Commission will not release information which the Commission considers to be confidential business information within the meaning of § 201.6(a) of this chapter unless the party submitting the confidential business information had notice, at the time of submission, that such information would be released by the Commission, or such party subsequently consents to the release of the information.

(b) *Exceptions.* (1) In calculating the estimated revenue loss required under the Act, the Commission may base its estimates in whole or in part on the estimated values of imports submitted by petitioners in their petitions.

(2) The Commission may disclose some or all of the confidential business information provided to the Commission in petitions and public comments to the U.S. Department of Commerce for use in preparing its report to the Commission and the Committees, and to the U.S. Department of Agriculture and CBP for use in providing information for Commerce's report.

§ 220.14 Application of other Commission rules.

Commission rules applicable to the initiation and conduct of investigations, including rules set out in subpart B of part 201 of this chapter (except § 201.9 (methods employed in obtaining information), § 201.14(a) (computation of time), and § 201.15 (attorneys or agents)), shall not apply to Commission proceedings under this part.

PARTS 221–299 [RESERVED]

CHAPTER III—INTERNATIONAL TRADE ADMINISTRATION, DEPARTMENT OF COMMERCE

Part		Page
300–350	[Reserved]	
351	Antidumping and countervailing duties	213
354	Procedures for imposing sanctions for violation of an antidumping or countervailing duty administrative protective order	320
356	Procedures and rules for implementing Article 1904 of the North American Free Trade Agreement	329
358	Supplies for use in emergency relief work	349
360	Steel import monitoring and analysis system	351
361–399	[Reserved]	

PARTS 300-350 [RESERVED]

PART 351—ANTIDUMPING AND COUNTERVAILING DUTIES

Subpart A—Scope and Definitions

Sec.
351.101 Scope.
351.102 Definitions.
351.103 Central Records Unit and Administrative Protective Order and Dockets Unit.
351.104 Record of proceedings.
351.105 Public, business proprietary, privileged, and classified information.
351.106 *De minimis* net countervailable subsidies and weighted-average dumping margins disregarded.
351.107 Cash deposit rates for nonproducing exporters; rates in antidumping proceedings involving a nonmarket economy country.

Subpart B—Antidumping and Countervailing Duty Procedures

351.201 Self-initiation.
351.202 Petition requirements.
351.203 Determination of sufficiency of petition.
351.204 Time periods and persons examined; voluntary respondents; exclusions.
351.205 Preliminary determination.
351.206 Critical circumstances.
351.207 Termination of investigation.
351.208 Suspension of investigation.
351.209 Violation of suspension agreement.
351.210 Final determination.
351.211 Antidumping order and countervailing duty order.
351.212 Assessment of antidumping and countervailing duties; provisional measures deposit cap; interest on certain overpayments and underpayments
351.213 Administrative review of orders and suspension agreements under section 751(a)(1) of the Act.
351.214 New shipper reviews under section 751(a)(2)(B) of the Act.
351.215 Expedited antidumping review and security in lieu of estimated duty under section 736(c) of the Act.
351.216 Changed circumstances review under section 751(b) of the Act.
351.217 Reviews to implement results of subsidies enforcement proceeding under section 751(g) of the Act.
351.218 Sunset reviews under section 751(c) of the Act.
351.219 Reviews of countervailing duty orders in connection with an investigation under section 753 of the Act.
351.220 Countervailing duty review at the direction of the President under section 762 of the Act.
351.221 Review procedures.
351.222 Revocation of orders; termination of suspended investigations.
351.223 Procedures for initiation of downstream product monitoring.
351.224 Disclosure of calculations and procedures for the correction of ministerial errors.
351.225 Scope rulings.

Subpart C—Information and Argument

351.301 Time limits for submission of factual information.
351.302 Extension of time limits; return of untimely filed or unsolicited material.
351.303 Filing, document identification, format, translation, service, and certification of documents.
351.304 Establishing business proprietary treatment of information.
351.305 Access to business proprietary information.
351.306 Use of business proprietary information.
351.307 Verification of information.
351.308 Determinations on the basis of the facts available.
351.309 Written argument.
351.310 Hearings.
351.311 Countervailable subsidy practice discovered during investigation or review.
351.312 Industrial users and consumer organizations.
351.313 Attorneys or representatives.

Subpart D—Calculation of Export Price, Constructed Export Price, Fair Value, and Normal Value

351.401 In general.
351.402 Calculation of export price and constructed export price; reimbursement of antidumping and countervailing duties.
351.403 Sales used in calculating normal value; transactions between affiliated parties.
351.404 Selection of the market to be used as the basis for normal value.
351.405 Calculation of normal value based on constructed value.
351.406 Calculation of normal value if sales are made at less than cost of production.
351.407 Calculation of constructed value and cost of production.
351.408 Calculation of normal value of merchandise from nonmarket economy countries.
351.409 Differences in quantities.
351.410 Differences in circumstances of sale.
351.411 Differences in physical characteristics.
351.412 Levels of trade; adjustment for difference in level of trade; constructed export price offset.
351.413 Disregarding insignificant adjustments.

351.414 Comparison of normal value with export price (constructed export price).
351.415 Conversion of currency.

Subpart E—Identification and Measurement of Countervailable Subsidies

351.501 Scope.
351.502 Specificity of domestic subsidies.
351.503 Benefit.
351.504 Grants.
351.505 Loans.
351.506 Loan guarantees.
351.507 Equity.
351.508 Debt forgiveness.
351.509 Direct taxes.
351.510 Indirect taxes and import charges (other than export programs).
351.511 Provision of goods or services.
351.512 Purchase of goods. [Reserved]
351.513 Worker-related subsidies.
351.514 Export subsidies.
351.515 Internal transport and freight charges for export shipments.
351.516 Price preferences for inputs used in the production of goods for export.
351.517 Exemption or remission upon export of indirect taxes.
351.518 Exemption, remission, or deferral upon export of prior-stage cumulative indirect taxes.
351.519 Remission or drawback of import charges upon export.
351.520 Export insurance.
351.521 Import substitution subsidies. [Reserved]
351.522 Green light and green box subsidies.
351.523 Upstream subsidies.
351.524 Allocation of benefit to a particular time period.
351.525 Calculation of *ad valorem* subsidy rate and attribution of subsidy to a product.
351.526 Program-wide changes.
351.527 Transnational subsidies.

Subpart F—Subsidy Determinations Regarding Cheese Subject to an In-Quota Rate of Duty

351.601 Annual list and quarterly update of subsidies.
351.602 Determination upon request.
351.603 Complaint of price-undercutting by subsidized imports.
351.604 Access to information.

Subpart G—Applicability Dates

351.701 Applicability dates.
351.702 Applicability dates for countervailing duty regulations.
ANNEX I TO PART 351—DEADLINES FOR PARTIES IN COUNTERVAILING INVESTIGATIONS
ANNEX II TO PART 351—DEADLINES FOR PARTIES IN COUNTERVAILING ADMINISTRATIVE REVIEWS
ANNEX III TO PART 351—DEADLINES FOR PARTIES IN ANTIDUMPING INVESTIGATIONS
ANNEX IV TO PART 351—DEADLINES FOR PARTIES IN ANTIDUMPING ADMINISTRATIVE REVIEWS
ANNEX V TO PART 351—COMPARISON OF PRIOR AND NEW REGULATIONS
ANNEX VI TO PART 351—COUNTERVAILING INVESTIGATIONS TIMELINE
ANNEX VII TO PART 351—ANTIDUMPING INVESTIGATIONS TIMELINE
ANNEX VIII–A TO PART 351—SCHEDULE FOR 90–DAY SUNSET REVIEWS
ANNEX VIII–B TO PART 351—SCHEDULE FOR EXPEDITED SUNSET REVIEWS
ANNEX VIII–C TO PART 351—SCHEDULE FOR FULL SUNSET REVIEWS

AUTHORITY: 5 U.S.C. 301; 19 U.S.C. 1202 note; 19 U.S.C. 1303 note; 19 U.S.C. 1671 *et seq.*; and 19 U.S.C. 3538.

SOURCE: 62 FR 27379, May 19, 1997, unless otherwise noted.

EDITORIAL NOTE: Nomenclature changes to part 351 appear at 78 FR 62418, Oct. 22, 2013.

Subpart A—Scope and Definitions

§ 351.101 Scope.

(a) *In general.* This part contains procedures and rules applicable to antidumping and countervailing duty proceedings under title VII of the Act (19 U.S.C. 1671 *et seq.*), and also determinations regarding cheese subject to an in-quota rate of duty under section 702 of the Trade Agreements Act of 1979 (19 U.S.C. 1202 note). This part reflects statutory amendments made by titles I, II, and IV of the Uruguay Round Agreements Act, Pub. L. 103–465, which, in turn, implement into United States law the provisions of the following agreements annexed to the Agreement Establishing the World Trade Organization: Agreement on Implementation of Article VI of the General Agreement on Tariffs and Trade 1994; Agreement on Subsidies and Countervailing Measures; and Agreement on Agriculture.

(b) *Countervailing duty investigations involving imports not entitled to a material injury determination.* Under section 701(c) of the Act, certain provisions of the Act do not apply to countervailing duty proceedings involving imports from a country that is not a Subsidies Agreement country and is not entitled to a material injury determination by the Commission. Accordingly, certain provisions of this part referring to the

Commission may not apply to such proceedings.

(c) *Application to governmental importations.* To the extent authorized by section 771(20) of the Act, merchandise imported by, or for the use of, a department or agency of the United States Government is subject to the imposition of countervailing duties or antidumping duties under this part.

§351.102 **Definitions.**

(a) *Introduction.* The Act contains many technical terms applicable to antidumping and countervailing duty proceedings. In the case of terms that are not defined in this section or other sections of this part, readers should refer to the relevant provisions of the Act. This section:

(1) Defines terms that appear in the Act but are not defined in the Act;

(2) Defines terms that appear in this Part but do not appear in the Act; and

(3) Elaborates on the meaning of certain terms that are defined in the Act.

(b) *Definitions.* (1) *Act.* "Act" means the Tariff Act of 1930, as amended.

(2) *Administrative review.* "Administrative review" means a review under section 751(a)(1) of the Act.

(3) *Affiliated persons; affiliated parties.* "Affiliated persons" and "affiliated parties" have the same meaning as in section 771(33) of the Act. In determining whether control over another person exists, within the meaning of section 771(33) of the Act, the Secretary will consider the following factors, among others: Corporate or family groupings; franchise or joint venture agreements; debt financing; and close supplier relationships. The Secretary will not find that control exists on the basis of these factors unless the relationship has the potential to impact decisions concerning the production, pricing, or cost of the subject merchandise or foreign like product. The Secretary will consider the temporal aspect of a relationship in determining whether control exists; normally, temporary circumstances will not suffice as evidence of control.

(4) *Aggregate basis.* "Aggregate basis" means the calculation of a country-wide subsidy rate based principally on information provided by the foreign government.

(5) *Anniversary month.* "Anniversary month" means the calendar month in which the anniversary of the date of publication of an order or suspension of investigation occurs.

(6) *APO.* "APO" means an administrative protective order described in section 777(c)(1) of the Act.

(7) *Applicant.* "Applicant" means a representative of an interested party that has applied for access to business proprietary information under an administrative protective order.

(8) *Article 4/Article 7 review.* "Article 4/Article 7 review" means a review under section 751(g)(2) of the Act.

(9) *Article 8 violation review.* "Article 8 violation review" means a review under section 751(g)(1) of the Act.

(10) *Authorized applicant.* "Authorized applicant" means an applicant that the Secretary has authorized to receive business proprietary information under an APO under section 777(c)(1) of the Act.

(11) *Changed circumstances review.* "Changed circumstances review" means a review under section 751(b) of the Act.

(12) *Consumed in the production process.* Inputs "consumed in the production process" are inputs physically incorporated, energy, fuels and oil used in the production process and catalysts which are consumed in the course of their use to obtain the product.

(13) *Cumulative indirect tax.* "Cumulative indirect tax" means a multi-staged tax levied where there is no mechanism for subsequent crediting of the tax if the goods or services subject to tax at one stage of production are used in a succeeding stage of production.

(14) *Customs Service.* "Customs Service" means United States Customs and Border Protection of the United States Department of Homeland Security.

(15) *Department.* "Department" means the United States Department of Commerce.

(16) *Direct tax.* "Direct tax" means a tax on wages, profits, interests, rents, royalties, and all other forms of income, a tax on the ownership of real property, or a social welfare charge.

(17) *Domestic interested party.* "Domestic interested party" means an interested party described in subparagraph (C), (D), (E), (F), or (G) of section 771(9) of the Act.

(18) *Expedited antidumping review.* "Expedited antidumping review" means a review under section 736(c) of the Act.

(19) *Expedited sunset review.* "Expedited sunset review" means an expedited sunset review conducted by the Department where respondent interested parties provide inadequate responses to a notice of initiation under section 751(c)(3)(B) of the Act and § 351.218(e)(1)(ii).

(20) *Export insurance.* "Export insurance" includes, but is not limited to, insurance against increases in the cost of exported products, nonpayment by the customer, inflation, or exchange rate risks.

(21) *Factual information.* "Factual information" means:

(i) Evidence, including statements of fact, documents, and data submitted either in response to initial and supplemental questionnaires, or, to rebut, clarify, or correct such evidence submitted by any other interested party;

(ii) Evidence, including statements of fact, documents, and data submitted either in support of allegations, or, to rebut, clarify, or correct such evidence submitted by any other interested party;

(iii) Publicly available information submitted to value factors under § 351.408(c) or to measure the adequacy of remuneration under § 351.511(a)(2), or, to rebut, clarify, or correct such publicly available information submitted by any other interested party;

(iv) Evidence, including statements of fact, documents and data placed on the record by the Department, or, evidence submitted by any interested party to rebut, clarify or correct such evidence placed on the record by the Department; and

(v) Evidence, including statements of fact, documents, and data, other than factual information described in paragraphs (b)(21)(i)–(iv) of this section, in addition to evidence submitted by any other interested party to rebut, clarify, or correct such evidence.

(22) *Fair value.* "Fair value" is a term used during an antidumping investigation, and is an estimate of normal value.

(23) *Firm.* For purposes of subpart E (Identification and Measurement of Countervailable Subsidies), "firm" is used to refer to the recipient of an alleged countervailable subsidy, including any individual, company, partnership, corporation, joint venture, association, organization, or other entity.

(24) *Full sunset review.* "Full sunset review" means a full sunset review conducted by the Department under section 751(c)(5) of the Act where both domestic interested parties and respondent interested parties provide adequate response to a notice of initiation under section 751(c)(3)(B) of the Act and §§ 351.218(e)(1)(i) and 351.218(e)(1)(ii).

(25) *Government-provided.* "Government-provided" is a shorthand expression for an act or practice that is alleged to be a countervailable subsidy. The use of the term "government-provided" is not intended to preclude the possibility that a government may provide a countervailable subsidy indirectly in a manner described in section 771(5)(B)(iii) of the Act (indirect financial contribution).

(26) *Import charge.* "Import charge" means a tariff, duty, or other fiscal charge that is levied on imports, other than an indirect tax.

(27) *Importer.* "Importer" means the person by whom, or for whose account, subject merchandise is imported.

(28) *Indirect tax.* "Indirect tax" means a sales, excise, turnover, value added, franchise, stamp, transfer, inventory, or equipment tax, a border tax, or any other tax other than a direct tax or an import charge.

(29) *Interested party.* For the purpose of submitting an application for APO access (Form ITA–367), "Interested Party" means:

(i) A foreign manufacturer, producer, or exporter of subject merchandise,

(ii) The United States importer of subject merchandise,

(iii) A trade or business association a majority of the members of which are producers, exporters, or importers of subject merchandise,

(iv) The government of a country in which subject merchandise is produced or manufactured or from which such merchandise is exported,

(v) A manufacturer, producer, or wholesaler in the United States of a domestic like product,

(vi) A certified union or recognized union or group of workers which is representative of an industry engaged in the manufacture, production, or wholesale in the United States of a domestic like product,

(vii) A trade or business association a majority of whose members manufacture, produce, or wholesale a domestic like product in the United States,

(viii) An association, a majority of whose members is composed of interested parties described in subparagraph (C), (D), or (E) of section 771(9) of the Act with respect to a domestic like product, and

(ix) A coalition or trade association as described in section 771(9)(G) of the Act.

(30) *Investigation.* Under the Act and this part, there is a distinction between an antidumping or countervailing duty investigation and a proceeding. An "investigation" is that segment of a proceeding that begins on the date of publication of notice of initiation of investigation and ends on the date of publication of the earliest of:

(i) Notice of termination of investigation,

(ii) Notice of rescission of investigation,

(iii) Notice of a negative determination that has the effect of terminating the proceeding, or

(iv) An order.

(31) *Loan.* "Loan" means a loan or other form of debt financing, such as a bond.

(32) *Long-term loan.* "Long-term loan" means a loan, the terms of repayment for which are greater than one year.

(33) *New shipper review.* "New shipper review" means a review under section 751(a)(2) of the Act.

(34) *Order.* An "order" is an order issued by the Secretary under section 303, section 706, or section 736 of the Act or a finding under the Antidumping Act, 1921.

(35) *Ordinary course of trade.* "Ordinary course of trade" has the same meaning as in section 771(15) of the Act. The Secretary may consider sales or transactions to be outside the ordinary course of trade if the Secretary determines, based on an evaluation of all of the circumstances particular to the sales in question, that such sales or transactions have characteristics that are extraordinary for the market in question. Examples of sales that the Secretary might consider as being outside the ordinary course of trade are sales or transactions involving off-quality merchandise or merchandise produced according to unusual product specifications, merchandise sold at aberrational prices or with abnormally high profits, merchandise sold pursuant to unusual terms of sale, or merchandise sold to an affiliated party at a non-arm's length price.

(36) *Party to the proceeding.* "Party to the proceeding" means any interested party that actively participates, through written submissions of factual information or written argument, in a segment of a proceeding. Participation in a prior segment of a proceeding will not confer on any interested party "party to the proceeding" status in a subsequent segment.

(37) *Person.* "Person" includes any interested party as well as any other individual, enterprise, or entity, as appropriate.

(38) *Price adjustment.* "Price adjustment" means a change in the price charged for subject merchandise or the foreign like product, such as a discount, rebate, or other adjustment, including, under certain circumstances, a change that is made after the time of sale (*see* § 351.401(c)), that is reflected in the purchaser's net outlay.

(39) *Prior-stage indirect tax.* "Prior-stage indirect tax" means an indirect tax levied on goods or services used directly or indirectly in making a product.

(40) *Proceeding.* A "proceeding" begins on the date of the filing of a petition under section 702(b) or section 732(b) of the Act or the publication of a notice of initiation in a self-initiated investigation under section 702(a) or section 732(a) of the Act, and ends on the date of publication of the earliest notice of:

(i) Dismissal of petition,

(ii) Rescission of initiation,

(iii) Termination of investigation,

(iv) A negative determination that has the effect of terminating the proceeding,

(v) Revocation of an order, or

(vi) Termination of a suspended investigation.

(41) *Rates.* "Rates" means the individual weighted-average dumping margins, the individual countervailable subsidy rates, the country-wide subsidy rate, or the all-others rate, as applicable.

(42) *Respondent interested party.* "Respondent interested party" means an interested party described in subparagraph (A) or (B) of section 771(9) of the Act.

(43) *Sale.* A "sale" includes a contract to sell and a lease that is equivalent to a sale.

(44) *Secretary.* "Secretary" means the Secretary of Commerce or a designee. The Secretary has delegated to the Assistant Secretary for Enforcement and Compliance the authority to make determinations under title VII of the Act and this part.

(45) *Section 753 review.* "Section 753 review" means a review under section 753 of the Act.

(46) *Section 762 review.* "Section 762 review" means a review under section 762 of the Act.

(47) *Segment of proceeding—*(i) *In general.* An antidumping or countervailing duty proceeding consists of one or more segments. "Segment of a proceeding" or "segment of the proceeding" refers to a portion of the proceeding that is reviewable under section 516A of the Act.

(ii) *Examples.* An antidumping or countervailing duty investigation or a review of an order or suspended investigation, or a scope inquiry under § 351.225, each would constitute a segment of a proceeding.

(48) *Short-term loan.* "Short-term loan" means a loan, the terms of repayment for which are one year or less.

(49) *Sunset review.* "Sunset review" means a review under section 751(c) of the Act.

(50) *Suspension of liquidation.* "Suspension of liquidation" refers to a suspension of liquidation ordered by the Secretary under the authority of title

VII of the Act, the provisions of this Part, or section 516a(g)(5)(C) of the Act, or by a court of the United States in a lawsuit involving action taken, or not taken, by the Secretary under title VII of the Act or the provisions of this part.

(51) *Third country.* For purposes of subpart D, "third country" means a country other than the exporting country and the United States. Under section 773(a) of the Act and subpart D, in certain circumstances the Secretary may determine normal value on the basis of sales to a third country.

(52) *URAA.* "URAA" means the Uruguay Round Agreements Act.

[73 FR 3640, Jan. 22, 2008, as amended at 78 FR 21254, Apr. 10, 2013; 81 FR 15645, Mar. 24, 2016]

§ 351.103 **Central Records Unit and Administrative Protective Order and Dockets Unit.**

(a) Enforcement and Compliance's Central Records Unit maintains a Public File Room in Room 7046, U.S. Department of Commerce, 14th Street and Constitution Avenue, NW., Washington, DC 20230. The office hours of the Public File Room are between 8:30 a.m. and 5 p.m. Eastern Time on business days. Among other things, the Central Records Unit is responsible for maintaining an official and public record for each antidumping and countervailing duty proceeding (see § 351.104).

(b) Enforcement and Compliance's Administrative Protective Order and Dockets Unit (APO/Dockets Unit) is located in Room 18022, U.S. Department of Commerce, 14th Street and Constitution Avenue, NW., Washington, DC 20230. The office hours of the APO/ Dockets Unit are between 8:30 a.m. and 5 p.m. Eastern Time on business days. Among other things, the APO/Dockets Unit is responsible for receiving submissions from interested parties, issuing administrative protective orders (APOs), maintaining the APO service list and the public service list as provided for in paragraph (d) of this section, releasing business proprietary information under APO, and conducting APO violation investigations. The APO/Dockets Unit also is the contact point for questions and concerns regarding claims for business proprietary treatment of information and proper public versions of submissions under § 351.105 and § 351.304.

(c) *Filing of documents with the Department.* No document will be considered as having been received by the Secretary unless it is electronically filed in accordance with § 351.303(b)(2)(i) or, where applicable, in accordance with § 351.303(b)(2)(ii), it is manually submitted to the Enforcement and Compliance's APO/Dockets Unit in Room 18022 and is stamped with the date, and, where necessary, the time, of receipt. A manually filed document must be submitted with a cover sheet, in accordance with § 351.303(b)(3).

(d) *Service list.* The APO/Dockets Unit will maintain and make available a public service list for each segment of a proceeding. The service list for an application for a scope ruling is described in § 351.225(n).

(1) With the exception of a petitioner filing a petition in an investigation, all persons wishing to participate in a segment of a proceeding must file a letter of appearance. The letter of appearance must identify the name of the interested party, how that party qualifies as an interested party under § 351.102(b)(29) and section 771(9) of the Act, and the name of the firm, if any, representing the interested party in that particular segment of the proceeding. All persons who file a letter of appearance and qualify as an interested party will be included in the public service list for the segment of the proceeding in which the letter of appearance is submitted. The letter of appearance may be filed as a cover letter to an application for APO access. If the representative of the party is not requesting access to business proprietary information under APO, the letter of appearance must be filed separately from any other document filed with the Department. If the interested party is a coalition or association as defined in subparagraph (A), (E), (F) or (G) of section 771(9) of the Act, the letter of appearance must identify all of the members of the coalition or association.

(2) Each interested party that asks to be included on the public service list for a segment of a proceeding must des-ignate a person to receive service of documents filed in that segment.

[76 FR 39274, July 6, 2011, as amended at 80 FR 36473, June 25, 2015]

§ 351.104 Record of proceedings.

(a) *Official record*—(1) *In general.* The Secretary will maintain an official record of each antidumping and countervailing duty proceeding. The Secretary will include in the official record all factual information, written argument, or other material developed by, presented to, or obtained by the Secretary during the course of a proceeding that pertains to the proceeding. The official record will include government memoranda pertaining to the proceeding, memoranda of ex parte meetings, determinations, notices published in the FEDERAL REGISTER, and transcripts of hearings. The official record will contain material that is public, business proprietary, privileged, and classified. For purposes of section 516A(b)(2) of the Act, the record is the official record of each segment of the proceeding.

(2) *Material rejected.* (i) The Secretary, in making any determination under this part, will not use factual information, written argument, or other material that the Secretary rejects.

(ii) The official record will include a copy of a rejected document, solely for purposes of establishing and documenting the basis for rejecting the document, if the document was rejected because:

(A) The document, although otherwise timely, contains untimely filed new factual information (see § 351.301(b));

(B) The submitter made a nonconforming request for business proprietary treatment of factual information (see § 351.304);

(C) The Secretary denied a request for business proprietary treatment of factual information (see § 351.304);

(D) The submitter is unwilling to permit the disclosure of business proprietary information under APO (see § 351.304).

(iii) In no case will the official record include any document that the Secretary rejects as untimely filed, or any unsolicited questionnaire response unless the response is a voluntary response accepted under § 351.204(d) (see § 351.302(d)).

(b) *Public record.* The Secretary will maintain a public record of each proceeding. The record will consist of all material contained in the official record (see paragraph (a) of this section) that the Secretary decides is public information under § 351.105(b), government memoranda or portions of memoranda that the Secretary decides may be disclosed to the general public, and public versions of all determinations, notices, and transcripts. The public record will be available to the public for inspection and copying in the Central Records Unit (see § 351.103). The Secretary will charge an appropriate fee for providing copies of documents.

(c) *Protection of records.* Unless ordered by the Secretary or required by law, no record or portion of a record will be removed from the Department.

[62 FR 27379, May 19, 1997, as amended at 76 FR 39274, July 6, 2011]

§ 351.105 Public, business proprietary, privileged, and classified information.

(a) *Introduction.* There are four categories of information in an antidumping or countervailing duty proceeding: public, business proprietary, privileged, and classified. In general, public information is information that may be made available to the public, whereas business proprietary information may be disclosed (if at all) only to authorized applicants under an APO. Privileged and classified information may not be disclosed at all, even under an APO. This section describes the four categories of information.

(b) *Public information.* The Secretary normally will consider the following to be public information:

(1) Factual information of a type that has been published or otherwise made available to the public by the person submitting it;

(2) Factual information that is not designated as business proprietary by the person submitting it;

(3) Factual information that, although designated as business proprietary by the person submitting it, is in a form that cannot be associated with or otherwise used to identify activities of a particular person or that the Secretary determines is not properly designated as business proprietary;

(4) Publicly available laws, regulations, decrees, orders, and other official documents of a country, including English translations; and

(5) Written argument relating to the proceeding that is not designated as business proprietary.

(c) *Business proprietary information.* The Secretary normally will consider the following factual information to be business proprietary information, if so designated by the submitter:

(1) Business or trade secrets concerning the nature of a product or production process;

(2) Production costs (but not the identity of the production components unless a particular component is a trade secret);

(3) Distribution costs (but not channels of distribution);

(4) Terms of sale (but not terms of sale offered to the public);

(5) Prices of individual sales, likely sales, or other offers (but not components of prices, such as transportation, if based on published schedules, dates of sale, product descriptions (other than business or trade secrets described in paragraph (c)(1) of this section), or order numbers);

(6) Names of particular customers, distributors, or suppliers (but not destination of sale or designation of type of customer, distributor, or supplier, unless the destination or designation would reveal the name);

(7) In an antidumping proceeding, the exact amount of the dumping margin on individual sales;

(8) In a countervailing duty proceeding, the exact amount of the benefit applied for or received by a person from each of the programs under investigation or review (but not descriptions of the operations of the programs, or the amount if included in official public statements or documents or publications, or the *ad valorem* countervailable subsidy rate calculated for each person under a program);

(9) The names of particular persons from whom business proprietary information was obtained;

(10) The position of a domestic producer or workers regarding a petition; and

(11) Any other specific business information the release of which to the public would cause substantial harm to the competitive position of the submitter.

(d) *Privileged information.* The Secretary will consider information privileged if, based on principles of law concerning privileged information, the Secretary decides that the information should not be released to the public or to parties to the proceeding. Privileged information is exempt from disclosure to the public or to representatives of interested parties.

(e) *Classified information.* Classified information is information that is classified under Executive Order No. 12356 of April 2, 1982 (47 FR 14874 and 15557, 3 CFR 1982 Comp. p. 166) or successor executive order, if applicable. Classified information is exempt from disclosure to the public or to representatives of interested parties.

§351.106 *De minimis net countervailable subsidies and weighted-average dumping margins disregarded.*

(a) *Introduction.* Prior to the enactment of the URAA, the Department had a well-established and judicially sanctioned practice of disregarding net countervailable subsidies or weighted-average dumping margins that were *de minimis.* The URAA codified in the Act the particular *de minimis* standards to be used in antidumping and countervailing duty investigations. This section discussed the application of the *de minimis* standards in antidumping or countervailing duty proceedings.

(b) *Investigations*—(1) *In general.* In making a preliminary or final antidumping or countervailing duty determination in an investigation (*see* sections 703(b), 733(b), 705(a), and 735(a) of the Act), the Secretary will apply the *de minimis* standard set forth in section 703(b)(4) or section 733(b)(3) of the Act (whichever is applicable).

(2) *Transition rule.* (i) If:

(A) The Secretary resumes an investigation that has been suspended (*see* section 704(i)(1)(B) or section 734(i)(1)(B) of the Act); and

(B) The investigation was initiated before January 1, 1995, then

(ii) The Secretary will apply the *de minimis* standard in effect at the time that the investigation was initiated.

(c) *Reviews and other determinations*—(1) *In general.* In making any determination other than a preliminary or final antidumping or countervailing duty determination in an investigation (*see* paragraph (b) of this section), the Secretary will treat as *de minimis* any weighted-average dumping margin or countervailable subsidy rate that is less than 0.5 percent *ad valorem,* or the equivalent specific rate.

(2) *Assessment of antidumping duties.* The Secretary will instruct the Customs Service to liquidate without regard to antidumping duties all entries of subject merchandise during the relevant period of review made by any person for which the Secretary calculates an assessment rate under §351.212(b)(1) that is less than 0.5 percent *ad valorem,* or the equivalent specific rate.

§351.107 Cash deposit rates for nonproducing exporters; rates in antidumping proceedings involving a nonmarket economy country.

(a) *Introduction.* This section deals with the establishment of cash deposit rates in situations where the exporter is not the producer of subject merchandise, the selection of the appropriate cash deposit rate in situations where entry documents do not indicate the producer of subject merchandise, and the calculation of dumping margins in antidumping proceedings involving imports from a nonmarket economy country.

(b) *Cash deposit rates for nonproducing exporters*—(1) *Use of combination rates*—(i) *In general.* In the case of subject merchandise that is exported to the United States by a company that is not the producer of the merchandise, the Secretary may establish a "combination" cash deposit rate for each combination of the exporter and its supplying producer(s).

(ii) *Example.* A nonproducing exporter (Exporter A) exports to the United States subject merchandise produced by Producers X, Y, and Z. In such a situation, the Secretary may establish

221

cash deposit rates for Exporter A/Producer X, Exporter A/Producer Y, and Exporter A/Producer Z.

(2) *New supplier.* In the case of subject merchandise that is exported to the United States by a company that is not the producer of the merchandise, if the Secretary has not established previously a combination cash deposit rate under paragraph (b)(1)(i) of this section for the exporter and producer in question or a noncombination rate for the exporter in question, the Secretary will apply the cash deposit rate established for the producer. If the Secretary has not previously established a cash deposit rate for the producer, the Secretary will apply the "all-others rate" described in section 705(c)(5) or section 735(c)(5) of the Act, as the case may be.

(c) *Producer not identified*—(1) *In general.* In situations where entry documents do not identify the producer of subject merchandise, if the Secretary has not established previously a noncombination rate for the exporter, the Secretary may instruct the Customs Service to apply as the cash deposit rate the higher of:

(i) The highest of any combination cash deposit rate established for the exporter under paragraph (b)(1)(i) of this section;

(ii) The highest cash deposit rate established for any producer other than a producer for which the Secretary established a combination rate involving the exporter in question under paragraph (b)(1)(i) of this section; or

(iii) The "all-others rate" described in section 705(c)(5) or section 735(c)(5) of the Act, as the case may be.

(2) [Reserved]

(d) *Rates in antidumping proceedings involving nonmarket economy countries.* In an antidumping proceeding involving imports from a nonmarket economy country, "rates" may consist of a single dumping margin applicable to all exporters and producers.

Subpart B—Antidumping and Countervailing Duty Procedures

§ 351.201 Self-initiation.

(a) *Introduction.* Antidumping and countervailing duty investigations may be initiated as the result of a peti-

tion filed by a domestic interested party or at the Secretary's own initiative. This section contains rules regarding the actions the Secretary will take when the Secretary self-initiates an investigation.

(b) *In general.* When the Secretary self-initiates an investigation under section 702(a) or section 732(a) of the Act, the Secretary will publish in the FEDERAL REGISTER notice of "Initiation of Antidumping (Countervailing Duty) Investigation." In addition, the Secretary will notify the Commission at the time of initiation of the investigation, and will make available to employees of the Commission directly involved in the proceeding the information upon which the Secretary based the initiation and which the Commission may consider relevant to its injury determination.

(c) *Persistent dumping monitoring.* To the extent practicable, the Secretary will expedite any antidumping investigation initiated as the result of a monitoring program established under section 732(a)(2) of the Act.

§ 351.202 Petition requirements.

(a) *Introduction.* The Secretary normally initiates antidumping and countervailing duty investigations based on petitions filed by a domestic interested party. This section contains rules concerning the contents of a petition, filing requirements, notification of foreign governments, pre-initiation communications with the Secretary, and assistance to small businesses in preparing petitions. Petitioners are also advised to refer to the Commission's regulations concerning the contents of petitions, currently 19 CFR 207.11.

(b) *Contents of petition.* A petition requesting the imposition of antidumping or countervailing duties must contain the following, to the extent reasonably available to the petitioner:

(1) The name, address, and telephone number of the petitioner and any person the petitioner represents;

(2) The identity of the industry on behalf of which the petitioner is filing, including the names, addresses, and telephone numbers of all other known persons in the industry;

(3) Information relating to the degree of industry support for the petition, including:

(i) The total volume and value of U.S. production of the domestic like product; and

(ii) The volume and value of the domestic like product produced by the petitioner and each domestic producer identified;

(4) A statement indicating whether the petitioner has filed for relief from imports of the subject merchandise under section 337 of the Act (19 U.S.C. 1337, 1671a), sections 201 or 301 of the Trade Act of 1974 (19 U.S.C. 2251 or 2411), or section 232 of the Trade Expansion Act of 1962 (19 U.S.C. 1862);

(5) A detailed description of the subject merchandise that defines the requested scope of the investigation, including the technical characteristics and uses of the merchandise and its current U.S. tariff classification number;

(6) The name of the country in which the subject merchandise is manufactured or produced and, if the merchandise is imported from a country other than the country of manufacture or production, the name of any intermediate country from which the merchandise is imported;

(7)(i) In the case of an antidumping proceeding:

(A) The names and addresses of each person the petitioner believes sells the subject merchandise at less than fair value and the proportion of total exports to the United States that each person accounted for during the most recent 12-month period (if numerous, provide information at least for persons that, based on publicly available information, individually accounted for two percent or more of the exports);

(B) All factual information (particularly documentary evidence) relevant to the calculation of the export price and the constructed export price of the subject merchandise and the normal value of the foreign like product (if unable to furnish information on foreign sales or costs, provide information on production costs in the United States, adjusted to reflect production costs in the country of production of the subject merchandise);

(C) If the merchandise is from a country that the Secretary has found to be a nonmarket economy country, factual information relevant to the calculation of normal value, using a method described in §351.408; or

(ii) In the case of a countervailing duty proceeding:

(A) The names and addresses of each person the petitioner believes benefits from a countervailable subsidy and exports the subject merchandise to the United States and the proportion of total exports to the United States that each person accounted for during the most recent 12-month period (if numerous, provide information at least for persons that, based on publicly available information, individually accounted for two percent or more of the exports);

(B) The alleged countervailable subsidy and factual information (particularly documentary evidence) relevant to the alleged countervailable subsidy, including any law, regulation, or decree under which it is provided, the manner in which it is paid, and the value of the subsidy to exporters or producers of the subject merchandise;

(C) If the petitioner alleges an upstream subsidy under section 771A of the Act, factual information regarding:

(1) Countervailable subsidies, other than an export subsidy, that an authority of the affected country provides to the upstream supplier;

(2) The competitive benefit the countervailable subsidies bestow on the subject merchandise; and

(3) The significant effect the countervailable subsidies have on the cost of producing the subject merchandise;

(8) The volume and value of the subject merchandise imported during the most recent two-year period and any other recent period that the petitioner believes to be more representative or, if the subject merchandise was not imported during the two-year period, information as to the likelihood of its sale for importation;

(9) The name, address, and telephone number of each person the petitioner believes imports or, if there were no importations, is likely to import the subject merchandise;

(10) Factual information regarding material injury, threat of material injury, or material retardation, and causation;

(11) If the petitioner alleges "critical circumstances" under section 703(e)(1) or section 733(e)(1) of the Act and § 351.206, factual information regarding:

(i) Whether imports of the subject merchandise are likely to undermine seriously the remedial effect of any order issued under section 706(a) or section 736(a) of the Act;

(ii) Massive imports of the subject merchandise in a relatively short period; and

(iii) (A) In an antidumping proceeding, either:

(1) A history of dumping; or

(2) The importer's knowledge that the exporter was selling the subject merchandise at less than its fair value, and that there would be material injury by reason of such sales; or

(B) In a countervailing duty proceeding, whether the countervailable subsidy is inconsistent with the Subsidies Agreement; and

(12) Any other factual information on which the petitioner relies.

(c) *Simultaneous filing and certification.* The petitioner must file a copy of the petition with the Commission and the Secretary on the same day and so certify in submitting the petition to the Secretary. Factual information in the petition must be certified, as provided in § 351.303(g). Other filing requirements are set forth in § 351.303.

(d) *Business proprietary status of information.* The Secretary will treat as business proprietary any factual information for which the petitioner requests business proprietary treatment and which meets the requirements of § 351.304.

(e) *Amendment of petition.* The Secretary may allow timely amendment of the petition. The petitioner must file an amendment with the Commission and the Secretary on the same day and so certify in submitting the amendment to the Secretary. If the amendment consists of new allegations, the timeliness of the new allegations will be governed by § 351.301.

(f) *Notification of representative of the exporting country.* Upon receipt of a petition, the Secretary will deliver a public version of the petition (*see* § 351.304(c)) to a representative in Washington, DC, of the government of any exporting country named in the petition.

(g) *Petition based upon derogation of an international undertaking on official export credits.* In the case of a petition described in section 702(b)(3) of the Act, the petitioner must file a copy of the petition with the Secretary of the Treasury, as well as with the Secretary and the Commission, and must so certify in submitting the petition to the Secretary.

(h) *Assistance to small businesses; additional information.* (1) The Secretary will provide technical assistance to eligible small businesses, as defined in section 339 of the Act, to enable them to prepare and file petitions. The Secretary may deny assistance if the Secretary concludes that the petition, if filed, could not satisfy the requirements of section 702(c)(1)(A) or section 732(c)(1)(A) of the Act (whichever is applicable) (*see* § 351.203).

(2) For additional information concerning petitions, contact the Director for Policy and Analysis, Enforcement and Compliance, International Trade Administration, Room 3093, U.S. Department of Commerce, Pennsylvania Avenue and 14th Street, NW, Washington, DC 20230; (202) 482-1768.

(i) *Pre-initiation communications—*(1) *In general.* During the period before the Secretary's decision whether to initiate an investigation, the Secretary will not consider the filing of a notice of appearance to constitute a communication for purposes of section 702(b)(4)(B) or section 732(b)(3)(B) of the Act.

(2) *Consultations with foreign governments in countervailing duty proceedings.* In a countervailing duty proceeding, the Secretary will invite the government of any exporting country named in the petition for consultations with respect to the petition. (The information collection requirements in paragraph (a) of this section have been approved by the Office of Management and Budget under control number 0625-0105.)

§351.203 Determination of sufficiency of petition.

(a) *Introduction.* When a petition is filed under §351.202, the Secretary must determine that the petition satisfies the relevant statutory requirements before initiating an antidumping or countervailing duty investigation. This section sets forth rules regarding a determination as to the sufficiency of a petition (including the determination that a petition is supported by the domestic industry), the deadline for making the determination, and the actions to be taken once the Secretary has made the determination.

(b) *Determination of sufficiency*—(1) *In general.* Normally, not later than 20 days after a petition is filed, the Secretary, on the basis of sources readily available to the Secretary, will examine the accuracy and adequacy of the evidence provided in the petition and determine whether to initiate an investigation under section 702(c)(1)(A) or section 732(c)(1)(A) of the Act (whichever is applicable).

(2) *Extension where polling required.* If the Secretary is required to poll or otherwise determine support for the petition under section 702(c)(4)(D) or section 732(c)(4)(D) of the Act, the Secretary may, in exceptional circumstances, extend the 20-day period by the amount of time necessary to collect and analyze the required information. In no case will the period between the filing of a petition and the determination whether to initiate an investigation exceed 40 days.

(c) *Notice of initiation and distribution of petition*—(1) *Notice of initiation.* If the initiation determination of the Secretary under section 702(c)(1)(A) or section 732(c)(1)(A) of the Act is affirmative, the Secretary will initiate an investigation and publish in the FEDERAL REGISTER notice of "Initiation of Antidumping (Countervailing Duty) Investigation." The Secretary will notify the Commission at the time of initiation of the investigation and will make available to employees of the Commission directly involved in the proceeding the information upon which the Secretary based the initiation and which the Commission may consider relevant to its injury determinations.

(2) *Distribution of petition.* As soon as practicable after initiation of an investigation, the Secretary will provide a public version of the petition to all known exporters (including producers who sell for export to the United States) of the subject merchandise. If the Secretary determines that there is a particularly large number of exporters involved, instead of providing the public version to all known exporters, the Secretary may provide the public version to a trade association of the exporters or, alternatively, may consider the requirement of the preceding sentence to have been satisfied by the delivery of a public version of the petition to the government of the exporting country under §351.202(f).

(d) *Insufficiency of petition.* If an initiation determination of the Secretary under section 702(c)(1)(A) or section 732(c)(1)(A) of the Act is negative, the Secretary will dismiss the petition, terminate the proceeding, notify the petitioner in writing of the reasons for the determination, and publish in the FEDERAL REGISTER notice of "Dismissal of Antidumping (Countervailing Duty) Petition."

(e) *Determination of industry support.* In determining industry support for a petition under section 702(c)(4) or section 732(c)(4) of the Act, the following rules will apply:

(1) *Measuring production.* The Secretary normally will measure production over a twelve-month period specified by the Secretary, and may measure production based on either value or volume. Where a party to the proceeding establishes that production data for the relevant period, as specified by the Secretary, is unavailable, production levels may be established by reference to alternative data that the Secretary determines to be indicative of production levels.

(2) *Positions treated as business proprietary information.* Upon request, the Secretary may treat the position of a domestic producer or workers regarding the petition and any production information supplied by the producer or workers as business proprietary information under §351.105(c)(10).

(3) *Positions expressed by workers.* The Secretary will consider the positions of workers and management regarding

the petition to be of equal weight. The Secretary will assign a single weight to the positions of both workers and management according to the production of the domestic like product of the firm in which the workers and management are employed. If the management of a firm expresses a position in direct opposition to the position of the workers in that firm, the Secretary will treat the production of that firm as representing neither support for, nor opposition to, the petition.

(4) *Certain positions disregarded.* (i) The Secretary will disregard the position of a domestic producer that opposes the petition if such producer is related to a foreign producer or to a foreign exporter under section 771(4)(B)(ii) of the Act, unless such domestic producer demonstrates to the Secretary's satisfaction that its interests as a domestic producer would be adversely affected by the imposition of an antidumping order or a countervailing duty order, as the case may be; and

(ii) The Secretary may disregard the position of a domestic producer that is an importer of the subject merchandise, or that is related to such an importer, under section 771(4)(B)(ii) of the Act.

(5) *Polling the industry.* In conducting a poll of the industry under section 702(c)(4)(D)(i) or section 732(c)(4)(D)(i) of the Act, the Secretary will include unions, groups of workers, and trade or business associations described in paragraphs (9)(D) and (9)(E) of section 771 of the Act.

(f) *Time limits where petition involves same merchandise as that covered by an order that has been revoked.* Under section 702(c)(1)(C) or section 732(c)(1)(C) of the Act, and in expediting an investigation involving subject merchandise for which a prior order was revoked or a suspended investigation was terminated, the Secretary will consider "section 751(d)" as including a predecessor provision.

§ 351.204 **Time periods and persons examined; voluntary respondents; exclusions.**

(a) *Introduction.* Because the Act does not specify the precise period of time that the Secretary should examine in

an antidumping or countervailing duty investigation, this section sets forth rules regarding the period of investigation ("POI"). In addition, this section includes rules regarding the selection of persons to be examined, the treatment of voluntary respondents that are not selected for individual examination, and the exclusion of persons that the Secretary ultimately finds are not dumping or are not receiving countervailable subsidies.

(b) *Period of investigation—*(1) *Antidumping investigation.* In an antidumping investigation, the Secretary normally will examine merchandise sold during the four most recently completed fiscal quarters (or, in an investigation involving merchandise imported from a nonmarket economy country, the two most recently completed fiscal quarters) as of the month preceding the month in which the petition was filed or in which the Secretary self-initiated an investigation. However, the Secretary may examine merchandise sold during any additional or alternate period that the Secretary concludes is appropriate.

(2) *Countervailing duty investigation.* In a countervailing duty investigation, the Secretary normally will rely on information pertaining to the most recently completed fiscal year for the government and exporters or producers in question. If the exporters or producers have different fiscal years, the Secretary normally will rely on information pertaining to the most recently completed calendar year. If the investigation is conducted on an aggregate basis under section 777A(e)(2)(B) of the Act, the Secretary normally will rely on information pertaining to the most recently completed fiscal year for the government in question. However, the Secretary may rely on information for any additional or alternate period that the Secretary concludes is appropriate.

(c) *Exporters and producers examined—*(1) *In general.* In an investigation, the Secretary will attempt to determine an individual weighted-average dumping margin or individual countervailable subsidy rate for each known exporter or producer of the subject merchandise. However, the Secretary may decline to examine a particular exporter or producer if that exporter or producer and the petitioner agree.

(2) *Limited investigation.* Notwithstanding paragraph (c)(1) of this section, the Secretary may limit the investigation by using a method described in subsection (a), (c), or (e) of section 777A of the Act.

(d) *Voluntary respondents*—(1) *In general.* If the Secretary limits the number of exporters or producers to be individually examined under section 777A(c)(2) or section 777A(e)(2)(A) of the Act, the Secretary will examine voluntary respondents (exporters or producers, other than those initially selected for individual examination) in accordance with section 782(a) of the Act.

(2) *Acceptance of voluntary respondents.* The Secretary will determine, as soon as practicable, whether to examine a voluntary respondent individually. A voluntary respondent accepted for individual examination under subparagraph (d)(1) of this section will be subject to the same requirements as an exporter or producer initially selected by the Secretary for individual examination under section 777A(c)(2) or section 777A(e)(2)(A) of the Act, including the requirements of section 782(a) of the Act and, where applicable, the use of the facts available under section 776 of the Act and §351.308.

(3) *Exclusion of voluntary respondents' rates from all-others rate.* In calculating an all-others rate under section 705(c)(5) or section 735(c)(5) of the Act, the Secretary will exclude weighted-average dumping margins or countervailable subsidy rates calculated for voluntary respondents.

(4) *Requests for voluntary respondent treatment.* An interested party seeking treatment as a voluntary respondent must so indicate by including as a title on the first page of the first submission, "Request for Voluntary Respondent Treatment."

(e) *Exclusions*—(1) *In general.* The Secretary will exclude from an affirmative final determination under section 705(a) or section 735(a) of the Act or an order under section 706(a) or section 736(a) of the Act, any exporter or producer for which the Secretary determines an individual weighted-average dumping margin or individual net countervailable subsidy rate of zero or *de minimis*.

(2) *Preliminary determinations.* In an affirmative preliminary determination under section 703(b) or section 733(b) of the Act, an exporter or producer for which the Secretary preliminarily determines an individual weighted-average dumping margin or individual net countervailable subsidy of zero or *de minimis* will not be excluded from the preliminary determination or the investigation. However, the exporter or producer will not be subject to provisional measures under section 703(d) or section 733(d) of the Act.

(3) *Exclusion of nonproducing exporter*—(i) *In general.* In the case of an exporter that is not the producer of subject merchandise, the Secretary normally will limit an exclusion of the exporter to subject merchandise of those producers that supplied the exporter during the period of investigation.

(ii) *Example.* During the period of investigation, Exporter A exports to the United States subject merchandise produced by Producer X. Based on an examination of Exporter A, the Secretary determines that the dumping margins with respect to these exports are *de minimis*, and the Secretary excludes Exporter A. Normally, the exclusion of Exporter A would be limited to subject merchandise produced by Producer X. If Exporter A began to export subject merchandise produced by Producer Y, this merchandise would be subject to the antidumping duty order, if any.

(4) *Countervailing duty investigations conducted on an aggregate basis and requests for exclusion from countervailing duty order.* Where the Secretary conducts a countervailing duty investigation on an aggregate basis under section 777A(e)(2)(B) of the Act, the Secretary will consider and investigate requests for exclusion to the extent practicable. An exporter or producer that desires exclusion from an order must submit:

(i) A certification by the exporter or producer that it received zero or *de minimis* net countervailable subsidies during the period of investigation;

(ii) If the exporter or producer received a countervailable subsidy, calculations demonstrating that the amount of net countervailable subsidies received was *de minimis* during the period of investigation;

(iii) If the exporter is not the producer of the subject merchandise, certifications from the suppliers and producers of the subject merchandise that those persons received zero or *de minimis* net countervailable subsidies during the period of the investigation; and

(iv) A certification from the government of the affected country that the government did not provide the exporter (or the exporter's supplier) or producer with more than *de minimis* net countervailable subsidies during the period of investigation.

[62 FR 27379, May 19, 1997, as amended at 73 FR 3643, Jan. 22, 2008]

§ 351.205 Preliminary determination.

(a) *Introduction.* A preliminary determination in an antidumping or countervailing duty investigation constitutes the first point at which the Secretary may provide a remedy (sometimes referred to as "provisional measures") if the Secretary preliminarily finds that dumping or countervailable subsidization has occurred. Whether the Secretary's preliminary determination is affirmative or negative, the investigation continues. This section contains rules regarding deadlines for preliminary determinations, postponement of preliminary determinations, notices of preliminary determinations, and the effects of affirmative preliminary determinations.

(b) *Deadline for preliminary determination.* The deadline for a preliminary determination under section 703(b) or section 733(b) of the Act will be:

(1) Normally not later than 140 days in an antidumping investigation (65 days in a countervailing duty investigation) after the date on which the Secretary initiated the investigation (*see* section 703(b)(1) or section 733(b)(1)(A) of the Act);

(2) Not later than 190 days in an antidumping investigation (130 days in a countervailing duty investigation) after the date on which the Secretary initiated the investigation if the Secretary postpones the preliminary determination at petitioner's request or because the Secretary determines that

the investigation is extraordinarily complicated (*see* section 703(c)(1) or section 733(c)(1) of the Act);

(3) In a countervailing duty investigation, not later than 250 days after the date on which the proceeding began if the Secretary postpones the preliminary determination due to an upstream subsidy allegation (up to 310 days if the Secretary also postponed the preliminary determination at the request of the petitioner or because the Secretary determined that the investigation is extraordinarily complicated) (*see* section 703(c)(1) and section 703(g)(1) of the Act);

(4) Within 90 days after initiation in an antidumping investigation, and on an expedited basis in a countervailing duty investigation, where verification has been waived (*see* section 703(b)(3) or section 733(b)(2) of the Act);

(5) In a countervailing duty investigation, on an expedited basis and within 65 days after the date on which the Secretary initiated the investigation if the sole subsidy alleged in the petition was the derogation of an international undertaking on official export credits (*see* section 702(b)(3) and section 703(b)(2) of the Act);

(6) In a countervailing duty investigation, not later than 60 days after the date on which the Secretary initiated the investigation if the only subsidy under investigation is a subsidy with respect to which the Secretary received notice from the United States Trade Representative of a violation of Article 8 of the Subsidies Agreement (*see* section 703(b)(5) of the Act); and

(7) In an antidumping investigation, within the deadlines set forth in section 733(b)(1)(B) of the Act if the investigation involves short life cycle merchandise (*see* section 733(b)(1)(B) and section 739 of the Act).

(c) *Contents of preliminary determination and publication of notice.* A preliminary determination will include a preliminary finding on critical circumstances, if appropriate, under section 703(e)(1) or section 733(e)(1) of the Act (whichever is applicable). The Secretary will publish in the FEDERAL

REGISTER notice of "Affirmative (Negative) Preliminary Antidumping (Countervailing Duty) Determination," including the rates, if any, and an invitation for argument consistent with §351.309.

(d) *Effect of affirmative preliminary determination.* If the preliminary determination is affirmative, the Secretary will take the actions described in section 703(d) or section 733(d) of the Act (whichever is applicable). With respect to section 703(d)(1)(B) and 733(d)(1)(B) of the Act, the Secretary will normally order the posting of cash deposits to ensure payment if antidumping or countervailing duties ultimately are imposed. In making information available to the Commission under section 703(d)(3) or section 733(d)(3) of the Act, the Secretary will make available to the Commission and to employees of the Commission directly involved in the proceeding the information upon which the Secretary based the preliminary determination and which the Commission may consider relevant to its injury determination.

(e) *Postponement at the request of the petitioner.* A petitioner must submit a request for postponement of the preliminary determination (*see* section 703(c)(1)(A) or section 733(c)(1)(A) of the Act) 25 days or more before the scheduled date of the preliminary determination, and must state the reasons for the request. The Secretary will grant the request, unless the Secretary finds compelling reasons to deny the request.

(f) *Notice of postponement.* (1) If the Secretary decides to postpone the preliminary determination at the request of the petitioner or because the investigation is extraordinarily complicated, the Secretary will notify all parties to the proceeding not later than 20 days before the scheduled date of the preliminary determination, and will publish in the FEDERAL REGISTER notice of "Postponement of Preliminary Antidumping (Countervailing Duty) Determination," stating the reasons for the postponement (*see* section 703(c)(2) or section 733(c)(2) of the Act).

(2) If the Secretary decides to postpone the preliminary determination due to an allegation of upstream subsidies, the Secretary will notify all parties to the proceeding not later than the scheduled date of the preliminary determination and will publish in the FEDERAL REGISTER notice of "Postponement of Preliminary Countervailing Duty Determination," stating the reasons for the postponement.

[62 FR 27379, May 19, 1997, as amended at 76 FR 61045, Oct. 3, 2011]

§351.206 Critical circumstances.

(a) *Introduction.* Generally, antidumping or countervailing duties are imposed on entries of merchandise made on or after the date on which the Secretary first imposes provisional measures (most often the date on which notice of an affirmative preliminary determination is published in the FEDERAL REGISTER). However, if the Secretary finds that "critical circumstances" exist, duties may be imposed retroactively on merchandise entered up to 90 days before the imposition of provisional measures. This section contains procedural and substantive rules regarding allegations and findings of critical circumstances.

(b) *In general.* If a petitioner submits to the Secretary a written allegation of critical circumstances, with reasonably available factual information supporting the allegation, 21 days or more before the scheduled date of the Secretary's final determination, or on the Secretary's own initiative in a self-initiated investigation, the Secretary will make a finding whether critical circumstances exist, as defined in section 705(a)(2) or section 735(a)(3) of the Act (whichever is applicable).

(c) *Preliminary finding.* (1) If the petitioner submits an allegation of critical circumstances 30 days or more before the scheduled date of the Secretary's final determination, the Secretary, based on the available information, will make a preliminary finding whether there is a reasonable basis to believe or suspect that critical circumstances exist, as defined in section 703(e)(1) or section 733(e)(1) of the Act (whichever is applicable).

(2) The Secretary will issue the preliminary finding:

(i) Not later than the preliminary determination, if the allegation is submitted 20 days or more before the scheduled date of the preliminary determination; or

(ii) Within 30 days after the petitioner submits the allegation, if the allegation is submitted later than 20 days before the scheduled date of the preliminary determination; or

(iii) If, pursuant to paragraph (i) of this section, the period examined for purposes of determining whether critical circumstances exists is earlier than normal, the Secretary will issue the preliminary finding as early as possible after initiation of the investigation, but normally not less than 45 days after the petition was filed. The Secretary will notify the Commission and publish in the FEDERAL REGISTER notice of the preliminary finding.

(d) *Suspension of liquidation.* If the Secretary makes an affirmative preliminary finding of critical circumstances, the provisions of section 703(e)(2) or section 733(e)(2) of the Act (whichever is applicable) regarding the retroactive suspension of liquidation will apply.

(e) *Final finding.* For any allegation of critical circumstances submitted 21 days or more before the scheduled date of the Secretary's final determination, the Secretary will make a final finding on critical circumstances, and will take appropriate action under section 705(c)(4) or section 735(c)(4) of the Act (whichever is applicable).

(f) *Findings in self-initiated investigations.* In a self-initiated investigation, the Secretary will make preliminary and final findings on critical circumstances without regard to the time limits in paragraphs (c) and (e) of this section.

(g) *Information regarding critical circumstances.* The Secretary may request the Commissioner of Customs to compile information on an expedited basis regarding entries of the subject merchandise if, at any time after the initiation of an investigation, the Secretary makes the findings described in section 702(e) or section 732(e) of the Act (whichever is applicable) regarding the possible existence of critical circumstances.

(h) *Massive imports.* (1) In determining whether imports of the subject merchandise have been massive under section 705(a)(2)(B) or section 735(a)(3)(B) of the Act, the Secretary normally will examine:

(i) The volume and value of the imports;

(ii) Seasonal trends; and

(iii) The share of domestic consumption accounted for by the imports.

(2) In general, unless the imports during the "relatively short period" (*see* paragraph (i) of this section) have increased by at least 15 percent over the imports during an immediately preceding period of comparable duration, the Secretary will not consider the imports massive.

(i) *Relatively short period.* Under section 705(a)(2)(B) or section 735(a)(3)(B) of the Act, the Secretary normally will consider a "relatively short period" as the period beginning on the date the proceeding begins and ending at least three months later. However, if the Secretary finds that importers, or exporters or producers, had reason to believe, at some time prior to the beginning of the proceeding, that a proceeding was likely, then the Secretary may consider a period of not less than three months from that earlier time.

[62 FR 27379, May 19, 1997, as amended at 64 FR 48707, Sept. 8, 1999]

§ 351.207   **Termination of investigation.**

(a) *Introduction.* "Termination" is a term of art that refers to the end of an antidumping or countervailing duty proceeding in which an order has not yet been issued. The Act establishes a variety of mechanisms by which an investigation may be terminated, most of which are dealt with in this section. For rules regarding the termination of a suspended investigation following a review under section 751 of the Act, *see* § 351.222.

(b) *Withdrawal of petition; self-initiated investigations*—(1) *In general.* The Secretary may terminate an investigation under section 704(a)(1)(A) or section 734(a)(1)(A) (withdrawal of petition) or under section 704(k) or section 734(k) (self-initiated investigation) of the Act, provided that the Secretary concludes that termination is in the public interest. If the Secretary terminates an investigation, the Secretary will publish in the FEDERAL REGISTER notice of "Termination of Antidumping (Countervailing Duty) Investigation," together with, when appropriate, a copy of any correspondence with the petitioner forming the basis of the withdrawal and the termination. (For the treatment in a subsequent investigation of records compiled in an investigation in which the petition was withdrawn, *see* section 704(a)(1)(B) or section 734(a)(1)(B) of the Act.)

(2) *Withdrawal of petition based on acceptance of quantitative restriction agreements.* In addition to the requirements of paragraph (b)(1) of this section, if a termination is based on the acceptance of an understanding or other kind of agreement to limit the volume of imports into the United States of the subject merchandise, the Secretary will apply the provisions of section 704(a)(2) or section 734(a)(2) of the Act (whichever is applicable) regarding public interest and consultations with consuming industries and producers and workers.

(c) *Lack of interest.* The Secretary may terminate an investigation based upon lack of interest (*see* section 782(h)(1) of the Act). Where the Secretary terminates an investigation under this paragraph, the Secretary will publish the notice described in paragraph (b)(1) of this section.

(d) *Negative determination.* An investigation terminates automatically upon publication in the FEDERAL REGISTER of the Secretary's negative final determination or the Commission's negative preliminary or final determination.

(e) *End of suspension of liquidation.* When an investigation terminates, if the Secretary previously ordered suspension of liquidation, the Secretary will order the suspension ended on the date of publication of the notice of termination referred to in paragraph (b) of this section or on the date of publication of a negative determination referred to in paragraph (d) of this section, and will instruct the Customs Service to release any cash deposit or bond.

§351.208 **Suspension of investigation.**

(a) *Introduction.* In addition to the imposition of duties, the Act also permits the Secretary to suspend an antidumping or countervailing duty investigation by accepting a suspension agreement (referred to in the WTO Agreements as an "undertaking"). Briefly, in a suspension agreement, the exporters and producers or the foreign government agree to modify their behavior so as to eliminate dumping or subsidization or the injury caused thereby. If the Secretary accepts a suspension agreement, the Secretary will "suspend" the investigation and thereafter will monitor compliance with the agreement. This section contains rules for entering into suspension agreements and procedures for suspending an investigation.

(b) *In general.* The Secretary may suspend an investigation under section 704 or section 734 of the Act and this section.

(c) *Definition of "substantially all."* Under section 704 and section 734 of the Act, exporters that account for "substantially all" of the merchandise means exporters and producers that have accounted for not less than 85 percent by value or volume of the subject merchandise during the period for which the Secretary is measuring dumping or countervailable subsidization in the investigation or such other period that the Secretary considers representative.

(d) *Monitoring.* In monitoring a suspension agreement under section 704(c), section 734(c), or section 734(l) of the Act (agreements to eliminate injurious effects or to restrict the volume of imports), the Secretary will not be obliged to ascertain on a continuing basis the prices in the United States of the subject merchandise or of domestic like products.

(e) *Exports not to increase during interim period.* The Secretary will not accept a suspension agreement under section 704(b)(2) or section 734(b)(1) of the Act (the cessation of exports) unless the agreement ensures that the quantity of the subject merchandise exported during the interim period set forth in the agreement does not exceed the quantity of the merchandise exported during a period of comparable duration that the Secretary considers representative.

(f) *Procedure for suspension of investigation—(1) Submission of proposed suspension agreement—(i) In general.* As appropriate, the exporters and producers or, in an antidumping investigation involving a nonmarket economy country or a countervailing duty investigation, the government, must submit to the Secretary a proposed suspension agreement within:

(A) In an antidumping investigation, 15 days after the date of issuance of the preliminary determination, or

(B) In a countervailing duty investigation, 7 days after the date of issuance of the preliminary determination.

(ii) *Postponement of final determination.* Where a proposed suspension agreement is submitted in an antidumping investigation, an exporter or producer or, in an investigation involving a nonmarket economy country, the government, may request postponement of the final determination under section 735(a)(2) of the Act (*see* § 351.210(e)). Where the final determination in a countervailing duty investigation is postponed under section 703(g)(2) or section 705(a)(1) of the Act (*see* § 351.210(b)(3) and § 351.210(i)), the time limits in paragraphs (f)(1)(i), (f)(2)(i), (f)(3), and (g)(1) of this section applicable to countervailing duty investigations will be extended to coincide with the time limits in such paragraphs applicable to antidumping investigations.

(iii) *Special rule for regional industry determination.* If the Commission makes a regional industry determination in its final affirmative determination under section 705(b) or section 735(b) of the Act but not in its preliminary affirmative determination under section 703(a) or section 733(a) of the Act, the exporters and producers or, in an antidumping investigation involving a nonmarket economy country or a countervailing duty investigation, the government, must submit to the Secretary any proposed suspension agreement within 15 days of the publication in the FEDERAL REGISTER of the antidumping or countervailing duty order.

(2) *Notification and consultation.* In fulfilling the requirements of section 704 or section 734 of the Act (whichever is applicable), the Secretary will take the following actions:

(i) *In general.* The Secretary will notify all parties to the proceeding of the proposed suspension of an investigation and provide to the petitioner a copy of the suspension agreement preliminarily accepted by the Secretary (the agreement must contain the procedures for monitoring compliance and a statement of the compatibility of the agreement with the requirements of section 704 or section 734 of the Act) within:

(A) In an antidumping investigation, 30 days after the date of issuance of the preliminary determination, or

(B) In a countervailing duty investigation, 15 days after the date of issuance of the preliminary determination; or

(ii) *Special rule for regional industry determination.* If the Commission makes a regional industry determination in its final affirmative determination under section 705(b) or section 735(b) of the Act but not in its preliminary affirmative determination under section 703(a) or section 733(a) of the Act, the Secretary, within 15 days of the submission of a proposed suspension agreement under paragraph (f)(1)(iii) of this section, will notify all parties to the proceeding of the proposed suspension agreement and provide to the petitioner a copy of the agreement preliminarily accepted by the Secretary (such agreement must contain the procedures for monitoring compliance and a statement of the compatibility of the agreement with the requirements of section 704 or section 734 of the Act); and

(iii) *Consultation.* The Secretary will consult with the petitioner concerning the proposed suspension of the investigation.

(3) *Opportunity for comment.* The Secretary will provide all interested parties, an industrial user of the subject merchandise or a representative consumer organization, as described in section 777(h) of the Act, and United States government agencies an opportunity to submit written argument and factual information concerning the proposed suspension of the investigation within:

(i) In an antidumping investigation, 50 days after the date of issuance of the preliminary determination,

(ii) In a countervailing duty investigation, 35 days after the date of issuance of the preliminary determination, or

(iii) In a regional industry case described in paragraph (f)(1)(iii) of this section, 35 days after the date of issuance of an order.

(g) *Acceptance of suspension agreement.* (1) The Secretary may accept an agreement to suspend an investigation within:

(i) In an antidumping investigation, 60 days after the date of issuance of the preliminary determination,

(ii) In a countervailing duty investigation, 45 days after the date of issuance of the preliminary determination, or

(iii) In a regional industry case described in paragraph (f)(1)(iii) of this section, 45 days after the date of issuance of an order.

(2) If the Secretary accepts an agreement to suspend an investigation, the Secretary will take the actions described in section 704(f), section 704(m)(3), section 734(f), or section 734(l)(3) of the Act (whichever is applicable), and will publish in the FEDERAL REGISTER notice of "Suspension of Antidumping (Countervailing Duty) Investigation," including the text of the agreement. If the Secretary has not already published notice of an affirmative preliminary determination, the Secretary will include that notice. In accepting an agreement, the Secretary may rely on factual or legal conclusions the Secretary reached in or after the affirmative preliminary determination.

(h) *Continuation of investigation.* (1) A request to the Secretary under section 704(g) or section 734(g) of the Act for the continuation of the investigation must be made in writing. In addition, the request must be simultaneously filed with the Commission, and the requester must so certify in submitting the request to the Secretary.

(2) If the Secretary and the Commission make affirmative final determinations in an investigation that has been continued, the suspension agreement will remain in effect in accordance with the factual and legal conclusions in the Secretary's final determination. If either the Secretary or the Commission makes a negative final determination, the agreement will have no force or effect.

(i) *Merchandise imported in excess of allowed quantity.* (1) The Secretary may instruct the Customs Service not to accept entries, or withdrawals from warehouse, for consumption of subject merchandise in excess of any quantity allowed by a suspension agreement under section 704 or section 734 of the Act, including any quantity allowed during the interim period (*see* paragraph (e) of this section).

(2) Imports in excess of the quantity allowed by a suspension agreement, including any quantity allowed during the interim period (*see* paragraph (e) of this section), may be exported or destroyed under Customs Service supervision, except that if the agreement is under section 704(c)(3) or section 734(l) of the Act (restrictions on the volume of imports), the excess merchandise, with the approval of the Secretary, may be held for future opening under the agreement by placing it in a foreign trade zone or by entering it for warehouse.

§ 351.209 Violation of suspension agreement.

(a) *Introduction.* A suspension agreement remains in effect until the underlying investigation is terminated (*see* §§ 351.207 and 351.222). However, if the Secretary finds that a suspension agreement has been violated or no longer meets the requirements of the Act, the Secretary may either cancel or revise the agreement. This section contains rules regarding cancellation and revision of suspension agreements.

(b) *Immediate determination.* If the Secretary determines that a signatory has violated a suspension agreement, the Secretary, without providing interested parties an opportunity to comment, will:

(1) Order the suspension of liquidation in accordance with section 704(i)(1)(A) or section 734(i)(1)(A) of the Act (whichever is applicable) of all entries of the subject merchandise entered, or withdrawn from warehouse, for consumption on or after the later of:

(i) 90 days before the date of publication of the notice of cancellation of the agreement; or

(ii) The date of first entry, or withdrawal from warehouse, for consumption of the merchandise the sale or export of which was in violation of the agreement;

(2) If the investigation was not completed under section 704(g) or section 734(g) of the Act, resume the investigation as if the Secretary had made an affirmative preliminary determination on the date of publication of the notice of cancellation and impose provisional measures by instructing the Customs Service to require for each entry of the subject merchandise suspended under paragraph (b)(1) of this section a cash deposit or bond at the rates determined in the affirmative preliminary determination;

(3) If the investigation was completed under section 704(g) or section 734(g) of the Act, issue an antidumping order or countervailing duty order (whichever is applicable) and, for all entries subject to suspension of liquidation under paragraph (b)(1) of this section, instruct the Customs Service to require for each entry of the merchandise suspended under this paragraph a cash deposit at the rates determined in the affirmative final determination;

(4) Notify all persons who are or were parties to the proceeding, the Commission, and, if the Secretary determines that the violation was intentional, the Commissioner of Customs; and

(5) Publish in the FEDERAL REGISTER notice of "Antidumping (Countervailing Duty) Order (Resumption of Antidumping (Countervailing Duty) Investigation); Cancellation of Suspension Agreement."

(c) *Determination after notice and comment.* (1) If the Secretary has reason to believe that a signatory has violated a suspension agreement, or that an agreement no longer meets the requirements of section 704(d)(1) or section 734(d) of the Act, but the Secretary does not have sufficient information to determine that a signatory has violated the agreement (*see* paragraph (b) of this section), the Secretary will publish in the FEDERAL REGISTER notice of "Invitation for Comment on Antidumping (Countervailing Duty) Suspension Agreement."

(2) After publication of the notice inviting comment and after consideration of comments received the Secretary will:

(i) Determine whether any signatory has violated the suspension agreement; or

(ii) Determine whether the suspension agreement no longer meets the requirements of section 704(d)(1) or section 734(d) of the Act.

(3) If the Secretary determines that a signatory has violated the suspension agreement, the Secretary will take appropriate action as described in paragraphs (b)(1) through (b)(5) of this section.

(4) If the Secretary determines that a suspension agreement no longer meets the requirements of section 704(d)(1) or section 734(d) of the Act, the Secretary will:

(i) Take appropriate action as described in paragraphs (b)(1) through (b)(5) of this section; except that, under paragraph (b)(1)(ii) of this section, the Secretary will order the suspension of liquidation of all entries of the subject merchandise entered, or withdrawn from warehouse, for consumption on or after the later of:

(A) 90 days before the date of publication of the notice of suspension of liquidation; or

(B) The date of first entry, or withdrawal from warehouse, for consumption of the merchandise the sale or export of which does not meet the requirements of section 704(d)(1) of the Act;

(ii) Continue the suspension of investigation by accepting a revised suspension agreement under section 704(b) or section 734(b) of the Act (whether or not the Secretary accepted the original agreement under such section) that, at the time the Secretary accepts the revised agreement, meets the applicable requirements of section 704(d)(1) or section 734(d) of the Act, and publish in the FEDERAL REGISTER notice of "Revision of Agreement Suspending Antidumping (Countervailing Duty) Investigation"; or

(iii) Continue the suspension of investigation by accepting a revised suspension agreement under section 704(c), section 734(c), or section 734(l) of the Act (whether or not the Secretary accepted the original agreement under such section) that, at the time the Secretary accepts the revised agreement, meets the applicable requirements of section 704(d)(1) or section 734(d) of the Act, and publish in the FEDERAL REGISTER notice of "Revision of Agreement Suspending Antidumping (Countervailing Duty) Investigation." If the Secretary continues to suspend an investigation based on a revised agreement accepted under section 704(c), section 734(c), or section 734(l) of the Act, the Secretary will order suspension of liquidation to begin. The suspension will not end until the Commission completes any requested review of the revised agreement under section 704(h) or section 734(h) of the Act. If the Commission receives no request for review within 20 days after the date of publication of the notice of the revision, the Secretary will order the suspension of liquidation ended on the 21st day after the date of publication, and will instruct the Customs Service to release any cash deposit or bond. If the Commission undertakes a review under section 704(h) or section 734(h) of the Act, the provisions of sections 704(h)(2) and (3) and sections 734(h)(2) and (3) of the Act will apply.

(5) If the Secretary decides neither to consider the suspension agreement violated nor to revise the agreement, the Secretary will publish in the FEDERAL REGISTER notice of the Secretary's decision under paragraph (c)(2) of this section, including a statement of the factual and legal conclusions on which the decision is based.

(d) *Additional signatories.* If the Secretary decides that a suspension agreement no longer will completely eliminate the injurious effect of exports to the United States of subject merchandise under section 704(c)(1) or section 734(c)(1) of the Act, or that the signatory exporters no longer account for substantially all of the subject merchandise, the Secretary may revise the agreement to include additional signatory exporters.

(e) *Definition of "violation."* Under this section, "violation" means noncompliance with the terms of a suspension agreement caused by an act or omission of a signatory, except, at the discretion of the Secretary, an act or omission which is inadvertent or inconsequential.

§351.210 Final determination.

(a) *Introduction.* A "final determination" in an antidumping or countervailing duty investigation constitutes a final decision by the Secretary as to whether dumping or countervailable subsidization is occurring. If the Secretary's final determination is affirmative, in most instances the Commission will issue a final injury determination (except in certain countervailing duty investigations). Also, if the Secretary's preliminary determination was negative but the final determination is affirmative, the Secretary will impose provisional measures. If the Secretary's final determination is negative, the proceeding, including the injury investigation conducted by the Commission, terminates. This section contains rules regarding deadlines for, and postponement of, final determinations, contents of final determinations, and the effects of final determinations.

(b) *Deadline for final determination.* The deadline for a final determination under section 705(a)(1) or section 735(a)(1) of the Act will be:

(1) Normally, not later than 75 days after the date of the Secretary's preliminary determination (*see* section 705(a)(1) or section 735(a)(1) of the Act);

(2) In an antidumping investigation, not later than 135 days after the date of publication of the preliminary determination if the Secretary postpones the final determination at the request of:

(i) The petitioner, if the preliminary determination was negative (*see* section 735(a)(2)(B) of the Act); or

(ii) Exporters or producers who account for a significant proportion of exports of the subject merchandise, if the preliminary determination was affirmative (*see* section 735(a)(2)(A) of the Act);

(3) In a countervailing duty investigation, not later than 165 days after the preliminary determination, if, after the preliminary determination, the Secretary decides to investigate an upstream subsidy allegation and concludes that additional time is needed to investigate the allegation (*see* section 703(g)(2) of the Act); or

(4) In a countervailing duty investigation, the same date as the date of the final antidumping determination, if:

(i) In a situation where the Secretary simultaneously initiated antidumping and countervailing duty investigations on the subject merchandise (from the same or other countries), the petitioner requests that the final countervailing duty determination be postponed to the date of the final antidumping determination; and

(ii) If the final countervailing duty determination is not due on a later date because of postponement due to an allegation of upstream subsidies under section 703(g) of the Act (see section 705(a)(1) of the Act).

(c) *Contents of final determination and publication of notice.* The final determination will include, if appropriate, a final finding on critical circumstances under section 705(a)(2) or section 735(a)(3) of the Act (whichever is applicable). The Secretary will publish in the FEDERAL REGISTER notice of "Affirmative (Negative) Final Antidumping (Countervailing Duty) Determination," including the rates, if any.

(d) *Effect of affirmative final determination.* If the final determination is affirmative, the Secretary will take the actions described in section 705(c)(1) or section 735(c)(1) of the Act (whichever is applicable). In addition, in the case of a countervailing duty investigation involving subject merchandise from a country that is not a Subsidies Agreement country, the Secretary will instruct the Customs Service to require a cash deposit, as provided in section 706(a)(3) of the Act, for each entry of the subject merchandise entered, or withdrawn from warehouse, for consumption on or after the date of publication of the order under section 706(a) of the Act.

(e) *Request for postponement of final antidumping determination*—(1) *In general.* A request to postpone a final antidumping determination under section 735(a)(2) of the Act (see paragraph (b)(2) of this section) must be submitted in writing within the scheduled date of the final determination. The Secretary may grant the request, unless the Secretary finds compelling reasons to deny the request.

(2) *Requests by exporters.* In the case of a request submitted under paragraph (e)(1) of this section by exporters who account for a significant proportion of exports of subject merchandise (see section 735(a)(2)(A) of the Act), the Secretary will not grant the request unless those exporters also submit a request described in the last sentence of section 733(d) of the Act (extension of provisional measures from a 4-month period to not more than 6 months).

(f) *Deferral of decision concerning upstream subsidization to review.* Notwithstanding paragraph (b)(3) of this section, if the petitioner so requests in writing and the preliminary countervailing duty determination was affirmative, the Secretary, instead of postponing the final determination, may defer a decision concerning upstream subsidization until the conclusion of the first administrative review of a countervailing duty order, if any (see section 703(g)(2)(B)(i) of the Act).

(g) *Notification of postponement.* If the Secretary postpones a final determination under paragraph (b)(2), (b)(3), or (b)(4) of this section, the Secretary will notify promptly all parties to the proceeding of the postponement, and will publish in the FEDERAL REGISTER notice of "Postponement of Final Antidumping (Countervailing Duty) Determination," stating the reasons for the postponement.

(h) *Termination of suspension of liquidation in a countervailing duty investigation.* If the Secretary postpones a final countervailing duty determination, the Secretary will end any suspension of liquidation ordered in the preliminary determination not later than 120 days after the date of publication of the preliminary determination, and will not resume it unless and until the Secretary publishes a countervailing duty order.

(i) *Postponement of final countervailing duty determination for simultaneous investigations.* A request by the petitioner to postpone a final countervailing duty determination to the date of the final antidumping determination must be submitted in writing within five days of the date of publication of the preliminary countervailing duty determination (see section 705(a)(1) and paragraph (b)(4) of this section).

(j) *Commission access to information.* If the final determination is affirmative, the Secretary will make available to the Commission and to employees of the Commission directly involved in the proceeding the information upon which the Secretary based the final determination and that the Commission may consider relevant to its injury determination (*see* section 705(c)(1)(A) or section 735(c)(1)(A) of the Act).

(k) *Effect of negative final determination.* An investigation terminates upon publication in the FEDERAL REGISTER of the Secretary's or the Commission's negative final determination, and the Secretary will take the relevant actions described in section 705(c)(2) or section 735(c)(2) of the Act (whichever is applicable).

§351.211 Antidumping order and countervailing duty order.

(a) *Introduction.* The Secretary issues an order when both the Secretary and the Commission (except in certain countervailing duty investigations) have made final affirmative determinations. The issuance of an order ends the investigative phase of a proceeding. Generally, upon the issuance of an order, importers no longer may post bonds as security for antidumping or countervailing duties, but instead must make a cash deposit of estimated duties. An order remains in effect until it is revoked. This section contains rules regarding the issuance of orders in general, as well as special rules for orders where the Commission has found a regional industry to exist.

(b) *In general.* Not later than seven days after receipt of notice of an affirmative final injury determination by the Commission under section 705(b) or section 735(b) of the Act, or, in a countervailing duty proceeding involving subject merchandise from a country not entitled to an injury test (*see* §351.101(b)), simultaneously with publication of an affirmative final countervailing duty determination by the Secretary, the Secretary will publish in the FEDERAL REGISTER an "Antidumping Order" or "Countervailing Duty Order" that:

(1) Instructs the Customs Service to assess antidumping duties or countervailing duties (whichever is applicable) on the subject merchandise, in accordance with the Secretary's instructions at the completion of each review requested under §351.213(b) (administrative review), §351.214(b) (new shipper review), or §351.215(b) (expedited antidumping review), or if a review is not requested, in accordance with the Secretary's assessment instructions under §351.212(c);

(2) Instructs the Customs Service to require a cash deposit of estimated antidumping or countervailing duties at the rates included in the Secretary's final determination; and

(3) Orders the suspension of liquidation ended for all entries of the subject merchandise entered, or withdrawn from warehouse, for consumption before the date of publication of the Commission's final determination, and instructs the Customs Service to release the cash deposit or bond on those entries, if in its final determination, the Commission found a threat of material injury or material retardation of the establishment of an industry, unless the Commission in its final determination also found that, absent the suspension of liquidation ordered under section 703(d)(2) or section 733(d)(2) of the Act, it would have found material injury (*see* section 706(b) or section 736(b) of the Act).

§351.212 Assessment of antidumping and countervailing duties; provisional measures deposit cap; interest on certain overpayments and underpayments.

(a) *Introduction.* Unlike the systems of some other countries, the United States uses a "retrospective" assessment system under which final liability for antidumping and countervailing duties is determined after merchandise is imported. Generally, the amount of duties to be assessed is determined in a review of the order covering a discrete period of time. If a review is not requested, duties are assessed at the rate established in the completed review covering the most recent prior period or, if no review has been completed, the cash deposit rate applicable at the time merchandise was entered. This section contains rules regarding the assessment of duties, the provisional measures deposit cap, and interest on over- or undercollections of estimated duties.

(b) *Assessment of antidumping and countervailing duties as the result of a review*—(1) *Antidumping duties.* If the Secretary has conducted a review of an antidumping order under § 351.213 (administrative review), § 351.214 (new shipper review), or § 351.215 (expedited antidumping review), the Secretary normally will calculate an assessment rate for each importer of subject merchandise covered by the review. The Secretary normally will calculate the assessment rate by dividing the dumping margin found on the subject merchandise examined by the entered value of such merchandise for normal customs duty purposes. The Secretary then will instruct the Customs Service to assess antidumping duties by applying the assessment rate to the entered value of the merchandise.

(2) *Countervailing duties.* If the Secretary has conducted a review of a countervailing duty order under § 351.213 (administrative review) or § 351.214 (new shipper review), the Secretary normally will instruct the Customs Service to assess countervailing duties by applying the rates included in the final results of the review to the entered value of the merchandise.

(c) *Automatic assessment of antidumping and countervailing duties if no review is requested.* (1) If the Secretary does not receive a timely request for an administrative review of an order (*see* paragraph (b)(1), (b)(2), or (b)(3) of § 351.213), the Secretary, without additional notice, will instruct the Customs Service to:

(i) Assess antidumping duties or countervailing duties, as the case may be, on the subject merchandise described in § 351.213(e) at rates equal to the cash deposit of, or bond for, estimated antidumping duties or countervailing duties required on that merchandise at the time of entry, or withdrawal from warehouse, for consumption; and

(ii) To continue to collect the cash deposits previously ordered.

(2) If the Secretary receives a timely request for an administrative review of an order (*see* paragraph (b)(1), (b)(2), or (b)(3) of § 351.213), the Secretary will instruct the Customs Service to assess antidumping duties or countervailing duties, and to continue to collect cash deposits, on the merchandise not covered by the request in accordance with paragraph (c)(1) of this section.

(3) The automatic assessment provisions of paragraphs (c)(1) and (c)(2) of this section will not apply to subject merchandise that is the subject of a new shipper review (*see* § 351.214) or an expedited antidumping review (*see* § 351.215).

(d) *Provisional measures deposit cap.* This paragraph applies to subject merchandise entered, or withdrawn from warehouse, for consumption before the date of publication of the Commission's notice of an affirmative final injury determination or, in a countervailing duty proceeding that involves merchandise from a country that is not entitled to an injury test, the date of the Secretary's notice of an affirmative final countervailing duty determination. If the amount of duties that would be assessed by applying the rates included in the Secretary's affirmative preliminary or affirmative final antidumping or countervailing duty determination ("provisional duties") is different from the amount of duties that would be assessed by applying the assessment rate under paragraphs (b)(1) and (b)(2) of this section ("final duties"), the Secretary will instruct the Customs Service to disregard the difference to the extent that the provisional duties are less than the final duties, and to assess antidumping or countervailing duties at the assessment rate if the provisional duties exceed the final duties.

(e) *Interest on certain overpayments and underpayments.* Under section 778 of the Act, the Secretary will instruct the Customs Service to calculate interest for each entry on or after the publication of the order from the date that a cash deposit is required to be deposited for the entry through the date of liquidation of the entry.

(f) *Special rule for regional industry cases*—(1) *In general.* If the Commission, in its final injury determination, found a regional industry under section 771(4)(C) of the Act, the Secretary may direct that duties not be assessed on subject merchandise of a particular exporter or producer if the Secretary determines that:

(i) The exporter or producer did not export subject merchandise for sale in the region concerned during or after the Department's period of investigation;

(ii) The exporter or producer has certified that it will not export subject merchandise for sale in the region concerned in the future so long as the antidumping or countervailing duty order is in effect; and

(iii) No subject merchandise of the exporter or producer was entered into the United States outside of the region and then sold into the region during or after the Department's period of investigation.

(2) *Procedures for obtaining an exception from the assessment of duties*—(i) *Request for exception.* An exporter or producer seeking an exception from the assessment of duties under paragraph (f)(1) of this section must request, subject to the provisions of § 351.213 or § 351.214, an administrative review or a new shipper review to determine whether subject merchandise of the exporter or producer in question should be excepted from the assessment of duties under paragraph (f)(1) of this section. The exporter or producer making the request may request that the review be limited to a determination as to whether the requirements of paragraph (f)(1) of this section are satisfied. The request for a review must be accompanied by:

(A) A certification by the exporter or producer that it did not export subject merchandise for sale in the region concerned during or after the Department's period of investigation, and that it will not do so in the future so long as the antidumping or countervailing duty order is in effect; and

(B) A certification from each of the exporter's or producer's U.S. importers of the subject merchandise that no subject merchandise of that exporter or producer was entered into the United States outside such region and then sold into the region during or after the Department's period of investigation.

(ii) *Limited review.* If the Secretary initiates an administrative review or a new shipper review based on a request for review that includes a request for an exception from the assessment of duties under paragraph (f)(2)(i) of this section, the Secretary, if requested, may limit the review to a determination as to whether an exception from the assessment of duties should be granted under paragraph (f)(1) of this section.

(3) *Exception granted.* If, in the final results of the administrative review or the new shipper review, the Secretary determines that the requirements of paragraph (f)(1) of this section are satisfied, the Secretary will instruct the Customs Service to liquidate, without regard to antidumping or countervailing duties (whichever is appropriate), entries of subject merchandise of the exporter or producer concerned.

(4) *Exception not granted.* If, in the final results of the administrative review or the new shipper review, the Secretary determines that the requirements of paragraph (f)(1) are not satisfied, the Secretary:

(i) Will issue assessment instructions to the Customs Service in accordance with paragraph (b) of this section; or

(ii) If the review was limited to a determination as to whether an exception from the assessment of duties should be granted, the Secretary will instruct the Customs Service to assess duties in accordance with paragraph (f)(1) or (f)(2) of this section, whichever is appropriate (automatic assessment if no review is requested).

§ 351.213 Administrative review of orders and suspension agreements under section 751(a)(1) of the Act.

(a) *Introduction.* As noted in § 351.212(a), the United States has a "retrospective" assessment system under which final liability for antidumping and countervailing duties is determined after merchandise is imported. Although duty liability may be determined in the context of other types of reviews, the most frequently used procedure for determining final duty liability is the administrative review procedure under section 751(a)(1) of the Act. This section contains rules regarding requests for administrative reviews and the conduct of such reviews.

(b) *Request for administrative review.* (1) Each year during the anniversary month of the publication of an antidumping or countervailing duty order, a domestic interested party or an interested party described in section 771(9)(B) of the Act (foreign government) may request in writing that the Secretary conduct an administrative review under section 751(a)(1) of the Act of specified individual exporters or producers covered by an order (except for a countervailing duty order in which the investigation or prior administrative review was conducted on an aggregate basis), if the requesting person states why the person desires the Secretary to review those particular exporters or producers.

(2) During the same month, an exporter or producer covered by an order (except for a countervailing duty order in which the investigation or prior administrative review was conducted on an aggregate basis) may request in writing that the Secretary conduct an administrative review of only that person.

(3) During the same month, an importer of the merchandise may request in writing that the Secretary conduct an administrative review of only an exporter or producer (except for a countervailing duty order in which the investigation or prior administrative review was conducted on an aggregate basis) of the subject merchandise imported by that importer.

(4) Each year during the anniversary month of the publication of a suspension of investigation, an interested party may request in writing that the Secretary conduct an administrative review of all producers or exporters covered by an agreement on which the suspension of investigation was based.

(c) *Deferral of administrative review—* (1) *In general.* The Secretary may defer the initiation of an administrative review, in whole or in part, for one year if:

(i) The request for administrative review is accompanied by a request that the Secretary defer the review, in whole or in part; and

(ii) None of the following persons objects to the deferral: the exporter or producer for which deferral is requested, an importer of subject merchandise of that exporter or producer, a domestic interested party and, in a countervailing duty proceeding, the foreign government.

(2) *Timeliness of objection to deferral.* An objection to a deferral of the initiation of administrative review under paragraph (c)(1)(ii) of this section must be submitted within 15 days after the end of the anniversary month in which the administrative review is requested.

(3) *Procedures and deadlines.* If the Secretary defers the initiation of an administrative review, the Secretary will publish notice of the deferral in the FEDERAL REGISTER. The Secretary will initiate the administrative review in the month immediately following the next anniversary month, and the deadline for issuing preliminary results of review (*see* paragraph (h)(1) of this section) and submitting factual information (*see* § 351.302(b)(2)) will run from the last day of the next anniversary month.

(d) *Rescission of administrative review—* (1) *Withdrawal of request for review.* The Secretary will rescind an administrative review under this section, in whole or in part, if a party that requested a review withdraws the request within 90 days of the date of publication of notice of initiation of the requested review. The Secretary may extend this time limit if the Secretary decides that it is reasonable to do so.

(2) *Self-initiated review.* The Secretary may rescind an administrative review that was self-initiated by the Secretary.

(3) *No shipments.* The Secretary may rescind an administrative review, in whole or only with respect to a particular exporter or producer, if the Secretary concludes that, during the period covered by the review, there were no entries, exports, or sales of the subject merchandise, as the case may be.

(4) *Notice of rescission.* If the Secretary rescinds an administrative review (in whole or in part), the Secretary will publish in the FEDERAL REGISTER notice of "Rescission of Antidumping (Countervailing Duty) Administrative Review" or, if appropriate, "Partial Rescission of Antidumping (Countervailing Duty) Administrative Review."

(e) *Period of review*—(1) *Antidumping proceedings.* (i) Except as provided in paragraph (e)(1)(ii) of this section, an administrative review under this section normally will cover, as appropriate, entries, exports, or sales of the subject merchandise during the 12 months immediately preceding the most recent anniversary month.

(ii) For requests received during the first anniversary month after publication of an order or suspension of investigation, an administrative review under this section will cover, as appropriate, entries, exports, or sales during the period from the date of suspension of liquidation under this part or suspension of investigation to the end of the month immediately preceding the first anniversary month.

(2) *Countervailing duty proceedings.* (i) Except as provided in paragraph (e)(2)(ii) of this section, an administrative review under this section normally will cover entries or exports of the subject merchandise during the most recently completed calendar year. If the review is conducted on an aggregate basis, the Secretary normally will cover entries or exports of the subject merchandise during the most recently completed fiscal year for the government in question.

(ii) For requests received during the first anniversary month after publication of an order or suspension of investigation, an administrative review under this section will cover entries or exports, as appropriate, during the period from the date of suspension of liquidation under this part or suspension of investigation to the end of the most recently completed calendar or fiscal year as described in paragraph (e)(2)(i) of this section.

(f) *Voluntary respondents.* In an administrative review, the Secretary will examine voluntary respondents in accordance with section 782(a) of the Act and § 351.204(d).

(g) *Procedures.* The Secretary will conduct an administrative review under this section in accordance with § 351.221.

(h) *Time limits*—(1) *In general.* The Secretary will issue preliminary results of review (*see* § 351.221(b)(4)) within 245 days after the last day of the anniversary month of the order or sus-

pension agreement for which the administrative review was requested, and final results of review (*see* § 351.221(b)(5)) within 120 days after the date on which notice of the preliminary results was published in the FEDERAL REGISTER.

(2) *Exception.* If the Secretary determines that it is not practicable to complete the review within the time specified in paragraph (h)(1) of this section, the Secretary may extend the 245-day period to 365 days and may extend the 120-day period to 180 days. If the Secretary does not extend the time for issuing preliminary results, the Secretary may extend the time for issuing final results from 120 days to 300 days.

(i) *Possible cancellation or revision of suspension agreement.* If during an administrative review the Secretary determines or has reason to believe that a signatory has violated a suspension agreement or that the agreement no longer meets the requirements of section 704 or section 734 of the Act (whichever is applicable), the Secretary will take appropriate action under section 704(i) or section 734(i) of the Act and § 351.209. The Secretary may suspend the time limit in paragraph (h) of this section while taking action under § 351.209.

(j) *Absorption of antidumping duties.* (1) During any administrative review covering all or part of a period falling between the first and second or third and fourth anniversary of the publication of an antidumping order under § 351.211, or a determination under § 351.218(d) (sunset review), the Secretary, if requested by a domestic interested party within 30 days of the date of publication of the notice of initiation of the review, will determine whether antidumping duties have been absorbed by an exporter or producer subject to the review if the subject merchandise is sold in the United States through an importer that is affiliated with such exporter or producer. The request must include the name(s) of the exporter or producer for which the inquiry is requested.

(2) For transition orders defined in section 751(c)(6) of the Act, the Secretary will apply paragraph (j)(1) of this section to any administrative review initiated in 1996 or 1998.

(3) In determining under paragraph (j)(1) of this section whether antidumping duties have been absorbed, the Secretary will examine the antidumping duties calculated in the administrative review in which the absorption inquiry is requested.

(4) The Secretary will notify the Commission of the Secretary's determination if:

(i) In the case of an administrative review other than one to which paragraph (j)(2) of this section applies, the administrative review covers all or part of a time period falling between the third and fourth anniversary month of an order; or

(ii) In the case of an administrative review to which paragraph (j)(2) of this section applies, the Secretary initiated the administrative review in 1998.

(k) *Administrative reviews of countervailing duty orders conducted on an aggregate basis*—(1) *Request for zero rate.* Where the Secretary conducts an administrative review of a countervailing duty on an aggregate basis under section 777A(e)(2)(B) of the Act, the Secretary will consider and review requests for individual assessment and cash deposit rates of zero to the extent practicable. An exporter or producer that desires a zero rate must submit:

(i) A certification by the exporter or producer that it received zero or *de minimis* net countervailable subsidies during the period of review;

(ii) If the exporter or producer received a countervailable subsidy, calculations demonstrating that the amount of net countervailable subsidies received was *de minimis* during the period of review;

(iii) If the exporter is not the producer of the subject merchandise, certifications from the suppliers and producers of the subject merchandise that those persons received zero or *de minimis* net countervailable subsidies during the period of the review; and

(iv) A certification from the government of the affected country that the government did not provide the exporter (or the exporter's supplier) or producer with more than *de minimis* net countervailable subsidies during the period of review.

(2) *Application of country-wide subsidy rate.* With the exception of assessment and cash deposit rates of zero determined under paragraph (k)(1) of this section, if, in the final results of an administrative review under this section of a countervailing duty order, the Secretary calculates a single country-wide subsidy rate under section 777A(e)(2)(B) of the Act, that rate will supersede, for cash deposit purposes, all rates previously determined in the countervailing duty proceeding in question.

(l) *Exception from assessment in regional industry cases.* For procedures relating to a request for the exception from the assessment of antidumping or countervailing duties in a regional industry case, see § 351.212(f).

§ 351.214 New shipper reviews under section 751(a)(2)(B) of the Act.

(a) *Introduction.* The URAA established a new procedure by which so-called "new shippers" can obtain their own individual dumping margin or countervailable subsidy rate on an expedited basis. In general, a new shipper is an exporter or producer that did not export, and is not affiliated with an exporter or producer that did export, to the United States during the period of investigation. This section contains rules regarding requests for new shipper reviews and procedures for conducting such reviews. In addition, this section contains rules regarding requests for expedited reviews by noninvestigated exporters in certain countervailing duty proceedings and procedures for conducting such reviews.

(b) *Request for new shipper review*—(1) *Requirement of sale or export.* Subject to the requirements of section 751(a)(2)(B) of the Act and this section, an exporter or producer may request a new shipper review if it has exported, or sold for export, subject merchandise to the United States.

(2) *Contents of request.* A request for a new shipper review must contain the following:

(i) If the person requesting the review is both the exporter and producer of the merchandise, a certification that the person requesting the review did not export subject merchandise to the United States (or, in the case of a regional industry, did not export the subject merchandise for sale in the region concerned) during the period of investigation;

(ii) If the person requesting the review is the exporter, but not the producer, of the subject merchandise:

(A) The certification described in paragraph (b)(2)(i) of this section; and

(B) A certification from the person that produced or supplied the subject merchandise to the person requesting the review that that producer or supplier did not export the subject merchandise to the United States (or, in the case of a regional industry, did not export the subject merchandise for sale in the region concerned) during the period of investigation;

(iii)(A) A certification that, since the investigation was initiated, such exporter or producer has never been affiliated with any exporter or producer who exported the subject merchandise to the United States (or in the case of a regional industry, who exported the subject merchandise for sale in the region concerned) during the period of investigation, including those not individually examined during the investigation;

(B) In an antidumping proceeding involving imports from a nonmarket economy country, a certification that the export activities of such exporter or producer are not controlled by the central government;

(iv) Documentation establishing:

(A) The date on which subject merchandise of the exporter or producer making the request was first entered, or withdrawn from warehouse, for consumption, or, if the exporter or producer cannot establish the date of first entry, the date on which the exporter or producer first shipped the subject merchandise for export to the United States;

(B) The volume of that and subsequent shipments; and

(C) The date of the first sale to an unaffiliated customer in the United States; and

(v) In the case of a review of a countervailing duty order, a certification that the exporter or producer has informed the government of the exporting country that the government will be required to provide a full response to the Department's questionnaire.

(c) *Deadline for requesting review.* An exporter or producer may request a new shipper review within one year of the date referred to in paragraph (b)(2)(iv)(A) of this section.

(d) *Time for new shipper review*—(1) *In general.* The Secretary will initiate a new shipper review under this section in the calendar month immediately following the anniversary month or the semiannual anniversary month if the request for the review is made during the 6-month period ending with the end of the anniversary month or the semiannual anniversary month (whichever is applicable).

(2) *Semiannual anniversary month.* The semiannual anniversary month is the calendar month which is 6 months after the anniversary month.

(3) *Example.* An order is published in January. The anniversary month would be January, and the semiannual anniversary month would be July. If the Secretary received a request for a new shipper review at any time during the period February-July, the Secretary would initiate a new shipper review in August. If the Secretary received a request for a new shipper review at any time during the period August-January, the Secretary would initiate a new shipper review in February.

(e) *Suspension of liquidation; posting bond or security.* When the Secretary initiates a new shipper review under this section, the Secretary will direct the Customs Service to suspend liquidation of any unliquidated entries of the subject merchandise from the relevant exporter or producer, and to allow, at the option of the importer, the posting, until the completion of the review, of a bond or security in lieu of a cash deposit for each entry of the subject merchandise.

(f) *Rescission of new shipper review*—(1) *Withdrawal of request for review.* The Secretary may rescind a new shipper review under this section, in whole or in part, if a party that requested a review withdraws its request not later than 60 days after the date of publication of notice of initiation of the requested review.

(2) *Absence of entry and sale to an unaffiliated customer.* The Secretary may rescind a new shipper review, in whole

or in part, if the Secretary concludes that:

(i) As of the end of the normal period of review referred to in paragraph (g) of this section, there has not been an entry and sale to an unaffiliated customer in the United States of subject merchandise; and

(ii) An expansion of the normal period of review to include an entry and sale to an unaffiliated customer in the United States of subject merchandise would be likely to prevent the completion of the review within the time limits set forth in paragraph (i) of this section.

(3) *Notice of Rescission.* If the Secretary rescinds a new shipper review (in whole or in part), the Secretary will publish in the FEDERAL REGISTER notice of "Rescission of Antidumping (Countervailing Duty) New Shipper Review" or, if appropriate, "Partial Rescission of Antidumping (Countervailing Duty) New Shipper Review."

(g) *Period of review*—(1) *Antidumping proceeding*—(i) *In general.* Except as provided in paragraph (g)(1)(ii) of this section, in an antidumping proceeding, a new shipper review under this section normally will cover, as appropriate, entries, exports, or sales during the following time periods:

(A) If the new shipper review was initiated in the month immediately following the anniversary month, the twelve-month period immediately preceding the anniversary month; or

(B) If the new shipper review was initiated in the month immediately following the semiannual anniversary month, the period of review will be the six-month period immediately preceding the semiannual anniversary month.

(ii) *Exceptions.* (A) If the Secretary initiates a new shipper review under this section in the month immediately following the first anniversary month, the review normally will cover, as appropriate, entries, exports, or sales during the period from the date of suspension of liquidation under this part to the end of the month immediately preceding the first anniversary month.

(B) If the Secretary initiates a new shipper review under this section in the month immediately following the first semiannual anniversary month, the review normally will cover, as appropriate, entries, exports, or sales during the period from the date of suspension of liquidation under this part to the end of the month immediately preceding the first semiannual anniversary month.

(2) *Countervailing duty proceeding.* In a countervailing duty proceeding, the period of review for a new shipper review under this section will be the same period as that specified in § 351.213(e)(2) for an administrative review.

(h) *Procedures.* The Secretary will conduct a new shipper review under this section in accordance with § 351.221.

(i) *Time limits*—(1) *In general.* Unless the time limit is waived under paragraph (j)(3) of this section, the Secretary will issue preliminary results of review (*see* § 351.221(b)(4)) within 180 days after the date on which the new shipper review was initiated, and final results of review (*see* § 351.221(b)(5)) within 90 days after the date on which the preliminary results were issued.

(2) *Exception.* If the Secretary concludes that a new shipper review is extraordinarily complicated, the Secretary may extend the 180-day period to 300 days, and may extend the 90-day period to 150 days.

(j) *Multiple reviews.* Notwithstanding any other provision of this subpart, if a review (or a request for a review) under § 351.213 (administrative review), § 351.214 (new shipper review), § 351.215 (expedited antidumping review), or § 351.216 (changed circumstances review) covers merchandise of an exporter or producer subject to a review (or to a request for a review) under this section, the Secretary may, after consulting with the exporter or producer:

(1) Rescind, in whole or in part, a review in progress under this subpart;

(2) Decline to initiate, in whole or in part, a review under this subpart; or

(3) Where the requesting party agrees in writing to waive the time limits of paragraph (i) of this section, conduct concurrent reviews, in which case all other provisions of this section will continue to apply with respect to the exporter or producer.

(k) *Expedited reviews in countervailing duty proceedings for noninvestigated exporters*—(1) *Request for review.* If, in a

244

countervailing duty investigation, the Secretary limited the number of exporters or producers to be individually examined under section 777A(e)(2)(A) of the Act, an exporter that the Secretary did not select for individual examination or that the Secretary did not accept as a voluntary respondent (*see* § 351.204(d)) may request a review under this paragraph (k). An exporter must submit a request for review within 30 days of the date of publication in the FEDERAL REGISTER of the countervailing duty order. A request must be accompanied by a certification that:

(i) The requester exported the subject merchandise to the United States during the period of investigation;

(ii) The requester is not affiliated with an exporter or producer that the Secretary individually examined in the investigation; and

(iii) The requester has informed the government of the exporting country that the government will be required to provide a full response to the Department's questionnaire.

(2) *Initiation of review*—(i) *In general.* The Secretary will initiate a review in the month following the month in which a request for review is due under paragraph (k)(1) of this section.

(ii) *Example.* The Secretary publishes a countervailing duty order on January 15. An exporter would have to submit a request for a review by February 14. The Secretary would initiate a review in March.

(3) *Conduct of review.* The Secretary will conduct a review under this paragraph (k) in accordance with the provisions of this section applicable to new shipper reviews, subject to the following exceptions:

(i) The period of review will be the period of investigation used by the Secretary in the investigation that resulted in the publication of the countervailing duty order (*see* § 351.204(b)(2));

(ii) The Secretary will not permit the posting of a bond or security in lieu of a cash deposit under paragraph (e) of this section;

(iii) The final results of a review under this paragraph (k) will not be the basis for the assessment of countervailing duties; and

(iv) The Secretary may exclude from the countervailing duty order in question any exporter for which the Secretary determines an individual net countervailable subsidy rate of zero or *de minimis* (*see* § 351.204(e)(1)), provided that the Secretary has verified the information on which the exclusion is based.

(l) *Exception from assessment in regional industry cases.* For procedures relating to a request for the exception from the assessment of antidumping or countervailing duties in a regional industry case, see § 351.212(f).

§ 351.215 Expedited antidumping review and security in lieu of estimated duty under section 736(c) of the Act.

(a) *Introduction.* Exporters and producers individually examined in an investigation normally cannot obtain a review of entries until an administrative review is requested. In addition, when an antidumping order is published, importers normally must begin to make a cash deposit of estimated antidumping duties upon the entry of subject merchandise. Section 736(c), however, establishes a special procedure under which exporters or producers may request an expedited review, and bonds, rather than cash deposits, may continue to be posted for a limited period of time if several criteria are satisfied. This section contains rules regarding requests for expedited antidumping reviews and the procedures applicable to such reviews.

(b) *In general.* If the Secretary determines that the criteria of section 736(c)(1) of the Act are satisfied, the Secretary:

(1) May permit, for not more than 90 days after the date of publication of an antidumping order, the posting of a bond or other security instead of the deposit of estimated antidumping duties required under section 736(a)(3) of the Act; and

(2) Will initiate an expedited antidumping review. Before making such a determination, the Secretary will make business proprietary information available, and will provide interested parties with an opportunity to file written comments, in accordance with section 736(c)(4) of the Act.

(c) *Procedures.* The Secretary will conduct an expedited antidumping review under this section in accordance with § 351.221.

§ 351.216 Changed circumstances review under section 751(b) of the Act.

(a) *Introduction.* Section 751(b) of the Act provides for what is known as a "changed circumstances" review. This section contains rules regarding requests for changed circumstances reviews and procedures for conducting such reviews.

(b) *Requests for changed circumstances review.* At any time, an interested party may request a changed circumstances review, under section 751(b) of the Act, of an order or a suspended investigation. Within 45 days after the date on which a request is filed, the Secretary will determine whether to initiate a changed circumstances review.

(c) *Limitation on changed circumstances review.* Unless the Secretary finds that good cause exists, the Secretary will not review a final determination in an investigation (*see* section 705(a) or section 735(a) of the Act) or a suspended investigation (*see* section 704 or section 734 of the Act) less than 24 months after the date of publication of notice of the final determination or the suspension of the investigation.

(d) *Procedures.* If the Secretary decides that changed circumstances sufficient to warrant a review exist, the Secretary will conduct a changed circumstances review in accordance with § 351.221.

(e) *Time limits.* The Secretary will issue final results of review (*see* § 351.221(b)(5)) within 270 days after the date on which the changed circumstances review is initiated, or within 45 days if all parties to the proceeding agree to the outcome of the review.

§ 351.217 Reviews to implement results of subsidies enforcement proceeding under section 751(g) of the Act.

(a) *Introduction.* Section 751(g) provides a mechanism for incorporating into an ongoing countervailing duty proceeding the results of certain sub-sidy-related disputes under the WTO Subsidies Agreement. Where the United States, in the WTO, has successfully challenged the "nonactionable" (*e.g.,* noncountervailable) status of a foreign subsidy, or where the United States has successfully challenged a prohibited or actionable subsidy, the Secretary may conduct a review to determine the effect, if any, of the successful outcome on an existing countervailing duty order or suspended investigation. This section contains rules regarding the initiation and conduct of reviews under section 751(g).

(b) *Violations of Article 8 of the Subsidies Agreement.* If:

(1) The Secretary receives notice from the Trade Representative of a violation of Article 8 of the Subsidies Agreement;

(2) The Secretary has reason to believe that merchandise subject to an existing countervailing duty order or suspended investigation is benefiting from the subsidy or subsidy program found to have been in violation of Article 8; and

(3) No administrative review is in progress, the Secretary will initiate an Article 8 violation review of the order or suspended investigation to determine whether the subject merchandise benefits from the subsidy or subsidy program found to have been in violation of Article 8 of the Subsidies Agreement.

(c) *Withdrawal of subsidy or imposition of countermeasures.* If the Trade Representative notifies the Secretary that, under Article 4 or Article 7 of the Subsidies Agreement:

(1)(i)(A) The United States has imposed countermeasures; and

(B) Such countermeasures are based on the effects in the United States of imports of merchandise that is the subject of a countervailing duty order; or

(ii) A WTO member country has withdrawn a countervailable subsidy provided with respect to merchandise subject to a countervailing duty order, then

(2) The Secretary will initiate an Article 4/Article 7 review of the order to determine if the amount of estimated duty to be deposited should be adjusted or the order should be revoked.

(d) *Procedures.* The Secretary will conduct an Article 8 violation review or an Article 4/Article 7 review under this section in accordance with §351.221.

(e) *Expedited reviews.* The Secretary will conduct reviews under this section on an expedited basis.

§351.218 Sunset reviews under section 751(c) of the Act.

(a) *Introduction.* The URAA added a new procedure, commonly referred to as "sunset reviews," in section 751(c) of the Act. In general, no later than once every five years, the Secretary must determine whether dumping or countervailable subsidies would be likely to continue or resume if an order were revoked or a suspended investigation were terminated. The Commission must conduct a similar review to determine whether injury would be likely to continue or resume in the absence of an order or suspended investigation. If the determinations under section 751(c) of both the Secretary and the Commission are affirmative, the order (or suspended investigation) remains in place. If either determination is negative, the order will be revoked (or the suspended investigation will be terminated). This section contains rules regarding the procedures for sunset reviews.

(b) *In general.* The Secretary will conduct a sunset review, under section 751(c) of the Act, of each antidumping and countervailing duty order and suspended investigation, and, under section 752(b) or section 752(c) (whichever is applicable), will determine whether revocation of an antidumping or countervailing duty order or termination of a suspended investigation would be likely to lead to continuation or recurrence of dumping or a countervailable subsidy.

(c) *Notice of initiation of review; early initiation*—(1) *Initial sunset review.* No later than 30 days before the fifth anniversary date of an order or suspension of an investigation (*see* section 751(c)(1) of the Act), the Secretary will publish a notice of initiation of a sunset review (*see* section 751(c)(2) of the Act).

(2) *Subsequent sunset reviews.* In the case of an order or suspended investigation that is continued following a sunset review initiated under paragraph

(c)(1) of this section, no later than 30 days before the fifth anniversary of the date of the last determination by the Commission to continue the order or suspended investigation, the Secretary will publish a notice of initiation of a sunset review (*see* section 751(c)(2) of the Act).

(3) *Early initiation.* The Secretary may publish a notice of initiation at an earlier date than the dates described in paragraph (c) (1) and (2) of this section if a domestic interested party demonstrates to the Secretary's satisfaction that an early initiation would promote administrative efficiency. However, if the Secretary determines that the domestic interested party that requested early initiation is a related party or an importer under section 771(4)(B) of the Act and §351.203(e)(4), the Secretary may decline the request for early initiation.

(4) *Transition orders.* The Secretary will initiate sunset reviews of transition orders, as defined in section 751(c)(6)(C) of the Act, in accordance with section 751(c)(6) of the Act.

(d) *Participation in sunset review*—(1) *Domestic interested party notification of intent to participate*—(i) *Filing of notice of intent to participate.* Where a domestic interested party intends to participate in a sunset review, the interested party must, not later than 15 days after the date of publication in the FEDERAL REGISTER of the notice of initiation, file a notice of intent to participate in a sunset review with the Secretary.

(ii) *Contents of notice of intent to participate.* Every notice of intent to participate in a sunset review must include a statement expressing the domestic interested party's intent to participate in the sunset review and the following information:

(A) The name, address, and phone number of the domestic interested party (and its members, if applicable) that intends to participate in the sunset review and the statutory basis (under section 771(9) of the Act) for interested party status;

(B) A statement indicating whether the domestic producer:

(*1*) Is related to a foreign producer or to a foreign exporter under section 771(4)(B) of the Act; or

(2) Is an importer of the subject merchandise or is related to such an importer under section 771(4)(B) of the Act;

(C) The name, address, and phone number of legal counsel or other representative, if any;

(D) The subject merchandise and country subject to the sunset review; and

(E) The citation and date of publication in the FEDERAL REGISTER of the notice of initiation.

(iii) *Failure of domestic interested party to file notice of intent to participate in the sunset review.* (A) A domestic interested party that does not file a notice of Intent to participate in the sunset review will be considered not willing to participate in the review and the Secretary will not accept or consider any unsolicited submissions from that party during the course of the review.

(B) If no domestic interested party files a notice of intent to participate in the sunset review, the Secretary will:

(1) Conclude that no domestic interested party has responded to the notice of initiation under section 751(c)(3)(A) of the Act;

(2) Notify the International Trade Commission in writing as such normally not later than 20 days after the date of publication in the FEDERAL REGISTER of the notice of initiation; and

(3) Not later than 90 days after the date of publication in the FEDERAL REGISTER of the Notice of Initiation, issue a final determination revoking the order or terminating the suspended investigation (*see* §§ 351.221(c)(5)(ii) and 351.222(i)).

(2) *Waiver of response by a respondent interested party to a notice of initiation—* (i) *Filing of statement of waiver.* A respondent interested party may waive participation in a sunset review before the Department under section 751(c)(4) of the Act by filing a statement of waiver with the Department, not later than 30 days after the date of publication in the FEDERAL REGISTER of the notice of initiation. If a respondent interested party waives participation in a sunset review before the Department, the Secretary will not accept or consider any unsolicited submissions from that party during the course of the re-

view. Waiving participation in a sunset review before the Department will not affect a party's opportunity to participate in the sunset review conducted by the International Trade Commission.

(ii) *Contents of statement of waiver.* Every statement of waiver must include a statement indicating that the respondent interested party waives participation in the sunset review before the Department; a statement that the respondent interested party is likely to dump or benefit from a countervailable subsidy (as the case may be) if the order is revoked or the investigation is terminated; in the case of a foreign government in a CVD sunset review, a statement that the government is likely to provide a countervailable subsidy if the order is revoked or the investigation is terminated; and the following information:

(A) The name, address, and phone number of the respondent interested party waiving participation in the sunset review before the Department;

(B) The name, address, and phone number of legal counsel or other representative, if any;

(C) The subject merchandise and country subject to the sunset review; and

(D) The citation and date of publication in the FEDERAL REGISTER of the notice of initiation.

(iii) [Reserved]

(iv) *Waiver of participation by a foreign government in a CVD sunset review.* Where a foreign government waives participation in a CVD sunset review under paragraph (d)(2)(i) or (d)(2)(iii) of this section, the Secretary will:

(A) Conclude that respondent interested parties have provided inadequate response to the notice of initiation under section 751(c)(3)(B) of the Act;

(B) Notify the International Trade Commission and conduct an expedited sunset review and issue final results of review in accordance with paragraph (e)(1)(ii)(C) of this section; and

(C) Base the final results of review on the facts available in accordance with 351.308(f).

(3) *Substantive response to a notice of initiation—*(i) *Time limit for substantive response to a notice of initiation.* A complete substantive response to a notice of initiation, filed under this section,

248

must be submitted to the Department not later than 30 days after the date of publication in the FEDERAL REGISTER of the notice of initiation.

(ii) *Required information to be filed by all interested parties in substantive response to a notice of initiation.* Except as provided in paragraph (d)(3)(v)(A) of this section, each interested party that intends to participate in a sunset review must file a submission with the Department containing the following:

(A) The name, address, and phone number of the interested party (and its members, if applicable) that intends to participate in the sunset review and the statutory basis (under section 771(9) of the Act) for interested party status;

(B) The name, address, and phone number of legal counsel or other representative, if any;

(C) The subject merchandise and country subject to the sunset review;

(D) The citation and date of publication in the FEDERAL REGISTER of the notice of initiation;

(E) A statement expressing the interested party's willingness to participate in the review by providing information requested by the Department, which must include a summary of that party's historical participation in any segment of the proceeding before the Department related to the subject merchandise;

(F) A statement regarding the likely effects of revocation of the order or termination of the suspended investigation under review, which must include any factual information, argument, and reason to support such statement;

(G) Factual information, argument, and reason concerning the dumping margin or countervailing duty rate, as applicable, that is likely to prevail if the Secretary revokes the order or terminates the suspended investigation, that the Department should select for a particular interested party(s);

(H) A summary of the Department's findings regarding duty absorption, if any, including a citation to the FEDERAL REGISTER notice in which the Department's findings are set forth; and

(I) A description of any relevant scope clarification or ruling, including a circumvention determination, or

changed circumstances determination issued by the Department during the proceeding with respect to the subject merchandise.

(iii) *Additional required information to be filed by respondent interested parties in substantive response to a notice of initiation.* Except as provided in paragraph (d)(3)(v)(A) of this section, the submission from each respondent interested party that intends to participate in a sunset review must also contain the following:

(A) That party's individual weighted average dumping margin or countervailing duty rate, as applicable, from the investigation and each subsequent completed administrative review, including the final margin or rate, as applicable, where such margin or rate was changed as a result of a final and conclusive court order;

(B) For each of the five calendar years (or fiscal years, if more appropriate) preceding the year of publication of the notice of initiation, that party's volume and value (normally on an FOB basis) of exports of subject merchandise to the United States;

(C) As applicable, for the calendar year (or fiscal year, if more appropriate) preceding the year of initiation of the dumping investigation, that party's volume and value (normally on an FOB basis) of exports of subject merchandise to the United States;

(D) For each of the five calendar years (or fiscal years, if more appropriate) preceding the year of publication of the notice of initiation, on a volume basis (or value basis, if more appropriate), that party's percentage of the total exports of subject merchandise (defined in section 771(25) of the Act) to the United States; and

(E) For each of the three most recent years, including the year of publication of the notice of initiation, that party's volume and value (normally on an FOB basis) of exports of subject merchandise to the United States during the two fiscal quarters as of the month preceding the month in which the notice of initiation was published.

(iv) *Optional information to be filed by interested parties in substantive response to a notice of initiation*—(A) *Showing good cause.* An interested party may submit information or evidence to show good cause for the Secretary to consider other factors under section 752(b)(2) (CVD) or section 752(c)(2) (AD) of the Act and paragraph (e)(2)(ii) of this section. Such information or evidence must be submitted in the party's substantive response to the notice of initiation under paragraph (d)(3) of this section.

(B) *Other information.* A substantive response from an interested party under paragraph (d)(3) of this section also may contain any other relevant information or argument that the party would like the Secretary to consider.

(v) *Required information to be filed by a foreign government in substantive response to the notice of initiation in a CVD sunset review*—(A) *In general.* The foreign government of a country subject to a CVD sunset review (*see* section 771(9)(B) of the Act) that intends to participate in a CVD sunset review must file a submission with the Department under paragraph (d)(3)(i) of this section containing the information required under paragraphs (d)(3)(ii) (A) through (E) of this section.

(B) *Additional required information to be filed by a foreign government in a CVD sunset review involving an order where the investigation was conducted on an aggregate basis.* The submission from the foreign government of a country subject to a CVD sunset review, involving an order where the investigation was conducted on an aggregate basis, must also contain:

(*1*) The information required under paragraphs (d)(3)(ii)(F), (d)(3)(ii)(G), and (d)(3)(ii)(I) of this section;

(*2*) The countervailing duty rate from the investigation and each subsequent completed administrative review, including the final rate where such rate was changed as a result of a final and conclusive court order; and

(*3*) For each of the five calendar years (or fiscal years, if more appropriate) preceding the year of publication of the notice of initiation, the volume and value (normally on an FOB basis) of exports of subject merchandise to the United States.

(vi) *Substantive responses from industrial users and consumers.* An industrial user of the subject merchandise or a representative consumer organization,

as described in section 777(h) of the Act, that intends to participate in a sunset review must file a submission with the Department under paragraph (d)(3)(i) of this section containing the information required under paragraphs (d)(3)(ii) (A) through (D) of this section and may submit other relevant information under paragraphs (d)(3)(ii) and (d)(3)(iv) of this section.

(4) *Rebuttal to substantive response to a notice of initiation.* Any interested party that files a substantive response to a notice of initiation under paragraph (d)(3) of this section may file a rebuttal to any other party's substantive response to a notice of initiation not later than five days after the date the substantive response is filed with the Department. Except as provided in § 351.309(e), the Secretary normally will not accept or consider any additional information from a party after the time for filing rebuttals has expired, unless the Secretary requests additional information from parties after determining to proceed to a full sunset review under paragraph (e)(2) of this section.

(e) *Conduct of sunset review*—(1) *Adequacy of response to a notice of initiation*—(i) *Adequacy of response from domestic interested parties*—(A) *In general.* The Secretary will make its determination of adequacy of response on a case-by-case basis; however, the Secretary normally will conclude that domestic interested parties have provided adequate response to a notice of initiation where it receives a complete substantive response under paragraph (d)(3) of this section from at least one domestic interested party.

(B) *Disregarding response from a domestic interested party.* In making its determination concerning the adequacy of response from domestic interested parties under paragraph (e)(1)(i)(A) of this section, the Secretary may disregard a response from a domestic producer:

(*1*) Related to a foreign producer or to a foreign exporter under section 771(4)(B) of the Act; or

(*2*) That is an importer of the subject merchandise or is related to such an importer under section 771(4)(B) of the Act (*see* paragraph (d)(1)(ii)(B) of this section).

(C) *Inadequate response from domestic interested parts.* Where the Secretary determines to disregard a response from a domestic interested party(s) under paragraph (e)(1)(i)(A) or (e)(1)(i)(B) of this section and no other domestic interested party has filed a complete substantive response to the notice of initiation under paragraph (d)(3) of this section, the Secretary will:

(1) Conclude that no domestic interested party has responded to the notice of initiation under section 751(c)(3)(A) of the Act;

(2) Notify the International Trade Commission in writing as such normally not later than 40 days after the date of publication in the FEDERAL REGISTER of the Notice of Initiation; and

(3) Not later than 90 days after the date of publication in the FEDERAL REGISTER of the Notice of Initiation, issue a final determination revoking the order or terminating the suspended investigation (see §§ 351.221(c)(5)(ii) and 351.222(i)).

(ii) *Adequacy of response from respondent interested parties*—(A) *In general.* The Secretary will makes its determination of adequacy of response on a case-by-case basis; however, the Secretary normally will conclude that respondent interested parties have provided adequate response to a notice of initiation where it receives complete substantive responses under paragraph (d)(3) of this section from respondent interested parties accounting on average for more than 50 percent, on a volume basis (or value basis, if appropriate), of the total exports of subject merchandise to the United States over the five calendar years preceding the year of publication of the notice of initiation.

(B) *Failure of a foreign government to file a substantive response to a notice of initiation in a CVD sunset review.* If a foreign government fails to file a complete substantive response to a notice of initiation in a CVD sunset review under paragraph (d)(3)(v) of this section or waives participation in a CVD sunset review under paragraph (d)(2)(i) of this section, the Secretary will:

(1) Conclude that respondent interested parties have provided inadequate response to the Notice of Initiation under section 751(c)(3)(B) of the Act;

(2) Notify the International Trade Commission and conduct an expedited sunset review and issue final results of review in accordance with paragraph (e)(1)(ii)(C) of this section; and

(3) Base the final results of review on the facts available in accordance with 351.308(f).

(C) *Inadequate response from respondent interested parties.* If the Secretary determines that respondent interested parties provided inadequate response to a notice of initiation under paragraph (d)(2)(iv), (e)(1)(ii)(A), or (e)(1)(ii)(B) of this section, the Secretary:

(1) Will notify the International Trade Commission in writing as such normally not later than 50 days after the date of publication in the FEDERAL REGISTER of the Notice of Initiation; and

(2) Normally will conduct an expedited sunset review and, not later than 120 days after the date of publication in the FEDERAL REGISTER of the notice of initiation, issue final results of review based on the facts available in accordance with § 351.308(f) (see section 751(c)(3)(B) of the Act and § 351.221(c)(5)(ii)).

(2) *Full sunset review upon adequate response from domestic and respondent interested parties*—(i) *In general.* Normally, only where the Department receives adequate response to the notice of initiation from domestic interested parties under paragraph (e)(1)(i)(A) of this section and from respondent interested parties under paragraph (e)(1)(ii)(A) of this section, will the Department conduct a full sunset review. Even where the Department conducts a full sunset review, only under the most extraordinary circumstances will the Secretary rely on a countervailing duty rate or a dumping margin other than those it calculated and published in its prior determinations, and in no case will the Secretary calculate a net countervailable subsidy or a dumping margin for a new shipper in the context of a sunset review.

(ii) [Reserved]

(iii) *Consideration of other factors under section 752(b)(2) (CVD) or section 752(c)(2) (AD) of the Act.* The Secretary will consider other factors under section 752(b)(2) (CVD) or section 752(c)(2) (AD) of the Act if the Secretary determines that good cause to consider such other factors exists. The Secretary normally will consider such other factors only where it conducts a full sunset review under paragraph (e)(2)(i) of this section.

(f) *Time limits*—(1) *Preliminary results of full sunset review.* The Department normally will issue its preliminary results in a full sunset review not later than 110 days after the date of publication in the FEDERAL REGISTER of the notice of initiation.

(2) *Verification*—(i) *In general.* The Department will verify factual information relied upon in making its final determination normally only in a full sunset review (*see* section 782(i)(2) of the Act and § 351.307(b)(1)(iii)) and only where needed. The Department will conduct verification normally only if, in its preliminary results, the Department determines that revocation of the order or termination of the suspended investigation, as applicable, is not likely to lead to continuation or recurrence of a countervailable subsidy or dumping (*see* section 752(b) and section 752(c) of the Act), as applicable, and the Department's preliminary results are not based on countervailing duty rates or dumping margins, as applicable, determined in the investigation or subsequent reviews.

(ii) *Timing of verification.* The Department normally will conduct verification, under paragraph (f)(2)(i) of this section and § 351.307, approximately 120 days after the date of publication in the FEDERAL REGISTER of the notice of initiation.

(3) *Final results of full sunset review and notification to the International Trade Commission*—(i) *Timing of final results of review and notification to the International Trade Commission.* The Department normally will issue its final results in a full sunset review and notify the International Trade Commission of its results of review not later than 240 days after the date of publication in the FEDERAL REGISTER of the notice of initiation (*see* section 751(c)(5)(A) of the Act).

(ii) *Extension of time limit.* If the Secretary determines that a full sunset re-

view is extraordinarily complicated under section 751(c)(5)(C) of the Act, the Secretary may extend the period for issuing final results by not more than 90 days (*see* section 751(c)(5)(B) of the Act).

(4) *Notice of continuation of an order or suspended investigation; notice of revocation of an order or termination of a suspended investigation.* Except as provided in paragraph (d)(1)(iii)(B)(*3*) of this section and § 351.222(i)(1)(i), the Department normally will issue its determination to continue an order or suspended investigation, or to revoke an order or terminate a suspended investigation, as applicable, not later than seven days after the date of publication in the FEDERAL REGISTER of the International Trade Commission's determination concluding the sunset review. The Department immediately thereafter will publish notice of its determination in the FEDERAL REGISTER.

[62 FR 27379, May 19, 1997, as amended at 63 FR 13520, Mar. 20, 1998; 70 FR 62064, Oct. 28, 2005]

§ 351.219 Reviews of countervailing duty orders in connection with an investigation under section 753 of the Act.

(a) *Introduction.* Section 753 of the Act is a transition provision for countervailing duty orders that were issued under section 303 of the Act without an injury determination by the Commission. Under the Subsidies Agreement, one country may not impose countervailing duties on imports from another WTO Member without first making a determination that such imports have caused injury to a domestic industry. Section 753 provides a mechanism for providing an injury test with respect to those "no-injury" orders under section 303 that apply to merchandise from WTO Members. This section contains rules regarding requests for section 753 investigations by a domestic interested party; and the procedures that the Department will follow in reviewing a countervailing duty order and providing the Commission with advice regarding the amount and nature of a countervailable subsidy.

(b) *Notification of domestic interested parties.* The Secretary will notify directly domestic interested parties as soon as possible after the opportunity arises for requesting an investigation by the Commission under section 753 of the Act.

(c) *Initiation and conduct of section 753 review.* Where the Secretary deems it necessary in order to provide to the Commission information on the amount or nature of a countervailable subsidy (*see* section 753(b)(2) of the Act), the Secretary may initiate a section 753 review of the countervailing duty order in question. The Secretary will conduct a section 753 review in accordance with §351.221.

§351.220 Countervailing duty review at the direction of the President under section 762 of the Act.

At the direction of the President or a designee, the Secretary will conduct a review under section 762(a)(1) of the Act to determine if a countervailable subsidy is being provided with respect to merchandise subject to an understanding or other kind of quantitative restriction agreement accepted under section 704(a)(2) or section 704(c)(3) of the Act. The Secretary will conduct a review under this section in accordance with §351.221. If the Secretary's final results of review under this section and the Commission's final results of review under section 762(a)(2) of the Act are both affirmative, the Secretary will issue a countervailing duty order and order suspension of liquidation in accordance with section 762(b) of the Act.

§351.221 Review procedures.

(a) *Introduction.* The procedures for reviews are similar to those followed in investigations. This section details the procedures applicable to reviews in general, as well as procedures that are unique to certain types of reviews.

(b) *In general.* After receipt of a timely request for a review, or on the Secretary's own initiative when appropriate, the Secretary will:

(1) Promptly publish in the FEDERAL REGISTER notice of initiation of the review;

(2) Before or after publication of notice of initiation of the review, send to appropriate interested parties or other persons (or, if appropriate, a sample of interested parties or other persons) questionnaires requesting factual information for the review;

(3) Conduct, if appropriate, a verification under §351.307;

(4) Issue preliminary results of review, based on the available information, and publish in the FEDERAL REGISTER notice of the preliminary results of review that include:

(i) The rates determined, if the review involved the determination of rates; and

(ii) An invitation for argument consistent with §351.309;

(5) Issue final results of review and publish in the FEDERAL REGISTER notice of the final results of review that include the rates determined, if the review involved the determination of rates;

(6) If the type of review in question involves a determination as to the amount of duties to be assessed, promptly after publication of the notice of final results instruct the Customs Service to assess antidumping duties or countervailing duties (whichever is applicable) on the subject merchandise covered by the review, except as otherwise provided in §351.106(c) with respect to *de minimis* duties; and

(7) If the review involves a revision to the cash deposit rates for estimated antidumping duties or countervailing duties, instruct the Customs Service to collect cash deposits at the revised rates on future entries.

(c) *Special rules*—(1) *Administrative reviews and new shipper reviews.* In an administrative review under section 751(a)(1) of the Act and §351.213 and a new shipper review under section 751(a)(2)(B) of the Act and §351.214 the Secretary:

(i) Will publish the notice of initiation of the review no later than the last day of the month following the anniversary month or the semiannual anniversary month (as the case may be); and

(ii) Normally will send questionnaires no later than 30 days after the date of publication of the notice of initiation.

(2) *Expedited antidumping review.* In an expedited antidumping review under section 736(c) of the Act and §351.215, the Secretary:

(i) Will include in the notice of initiation of the review an invitation for argument consistent with § 351.309, and a statement that the Secretary is permitting the posting of a bond or other security instead of a cash deposit of estimated antidumping duties;

(ii) Will instruct the Customs Service to accept, instead of the cash deposit of estimated antidumping duties under section 736(a)(3) of the Act, a bond for each entry of the subject merchandise entered, or withdrawn from warehouse, for consumption on or after the date of publication of the notice of initiation of the investigation and through the date not later than 90 days after the date of publication of the order; and

(iii) Will not issue preliminary results of review.

(3) *Changed circumstances review.* In a changed circumstances review under section 751(b) of the Act and § 351.216, the Secretary:

(i) Will include in the preliminary results of review and the final results of review a description of any action the Secretary proposed based on the preliminary or final results;

(ii) May combine the notice of initiation of the review and the preliminary results of review in a single notice if the Secretary concludes that expedited action is warranted; and

(iii) May refrain from issuing questionnaires under paragraph (b)(2) of this section.

(4) *Article 8 Violation review and Article 4/Article 7 review.* In an Article 8 Violation review or an Article 4/Article 7 review under section 751(g) of the Act and § 351.217, the Secretary:

(i) Will include in the notice of initiation of the review an invitation for argument consistent with § 351.309 and will notify all parties to the proceeding at the time the Secretary initiates the review;

(ii) Will not issue preliminary results of review; and

(iii) In the final results of review will indicate the amount, if any, by which the estimated duty to be deposited should be adjusted, and, in an Article 4/Article 7 review, any action, including revocation, that the Secretary will take based on the final results.

(5) *Sunset review.* In a sunset review under section 751(c) of the Act and § 351.218:

(i) The notice of initiation of a sunset review will contain a request for the information described in § 351.218(d); and

(ii) The Secretary, without issuing preliminary results of review, may issue final results of review under paragraphs (3) or (4) of subsection 751(c) of the Act if the conditions of those paragraphs are satisfied.

(6) *Section 753 review.* In a section 753 review under section 753 of the Act and § 351.219, the Secretary:

(i) Will include in the notice of initiation of the review an invitation for argument consistent with § 351.309, and will notify all parties to the proceeding at the time the Secretary initiates the review; and

(ii) May decline to issue preliminary results of review.

(7) *Countervailing duty review at the direction of the President.* In a countervailing duty review at the direction of the President under section 762 of the Act and § 351.220, the Secretary will:

(i) Include in the notice of initiation of the review a description of the merchandise, the period under review, and a summary of the available information which, if accurate, would support the imposition of countervailing duties;

(ii) Notify the Commission of the initiation of the review and the preliminary results of review;

(iii) Include in the preliminary results of review the countervailable subsidy, if any, during the period of review and a description of official changes in the subsidy programs made by the government of the affected country that affect the estimated countervailable subsidy; and

(iv) Include in the final results of review the countervailable subsidy, if any, during the period of review and a description of official changes in subsidy programs, made by the government of the affected country not later than the date of publication of the notice of preliminary results, that affect the estimated countervailable subsidy.

[62 FR 27379, May 19, 1997, as amended at 63 FR 13525, Mar. 20, 1998]

§351.222 Revocation of orders; termination of suspended investigations.

(a) *Introduction.* "Revocation" is a term of art that refers to the end of an antidumping or countervailing proceeding in which an order has been issued. "Termination" is the companion term for the end of a proceeding in which the investigation was suspended due to the acceptance of a suspension agreement. Generally, a revocation or termination may occur only after the Department or the Commission has conducted one or more reviews under section 751 of the Act. This section contains rules regarding requirements for a revocation or termination; and procedures that the Department will follow in determining whether to revoke an order or terminate a suspended investigation.

(b) *Revocation or termination based on absence of dumping.* (1) In determining whether to revoke an antidumping duty order or terminate a suspended antidumping investigation, the Secretary will consider:

(i) Whether all exporters and producers covered at the time of revocation by the order or the suspension agreement have sold the subject merchandise at not less than normal value for a period of at least three consecutive years; and

(ii) Whether the continued application of the antidumping duty order is otherwise necessary to offset dumping.

(2) If the Secretary determines, based upon the criteria in paragraphs (b)(1)(i) and (ii) of this section, that the antidumping duty order or suspension of the antidumping duty investigation is no longer warranted, the Secretary will revoke the order or terminate the investigation.

(c) *Revocation or termination based on absence of countervailable subsidy.* (1)(i) In determining whether to revoke a countervailing duty order or terminate a suspended countervailing duty investigation, the Secretary will consider:

(A) Whether the government of the affected country has eliminated all countervailable subsidies on the subject merchandise by abolishing for the subject merchandise, for a period of at least three consecutive years, all programs that the Secretary has found countervailable;

(B) Whether exporters and producers of the subject merchandise are continuing to receive any net countervailable subsidy from an abolished program referred to in paragraph (c)(1)(i)(A) of this section; and

(C) Whether the continued application of the countervailing duty order or suspension of countervailing duty investigation is otherwise necessary to offset subsidization.

(ii) If the Secretary determines, based upon the criteria in paragraphs (c)(1)(i)(A) through (C) of this section, that the countervailing duty order or suspension of the countervailing duty investigation is no longer warranted, the Secretary will revoke the order or terminate the suspended investigation.

(2)(i) In determining whether to revoke a countervailing duty order or terminate a suspended countervailing duty investigation, the Secretary will consider:

(A) Whether all exporters and producers covered at the time of revocation by the order or the suspension agreement have not applied for or received any net countervailable subsidy on the subject merchandise for a period of at least five consecutive years; and

(B) Whether the continued application of the countervailing duty order or suspension of the countervailing duty investigation is otherwise necessary to offset subsidization.

(ii) If the Secretary determines, based upon the criteria in paragraphs (c)(2)(i)(A) and (B) of this section, that the countervailing duty order or the suspension of the countervailing duty investigation is no longer warranted, the Secretary will revoke the order or terminate the suspended investigation.

(d) *Treatment of unreviewed intervening years—*(1) *In general.* The Secretary will not revoke an order or terminate a suspended investigation under paragraphs (b) or (c) of this section unless the Secretary has conducted a review under this subpart of the first and third (or fifth) years of the three-and five-year consecutive time periods referred to in those paragraphs. The Secretary need not have conducted a review of an intervening year (*see* paragraph (d)(2) of this section). However, except in the case of a revocation or termination under paragraph (c)(1) of this section (government abolition of countervailable subsidy programs), before revoking an order or terminating a suspended investigation, the Secretary must be satisfied that, during each of the three (or five) years, there were exports to the United States in commercial quantities of the subject merchandise to which a revocation or termination will apply.

(2) *Intervening year.* "Intervening year" means any year between the first and final year of the consecutive period on which revocation or termination is conditioned.

(e) Request for revocation or termination—(1) *Antidumping proceeding.* During the third and subsequent annual anniversary months of the publication of an antidumping order or suspension of an antidumping investigation, any exporter or producer may request in writing that the Secretary revoke an order or terminate a suspended investigation under paragraph (b) of this section if the person submits with the request:

(i) Certifications for all exporters and producers covered by the order or suspension agreement that they sold the subject merchandise at not less than normal value during the period of review described in § 351.213(e)(1), and that in the future they will not sell the merchandise at less than normal value; and

(ii) Certifications for all exporters and producers covered by the order or suspension agreement that, during each of the consecutive years referred to in paragraph (b) of this section, they sold the subject merchandise to the United States in commercial quantities.

(2) *Countervailing duty proceeding.* (i) During the third and subsequent annual anniversary months of the publication of a countervailing duty order or suspension of a countervailing duty investigation, the government of the affected country may request in writing that the Secretary revoke an order or terminate a suspended investigation under paragraph (c)(1) of this section if the government submits with the request its certification that it has satisfied, during the period of review described in § 351.213(e)(2), the require-

ments of paragraph (c)(1)(i) of this section regarding the abolition of countervailable subsidy programs, and that it will not reinstate for the subject merchandise those programs or substitute other countervailable subsidy programs;

(ii) During the fifth and subsequent annual anniversary months of the publication of a countervailing duty order or suspended countervailing duty investigation, the government of the affected country may request in writing that the Secretary revoke an order or terminate a suspended investigation under paragraph (c)(2) of this section if the government submits with the request:

(A) Certifications for all exporters and producers covered by the order or suspension agreement that they have not applied for or received any net countervailable subsidy on the subject merchandise for a period of at least five consecutive years (see paragraph (c)(2)(i) of this section);

(B) Those exporters' and producers' certifications that they will not apply for or receive any net countervailable subsidy on the subject merchandise from any program the Secretary has found countervailable in any proceeding involving the affected country or from other countervailable programs (see paragraph (c)(2)(ii) of this section); and

(C) A certification from each exporter or producer that, during each of the consecutive years referred to in paragraph (c)(2) of this section, that person sold the subject merchandise to the United States in commercial quantities.

(f) *Procedures.* (1) Upon receipt of a timely request for revocation or termination under paragraph (e) of this section, the Secretary will consider the request as including a request for an administrative review and will initiate and conduct a review under § 351.213.

(2) When the Secretary is considering a request for revocation or termination under paragraph (e) of this section, in addition to the requirements of § 351.221 regarding the conduct of an administrative review, the Secretary will:

(i) Publish with the notice of initiation under § 351.221(b)(1), notice of "Request for Revocation of Order" or

"Request for Termination of Suspended Investigation" (whichever is applicable);

(ii) Conduct a verification under §351.307;

(iii) Include in the preliminary results of review under §351.221(b)(4) the Secretary's decision whether there is a reasonable basis to believe that the requirements for revocation or termination are met;

(iv) If the Secretary decides that there is a reasonable basis to believe that the requirements for revocation or termination are met, publish with the notice of preliminary results of review under §351.221(b)(4) notice of "Intent To Revoke Order" or "Intent To Terminate Suspended Investigation" (whichever is applicable);

(v) Include in the final results of review under §351.221(b)(5) the Secretary's final decision whether the requirements for revocation or termination are met; and

(vi) If the Secretary determines that the requirements for revocation or termination are met, publish with the notice of final results of review under §351.221(b)(5) notice of "Revocation of Order" or "Termination of Suspended Investigation" (whichever is applicable).

(3) If the Secretary revokes an order, the Secretary will order the suspension of liquidation terminated for the merchandise covered by the revocation on the first day after the period under review, and will instruct the Customs Service to release any cash deposit or bond.

(g) *Revocation or termination based on changed circumstances.* (1) The Secretary may revoke an order, in whole or in part, or terminate a suspended investigation if the Secretary concludes that:

(i) Producers accounting for substantially all of the production of the domestic like product to which the order (or the part of the order to be revoked) or suspended investigation pertains have expressed a lack of interest in the order, in whole or in part, or suspended investigation (*see* section 782(h) of the Act); or

(ii) Other changed circumstances sufficient to warrant revocation or termination exist.

(2) If at any time the Secretary concludes from the available information that changed circumstances sufficient to warrant revocation or termination may exist, the Secretary will conduct a changed circumstances review under §351.216.

(3) In addition to the requirements of §351.221, the Secretary will:

(i) Publish with the notice of initiation (*see* §353.221(b)(1), notice of "Consideration of Revocation of Order (in Part)" or "Consideration of Termination of Suspended Investigation" (whichever is applicable);

(ii) If the Secretary's conclusion regarding the possible existence of changed circumstances (*see* paragraph (g)(2) of this section), is not based on a request, the Secretary, not later than the date of publication of the notice of "Consideration of Revocation of Order (in Part)" or "Consideration of Termination of Suspended Investigation" (whichever is applicable) (*see* paragraph (g)(3)(i) of this section), will serve written notice of the consideration of revocation or termination on each interested party listed on the Department's service list and on any other person that the Secretary has reason to believe is a domestic interested party;

(iii) Conduct a verification, if appropriate, under §351.307;

(iv) Include in the preliminary results of review, under §351.221(b)(4), the Secretary's decision whether there is a reasonable basis to believe that changed circumstances warrant revocation or termination;

(v) If the Secretary's preliminary decision is that changed circumstances warrant revocation or termination, publish with the notice of preliminary results of review, under §351.221(b)(4), notice of "Intent to Revoke Order (in Part)" or "Intent to Terminate Suspended Investigation" (whichever is applicable);

(vi) Include in the final results of review, under §351.221(b)(5), the Secretary's final decision whether changed circumstances warrant revocation or termination; and

(vii) If the Secretary's determines that changed circumstances warrant revocation or termination, publish with the notice of final results of review, under §351.221(b)(5), notice of

"Revocation of Order (in Part)" or "Termination of Suspended Investigation" (whichever is applicable).

(4) If the Secretary revokes an order, in whole or in part, under paragraph (g) of this section, the Secretary will order the suspension of liquidation ended for the merchandise covered by the revocation on the effective date of the notice of revocation, and will instruct the Customs Service to release any cash deposit or bond.

(h) *Revocation or termination based on injury reconsideration.* If the Commission determines in a changed circumstances review under section 751(b)(2) of the Act that the revocation of an order or termination of a suspended investigation is not likely to lead to continuation or recurrence of material injury, the Secretary will revoke, in whole or in part, the order or terminate the suspended investigation, and will publish in the FEDERAL REGISTER notice of "Revocation of Order (in Part)" or "Termination of Suspended Investigation" (whichever is applicable).

(i) *Revocation or termination based on sunset review—*(1) *Circumstances under which the Secretary will revoke an order or terminate a suspended investigation.* In the case of a sunset review under § 351.218, the Secretary will revoke an order or terminate a suspended investigation:

(i) Under section 751(c)(3)(A) of the Act, where no domestic interested party files a Notice of Intent to Participate in the sunset review under § 351.218(d)(1), or where the Secretary determines under § 351.218(e)(1)(i)(C) that domestic interested parties have provided inadequate response to the Notice of Initiation, not later than 90 days after the date of publication in the FEDERAL REGISTER of the notice of initiation;

(ii) Under section 751(d)(2) of the Act, where the Secretary determines that revocation or termination is not likely to lead to continuation or recurrence of a countervailable subsidy or dumping (*see* section 752(b) and section 752(c) of the Act), as applicable, not later than 240 days (or 330 days where a full sunset review is fully extended) after the date of publication in the FEDERAL REGISTER of the notice of initiation; or

(iii) Under section 751(d)(2) of the Act, where the International Trade Commission makes a determination, under section 752(a) of the Act, that revocation or termination is not likely to lead to continuation or recurrence of material injury, not later than seven days after the date of publication in the FEDERAL REGISTER of the International Trade Commission's determination concluding the sunset review.

(2) *Effective date of revocation—*(i) *In general.* Except as provided in paragraph (i)(2)(ii) of this section, where the Secretary revokes an order or terminates a suspended investigation, pursuant to section 751(c)(3)(A) or section 751(d)(2) of the Act (*see* paragraph (i)(1) of this section), the revocation or termination will be effective on the fifth anniversary of the date of publication in the FEDERAL REGISTER of the order or suspended investigation, as applicable. This paragraph also applies to subsequent sunset reviews of transition orders (*see* paragraph (i)(2)(ii) of this section and section 751(c)(6)(A)(iii) of the Act).

(ii) *Transition orders.* Where the Secretary revokes a transition order (defined in section 751(c)(6)(C) of the Act) pursuant to section 751(c)(3)(A) or section 751(d)(2) of the Act (*see* paragraph (i)(1) of this section), the revocation or termination will be effective on January 1, 2000. This paragraph does not apply to subsequent sunset reviews of transition orders (*see* section 751(c)(6)(A)(iii) of the Act).

(j) *Revocation of countervailing duty order based on Commission negative determination under section 753 of the Act.* The Secretary will revoke a countervailing duty order, and will order the refund, with interest, of any estimated countervailing duties collected during the period liquidation was suspended under section 753(a)(4) of the Act upon being notified by the Commission that:

(1) The Commission has determined that an industry in the United States is not likely to be materially injured if the countervailing duty order in question is revoked (*see* section 753(a)(1) of the Act); or

(2) A domestic interested party did not make a timely request for an investigation under section 753(a) of the Act (*see* section 753(a)(3) of the Act).

(k) *Revocation based on Article 4/Article 7 review*—(1) *In general.* The Secretary may revoke a countervailing duty order, in whole or in part, following an Article 4/Article 7 review under §351.217(c), due to the imposition of countermeasures by the United States or the withdrawal of a countervailable subsidy by a WTO member country (*see* section 751(g)(2) of the Act).

(2) *Additional requirements.* In addition to the requirements of §351.221, if the Secretary determines to revoke an order as the result of an Article 4/Article 7 review, the Secretary will:

(i) Conduct a verification, if appropriate, under §351.307;

(ii) Include in the final results of review, under §351.221(b)(5), the Secretary's final decision whether the order should be revoked;

(iii) If the Secretary's final decision is that the order should be revoked:

(A) Determine the effective date of the revocation;

(B) Publish with the notice of final results of review, under §351.221(b)(5), a notice of "Revocation of Order (in Part)," that will include the effective date of the revocation; and

(C) Order any suspension of liquidation ended for merchandise covered by the revocation that was entered on or after the effective date of the revocation, and instruct the Customs Service to release any cash deposit or bond.

(l) *Revocation under section 129.* The Secretary may revoke an order under section 129 of the URAA (implementation of WTO dispute settlement).

(m) *Cross-reference.* For the treatment in a subsequent investigation of business proprietary information submitted to the Secretary in connection with a changed circumstances review under §351.216 or a sunset review under §351.218 that results in the revocation of an order (or termination of a suspended investigation), see section 777(b)(3) of the Act.

[62 FR 27379, May 19, 1997, as amended at 63 FR 13523, Mar. 20, 1998; 64 FR 51240, Sept. 22, 1999; 77 FR 29883, May 21, 2012]

§351.223 Procedures for initiation of downstream product monitoring.

(a) *Introduction.* Section 780 of the Act establishes a mechanism for monitoring imports of "downstream products." In general, section 780 is aimed at situations where, following the issuance of an antidumping or countervailing duty order on a product that is used as a component in another product, exports to the United States of that other (or "downstream") product increase. Although the Department is responsible for determining whether trade in the downstream product should be monitored, the Commission is responsible for conducting the actual monitoring. The Commission must report the results of its monitoring to the Department, and the Department must consider the reports in determining whether to self-initiate an antidumping or countervailing duty investigation on the downstream product. This section contains rules regarding applications for the initiation of downstream product monitoring and decisions regarding such applications.

(b) *Contents of application.* An application to designate a downstream product for monitoring under section 780 of the Act must contain the following information, to the extent reasonably available to the applicant:

(1) The name and address of the person requesting the monitoring and a description of the article it produces which is the basis for filing its application;

(2) A detailed description of the downstream product in question;

(3) A detailed description of the component product that is incorporated into the downstream product, including the value of the component part in relation to the value of the downstream product, and the extent to which the component part has been substantially transformed as a result of its incorporation into the downstream product;

(4) The name of the country of production of both the downstream and component products and the name of any intermediate country from which the merchandise is imported;

(5) The name and address of all known producers of component parts and downstream products in the relevant countries and a detailed description of any relationship between such producers;

(6) Whether the component part is already subject to monitoring to aid in

the enforcement of a bilateral arrangement within the meaning of section 804 of the Trade and Tariff Act of 1984;

(7) A list of all antidumping or countervailing duty investigations that have been suspended, or antidumping or countervailing duty orders that have been issued, on merchandise that is related to the component part and that is manufactured in the same foreign country in which the component part is manufactured;

(8) A list of all antidumping or countervailing duty investigations that have been suspended, or antidumping or countervailing duty orders that have been issued, on merchandise that is manufactured or exported by the manufacturer or exporter of the component part and that is similar in description and use to the component part; and

(9) The reasons for suspecting that the imposition of antidumping or countervailing duties has resulted in a diversion of exports of the component part into increased production and exportation to the United States of the downstream product.

(c) *Determination of sufficiency of application.* Within 14 days after an application is filed under paragraph (b) of this section, the Secretary will rule on the sufficiency of the application by making the determinations described in section 780(a)(2) of the Act.

(d) *Notice of determination.* The Secretary will publish in the FEDERAL REGISTER notice of each affirmative or negative "monitoring" determination made under section 780(a)(2) of the Act, and if the determination under section 780(a)(2)(A) of the Act and a determination made under any clause of section 780(a)(2)(B) of the Act are affirmative, will transmit to the Commission a copy of the determination and the application. The Secretary will make available to the Commission, and to its employees directly involved in the monitoring, the information upon which the Secretary based the initiation.

§ 351.224   Disclosure of calculations and procedures for the correction of ministerial errors.

(a) *Introduction.* In the interests of transparency, the Department has long had a practice of providing parties with the details of its antidumping and countervailing duty calculations. This practice has come to be referred to as a "disclosure." This section contains rules relating to requests for disclosure and procedures for correcting ministerial errors.

(b) *Disclosure.* The Secretary will disclose to a party to the proceeding calculations performed, if any, in connection with a preliminary determination under section 703(b) or section 733(b) of the Act, a final determination under section 705(a) or section 735(a) of the Act, and a final results of a review under section 736(c), section 751, or section 753 of the Act, normally within five days after the date of any public announcement or, if there is no public announcement of, within five days after the date of publication of, the preliminary determination, final determination, or final results of review (whichever is applicable). The Secretary will disclose to a party to the proceeding calculations performed, if any, in connection with a preliminary results of review under section 751 or section 753 of the Act, normally not later than ten days after the date of the public announcement of, or, if there is no public announcement, within five days after the date of publication of, the preliminary results of review.

(c) *Comments regarding ministerial errors*—(1) *In general.* A party to the proceeding to whom the Secretary has disclosed calculations performed in connection with a preliminary determination may submit comments concerning a significant ministerial error in such calculations. A party to the proceeding to whom the Secretary has disclosed calculations performed in connection with a final determination or the final results of a review may submit comments concerning any ministerial error in such calculations. Comments concerning ministerial errors made in the preliminary results of a review should be included in a party's case brief.

(2) *Time limits for submitting comments.* A party to the proceeding must file comments concerning ministerial errors within five days after the earlier of:

(i) The date on which the Secretary released disclosure documents to that party; or

(ii) The date on which the Secretary held a disclosure meeting with that party.

(3) *Replies to comments.* Replies to comments submitted under paragraph (c)(1) of this section must be filed within five days after the date on which the comments were filed with the Secretary. The Secretary will not consider replies to comments submitted in connection with a preliminary determination.

(4) *Extensions.* A party to the proceeding may request an extension of the time limit for filing comments concerning a ministerial error in a final determination or final results of review under §351.302(c) within three days after the date of any public announcement, or, if there is no public announcement, within five days after the date of publication of the final determination or final results of review, as applicable. The Secretary will not extend the time limit for filing comments concerning a significant ministerial error in a preliminary determination.

(d) *Contents of comments and replies.* Comments filed under paragraph (c)(1) of this section must explain the alleged ministerial error by reference to applicable evidence in the official record, and must present what, in the party's view, is the appropriate correction. In addition, comments concerning a preliminary determination must demonstrate how the alleged ministerial error is significant (*see* paragraph (g) of this section) by illustrating the effect on individual weighted-average dumping margin or countervailable subsidy rate, the all-others rate, or the country-wide subsidy rate (whichever is applicable). Replies to any comments must be limited to issues raised in such comments.

(e) *Corrections.* The Secretary will analyze any comments received and, if appropriate, correct any significant ministerial error by amending the preliminary determination, or correct any ministerial error by amending the final determination or the final results of review (whichever is applicable). Where practicable, the Secretary will an-nounce publicly the issuance of a correction notice, and normally will do so within 30 days after the date of public announcement, or, if there is no public announcement, within 30 days after the date of publication, of the preliminary determination, final determination, or final results of review (whichever is applicable). In addition, the Secretary will publish notice of such corrections in the FEDERAL REGISTER. A correction notice will not alter the anniversary month of an order or suspended investigation for purposes of requesting an administrative review (*see* §351.213) or a new shipper review (*see* §351.214) or initiating a sunset review (*see* §351.218).

(f) *Definition of "ministerial error."* Under this section, *ministerial error* means an error in addition, subtraction, or other arithmetic function, clerical error resulting from inaccurate copying, duplication, or the like, and any other similar type of unintentional error which the Secretary considers ministerial.

(g) *Definition of "significant ministerial error."* Under this section, *significant ministerial error* means a ministerial error (*see* paragraph (f) of this section), the correction of which, either singly or in combination with other errors:

(1) Would result in a change of at least five absolute percentage points in, but not less than 25 percent of, the weighted-average dumping margin or the countervailable subsidy rate (whichever is applicable) calculated in the original (erroneous) preliminary determination; or

(2) Would result in a difference between a weighted-average dumping margin or countervailable subsidy rate (whichever is applicable) of zero (or *de minimis*) and a weighted-average dumping margin or countervailable subsidy rate of greater than *de minimis*, or vice versa.

§351.225 Scope rulings.

(a) *Introduction.* Issues arise as to whether a particular product is included within the scope of an antidumping or countervailing duty order or a suspended investigation. Such issues can arise because the descriptions of subject merchandise contained in the Department's determinations must be written in general terms. At other times, a domestic interested party may allege that changes to an imported product or the place where the imported product is assembled constitutes circumvention under section 781 of the Act. When such issues arise, the Department issues "scope rulings" that clarify the scope of an order or suspended investigation with respect to particular products. This section contains rules regarding scope rulings, requests for scope rulings, procedures for scope inquiries, and standards used in determining whether a product is within the scope of an order or suspended investigation.

(b) *Self-initiation.* If the Secretary determines from available information that an inquiry is warranted to determine whether a product is included within the scope of an antidumping or countervailing duty order or a suspended investigation, the Secretary will initiate an inquiry, and will notify all parties on the Department's scope service list of its initiation of a scope inquiry.

(c) *By application*—(1) *Contents and service of application.* Any interested party may apply for a ruling as to whether a particular product is within the scope of an order or a suspended investigation. The application must be served upon all parties on the scope service list described in paragraph (n) of this section, and must contain the following, to the extent reasonably available to the interested party:

(i) A detailed description of the product, including its technical characteristics and uses, and its current U.S. Tariff Classification number;

(ii) A statement of the interested party's position as to whether the product is within the scope of an order or a suspended investigation, including:

(A) A summary of the reasons for this conclusion,

(B) Citations to any applicable statutory authority, and

(C) Any factual information supporting this position, including excerpts from portions of the Secretary's or the Commission's investigation, and relevant prior scope rulings.

(2) *Deadline for action on application.* Within 45 days of the date of receipt of an application for a scope ruling, the Secretary will issue a final ruling under paragraph (d) of this section or will initiate a scope inquiry under paragraph (e) of this section.

(d) *Ruling based upon the application.* If the Secretary can determine, based solely upon the application and the descriptions of the merchandise referred to in paragraph (k)(1) of this section, whether a product is included within the scope of an order or a suspended investigation, the Secretary will issue a final ruling as to whether the product is included within the order or suspended investigation. The Secretary will notify all persons on the Department's scope service list (*see* paragraph (n) of this section) of the final ruling.

(e) *Ruling where further inquiry is warranted.* If the Secretary finds that the issue of whether a product is included within the scope of an order or a suspended investigation cannot be determined based solely upon the application and the descriptions of the merchandise referred to in paragraph (k)(1) of this section, the Secretary will notify by mail all parties on the Department's scope service list of the initiation of a scope inquiry.

(f) *Notice and procedure.* (1) Notice of the initiation of a scope inquiry issued under paragraph (b) or (e) of this section will include:

(i) A description of the product that is the subject of the scope inquiry; and

(ii) An explanation of the reasons for the Secretary's decision to initiate a scope inquiry;

(iii) A schedule for submission of comments that normally will allow interested parties 20 days in which to provide comments on, and supporting factual information relating to, the inquiry, and 10 days in which to provide any rebuttal to such comments.

(2) The Secretary may issue questionnaires and verify submissions received, where appropriate.

(3) Whenever the Secretary finds that a scope inquiry presents an issue of significant difficulty, the Secretary will issue a preliminary scope ruling, based upon the available information at the time, as to whether there is a reasonable basis to believe or suspect that the product subject to a scope inquiry is included within the order or suspended

investigation. The Secretary will notify all parties on the Department's scope service list (see paragraph (n) of this section) of the preliminary scope ruling, and will invite comment. Unless otherwise specified, interested parties will have within twenty days from the date of receipt of the notification in which to submit comments, and ten days thereafter in which to submit rebuttal comments.

(4) The Secretary will issue a final ruling as to whether the product which is the subject of the scope inquiry is included within the order or suspended investigation, including an explanation of the factual and legal conclusions on which the final ruling is based. The Secretary will notify all parties on the Department's scope service list (see paragraph (n) of this section) of the final scope ruling.

(5) The Secretary will issue a final ruling under paragraph (k) of this section (other scope rulings) normally within 120 days of the initiation of the inquiry under this section. The Secretary will issue a final ruling under paragraph (g), (h), (i), or (j) of this section (circumvention rulings under section 781 of the Act) normally within 300 days from the date of the initiation of the scope inquiry.

(6) When an administrative review under §351.213, a new shipper review under §351.214, or an expedited antidumping review under §351.215 is in progress at the time the Secretary provides notice of the initiation of a scope inquiry (see paragraph (e)(1) of this section), the Secretary may conduct the scope inquiry in conjunction with that review.

(7)(i) The Secretary will notify the Commission in writing of the proposed inclusion of products in an order prior to issuing a final ruling under paragraph (f)(4) of this section based on a determination under:

(A) Section 781(a) of the Act with respect to merchandise completed or assembled in the United States (other than minor completion or assembly);

(B) Section 781(b) of the Act with respect to merchandise completed or assembled in other foreign countries; or

(C) Section 781(d) of the Act with respect to later-developed products which incorporate a significant technological advance or significant alteration of an earlier product.

(ii) If the Secretary notifies the Commission under paragraph (f)(7)(i) of this section, upon the written request of the Commission, the Secretary will consult with the Commission regarding the proposed inclusion, and any such consultation will be completed within 15 days after the date of such request. If, after consultation, the Commission believes that a significant injury issue is presented by the proposed inclusion of a product within an order, the Commission may provide written advice to the Secretary as to whether the inclusion would be inconsistent with the affirmative injury determination of the Commission on which the order is based.

(g) *Products completed or assembled in the United States.* Under section 781(a) of the Act, the Secretary may include within the scope of an antidumping or countervailing duty order imported parts or components referred to in section 781(a)(1)(B) of the Act that are used in the completion or assembly of the merchandise in the United States at any time such order is in effect. In making this determination, the Secretary will not consider any single factor of section 781(a)(2) of the Act to be controlling. In determining the value of parts or components purchased from an affiliated person under section 781(a)(1)(D) of the Act, or of processing performed by an affiliated person under section 781(a)(2)(E) of the Act, the Secretary may determine the value of the part or component on the basis of the cost of producing the part or component under section 773(f)(3) of the Act.

(h) *Products completed or assembled in other foreign countries.* Under section 781(b) of the Act, the Secretary may include within the scope of an antidumping or countervailing duty order, at any time such order is in effect, imported merchandise completed or assembled in a foreign country other than the country to which the order applies. In making this determination, the Secretary will not consider any single factor of section 781(b)(2) of the Act to be controlling. In determining the value of parts or components purchased from an affiliated person under section 781(b)(1)(D) of the Act, or of processing performed by an affiliated person under section 781(b)(2)(E) of the Act, the Secretary may determine the value of the part or component on the basis of the cost of producing the part or component under section 773(f)(3) of the Act.

(i) *Minor alterations of merchandise.* Under section 781(c) of the Act, the Secretary may include within the scope of an antidumping or countervailing duty order articles altered in form or appearance in minor respects.

(j) *Later-developed merchandise.* In determining whether later-developed merchandise is within the scope of an antidumping or countervailing duty order, the Secretary will apply section 781(d) of the Act.

(k) *Other scope determinations.* With respect to those scope determinations that are not covered under paragraphs (g) through (j) of this section, in considering whether a particular product is included within the scope of an order or a suspended investigation, the Secretary will take into account the following:

(1) The descriptions of the merchandise contained in the petition, the initial investigation, and the determinations of the Secretary (including prior scope determinations) and the Commission.

(2) When the above criteria are not dispositive, the Secretary will further consider:

(i) The physical characteristics of the product;

(ii) The expectations of the ultimate purchasers;

(iii) The ultimate use of the product;

(iv) The channels of trade in which the product is sold; and

(v) The manner in which the product is advertised and displayed.

(l) *Suspension of liquidation.* (1) When the Secretary conducts a scope inquiry under paragraph (b) or (e) of this section, and the product in question is already subject to suspension of liquidation, that suspension of liquidation will be continued, pending a preliminary or a final scope ruling, at the cash deposit rate that would apply if the product were ruled to be included within the scope of the order.

(2) If the Secretary issues a preliminary scope ruling under paragraph (f)(3) of this section to the effect that the product in question is included within the scope of the order, any suspension of liquidation described in paragraph (l)(1) of this section will continue. If liquidation has not been suspended, the Secretary will instruct the Customs Service to suspend liquidation and to require a cash deposit of estimated duties, at the applicable rate, for each unliquidated entry of the product entered, or withdrawn from warehouse, for consumption on or after the date of initiation of the scope inquiry. If the Secretary issues a preliminary scope ruling to the effect that the product in question is not included within the scope of the order, the Secretary will order any suspension of liquidation on the product ended, and will instruct the Customs Service to refund any cash deposits or release any bonds relating to that product.

(3) If the Secretary issues a final scope ruling, under either paragraph (d) or (f)(4) of this section, to the effect that the product in question is included within the scope of the order, any suspension of liquidation under paragraph (l)(1) or (l)(2) of this section will continue. Where there has been no suspension of liquidation, the Secretary will instruct the Customs Service to suspend liquidation and to require a cash deposit of estimated duties, at the applicable rate, for each unliquidated entry of the product entered, or withdrawn from warehouse, for consumption on or after the date of initiation of the scope inquiry. If the Secretary's final scope ruling is to the effect that the product in question is not included within the scope of the order, the Secretary will order any suspension of liquidation on the subject product ended and will instruct Customs Service to refund any cash deposits or release any bonds relating to this product.

(4) If, within 90 days of the initiation of a review of an order or a suspended investigation under this subpart, the Secretary issues a final ruling that a product is included within the scope of the order or suspended investigation that is the subject of the review, the Secretary, where practicable, will include sales of that product for purposes of the review and will seek information

regarding such sales. If the Secretary issues a final ruling after 90 days of the initiation of the review, the Secretary may consider sales of the product for purposes of the review on the basis of non-adverse facts available. However, notwithstanding the pendency of a scope inquiry, if the Secretary considers it appropriate, the Secretary may request information concerning the product that is the subject of the scope inquiry for purposes of a review under this subpart.

(m) *Orders covering identical products.* Except for a scope inquiry and a scope ruling that involves section 781(a) or section 781(b) of the Act (assembly of parts or components in the United States or in a third country), if more than one order or suspended investigation cover the same subject merchandise, and if the Secretary considers it appropriate, the Secretary may conduct a single inquiry and issue a single scope ruling that applies to all such orders or suspended investigations.

(n) *Service of applications; scope service list.* The requirements of §351.303(f) apply to this section, except that an application for a scope ruling must be served on all persons on the Department's scope service list. For purposes of this section, the "scope service list" will include all persons that have participated in any segment of the proceeding. If an application for a scope ruling in one proceeding results in a single inquiry that will apply to another proceeding (*see* paragraph (m) of this section), the Secretary will notify persons on the scope service list of the other proceeding of the application for a scope ruling.

(o) *Publication of list of scope rulings.* On a quarterly basis, the Secretary will publish in the FEDERAL REGISTER a list of scope rulings issued within the last three months. This list will include the case name, reference number, and a brief description of the ruling.

Subpart C—Information and Argument

§351.301 Time limits for submission of factual information.

(a) *Introduction.* This section sets forth the time limits for submitting factual information, as defined by §351.102(b)(21). The Department obtains most of its factual information in antidumping and countervailing duty proceedings from submissions made by interested parties during the course of the proceeding. Notwithstanding paragraph (b) of this section, the Secretary may request any person to submit factual information at any time during a proceeding or provide additional opportunities to submit factual information. Section 351.302 sets forth the procedures for requesting an extension of such time limits, and provides that, unless expressly precluded by statute, the Secretary may, for good cause, extend any time limit established in the Department's regulations. Section 351.303 contains the procedural rules regarding filing (including procedures for filing on non-business days), format, translation, service, and certification of documents. In the Secretary's written request to an interested party for a response to a questionnaire or for other factual information, the Secretary will specify the following: The time limit for the response; the information to be provided; the form and manner in which the interested party must submit the information; and that failure to submit the requested information in the requested form and manner by the date specified may result in use of the facts available under section 776 of the Act and §351.308.

(b) *Submission of factual information.* Every submission of factual information must be accompanied by a written explanation identifying the subsection of §351.102(b)(21) under which the information is being submitted.

(1) If an interested party states that the information is submitted under §351.102(b)(21)(v), the party must explain why the information does not satisfy the definitions described in §351.102(b)(21)(i)–(iv).

(2) If the factual information is being submitted to rebut, clarify, or correct factual information on the record, the submitter must provide a written explanation identifying the information which is already on the record that the factual information seeks to rebut, clarify, or correct, including the name of the interested party that submitted the information and the date on which the information was submitted.

(c) *Time limits.* The type of factual information determines the time limit for submission to the Department.

(1) *Factual information submitted in response to questionnaires.* During a proceeding, the Secretary may issue to any person questionnaires, which includes both initial and supplemental questionnaires. The Secretary will not consider or retain in the official record of the proceeding unsolicited questionnaire responses, except as provided under § 351.204(d)(2), or untimely filed questionnaire responses. The Secretary will reject any untimely filed or unsolicited questionnaire response and provide, to the extent practicable, written notice stating the reasons for rejection (see § 351.302(d)).

(i) Initial questionnaire responses are due 30 days from the date of receipt of such questionnaire. The time limit for response to individual sections of the questionnaire, if the Secretary requests a separate response to such sections, may be less than the 30 days allotted for response to the full questionnaire. In general, the date of receipt will be considered to be seven days from the date on which the initial questionnaire was transmitted.

(ii) Supplemental questionnaire responses are due on the date specified by the Secretary.

(iii) A notification by an interested party, under section 782(c)(1) of the Act, of difficulties in submitting information in response to a questionnaire issued by the Secretary is to be submitted in writing within 14 days after the date of the questionnaire or, if the questionnaire is due in 14 days or less, within the time specified by the Secretary.

(iv) A respondent interested party may request in writing that the Secretary conduct a questionnaire presentation. The Secretary may conduct a questionnaire presentation if the Secretary notifies the government of the affected country and that government does not object.

(v) *Factual information submitted to rebut, clarify, or correct questionnaire responses.* Within 14 days after an initial questionnaire response and within 10 days after a supplemental questionnaire response has been filed with the Department, an interested party other than the original submitter is permitted one opportunity to submit factual information to rebut, clarify, or correct factual information contained in the questionnaire response. Within seven days of the filing of such rebuttal, clarification, or correction to a questionnaire response, the original submitter of the questionnaire response is permitted one opportunity to submit factual information to rebut, clarify, or correct factual information submitted in the interested party's rebuttal, clarification or correction. The Secretary will reject any untimely filed rebuttal, clarification, or correction submission and provide, to the extent practicable, written notice stating the reasons for rejection (see § 351.302). If insufficient time remains before the due date for the final determination or final results of review, the Secretary may specify shorter deadlines under this section.

(2) *Factual information submitted in support of allegations.* Factual information submitted in support of allegations must be accompanied by a summary, not to exceed five pages, of the allegation and supporting data.

(i) *Market viability and the basis for determining normal value.* Allegations regarding market viability in an antidumping investigation or administrative review, including the exceptions in § 351.404(c)(2), are due, with all supporting factual information, 10 days after the respondent interested party files the response to the relevant section of the questionnaire, unless the Secretary alters this time limit.

(ii) *Sales at prices below the cost of production.* Allegations of sales at prices below the cost of production made by the petitioner or other domestic interested party are due within:

(A) In an antidumping investigation, on a country-wide basis, 20 days after the date on which the initial questionnaire was issued to any person, unless the Secretary alters this time limit; or, on a company-specific basis, 20 days after a respondent interested party files the response to the relevant section of the questionnaire, unless the relevant questionnaire response is, in the Secretary's view, incomplete, in which case the Secretary will determine the time limit;

(B) In an administrative review, new shipper review, or changed circumstances review, on a company-specific basis, 20 days after a respondent interested party files the response to the relevant section of the questionnaire, unless the relevant questionnaire response is, in the Secretary's view, incomplete, in which case the Secretary will determine the time limit; or

(C) In an expedited antidumping review, on a company-specific basis, 10 days after the date of publication of the notice of initiation of the review.

(iii) *Purchases of major inputs from an affiliated party at prices below the affiliated party's cost of production.* An allegation of purchases of major inputs from an affiliated party at prices below the affiliated party's cost of production made by the petitioner or other domestic interested party is due within 20 days after a respondent interested party files the response to the relevant section of the questionnaire, unless the relevant questionnaire response is, in the Secretary's view, incomplete, in which case the Secretary will determine the time limits.

(iv) *Countervailable subsidy; upstream subsidy.* A countervailable subsidy allegation made by the petitioner or other domestic interested party is due no later than:

(A) In a countervailing duty investigation, 40 days before the scheduled date of the preliminary determination, unless the Secretary extends this time limit for good cause; or

(B) In an administrative review, new shipper review, or changed circumstances review, 20 days after all responses to the initial questionnaire are filed with the Department, unless the Secretary alters this time limit.

(C) Exception for upstream subsidy allegation in an investigation. In a countervailing duty investigation, an allegation of upstream subsidies made by the petitioner or other domestic interested party is due no later than 60 days after the date of the preliminary determination.

(v) *Other allegations.* An interested party may submit factual information in support of other allegations not specified in paragraphs (c)(2)(i)–(iv) of this section. Upon receipt of factual in-

formation under this subsection, the Secretary will issue a memorandum accepting or rejecting the information and, to the extent practicable, will provide written notice stating the reasons for rejection. If the Secretary accepts the information, the Secretary will issue a schedule providing deadlines for submission of factual information to rebut, clarify or correct the factual information.

(vi) *Rebuttal, clarification, or correction of factual information submitted in support of allegations.* An interested party is permitted one opportunity to submit factual information to rebut, clarify, or correct factual information submitted in support of allegations 10 days after the date such factual information is served on an interested party.

(3) *Factual information submitted to value factors under § 351.408(c) or to measure the adequacy of remuneration under § 351.511(a)(2).*

(i) *Antidumping or countervailing duty investigations.* All submissions of factual information to value factors of production under § 351.408(c) in an antidumping investigation, or to measure the adequacy of remuneration under § 351.511(a)(2) in a countervailing duty investigation, are due no later than 30 days before the scheduled date of the preliminary determination.

(ii) *Administrative review, new shipper review, or changed circumstances review.* All submissions of factual information to value factors under § 351.408(c), or to measure the adequacy of remuneration under § 351.511(a)(2), are due no later than 30 days before the scheduled date of the preliminary results of review; and

(iii) *Expedited antidumping review.* All submissions of factual information to value factors under § 351.408(c) are due on a date specified by the Secretary.

(iv) *Rebuttal, clarification, or correction of factual information submitted to value factors under § 351.408(c) or to measure the adequacy of remuneration under § 351.511(a)(2).* An interested party is permitted one opportunity to submit publicly available information to rebut, clarify, or correct such factual information submitted pursuant to § 351.408(c) or § 351.511(a)(2) 10 days after the date such factual information is served on the interested party. An interested party may not submit additional, previously absent-from-the-record alternative surrogate value information under this subsection. Additionally, all factual information submitted under this subsection must be accompanied by a written explanation identifying what information already on the record of the ongoing proceeding the factual information is rebutting, clarifying, or correcting. Information submitted to rebut, clarify, or correct factual information submitted pursuant to § 351.408(c) will not be used to value factors under § 351.408(c).

(4) *Factual information placed on the record of the proceeding by the Department.* The Department may place factual information on the record of the proceeding at any time. An interested party is permitted one opportunity to submit factual information to rebut, clarify, or correct factual information placed on the record of the proceeding by the Department by a date specified by the Secretary.

(5) *Factual information not directly responsive to or relating to paragraphs (c)(1)–(4) of this section).* Paragraph (c)(5) applies to factual information other than that described in § 351.102(b)(21)(i)–(iv). The Secretary will reject information filed under paragraph (c)(5) that satisfies the definition of information described in § 351.102(b)(21)(i)–(iv) and that was not filed within the deadlines specified above. All submissions of factual information under this subsection are required to clearly explain why the information contained therein does not meet the definition of factual information described in § 351.102(b)(21)(i)–(iv), and must provide a detailed narrative of exactly what information is contained in the submission and why it should be considered. The deadline for filing such information will be 30 days before the scheduled date of the preliminary determination in an investigation, or 14 days before verification, whichever is earlier, and 30 days before the scheduled date of the preliminary results in an administrative review, or 14 days before verification, whichever is earlier.

(i) Upon receipt of factual information under this subsection, the Sec-

retary will issue a memorandum accepting or rejecting the information and, to the extent practicable, will provide written notice stating the reasons for rejection.

(ii) If the Secretary accepts the information, the Secretary will issue a schedule providing deadlines for submission of factual information to rebut, clarify or correct the factual information.

[78 FR 21254, Apr. 10, 2013]

§ 351.302 Extension of time limits; return of untimely filed or unsolicited material.

(a) *Introduction.* This section sets forth the procedures for requesting an extension of a time limit. In addition, this section explains that certain untimely filed or unsolicited material will be rejected together with an explanation of the reasons for the rejection of such material.

(b) *Extension of time limits.* Unless expressly precluded by statute, the Secretary may, for good cause, extend any time limit established by this part.

(c) *Requests for extension of specific time limit.* Before the applicable time limit established under this part expires, a party may request an extension pursuant to paragraph (b) of this section. An untimely filed extension request will not be considered unless the party demonstrates that an extraordinary circumstance exists. The request must be in writing, in a separate, stand-alone submission, filed consistent with § 351.303, and state the reasons for the request. An extension granted to a party must be approved in writing.

(1) An extension request will be considered untimely if it is received after the applicable time limit expires or as otherwise specified by the Secretary.

(2) An extraordinary circumstance is an unexpected event that:

(i) Could not have been prevented if reasonable measures had been taken, and

(ii) Precludes a party or its representative from timely filing an extension request through all reasonable means.

(d) *Rejection of untimely filed or unsolicited material.* (1) Unless the Secretary extends a time limit under paragraph

(b) of this section, the Secretary will not consider or retain in the official record of the proceeding:

(i) Untimely filed factual information, written argument, or other material that the Secretary rejects, except as provided under § 351.104(a)(2); or

(ii) Unsolicited questionnaire responses, except as provided under § 351.204(d)(2).

(2) The Secretary will reject such information, argument, or other material, or unsolicited questionnaire response with, to the extent practicable, written notice stating the reasons for rejection.

[62 FR 27379, May 19, 1997, as amended at 76 FR 39275, July 6, 2011; 78 FR 57795, Sept. 20, 2013]

§ 351.303 Filing, document identification, format, translation, service, and certification of documents.

(a) *Introduction.* This section contains the procedural rules regarding filing, document identification, format, service, translation, and certification of documents and applies to all persons submitting documents to the Department for consideration in an antidumping or countervailing duty proceeding.

(b) *Filing*—(1) *In general.* Persons must address all documents to the Secretary of Commerce, Attention: Enforcement and Compliance, APO/Dockets Unit, Room 18022, U.S. Department of Commerce, 14th Street and Constitution Avenue, NW., Washington, DC 20230. An electronically filed document must be received successfully in its entirety by the Department's electronic records system, ACCESS, by 5 p.m. Eastern Time on the due date. Where applicable, a submitter must manually file a document between the hours of 8:30 a.m. and 5 p.m. Eastern Time on business days (see § 351.103(b)). For both electronically filed and manually filed documents, if the applicable due date falls on a non-business day, the Secretary will accept documents that are filed on the next business day. A manually filed document must be accompanied by a cover sheet generated in ACCESS, in accordance with § 351.303(b)(3).

(2) *Filing of documents and databases*—(i) *Electronic filing.* A person must file all documents and databases electronically using ACCESS at *https://access.trade.gov*. A person making a filing must comply with the procedures set forth in the ACCESS Handbook on Electronic Filing Procedures, which is available on the ACCESS Web site at *https://access.trade.gov*.

(ii) *Manual filing.* (A) Notwithstanding § 351.303(b)(2)(i), a person must manually file a data file that exceeds the file size limit specified in the ACCESS Handbook on Electronic Filing Procedures and as referenced in § 351.303(c)(3), and the data file must be accompanied by a cover sheet described in § 351.303(b)(3). A person may manually file a bulky document. If a person elects to manually file a bulky document, it must be accompanied by a cover sheet described in § 351.303(b)(3). The Department both provides specifications for large data files and defines bulky document standards in the ACCESS Handbook on Electronic Filing Procedures, which is available on the ACCESS Web site at *https://access.trade.gov*.

(B) [Reserved]

(3) *Cover sheet.* When manually filing a document, parties must complete the cover sheet (as described in the ACCESS Handbook on Electronic Filing Procedures) online at *https://access.trade.gov* and print the cover sheet for submission to the APO/Dockets Unit.

(4) *Document identification.* Each document must be clearly identified as one of the following five document classifications and must conform with the requirements under paragraph (d)(2) of this section. Business proprietary document or business proprietary/APO version, as applicable, means a document or a version of a document containing information for which a person claims business proprietary treatment under § 351.304.

(i) Business Proprietary Document— May be Released Under APO. This business proprietary document contains single-bracketed business proprietary information that the submitter agrees to release under APO. It must contain the statement "May be Released Under APO" in accordance with the requirements under paragraph (d)(2)(v) of this section.

(ii) Business Proprietary Document—May Not be Released Under APO. This business proprietary document contains double-bracketed business proprietary information that the submitter does not agree to release under APO. This document must contain the statement "May Not be Released Under APO" in accordance with the requirements under paragraph (d)(2)(v) of this section. This type of document may contain single-bracketed business proprietary information in addition to double-bracketed business proprietary information.

(iii) Business Proprietary/APO Version—May be Released Under APO. In the event that a business proprietary document contains both single- and double-bracketed business proprietary information, the submitting person must submit a version of the document with the double-bracketed business proprietary information omitted. This version must contain the single-bracketed business proprietary information that the submitter agrees to release under APO. This version must be identified as "Business Proprietary/APO Version" and must contain the statement "May be Released Under APO" in accordance with the requirements under paragraph (d)(2)(v) of this section.

(iv) *Public version.* The public version excludes all business proprietary information, whether single- or double-bracketed. Specific filing requirements for public version submissions are discussed in § 351.304(c).

(v) *Public document.* The public document contains only public information. There is no corresponding business proprietary document for a public document.

(c) Filing of business proprietary documents and public versions under the one-day lag rule; information in double brackets.

(1) *In general.* If a submission contains information for which the submitter claims business proprietary treatment, the submitter may elect to file the submission under the one-day lag rule described in paragraph (c)(2) of this section. A petition, an amendment to a petition, and any other submission filed prior to the initiation of an investigation shall not be filed under the one-day lag rule. The business proprietary document and public version of such pre-initiation submissions must be filed simultaneously on the same day.

(2) *Application of the one-day lag rule—* (i) *Filing the business proprietary document.* A person must file a business proprietary document with the Department within the applicable time limit.

(ii) Filing of final business proprietary document; bracketing corrections. By the close of business one business day after the date the business proprietary document is filed under paragraph (c)(2)(i) of this section, a person must file the complete final business proprietary document with the Department. The final business proprietary document must be identical in all respects to the business proprietary document filed on the previous day except for any bracketing corrections and the omission of the warning "Bracketing of Business Proprietary Information Is Not Final for One Business Day After Date of Filing" in accordance with paragraph (d)(2)(v) of this section. A person must serve other persons with the complete final business proprietary document if there are bracketing corrections. If there are no bracketing corrections, a person need not serve a copy of the final business proprietary document.

(iii) *Filing the public version.* Simultaneously with the filing of the final business proprietary document under paragraph (c)(2)(ii) of this section, a person also must file the public version of such document (see § 351.304(c)) with the Department.

(iv) *Information in double brackets.* If a person serves authorized applicants with a business proprietary/APO version of a document that excludes information in double brackets pursuant to §§ 351.303(b)(4)(iii) and 351.304(b)(2), the person simultaneously must file with the Department the complete business proprietary/APO version of the document from which information in double brackets has been excluded.

(3) *Sales files, cost of production files and other electronic databases.* When a submission includes sales files, cost of production files or other electronic databases, such electronic databases

must be filed electronically in accordance with paragraph (b)(2) of this section. If a submitter must file the database manually pursuant to §351.303(b)(2)(ii)(A), the submitter must file such information on the computer medium specified by the Department's request for such information. The submitter need not accompany the computer medium with a paper printout. All electronic database information must be releasable under APO (see §351.305). A submitter need not include brackets in an electronic database containing business proprietary information. The submitter's selection of the security classification "Business Proprietary Document—May Be Released Under APO" at the time of filing indicates the submitter's request for business proprietary treatment of the information contained in the database. Where possible, the submitter must insert headers or footers requesting business proprietary treatment of the information on the databases for printing purposes. A submitter must submit a public version of a database in pdf format. The public version of the database must be publicly summarized and ranged in accordance with §351.304(c).

(d) *Format of submissions*—(1) *In general.* Unless the Secretary alters the requirements of this section, a document filed with the Department must conform to the specification and marking requirements under paragraph (d)(2) of this section or the Secretary may reject such document in accordance with §351.104(a).

(2) *Specifications and markings.* If a document is filed manually, it must be on letter-size (8½ × 11 inch) paper, single-sided and double-spaced, bound with a paper clip, butterfly/binder clip, or rubber band. The filing of stapled, spiral, velo, or other type of solid binding is not permitted. In accordance with paragraph (b)(3) of this section, a cover sheet must be placed before the first page of the document. Electronically filed documents must be formatted to print on letter-size (8½ × 11 inch) paper and double-spaced. Spreadsheets, unusually sized exhibits, and databases are best utilized in their original printing format and should not be reformatted for submission. A submitter must mark the first page of each document in the upper right-hand corner with the following information in the following format:

(i) On the first line, except for a petition, indicate the Department case number;

(ii) On the second line, indicate the total number of pages in the document including cover pages, appendices, and any unnumbered pages;

(iii) On the third line, indicate the specific segment of the proceeding, (*e.g.*, investigation, administrative review, scope inquiry, suspension agreement, *etc.*) and, if applicable, indicate the complete period of review (MM/DD/YY–MM/DD/YY);

(iv) On the fourth line, except for a petition, indicate the Department office conducting the proceeding;

(v) On the fifth and subsequent lines, indicate whether any portion of the document contains business proprietary information and, if so, list the applicable page numbers and state either: "Business Proprietary Document—May Be Released Under APO," "Business Proprietary Document—May Not Be Released Under APO," or "Business Proprietary/APO Version—May Be Released Under APO," as applicable, and consistent with §351.303(b)(4). Indicate "Business Proprietary Treatment Requested" on the top of each page containing business proprietary information. In addition, include the warning "Bracketing of Business Proprietary Information Is Not Final for One Business Day After Date of Filing" on the top of each page containing business proprietary information in the business proprietary document filed under paragraph (c)(2)(i) of this section (one-day lag rule). Do not include this warning in the final business proprietary document filed on the next business day under paragraph (c)(2)(ii) of this section (see §351.303(c)(2) and §351.304(c)); and

(vi) For the public version of a business proprietary document required under §351.304(c), complete the marking as required in paragraphs (d)(2)(i)–(v) of this section for the business proprietary document, but conspicuously mark the first page "Public Version."

(vii) For a public document, complete the marking as required in paragraphs (d)(2)(i)–(v) of this section for the business proprietary document or version, as applicable, but conspicuously mark the first page "Public Document."

(e) *Translation to English.* A document submitted in a foreign language must be accompanied by an English translation of the entire document or of only pertinent portions, where appropriate, unless the Secretary waives this requirement for an individual document. A party must obtain the Department's approval for submission of an English translation of only portions of a document prior to submission to the Department.

(f) *Service of copies on other persons—* (1)(i) *In general.* Except as provided in §351.202(c) (filing of petition), §351.208(f)(1) (submission of proposed suspension agreement), and paragraph (f)(3) of this section, a person filing a document with the Department simultaneously must serve a copy of the document on all other persons on the service list by personal service or first class mail.

(ii) *Service of public versions, public documents, or a party's own business proprietary information.* Notwithstanding paragraphs (f)(1)(i) and (f)(3) of this section, service of a business proprietary document containing only the server's own business proprietary information, on persons on the APO service list, or the public version of such a document, or a public document on persons on the public service list, may be made by facsimile transmission or other electronic transmission process, with the consent of the person to be served.

(2) *Certificate of service.* Each document filed with the Department must include a certificate of service listing each person served (including agents), the type of document served, and the date and method of service on each person. The Secretary may refuse to accept any document that is not accompanied by a certificate of service.

(3) *Service requirements for certain documents—*(i) *Briefs.* In addition to the certificate of service requirements contained in paragraph (f)(2) of this section, a person filing a case or rebuttal brief with the Department simultaneously must serve a copy of that brief on all persons on the service list and on any U.S. Government agency that has submitted a case or rebuttal brief in the segment of the proceeding. If, under §351.103(c), a person has designated an agent to receive service that is located in the United States, service on that person must be either by personal service on the same day the brief is filed or by overnight mail or courier on the next day. If the person has designated an agent to receive service that is located outside the United States, service on that person must be by first class airmail.

(ii) *Request for review.* In addition to the certificate of service requirements under paragraph (f)(2) of this section, an interested party that files with the Department a request for an expedited antidumping review, an administrative review, a new shipper review, or a changed circumstances review must serve a copy of the request by personal service or first class mail on each exporter or producer specified in the request and on the petitioner by the end of the anniversary month or within ten days of filing the request for review, whichever is later. If the interested party that files the request is unable to locate a particular exporter or producer, or the petitioner, the Secretary may accept the request for review if the Secretary is satisfied that the party made a reasonable attempt to serve a copy of the request on such person.

(g) *Certifications.* Each submission containing factual information must include the following certification from the person identified in paragraph (g)(1) of this section and, in addition, if the person has legal counsel or another representative, the certification in paragraph (g)(2) of this section. The certifying party must maintain the original signed certification for a period of five years from the date of filing the submission to which the certification pertains. The original signed certification must be available for inspection by U.S. Department of Commerce officials. Copies of the certifications must be included in the submission filed at the Department.

(1) For the person(s) officially responsible for presentation of the factual information:

(i) COMPANY CERTIFICATION *

I, (PRINTED NAME AND TITLE), currently employed by (COMPANY NAME), certify that I prepared or otherwise supervised the preparation of the attached submission of (IDENTIFY THE SPECIFIC SUBMISSION BY TITLE) due on (DATE) OR filed on (DATE) pursuant to the (INSERT ONE OF THE FOLLOWING OPTIONS IN { }: {THE (ANTIDUMPING OR COUNTERVAILING) DUTY INVESTIGATION OF (PRODUCT) FROM (COUNTRY) (CASE NUMBER)} or {THE (DATES OF PERIOD OF REVIEW) (ADMINISTRATIVE OR NEW SHIPPER) REVIEW UNDER THE (ANTIDUMPING OR COUNTERVAILING) DUTY ORDER ON (PRODUCT) FROM (COUNTRY) (CASE NUMBER)} or {THE (SUNSET REVIEW OR CHANGED CIRCUMSTANCE REVIEW OR SCOPE RULING OR CIRCUMVENTION INQUIRY) OF THE (ANTIDUMPING OR COUNTERVAILING) DUTY ORDER ON (PRODUCT) FROM (COUNTRY) (CASE NUMBER)}). I certify that the public information and any business proprietary information of (CERTIFIER'S COMPANY NAME) contained in this submission is accurate and complete to the best of my knowledge. I am aware that the information contained in this submission may be subject to verification or corroboration (as appropriate) by the U.S. Department of Commerce. I am also aware that U.S. law (including, but not limited to, 18 U.S.C. 1001) imposes criminal sanctions on individuals who knowingly and willfully make material false statements to the U.S. Government. In addition, I am aware that, even if this submission may be withdrawn from the record of the AD/CVD proceeding, the U.S. Department of Commerce may preserve this submission, including a business proprietary submission, for purposes of determining the accuracy of this certification. I certify that a copy of this signed certification will be filed with this submission to the U.S. Department of Commerce.

Signature: _____

Date: _____

*For multiple person certifications, all persons should be listed in the first sentence of the certification and all persons should sign and date the certification. In addition, singular pronouns and possessive adjectives should be changed accordingly, e.g., "I" should be changed to "we" and "my knowledge" should be changed to "our knowledge."

(ii) GOVERNMENT CERTIFICATION**

I, (PRINTED NAME AND TITLE), currently employed by the government of (COUNTRY), certify that I prepared or otherwise supervised the preparation of the attached submission of (IDENTIFY THE SPECIFIC SUBMISSION BY TITLE) due on (DATE) OR filed on (DATE) pursuant to the (INSERT ONE OF THE FOLLOWING OPTIONS IN { }: {THE (ANTIDUMPING OR COUNTERVAILING) DUTY INVESTIGATION OF (PRODUCT) FROM (COUNTRY) (CASE NUMBER)} or {THE (DATES OF PERIOD OF REVIEW) (ADMINISTRATIVE OR NEW SHIPPER) REVIEW UNDER THE (ANTIDUMPING OR COUNTERVAILING) DUTY ORDER ON (PRODUCT) FROM (COUNTRY) (CASE NUMBER)} or {THE (SUNSET REVIEW OR CHANGED CIRCUMSTANCE REVIEW OR SCOPE RULING OR CIRCUMVENTION INQUIRY) OF THE (ANTIDUMPING OR COUNTERVAILING) DUTY ORDER ON (PRODUCT) FROM (COUNTRY) (CASE NUMBER)}). I certify that the public information and any business proprietary information of the government of (COUNTRY) contained in this submission is accurate and complete to the best of my knowledge. I am aware that the information contained in this submission may be subject to verification or corroboration (as appropriate) by the U.S. Department of Commerce. In addition, I am aware that, even if this submission may be withdrawn from the record of the AD/CVD proceeding, the U.S. Department of Commerce may preserve this submission, including a business proprietary submission, for purposes of determining the accuracy of this certification. I certify that a copy of this signed certification will be filed with this submission to the U.S. Department of Commerce.

Signature: _____

Date: _____

**For multiple person certifications, all persons should be listed in the first sentence of the certification and all persons should sign and date the certification. In addition, singular pronouns and possessive adjectives should be changed accordingly, e.g., "I" should be changed to "we" and "my knowledge" should be changed to "our knowledge."

(2) For the legal counsel or other representative:

REPRESENTATIVE CERTIFICATION * * *

I, (PRINTED NAME), with (LAW FIRM or OTHER FIRM), (INSERT ONE OF THE FOLLOWING OPTIONS IN { }: {COUNSEL TO} or {REPRESENTATIVE OF}) (COMPANY NAME, OR GOVERNMENT OF COUNTRY, OR NAME OF ANOTHER PARTY), certify that I have read the attached submission of (IDENTIFY THE SPECIFIC SUBMISSION BY TITLE) due on (DATE) OR filed on (DATE) pursuant to the (INSERT ONE OF THE FOLLOWING OPTIONS IN { }: {THE (ANTIDUMPING OR COUNTERVAILING) DUTY) INVESTIGATION OF (PRODUCT) FROM (COUNTRY) (CASE NUMBER)} or

{THE (DATES OF PERIOD OF REVIEW) (ADMINISTRATIVE OR NEW SHIPPER) REVIEW UNDER THE (ANTIDUMPING OR COUNTERVAILING) DUTY ORDER ON (PRODUCT) FROM (COUNTRY) (CASE NUMBER)} or {THE (SUNSET REVIEW OR CHANGED CIRCUMSTANCE REVIEW OR SCOPE RULING OR CIRCUMVENTION INQUIRY) OF THE (ANTIDUMPING OR COUNTERVAILING) DUTY ORDER ON (PRODUCT) FROM (COUNTRY) (CASE NUMBER)}). In my capacity as (INSERT ONE OF THE FOLLOWING OPTIONS IN { }: {COUNSEL} or {ADVISER, PREPARER, OR REVIEWER}) of this submission, I certify that the information contained in this submission is accurate and complete to the best of my knowledge. I am aware that U.S. law (including, but not limited to, 18 U.S.C. 1001) imposes criminal sanctions on individuals who knowingly and willfully make material false statements to the U.S. Government. In addition, I am aware that, even if this submission may be withdrawn from the record of the AD/CVD proceeding, the U.S. Department of Commerce may preserve this submission, including a business proprietary submission, for purposes of determining the accuracy of this certification. I certify that a copy of this signed certification will be filed with this submission to the U.S. Department of Commerce.

Signature: _____

Date: _____

*** For multiple representative certifications, all representatives and their firms should be listed in the first sentence of the certification and all representatives should sign and date the certification. In addition, singular pronouns and possessive adjectives should be changed accordingly, e.g., "I" should be changed to "we" and "my knowledge" should be changed to "our knowledge."

[62 FR 27379, May 19, 1997, as amended at 73 FR 3643, Jan. 22, 2008; 76 FR 7499, Feb. 10, 2011; 76 FR 39275, July 6, 2011; 76 FR 54699, Sept. 2, 2011; 78 FR 42691, July 17, 2013; 79 FR 69047, Nov. 20, 2014; 80 FR 36473, June 25, 2015]

§ 351.304 Establishing business proprietary treatment of information.

(a) *Claim for business proprietary treatment.* (1) Any person that submits factual information to the Secretary in connection with a proceeding may:

(i) Request that the Secretary treat any part of the submission as business proprietary information that is subject to disclosure only under an administrative protective order,

(ii) Claim that there is a clear and compelling need to withhold certain business proprietary information from disclosure under an administrative protective order, or

(iii) In an investigation, identify customer names that are exempt from disclosure under administrative protective order under section 777(c)(1)(A) of the Act.

(2) The Secretary will require that all business proprietary information presented to, or obtained or generated by, the Secretary during a segment of a proceeding be disclosed to authorized applicants, except for

(i) Customer names submitted in an investigation,

(ii) Information for which the Secretary finds that there is a clear and compelling need to withhold from disclosure, and

(iii) Privileged or classified information.

(b) *Identification of business proprietary information*—(1) *Information releasable under administrative protective order*—(i) *In general.* A person submitting information must identify the information for which it claims business proprietary treatment by enclosing the information within single brackets. The submitting person must provide with the information an explanation of why each item of bracketed information is entitled to business proprietary treatment. A person submitting a request for business proprietary treatment also must include an agreement to permit disclosure under an administrative protective order, unless the submitting party claims that there is a clear and compelling need to withhold the information from disclosure under an administrative protective order.

(ii) *Electronic databases.* In accordance with § 351.303(c)(3), an electronic database need not contain brackets. The submitter must select the security classification "Business Proprietary Document—May Be Released Under APO" at the time of filing to request business proprietary treatment of the information contained in the database. The public version of the database must be publicly summarized and ranged in accordance with § 351.304(c).

(2) *Information claimed to be exempt from disclosure under administrative protective order.* (i) If the submitting person claims that there is a clear and

274

compelling need to withhold certain information from disclosure under an administrative protective order (see paragraph (a)(1)(ii) of this section), the submitting person must identify the information by enclosing the information within double brackets, and must include a full explanation of the reasons for the claim.

(ii) In an investigation, the submitting person may enclose business proprietary customer names within double brackets (see paragraph (a)(1)(iii) of this section).

(iii) The submitting person may exclude the information in double brackets from the business proprietary/APO version of the submission served on authorized applicants. See §351.303 for filing and service requirements.

(c) *Public version.* (1) A person filing a submission that contains information for which business proprietary treatment is claimed must file a public version of the submission. The public version must be filed on the first business day after the filing deadline for the business proprietary document (see §351.303(b)). The public version must contain a summary of the bracketed information in sufficient detail to permit a reasonable understanding of the substance of the information. If the submitting person claims that summarization is not possible, the claim must be accompanied by a full explanation of the reasons supporting that claim. Generally, numerical data will be considered adequately summarized if grouped or presented in terms of indices or figures within 10 percent of the actual figure. If an individual portion of the numerical data is voluminous, at least one percent representative of that portion must be summarized. A submitter should not create a public summary of business proprietary information of another person.

(2) If a submitting party discovers that it has failed to bracket information correctly, the submitter may file a complete, corrected business proprietary document along with the public version (see §351.303(b)). At the close of business on the day on which the public version of a submission is due under paragraph (c)(2) of this section, however, the bracketing of business proprietary information in the original business proprietary document or, if a corrected version is timely filed, the corrected business proprietary document will become final. Once bracketing has become final, the Secretary will not accept any further corrections to the bracketing of information in a submission, and the Secretary will treat nonbracketed information as public information.

(d) *Nonconforming submissions*—(1) *In general.* The Secretary will reject a submission that does not meet the requirements of section 777(b) of the Act and this section with a written explanation. The submitting person may take any of the following actions within two business days after receiving the Secretary's explanation:

(i) Correct the problems and resubmit the information;

(ii) If the Secretary denied a request for business proprietary treatment, agree to have the information in question treated as public information;

(iii) If the Secretary granted business proprietary treatment but denied a claim that there was a clear and compelling need to withhold information under an administrative protective order, agree to the disclosure of the information in question under an administrative protective order; or

(iv) Submit other material concerning the subject matter of the rejected information. If the submitting person does not take any of these actions, the Secretary will not consider the rejected submission.

(2) *Timing.* The Secretary normally will determine the status of information within 30 days after the day on which the information was submitted. If the business proprietary status of information is in dispute, the Secretary will treat the relevant portion of the submission as business proprietary information until the Secretary decides the matter.

[63 FR 24401, May 4, 1998, as amended at 76 FR 39277, July 6, 2011]

§351.305   Access to business proprietary information.

(a) *The administrative protective order.* The Secretary will place an administrative protective order on the record within two business days after the day on which a petition is filed or an investigation is self-initiated, within five business days after the day on which a request for a new shipper review is properly filed in accordance with §§ 351.214 and 351.303 or an application for a scope ruling is properly filed in accordance with §§ 351.225 and 351.303, within five business days after the day on which a request for a changed circumstances review is properly filed in accordance with §§ 351.216 and 351.303 or a changed circumstances review is self-initiated, or five business days after initiating any other segment of a proceeding. The administrative protective order will require the authorized applicant to:

(1) Establish and follow procedures to ensure that no employee of the authorized applicant's firm releases business proprietary information to any person other than the submitting party, an authorized applicant, or an appropriate Department official identified in section 777(b) of the Act;

(2) Notify the Secretary of any changes in the facts asserted by the authorized applicant in its administrative protective order application;

(3) Destroy business proprietary information by the time required under the terms of the administrative protective order;

(4) Immediately report to the Secretary any apparent violation of the administrative protective order; and

(5) Acknowledge that any unauthorized disclosure may subject the authorized applicant, the firm of which the authorized applicant is a partner, associate, or employee, and any partner, associate, or employee of the authorized applicant's firm to sanctions listed in part 354 of this chapter (19 CFR part 354).

(b) *Application for access under administrative protective order.* (1) Generally, no more than two independent representatives of a party to the proceeding may have access to business proprietary information under an administrative protective order. A party must designate a lead firm if the party has more than one independent authorized applicant firm.

(2) A representative of a party to the proceeding may apply for access to business proprietary information under

the administrative protective order by submitting Form ITA–367 to the Secretary. Form ITA–367 must identify the applicant and the segment of the proceeding involved, state the basis for eligibility of the applicant for access to business proprietary information, and state the agreement of the applicant to be bound by the administrative protective order. Form ITA–367 may be prepared on the applicant's own wordprocessing system, and must be accompanied by a certification that the application is consistent with Form ITA–367 and an acknowledgment that any discrepancies will be interpreted in a manner consistent with Form ITA–367. An applicant must apply to receive all business proprietary information on the record of the segment of a proceeding in question, but may waive service of business proprietary information it does not wish to receive from other parties to the proceeding. An applicant must serve an APO application on the other parties by the most expeditious manner possible at the same time that it files the application with the Department.

(3) With respect to proprietary information submitted to the Secretary on or before the date on which the Secretary grants access to a qualified applicant, except as provided in paragraph (b)(4) of this section, within two business days the submitting party shall serve the party which has been granted access, in accordance with paragraph (c) of this section.

(4) To minimize the disruption caused by late applications, an application should be filed before the first questionnaire response has been submitted. Where justified, however, applications may be filed up to the date on which the case briefs are due, but any applicant filing after the first questionnaire response is submitted will be liable for costs associated with the additional production and service of business proprietary information already on the record. Parties have five business days to serve their business proprietary information already on the record to a party who has filed an application after

the submission of the first questionnaire response and is authorized to receive such information after such information has been placed on the record.

(c) *Approval of access under administrative protective order; administrative protective order service list.* The Secretary will grant access to a qualified applicant by including the name of the applicant on an administrative protective order service list. Access normally will be granted within five days of receipt of the application unless there is a question regarding the eligibility of the applicant to receive access. In that case, the Secretary will decide whether to grant the applicant access within 30 days of receipt of the application. The Secretary will provide by the most expeditious means available the administrative protective order service list to parties to the proceeding on the day the service list is issued or amended.

(d) *Additional filing requirements for importers.* If an applicant represents a party claiming to be an interested party by virtue of being an importer, then the applicant shall submit, along with the Form ITA–367, documentary evidence demonstrating that during the applicable period of investigation or period of review the party imported subject merchandise. For a scope inquiry, the applicant must present documentary evidence that it imported subject merchandise, or that it has taken steps towards importing the merchandise subject to the scope inquiry.

[63 FR 24402, May 4, 1998, as amended at 73 FR 3643, Jan. 22, 2008; 76 FR 39277, July 6, 2011]

§351.306 Use of business proprietary information.

(a) *By the Secretary.* The Secretary may disclose business proprietary information submitted to the Secretary only to:

(1) An authorized applicant;

(2) An employee of the Department of Commerce or the International Trade Commission directly involved in the proceeding in which the information is submitted;

(3) An employee of the Customs Service directly involved in conducting a fraud investigation relating to an antidumping or countervailing duty proceeding;

(4) The U.S. Trade Representative as provided by 19 U.S.C. 3571(i);

(5) Any person to whom the submitting person specifically authorizes disclosure in writing; and

(6) A charged party or counsel for the charged party under 19 CFR part 354.

(b) *By an authorized applicant.* An authorized applicant may retain business proprietary information for the time authorized by the terms of the administrative protective order. An authorized applicant may use business proprietary information for purposes of the segment of a proceeding in which the information was submitted. If business proprietary information that was submitted in a segment of the proceeding is relevant to an issue in a different segment of the proceeding, an authorized applicant may place such information on the record of the subsequent segment as authorized by the APO.

(c) *Identifying parties submitting business proprietary information.* (1) If a party submits a document containing business proprietary information of another person, the submitting party must identify, contiguously with each item of business proprietary information, the person that originally submitted the item (e.g., Petitioner, Respondent A, Respondent B). Business proprietary information not identified will be treated as information of the person making the submission. If the submission contains business proprietary information of only one person, it shall so state on the first page and identify the person that originally submitted the business proprietary information on the first page.

(2) If a party to a proceeding is not represented by an authorized applicant, a party submitting a document containing the unrepresented party's business proprietary information must serve the unrepresented party with a version of the document that contains only the unrepresented party's business proprietary information. The document must not contain the business proprietary information of other parties.

(d) *Disclosure to parties not authorized to receive business proprietary information.* No person, including an authorized applicant, may disclose the business proprietary information of another person to any other person except another authorized applicant or a Department official described in paragraph (a)(2) of this section. Any person that is not an authorized applicant and that is served with business proprietary information must return it to the sender immediately, to the extent possible without reading it, and must notify the Department. An allegation of an unauthorized disclosure will subject the person that made the alleged unauthorized disclosure to an investigation and possible sanctions under 19 CFR part 354.

[63 FR 24403, May 4, 1998]

§ 351.307 Verification of information.

(a) *Introduction.* Prior to making a final determination in an investigation or issuing final results of review, the Secretary may verify relevant factual information. This section clarifies when verification will occur, the contents of a verification report, and the procedures for verification.

(b) *In general.* (1) Subject to paragraph (b)(4) of this section, the Secretary will verify factual information upon which the Secretary relies in:

(i) A final determination in a continuation of a previously suspended countervailing duty investigation (section 704(g) of the Act), countervailing duty investigation, continuation of a previously suspended antidumping investigation (section 705(a) of the Act), or antidumping investigation;

(ii) The final results of an expedited antidumping review;

(iii) A revocation under section 751(d) of the Act;

(iv) The final results of an administrative review, new shipper review, or changed circumstances review, if the Secretary decides that good cause for verification exists; and

(v) The final results of an administrative review if:

(A) A domestic interested party, not later than 100 days after the date of publication of the notice of initiation of review, submits a written request for verification; and

(B) The Secretary conducted no verification under this paragraph during either of the two immediately preceding administrative reviews.

(2) The Secretary may verify factual information upon which the Secretary relies in a proceeding or a segment of a proceeding not specifically provided for in paragraph (b)(1) of this section.

(3) If the Secretary decides that, because of the large number of exporters or producers included in an investigation or administrative review, it is impractical to verify relevant factual information for each person, the Secretary may select and verify a sample.

(4) The Secretary may conduct verification of a person if that person agrees to verification and the Secretary notifies the government of the affected country and that government does not object. If the person or the government objects to verification, the Secretary will not conduct verification and may disregard any or all information submitted by the person in favor of use of the facts available under section 776 of the Act and § 351.308.

(c) *Verification report.* The Secretary will report the methods, procedures, and results of a verification under this section prior to making a final determination in an investigation or issuing final results in a review.

(d) *Procedures for verification.* The Secretary will notify the government of the affected country that employees of the Department will visit with the persons listed below in order to verify the accuracy and completeness of submitted factual information. The notification will, where practicable, identify any member of the verification team who is not an officer of the U.S. Government. As part of the verification, employees of the Department will request access to all files, records, and personnel which the Secretary considers relevant to factual information submitted of:

(1) Producers, exporters, or importers;

(2) Persons affiliated with the persons listed in paragraph (d)(1) of this section, where applicable;

(3) Unaffiliated purchasers, or

(4) The government of the affected country as part of verification in a countervailing duty proceeding.

§351.308 Determinations on the basis of the facts available.

(a) *Introduction.* The Secretary may make determinations on the basis of the facts available whenever necessary information is not available on the record, an interested party or any other person withholds or fails to provide information requested in a timely manner and in the form required or significantly impedes a proceeding, or the Secretary is unable to verify submitted information. If the Secretary finds that an interested party "has failed to cooperate by not acting to the best of its ability to comply with a request for information," the Secretary may use an inference that is adverse to the interests of that party in selecting from among the facts otherwise available. This section lists some of the sources of information upon which the Secretary may base an adverse inference and explains the actions the Secretary will take with respect to corroboration of information.

(b) *In general.* The Secretary may make a determination under the Act and this part based on the facts otherwise available in accordance with section 776(a) of the Act.

(c) *Adverse inferences.* For purposes of section 776(b) of the Act, an adverse inference may include reliance on:

(1) Secondary information, such as information derived from:

(i) The petition;

(ii) A final determination in a countervailing duty investigation or an antidumping investigation;

(iii) Any previous administrative review, new shipper review, expedited antidumping review, section 753 review, or section 762 review; or

(2) Any other information placed on the record.

(d) *Corroboration of secondary information.* Under section 776(c) of the Act, when the Secretary relies on secondary information, the Secretary will, to the extent practicable, corroborate that information from independent sources that are reasonably at the Secretary's disposal. Independent sources may include, but are not limited to, published price lists, official import statistics and customs data, and information obtained from interested parties during the instant investigation or review.

Corroborate means that the Secretary will examine whether the secondary information to be used has probative value. The fact that corroboration may not be practicable in a given circumstance will not prevent the Secretary from applying an adverse inference as appropriate and using the secondary information in question.

(e) *Use of certain information.* In reaching a determination under the Act and this part, the Secretary will not decline to consider information that is submitted by an interested party and is necessary to the determination but does not meet all the applicable requirements established by the Secretary if the conditions listed under section 782(e) of the Act are met.

(f) *Use of facts available in a sunset review.* Where the Secretary determines to issue final results of sunset review on the basis of facts available, the Secretary normally will rely on:

(1) Calculated countervailing duty rates or dumping margins, as applicable, from prior Department determinations; and

(2) Information contained in parties' substantive responses to the Notice of Initiation filed under §351.218(d)(3), consistent with section 752(b) or 752(c) of the Act, as applicable.

[62 FR 27379, May 19, 1997, as amended at 63 FR 13524, Mar. 20, 1998]

§351.309 Written argument.

(a) *Introduction.* Written argument may be submitted during the course of an antidumping or countervailing duty proceeding. This section sets forth the time limits for submission of case and rebuttal briefs and provides guidance on what should be contained in these documents.

(b) *Written argument*—(1) *In general.* In making the final determination in a countervailing duty investigation or antidumping investigation or the final results of an administrative review, new shipper review, expedited antidumping review, section 753 review, or section 762 review, the Secretary will consider written arguments in case or rebuttal briefs filed within the time limits in this section.

(2) *Written argument on request.* Notwithstanding paragraph (b)(1) of this section, the Secretary may request

written argument on any issue from any person or U.S. Government agency at any time during a proceeding.

(c) *Case brief.* (1) Any interested party or U.S. Government agency may submit a "case brief" within:

(i) For a final determination in a countervailing duty investigation or antidumping investigation, or for the final results of a full sunset review, 50 days after the date of publication of the preliminary determination or results of review, as applicable, unless the Secretary alters the time limit;

(ii) For the final results of an administrative review, new shipper review, changed circumstances review, or section 762 review, 30 days after the date of publication of the preliminary results of review, unless the Secretary alters the time limit; or

(iii) For the final results of an expedited sunset review, expedited antidumping review, Article 8 violation review, Article 4/Article 7 review, or section 753 review, a date specified by the Secretary.

(2) The case brief must present all arguments that continue in the submitter's view to be relevant to the Secretary's final determination or final results, including any arguments presented before the date of publication of the preliminary determination or preliminary results. As part of the case brief, parties are encouraged to provide a summary of the arguments not to exceed five pages and a table of statutes, regulations, and cases cited.

(d) *Rebuttal brief.* (1) Any interested party or U.S. Government agency may submit a "rebuttal brief" within five days after the time limit for filing the case brief, unless the Secretary alters this time limit.

(2) The rebuttal brief may respond only to arguments raised in case briefs and should identify the arguments to which it is responding. As part of the rebuttal brief, parties are encouraged to provide a summary of the arguments not to exceed five pages and a table of statutes, regulations, and cases cited.

(e) *Comments on adequacy of response and appropriateness of expedited sunset review*—(i) *In general.* Where the Secretary determines that respondent interested parties provided inadequate response to a Notice of Initiation (*see*

§ 351.218(e)(1)(ii)) and has notified the International Trade Commission as such under § 351.218(e)(1)(ii)(C), interested parties (and industrial users and consumer organizations) that submitted a complete substantive response to the Notice of Initiation under § 351.218(d)(3) may file comments on whether an expedited sunset review under section 751(c)(3)(B) of the Act and § 351.218(e)(1)(ii)(B) or 351.218(e)(1)(ii)(C) is appropriate based on the adequacy of responses to the notice of initiation. These comments may not include any new factual information or evidence (such as supplementation of a substantive response to the notice of initiation) and are limited to five pages.

(ii) *Time limit for filing comments.* Comments on adequacy of response and appropriateness of expedited sunset review must be filed not later than 70 days after the date publication in the FEDERAL REGISTER of the notice of initiation.

[62 FR 27379, May 19, 1997, as amended at 63 FR 13524, Mar. 20, 1998; 70 FR 62064, Oct. 28, 2005]

§ 351.310   Hearings.

(a) *Introduction.* This section sets forth the procedures for requesting a hearing, indicates that the Secretary may consolidate hearings, and explains when the Secretary may hold closed hearing sessions.

(b) *Pre-hearing conference.* The Secretary may conduct a telephone pre-hearing conference with representatives of interested parties to facilitate the conduct of the hearing.

(c) *Request for hearing.* Any interested party may request that the Secretary hold a public hearing on arguments to be raised in case or rebuttal briefs within 30 days after the date of publication of the preliminary determination or preliminary results of review, unless the Secretary alters this time limit, or in a proceeding where the Secretary will not issue a preliminary determination, not later than a date specified by the Secretary. To the extent practicable, a party requesting a hearing must identify arguments to be raised at the hearing. At the hearing, an interested party may make an affirmative presentation only on arguments included in that party's case brief and may make a rebuttal presentation only on arguments included in that party's rebuttal brief.

(d) *Hearings in general.* (1) If an interested party submits a request under paragraph (c) of this section, the Secretary will hold a public hearing on the date stated in the notice of the Secretary's preliminary determination or preliminary results of administrative review (or otherwise specified by the Secretary in an expedited antidumping review), unless the Secretary alters the date. Ordinarily, the hearing will be held two days after the scheduled date for submission of rebuttal briefs.

(2) The hearing is not subject to 5 U.S.C. §§ 551–559, and § 702 (Administrative Procedure Act). Witness testimony, if any, will not be under oath or subject to cross-examination by another interested party or witness. During the hearing, the chair may question any person or witness and may request persons to present additional written argument.

(e) *Consolidated hearings.* At the Secretary's discretion, the Secretary may consolidate hearings in two or more cases.

(f) *Closed hearing sessions.* An interested party may request a closed session of the hearing no later than the date the case briefs are due in order to address limited issues during the course of the hearing. The requesting party must identify the subjects to be discussed, specify the amount of time requested, and justify the need for a closed session with respect to each subject. If the Secretary approves the request for a closed session, only authorized applicants and other persons authorized by the regulations may be present for the closed session (*see* § 351.305).

(g) *Transcript of hearing.* The Secretary will place a verbatim transcript of the hearing in the public and official records of the proceeding and will announce at the hearing how interested parties may obtain copies of the transcript.

§ 351.311 Countervailable subsidy practice discovered during investigation or review.

(a) *Introduction.* During the course of a countervailing duty investigation or review, Department officials may discover or receive notice of a practice that appears to provide a countervailable subsidy. This section explains when the Secretary will examine such a practice.

(b) *Inclusion in proceeding.* If during a countervailing duty investigation or a countervailing duty administrative review the Secretary discovers a practice that appears to provide a countervailable subsidy with respect to the subject merchandise and the practice was not alleged or examined in the proceeding, or if, pursuant to section 775 of the Act, the Secretary receives notice from the United States Trade Representative that a subsidy or subsidy program is in violation of Article 8 of the Subsidies Agreement, the Secretary will examine the practice, subsidy, or subsidy program if the Secretary concludes that sufficient time remains before the scheduled date for the final determination or final results of review.

(c) *Deferral of examination.* If the Secretary concludes that insufficient time remains before the scheduled date for the final determination or final results of review to examine the practice, subsidy, or subsidy program described in paragraph (b) of this section, the Secretary will:

(1) During an investigation, allow the petitioner to withdraw the petition without prejudice and resubmit it with an allegation with regard to the newly discovered practice, subsidy, or subsidy program; or

(2) During an investigation or review, defer consideration of the newly discovered practice, subsidy, or subsidy program until a subsequent administrative review, if any.

(d) *Notice.* The Secretary will notify the parties to the proceeding of any practice the Secretary discovers, or any subsidy or subsidy program with respect to which the Secretary receives notice from the United States Trade Representative, and whether or not it will be included in the then ongoing proceeding.

§ 351.312 Industrial users and consumer organizations.

(a) *Introduction.* The URAA provides for opportunity for comment by consumer organizations and industrial users on matters relevant to a particular determination of dumping, subsidization, or injury. This section indicates under what circumstances such persons may submit relevant information and argument.

(b) *Opportunity to submit relevant information and argument.* In an antidumping or countervailing duty proceeding under title VII of the Act and this part, an industrial user of the subject merchandise or a representative consumer organization, as described in section 777(h) of the Act, may submit relevant factual information and written argument to the Department under paragraphs (d)(3)(ii), and (d)(3)(vi), and (d)(4) of § 351.218, paragraphs (b), (c)(1), and (c)(3) of § 351.301, and paragraphs (c), (d), and (e) of § 351.309 concerning dumping or a countervailing subsidy. All such submissions must be filed in accordance with § 351.303.

(c) *Business proprietary information.* Persons described in paragraph (b) of this section may request business proprietary treatment of information under § 351.304, but will not be granted access under § 351.305 to business proprietary information submitted by other persons.

[62 FR 27379, May 19, 1997, as amended at 63 FR 13524, Mar. 20, 1998]

§ 351.313 Attorneys or representatives.

In general. No register of attorneys or representatives who may practice before the Department is maintained. No application for admission to practice is required. Any person desiring to appear as attorney or representative before the Department may be required to show to the satisfaction of the Secretary his acceptability in that capacity. Any attorney or representative practicing before the Department, or desiring so to practice, may for good cause shown be suspended or barred from practicing before the Department, or have imposed on him such lesser sanctions (e.g., public or private reprimand) as the Secretary deems appropriate, but only after he has been accorded an opportunity to present his views in the matter. The Department will maintain a public register of attorneys and representatives suspended or barred from practice. "Attorney" pursuant to this subpart and "legal counsel" in § 351.303(g) have the same meaning. "Representative" pursuant to this subpart and in § 351.303(g) has the same meaning.

[78 FR 22777, Apr. 17, 2013]

Subpart D—Calculation of Export Price, Constructed Export Price, Fair Value, and Normal Value

§ 351.401 In general.

(a) *Introduction.* In general terms, an antidumping analysis involves a comparison of export price or constructed export price in the United States with normal value in the foreign market. This section establishes certain general rules that apply to the calculation of export price, constructed export price and normal value. (*See* section 772, section 773, and section 773A of the Act.)

(b) *Adjustments in general.* In making adjustments to export price, constructed export price, or normal value, the Secretary will adhere to the following principles:

(1) The interested party that is in possession of the relevant information has the burden of establishing to the satisfaction of the Secretary the amount and nature of a particular adjustment; and

(2) The Secretary will not double-count adjustments.

(c) *Use of price net of price adjustments.* In calculating export price, constructed export price, and normal value (where normal value is based on price), the Secretary normally will use a price that is net of price adjustments, as defined in § 351.102(b), that are reasonably attributable to the subject merchandise or the foreign like product (whichever is applicable). The Secretary will not accept a price adjustment that is made after the time of sale unless the interested party demonstrates, to the satisfaction of the Secretary, its entitlement to such an adjustment.

(d) *Delayed payment or pre-payment of expenses.* Where cost is the basis for determining the amount of an adjustment to export price, constructed export price, or normal value, the Secretary will not factor in any delayed payment or pre-payment of expenses by the exporter or producer.

(e) *Adjustments for movement expenses*—(1) *Original place of shipment.* In making adjustments for movement expenses to establish export price or constructed export price under section 772(c)(2)(A) of the Act, or normal value under section 773(a)(6)(B)(ii) of the Act, the Secretary normally will consider the production facility as being the "original place of shipment. However, where the Secretary bases export price, constructed export price, or normal value on a sale by an unaffiliated reseller, the Secretary may treat the original place from which the reseller shipped the merchandise as the "original place of shipment."

(2) *Warehousing.* The Secretary will consider warehousing expenses that are incurred after the subject merchandise or foreign like product leaves the original place of shipment as movement expenses.

(f) *Treatment of affiliated producers in antidumping proceedings*—(1) *In general.* In an antidumping proceeding under this part, the Secretary will treat two or more affiliated producers as a single entity where those producers have production facilities for similar or identical products that would not require substantial retooling of either facility in order to restructure manufacturing priorities and the Secretary concludes that there is a significant potential for the manipulation of price or production.

(2) *Significant potential for manipulation.* In identifying a significant potential for the manipulation of price or production, the factors the Secretary may consider include:

(i) The level of common ownership;

(ii) The extent to which managerial employees or board members of one firm sit on the board of directors of an affiliated firm; and

(iii) Whether operations are intertwined, such as through the sharing of sales information, involvement in production and pricing decisions, the shar-

ing of facilities or employees, or significant transactions between the affiliated producers.

(g) *Allocation of expenses and price adjustments*—(1) *In general.* The Secretary may consider allocated expenses and price adjustments when transaction-specific reporting is not feasible, provided the Secretary is satisfied that the allocation method used does not cause inaccuracies or distortions.

(2) *Reporting allocated expenses and price adjustments.* Any party seeking to report an expense or a price adjustment on an allocated basis must demonstrate to the Secretary's satisfaction that the allocation is calculated on as specific a basis as is feasible, and must explain why the allocation methodology used does not cause inaccuracies or distortions.

(3) *Feasibility.* In determining the feasibility of transaction-specific reporting or whether an allocation is calculated on as specific a basis as is feasible, the Secretary will take into account the records maintained by the party in question in the ordinary course of its business, as well as such factors as the normal accounting practices in the country and industry in question and the number of sales made by the party during the period of investigation or review.

(4) *Expenses and price adjustments relating to merchandise not subject to the proceeding.* The Secretary will not reject an allocation method solely because the method includes expenses incurred, or price adjustments made, with respect to sales of merchandise that does not constitute subject merchandise or a foreign like product (whichever is applicable).

(h) [Reserved]

(i) *Date of sale.* In identifying the date of sale of the subject merchandise or foreign like product, the Secretary normally will use the date of invoice, as recorded in the exporter or producer's records kept in the ordinary course of business. However, the Secretary may use a date other than the date of invoice if the Secretary is satisfied that a different date better reflects the date on which the exporter or producer establishes the material terms of sale.

[62 FR 27379, May 19, 1997, as amended at 73 FR 16518, Mar. 28, 2008; 81 FR 15645, Mar. 24, 2016]

§ 351.402 Calculation of export price and constructed export price; reimbursement of antidumping and countervailing duties.

(a) *Introduction.* In order to establish export price, constructed export price, and normal value, the Secretary must make certain adjustments to the price to the unaffiliated purchaser (often called the "starting price") in both the United States and foreign markets. This regulation clarifies how the Secretary will make certain of the adjustments to the starting price in the United States that are required by section 772 of the Act.

(b) *Additional adjustments to constructed export price.* In establishing constructed export price under section 772(d) of the Act, the Secretary will make adjustments for expenses associated with commercial activities in the United States that relate to the sale to an unaffiliated purchaser, no matter where or when paid. The Secretary will not make an adjustment for any expense that is related solely to the sale to an affiliated importer in the United States, although the Secretary may make an adjustment to normal value for such expenses under section 773(a)(6)(C)(iii) of the Act.

(c) *Special rule for merchandise with value added after importation*—(1) *Merchandise imported by affiliated persons.* In applying section 772(e) of the Act, merchandise imported by and value added by a person affiliated with the exporter or producer includes merchandise imported and value added for the account of such an affiliated person.

(2) *Estimation of value added.* The Secretary normally will determine that the value added in the United States by the affiliated person is likely to exceed substantially the value of the subject merchandise if the Secretary estimates the value added to be at least 65 percent of the price charged to the first unaffiliated purchaser for the merchandise as sold in the United States. The Secretary normally will estimate the value added based on the difference between the price charged to the first unaffiliated purchaser for the merchandise as sold in the United States and the price paid for the subject merchandise by the affiliated person. The Secretary normally will base this determination on averages of the prices and the value added to the subject merchandise.

(3) *Determining dumping margins.* For purposes of determining dumping margins under paragraphs (1) and (2) of section 772(e) of the Act, the Secretary may use the weighted-average dumping margins calculated on sales of identical or other subject merchandise sold to unaffiliated persons.

(d) *Special rule for determining profit.* This paragraph sets forth rules for calculating profit in establishing constructed export price under section 772(f) of the Act.

(1) *Basis for total expenses and total actual profit.* In calculating total expenses and total actual profit, the Secretary normally will use the aggregate of expenses and profit for all subject merchandise sold in the United States and all foreign like products sold in the exporting country, including sales that have been disregarded as being below the cost of production. (*See* section 773(b) of the Act (sales at less than cost of production).)

(2) *Use of financial reports.* For purposes of determining profit under section 772(d)(3) of the Act, the Secretary may rely on any appropriate financial reports, including public, audited financial statements, or equivalent financial reports, and internal financial reports prepared in the ordinary course of business.

(3) *Voluntary reporting of costs of production.* The Secretary will not require the reporting of costs of production solely for purposes of determining the amount of profit to be deducted from the constructed export price. The Secretary will base the calculation of profit on costs of production if such costs are reported voluntarily by the date established by the Secretary, and provided that it is practicable to do so and the costs of production are verifiable.

(e) *Treatment of payments between affiliated persons.* Where a person affiliated with the exporter or producer incurs any of the expenses deducted from constructed export price under section 772(d) of the Act and is reimbursed for such expenses by the exporter, producer or other affiliate, the Secretary normally will make an adjustment based on the actual cost to the affiliated person. If the Secretary is satisfied that information regarding the actual cost to the affiliated person is unavailable to the exporter or producer, the Secretary may determine the amount of the adjustment on any other reasonable basis, including the amount of the reimbursement to the affiliated person if the Secretary is satisfied that such amount reflects the amount usually paid in the market under consideration.

(f) *Reimbursement of antidumping duties and countervailing duties*—(1) *In general.* (i) In calculating the export price (or the constructed export price), the Secretary will deduct the amount of any antidumping duty or countervailing duty which the exporter or producer:

(A) Paid directly on behalf of the importer; or

(B) Reimbursed to the importer.

(ii) The Secretary will not deduct the amount of any antidumping duty or countervailing duty paid or reimbursed if the exporter or producer granted to the importer before initiation of the antidumping investigation in question a warranty of nonapplicability of antidumping duties or countervailing duties with respect to subject merchandise which was:

(A) Sold before the date of publication of the Secretary's order applicable to the merchandise in question; and

(B) Exported before the date of publication of the Secretary's final antidumping determination.

(iii) Ordinarily, under paragraph (f)(1)(i) of this section, the Secretary will deduct the amount reimbursed only once in the calculation of the export price (or constructed export price).

(2) *Certificate.* The importer must file prior to liquidation a certificate in the following form with the appropriate District Director of Customs:

I hereby certify that I (have) (have not) entered into any agreement or understanding for the payment or for the refunding to me, by the manufacturer, producer, seller, or exporter, of all or any part of the antidumping duties or countervailing duties assessed upon the following importations of (commodity) from (country): (List entry numbers) which have been purchased on or after (date of publication of antidumping notice suspending liquidation in the FEDERAL REGISTER) or purchased before (same date) but exported on or after (date of final determination of sales at less than fair value).

(3) *Presumption.* The Secretary may presume from an importer's failure to file the certificate required in paragraph (f)(2) of this section that the exporter or producer paid or reimbursed the antidumping duties or countervailing duties.

§351.403 Sales used in calculating normal value; transactions between affiliated parties.

(a) *Introduction.* This section clarifies when the Secretary may use offers for sale in determining normal value. Additionally, this section clarifies the authority of the Secretary to use sales to or through an affiliated party as a basis for normal value. (*See* section 773(a)(5) of the Act (indirect sales or offers for sale).)

(b) *Sales and offers for sale.* In calculating normal value, the Secretary normally will consider offers for sale only in the absence of sales and only if the Secretary concludes that acceptance of the offer can be reasonably expected.

(c) *Sales to an affiliated party.* If an exporter or producer sold the foreign like product to an affiliated party, the Secretary may calculate normal value based on that sale only if satisfied that the price is comparable to the price at which the exporter or producer sold the foreign like product to a person who is not affiliated with the seller.

(d) *Sales through an affiliated party.* If an exporter or producer sold the foreign like product through an affiliated party, the Secretary may calculate normal value based on the sale by such affiliated party. However, the Secretary normally will not calculate normal value based on the sale by an affiliated party if sales of the foreign like product by an exporter or producer to affiliated parties account for less than five percent of the total value (or quantity) of the exporter's or producer's sales of the foreign like product in the market in question or if sales to the affiliated party are comparable, as defined in paragraph (c) of this section.

§ 351.404 **Selection of the market to be used as the basis for normal value.**

(a) *Introduction.* Although in most circumstances sales of the foreign like product in the home market are the most appropriate basis for determining normal value, section 773 of the Act also permits use of sales to a third country or constructed value as the basis for normal value. This section clarifies the rules for determining the basis for normal value.

(b) *Determination of viable market*—(1) *In general.* The Secretary will consider the exporting country or a third country as constituting a viable market if the Secretary is satisfied that sales of the foreign like product in that country are of sufficient quantity to form the basis of normal value.

(2) *Sufficient quantity.* "Sufficient quantity" normally means that the aggregate quantity (or, if quantity is not appropriate, value) of the foreign like product sold by an exporter or producer in a country is 5 percent or more of the aggregate quantity (or value) of its sales of the subject merchandise to the United States.

(c) *Calculation of price-based normal value in viable market*—(1) *In general.* Subject to paragraph (c)(2) of this section:

(i) If the exporting country constitutes a viable market, the Secretary will calculate normal value on the basis of price in the exporting country (*see* section 773(a)(1)(B)(i) of the Act (price used for determining normal value)); or

(ii) If the exporting country does not constitute a viable market, but a third country does constitute a viable market, the Secretary may calculate normal value on the basis of price to a third country (*see* section 773(a)(1)(B)(ii) of the Act (use of third country prices in determining normal value)).

(2) *Exception.* The Secretary may decline to calculate normal value in a particular market under paragraph

(c)(1) of this section if it is established to the satisfaction of the Secretary that:

(i) In the case of the exporting country or a third country, a particular market situation exists that does not permit a proper comparison with the export price or constructed export price (*see* section 773(a)(1)(B)(ii)(III) or section 773(a)(1)(C)(iii) of the Act); or

(ii) In the case of a third country, the price is not representative (*see* section 773(a)(1)(B)(ii)(I) of the Act).

(d) *Allegations concerning market viability and the basis for determining a price-based normal value.* In an antidumping investigation or review, allegations regarding market viability or the exceptions in paragraph (c)(2) of this section, must be filed, with all supporting factual information, in accordance with § 351.301(d)(1).

(e) *Selection of third country.* For purposes of calculating normal value based on prices in a third country, where prices in more than one third country satisfy the criteria of section 773(a)(1)(B)(ii) of the Act and this section, the Secretary generally will select the third country based on the following criteria:

(1) The foreign like product exported to a particular third country is more similar to the subject merchandise exported to the United States than is the foreign like product exported to other third countries;

(2) The volume of sales to a particular third country is larger than the volume of sales to other third countries;

(3) Such other factors as the Secretary considers appropriate.

(f) *Third country sales and constructed value.* The Secretary normally will calculate normal value based on sales to a third country rather than on constructed value if adequate information is available and verifiable (*see* section 773(a)(4) of the Act (use of constructed value)).

§ 351.405 **Calculation of normal value based on constructed value.**

(a) *Introduction.* In certain circumstances, the Secretary may determine normal value by constructing a value based on the cost of manufacture, selling general and administrative expenses, and profit. The Secretary may use constructed value as the basis for normal value where: neither the home market nor a third country market is viable; sales below the cost of production are disregarded; sales outside the ordinary course of trade, or sales the prices of which are otherwise unrepresentative, are disregarded; sales used to establish a fictitious market are disregarded; no contemporaneous sales of comparable merchandise are available; or in other circumstances where the Secretary determines that home market or third country prices are inappropriate. (*See* section 773(e) and section 773(f) of the Act.) This section clarifies the meaning of certain terms relating to constructed value.

(b) *Profit and selling, general, and administrative expenses.* In determining the amount to be added to constructed value for profit and for selling, general, and administrative expenses, the following rules will apply:

(1) Under section 773(e)(2)(A) of the Act, "foreign country" means the country in which the merchandise is produced or a third country selected by the Secretary under § 351.404(e), as appropriate.

(2) Under section 773(e)(2)(B) of the Act, "foreign country" means the country in which the merchandise is produced.

§ 351.406 Calculation of normal value if sales are made at less than cost of production.

(a) *Introduction.* In determining normal value, the Secretary may disregard sales of the foreign like product made at prices that are less than the cost of production of that product. However, such sales will be disregarded only if they are made within an extended period of time, in substantial quantities, and are not at prices which permit recovery of costs within a reasonable period of time. (*See* section 773(b) of the Act.) This section clarifies the meaning of the term "extended period of time" as used in the Act.

(b) *Extended period of time.* The "extended period of time" under section 773(b)(1)(A) of the Act normally will co-incide with the period in which the sales under consideration for the determination of normal value were made.

§ 351.407 Calculation of constructed value and cost of production.

(a) *Introduction.* This section sets forth certain rules that are common to the calculation of constructed value and the cost of production. (*See* section 773(f) of the Act.)

(b) *Determination of value under the major input rule.* For purposes of section 773(f)(3) of the Act, the Secretary normally will determine the value of a major input purchased from an affiliated person based on the higher of:

(1) The price paid by the exporter or producer to the affiliated person for the major input;

(2) The amount usually reflected in sales of the major input in the market under consideration; or

(3) The cost to the affiliated person of producing the major input.

(c) *Allocation of costs.* In determining the appropriate method for allocating costs among products, the Secretary may take into account production quantities, relative sales values, and other quantitative and qualitative factors associated with the manufacture and sale of the subject merchandise and the foreign like product.

(d) *Startup costs.* (1) In identifying startup operations under section 773(f)(1)(C)(ii) of the Act:

(i) "New production facilities" includes the substantially complete retooling of an existing plant. Substantially complete retooling involves the replacement of nearly all production machinery or the equivalent rebuilding of existing machinery.

(ii) A "new product" is one requiring substantial additional investment, including products which, though sold under an existing nameplate, involve the complete revamping or redesign of the product. Routine model year changes will not be considered a new product.

(iii) Mere improvements to existing products or ongoing improvements to existing facilities will not be considered startup operations.

(iv) An expansion of the capacity of an existing production line will not qualify as a startup operation unless the expansion constitutes such a major undertaking that it requires the construction of a new facility and results in a depression of production levels due to technical factors associated with the initial phase of commercial production of the expanded facilities.

(2) In identifying the end of the startup period under clauses (ii) and (iii) of section 773(f)(1)(C) of the Act:

(i) The attainment of peak production levels will not be the standard for identifying the end of the startup period, because the startup period may end well before a company achieves optimum capacity utilization.

(ii) The startup period will not be extended to cover improvements and cost reductions that may occur over the entire life cycle of a product.

(3) In determining when a producer reaches commercial production levels under section 773(f)(1)(C)(ii) of the Act:

(i) The Secretary will consider the actual production experience of the merchandise in question, measuring production on the basis of units processed.

(ii) To the extent necessary, the Secretary will examine factors in addition to those specified in section 773(f)(1)(C)(ii) of the Act, including historical data reflecting the same producer's or other producers' experiences in producing the same or similar products. A producer's projections of future volume or cost will be accorded little weight.

(4) In making an adjustment for startup operations under section 773(f)(1)(C)(iii) of the Act:

(i) The Secretary will determine the duration of the startup period on a case-by-case basis.

(ii) The difference between actual costs and the costs of production calculated for startup costs will be amortized over a reasonable period of time subsequent to the startup period over the life of the product or machinery, as appropriate.

(iii) The Secretary will consider unit production costs to be items such as depreciation of equipment and plant, labor costs, insurance, rent and lease expenses, material costs, and factory overhead. The Secretary will not consider sales expenses, such as advertising costs, or other general and ad-

ministrative or non-production costs (such as general research and development costs), as startup costs.

§ 351.408 Calculation of normal value of merchandise from nonmarket economy countries.

(a) *Introduction.* In identifying dumping from a nonmarket economy country, the Secretary normally will calculate normal value by valuing the nonmarket economy producers' factors of production in a market economy country. (*See* section 773(c) of the Act.) This section clarifies when and how this special methodology for nonmarket economies will be applied.

(b) *Economic Comparability.* In determining whether a country is at a level of economic development comparable to the nonmarket economy under section 773(c)(2)(B) or section 773(c)(4)(A) of the Act, the Secretary will place primary emphasis on *per capita* GDP as the measure of economic comparability.

(c) *Valuation of Factors of Production.* For purposes of valuing the factors of production, general expenses, profit, and the cost of containers, coverings, and other expenses (referred to collectively as "factors") under section 773(c)(1) of the Act the following rules will apply:

(1) *Information used to value factors.* The Secretary normally will use publicly available information to value factors. However, where a factor is produced in one or more market economy countries, purchased from one or more market economy suppliers and paid for in market economy currency, the Secretary normally will use the price(s) paid to the market economy supplier(s) if substantially all of the total volume of the factor is purchased from the market economy supplier(s). For purposes of this provision, the Secretary defines the term "substantially all" to be 85 percent or more of the total volume purchased of the factor used in the production of subject merchandise. In those instances where less than substantially all of the total volume of the factor is produced in one or more market economy countries and purchased from one or more market economy suppliers, the Secretary normally will weight-average the actual price(s) paid

for the market economy portion and the surrogate value for the nonmarket economy portion by their respective quantities.

(2) *Valuation in a single country.* Except for labor, as provided in paragraph (d)(3) of this section, the Secretary normally will value all factors in a single surrogate country.

(3) *Labor.* For labor, the Secretary will use regression-based wage rates reflective of the observed relationship between wages and national income in market economy countries. The Secretary will calculate the wage rate to be applied in nonmarket economy proceedings each year. The calculation will be based on current data, and will be made available to the public.

(4) *Manufacturing overhead, general expenses, and profit.* For manufacturing overhead, general expenses, and profit, the Secretary normally will use nonproprietary information gathered from producers of identical or comparable merchandise in the surrogate country.

[62 FR 27379, May 19, 1997, as amended at 78 FR 46804, Aug. 2, 2013]

§351.409 Differences in quantities.

(a) *Introduction.* Because the quantity of merchandise sold may affect the price, in comparing export price or constructed export price with normal value, the Secretary will make a reasonable allowance for any difference in quantities to the extent the Secretary is satisfied that the amount of any price differential (or lack thereof) is wholly or partly due to that difference in quantities. (*See* section 773(a)(6)(C)(i) of the Act.)

(b) *Sales with quantity discounts in calculating normal value.* The Secretary normally will calculate normal value based on sales with quantity discounts only if:

(1) During the period examined, or during a more representative period, the exporter or producer granted quantity discounts of at least the same magnitude on 20 percent or more of sales of the foreign like product for the relevant country; or

(2) The exporter or producer demonstrates to the Secretary's satisfaction that the discounts reflect savings specifically attributable to the production of the different quantities.

(c) *Sales with quantity discounts in calculating weighted-average normal value.* If the exporter or producer does not satisfy the conditions of paragraph (b) of this section, the Secretary will calculate normal value based on weighted-average prices that include sales at a discount.

(d) *Price lists.* In determining whether a discount has been granted, the existence or lack of a published price list reflecting such a discount will not be controlling. Ordinarily, the Secretary will give weight to a price list only if, in the line of trade and market under consideration, the exporter or producer demonstrates that it has adhered to its price list.

(e) *Relationship to level of trade adjustment.* If adjustments are claimed for both differences in quantities and differences in level of trade, the Secretary will not make an adjustment for differences in quantities unless the Secretary is satisfied that the effect on price comparability of differences in quantities has been identified and established separately from the effect on price comparability of differences in the levels of trade.

§351.410 Differences in circumstances of sale

(a) *Introduction.* In calculating normal value the Secretary may make adjustments to account for certain differences in the circumstances of sales in the United States and foreign markets. (*See* section 773(a)(6)(C)(iii) of the Act.) This section clarifies certain terms used in the statute regarding circumstances of sale adjustments and describes the adjustment when commissions are paid only in one market.

(b) *In general.* With the exception of the allowance described in paragraph (e) of this section concerning commissions paid in only one market, the Secretary will make circumstances of sale adjustments under section 773(a)(6)(C)(iii) of the Act only for direct selling expenses and assumed expenses.

(c) *Direct selling expenses.* "Direct selling expenses" are expenses, such as commissions, credit expenses, guarantees, and warranties, that result from, and bear a direct relationship to, the particular sale in question.

(d) *Assumed expenses.* Assumed expenses are selling expenses that are assumed by the seller on behalf of the buyer, such as advertising expenses.

(e) *Commissions paid in one market.* The Secretary normally will make a reasonable allowance for other selling expenses if the Secretary makes a reasonable allowance for commissions in one of the markets under considerations, and no commission is paid in the other market under consideration. The Secretary will limit the amount of such allowance to the amount of the other selling expenses incurred in the one market or the commissions allowed in the other market, whichever is less.

(f) *Reasonable allowance.* In deciding what is a reasonable allowance for any difference in circumstances of sale, the Secretary normally will consider the cost of such difference to the exporter or producer but, if appropriate, may also consider the effect of such difference on the market value of the merchandise.

§ 351.411 Differences in physical characteristics.

(a) *Introduction.* In comparing United States sales with foreign market sales, the Secretary may determine that the merchandise sold in the United States does not have the same physical characteristics as the merchandise sold in the foreign market, and that the difference has an effect on prices. In calculating normal value, the Secretary will make a reasonable allowance for such differences. (*See* section 773(a)(6)(C)(ii) of the Act.)

(b) *Reasonable allowance.* In deciding what is a reasonable allowance for differences in physical characteristics, the Secretary will consider only differences in variable costs associated with the physical differences. Where appropriate, the Secretary may also consider differences in the market value. The Secretary will not consider differences in cost of production when compared merchandise has identical physical characteristics.

§ 351.412 Levels of trade; adjustment for difference in level of trade; constructed export price offset.

(a) *Introduction.* In comparing United States sales with foreign market sales, the Secretary may determine that sales in the two markets were not made at the same level of trade, and that the difference has an effect on the comparability of the prices. The Secretary is authorized to adjust normal value to account for such a difference. (*See* section 773(a)(7) of the Act.)

(b) *Adjustment for difference in level of trade.* The Secretary will adjust normal value for a difference in level of trade if:

(1) The Secretary calculates normal value at a different level of trade from the level of trade of the export price or the constructed export price (whichever is applicable); and

(2) The Secretary determines that the difference in level of trade has an effect on price comparability.

(c) *Identifying levels of trade and differences in levels of trade*—(1) *Basis for identifying levels of trade.* The Secretary will identify the level of trade based on:

(i) In the case of export price, the starting price;

(ii) In the case of constructed export price, the starting price, as adjusted under section 772(d) of the Act; and

(iii) In the case of normal value, the starting price or constructed value.

(2) *Differences in levels of trade.* The Secretary will determine that sales are made at different levels of trade if they are made at different marketing stages (or their equivalent). Substantial differences in selling activities are a necessary, but not sufficient, condition for determining that there is a difference in the stage of marketing. Some overlap in selling activities will not preclude a determination that two sales are at different stages of marketing.

(d) *Effect on price comparability*—(1) *In general.* The Secretary will determine that a difference in level of trade has an effect on price comparability only if it is established to the satisfaction of the Secretary that there is a pattern of consistent price differences between sales in the market in which normal value is determined:

(i) At the level of trade of the export price or constructed export price (whichever is appropriate); and

(ii) At the level of trade at which normal value is determined.

(2) *Relevant sales.* Where possible, the Secretary will make the determination under paragraph (d)(1) of this section on the basis of sales of the foreign like product by the producer or exporter. Where this is not possible, the Secretary may use sales of different or broader product lines, sales by other companies, or any other reasonable basis.

(e) *Amount of adjustment.* The Secretary normally will calculate the amount of a level of trade adjustment by:

(1) Calculating the weighted-averages of the prices of sales at the two levels of trade identified in paragraph (d), after making any other adjustments to those prices appropriate under section 773(a)(6) of the Act and this subpart;

(2) Calculating the average of the percentage differences between those weighted-average prices; and

(3) Applying the percentage difference to normal value, where it is at a different level of trade from the export price or constructed export price (whichever is applicable), after making any other adjustments to normal value appropriate under section 773(a)(6) of the Act and this subpart.

(f) *Constructed export price offset*—(1) *In general.* The Secretary will grant a constructed export price offset only where:

(i) Normal value is compared to constructed export price;

(ii) Normal value is determined at a more advanced level of trade than the level of trade of the constructed export price; and

(iii) Despite the fact that a person has cooperated to the best of its ability, the data available do not provide an appropriate basis to determine under paragraph (d) of this section whether the difference in level of trade affects price comparability.

(2) *Amount of the offset.* The amount of the constructed export price offset will be the amount of indirect selling expenses included in normal value, up to the amount of indirect selling expenses deducted in determining constructed export price. In making the constructed export price offset, "indirect selling expenses" means selling expenses, other than direct selling expenses or assumed selling expenses (*see* §351.410), that the seller would incur regardless of whether particular sales were made, but that reasonably may be attributed, in whole or in part, to such sales.

(3) *Where data permit determination of affect on price comparability.* Where available data permit the Secretary to determine under paragraph (d) of this section whether the difference in level of trade affects price comparability, the Secretary will not grant a constructed export price offset. In such cases, if the Secretary determines that price comparability has been affected, the Secretary will make a level of trade adjustment. If the Secretary determines that price comparability has not been affected, the Secretary will not grant either a level of trade adjustment or a constructed export price offset.

§351.413 Disregarding insignificant adjustments.

Ordinarily, under section 777A(a)(2) of the Act, an "insignificant adjustment" is any individual adjustment having an *ad valorem* effect of less than 0.33 percent, or any group of adjustments having an *ad valorem* effect of less than 1.0 percent, of the export price, constructed export price, or normal value, as the case may be. Groups of adjustments are adjustments for differences in circumstances of sale under §351.410, adjustments for differences in the physical characteristics of the merchandise under §351.411, and adjustments for differences in the levels of trade under §351.412.

§351.414 Comparison of normal value with export price (constructed export price).

(a) *Introduction.* This section explains when and how the Secretary will average prices in making comparisons of export price or constructed export price with normal value. (*See* section 777A(d) of the Act.)

(b) *Description of methods of comparison*—(1) *Average-to-average method.* The "average-to-average" method involves

291

a comparison of the weighted average of the normal values with the weighted average of the export prices (and constructed export prices) for comparable merchandise.

(2) *Transaction-to-transaction method.* The "transaction-to-transaction" method involves a comparison of the normal values of individual transactions with the export prices (or constructed export prices) of individual transactions for comparable merchandise.

(3) *Average-to-transaction method.* The "average-to-transaction" method involves a comparison of the weighted average of the normal values to the export prices (or constructed export prices) of individual transactions for comparable merchandise.

(c) *Choice of method.* (1) In an investigation or review, the Secretary will use the average-to-average method unless the Secretary determines another method is appropriate in a particular case.

(2) The Secretary will use the transaction-to-transaction method only in unusual situations, such as when there are very few sales of subject merchandise and the merchandise sold in each market is identical or very similar or is custom-made.

(d) *Application of the average-to-average method*—(1) *In general.* In applying the average-to-average method, the Secretary will identify those sales of the subject merchandise to the United States that are comparable, and will include such sales in an "averaging group." The Secretary will calculate a weighted average of the export prices and the constructed export prices of the sales included in the averaging group, and will compare this weighted average to the weighted average of the normal values of such sales.

(2) *Identification of the averaging group.* An averaging group will consist of subject merchandise that is identical or virtually identical in all physical characteristics and that is sold to the United States at the same level of trade. In identifying sales to be included in an averaging group, the Secretary also will take into account, where appropriate, the region of the United States in which the merchandise is sold, and such other factors as the Secretary considers relevant.

(3) *Time period over which weighted average is calculated.* When applying the average-to-average method in an investigation, the Secretary normally will calculate weighted averages for the entire period of investigation. However, when normal values, export prices, or constructed export prices differ significantly over the course of the period of investigation, the Secretary may calculate weighted averages for such shorter period as the Secretary deems appropriate. When applying the average-to-average method in a review, the Secretary normally will calculate weighted averages on a monthly basis and compare the weighted-average monthly export price or constructed export price to the weighted-average normal value for the contemporaneous month.

(e) *Application of the average-to-transaction method*—In applying the average-to-transaction method in a review, when normal value is based on the weighted average of sales of the foreign like product, the Secretary will limit the averaging of such prices to sales incurred during the contemporaneous month.

(f) *Contemporaneous Month.* Normally, the Secretary will select as the contemporaneous month the first of the following months which applies:

(1) The month during which the particular U.S. sales under consideration were made;

(2) If there are no sales of the foreign like product during this month, the most recent of the three months prior to the month of the U.S. sales in which there was a sale of the foreign like product.

(3) If there are no sales of the foreign like product during any of these months, the earlier of the two months following the month of the U.S. sales in which there was a sale of the foreign like product.

[77 FR 8114, Feb. 14, 2012]

§ 351.415 **Conversion of currency.**

(a) *In general.* In an antidumping proceeding, the Secretary will convert foreign currencies into United States dollars using the rate of exchange on the date of sale of the subject merchandise.

(b) *Exception.* If the Secretary establishes that a currency transaction on forward markets is directly linked to an export sale under consideration, the Secretary will use the exchange rate specified with respect to such foreign currency in the forward sale agreement to convert the foreign currency.

(c) *Exchange rate fluctuations.* The Secretary will ignore fluctuations in exchange rates.

(d) *Sustained movement in foreign currency value.* In an antidumping investigation, if there is a sustained movement increasing the value of the foreign currency relative to the United States dollar, the Secretary will allow exporters 60 days to adjust their prices to reflect such sustained movement.

Subpart E—Identification and Measurement of Countervailable Subsidies

SOURCE: 63 FR 65407, Nov. 25, 1998, unless otherwise noted.

§ 351.501 Scope.

The provisions of this subpart E set forth rules regarding the identification and measurement of countervailable subsidies. Where this subpart E does not expressly deal with a particular type of alleged subsidy, the Secretary will identify and measure the subsidy, if any, in accordance with the underlying principles of the Act and this subpart E.

§ 351.502 Specificity of domestic subsidies.

(a) *Sequential analysis.* In determining whether a subsidy is *de facto* specific, the Secretary will examine the factors contained in section 771(5A)(D)(iii) of the Act sequentially in order of their appearance. If a single factor warrants a finding of specificity, the Secretary will not undertake further analysis.

(b) *Characteristics of a "group."* In determining whether a subsidy is being provided to a "group" of enterprises or industries within the meaning of section 751(5A)(D) of the Act, the Secretary is not required to determine whether there are shared characteristics among the enterprises or industries that are eligible for, or actually receive, a subsidy.

(c) *Integral linkage.* Unless the Secretary determines that two or more programs are integrally linked, the Secretary will determine the specificity of a program under section 771(5A)(D) of the Act solely on the basis of the availability and use of the particular program in question. The Secretary may find two or more programs to be integrally linked if:

(1) The subsidy programs have the same purpose;

(2) The subsidy programs bestow the same type of benefit;

(3) The subsidy programs confer similar levels of benefits on similarly situated firms; and

(4) The subsidy programs were linked at inception.

(d) *Agricultural subsidies.* The Secretary will not regard a subsidy as being specific under section 771(5A)(D) of the Act solely because the subsidy is limited to the agricultural sector (domestic subsidy).

(e) *Subsidies to small-and medium-sized businesses.* The Secretary will not regard a subsidy as being specific under section 771(5A)(D) of the Act solely because the subsidy is limited to small firms or small-and medium-sized firms.

(f) *Disaster relief.* The Secretary will not regard disaster relief as being specific under section 771(5A)(D) of the Act if such relief constitutes general assistance available to anyone in the area affected by the disaster.

§ 351.503 Benefit.

(a) *Specific rules.* In the case of a government program for which a specific rule for the measurement of a benefit is contained in this subpart E, the Secretary will measure the extent to which a financial contribution (or income or price support) confers a benefit as provided in that rule. For example, § 351.504(a) prescribes the specific rule for measurement of the benefit of grants.

(b) *Other subsidies*—(1) *In general.* For other government programs, the Secretary normally will consider a benefit to be conferred where a firm pays less for its inputs (*e.g.,* money, a good, or a service) than it otherwise would pay in the absence of the government program, or receives more revenues than it otherwise would earn.

(2) *Exception.* Paragraph (b)(1) of this section is not intended to limit the ability of the Secretary to impose countervailing duties when the facts of a particular case establish that a financial contribution (or income or price support) has conferred a benefit, even if that benefit does not take the form of a reduction in input costs or an enhancement of revenues. When paragraph (b)(1) of this section is not applicable, the Secretary will determine whether a benefit is conferred by examining whether the alleged program or practice has common or similar elements to the four illustrative examples in sections 771(5)(E)(i) through (iv) of the Act.

(c) *Distinction from effect of subsidy.* In determining whether a benefit is conferred, the Secretary is not required to consider the effect of the government action on the firm's performance, including its prices or output, or how the firm's behavior otherwise is altered.

(d) *Varying financial contribution levels*—(1) *In general.* Where a government program provides varying levels of financial contributions based on different eligibility criteria, and one or more of such levels is not specific within the meaning of § 351.502, a benefit is conferred to the extent that a firm receives a greater financial contribution than the financial contributions provided at a non-specific level under the program. The preceding sentence shall apply only to the extent the Secretary determines that the varying levels of financial contributions are set forth in a statute, decree, regulation, or other official act; that the levels are clearly delineated and identifiable; and that the firm would have been eligible for the non-specific level of contributions.

(2) *Exception.* Paragraph (d)(1) of this section shall not apply where the statute specifies a commercial test for determining the benefit.

(e) *Tax consequences.* In calculating the amount of a benefit, the Secretary will not consider the tax consequences of the benefit.

§ 351.504 Grants.

(a) *Benefit.* In the case of a grant, a benefit exists in the amount of the grant.

(b) *Time of receipt of benefit.* In the case of a grant, the Secretary normally will consider a benefit as having been received on the date on which the firm received the grant.

(c) *Allocation of a grant to a particular time period.* The Secretary will allocate the benefit from a grant to a particular time period in accordance with § 351.524.

§ 351.505 Loans.

(a) *Benefit*—(1) *In general.* In the case of a loan, a benefit exists to the extent that the amount a firm pays on the government-provided loan is less than the amount the firm would pay on a comparable commercial loan(s) that the firm could actually obtain on the market. *See* section 771(5)(E)(ii) of the Act. In making the comparison called for in the preceding sentence, the Secretary normally will rely on effective interest rates.

(2) *"Comparable commercial loan" defined*—(i) *"Comparable" defined.* In selecting a loan that is "comparable" to the government-provided loan, the Secretary normally will place primary emphasis on similarities in the structure of the loans (*e.g.*, fixed interest rate v. variable interest rate), the maturity of the loans (*e.g.*, short-term v. long-term), and the currency in which loans are denominated.

(ii) *"Commercial" defined.* In selecting a "commercial" loan, the Secretary normally will use a loan taken out by the firm from a commercial lending institution or a debt instrument issued by the firm in a commercial market. Also, the Secretary will treat a loan from a government-owned bank as a commercial loan, unless there is evidence that the loan from a government-owned bank is provided on non-commercial terms or at the direction of the government. However, the Secretary will not consider a loan provided under a government program, or a loan provided by a government-owned special purpose bank, to be a commercial loan for purposes of selecting a loan to compare with a government-provided loan.

(iii) *Long-term loans.* In selecting a comparable loan, if the government-provided loan is a long-term loan, the Secretary normally will use a loan the terms of which were established during, or immediately before, the year in which the terms of the government-provided loan were established.

(iv) *Short-term loans.* In making the comparison required under paragraph (a)(1) of this section, if the government-provided loan is a short-term loan, the Secretary normally will use an annual average of the interest rates on comparable commercial loans during the year in which the government-provided loan was taken out, weighted by the principal amount of each loan. However, if the Secretary finds that interest rates fluctuated significantly during the period of investigation or review, the Secretary will use the most appropriate interest rate based on the circumstances presented.

(3) *"Could actually obtain on the market" defined*—(i) *In general.* In selecting a comparable commercial loan that the recipient "could actually obtain on the market," the Secretary normally will rely on the actual experience of the firm in question in obtaining comparable commercial loans for both short-term and long-term loans.

(ii) *Where the firm has no comparable commercial loans.* If the firm did not take out any comparable commercial loans during the period referred to in paragraph (a)(2)(iii) or (a)(2)(iv) of this section, the Secretary may use a national average interest rate for comparable commercial loans.

(iii) *Exception for uncreditworthy companies.* If the Secretary finds that a firm that received a government-provided long-term loan was uncreditworthy, as defined in paragraph (a)(4) of this section, the Secretary normally will calculate the interest rate to be used in making the comparison called for by paragraph (a)(1) of this section according to the following formula:

$$i_b = [(1 - q_n)(1 + i_f)^n / (1 - p_n)]^{1/n} - 1,$$

where:

n = the term of the loan;
i_b = the benchmark interest rate for uncreditworthy companies;
i_f = the long-term interest rate that would be paid by a creditworthy company;
p_n = the probability of default by an uncreditworthy company within n years; and

q_n = the probability of default by a creditworthy company within n years.

"Default" means any missed or delayed payment of interest and/or principal, bankruptcy, receivership, or distressed exchange. For values of p_n, the Secretary will normally rely on the average cumulative default rates reported for the Caa to C-rated category of companies in Moody's study of historical default rates of corporate bond issuers. For values of q_n, the Secretary will normally rely on the average cumulative default rates reported for the Aaa to Baa-rated categories of companies in Moody's study of historical default rates of corporate bond issuers.

(4) *Uncreditworthiness*—(i) *In general.* The Secretary will consider a firm to be uncreditworthy if the Secretary determines that, based on information available at the time of the government-provided loan, the firm could not have obtained long-term loans from conventional commercial sources. The Secretary will determine uncreditworthiness on a case-by-case basis, and may, in appropriate circumstances, focus its creditworthiness analysis on the project being financed rather than the company as a whole. In making the creditworthiness determination, the Secretary may examine, among other factors, the following:

(A) The receipt by the firm of comparable commercial long-term loans;

(B) The present and past financial health of the firm, as reflected in various financial indicators calculated from the firm's financial statements and accounts;

(C) The firm's recent past and present ability to meet its costs and fixed financial obligations with its cash flow; and

(D) Evidence of the firm's future financial position, such as market studies, country and industry economic forecasts, and project and loan appraisals prepared prior to the agreement between the lender and the firm on the terms of the loan.

(ii) *Significance of long-term commercial loans.* In the case of firms not owned by the government, the receipt by the firm of comparable long-term commercial loans, unaccompanied by a government-provided guarantee, will normally constitute dispositive evidence that the firm is not uncreditworthy.

(iii) *Significance of prior subsidies.* In determining whether a firm is uncreditworthy, the Secretary will ignore current and prior subsidies received by the firm.

(iv) *Discount rate.* When the creditworthiness of a firm is considered in connection with the allocation of non-recurring benefits, the Secretary will rely on information available in the year in which the government agreed to provide the subsidy conferring a non-recurring benefit.

(5) *Long-term variable rate loans—(i) In general.* In the case of a long-term variable rate loan, the Secretary normally will make the comparison called for by paragraph (a)(1) of this section by relying on a comparable commercial loan with a variable interest rate. The Secretary then will compare the variable interest rates on the comparable commercial loan and the government-provided loan for the year in which the terms of the government-provided loan were established. If the comparison shows that the interest rate on the government-provided loan was equal to or higher than the interest rate on the comparable commercial loan, the Secretary will not consider the government-provided loan as having conferred a benefit. If the comparison shows that the interest rate on the government-provided loan was lower, the Secretary will consider the government-provided loan as having conferred a benefit, and, if the other criteria for a countervailable subsidy are satisfied, will calculate the amount of the benefit in accordance with paragraph (c)(4) of this section.

(ii) *Exception.* If the Secretary is unable to make the comparison described in paragraph (a)(5)(i) of this section or if the comparison described in paragraph (a)(5)(i) of this section would yield an inaccurate measure of the benefit, the Secretary may modify the method described in paragraph (a)(5)(i) of this section.

(6) *Allegations—(i) Allegation of uncreditworthiness required.* Normally, the Secretary will not consider the uncreditworthiness of a firm absent a specific allegation by the petitioner that is supported by information establishing a reasonable basis to believe or suspect that the firm is uncreditworthy.

(ii) *Government-owned banks.* The Secretary will not investigate a loan provided by a government-owned bank absent a specific allegation that is supported by information reasonably available to petitioners indicating that:

(A) The loan meets the specificity criteria in accordance with section 771(5A) of the Act; and

(B) A benefit exists within the meaning of paragraph (a)(1) of this section.

(b) *Time of receipt of benefit.* In the case of loans described in paragraphs (c)(1), (c)(2), and (c)(4) of this section, the Secretary normally will consider a benefit as having been received in the year in which the firm otherwise would have had to make a payment on the comparable commercial loan. In the case of a loan described in paragraph (c)(3) of this section, the Secretary normally will consider the benefit as having been received in the year in which the firm receives the proceeds of the loan.

(c) *Allocation of benefit to a particular time period—(1) Short-term loans.* The Secretary will allocate (expense) the benefit from a short-term loan to the year(s) in which the firm is due to make interest payments on the loan. In no event may the present value (in the year of receipt of the loan) of the amounts calculated under the preceding sentence exceed the principal of the loan.

(2) *Long-term fixed-rate loans with concessionary interest rates.* Except as provided in paragraph (c)(3) of this section, the Secretary normally will calculate the subsidy amount to be assigned to a particular year by calculating the difference in interest payments for that year, i.e., the difference between the interest paid by the firm in that year on the government-provided loan and the interest the firm would have paid on the comparison loan. However, in no event may the present value (in the year of receipt of the loan) of the amounts calculated under the preceding sentence exceed the principal of the loan.

(3) *Long-term fixed-rate loans with different repayment schedules*—(i) *Calculation of present value of benefit.* Where the government-provided loan and the loan to which it is compared under paragraph (a) of this section are both long-term, fixed-interest rate loans, but have different grace periods or maturities, or where the shapes of the repayment schedules differ, the Secretary will determine the total benefit by calculating the present value, in the year that repayment would begin on the comparable commercial loan, of the difference between the amount that the firm is to pay on the government-provided loan and the amount that the firm would have paid on the comparison loan. In no event may the total benefit calculated under the preceding sentence exceed the principal of the loan.

(ii) *Calculation of annual benefit.* With respect to the benefit calculated under paragraph (c)(3)(i) of this section, the Secretary will determine the portion of that benefit to be assigned to a particular year by using the formula set forth in § 351.524(d)(1) and the following parameters:

A_k = the amount countervailed in year k,
y = the present value of the benefit (*see* paragraph (c)(3)(i) of this section),
n = the number of years in the life of the loan,
d = the interest rate on the comparison loan selected under paragraph (a) of this section, and
k = the year of allocation, where the year that repayment would begin on the comparable commercial loan = 1.

(4) *Long-term variable interest rate loans.* In the case of a government-provided long-term variable-rate loan, the Secretary normally will determine the amount of the benefit attributable to a particular year by calculating the difference in payments for that year, *i.e.,* the difference between the amount paid by the firm in that year on the government-provided loan and the amount the firm would have paid on the comparison loan. However, in no event may the present value (in the year of receipt of the loan) of the amounts calculated under the preceding sentence exceed the principal of the loan.

(d) *Contingent liability interest-free loans*—(1) *Treatment as loans.* In the case of an interest-free loan, for which the repayment obligation is contingent upon the company taking some future action or achieving some goal in fulfillment of the loan's requirements, the Secretary normally will treat any balance on the loan outstanding during a year as an interest-free, short-term loan in accordance with paragraphs (a), (b), and (c)(1) of this section. However, if the event upon which repayment of the loan depends will occur at a point in time more than one year after the receipt of the contingent liability loan, the Secretary will use a long-term interest rate as the benchmark in accordance with paragraphs (a), (b), and (c)(2) of this section. In no event may the present value (in the year of receipt of the contingent liability loan) of the amounts calculated under this paragraph exceed the principal of the loan.

(2) *Treatment as grants.* If, at any point in time, the Secretary determines that the event upon which repayment depends is not a viable contingency, the Secretary will treat the outstanding balance of the loan as a grant received in the year in which this condition manifests itself.

§ 351.506 Loan guarantees.

(a) *Benefit*—(1) *In general.* In the case of a loan guarantee, a benefit exists to the extent that the total amount a firm pays for the loan with the government-provided guarantee is less than the total amount the firm would pay for a comparable commercial loan that the firm could actually obtain on the market absent the government-provided guarantee, including any difference in guarantee fees. *See* section 771(5)(E)(iii) of the Act. The Secretary will select a comparable commercial loan in accordance with § 351.505(a).

(2) *Government acting as owner.* In situations where a government, acting as the owner of a firm, provides a loan guarantee to that firm, the guarantee does not confer a benefit if the respondent provides evidence demonstrating that it is normal commercial practice in the country in question for shareholders to provide guarantees to their firms under similar circumstances and on comparable terms.

(b) *Time of receipt of benefit.* In the case of a loan guarantee, the Secretary normally will consider a benefit as having been received in the year in which the firm otherwise would have had to make a payment on the comparable commercial loan.

(c) *Allocation of benefit to a particular time period.* In allocating the benefit from a government-provided loan guarantee to a particular time period, the Secretary will use the methods set forth in § 351.505(c) regarding loans.

§ 351.507 Equity.

(a) *Benefit*—(1) *In general.* In the case of a government-provided equity infusion, a benefit exists to the extent that the investment decision is inconsistent with the usual investment practice of private investors, including the practice regarding the provision of risk capital, in the country in which the equity infusion is made. *See* section 771(5)(E)(i) of the Act.

(2) *Private investor prices available*—(i) *In general.* Except as provided in paragraph (a)(2)(iii) of this section, the Secretary will consider an equity infusion as being inconsistent with usual investment practice (*see* paragraph (a)(1) of this section) if the price paid by the government for newly issued shares is greater than the price paid by private investors for the same (or similar form of) newly issued shares.

(ii) *Timing of private investor prices.* In selecting a private investor price under paragraph (a)(2)(i) of this section, the Secretary will rely on sales of newly issued shares made reasonably concurrently with the newly issued shares purchased by the government.

(iii) *Significant private sector participation required.* The Secretary will not use private investor prices under paragraph (a)(2)(i) of this section if the Secretary concludes that private investor purchases of newly issued shares are not significant.

(iv) *Adjustments for "similar" form of equity.* Where the Secretary uses private investor prices for a form of shares that is similar to the newly issued shares purchased by the government (*see* paragraph (a)(2)(i) of this section), the Secretary, where appropriate, will adjust the prices to reflect the differences in the forms of shares.

(3) *Actual private investor prices unavailable*—(i) *In general.* If actual private investor prices are not available under paragraph (a)(2) of this section, the Secretary will determine whether the firm funded by the government-provided equity was equityworthy or unequityworthy at the time of the equity infusion (*see* paragraph (a)(4) of this section). If the Secretary determines that the firm was equityworthy, the Secretary will apply paragraph (a)(5) of this section to determine whether the equity infusion was inconsistent with the usual investment practice of private investors. A determination by the Secretary that the firm was unequityworthy will constitute a determination that the equity infusion was inconsistent with usual investment practice of private investors, and the Secretary will apply paragraph (a)(6) of this section to measure the benefit attributable to the equity infusion.

(4) *Equityworthiness*—(i) *In general.* The Secretary will consider a firm to have been equityworthy if the Secretary determines that, from the perspective of a reasonable private investor examining the firm at the time the government-provided equity infusion was made, the firm showed an ability to generate a reasonable rate of return within a reasonable period of time. The Secretary may, in appropriate circumstances, focus its equityworthiness analysis on a project rather than the company as a whole. In making the equityworthiness determination, the Secretary may examine the following factors, among others:

(A) Objective analyses of the future financial prospects of the recipient firm or the project as indicated by, *inter alia*, market studies, economic forecasts, and project or loan appraisals prepared prior to the government-provided equity infusion in question;

(B) Current and past indicators of the recipient firm's financial health calculated from the firm's statements and accounts, adjusted, if appropriate, to conform to generally accepted accounting principles;

(C) Rates of return on equity in the three years prior to the government equity infusion; and

(D) Equity investment in the firm by private investors.

(ii) *Significance of a pre-infusion objective analysis.* For purposes of making an equityworthiness determination, the Secretary will request and normally require from the respondents the information and analysis completed prior to the infusion, upon which the government based its decision to provide the equity infusion (*see,* paragraph (a)(4)(i)(A) of this section). Absent the existence or provision of an objective analysis, containing information typically examined by potential private investors considering an equity investment, the Secretary will normally determine that the equity infusion received provides a countervailable benefit within the meaning of paragraph (a)(1) of this section. The Secretary will not necessarily make such a determination if the absence of an objective analysis is consistent with the actions of reasonable private investors in the country in question.

(iii) *Significance of prior subsidies.* In determining whether a firm was equityworthy, the Secretary will ignore current and prior subsidies received by the firm.

(5) *Benefit where firm is equityworthy.* If the Secretary determines that the firm or project was equityworthy (*see* paragraph (a)(4) of this section), the Secretary will examine the terms and the nature of the equity purchased to determine whether the investment was otherwise inconsistent with the usual investment practice of private investors. If the Secretary determines that the investment was inconsistent with usual private investment practice, the Secretary will determine the amount of the benefit conferred on a case-by-case basis.

(6) *Benefit where firm is unequityworthy.* If the Secretary determines that the firm or project was unequityworthy (*see* paragraph (a)(4) of this section), a benefit to the firm exists in the amount of the equity infusion.

(7) *Allegations.* The Secretary will not investigate an equity infusion in a firm absent a specific allegation by the petitioner which is supported by information establishing a reasonable basis to believe or suspect that the firm received an equity infusion that provides a countervailable benefit within the meaning of paragraph (a)(1) of this section.

(b) *Time of receipt of benefit.* In the case of a government-provided equity infusion, the Secretary normally will consider the benefit to have been received on the date on which the firm received the equity infusion.

(c) *Allocation of benefit to a particular time period.* The benefit conferred by an equity infusion shall be allocated over the same time period as a non-recurring subsidy. *See* §351.524(d).

§351.508 Debt forgiveness.

(a) *Benefit.* In the case of an assumption or forgiveness of a firm's debt obligation, a benefit exists equal to the amount of the principal and/or interest (including accrued, unpaid interest) that the government has assumed or forgiven. In situations where the entity assuming or forgiving the debt receives shares in a firm in return for eliminating or reducing the firm's debt obligation, the Secretary will determine the existence of a benefit under §351.507 (equity infusions).

(b) *Time of receipt of benefit.* In the case of a debt or interest assumption or forgiveness, the Secretary normally will consider the benefit as having been received as of the date on which the debt or interest was assumed or forgiven.

(c) *Allocation of benefit to a particular time period*—(1) *In general.* The Secretary will treat the benefit determined under paragraph (a) of this section as a non-recurring subsidy, and will allocate the benefit to a particular year in accordance with §351.524(d).

(2) *Exception.* Where an interest assumption is tied to a particular loan and where a firm can reasonably expect to receive the interest assumption at the time it applies for the loan, the Secretary will normally treat the interest assumption as a reduced-interest loan and allocate the benefit to a particular year in accordance with §351.505(c) (loans).

§351.509 Direct taxes.

(a) *Benefit*—(1) *Exemption or remission of taxes.* In the case of a program that provides for a full or partial exemption or remission of a direct tax (*e.g.*, an income tax), or a reduction in the base used to calculate a direct tax, a benefit exists to the extent that the tax paid by a firm as a result of the program is less than the tax the firm would have paid in the absence of the program.

(2) *Deferral of taxes.* In the case of a program that provides for a deferral of direct taxes, a benefit exists to the extent that appropriate interest charges are not collected. Normally, a deferral of direct taxes will be treated as a government-provided loan in the amount of the tax deferred, according to the methodology described in § 351.505. The Secretary will use a short-term interest rate as the benchmark for tax deferrals of one year or less. The Secretary will use a long-term interest rate as the benchmark for tax deferrals of more than one year.

(b) *Time of receipt of benefit*—(1) *Exemption or remission of taxes.* In the case of a full or partial exemption or remission of a direct tax, the Secretary normally will consider the benefit as having been received on the date on which the recipient firm would otherwise have had to pay the taxes associated with the exemption or remission. Normally, this date will be the date on which the firm filed its tax return.

(2) *Deferral of taxes.* In the case of a tax deferral of one year or less, the Secretary normally will consider the benefit as having been received on the date on which the deferred tax becomes due. In the case of a multi-year deferral, the Secretary normally will consider the benefit as having been received on the anniversary date(s) of the deferral.

(c) *Allocation of benefit to a particular time period.* The Secretary normally will allocate (expense) the benefit of a full or partial exemption, remission, or deferral of a direct tax to the year in which the benefit is considered to have been received under paragraph (b) of this section.

§ 351.510 Indirect taxes and import charges (other than export programs).

(a) *Benefit*—(1) *Exemption or remission of taxes.* In the case of a program, other than an export program, that provides for the full or partial exemption or remission of an indirect tax or an import charge, a benefit exists to the extent

that the taxes or import charges paid by a firm as a result of the program are less than the taxes the firm would have paid in the absence of the program.

(2) *Deferral of taxes.* In the case of a program, other than an export program, that provides for a deferral of indirect taxes or import charges, a benefit exists to the extent that appropriate interest charges are not collected. Normally, a deferral of indirect taxes or import charges will be treated as a government-provided loan in the amount of the taxes deferred, according to the methodology described in § 351.505. The Secretary will use a short-term interest rate as the benchmark for tax deferrals of one year or less. The Secretary will use a long-term interest rate as the benchmark for tax deferrals of more than one year.

(b) *Time of receipt of benefit*—(1) *Exemption or remission of taxes.* In the case of a full or partial exemption or remission of an indirect tax or import charge, the Secretary normally will consider the benefit as having been received at the time the recipient firm otherwise would be required to pay the indirect tax or import charge.

(2) *Deferral of taxes.* In the case of the deferral of an indirect tax or import charge of one year or less, the Secretary normally will consider the benefit as having been received on the date on which the deferred tax becomes due. In the case of a multi-year deferral, the Secretary normally will consider the benefit as having been received on the anniversary date(s) of the deferral.

(c) *Allocation of benefit to a particular time period.* The Secretary normally will allocate (expense) the benefit of a full or partial exemption, remission, or deferral described in paragraph (a) of this section to the year in which the benefit is considered to have been received under paragraph (b) of this section.

§ 351.511 Provision of goods or services.

(a) *Benefit*—(1) *In general.* In the case where goods or services are provided, a benefit exists to the extent that such goods or services are provided for less than adequate remuneration. *See* section 771(5)(E)(iv) of the Act.

(2) *"Adequate Remuneration" defined*— (i) *In general.* The Secretary will normally seek to measure the adequacy of remuneration by comparing the government price to a market-determined price for the good or service resulting from actual transactions in the country in question. Such a price could include prices stemming from actual transactions between private parties, actual imports, or, in certain circumstances, actual sales from competitively run government auctions. In choosing such transactions or sales, the Secretary will consider product similarity; quantities sold, imported, or auctioned; and other factors affecting comparability.

(ii) *Actual market-determined price unavailable.* If there is no useable market-determined price with which to make the comparison under paragraph (a)(2)(i) of this section, the Secretary will seek to measure the adequacy of remuneration by comparing the government price to a world market price where it is reasonable to conclude that such price would be available to purchasers in the country in question. Where there is more than one commercially available world market price, the Secretary will average such prices to the extent practicable, making due allowance for factors affecting comparability.

(iii) *World market price unavailable.* If there is no world market price available to purchasers in the country in question, the Secretary will normally measure the adequacy of remuneration by assessing whether the government price is consistent with market principles.

(iv) *Use of delivered prices.* In measuring adequate remuneration under paragraph (a)(2)(i) or (a)(2)(ii) of this section, the Secretary will adjust the comparison price to reflect the price that a firm actually paid or would pay if it imported the product. This adjustment will include delivery charges and import duties.

(b) *Time of receipt of benefit.* In the case of the provision of a good or service, the Secretary normally will consider a benefit as having been received as of the date on which the firm pays or, in the absence of payment, was due to pay for the government-provided good or service.

(c) *Allocation of benefit to a particular time period.* In the case of the provision of a good or service, the Secretary will normally allocate (expense) the benefit to the year in which the benefit is considered to have been received under paragraph (b) of this section. In the case of the provision of infrastructure, the Secretary will normally treat the benefit as non-recurring and will allocate the benefit to a particular year in accordance with §351.524(d).

(d) *Exception for general infrastructure.* A financial contribution does not exist in the case of the government provision of general infrastructure. General infrastructure is defined as infrastructure that is created for the broad societal welfare of a country, region, state or municipality.

§351.512 Purchase of goods. [Reserved]

§351.513 Worker-related subsidies.

(a) *Benefit.* In the case of a program that provides assistance to workers, a benefit exists to the extent that the assistance relieves a firm of an obligation that it normally would incur.

(b) *Time of receipt of benefit.* In the case of assistance provided to workers, the Secretary normally will consider the benefit as having been received by the firm on the date on which the payment is made that relieves the firm of the relevant obligation.

(c) *Allocation of benefit to a particular time period.* Normally, the Secretary will allocate (expense) the benefit from assistance provided to workers to the year in which the benefit is considered to have been received under paragraph (b) of this section.

§351.514 Export subsidies.

(a) *In general.* The Secretary will consider a subsidy to be an export subsidy if the Secretary determines that eligibility for, approval of, or the amount of, a subsidy is contingent upon export performance. In applying this section, the Secretary will consider a subsidy to be contingent upon export performance if the provision of the subsidy is, in law or in fact, tied to actual or anticipated exportation or export earnings, alone or as one of two or more conditions.

(b) *Exception.* In the case of export promotion activities of a government, a benefit does not exist if the Secretary determines that the activities consist of general informational activities that do not promote particular products over others.

§ 351.515 Internal transport and freight charges for export shipments.

(a) *Benefit*—(1) *In general.* In the case of internal transport and freight charges on export shipments, a benefit exists to the extent that the charges paid by a firm for transport or freight with respect to goods destined for export are less than what the firm would have paid if the goods were destined for domestic consumption. The Secretary will consider the amount of the benefit to equal the difference in amounts paid.

(2) *Exception.* For purposes of paragraph (a)(1) of this section, a benefit does not exist if the Secretary determines that:

(i) Any difference in charges is the result of an arm's-length transaction between the supplier and the user of the transport or freight service; or

(ii) The difference in charges is commercially justified.

(b) *Time of receipt of benefit.* In the case of internal transport and freight charges for export shipments, the Secretary normally will consider the benefit as having been received by the firm on the date on which the firm paid, or in the absence of payment was due to pay, the charges.

(c) *Allocation of benefit to a particular time period.* Normally, the Secretary will allocate (expense) the benefit from internal transport and freight charges for export shipments to the year in which the benefit is considered to have been received under paragraph (b) of this section.

§ 351.516 Price preferences for inputs used in the production of goods for export.

(a) *Benefit*—(1) *In general.* In the case of a program involving the provision by

governments or their agencies, either directly or indirectly through government-mandated schemes, of imported or domestic products or services for use in the production of exported goods, a benefit exists to the extent that the Secretary determines that the terms or conditions on which the products or services are provided are more favorable than the terms or conditions applicable to the provision of like or directly competitive products or services for use in the production of goods for domestic consumption unless, in the case of products, such terms or conditions are not more favorable than those commercially available on world markets to exporters.

(2) *Amount of benefit.* In the case of products provided under such schemes, the Secretary will determine the amount of the benefit by comparing the price of products used in the production of exported goods to the commercially available world market price of such products, inclusive of delivery charges.

(3) *Commercially available.* For purposes of paragraph (a)(2) of this section, *commercially available* means that the choice between domestic and imported products is unrestricted and depends only on commercial considerations.

(b) *Time of receipt of benefit.* In the case of a benefit described in paragraph (a)(1) of this section, the Secretary normally will consider the benefit to have been received as of the date on which the firm paid, or in the absence of payment was due to pay, for the product.

(c) *Allocation of benefit to a particular time period.* Normally, the Secretary will allocate (expense) benefits described in paragraph (a)(1) of this section to the year in which the benefit is considered to have been received under paragraph (b) of this section.

§ 351.517 Exemption or remission upon export of indirect taxes.

(a) *Benefit.* In the case of the exemption or remission upon export of indirect taxes, a benefit exists to the extent that the Secretary determines that the amount remitted or exempted exceeds the amount levied with respect to the production and distribution of like products when sold for domestic consumption.

(b) *Time of receipt of benefit.* In the case of the exemption or remission upon export of an indirect tax, the Secretary normally will consider the benefit as having been received as of the date of exportation.

(c) *Allocation of benefit to a particular time period.* Normally, the Secretary will allocate (expense) the benefit from the exemption or remission upon export of indirect taxes to the year in which the benefit is considered to have been received under paragraph (b) of this section.

§351.518 Exemption, remission, or deferral upon export of prior-stage cumulative indirect taxes.

(a) *Benefit*—(1) *Exemption of prior-stage cumulative indirect taxes.* In the case of a program that provides for the exemption of prior-stage cumulative indirect taxes on inputs used in the production of an exported product, a benefit exists to the extent that the exemption extends to inputs that are not consumed in the production of the exported product, making normal allowance for waste, or if the exemption covers taxes other than indirect taxes that are imposed on the input. If the Secretary determines that the exemption of prior-stage cumulative indirect taxes confers a benefit, the Secretary normally will consider the amount of the benefit to be the prior-stage cumulative indirect taxes that otherwise would have been paid on the inputs not consumed in the production of the exported product, making normal allowance for waste, and the amount of charges other than import charges covered by the exemption.

(2) *Remission of prior-stage cumulative indirect taxes.* In the case of a program that provides for the remission of prior-stage cumulative indirect taxes on inputs used in the production of an exported product, a benefit exists to the extent that the amount remitted exceeds the amount of prior-stage cumulative indirect taxes paid on inputs that are consumed in the production of the exported product, making normal allowance for waste. If the Secretary determines that the remission of prior-stage cumulative indirect taxes confers

a benefit, the Secretary normally will consider the amount of the benefit to be the difference between the amount remitted and the amount of the prior-stage cumulative indirect taxes on inputs that are consumed in the production of the export product, making normal allowance for waste.

(3) *Deferral of prior-stage cumulative indirect taxes.* In the case of a program that provides for a deferral of prior-stage cumulative indirect taxes on an exported product, a benefit exists to the extent that the deferral extends to inputs that are not consumed in the production of the exported product, making normal allowance for waste, and the government does not charge appropriate interest on the taxes deferred. If the Secretary determines that a benefit exists, the Secretary will normally treat the deferral as a government-provided loan in the amount of the tax deferred, according to the methodology described in §351.505. The Secretary will use a short-term interest rate as the benchmark for tax deferrals of one year or less. The Secretary will use a long-term interest rate as the benchmark for tax deferrals of more than one year.

(4) *Exception.* Notwithstanding the provisions in paragraphs (a)(1), (a)(2), and (a)(3) of this action, the Secretary will consider the entire amount of the exemption, remission or deferral to confer a benefit, unless the Secretary determines that:

(i) The government in question has in place and applies a system or procedure to confirm which inputs are consumed in the production of the exported products and in what amounts, and to confirm which indirect taxes are imposed on these inputs, and the system or procedure is reasonable, effective for the purposes intended, and is based on generally accepted commercial practices in the country of export; or

(ii) If the government in question does not have a system or procedure in place, if the system or procedure is not reasonable, or if the system or procedure is instituted and considered reasonable, but is found not to be applied or not to be applied effectively, the government in question has carried out an examination of actual inputs involved to confirm which inputs are consumed in the production of the exported product, in what amounts, and which indirect taxes are imposed on the inputs.

(b) *Time of receipt of benefit*. In the case of the exemption, remission, or deferral of priorstage cumulative indirect taxes, the Secretary normally will consider the benefit as having been received:

(1) In the case of an exemption, as of the date of exportation;

(2) In the case of a remission, as of the date of exportation;

(3) In the case of a deferral of one year or less, on the date the deferred tax became due; and

(4) In the case of a multi-year deferral, on the anniversary date(s) of the deferral.

(c) *Allocation of benefit to a particular time period*. The Secretary normally will allocate (expense) the benefit of the exemption, remission or deferral of prior-stage cumulative indirect taxes to the year in which the benefit is considered to have been received under paragraph (b) of this section.

§ 351.519   Remission or drawback of import charges upon export.

(a) *Benefit*—(1) *In general*. The term "remission or drawback" includes full or partial exemptions and deferrals of import charges.

(i) *Remission or drawback of import charges*. In the case of the remission or drawback of import charges upon export, a benefit exists to the extent that the Secretary determines that the amount of the remission or drawback exceeds the amount of import charges on imported inputs that are consumed in the production of the exported product, making normal allowances for waste.

(ii) *Exemption of import charges*. In the case of an exemption of import charges upon export, a benefit exists to the extent that the exemption extends to inputs that are not consumed in the production of the exported product, making normal allowances for waste, or if the exemption covers charges other than import charges that are imposed on the input.

(iii) *Deferral of import charges*. In the case of a deferral, a benefit exists to the extent that the deferral extends to inputs that are not consumed in the production of the exported product, making normal allowance for waste, and the government does not charge appropriate interest on the import charges deferred.

(2) *Substitution drawback*. "Substitution drawback" involves a situation in which a firm uses a quantity of home market inputs equal to, and having the same quality and characteristics as, the imported inputs as a substitute for them. Substitution drawback does not necessarily result in the conferral of a benefit. However, a benefit exists if the Secretary determines that:

(i) The import and the corresponding export operations both did not occur within a reasonable time period, not to exceed two years; or

(ii) The amount drawn back exceeds the amount of the import charges levied initially on the imported inputs for which drawback is claimed.

(3) *Amount of the benefit*—(i) *Remission or drawback of import charges*. If the Secretary determines that the remission or drawback, including substitution drawback, of import charges confers a benefit under paragraph (a)(1) or (a)(2) of this section, the Secretary normally will consider the amount of the benefit to be the difference between the amount of import charges remitted or drawn back and the amount paid on imported inputs consumed in production for which remission or drawback was claimed.

(ii) *Exemption of import charges*. If the Secretary determines that the exemption of import charges upon export confers a benefit, the Secretary normally will consider the amount of the benefit to be the import charges that otherwise would have been paid on the inputs not consumed in the production of the exported product, making normal allowance for waste, and the amount of charges other than import charges covered by the exemption.

(iii) *Deferral of import charges*. If the Secretary determines that the deferral of import charges upon export confers a benefit, the Secretary will normally treat a deferral as a government-provided loan in the amount of the import charges deferred on the inputs not consumed in the production of the exported product, making normal allowance for waste, according to the methodology described in §351.505. The Secretary will use a short-term interest rate as the benchmark for deferrals of one year or less. The Secretary will use a long-term interest rate as the benchmark for deferrals of more than one year.

(4) *Exception.* Notwithstanding paragraph (a)(3) of this section, the Secretary will consider the entire amount of an exemption, deferral, remission or drawback to confer a benefit, unless the Secretary determines that:

(i) The government in question has in place and applies a system or procedure to confirm which inputs are consumed in the production of the exported products and in what amounts, and the system or procedure is reasonable, effective for the purposes intended, and is based on generally accepted commercial practices in the country of export; or

(ii) If the government in question does not have a system or procedure in place, if the system or procedure is not reasonable, or if the system or procedure is instituted and considered reasonable, but is found not to be applied or not to be applied effectively, the government in question has carried out an examination of actual inputs involved to confirm which inputs are consumed in the production of the exported product, and in what amounts.

(b) *Time of receipt of benefit.* In the case of the exemption, deferral, remission or drawback, including substitution drawback, of import charges, the Secretary normally will consider the benefit as having been received:

(1) In the case of remission or drawback, as of the date of exportation;

(2) In the case of an exemption, as of the date of the exportation;

(3) In the case of a deferral of one year or less, on the date the import charges became due; and (4) In the case of a multi-year deferral, on the anniversary date(s) of the deferral.

(c) *Allocation of benefit to a particular time period.* The Secretary normally will allocate (expense) the benefit from the exemption, deferral, remission or drawback of import charges to the year

in which the benefit is considered to have been received under paragraph (b) of this section.

§351.520 Export insurance.

(a) *Benefit*—(1) *In general.* In the case of export insurance, a benefit exists if the premium rates charged are inadequate to cover the long-term operating costs and losses of the program.

(2) *Amount of the benefit.* If the Secretary determines under paragraph (a)(1) of this section that premium rates are inadequate, the Secretary normally will calculate the amount of the benefit as the difference between the amount of premiums paid by the firm and the amount received by the firm under the insurance program during the period of investigation or review.

(b) *Time of receipt of benefit.* In the case of export insurance, the Secretary normally will consider the benefit as having been received in the year in which the difference described in paragraph (a)(2) of this section occurs.

(c) *Allocation of benefit to a particular time period.* The Secretary normally will allocate (expense) the benefit from export insurance to the year in which the benefit is considered to have been received under paragraph (b) of this section.

§351.521 Import substitution subsidies. [Reserved]

§351.522 Green light and green box subsidies.

(a) *Certain agricultural subsidies.* The Secretary will treat as non-countervailable domestic support measures that are provided to certain agricultural products (*i.e.,* products listed in Annex 1 of the WTO Agreement on Agriculture) and that the Secretary determines conform to the criteria of Annex 2 of the WTO Agreement on Agriculture. *See* section 771(5B)(F) of the Act. The Secretary will determine that a particular domestic support measure conforms fully to the provisions of Annex 2 if the Secretary finds that the measure:

(1) Is provided through a publicly-funded government program (including government revenue foregone) not involving transfers from consumers;

(2) Does not have the effect of providing a price support to producers; and (3) Meets the relevant policy-specific criteria and conditions set out in paragraphs 2 through 13 of Annex 2.

(b) *Research subsidies.* In accordance with section 771(5B)(B)(iii)(II) of the Act, the Secretary will examine the total eligible costs to be incurred over the duration of a particular project to determine whether a subsidy for research activities exceeds 75 percent of the costs of industrial research, 50 percent of the costs of precompetitive development activity, or 62.5 percent of the costs for a project that includes both industrial research and precompetitive activity. If the Secretary determines that, at some point over the life of a particular project, these relevant thresholds will be exceeded, the Secretary will treat the entire amount of the subsidy as countervailable.

(c) *Subsidies for adaptation of existing facilities to new environmental requirements.* If the Secretary determines that a subsidy is given to upgrade existing facilities to environmental standards in excess of minimum statutory or regulatory requirements, the subsidy will not qualify for non-countervailable treatment under section 771(5B)(D) of the Act and the Secretary will treat the entire amount of the subsidy as countervailable.

§ 351.523 **Upstream subsidies.**

(a) *Investigation of upstream subsidies*—(1) *In general.* Before investigating the existence of an upstream subsidy (*see* section 771A of the Act), the Secretary must have a reasonable basis to believe or suspect that all of the following elements exist:

(i) A countervailable subsidy, other than an export subsidy, is provided with respect to an input product;

(ii) One of the following conditions exists:

(A) The supplier of the input product and the producer of the subject merchandise are affiliated;

(B) The price for the subsidized input product is lower than the price that the producer of the subject merchandise otherwise would pay another seller in an arm's-length transaction for an unsubsidized input product; or

(C) The government sets the price of the input product so as to guarantee that the benefit provided with respect to the input product is passed through to producers of the subject merchandise; and

(iii) The *ad valorem* countervailable subsidy rate on the input product, multiplied by the proportion of the total production costs of the subject merchandise accounted for by the input product, is equal to, or greater than, one percent.

(b) *Input product.* For purposes of this section, "input product" means any product used in the production of the subject merchandise.

(c) *Competitive benefit*—(1) *In general.* In evaluating whether a competitive benefit exists under section 771A(b) of the Act, the Secretary will determine whether the price for the subsidized input product is lower than the benchmark input price. For purposes of this section, the Secretary will use as a benchmark input price the following, in order of preference:

(i) The actual price paid by, or offered to, the producer of the subject merchandise for an unsubsidized input product, including an imported input product;

(ii) An average price for an unsubsidized input product, including an imported input product, based upon publicly available data;

(iii) The actual price paid by, or offered to, the producer of the subject merchandise for a subsidized input product, including an imported input product, that is adjusted to account for the countervailable subsidy;

(iv) An average price for a subsidized input product, including an imported input product, based upon publicly available data, that is adjusted to account for the countervailable subsidy; or

(v) An unadjusted price for a subsidized input product or any other surrogate price deemed appropriate by the Secretary.

For purposes of this section, such prices must be reflective of a time period that reasonably corresponds to the time of the purchase of the input.

(2) *Use of delivered prices.* The Secretary will use a delivered price whenever the Secretary uses the price of an

input product under paragraph (c)(1) of this section.

(d) *Significant effect*—(1) *Presumptions.* In evaluating whether an upstream subsidy has a significant effect on the cost of manufacturing or producing the subject merchandise (*see* section 771A(a)(3) of the Act), the Secretary will multiply the *ad valorem* countervailable subsidy rate on the input product by the proportion of the total production cost of the subject merchandise that is accounted for by the input product. If the product of that multiplication exceeds five percent, the Secretary will presume the existence of a significant effect. If the product is less than one percent, the Secretary will presume the absence of a significant effect. If the product is between one and five percent, there will be no presumption.

(2) *Rebuttal of presumptions.* A party to the proceeding may present information to rebut these presumptions. In evaluating such information, the Secretary will consider the extent to which factors other than price, such as quality differences, are important determinants of demand for the subject merchandise.

§351.524 Allocation of benefit to a particular time period.

Unless otherwise specified in §§351.504–351.523, the Secretary will allocate benefits to a particular time period in accordance with this section.

(a) *Recurring benefits.* The Secretary will allocate (expense) a recurring benefit to the year in which the benefit is received.

(b) *Non-recurring benefits*—(1) *In general.* The Secretary will normally allocate a non-recurring benefit to a firm over the number of years corresponding to the average useful life ("AUL") of renewable physical assets as defined in paragraph (d)(2) of this section.

(2) *Exception.* The Secretary will normally allocate (expense) non-recurring benefits provided under a particular subsidy program to the year in which the benefits are received if the total amount approved under the subsidy program is less than 0.5 percent of relevant sales (*e.g.*, total sales, export sales, the sales of a particular product, or the sales to a particular market) of

the firm in question during the year in which the subsidy was approved.

(c) *"Recurring" versus "non-recurring" benefits*—(1) *Non-binding illustrative lists of recurring and non-recurring benefits.* The Secretary normally will treat the following types of subsidies as providing recurring benefits: Direct tax exemptions and deductions; exemptions and excessive rebates of indirect taxes or import duties; provision of goods and services for less than adequate remuneration; price support payments; discounts on electricity, water, and other utilities; freight subsidies; export promotion assistance; early retirement payments; worker assistance; worker training; wage subsidies; and upstream subsidies. The Secretary normally will treat the following types of subsidies as providing non-recurring benefits: equity infusions, grants, plant closure assistance, debt forgiveness, coverage for operating losses, debt-to-equity conversions, provision of non-general infrastructure, and provision of plant and equipment.

(2) *The test for determining whether a benefit is recurring or non-recurring.* If a subsidy is not on the illustrative lists, or is not addressed elsewhere in these regulations, or if a party claims that a subsidy on the recurring list should be treated as non-recurring or a subsidy on the non-recurring list should be treated as recurring, the Secretary will consider the following criteria in determining whether the benefits from the subsidy should be considered recurring or non-recurring:

(i) Whether the subsidy is exceptional in the sense that the recipient cannot expect to receive additional subsidies under the same program on an ongoing basis from year to year;

(ii) Whether the subsidy required or received the government's express authorization or approval (*i.e.*, receipt of benefits is not automatic), or

(iii) Whether the subsidy was provided for, or tied to, the capital structure or capital assets of the firm.

(d) *Process for allocating non-recurring benefits over time*—(1) *In general.* For purposes of allocating a non-recurring benefit over time and determining the annual benefit amount that should be assigned to a particular year, the Secretary will use the following formula:

$$A_k = \frac{y/n + [y - (y/n)(k-1)]d}{1+d}$$

Where:

A_k = the amount of the benefit allocated to year k,
y = the face value of the subsidy,
n = the AUL (see paragraph (d)(2) of this section),
d = the discount rate (see paragraph (d)(3) of this section), and
k = the year of allocation, where the year of receipt = 1 and 1 ≤k ≤n.

(2) *AUL*—(i) *In general.* The Secretary will presume the allocation period for non-recurring subsidies to be the AUL of renewable physical assets for the industry concerned as listed in the Internal Revenue Service's ("IRS") 1977 Class Life Asset Depreciation Range System (Rev. Proc. 77–10, 1977–1, C.B. 548 (RR–38)), as updated by the Department of Treasury. The presumption will apply unless a party claims and establishes that the IRS tables do not reasonably reflect the company-specific AUL or the country-wide AUL for the industry under investigation, subject to the requirement, in paragraph (d)(2)(ii) of this section, that the difference between the company-specific AUL or country-wide AUL for the industry under investigation and the AUL in the IRS tables is significant. If this is the case, the Secretary will use company-specific or country-wide AULs to allocate non-recurring benefits over time (*see* paragraph (d)(2)(iii) of this section).

(ii) *Definition of "significant."* For purposes of this paragraph (d), *significant* means that a party has demonstrated that the company-specific AUL or country-wide AUL for the industry differs from AUL in the IRS tables by one year or more.

(iii) *Calculation of a company-specific or country-wide AUL.* A calculation of a company-specific AUL will not be accepted by the Secretary unless it satisfies the following requirements: the company must base its depreciation on an estimate of the actual useful lives of assets and it must use straight-line depreciation or demonstrate that its calculation is not distorted through irregular or uneven additions to the pool of fixed assets. A company-specific AUL is calculated by dividing the aggregate of the annual average gross book values of the firm's depreciable productive fixed assets by the firm's aggregated annual charge to accumulated depreciation, for a period considered appropriate by the Secretary, subject to appropriate normalizing adjustments. A country-wide AUL for the industry under investigation will not be accepted by the Secretary unless the respondent government demonstrates that it has a system in place to calculate AULs for its industries, and that this system provides a reliable representation of AUL.

(iv) *Exception.* Under certain extraordinary circumstances, the Secretary may consider whether an allocation period other than AUL is appropriate or whether the benefit stream begins at a date other than the date the subsidy was bestowed.

(3) *Selection of a discount rate.* (i) *In general.* The Secretary will select a discount rate based upon data for the year in which the government agreed to provide the subsidy. The Secretary will use as a discount rate the following, in order of preference:

(A) The cost of long-term, fixed-rate loans of the firm in question, excluding any loans that the Secretary has determined to be countervailable subsidies;

(B) The average cost of long-term, fixed-rate loans in the country in question; or

(C) A rate that the Secretary considers to be most appropriate.

(ii) *Exception for uncreditworthy firms.* In the case of a firm considered by the Secretary to be uncreditworthy (*see* § 351.505(a)(4)), the Secretary will use as a discount rate the interest rate described in § 351.505(a)(3)(iii).

§ 351.525 Calculation of *ad valorem* subsidy rate and attribution of subsidy to a product.

(a) *Calculation of ad valorem subsidy rate.* The Secretary will calculate an *ad valorem* subsidy rate by dividing the amount of the benefit allocated to the period of investigation or review by the sales value during the same period of the product or products to which the Secretary attributes the subsidy under paragraph (b) of this section. Normally, the Secretary will determine the sales value of a product on an f.o.b. (port) basis (if the product is exported) or on an f.o.b. (factory) basis (if the product is sold for domestic consumption). However, if the Secretary determines that countervailable subsidies are provided with respect to the movement of a product from the port or factory to the place of destination (*e.g.*, freight or insurance costs are subsidized), the Secretary may make appropriate adjustments to the sales value used in the denominator.

(b) *Attribution of subsidies*—(1) *In general.* In attributing a subsidy to one or more products, the Secretary will apply the rules set forth in paragraphs (b)(2) through (b)(7) of this section.

(2) *Export subsidies.* The Secretary will attribute an export subsidy only to products exported by a firm.

(3) *Domestic subsidies.* The Secretary will attribute a domestic subsidy to all products sold by a firm, including products that are exported.

(4) *Subsidies tied to a particular market.* If a subsidy is tied to sales to a particular market, the Secretary will attribute the subsidy only to products sold by the firm to that market.

(5) *Subsidies tied to a particular product.* (i) *In general.* If a subsidy is tied to the production or sale of a particular product, the Secretary will attribute the subsidy only to that product.

(ii) *Exception.* If a subsidy is tied to production of an input product, then the Secretary will attribute the subsidy to both the input and downstream products produced by a corporation.

(6) *Corporations with cross-ownership.* (i) *In general.* The Secretary normally will attribute a subsidy to the products produced by the corporation that received the subsidy.

(ii) *Corporations producing the same product.* If two (or more) corporations with cross-ownership produce the subject merchandise, the Secretary will attribute the subsidies received by either or both corporations to the products produced by both corporations.

(iii) *Holding or parent companies.* If the firm that received a subsidy is a holding company, including a parent company with its own operations, the Secretary will attribute the subsidy to the consolidated sales of the holding company and its subsidiaries. However, if the Secretary finds that the holding company merely served as a conduit for the transfer of the subsidy from the government to a subsidiary of the holding company, the Secretary will attribute the subsidy to products sold by the subsidiary.

(iv) *Input suppliers.* If there is cross-ownership between an input supplier and a downstream producer, and production of the input product is primarily dedicated to production of the downstream product, the Secretary will attribute subsidies received by the input producer to the combined sales of the input and downstream products produced by both corporations (excluding the sales between the two corporations).

(v) *Transfer of subsidy between corporations with cross-ownership producing different products.* In situations where paragraphs (b)(6)(i) through (iv) of this section do not apply, if a corporation producing non-subject merchandise received a subsidy and transferred the subsidy to a corporation with cross-ownership, the Secretary will attribute the subsidy to products sold by the recipient of the transferred subsidy.

(vi) *Cross-ownership defined.* Cross-ownership exists between two or more corporations where one corporation can use or direct the individual assets of the other corporation(s) in essentially the same ways it can use its own assets. Normally, this standard will be met where there is a majority voting ownership interest between two corporations or through common ownership of two (or more) corporations.

(7) *Multinational firms.* If the firm that received a subsidy has production facilities in two or more countries, the Secretary will attribute the subsidy to products produced by the firm within the country of the government that granted the subsidy. However, if it is demonstrated that the subsidy was tied to more than domestic production, the Secretary will attribute the subsidy to multinational production.

(c) *Trading companies.* Benefits from subsidies provided to a trading company which exports subject merchandise shall be cumulated with benefits from subsidies provided to the firm which is producing subject merchandise that is sold through the trading company, regardless of whether the trading company and the producing firm are affiliated.

§ 351.526 Program-wide changes.

(a) *In general*. The Secretary may take a program-wide change into account in establishing the estimated countervailing duty cash deposit rate if:

(1) The Secretary determines that subsequent to the period of investigation or review, but before a preliminary determination in an investigation (*see* § 351.205) or a preliminary result of an administrative review or a new shipper review (*see* §§ 351.213 and 351.214), a program-wide change has occurred; and

(2) The Secretary is able to measure the change in the amount of countervailable subsidies provided under the program in question.

(b) *Definition of program-wide change*. For purposes of this section, "program-wide change" means a change that:

(1) Is not limited to an individual firm or firms; and

(2) Is effectuated by an official act, such as the enactment of a statute, regulation, or decree, or contained in the schedule of an existing statute, regulation, or decree.

(c) *Effect limited to cash deposit rate—* (1) *In general*. The application of paragraph (a) of this section will not result in changing, in an investigation, an affirmative determination to a negative determination or a negative determination to an affirmative determination.

(2) *Example*. In a countervailing duty investigation, the Secretary determines that during the period of investigation a countervailable subsidy existed in the amount of 10 percent *ad valorem*. Subsequent to the period of investigation, but before the preliminary determination, the foreign government in question enacts a change to the program that reduces the amount of the subsidy to a *de minimis* level. In a final determination, the Secretary would issue an affirmative determination, but would establish a cash deposit rate of zero.

(d) *Terminated programs*. The Secretary will not adjust the cash deposit rate under paragraph (a) of this section if the program-wide change consists of the termination of a program and:

(1) The Secretary determines that residual benefits may continue to be bestowed under the terminated program; or

(2) The Secretary determines that a substitute program for the terminated program has been introduced and the Secretary is not able to measure the amount of countervailable subsidies provided under the substitute program.

§ 351.527 Transnational subsidies.

Except as otherwise provided in section 701(d) of the Act (subsidies provided to international consortia) and section 771A of the Act (upstream subsidies), a subsidy does not exist if the Secretary determines that the funding for the subsidy is supplied in accordance with, and as part of, a program or project funded:

(a) By a government of a country other than the country in which the recipient firm is located; or

(b) By an international lending or development institution.

Subpart F—Subsidy Determinations Regarding Cheese Subject to an In-Quota Rate of Duty

§ 351.601 Annual list and quarterly update of subsidies.

The Secretary will make the determinations called for by section 702(a) of the Trade Agreements Act of 1979, as amended (19 U.S.C. 1202 note) based on the available information, and will publish the annual list and quarterly updates described in such section in the FEDERAL REGISTER.

§ 351.602 Determination upon request.

(a) *Request for determination*. (1) Any person, including the Secretary of Agriculture, who has reason to believe there have been changes in or additions to the latest annual list published under § 351.601 may request in writing that the Secretary determine under section 702(a)(3) of the Trade Agreements Act of 1979 whether there are any changes or additions. The person must file the request with the Central Records Unit (*see* § 351.103). The request must allege either a change in the type or amount of any subsidy included in the latest annual list or quarterly update or an additional subsidy not included in that list or update provided by a foreign government, and must contain the following, to the extent reasonably available to the requesting person:

(i) The name and address of the person;

(ii) The article of cheese subject to an in-quota rate of duty allegedly benefitting from the changed or additional subsidy;

(iii) The country of origin of the article of cheese subject to an in-quota rate of duty; and

(iv) The alleged subsidy or changed subsidy and relevant factual information (particularly documentary evidence) regarding the alleged changed or additional subsidy including the authority under which it is provided, the manner in which it is paid, and the value of the subsidy to producers or exporters of the article.

(2) The requirements of §351.303 (c) and (d) apply to this section.

(b) *Determination.* Not later than 30 days after receiving an acceptable request, the Secretary will:

(1) In consultation with the Secretary of Agriculture, determine based on the available information whether there has been any change in the type or amount of any subsidy included in the latest annual list or quarterly update or an additional subsidy not included in that list or update is being provided by a foreign government;

(2) Notify the Secretary of Agriculture and the person making the request of the determination; and

(3) Promptly publish in the FEDERAL REGISTER notice of any changes or additions.

§351.603   Complaint of price-undercutting by subsidized imports.

Upon receipt of a complaint filed with the Secretary of Agriculture under section 702(b) of the Trade Agreements Act concerning price-undercutting by subsidized imports, the Secretary will promptly determine, under section 702(a)(3) of the Trade Agreements Act of 1979, whether or not the alleged subsidies are included in or should be added to the latest annual list or quarterly update.

§351.604   Access to information.

Subpart C of this part applies to factual information submitted in connection with this subpart.

Subpart G—Applicability Dates

§351.701   Applicability dates.

The regulations contained in this part 351 apply to all administrative reviews initiated on the basis of requests made on or after the first day of July, 1997, to all investigations and other segments of proceedings initiated on the basis of petitions filed or requests made after June 18, 1997 and to segments of proceedings self-initiated by the Department after June 18, 1997. Segments of proceedings to which part 351 do not apply will continue to be governed by the regulations in effect on the date the petitions were filed or requests were made for those segments, to the extent that those regulations were not invalidated by the URAA or replaced by the interim final regulations published on May 11, 1995 (60 FR 25130 (1995)). For segments of proceedings initiated on the basis of petitions filed or requests made after January 1, 1995, but before part 351 applies, part 351 will serve as a restatement of the Department's interpretation of the requirements of the Act as amended by the URAA.

§351.702   Applicability dates for countervailing duty regulations.

(a) Notwithstanding §351.701, the regulations in subpart E of this part apply to:

(1) All CVD investigations initiated on the basis of petitions filed after December 28, 1998;

(2) All CVD administrative reviews initiated on the basis of requests filed on or after the first day of January 1999; and

(3) To all segments of CVD proceedings self-initiated by the Department after December 28, 1998.

(b) Segments of CVD proceedings to which subpart E of this part does not apply will continue to be guided by the Department's previous methodology (in particular, as described in the 1989 Proposed Regulations), except to the extent that the previous methodology was invalidated by the URAA, in which case the Secretary will treat subpart E of this part as a restatement of the Department's interpretation of the requirements of the Act as amended by the URAA.

[63 FR 65417, Nov. 25, 1998]

ANNEX I TO PART 351—DEADLINES FOR PARTIES IN COUNTERVAILING INVESTIGATIONS

Day [1]	Event	Regulation
0 days	Initiation	
31 days [2]	Notification of difficulty in responding to questionnaire.	351.301(c)(2)(iv) (14 days after date of receipt of initial questionnaire)
37 days	Application for an administrative protective order.	351.305(b)(3)
40 days	Request for postponement by petitioner	351.205(e) (25 days or more before preliminary determination)
45 days	Allegation of critical circumstances	351.206(c)(2)(i) (20 days before preliminary determination)
47 days	Questionnaire response	351.301(c)(2)(iii) (30 days from date of receipt of initial questionnaire)
55 days	Allegation of upstream subsidies	351.301(d)(4)(ii)(A) (10 days before preliminary determination)
65 days (Can be extended)	Preliminary determination	351.205(b)(1)
72 days	Submission of proposed suspension agreement.	351.208(f)(1)(B) (7 days after preliminary determination)
75 days [3]	Submission of factual information	351.301(b)(1) (7 days before date on which verification is to commence)
75 days	Submission of ministerial error comments	351.224(c)(2) (5 days after release of disclosure documents)
77 days [4]	Request to align a CVD case with a concurrent AD case.	351.210(i) (5 days after date of publication of preliminary determination)
102 days	Request for a hearing	351.310(c) (30 days after date of publication of preliminary determination)
119 days	Critical circumstances allegation	351.206(e) (21 days or more before final determination)
122 days	Requests for closed hearing sessions	351.310(f) (No later than the date the case briefs are due)
122 days	Submission of briefs	351.309(c)(1)(i) (50 days after date of publication of preliminary determination)
125 days	Allegation of upstream subsidies	351.301(d)(4)(ii)(B) (15 days before final determination)
127 days	Submission of rebuttal briefs	351.309(d) (5 days after dead-line for filing case brief)
129 days	Hearing	351.310(d)(1) (2 days after submission of rebuttal briefs)
140 days (Can be extended)	Final determination	351.210(b)(1) (75 days after preliminary determination)
150 days	Submission of ministerial error comments	351.224(c)(2) (5 days after release of disclosure documents)
155 days	Submission of replies to ministerial error comments.	351.224(c)(3) (5 days after filing of comments)
192 days	Order issued	351.211(b)

[1] Indicates the number of days from the date of initiation. Most of the deadlines shown here are approximate. The actual deadline in any particular segment of a proceeding may depend on the date of an earlier event or be established by the Secretary.
[2] Assumes that the Department sends out the questionnaire within 10 days of the initiation and allows 7 days for receipt of the questionnaire from the date on which it was transmitted.
[3] Assumes about 17 days between the preliminary determination and verification.
[4] Assumes that the preliminary determination is published 7 days after issuance (i.e., signature).

ANNEX II TO PART 351—DEADLINES FOR PARTIES IN COUNTERVAILING ADMINISTRATIVE REVIEWS

Day [1]	Event	Regulation
0 days	Request for review	351.213(b) (Last day of the anniversary month)
30 days	Publication of initiation notice	351.221(c)(1)(i) (End of month following the anniversary month)
66 days [2]	Notification of difficulty in responding to questionnaire.	351.301(c)(2)(iv) (14 days after date of receipt of initial questionnaire)
75 days	Application for an administrative protective order.	351.305(b)(3)
90 days [3]	Questionnaire response	351.301(c)(2)(iii) (At least 30 days after date of receipt of initial questionnaire)

Day [1]	Event	Regulation
120 days	Withdrawal of request for review	351.213(d)(1) (90 days after date of publication of initiation)
130 days	Request for verification	351.307(b)(1)(v) (100 days after date of publication of initiation)
140 days	Submission of factual information	351.301(b)(2)
245 days (Can be extended) ..	Preliminary results of review	351.213(h)(1)
282 days [4]	Request for a hearing and/or closed hearing session.	351.310(c); 351.310(f) (30 days after date of publication of preliminary results)
282 days	Submission of briefs	351.309(c)(1)(ii) (30 days after date of publication of preliminary results)
287 days	Submission of rebuttal briefs	351.309(d)(1) (5 days after deadline for filing case briefs)
289 days	Hearing	351.310(d)(1) (2 days after submission of rebuttal briefs)
372 days (Can be extended) ..	Final results of review	351.213(h)(1) (120 days after date of publication of preliminary results)
382 days	Submission of ministerial error comments ...	351.224(c)(2) (5 days after release of disclosure documents)
387 days	Replies to ministerial error comments	351.224(c)(3) (5 days after filing of comments)

[1] Indicates the number of days from the end of the anniversary month. Most of the deadlines shown here are approximate. The actual deadline in any particular segment of a proceeding may depend on the date of an earlier event or be established by the Secretary.
[2] Assumes that the Department sends out the questionnaire 45 days after the last day of the anniversary month and allows 7 days for receipt of the questionnaire from the date on which it was transmitted.
[3] Assumes that the Department sends out the questionnaire on day 45 and the response is due 45 days later.
[4] Assumes that the preliminary results are published 7 days after issuance (i.e., signature).

ANNEX III TO PART 351—DEADLINES FOR PARTIES IN ANTIDUMPING INVESTIGATIONS

Day [1]	Event	Regulation
0 days	Initiation	
37 days	Application for an administrative protective order.	351.305(b)(3)
50 days	Country-wide cost allegation	351.301(d)(2)(i)(A) (20 days after date on which initial questionnaire was transmitted)
51 days [2]	Notification of difficulty in responding to questionnaire.	351.301(c)(2)(iv) (Within 14 days after date of receipt of initial questionnaire)
51 days	Section A response	None
67 days	Sections B, C, D, E responses	351.301(c)(2)(iii) (At least 30 days after date of receipt of initial questionnaire)
70 days	Viability arguments	351.301(d)(1) (40 days after date on which initial questionnaire was transmitted)
87 days	Company-specific cost allegations	351.301(d)(2)(i)(B)
87 days	Major input cost allegations	351.301(d)(3)
115 days	Request for postponement by petitioner	351.205(e) (25 days or more before preliminary determination)
120 days	Allegation of critical circumstances	351.206(c)(2)(i) (20 days before preliminary determination)
140 days (Can be extended) ..	Preliminary determination	351.205(b)(1)
150 days	Submission of ministerial error comments ...	351.224(c)(2) (5 days after release of disclosure documents)
155 days	Submission of proposed suspension agreement.	351.208(f)(1)(A) (15 days after preliminary determination)
161 days [3]	Submission of factual information	351.301(b)(1) (7 days before date on which verification is to commence)
177 days [4]	Request for a hearing	351.310(c) (30 days after date of publication of preliminary determination)
187 days	Submission of publicly available information to value factors (NME's).	351.301(c)(3)(i) (40 days after date of publication of preliminary determination)
194 days	Critical circumstance allegation	351.206(e) (21 days before final determination)
197 days (Can be changed) ...	Request for closed hearing sessions	351.310(f) (No later than the date the case briefs are due)
197 days (Can be changed) ...	Submission of briefs	351.309(c)(1)(i) (50 days after date of publication of preliminary determination)
202 days	Submission of rebuttal briefs	351.309(d) (5 days after deadline for filing case briefs)
204 days	Hearing	351.310(d)(1) (2 days after submission of rebuttal briefs)
215 days	Request for postponement of the final determination.	351.210(e)
215 days (Can be extended) ..	Final determination	351.210(b)(1) (75 days after preliminary determination)

Day[1]	Event	Regulation
225 days	Submission ministerial error comments	351.224(c)(2) (5 days after release of disclosure documents)
230 days	Replies to ministerial error comments	351.224(c)(3) (5 days after filing of comments)
267 days	Order issued	351.211(b)

[1] Indicates the number of days from the date of initiation. Most of the deadlines shown here are approximate. The actual deadline in any particular segment of a proceeding may depend on the date of an earlier event or be established by the Secretary.
[2] Assumes that the Department sends out the questionnaire 5 days after the ITC vote and allows 7 days for receipt of the questionnaire from the date on which it was transmitted.
[3] Assumes about 28 days between the preliminary determination and verification.
[4] Assumes that the preliminary determination is published 7 days after issuance (*i.e.*, signature).

ANNEX IV TO PART 351—DEADLINES FOR PARTIES IN ANTIDUMPING ADMINISTRATIVE REVIEWS

Day[1]	Event	Regulation
0 days	Request for review	351.213(b) (Last day of the anniversary month)
30 days	Publication of initiation	351.221 (c)(1)(i) (End of month following the anniversary month)
37 days	Application for an administrative protective order.	351.305(b)(3)
60 days	Request to examine absorption of duties (AD)	351.213(j) (30 days after date of publication of initiation)
66 days[2]	Notification of difficulty in responding to questionnaire.	351.301(c)(2)(iv) (14 days after date of receipt of initial questionnaire)
66 days	Section A response	None
85 days	Viability arguments	351.301(d)(1) (40 days after date of transmittal of initial questionnaire)
90 days[3]	Sections B, C, D, E response	351.301(c)(2)(iii) (At least 30 days after date of receipt of initial questionnaire)
110 days	Company-specific cost allegations	351.301(d)(2)(i)(B) (20 days after relevant section is filed)
110 days	Major input cost allegations	351.301(d)(3) (20 days after relevant section is filed)
120 days	Withdrawal of request for review	351.213(d)(1) (90 days after date of publication of initiation)
130 days	Request for verification	351.307(b)(1)(v) (100 days after date of publication of initiation)
140 days	Submission of factual information	351.301(b)(2)
245 days (Can be extended)	Preliminary results of review	351.213(h)(1)
272 days[4]	Submission of publicly available information to value factors (NME's).	351.301(c)(3)(ii) (20 days after date of publication of preliminary results)
282 days	Request for a hearing and/or closed hearing session.	351.310(c); 351.310(f) (30 days after date of publication of preliminary results)
282 days	Submission of briefs	351.309(c)(1)(ii) (30 days after date of publication of preliminary results)
287 days	Submission of rebuttal briefs	351.309(d)(1) (5 days after deadline for filing case briefs)
289 days	Hearing; closed hearing session	351.310(d)(1) (2 days after submission of rebuttal briefs)
372 days (Can be extended)	Final results of review	351.213(h)(1) (120 days after date of publication of preliminary results)
382 days	Ministerial error comments	351.224(c)(2) (5 days after release of disclosure documents)
387 days	Replies to ministerial error comments	351.224(c)(3) (5 days after filing of comments)

[1] Indicates the number of days from the end of the anniversary month. Most of the deadlines shown here are approximate. The actual deadline in any particular segment of a proceeding may depend on the date of an earlier event or be established by the Secretary.
[2] Assumes that the Department sends out the questionnaire 45 days after the last day of the anniversary month and allows 7 days for receipt of the questionnaire from the date on which it was transmitted.
[3] Assumes that the Department sends out the questionnaire on day 45 and the response is due 45 days later.
[4] Assumes that the preliminary results are published 7 days after issuance (*i.e.*, signature).

ANNEX V TO PART 351—COMPARISON OF PRIOR AND NEW REGULATIONS

Prior	New	Description
PART 353—ANTIDUMPING DUTIES		
Subpart A—Scope and Definitions		
353.1	351.101	Scope of regulations
353.2	351.102	Definitions
353.3	351.104	Record of proceedings

Prior	New	Description
353.4	351.105	Public, proprietary, privileged & classified
353.5	Removed	Trade and Tariff Act of 1984 amendments
353.6	351.106	*De minimis* weighted-average dumping margin

Subpart B—Antidumping Duty Procedures

Prior	New	Description
353.11	351.201	Self-initiation
353.12	351.202	Petition requirements
353.13	351.203	Determination of sufficiency of petition
353.14	351.204(e)	Exclusion from antidumping duty order
353.15	351.205	Preliminary determination
353.16	351.206	Critical circumstances
353.17	351.207	Termination of investigation
353.18	351.208	Suspension of investigation
353.19	351.209	Violation of suspension agreement
353.20	351.210	Final determination
353.21	351.211	Antidumping duty order
353.21(c)	351.204(e)	Exclusion from antidumping duty order
1353.22(a)–(d)	351.213, 351.221	Administrative reviews under 751(a) of the Act
353.22(e)	351.212(c)	Automatic assessment of duties
353.22(f)	351.216, 351.221(c)(3)	Changed circumstances reviews
353.22(g)	351.215, 351.221(c)(2)	Expedited antidumping review
353.23	351.212(d)	Provisional measures deposit cap
353.24	351.212(e)	Interest on overpayments and under-payments
353.25	351.222	Revocation of orders; termination of suspended investigations
353.26	351.402(f)	Reimbursement of duties
353.27	351.223	Downstream product monitoring
353.28	351.224	Correction of ministerial errors
353.29	351.225	Scope rulings

Subpart C—Information and Argument

Prior	New	Description
353.31(a)–(c)	351.301	Time Limits for submission of factual information
353.31(a)(3)	351.301(d), 351.104(a)(2) ..	Return of untimely material
353.31(b)(3)	351.302(c)	Request for extension of time
353.31(d)–(i)	351.303	Filing, format, translation, service and certification
353.32	351.304	Request for proprietary treatment of information
353.33	351.104, 351.304(a)(2)	Information exempt from disclosure
353.34	351.305, 351.306	Disclosure of information under protective order
353.35	Removed	*Ex parte* meeting
353.36	351.307	Verification
353.37	351.308	Determination on the basis of the facts available
353.38(a)–(e)	351.309	Written argument
353.38(f)	351.310	Hearings

Subpart D—Calculation of Export Price, Constructed Export Price, Fair Value and Normal Value

Prior	New	Description
353.41	351.402	Calculation of export price
353.42(a)	351.102	Fair value (definition)
353.42(b)	351.104(c)	Transaction and persons examined
353.43	351.403(b)	Sales used in calculating normal value
353.44	Removed	Sales at varying prices
353.45	351.403	Transactions between affiliated parties
353.46	351.404	Selection of home market as the basis for normal value
353.47	Removed	Intermediate countries
353.48	351.404	Basis for normal value if home market sales are inadequate
353.49	351.404	Sales to a third country
353.50	351.405, 351.407	Calculation of normal value based on constructed value
353.51	351.406, 351.407	Sales at less than the cost of production
353.52	351.408	Nonmarket economy countries
353.53	Removed	Multinational corporations
353.54	351.401(b)	Claims for adjustments
353.55	351.409	Differences in quantities
353.56	351.410	Differences in circumstances of sale
353.57	351.411	Differences in physical characteristics
353.58	351.412	Levels of trade
353.59(a)	351.413	Insignificant adjustments
353.59(b)	351.414	Use of averaging
353.60	351.415	Conversion of currency

PART 355—COUNTERVAILING DUTIES

Subpart A—Scope and Definitions

Prior	New	Description
355.1	351.001	Scope of regulations

Prior	New	Description
355.2	351.002	Definitions
355.3	351.004	Record of proceeding
355.4	351.005	Public, proprietary, privileged & classified
355.5	351.003(a)	Subsidy library
355.6	Removed	Trade and Tariff Act of 1984 amendments
355.7	351.006	*De minimis* net subsidies

Subpart B—Countervailing Duty Procedures

Prior	New	Description
355.11	351.101	Delf-initiation
355.12	351.102	Petition requirements
355.13	351.103	Determination of sufficiency of petition
355.14	351.104(e)	Exclusion from countervailing duty order
355.15	351.105	Preliminary determination
355.16	351.106	Critical circumstances
355.17	351.107	Termination of investigation
355.18	351.108	Suspension of investigation
355.19	351.109	Violation of agreement
355.20	351.110	Final determination
355.21	351.111	Countervailing duty order
355.21(c)	351.104(e)	Exclusion from countervailing duty order
355.22(a)–(c)	351.113, 351.121	Administrative reviews under 751(a) of the Act
355.22(d)	Removed	Calculation of individual rates
355.22(e)	351.113(h)	Possible cancellation or revision of suspension agreements
355.22(f)	Removed	Review of individual producer or exporter
355.22(g)	351.112(c)	Automatic assessment of duties
355.22(h)	351.116, 351.121(c)(3)	Changed circumstances review
355.22(i)	351.120, 351.221(c)(7)	Review at the direction of the President
355.23	351.112(d)	Provisional measures deposit cap
355.24	351.112(e)	Interest on overpayments and underpayments
355.25	351.112	Revocation of orders; termination of suspended investigations
355.27	351.123	Downstream product monitoring
355.28	351.124	Correction of ministerial errors
355.29	351.125	Scope determinations

Subpart C—Information and Argument

Prior	New	Description
355.31(a)–(c)	351.301	Time limits for submission of factual information
355.31(a)(3)	351.302(d), 351.104(a)(2)	Return of untimely material
355.31(b)(3)	351.302(c)	Request for extension of time
355.31(d)–(i)	351.303	Filing, format, translation, service and certification
355.32	351.304	Request for proprietary treatment of information
355.33	351.104, 351.304(a)(2)	Information exempt from disclosure
355.34	351.305, 351.306	Disclosure of information under protective order
355.35	Removed	*Ex parte* meeting
355.36	351.307	Verification
355.37	351.308	Determinations on the basis of the facts available
355.38(a)–(e)	351.309	Written argument
355.38(f)	351.310	Hearings
355.39	351.311	Subsidy practice discovered during investigation or review

Subpart D—Quota Cheese Subsidy Determinations

Prior	New	Description
355.41	Removed	Definition of subsidy
355.42	351.601	Annual list and quarterly update
355.43	351.602	Determination upon request
355.44	351.603	Complaint of price-undercutting
355.45	351.604	Access to information

ANNEX VI TO PART 351—COUNTERVAILING INVESTIGATIONS TIMELINE

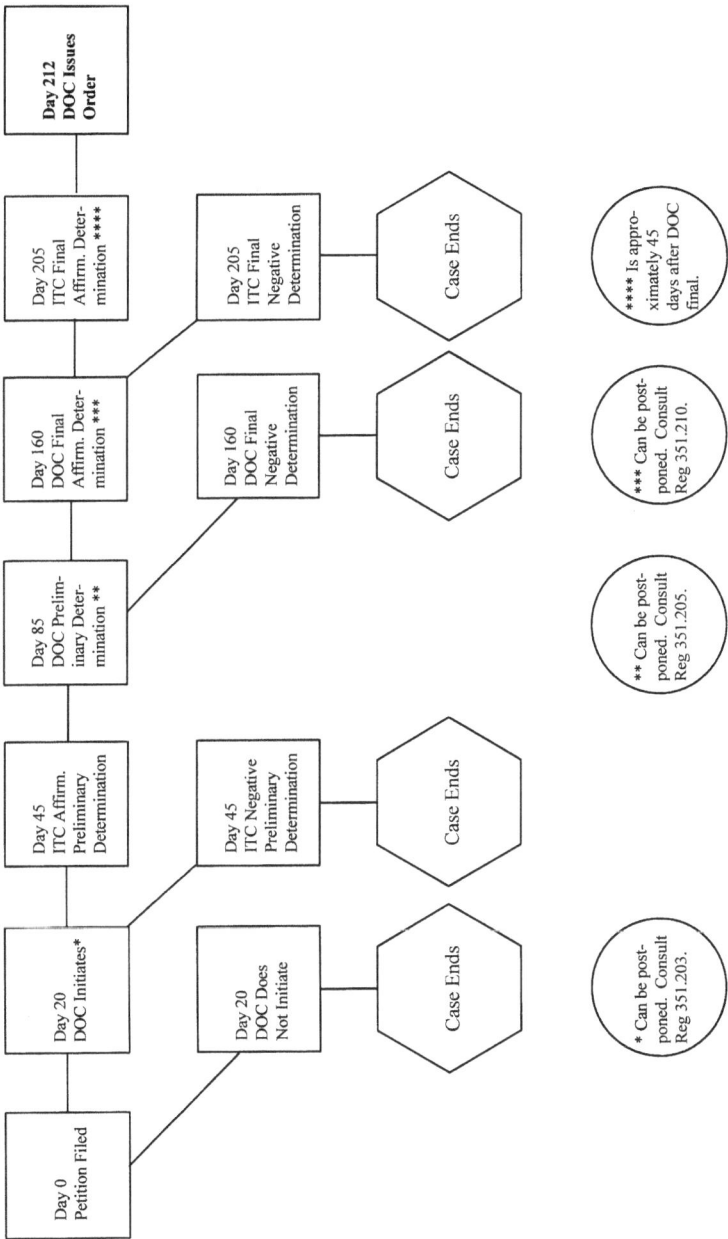

Countervailing Investigations Timeline

Day 0
Petition Filed

Day 20
DOC Initiates*

Day 20
DOC Does
Not Initiate

Case Ends

* Can be post-
poned. Consult
Reg 351.203.

Day 45
ITC Affirm.
Preliminary
Determination

Day 45
ITC Negative
Preliminary
Determination

Case Ends

Day 85
DOC Prelim-
inary Deter-
mination **

** Can be post-
poned. Consult
Reg 351.205.

Day 160
DOC Final
Affirm. Deter-
mination ***

Day 160
DOC Final
Negative
Determination

Case Ends

*** Can be post-
poned. Consult
Reg 351.210.

Day 205
ITC Final
Affirm. Deter-
mination ****

Day 205
ITC Final
Negative
Determination

Case Ends

**** Is appro-
ximately 45
days after DOC
final.

Day 212
DOC Issues
Order

317

ANNEX VII TO PART 351—ANTIDUMPING INVESTIGATIONS TIMELINE

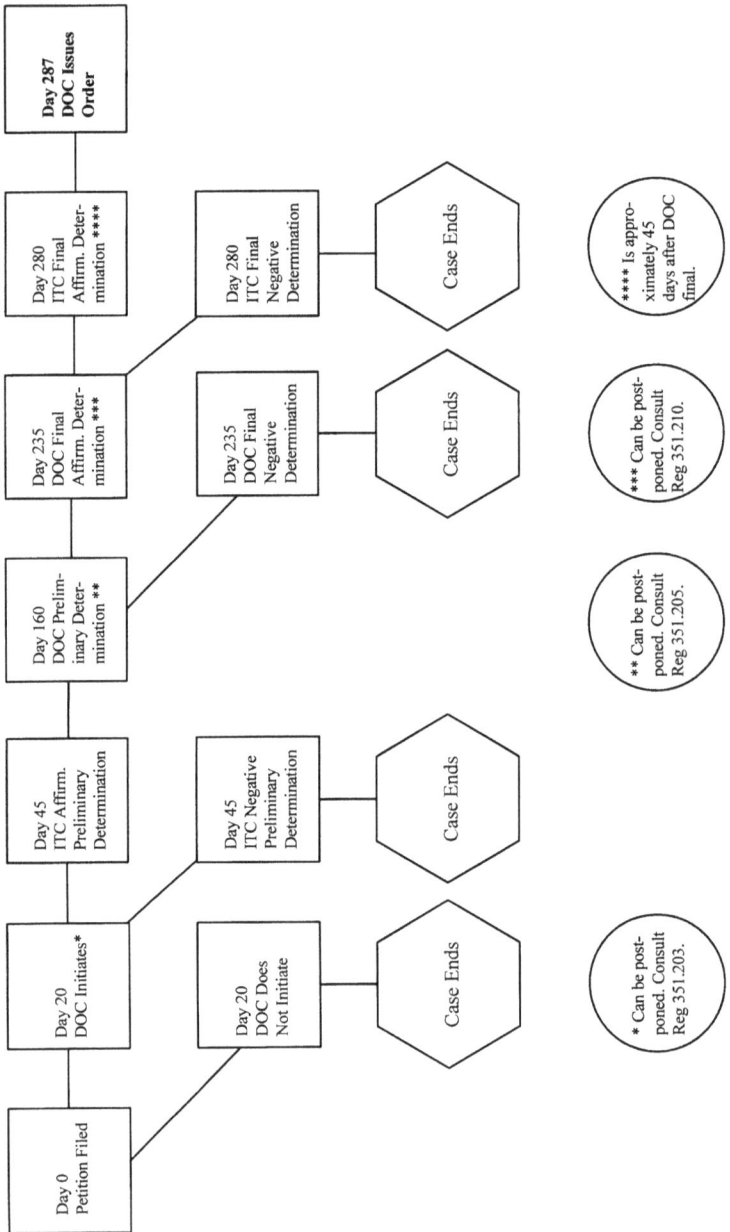

Antidumping Investigations Timeline

Day 287 DOC Issues Order	

Day 0 Petition Filed

Day 20 DOC Initiates*

Day 20 DOC Does Not Initiate → Case Ends

Day 45 ITC Affirm. Preliminary Determination

Day 45 ITC Negative Preliminary Determination → Case Ends

Day 160 DOC Preliminary Determination **

Day 235 DOC Final Affirm. Determination ***

Day 235 DOC Final Negative Determination → Case Ends

Day 280 ITC Final Affirm. Determination ****

Day 280 ITC Final Negative Determination → Case Ends

* Can be postponed. Consult Reg 351.203.

** Can be postponed. Consult Reg 351.205.

*** Can be postponed. Consult Reg 351.210.

**** Is approximately 45 days after DOC final.

ANNEX VIII–A TO PART 351—SCHEDULE FOR 90-DAY SUNSET REVIEWS

Day [1]	Event	Regulation
0	Initiation	§ 351.218(c)
15	Filing of Notice of Intent to Participate by domestic interested parties.	§ 351.218(d)(1)(i) (not later than 15 days after the date of publication of the Notice of Initiation)
20	Notification to the ITC that no domestic interested party has responded to the Notice of Initiation.	§ 351.218(d)(1)(iii)(B)(2) (normally not later than 20 days after the date of publication of the Notice of Initiation)
30	Filing of substantive response to the Notice of Initiation by all interested parties and industrial users and consumers.	§§ 351.218(d)(3)(i) and 351.218(d)(3)(vi) (not later than 30 days after the date of publication of the Notice of Initiation)
35	Filing of rebuttal to substantive response to the Notice of Initiation.	§ 351.218(d)(4) (not later than 5 days after the substantive response is filed with the Department)
40	Notification to the ITC that no domestic interested party has responded to the Notice of Initiation (based on inadequate response from domestic interested parties).	§ 351.218(e)(1)(i)(C)(2) (normally not later than 40 days after the date of publication of the Notice of Initiation)
90	Final determination revoking an order or terminating a suspended investigation where no domestic interested party responds to the Notice of Initiation.	§§ 351.218(d)(1)(iii)(B)(3) and 351.222(i)(1)(i) (not later than 90 days after the date of publication of the Notice of Initiation)

[1] Indicates the number of days from the date of publication in the FEDERAL REGISTER of the Notice of Initiation.

[63 FR 13524, Mar. 20, 1998]

ANNEX VIII–B TO PART 351—SCHEDULE FOR EXPEDITED SUNSET REVIEWS

Day [1]	Event	Regulation
0	Initiation	§ 351.218(c)
15	Filing of Notice of Intent to Participate by domestic interested parties.	§ 351.218(d)(1)(i) (not later than 15 days after the date of publication of the Notice of Initiation)
30	Filing of Statement of Waiver by respondent interested parties.	§ 351.218(d)(2)(i) (not later than 30 days after the date of publication of the Notice of Initiation)
30	Filing of substantive response to the Notice of Initiation by all interested parties and industrial users and consumers.	§§ 351.218(d)(3)(i) and 351.218(d)(3)(vi) (not later than 30 days after the date of publication of the Notice of Initiation)
35	Filing of rebuttal to substantive response to the Notice of Initiation.	§ 351.218(d)(4) (not later than 5 days after the substantive response is filed with the Department)
50	Notification to the ITC that respondent interested parties provided inadequate response to the Notice of Initiation.	§ 351.218(e)(1)(ii)(C)(1) (normally not later than 50 days after the date of publication of the Notice of Initiation)
70	Comments on adequacy of response and appropriateness of expedited sunset review.	§ 351.309(e)(ii) (not later than 70 days after the date of publication of the Notice of Initiation)
120	Final results of expedited sunset review where respondent interested parties provide inadequate response to the Notice of Initiation.	§§ 351.218(e)(1)(ii)(B) and 351.218(e)(1)(ii)(C)(2) (not later than 120 days after the date of publication of the Notice of Initiation)

[1] Indicates the number of days from the date of publication in the FEDERAL REGISTER of the Notice of Initiation.

[63 FR 13525, Mar. 20, 1998]

ANNEX VIII–C TO PART 351—SCHEDULE FOR FULL SUNSET REVIEWS

Day [1]	Event	Regulation
0	Initiation	§ 351.218(c)
15	Filing of Notice of Intent to Participate by domestic interested parties.	§ 351.218(d)(1)(i) (not later than 15 days after the date of publication of the Notice of Initiation)
30	Filing of Statement of Waiver by respondent interested parties.	§ 351.218(d)(2)(i) (not later than 30 days after the date of publication of the Notice of Initiation)
30	Filing of substantive response to the Notice of Initiation by all interested parties and industrial users and consumers.	§§ 351.218(d)(3)(i) and 351.218(d)(3)(vi) (not later than 30 days after the date of publication of the Notice of Initiation)
35	Filing of rebuttal to substantive response to the Notice of Initiation.	§ 351.218(d)(4) (not later than 5 days after the substantive response is filed with the Department)
110	Preliminary results of full sunset review	§ 351.218(f)(1) (normally not later than 110 days after the date of publication of the Notice of Initiation)
120	Verification in a full sunset review, where needed	§ 351.218(f)(2)(ii) (approximately 120 days after the date of publication of the Notice of Initiation)
160	Filing of case brief in full sunset review	§ 351.309(c)(1)(i) (50 days after the date of publication of the preliminary results of full sunset review)
165	Filing of rebuttal brief in full sunset review	§ 351.309(d)(1) (5 days after the time limit for filing a case brief)

Day [1]	Event	Regulation
167	Hearing in full sunset review if requested	§ 351.310(d)(i) (2 days after the time limit for filing a rebuttal brief)
240	Final results of full sunset review	§ 351.218(f)(3)(i) (not later than 240 days after the date of publication of the Notice of Initiation)
330	Final results of full sunset review if fully extended	§ 351.218(f)(3)(ii) (if full sunset review is extraordinarily complicated, period for issuing final results may be extended by not more than 90 days)

[1] Indicates the number of days from the date of publication in the FEDERAL REGISTER of the Notice of Initiation.

[63 FR 13525, Mar. 20, 1998]

PART 354—PROCEDURES FOR IMPOSING SANCTIONS FOR VIOLATION OF AN ANTIDUMPING OR COUNTERVAILING DUTY ADMINISTRATIVE PROTECTIVE ORDER

Sec.
354.1   Scope.
354.2   Definitions.
354.3   Sanctions.
354.4   Suspension of rules.
354.5   Report of violation and investigation.
354.6   Initiation of proceedings.
354.7   Charging letter.
354.8   Interim sanctions.
354.9   Request for a hearing.
354.10 Discovery.
354.11 Prehearing conference.
354.12 Hearing.
354.13 Proceeding without a hearing.
354.14 Initial decision.
354.15 Final decision.
354.16 Reconsideration.
354.17 Confidentiality.
354.18 Public notice of sanctions.
354.19 Sunset.

AUTHORITY: 5 U.S.C. 301, and 19 U.S.C. 1677.

SOURCE: 53 FR 47920, Nov. 28, 1988, unless otherwise noted.

EDITORIAL NOTE: Nomenclature changes to part 354 appear at 63 FR 24403, May 4, 1998.

EDITORIAL NOTE: Nomenclature changes to part 354 appear at 78 FR 62418, Oct. 22, 2013.

§ 354.1 Scope.

This part sets forth the procedures for imposing sanctions for violation of an administrative protective order issued under 19 CFR 351.306, or successor regulations, as authorized by 19 U.S.C. 1677f(c).

[53 FR 47920, Nov. 28, 1988, as amended at 63 FR 24403, May 4, 1998]

§ 354.2 Definitions.

For purposes of this part:

Administrative protective order (APO) means an administrative protective order described in section 777(c)(1) of the Tariff Act of 1930, as amended; APO Sanctions Board means the Administrative Protective Order Sanctions Board.

Business proprietary information means information the disclosure of which the Secretary has decided is limited under 19 CFR 351.105, or successor regulations;

Charged party means a person who is charged by the Deputy Under Secretary with violating a protective order;

Chief Counsel means the Chief Counsel for Trade Enforcement and Compliance or a designee;

Date of service means the day a document is deposited in the mail or delivered in person;

Days means calendar days, except that a deadline which falls on a weekend or holiday shall be extended to the next working day;

Department means the United States Department of Commerce;

Deputy Under Secretary means the Deputy Under Secretary for International Trade or a designee;

Director means the Senior APO Specialist or an office director under a Deputy Assistant Secretary, International Trade Administration, or a designee;

Lesser included sanction means a sanction of the same type but of more limited scope than the proposed sanction; thus a one-year bar on representations before the International Trade Administration is a lesser included sanction of a proposed seven-year bar;

Parties means the Department and the charged party or affected party in an action under this part;

Presiding official means the person authorized to conduct hearings in administrative proceedings or to rule on any motion or make any determination under this part, who may be an Administrative Law Judge, a Hearing Commissioner, or such other person who is not under the supervision or control of the Assistant Secretary for Enforcement and Compliance, the Deputy Under Secretary for International Trade, the Chief Counsel for Trade Enforcement and Compliance, or a member of the APO Sanctions Board;

Proprietary information means information the disclosure of which the Secretary has decided is limited under 19 CFR part 351 including business or trade secrets; production costs; distribution costs; terms of sale; prices of individual sales, likely sales, or offers; names of customers, distributors, or suppliers; exact amounts of the gross net subsidies received and used by a person; names of particular persons from whom proprietary information was obtained; and any other business information the release of which to the public would cause substantial harm to the competitive position of the submitter;

Secretary means the Secretary of Commerce or a designee;

Segment of the proceeding means a portion of an antidumping or countervailing duty proceeding that is reviewable under section 516A of the Tariff Act of 1930, as amended.

Senior APO Specialist means the Department employee under the Director for Policy and Analysis who leads the APO Unit and is responsible for directing Enforcement and Compliance's handling of business proprietary information;

Under Secretary means the Under Secretary for International Trade or a designee.

[63 FR 24403, May 4, 1998]

§354.3 Sanctions.

(a) A person determined under this part to have violated an administrative protective order may be subjected to any or all of the following sanctions:

(1) Barring such person from appearing before the International Trade Administration to represent another for a designated time period from the date of publication in the FEDERAL REGISTER of a notice that a violation has been determined to exist;

(2) Denying the person access to business proprietary information for a designated time period from the date of publication in the FEDERAL REGISTER of a notice that a violation has been determined to exist;

(3) Other appropriate administrative sanctions, including striking from the record any information or argument submitted by, or on behalf of, the violating party or the party represented by the violating party; terminating any proceeding then in progress; or revoking any order then in effect;

(4) Requiring the person to return material previously provided by the Secretary and all other materials containing the business proprietary information, such as briefs, notes, or charts based on any such information received under an administrative protective order; and

(5) Issuing a private letter of reprimand.

(b)(1) The firm of which a person determined to have violated an administrative protective order is a partner, associate or employee; any partner, associate, employer, or employee of such person; and any person represented by such person may be barred from appearing before the International Trade Administration for a designated time period from the date of publication in the FEDERAL REGISTER of notice that a violation has been determined to exist or may be subjected to the sanctions set forth in paragraph (a) of this section, as appropriate.

(2) Each person against whom sanctions are proposed under paragraph (b)(1) of this section is entitled to all the administrative rights set forth in this part separately and apart from rights provided to a person subject to sanctions under paragraph (a) of this section, including the right to a charging letter, right to representation, and right to a hearing, but subject to joinder or consolidation by a presiding official under §354.12(b).

[53 FR 47920, Nov. 28, 1988, as amended at 63 FR 24404, May 4, 1998]

§ 354.4 Suspension of rules.

Upon request by the Deputy Under Secretary, a charged or affected party, or the APO Sanctions Board, a presiding official may modify or waive any rule in the part upon determining that no party will be unduly prejudiced and the ends of justice will thereby be served and upon notice to all parties.

§ 354.5 Report of violation and investigation.

(a) An employee of the Department who has information indicating that the terms of an administrative protective order have been violated will provide the information to the Senior APO Specialist or the Chief Counsel.

(b) Upon receiving information which indicates that a person may have violated the terms of an administrative protective order from an employee of the Department or any other person, the director will conduct an investigation concerning whether there was a violation of an administrative protective order, and who was responsible for the violation, if any. No director shall investigate an alleged violation that arose out of a proceeding for which the director was responsible. For the purposes of this part, the director will be supervised by the Deputy Under Secretary for International Trade with guidance from the Chief Counsel. The director will conduct an investigation only if the information is received within 30 days after the alleged violation occurred or, as determined by the director, could have been discovered through the exercise of reasonable and ordinary care.

(c)(1) The director conducting the investigation will provide a report of the investigation to the Deputy Under Secretary for International Trade, after review by the Chief Counsel, no later than 90 days after receiving information concerning a violation if:

(i) The person alleged to have violated an administrative protective order personally notified the Secretary and reported the particulars surrounding the incident; and

(ii) The alleged violation did not result in any actual disclosure of business proprietary information. Upon the director's request, and if extraordinary circumstances exist, the Deputy Under

Secretary for International Trade may grant the director up to an additional 90 days to conduct the investigation and submit the report.

(2) In all other cases, the director will provide a report of the investigation to the Deputy Under Secretary for International Trade, after review by the Chief Counsel, no later than 180 days after receiving information concerning a violation. Upon the director's request, and if extraordinary circumstances exist, the Deputy Under Secretary for International Trade may grant the director up to an additional 180 days to conduct the investigation and submit the report.

(d) The following examples of actions that constitute violations of an administrative protective order shall serve as guidelines to each person subject to an administrative protective order. These examples do not represent an exhaustive list. Evidence that one of the acts described in the guidelines has been committed, however, shall be considered by the Deputy Under Secretary as reasonable cause to believe a person has violated an administrative protective order, within the meaning of § 354.6.

(1) Disclosure of business proprietary information to any person other than the submitting party, an authorized applicant, or an appropriate Department official identified in section 777(b) of the Tariff Act of 1930, including disclosure to an employee of any other United States Government agency or a member of Congress.

(2) Failure to follow the terms and conditions outlined in the administrative protective order for safeguarding business proprietary information.

(3) Loss of business proprietary information.

(4) Failure to return or destroy all copies of the original documents and all notes, memoranda, and submissions containing business proprietary information at the close of the proceeding for which the data were obtained by burning or shredding of the documents or by erasing electronic memory, computer disk, or tape memory, as set forth in the administrative protective order.

(5) Failure to delete business proprietary information from the public

version of a brief or other correspondence filed with the Department.

(6) Disclosure of business proprietary information during a public hearing.

(7) Use of business proprietary information submitted in one segment of a proceeding in another segment of the same proceeding or in another proceeding, except as authorized by the Tariff Act of 1930 or by an administrative protective order.

(8) Use of business proprietary information submitted for a countervailing duty investigation or administrative review during an antidumping duty investigation or administrative review, or vice versa.

[53 FR 47920, Nov. 28, 1988, as amended at 63 FR 24404, May 4, 1998]

§ 354.6 Initiation of proceedings.

(a) *In general.* After an investigation and report by the director under § 354.5(c) and consultation with the Chief Counsel, the Deputy Under Secretary for International Trade will determine whether there is reasonable cause to believe that a person has violated an administrative protective order. If the Deputy Under Secretary for International Trade determines that there is reasonable cause, the Deputy Under Secretary for International Trade also will determine whether sanctions under paragraph (b) or a warning under paragraph (c) is appropriate for the violation.

(b) *Sanctions.* In determining under paragraph (a) of this section whether sanctions are appropriate, and, if so, what sanctions to impose, the Deputy Under Secretary for International Trade will consider the nature of the violation, the resulting harm, and other relevant circumstances of the case. If the Deputy Under Secretary for International Trade determines that sanctions are appropriate, the Deputy Under Secretary for International Trade will initiate a proceeding under this part by issuing a charging letter under § 354.7. The Deputy Under Secretary for International Trade will determine whether to initiate a proceeding no later than 60 days after receiving a report of the investigation.

(c) *Warning.* If the Deputy Under Secretary for International Trade determines under paragraph (a) of this section that a warning is appropriate, the Deputy Under Secretary will issue a warning letter to the person believed to have violated an administrative protective order. Sanctions are not appropriate and a warning is appropriate if:

(1) The person took due care;

(2) The Secretary has not previously charged the person with violating an administrative protective order;

(3) The violation did not result in any disclosure of the business proprietary information or the Secretary is otherwise able to determine that the violation caused no harm to the submitter of the information; and

(4) The person cooperated fully in the investigation.

[63 FR 24404, May 4, 1998]

§ 354.7 Charging letter.

(a) *Contents of Letter.* The Deputy Under Secretary will initiate proceedings by issuing a charging letter to each charged party and affected party which includes:

(1) A statement of the allegation that an administrative protective order has been violated and the basis thereof;

(2) A statement of the proposed sanctions;

(3) A statement that the charged or affected party is entitled to review the documents or other physical evidence upon which the charge is based and the method for requesting access to, or copies of, such documents;

(4) A statement that the charged or affected party is entitled to a hearing before a presiding official if requested within 30 days of the date of service of the charging letter and the procedure for requesting a hearing, including the name, address, and telephone number of the person to contact if there are further questions;

(5) A statement that the charged or affected party has a right, if a hearing is not requested, to submit documentary evidence to the Deputy Under Secretary and an explanation of the method for submitting evidence and the date by which it must be received; and

(6) A statement that the charged or affected party has a right to retain counsel at the party's own expense for purposes of representation.

(b) Settlement and amending the charging letter. The Deputy Under Secretary for International Trade and a charged or affected party may settle a charge brought under this part by mutual agreement at any time after service of the charging letter; approval of the presiding official or the administrative protective order Sanctions Board is not necessary. The charged or affected party may request a hearing but at the same time request that a presiding official not be appointed pending settlement discussions. Settlement agreements may include sanctions for purposes of § 354.18. The Deputy Under Secretary for International Trade may amend, supplement, or withdraw the charging letter as follows:

(1) If there has been no request for a hearing, or if supporting information has not been submitted under § 354.13, the withdrawal will not preclude future actions on the same alleged violation.

(2) If a hearing has been requested but no presiding official has been appointed, withdrawal of the charging letter will preclude the Deputy Under Secretary for International Trade from seeking sanctions at a later date for the same alleged violation.

(3) The Deputy Under Secretary for International Trade may amend, supplement or withdraw the charging letter at any time after the appointment of a presiding official, if the presiding official determines that the interests of justice would thereby be served. If the presiding official so determines, the presiding official will also determine whether the withdrawal will preclude the Deputy Under Secretary for International Trade from seeking sanctions at a later date for the same alleged violation.

(c) *Service of charging letter on a resident of the United States.* (1) Service of a charging letter on a United States resident will be made by:

(i) Mailing a copy by registered or certified mail addressed to the charged or affected party at the party's last known address;

(ii) Leaving a copy with the charged or affected party or with an officer, a managing or general agent, or any other agent authorized by appointment or by law to receive service for the party; or

(iii) Leaving a copy with a person of suitable age and discretion who resides at the party's last known dwelling.

(2) Service made in the manner described in paragraph (c) (ii) or (iii) of this section shall be evidenced by a certificate of service signed by the person making such service, stating the method of service and the identity of the person with whom the charging letter was left.

(d) *Service of charging letter on a nonresident.* If applicable laws or intergovernmental agreements or understandings make the methods of service set forth in paragraph (c) of this section inappropriate or ineffective, service of the charging letter on a person who is not a resident of the United States may be made by any method that is permitted by the country in which the person resides and that satisfies the due process requirements under United States law with respect to notice in administrative proceedings.

[53 FR 47920, Nov. 28, 1988, as amended at 63 FR 24405, May 4, 1998]

§ 354.8 Interim sanctions.

(a) If the Deputy Under Secretary concludes, after issuing a charging letter under § 354.7 and before a final decision is rendered, that interim sanctions are necessary to protect the interests of the Department or others, including the protection of business proprietary information, the Deputy Under Secretary may petition a presiding official to impose such sanctions.

(b) The presiding official may impose interim sanctions against a person upon determining that:

(1) There is probable cause to believe that there was a violation of an administrative protective order and the Department is likely to prevail in obtaining sanctions under this part,

(2) The Department or others are likely to suffer irreparable harm if the interim sanctions are not imposed, and

(3) The interim sanctions are a reasonable means for protecting the rights of the Department or others while preserving to the greatest extent possible the rights of the person against whom the interim sanctions are proposed.

(c) Interim sanctions which may be imposed include any sanctions that are necessary to protect the rights of the Department or others, including, but not limited to:

(1) Denying a person further access to business proprietary information.

(2) Barring a person from representing another person before the International Trade Administration.

(3) Barring a person from appearing before the International Trade Administration, and

(4) Requiring the person to return material previously provided by the Department and all other materials containing the business proprietary information, such as briefs, notes, or charts based on any such information received under an administrative protective order.

(d) The Deputy Under Secretary will notify the person against whom interim sanctions are sought of the request for interim sanctions and provide to that person the material submitted to the presiding official to support the request. The notice will include a reference to the procedures of this section.

(e) A person against whom interim sanctions are proposed has a right to oppose the request through submission of material to the presiding official. The presiding official has discretion to permit oral presentations and to allow further submissions.

(f) The presiding official will notify the parties of the decision on interim sanctions and the basis therefor within five days of the conclusion of oral presentations or the date of final written submissions.

(g) If interim sanctions have been imposed, the investigation and any proceedings under this part will be conducted on an expedited basis.

(h) An order imposing interim sanctions may be revoked at any time by the presiding official and expires automatically upon the issuance of a final order.

(i) The presiding official may reconsider imposition of interim sanctions on the basis of new and material evidence or other good cause shown. The Deputy Under Secretary or a person against whom interim sanctions have been imposed may appeal a decision on interim sanctions to the APO Sanctions Board, if such an appeal is certified by the presiding official as necessary to prevent undue harm to the Department, a person against whom interim sanctions have been imposed or others, or is otherwise in the interests of justice. Interim sanctions which have been imposed remain in effect while an appeal is pending, unless the presiding official determines otherwise.

(j) The Deputy Under Secretary may request a presiding official to impose emergency interim sanctions to preserve the status quo. Emergency interim sanctions may last no longer than 48 hours, excluding weekends and holidays. The person against whom such emergency interim sanctions are proposed need not be given prior notice or an opportunity to oppose the request for sanctions. The presiding official may impose emergency interim sanctions upon determining that the Department is, or others are, likely to suffer irreparable harm if such sanctions are not imposed and that the interests of justice would thereby be served. The presiding official will promptly notify a person against whom emergency sanctions have been imposed of the sanctions and their duration.

(k) If a hearing has not been requested, the Deputy Under Secretary will ask the Under Secretary to appoint a presiding official for making determinations under this section.

§ 354.9 Request for a hearing.

(a) Any party may request a hearing by submitted a written request to the Under Secretary within 30 days after the date of service of the charging letter. However, the Deputy Under Secretary may request a hearing only if the interests of justice would thereby be served.

(b) Upon timely receipt of a request for a hearing, and unless the party requesting a hearing requests that the Under Secretary not appoint a presiding official, the Under Secretary will appoint a presiding official to conduct the hearing and render an initial decision.

[53 FR 47920, Nov. 28, 1988, as amended at 63 FR 24405, May 4, 1998]

§ 354.10 Discovery.

(a) *Voluntary discovery.* All parties are encouraged to engage in voluntary discovery procedures regarding any matter, not privileged, which is relevant to the subject matter of the pending proceeding.

(b) *Interrogatories and requests for admissions or production of documents.* A party may serve on any other party interrogatories, requests for admissions, or requests for production of documents for inspection and copying, and a party concerned may then apply to the presiding official for such enforcement or administrative protective order as that party deems warranted concerning such discovery. The party will serve a discovery request at least 20 days before the scheduled date of a hearing, if a hearing has been requested and scheduled, unless the presiding official specifies a shorter time period. Copies of interrogatories, requests for admissions, and requests for production of documents and responses thereto will be served on all parties. Matters of fact or law of which admission is requested will be deemed admitted unless, within a period designated in the request (at least 10 days after the date of service of the request, or within such further time as the presiding official may allow), the party to whom the request is directed serves upon the requesting party a sworn statement either admitting or denying specifically the matters of which admission is requested or setting forth in detail the reasons why the party cannot truthfully either admit or deny such matters.

(c) *Depositions.* Upon application of a party and for good cause shown, the presiding official may order the taking of the testimony of any person who is a party, or under the control or authority of a party, by deposition and the production of specified documents or materials by the person at the deposition. The application shall state the purpose of the deposition and shall set forth the facts sought to be established through the deposition.

(d) *Enforcement.* The presiding official may order a party to answer designated questions, to produce specified documents or items, or to take any other action in response to a proper discovery request. If a party does not comply with such an order, the presiding official may make any determination or enter any order in the proceedings as he or she deems reasonable and appropriate. The presiding official may strike related charges or defenses in whole or in part, or may take particular facts relating to the discovery request to which the party failed or refused to respond as being established for purposes of the proceeding in accordance with the contentions of the party seeking discovery. In issuing a discovery order, the presiding official will consider the necessity to protect business proprietary information and will not order the release of information in circumstances where it is reasonable to conclude that such release will lead to unauthorized dissemination of such information.

(e) *Role of the Under Secretary.* If a hearing has not been requested, the party seeking enforcement will ask the Under Secretary to appoint a presiding official to rule on motions under this section.

§ 354.11 Prehearing conference.

(a)(1) If an administrative hearing has been requested, the presiding official will direct the parties to attend a prehearing conference to consider:

(i) Simplification of issues;

(ii) Obtaining stipulations of fact and of documents to avoid unnecessary proof;

(iii) Settlement of the matter;

(iv) Discovery; and

(v) Such other matters as may expedite the disposition of the proceedings.

(2) Any relevant and significant stipulations or admissions will be incorporated into the initial decision.

(b) If a prehearing conference is impractical, the presiding official will direct the parties to correspond with each other or to confer by telephone or otherwise to achieve the purposes of such a conference.

§ 354.12 Hearing.

(a) *Scheduling of hearing.* The presiding official will schedule the hearing at a reasonable time, date, and place, which will be in Washington, DC, unless the presiding official determines otherwise based upon good cause shown that another location would better serve the interests of justice. In setting the date, the presiding official will give due regard to the need for the parties adequately to prepare for the hearing and the importance of expeditiously resolving the matter.

(b) *Joinder or consolidation.* The presiding official may order joinder or consolidation if sanctions are proposed against more than one party or if violations of more than one administrative protective order are alleged if to do so would expedite processing of the cases and not adversely affect the interests of the parties.

(c) *Hearing procedures.* Hearings will be conducted in a fair and impartial manner by the presiding official, who may limit attendance at any hearing or portion thereof if necessary or advisable in order to protect business proprietary information from improper disclosure. The rules of evidence prevailing in courts of law shall not apply, and all evidentiary material the presiding official determines to be relevant and material to the proceeding and not unduly repetitious may be received into evidence and given appropriate weight. The presiding official may make such orders and determinations regarding the admissibility of evidence, conduct of examination and cross-examination, and similar matters as are necessary or appropriate to ensure orderliness in the proceedings. The presiding official will ensure that a record of the hearing be taken by reporter or by electronic recording, and will order such part of the record to be sealed as is necessary to protect business proprietary information.

(d) *Rights of parties.* At a hearing each party shall have the right to:

(1) Introduce and examine witnesses and submit physical evidence,

(2) Confront and cross-examine adverse witnesses,

(3) Present oral argument, and

(4) Receive a transcript or recording of the proceedings, upon request, subject to the presiding official's orders regarding sealing the record.

(e) *Representation.* Each charged or affected party has a right to represent himself or herself or to retain private counsel for that purpose. The Chief Counsel will represent the Department,

unless the General Counsel determines otherwise. The presiding official may disallow a representative if such representation constitutes a conflict of interest or is otherwise not in the interests of justice and may debar a representative for contumacious conduct relating to the proceedings.

(f) *Ex parte communications.* The parties and their representatives may not make any *ex parte* communications to the presiding official concerning the merits of the allegations or any matters at issue, except as provided in §354.8 regarding emergency interim sanctions.

§354.13 Proceeding without a hearing.

If no party has requested a hearing, the Deputy Under Secretary, within 40 days after the date of service of a charging letter, will submit for inclusion into the record and provide each charged or affected party information supporting the allegations in the charging letter. Each charged or affected party has the right to file a written response to the information and supporting documentation within 30 days after the date of service of the information provided by the Deputy Under Secretary unless the Deputy Under Secretary alters the time period for good cause. The Deputy Under Secretary may allow the parties to submit further information and argument.

§354.14 Initial decision.

(a) *Initial decision.* The presiding official, if a hearing was requested, or the Deputy Under Secretary will submit an initial decision to the APO Sanctions Board, providing copies to the parties. The presiding official or Deputy Under Secretary will ordinarily issue the decision within 20 days of the conclusion of the hearing, if one was held, or within 15 days of the date of service of final written submissions. The initial decision will be based solely on evidence received into the record, and the pleadings of the parties.

(b) *Findings and conclusions.* The initial decision will state findings and conclusions as to whether a person has violated an administrative protective order; the basis for those findings and conclusions; and whether the sanctions proposed in the charging letter, or lesser included sanctions, should be imposed against the charged or affected party. The presiding official or Deputy Under Secretary may impose sanctions only upon determining that the preponderance of the evidence supports a finding of violation of an administrative protective order and that the sanctions are warranted against the charged or affected party. In determining whether sanctions are appropriate and, if so, what sanctions to impose, the presiding official or the Deputy Under Secretary will consider the nature of the violation, the resulting harm, and other relevant circumstances of the case.

(c) *Finality of decision.* If the APO Sanctions Board has not issued a decision on the matter within 60 days after issuance of the initial decision, the initial decision becomes the final decision of the Department.

§ 354.15   Final decision.

(a) *APO Sanctions Board.* Upon request of a party, the initial decision will be reviewed by the members of the APO Sanctions Board. The Board consists of the Under Secretary for International Trade, who shall serve as Chairperson, the Under Secretary for Economic Affairs, and the General Counsel.

(b) *Comments on initial decision.* Within 30 days after issuance of the initial decision, a party may submit written comments to the APO Sanctions Board on the initial decision, which the Board will consider when reviewing the initial decision. The parties have no right to an oral presentation, although the Board may allow oral argument in its discretion.

(c) *Final decision by the APO Sanctions Board.* Within 60 days but not sooner than 30 days after issuance of an initial decision, the APO Sanctions Board may issue a final decision which adopts the initial decision in its entirety; differs in whole or in part from the initial decision, including the imposition of lesser included sanctions; or remands the matter to the presiding official or Deputy Under Secretary for further consideration. The only sanctions that the Board can impose are those sanctions proposed in the charging letter or lesser included sanctions.

(d) *Contents of final decision.* If the final decision of the APO Sanctions Board does not remand the matter and differs from the initial decision, it will state findings and conclusions which differ from the initial decision, if any, the basis for those findings and conclusions, and the sanctions which are to be imposed, to the extent they differ from the sanctions in the initial decision.

[53 FR 47920, Nov. 28, 1988, as amended at 63 FR 24405, May 4, 1998]

§ 354.16   Reconsideration.

Any party may file a motion for reconsideration with the APO Sanctions Board. The party must state with particularity the grounds for the motion, including any facts or points of law which the party claims the APO Sanctions Board has overlooked or misapplied. The party may file the motion within 30 days of the issuance of the final decision or the adoption of the initial decision as the final decision, except that if the motion is based on the discovery of new and material evidence which was not known, and could not reasonably have been discovered through due diligence prior to the close of the record, the party shall file the motion within 15 days of the discovery of the new and material evidence. The party shall provide a copy of the motion to all other parties. Opposing parties may file a response within 30 days of the date of service of the motion. The response shall be considered as part of the record. The parties have no right to an oral presentation on a motion for reconsideration, but the Board may permit oral argument at its discretion. If the motion to reconsider is granted, the Board will review the record and affirm, modify, or reverse the original decision or remand the matter for further consideration to a presiding official or the Deputy Under Secretary, as warranted.

§ 354.17   Confidentiality.

(a) All proceedings involving allegations of a violation of an administrative protective order shall be kept confidential until such time as the Department makes a final decision under these regulations, no longer subject to reconsideration, imposing a sanction.

(b) The charged party or counsel for the charged party will be granted access to business proprietary information in these proceedings, as necessary, under administrative protective order, consistent with the provisions of 19 CFR 351.305(c), or their successor regulations.

[53 FR 47920, Nov. 28, 1988, as amended at 63 FR 24405, May 4, 1998]

§ 354.18 Public notice of sanctions.

If there is a final decision under § 354.15 to impose sanctions, or if a charging letter is settled under § 354.7(b), notice of the Secretary's decision or of the existence of a settlement will be published in the FEDERAL REGISTER. If a final decision is reached, such publication will be no sooner than 30 days after issuance of a final decision or after a motion to reconsider has been denied, if such a motion was filed. In addition, whenever the Deputy Under Secretary for International Trade subjects a charged or affected party to a sanction under § 354.3(a)(1), the Deputy Under Secretary for International Trade also will provide such information to the ethics panel or other disciplinary body of the appropriate bar associations or other professional associations and to any Federal agency likely to have an interest in the matter. The Deputy Under Secretary for International Trade will cooperate in any disciplinary actions by any association or agency. Whenever the Deputy Under Secretary for International Trade subjects a charged or affected party to a private letter of reprimand under § 354.3(a)(5), the Secretary will not make public the identity of the violator, nor will the Secretary make public the specifics of the violation in a manner that would reveal indirectly the identity of the violator.

[63 FR 24405, May 4, 1998]

§ 354.19 Sunset.

(a) If, after a period of three years from the date of issuance of a warning letter, a final decision or settlement in which sanctions were imposed, the charged or affected party has fully complied with the terms of the sanc-

tions and has not been found to have violated another administrative protective order, the party may request in writing that the Deputy Under Secretary for International Trade rescind the charging letter. A request for rescission must include:

(1) A description of the actions taken during the preceding three years in compliance with the terms of the sanctions; and

(2) A letter certifying that: the charged or affected party complied with the terms of the sanctions; the charged or affected party has not received another administrative protective order sanction during the three-year period; and the charged or affected party is not the subject of another investigation for a possible violation of an administrative protective order.

(b) Subject to the Chief Counsel's confirmation that the charged or affected party has complied with terms set forth in paragraph (a) of this section, the Deputy Under Secretary for International Trade will rescind the charging letter within 30 days after receiving the written request.

[63 FR 24405, May 4, 1998]

PART 356—PROCEDURES AND RULES FOR IMPLEMENTING ARTICLE 1904 OF THE NORTH AMERICAN FREE TRADE AGREEMENT

Subpart A—Scope and Definitions

Sec.
356.1 Scope.
356.2 Definitions.

Subpart B—Procedures for Commencing Review of Final Determinations

356.3 Notice of intent to commence judicial review.
356.4 Request for panel review.
356.5 [Reserved]
356.6 Receipt of notice of a scope determination by the Government of a FTA country.
356.7 Request to determine when the Government of a FTA country received notice of a scope determination.
356.8 Continued suspension of liquidation.

Subpart C—Proprietary and Privileged Information

356.9 Persons authorized to receive proprietary information.
356.10 Procedures for obtaining access to proprietary information.
356.11 Procedures for obtaining access to privileged information.

Subpart D—Violation of a Protective Order or a Disclosure Undertaking

356.12 Sanctions for violation of a protective order or disclosure undertaking.
356.13 Suspension of rules.
356.14 Report of violation and investigation.
356.15 Initiation of proceedings.
356.16 Charging letter.
356.17 Request to charge.
356.18 Interim sanctions.
356.19 Request for a hearing.
356.20 Discovery.
356.21 Subpoenas.
356.22 Prehearing conference.
356.23 Hearing.
356.24 Proceeding without a hearing.
356.25 Witnesses.
356.26 Initial decision.
356.27 Final decision.
356.28 Reconsideration.
356.29 Confidentiality.
356.30 Sanctions for violations of a protective order for privileged information.

AUTHORITY: 19 U.S.C. 1516a and 1677f(f), unless otherwise noted.

SOURCE: 59 FR 229, Jan. 3, 1994, unless otherwise noted.

EDITORIAL NOTE: Nomenclature changes to part 356 appear at 78 FR 62418, Oct. 22, 2013.

Subpart A—Scope and Definitions

§ 356.1 Scope.

This part sets forth procedures and rules for the implementation of Article 1904 of the North American Free Trade Agreement under the Tariff Act of 1930, as amended by title IV of the North American Free Trade Agreement Implementation Act of 1993 (19 U.S.C. 1516a and 1677f(f)). This part is authorized by section 402(g) of the North American Free Trade Agreement Implementation Act of 1993.

§ 356.2 Definitions.

For purposes of this part:
(a) *Act* means the Tariff Act of 1930, as amended;
(b) *Administrative law judge* means the person appointed under 5 U.S.C. 3105 who presides over the taking of evidence as provided by subpart D of this part;

(c) *Affected party* means a person against whom sanctions have been proposed for alleged violation of a protective order or disclosure undertaking but who is not a charged party;

(d) *Agreement* means the North American Free Trade Agreement between Canada, the United Mexican States and the United States, signed on December 17, 1992; or, with respect to binational panel or extraordinary challenge proceedings underway as of such date, or any binational panel or extraordinary challenge proceedings that may proceed between Canada and the United States following any withdrawal from the Agreement by Canada or the United States, the United States-Canada Free Trade Agreement between Canada and the United States, which came into force on January 1, 1989;

(e) *APO Sanctions Board* means the Administrative Protective Order Sanctions Board;

(f) *Article 1904 Panel Rules* means the NAFTA Article 1904 Panel Rules, negotiated pursuant to Article 1904 of the North American Free Trade Agreement between Canada, the United Mexican States and the United States, and any subsequent amendments; or, with respect to binational panel proceedings underway as of such date, or any binational panel proceedings that may proceed between the Canada and the United States following any withdrawal from the Agreement by Canada or the United States, the *Article 1904 Panel Rules*, as amended, which came into force on January 1, 1989;

(g) *Authorized agency of a free trade area country* means:
(1) In the case of Canada, any Canadian government agency that is authorized by Canadian law to request the Department to initiate proceedings to impose sanctions for an alleged violation of a disclosure undertaking; and
(2) In the case of Mexico, any Mexican government agency that is authorized by Mexican law to request the Department to initiate proceedings to impose sanctions for an alleged violation of a disclosure undertaking;

(h) *Binational panel* means a binational panel established pursuant to

Annex 1901.2 to Chapter Nineteen of the Agreement for the purpose of reviewing a final determination;

(i) *Charged party* means a person who is charged by the Deputy Under Secretary with violating a protective order or a disclosure undertaking;

(j) *Chief Counsel* means the Chief Counsel for Trade Enforcement and Compliance, U.S. Department of Commerce, or designee;

(k) *Days* means calendar days, except that a deadline which falls on a weekend or holiday shall be extended to the next working day;

(l) *Department* means the U.S. Department of Commerce;

(m) *Deputy Under Secretary* means the Deputy Under Secretary for International Trade, U.S. Department of Commerce;

(n) *Director* means an Office Director under the Deputy Assistant Secretary for Investigations, U.S. Department of Commerce, or designee, if the panel review is of a final determination by the Department under section 751 of the Act, or an Office Director under the Deputy Assistant Secretary for Compliance, or designee, if the panel review is of a final determination by the Department under section 705(a) or 735(a) of the Act;

(o) *Disclosure undertaking* means:

(1) In the case of Canada, the Canadian mechanism for protecting proprietary or privileged information during proceedings pursuant to Article 1904 of the Agreement, as prescribed by subsection 77.21(2) of the Special Import Measures Act, as amended; and

(2) In the case of Mexico, the Mexican mechanism for protecting proprietary or privileged information during proceedings pursuant to Article 1904 of the Agreement, as prescribed by the Ley de Comercio Exterior and its regulations;

(p) *Extraordinary challenge committee* means the committee established pursuant to Annex 1904.13 to Chapter Nineteen of the Agreement to review decisions of a panel or conduct of a panelist;

(q) *Final determination* means "final determination" as defined by Article 1911 of the Agreement;

(r) *Free trade area country* or *FTA country* means "free trade area country" as defined by section 516A(f)(10) of the Act (19 U.S.C. 1516a(f)(10));

(s) *Investigating authority* means the competent investigating authority that issued the final determination subject to review and includes, in respect of the issuance, amendment, modification or revocation of a protective order or disclosure undertaking, any person authorized by the investigating authority;

(t) *Lesser-included sanction* means a sanction of the same type but of more limited scope than the proposed sanction for violation of a protective order or disclosure undertaking; thus, a one-year bar on representation before the Department is a lesser-included sanction of a proposed seven-year bar;

(u) *Letter of transmittal* means a document marked according to the requirements of 19 CFR 353.31(e)(2)(i)–(v) or 355.31(e)(2)(i)–(v);

(v) *Official publication* means:

(1) In the case of Canada, the *Canada Gazette;*

(2) In the case of Mexico, the Diario Oficial de la Federacion; and

(3) In the case of the United States, the FEDERAL REGISTER;

(w) *Panel review* means review of a final determination pursuant to Chapter Nineteen of the Agreement;

(x) *Party to the proceeding* means a person that would be entitled, under section 516A of the Act (19 U.S.C. 1516a), to commence proceedings for judicial review of a final determination;

(y) *Participant* means a party to the proceeding that files a Complaint or a Notice of Appearance in a panel review, and the Department;

(z) *Parties* means, in an action under subpart D of this part, the Department and the charged party or affected party;

(aa) *Person* means, an individual, partnership, corporation, association, organization, or other entity;

(bb) *Privileged information* means:

(1) With respect to a panel review of a final determination made in Canada, information of the investigating authority that is subject to the solicitor-client privilege under the laws of Canada, or that constitutes part of the deliberative process with respect to the final determination, and with respect

to which the privilege has not been waived;

(2) With respect to a panel review of a final determination made in Mexico:

(i) Information of the investigating authority that is subject to attorney-client privilege under the laws of Mexico; or

(ii) Internal communications between officials of the Secretaria de Comercio y Fomento Industrial in charge of antidumping and countervailing duty investigations or communications between those officials and other government officials, where those communications constitute part of the deliberative process with respect to the final determination; and

(3) With respect to a panel review of a final determination made in the United States, information of the investigating authority that is subject to the attorney-client, attorney work product or government deliberative process privilege under the laws of the United States and with respect to which the privilege has not been waived;

(cc) *Proprietary information* means:

(1) With respect to a panel review of a final determination made in Canada, information referred to in subsection 84(3) of the Special Import Measures Act, as amended, or subsection 45(3) of the Canadian International Trade Tribunal Act, as amended, with respect to which the person who designated or submitted the information has not withdrawn the person's claim as to the confidentiality of the information;

(2) With respect to a panel review of a final determination made in Mexico, informacion confidencial, as defined under article 80 of the Ley de Comercio Exterior and its regulations; and

(3) With respect to a panel review of a final determination made in the United States, business proprietary information under section 777(f) of the Act (19 U.S.C. 1677f(f)) and information the disclosure of which the Department has decided is limited under the procedures adopted pursuant to Article 1904.14 of the Agreement, including business or trade secrets; production costs; terms of sale; prices of individual sales, likely sales, or offers; names of customers, distributors, or suppliers; exact amounts of the subsidies received and used by a person; names of particular persons from whom proprietary information was obtained; and any other business information the release of which to the public would cause substantial harm to the competitive position of the submitter;

(dd) *Protective order* means a protective order issued by the Department under 19 CFR 356.10(c) or 356.11(c);

(ee) *Scope determination* means a determination by the Department, reviewable under section 516A(a)(2)(B)(vi) of the Act (19 U.S.C. 1516a(a)(2)(B)(vi), as to whether a particular type of merchandise is within the class or kind of merchandise described in an existing finding of dumping or an antidumping or countervailing duty order covering free trade area country merchandise;

(ff) *Secretariat* means the Secretariat established pursuant to Article 2002 of the Agreement and includes the Secretariat sections located in Canada, Mexico and the United States;

(gg) *Secretary* means the Secretary of the Canadian section of the Secretariat, the Secretary of the Mexican section of the Secretariat, or the Secretary of the United States section of the Secretariat and includes any person authorized to act on behalf of the Secretary;

(hh) *Service address* means the address of the counsel of record for a person, including any facsimile number submitted with that address, or, where a person is not represented by counsel, the address set out by the person in a Request for Panel Review, Complaint or Notice of Appearance as the address at which the person may be served, including any facsimile number submitted with that address, or where a Change of Service Address has been filed by a person, the new service address set out as the service address in that form, including any facsimile number submitted with that address;

(ii) *Service list* means, with respect to a panel review of a final determination made in the United States, the list maintained by the investigating authority of persons who have been served in the proceeding leading to the final determination;

(jj) *Under Secretary* means the Under Secretary for International Trade, U.S. Department of Commerce, or designee;

(kk) *United States section of the Secretariat* means, for the purposes of filing, United States Secretary, NAFTA Secretariat, room 2061, U.S. Department of Commerce, 14th and Constitution Avenue, NW., Washington, DC 20230.

Subpart B—Procedures for Commencing Review of Final Determinations

§356.3 Notice of intent to commence judicial review.

A party to a proceeding who intends to commence judicial review of a final determination made in the United States shall file a Notice of Intent to Commence Judicial Review, which shall contain such information, and be in such form, manner, and style, including service requirements, as prescribed by the Article 1904 Panel Rules, within 20 days after:

(a) The date of publication in the FEDERAL REGISTER of the final determination; or

(b) The date on which the notice of the final determination was received by the Government of the FTA country if the final determination was not published in the FEDERAL REGISTER.

§356.4 Request for panel review.

A party to a proceeding who seeks panel review of a final determination shall file a Request for Panel Review, which shall contain such information, and be in such form, manner, and style, including service requirements, as prescribed by the Article 1904 Panel Rules, within 30 days after:

(a) The date of publication in the official publication of the final determination; or

(b) The date on which the notice of the final determination was received by the United States Government or the Government of the FTA country if the final determination was not published in the official publication.

§356.5 [Reserved]

§356.6 Receipt of notice of a scope determination by the Government of a FTA country.

(a) Where the Department has made a scope determination, notice of such determination shall be deemed received by the Government of a FTA country when a certified copy of the determination is delivered to the chancery of the Embassy of the FTA country during its normal business hours.

(b) Where feasible, the Department, or an agent therefor, will obtain a certificate of receipt signed by a person authorized to accept delivery of documents to the Embassy of the FTA country acknowledging receipt of the scope determination. The certificate will describe briefly the document being delivered to the Embassy of the FTA country, state the date and time of receipt, and include the name and title of the person who signs the certificate. The certificate will be retained by the Department in its public files pertaining to the scope determination at issue.

§356.7 Request to determine when the Government of a FTA country received notice of a scope determination.

(a) Pursuant to section 516A(g)(10) of the Act (19 U.S.C. 1516a(g)(10)), any party to the proceeding may request in writing from the Department the date on which the Government of a FTA country received notice of a scope determination made by the Department.

(b) A request shall be made by filing a written request and the correct number of copies in accordance with the requirements set forth in 19 CFR 353.31(d) and (e)(2) or 355.31(d) and (e)(2) with the Secretary of Commerce, Attention: Enforcement and Compliance, Central Records Unit, room B–099, U.S. Department of Commerce, 14th and Constitution Avenue, NW., Washington, DC 20230. A letter of transmittal must be bound to the original and each copy as the first page of the request.

(c) The requesting party shall serve a copy of the Request to Determine When the Government of [insert name of applicable FTA country] Received Notice of a Scope Determination by first class mail or personal service on any interested party on the Department's service list in accordance with the service requirements listed in 19 CFR 353.31(g) or 355.31(g).

(d) The Department will respond to the request referred to in paragraph (b) of this section within five business days of receipt.

§ 356.8 Continued suspension of liquidation.

(a) *In general.* In the case of an administrative determination specified in clause (iii) or (vi) of section 516A(a)(2)(B) of the Act (19 U.S.C. 1516a(a)(2)(B)(iii) and (vi)) and involving free trade area country merchandise, the Department shall not order liquidation of entries of merchandise covered by such a determination until the forty-first day after the date of publication of the notice described in clause (iii) or receipt of the determination described in clause (vi), as appropriate. If requested, the Department will order the continued suspension of liquidation of such entries in accordance with the terms of paragraphs (b), (c), and (d) of this section.

(b) *Eligibility to request continued suspension of liquidation.* (1) A participant in a binational panel review that was a domestic party to the proceeding, as described in section 771(9)(C), (D), (E), (F), or (G) of the Act (19 U.S.C. 1677(9)(C), (D), (E), (F) and (G)), may request continued suspension of liquidation of entries of merchandise covered by the administrative determination under review by the panel and that would be affected by the panel review.

(2) A participant in a binational panel review that was a party to the proceeding, as described in section 771(9)(A) of the Act (19 U.S.C. 1677(9)(A)), may request continued suspension of liquidation of the merchandise which it manufactured, produced, exported, or imported and which is covered by the administrative determination under review by the panel.

(c) *Request for continued suspension of liquidation.* A request for continued suspension of liquidation must include:

(1) The name of the final determination subject to binational panel review and the case number assigned by the Department;

(2) The caption of the binational panel proceeding;

(3) The name of the requesting participant;

(4) The requestor's status as a party to the proceeding and as a participant in the binational panel review; and

(5) The specific entries to be suspended by name of manufacturer, producer, exporter, or U.S. importer.

(d) *Filing and service.* (1) A request for Continued Suspension of Liquidation must be filed with the Assistant Secretary for Enforcement and Compliance, room B–099, 14th and Constitution Avenue, NW., Washington, DC 20230, in accordance with the requirements set forth in 19 CFR 353.31(d) and (e)(2) or 355.31(d) and (e)(2). A letter of transmittal must be bound to the original and each copy as the first page of the request. The envelope and the first page of the request must be marked: Panel Review—Request for Continued Suspension of Liquidation. The request may be made no earlier than the date on which the first request for binational panel review is filed.

(2) The requesting party shall serve a copy of the Request for Continued Suspension of Liquidation on the United States Secretary and all parties to the proceeding in accordance with the requirements of 19 CFR 353.31(g) or 19 CFR 355.31(g).

(e) *Termination of Continued Suspension.* Upon completion of the panel review, including any panel review of remand determinations and any review by an extraordinary challenge committee, the Department will order liquidation of entries, the suspension of which was continued pursuant to this section.

Subpart C—Proprietary and Privileged Information

§ 356.9 Persons authorized to receive proprietary information.

Persons described in paragraphs (a), (d), (e), (f) and (g) of this section shall, and persons described in paragraphs (b) and (c) of this section may, be authorized by the Department to receive access to proprietary information if they comply with this subpart and such other conditions imposed upon them by the Department:

(a) The members of, and appropriate staff of, a binational panel or extraordinary challenge committee;

(b) Counsel to participants in panel reviews and professionals retained by, or under the direction or control of such counsel, provided that the counsel or professional does not participate in competitive decision-making activity (such as advice on production, sales, operations, or investments, but not legal advice) for the participant represented or for any person who would gain competitive advantage through knowledge of the proprietary information sought;

(c) Other persons who are retained or employed by and under the direction or control of a counsel or professional, panelist, or committee member who has been issued a protective order, such as paralegals, law clerks, and secretaries, if such other persons are:

(1) Not involved in the competitive decision-making of a participant to the panel review or for any person who would gain competitive advantage through knowledge of the proprietary information sought; and

(2) Have agreed to be bound by the terms set forth on the application for protective order of the counsel or professional, panelist, or committee member;

(d) Each Secretary and every member of the staff of the Secretariat;

(e) Such officials of the United States Government (other than an officer or employee of the investigating authority that issued the final determination subject to review) as the United States Trade Representative informs the Department require access to proprietary information for the purpose of evaluating whether the United States should seek an extraordinary challenge committee review of a panel determination;

(f) Such officials of the Government of a FTA country as an authorized agency of the FTA country informs the Department require access to proprietary information for the purpose of evaluating whether the FTA country should seek an extraordinary challenge committee review of a panel determination; and

(g) Every court reporter, interpreter and translator employed in a panel or extraordinary challenge committee review.

§ 356.10 Procedures for obtaining access to proprietary information.

(a) *Persons who must file an application for disclosure under protective order.*

In order to be permitted access to proprietary information in the administrative record of a final determination under review by a panel, all persons described in §§ 356.9 (a), (b), (d), (e), (f) and (g) shall file an application for a protective order. The procedures for applying for a protective order described in paragraph (b) of this section apply as well to amendments or modifications filed by persons described in § 356.9.

(b) *Procedures for applying for a protective order*—(1) *Contents of applications.* (i) The Department has adopted application forms for disclosure of proprietary information which are available from the United States section of the Secretariat or the Central Records Unit, room B–099, U.S. Department of Commerce, 14th and Constitution Avenue, NW., Washington, DC 20230. The application forms may be amended from time to time.

(ii) Such forms require the applicant to submit a personal sworn statement stating, in addition to such other terms as the Department may require, that the applicant shall:

(A) Not disclose any proprietary information obtained under protective order and not otherwise available to the applicant, to any person other than:

(*1*) An official of the Department involved in the particular panel review in which the proprietary information is part of the administrative record;

(*2*) The person from whom the information was obtained;

(*3*) A person who has been granted access to the proprietary information at issue under § 356.9; and

(*4*) A person employed by and under the direction or control of a counsel or professional, panelist, or committee member who has been issued a protective order, such as a paralegal, law clerk, or secretary if such person:

(*i*) Is not involved in competitive decision-making for a participant in the panel review or for any person that would gain competitive advantage through knowledge of the proprietary information sought; and

(*ii*) Has agreed to be bound by the terms set forth in the application for protective order by the counsel, professional, panelist, or committee member;

(B) Not use any of the proprietary information not otherwise available to the applicant for purposes other than proceedings pursuant to Article 1904 of the Agreement;

(C) Upon completion of the panel review, or at such earlier date as may be determined by the Department, return to the Department or certify to the Department the destruction of all documents released under the protective order and all other documents containing the proprietary information (such as briefs, notes, or charts based on any such information received under the protective order); and

(D) Acknowledge that breach thereof may subject the signatory to sanctions under § 356.12.

(2) *Timing of application for disclosure under protective order*—(i) *Persons described in § 356.9(a) (panelists, etc.).* A person described in § 356.9(a) may file an application after a Notice of Request for Panel Review has been filed with the Secretariat.

(ii) *Persons described in § 356.9(b) (counsel, etc.).* A person described in § 356.9(b) may file an application at any time but not before that person files a Complaint or a Notice of Appearance.

(iii) *Persons described in § 356.9(d) (Secretaries, etc.).* A person described in § 356.9(d) shall file an application immediately upon assuming official responsibilities in the Secretariat.

(iv) *Persons described in § 356.9 (e), (f) or (g) (designated Government officials or court reporters, etc.).* A person described in § 356.9 (e), (f) or (g) shall file an application before seeking or obtaining access to proprietary information.

(3) *Filing of applications.* A person described in § 356.9 (a), (b), (d), (e), (f) or (g) shall file the completed original and five copies of an application with the United States section of the Secretariat which, in turn, shall submit the original and one copy of the application to the Department. A letter of transmittal must be bound to the original and each copy as the first page of the document.

(4) *Service of applications*—(i) *Persons described in §§ 356.9(b) (counsel, etc.).* A person described in § 356.9(b) who files an application before the expiration of the time period fixed under the Article 1904 Panel Rules for filing a Notice of Appearance in the panel review shall serve one copy of the application on each person listed on the service list in accordance with paragraphs (b)(4) (ii) and (iii) of this section. In any other case, such person shall serve one copy of the application on each participant, other than the investigating authority, in accordance with paragraphs (b)(4) (ii) and (iii) of this section.

(ii) *Method of service.* A document may be served by:

(A) Delivering a copy of the document to the service address of the participant;

(B) Sending a copy of the document to the service address of the participant by facsimile transmission or by expedited delivery courier or expedited mail service; or

(C) Personal service on the participant.

(iii) *Proof and date of service.* A proof of service shall appear on, or be affixed to, the document. Where a document is served by expedited delivery courier or expedited mail service, the date of service set out in the affidavit of service or certificate of service shall be the day on which the document is consigned to the expedited delivery courier service or expedited mail service.

(5) *Release to employees of panelists, committee members, and counsel or professionals.* A person described in § 356.9(c), including a paralegal, law clerk, or secretary, may be permitted access to proprietary information disclosed under protective order by the counsel, professional, panelist, or extraordinary challenge committee member who retains or employs such person, if such person has agreed to the terms of the protective order issued to the counsel, professional, panelist, or extraordinary challenge committee member, by signing and dating a completed copy of the application for protective order of the representative counsel, professional, panelist or extraordinary challenge committee member in the location indicated in that application.

(6) *Counsel or professional who retains access to proprietary information under a protective order issued during the administrative proceeding.* A person described in § 356.9(b) who has been granted access to proprietary information under

protective order during an administrative proceeding that resulted in a final determination that becomes the subject of panel review may, if permitted by the terms of the protective order previously issued by the Department, retain such information until the applicant receives a protective order under this part.

(c) *Issuance and service of protective orders*—(1) *Persons described in § 356.9(a) (panelists, etc.).* (i) Upon receipt by the Department of an application from a person described in §356.9(a), the Department will issue a protective order authorizing disclosure of proprietary information included in the administrative record of the final determination that is the subject of the panel review at issue. The Department shall transmit the original and four copies of the protective order to the United States section of the Secretariat which, in turn, shall transmit the original to the applicant and serve one copy of the order on each participant, other than the investigating authority, in accordance with paragraphs (b)(4) (ii) and (iii) of this section.

(ii) A member of a binational panel or extraordinary challenge committee proceeding initiated under the United States-Canada Free Trade Agreement to whom the Department issues a protective order must countersign the protective order and return one copy of the countersigned protective order to the United States section of the Secretariat.

(2) *Persons described in §§ 356.9 (b) or (c) (counsel, etc., or paralegals, etc.)*—(i) *Opportunity to object to disclosure.* The Department will not rule on an application filed by a person described in §356.9(b) until at least ten days after the request is filed, unless there is compelling need to rule more expeditiously. Unless the Department has indicated otherwise, any person may file an objection to the application within seven days of filing of the application. Any such objection shall state the specific reasons in the view of such person why the application should not be granted. One copy of the objection shall be served on the applicant and on all persons who were served with the application. Service shall be made in accordance with paragraphs (b)(4) (ii)

and (iii) of this section. Any reply to an objection will be considered if it is filed before the Department renders a decision.

(ii) *Timing of decisions on applications.* Normally, the Department will render a decision to approve or deny an application within 14 days. If any person files an objection, the Department will normally render the decision within 30 days.

(iii) *Approval of applications.* If appropriate, the Department will issue a protective order permitting the release of proprietary information to the applicant.

(iv) *Denial of applications.* If the Department denies an application, it shall issue a letter notifying the applicant of its decision and the reasons therefor.

(v) *Issuance of protective orders.* If the Department issues a protective order to a person described in § 356.9(b), that person shall immediately file four copies of the protective order with the United States section of the Secretariat and shall serve one copy of the order on each participant, other than the investigating authority, in accordance with paragraphs (b)(4) (ii) and (iii) of this section.

(3) *Persons described in § 356.9 (d) or (g) (Secretaries, etc., or court reporters, etc.).* Upon receipt by the Department of an application from a person described in §356.9 (d) or (g), the Department will issue a protective order authorizing disclosure of proprietary information to the applicant. The Department shall transmit the original and four copies of the protective order to the United States section of the Secretariat.

(4) *Persons described in § 356.9 (e) or (f) (designated Government officials).* (i) Upon receipt by the Department of an application from a person described in §356.9 (e) or (f), the Department will issue a protective order authorizing disclosure of proprietary information included in the record of the panel review at issue. The Department shall transmit the original and four copies of the protective order to the United States section of the Secretariat which, in turn, shall transmit the original to the applicant and serve one

copy of the document on each participant, other than the investigating authority, in accordance with paragraphs (b)(4) (ii) and (iii) of this section.

(d) *Modification or revocation of protective orders*—(1) *Notification.* If any person believes that changed conditions of fact or law, or the public interest, may require that a protective order issued pursuant to paragraph (c) of this section be modified or revoked, in whole or in part, such person may notify the Department in writing. The notification shall state the changes desired and the changed circumstances warranting such action and shall include materials and argument in support thereof. Such notification shall be served by the person submitting it upon the person to whom the protective order was issued. Responses to the notification may be filed within 20 days after the notification is filed unless the Department indicates otherwise. The Department may also consider such action on its own initiative.

(2) *Issuance of modification or revocation.* If the Department modifies or revokes a protective order pursuant to paragraph (d) of this section, the Department shall transmit the original and four copies of the modification or Notice of Revocation to the United States section of the Secretariat which, in turn, shall transmit the original to the person to whom the protective order was issued and serve one copy on each participant, other than the investigating authority, in accordance with paragraphs (b)(4) (ii) and (iii) of this section.

§ 356.11 **Procedures for obtaining access to privileged information.**

(a) *Persons who may apply for access to privileged information under protective order and filing of applications*—(1) *Panelists.* (i) If a panel decides that *in camera* examination of a document containing privileged information in an administrative record is necessary in order for the panel to determine whether the document, or portions thereof, should be disclosed under a Protective Order for Privileged Information, each panelist who is to conduct the *in camera* review, pursuant to the rules of procedure adopted by the United States and the free trade area countries to im-

plement Article 1904 of the Agreement, shall submit an application for disclosure of the privileged information under Protective Order for Privileged Information to the United States section of the Secretariat for filing with the Department; and

(ii) If a panel orders disclosure of a document containing privileged information, any panelist who has not filed an application pursuant to paragraph (a)(1)(i) of this section shall submit an application for disclosure of the privileged information under a Protective Order for Privileged Information to the United States section of the Secretariat for filing with the Department.

(2) *Designated officials of the United States Government.* Where, in the course of a panel review, the panel has reviewed privileged information under a Protective Order for Privileged Information, and the issue to which such information pertains is relevant to the evaluation of whether the United States should request an extraordinary challenge committee, each official of the United States Government (other than an officer or employee of the investigating authority that issued the final determination subject to review) whom the United States Trade Representative informs the Department requires access for the purpose of such evaluation shall file the completed original and five copies of an application for a Protective Order for Privileged Information with the United States section of the Secretariat which, in turn, shall submit the original and one copy of the application to the Department.

(3) *Designated officials of the government of a FTA country.* Where, in the course of a panel review, the panel has reviewed privileged information under a Protective Order for Privileged Information, and the issue to which such information pertains is relevant to the evaluation of whether the Government of an involved FTA country should request an extraordinary challenge committee, each official of the Government of the involved FTA country whom an authorized agency of the involved FTA country informs the Department requires access for the purpose of such evaluation shall file the completed

original and five copies of an application for a Protective Order for Privileged Information with the United States section of the Secretariat which, in turn, shall submit the original and one copy of the application to the Department.

(4) *Members of an extraordinary challenge committee.* Where an extraordinary challenge record contains privileged information and a Protective Order for Privileged Information was issued to counsel or professionals representing participants in the panel review at issue, each member of the extraordinary challenge committee shall submit an application for a Protective Order for Privileged Information to the United States section of the Secretariat for filing with the Department.

(5) *Counsel or a professional under the direction or control of counsel.* If the panel decides, in accordance with the Article 1904 Rules, that disclosure of a document containing privileged information is appropriate, a counsel or a professional under the direction or control of counsel identified in such a decision as entitled to release of information under a Protective Order for Privileged Information shall submit an application for a Protective Order for Privileged Information. Any such person shall:

(i) File the completed original and five copies of an application with the United States section of the Secretariat which, in turn, shall submit the original and one copy of the application to the Department; and

(ii) As soon as the deadline fixed under the Article 1904 Panel Rules for filing a Notice of Appearance in the panel review has passed, shall serve a copy of the application on each participant, other than the investigating authority, in accordance with paragraphs (b)(4) (ii) and (iii) of this section.

(6) *Other designated persons.* If the panel decides, in accordance with the Article 1904 Panel Rules, that disclosure of a document containing privileged information is appropriate, any person identified in such a decision as entitled to release of information under a Protective Order for Privileged Information, *e.g.,* a Secretary, Secretariat staff, court reporters, interpreters and translators, or a member of

the staff of a panelist or extraordinary challenge committee member, shall submit an application for release under Protective Order for Privileged Information to the United States section of the Secretariat for filing with the Department.

(b) *Contents of applications for release under protective order for privileged information.* (1) The Department has adopted application forms for disclosure of privileged information which are available from the United States section of the Secretariat and the Central Records Unit, room B–099, U.S. Department of Commerce, 14th and Constitution Avenue NW., Washington, DC 20230. These forms may be amended from time to time.

(2) Such forms require the applicant for release of privileged information under Protective Order for Privileged Information to submit a personal sworn statement stating, in addition to such other conditions as the Department may require, that the applicant shall:

(i) Not disclose any privileged information obtained under protective order to any person other than:

(A) An official of the Department involved in the particular panel review in which the privileged information is part of the record;

(B) A person who has furnished a similar application and who has been issued a Protective Order for Privileged Information concerning the privileged information at issue; and

(C) A person retained or employed by counsel, a professional, a panelist or extraordinary challenge committee member who has been issued a Protective Order for Privileged Information, such as a paralegal, law clerk, or secretary, if such person has agreed to be bound by the terms set forth in the application for Protective Order for Privileged Information of the counsel, professional, panelist or extraordinary challenge committee member by signing and dating the completed application at the location indicated in such application;

(ii) Use such information solely for purposes of the proceedings under Article 1904 of the Agreement;

(iii) Upon completion of the panel review, or at such earlier date as may be determined by the Department, return to the Department or certify to the Department the destruction of all documents released under the Protective Order for Privileged Information and all other documents containing the privileged information (such as briefs, notes, or charts based on any such information received under the Protective Order for Privileged Information); and

(iv) Acknowledge that breach thereof may subject the signatory to sanctions under §§ 356.12 and 356.30.

(c) *Issuance of protective orders for privileged information*—(1) *Panelists, designated government officials and members of an extraordinary challenge committee.* (i) Upon receipt of an application for protective order under this section from a panelist, designated government official or member of an extraordinary challenge committee, the Department shall issue a Protective Order for Privileged Information. The Department shall transmit the original and four copies of the protective order to the United States section of the Secretariat which, in turn, shall transmit the original to the applicant and serve one copy of the order on each participant, other than the investigating authority, in accordance with §§ 356.10(b)(4) (ii) and (iii).

(ii) If the Department issues a Protective Order for Privileged Information to a member of a binational panel or extraordinary challenge proceeding initiated under the United States-Canada Free Trade Agreement, that person must countersign the protective order and return one copy of the countersigned protective order to the United States section of the Secretariat.

(2) *Counsel or a professional under the direction or control of counsel.* Upon receipt of an application for protective order under this section from a counsel or a professional under the direction or control of counsel, the Department shall issue a Protective Order for Privileged Information. If the Department issues a protective order to such person, that person shall immediately file four copies of the protective order with the United States section of the Secretariat and shall serve one copy of the order on each participant, other than

the investigating authority, in accordance with §§ 356.10(b)(4) (ii) and (iii).

(3) *Other designated persons described paragraph (a)(6) of this section.* Upon receipt of an application for protective order under this section from a designated person described in paragraph (a)(6) of this section, the Department shall issue a Protective Order for Privileged Information. The Department shall transmit the original and four copies of the protective order to the United States section of the Secretariat.

(d) *Modification or revocation of protective order for privileged information*—(1) *Notification.* If any person believes that changed conditions of fact or law, or the public interest, may require that a Protective Order for Privileged Information be modified or revoked, in whole or in part, such person may notify the Department in writing. The notification shall state the changes desired and the changed circumstances warranting such action and shall include materials and argument in support thereof. Such notification shall be served by the person submitting it upon the person to whom the Protective Order for Privileged Information was issued. Responses to the notification may be filed within 20 days after the notification is filed unless the Department indicates otherwise. The Department may also consider such action on its own initiative.

(2) *Issuance of modification or revocation.* If the Department modifies or revokes a Protective Order for Privileged Information pursuant to paragraph (d) of this section, the Department shall transmit the original and four copies of the modification or Notice of Revocation to the United States section of the Secretariat which, in turn, shall transmit the original to the person to whom the protective order was issued and serve one copy on each participant, other than the investigating authority, in accordance with §§ 356.10(b)(4) (ii) and (iii).

Subpart D—Violation of a Protective Order or a Disclosure Undertaking

§ 356.12 Sanctions for violation of a protective order or disclosure undertaking.

(a) A person, other than a person exempted from this part by the provisions of section 777f(f)(4) of the Act (19 U.S.C. 1677f(f)(4)), determined under this part to have violated a protective order or a disclosure undertaking may be subjected to any or all or the following sanctions:

(1) Liable to the United States for a civil penalty not to exceed $100,000 for each violation;

(2) Barred from appearing before the Department to represent another for a designated time period from the date of publication in an official publication of a notice that a violation has been determined to exist;

(3) Denied access to proprietary information for a designated time period from the date of publication in an official publication of a notice that a violation has been determined to exist;

(4) Other appropriate administrative sanctions, including striking from the record of the panel review any information or argument submitted by, or on behalf of, the violating party or the party represented by the violating party; terminating any proceeding then in progress; or revoking any order then in effect; and

(5) Required to return material previously provided by the investigating authority, and all other materials containing the proprietary information, such as briefs, notes, or charts based on any such information received under a protective order or a disclosure undertaking.

(b)(1) The firm of which a person determined to have violated a protective order or a disclosure undertaking is a partner, associate, or employee; any partner, associate, employer, or employee of such person; and any person represented by such person may be barred from appearing before the Department for a designated time period from the date of publication in an official publication of notice that a violation has been determined to exist or may be subjected to the sanctions set forth in paragraph (a) of this section, as appropriate.

(2) Each person against whom sanctions are proposed under paragraph (b)(1) of this section is entitled to all the administrative rights set forth in this subpart separately and apart from rights provided to a person subject to sanctions under paragraph (a) of this section, including the right to a charging letter, right to representation, and right to a hearing, but subject to joinder or consolidation by the administrative law judge under § 356.23(b).

§ 356.13 Suspension of rules.

Upon request by the Deputy Under Secretary, a charged or affected party, or the APO Sanctions Board, the administrative law judge may modify or waive any rule in this subpart upon determining that no party will be unduly prejudiced and the ends of justice will thereby be served and upon notice to all parties.

§ 356.14 Report of violation and investigation.

(a) An employee of the Department or any other person who has information indicating that the terms of a protective order or a disclosure undertaking have been violated will provide the information to a Director or the Chief Counsel.

(b) Upon receiving information which indicates that a person may have violated the terms of a protective order or an undertaking, the Director will conduct an investigation concerning whether there was a violation of a protective order or a disclosure undertaking, and who was responsible for the violation, if any. For purposes of this subpart, the Director will be supervised by the Deputy Under Secretary with guidance from the Chief Counsel. The Director will conduct an investigation only if the information is received within 30 days after the alleged violation occurred or, as determined by the Director, could have been discovered through the exercise of reasonable and ordinary care.

(c) The Director will provide a report of the investigation to the Deputy Under Secretary, after review by the Chief Counsel, no later than 180 days after receiving information concerning a violation. Upon the Director's request, and if extraordinary circumstances exist, the Deputy Under Secretary may grant the Director up to an additional 180 days to conduct the investigation and submit the report.

(d) The following examples of actions that constitute violations of an administrative protective order shall serve as guidelines to each person subject to a protective order. These examples do not represent an exhaustive list. Evidence that one of the acts described in the guidelines has been committed, however, shall be considered by the Director as reasonable cause to believe a person has violated a protective order within the meaning of § 356.15.

(1) Disclosure of proprietary information to any person not granted access to that information by protective order, including an official of the Department or member of the Secretariat staff not directly involved with the panel review pursuant to which the proprietary information was released, an employee of any other United States, foreign government or international agency, or a member of the United States Congress, the Canadian Parliament, or the Mexican Congress.

(2) Failure to follow the detailed procedures outlined in the protective order for safeguarding proprietary information, including maintaining a log showing when each proprietary document is used, and by whom, and requiring all employees who obtain access to proprietary information (under the terms of a protective order granted their employer) to sign and date a copy of that protective order.

(3) Loss of proprietary information.

(4) Failure to return or destroy all copies of the original documents and all notes, memoranda, and submissions containing proprietary information at the close of the proceeding for which the data were obtained by burning or shredding of the documents or by erasing electronic memory, computer disk, or tape memory, as set forth in the protective order.

(5) Failure to delete proprietary information from the public version of a brief or other correspondence filed with the Secretariat.

(6) Disclosure of proprietary information during a public hearing.

(e) Each day of a continuing violation shall constitute a separate violation.

§ 356.15   Initiation of proceedings.

(a) If the Deputy Under Secretary concludes, after an investigation and report by the Director under § 356.14(c) and consultation with the Chief Counsel, that there is reasonable cause to believe that a person has violated a protective order or a disclosure undertaking and that sanctions are appropriate for the violation, the Deputy Under Secretary will, at the Deputy Under Secretary's discretion, either initiate a proceeding under this subpart by issuing a charging letter as set forth in § 356.16 or request that the authorized agency of the involved FTA country initiate a proceeding by issuing a request to charge as set forth in § 356.17. In determining whether sanctions are appropriate and, if so, what sanctions to impose, the Deputy Under Secretary will consider the nature of the violation, the resulting harm, and other relevant circumstances of the case. The Deputy Under Secretary will decide whether to initiate a proceeding no later than 60 days after receiving a report of the investigation.

(b) If the Department receives a request to charge from an authorized agency of a FTA country, the Deputy Under Secretary will promptly initiate proceedings under this part by issuing a charging letter as set forth in § 356.16.

§ 356.16   Charging letter.

(a) *Contents of letter.* The Deputy Under Secretary will initiate proceedings by issuing a charging letter to each charged party and affected party which includes:

(1) A statement of the allegation that a protective order or a disclosure undertaking has been violated and the basis thereof;

(2) A statement of the proposed sanctions;

(3) A statement that the charged or affected party is entitled to review the documents or other physical evidence upon which the charge is based and the method for requesting access to, or copies of, such documents;

(4) A statement that the charged or affected party is entitled to a hearing before an administrative law judge if requested within 30 days of the date of service of the charging letter and the procedure for requesting a hearing, including the name, address, and telephone number of the person to contact if there are further questions;

(5) A statement that the charged or affected party has a right, if a hearing is not requested, to submit documentary evidence to the Deputy Under Secretary and an explanation of the method for submitting evidence and the date by which it must be received; and

(6) A statement that the charged or affected party has a right to retain counsel at the party's own expense for purposes of representation.

(b) *Settlement and amendment of the charging letter.* The Deputy Under Secretary may amend, supplement, or withdraw the charging letter at any time with the approval of an administrative law judge if the interests of justice would thereby be served. If a hearing has not been requested, the Deputy Under Secretary will ask the Under Secretary to appoint an administrative law judge to make this determination. If a charging letter is withdrawn after a request for a hearing, the administrative law judge will determine whether the withdrawal will bar the Deputy Under Secretary from seeking sanctions at a later date for the same alleged violation. If there has been no request for a hearing, or if supporting information has not been submitted under §356.28, the withdrawal will not bar future actions on the same alleged violation. The Deputy Under Secretary and a charged or affected party may settle a charge brought under this subpart by mutual agreement at any time after service of the charging letter; approval of the administrative law judge or the APO Sanctions Board is not necessary.

(c) *Service of charging letter on a resident of the United States.* (1) Service of a charging letter on a United States resident will be made by:

(i) Mailing a copy by registered or certified mail addressed to the charged or affected party at the party's last known address;

(ii) Leaving a copy with the charged or affected party or with an officer, a managing or general agent, or any other agent authorized by appointment or by law to receive service for the party; or

(iii) Leaving a copy with a person of suitable age and discretion who resides at the party's last known dwelling.

(2) Service made in the manner described in paragraph (c)(1) (ii) or (iii) of this section shall be evidenced by a certificate of service signed by the person making such service, stating the method of service and the identity of the person with whom the charging letter was left.

(d) *Service of charging letter on a nonresident.* If applicable laws or intergovernmental agreements or understandings make the methods of service set forth in paragraph (c) of this section inappropriate or ineffective, service of the charging letter on a person who is not a resident of the United States may be made by any method that is permitted by the country in which the person resides and that, in the opinion of the Deputy Under Secretary, satisfies due process requirements under United States law with respect to notice in administrative proceedings.

§356.17 Request to charge.

Upon deciding to initiate a proceeding pursuant to §356.15, the Deputy Under Secretary will request the authorized agency of the involved FTA country to initiate a proceeding for imposing sanctions for violation of a protective order or a disclosure undertaking by issuing a letter of request to charge that includes a statement of the allegation that a protective order or a disclosure undertaking has been violated and the basis thereof.

§356.18 Interim sanctions.

(a) If the Deputy Under Secretary concludes, after issuing a charging letter under §356.16 and before a final decision is rendered, that interim sanctions are necessary to protect the interests of the Department, an authorized agency of the involved FTA country, or others, including the protection of proprietary information, the Deputy

Under Secretary may petition an administrative law judge to impose such sanctions.

(b) The administrative law judge may impose interim sanctions against a person upon determining that:

(1) There is probable cause to believe that there was a violation of a protective order or a disclosure undertaking and the Department is likely to prevail in obtaining sanctions under this subpart;

(2) The Department, authorized agency of the involved FTA country, or others are likely to suffer irreparable harm if the interim sanctions are not imposed; and

(3) The interim sanctions are a reasonable means for protecting the rights of the Department, authorized agency of the involved FTA country, or others while preserving to the greatest extent possible the rights of the person against whom the interim sanctions are proposed.

(c) Interim sanctions which may be imposed include any sanctions that are necessary to protect the rights of the Department, authorized agency of the involved FTA country, or others, including, but not limited to:

(1) Denying a person further access to proprietary information;

(2) Barring a person from representing another person before the Department;

(3) Barring a person from appearing before the Department; and

(4) Requiring the person to return material previously provided by the Department or the investigating authority of the involved FTA country, and all other materials containing the proprietary information, such as briefs, notes, or charts based on any such information received under a protective order or disclosure undertaking.

(d) The Deputy Under Secretary will notify the person against whom interim sanctions are sought of the request for interim sanctions and provide to that person the material submitted to the administrative law judge to support the request. The notice will include a reference to the procedures of this section.

(e) A person against whom interim sanctions are proposed has a right to oppose the request through submission of material to the administrative law judge. The administrative law judge has discretion to permit oral presentations and to allow further submissions.

(f) The administrative law judge will notify the parties of the decision on interim sanctions and the basis therefor within five days of the conclusion of oral presentations or the date of final written submissions.

(g) If interim sanctions have been imposed, the investigation and any proceedings under this subpart will be conducted on an expedited basis.

(h) An order imposing interim sanctions may be revoked at any time by the administrative law judge and expires automatically upon the issuance of a final order.

(i) The administrative law judge may reconsider imposition of interim sanctions on the basis of new and material evidence or other good cause shown. The Deputy Under Secretary or a person against whom interim sanctions have been imposed may appeal a decision on interim sanctions to the APO Sanctions Board, if such an appeal is certified by the administrative law judge as necessary to prevent undue harm to the Department or authorized agency of the involved FTA country, a person against whom interim sanctions have been imposed or others, or is otherwise in the interests of justice. Interim sanctions which have been imposed remain in effect while an appeal is pending, unless the administrative law judge determines otherwise.

(j) The Deputy Under Secretary may request an administrative law judge to impose emergency interim sanctions to preserve the status quo. Emergency interim sanctions may last no longer than 48 hours, excluding weekends and holidays. The person against whom such emergency interim sanctions are proposed need not be given prior notice or an opportunity to oppose the request for sanctions. The administrative law judge may impose emergency interim sanctions upon determining that the Department or authorized agency of the involved FTA country is, or others are, likely to suffer irreparable harm if such sanctions are not imposed and that the interests of justice would thereby be served. The administrative law judge will promptly notify a person against whom emergency sanctions have been imposed of the sanctions and their duration.

(k) If a hearing has not been requested, the Deputy Under Secretary will request that the Under Secretary appoint an administrative law judge for making determinations under this section.

(l) The Deputy Under Secretary will notify the Secretariat concerning the imposition or revocation of interim sanctions or emergency interim sanctions.

§356.19 Request for a hearing.

(a) Any party may request a hearing by submitting a written request to the Under Secretary within 30 days after the date of service of the charging letter. However, the Deputy Under Secretary may request a hearing only if the interests of justice would thereby be served.

(b) Upon timely receipt of a request for a hearing, the Under Secretary will appoint an administrative law judge to conduct the hearing and render an initial decision.

§356.20 Discovery.

(a) *Voluntary discovery.* All parties are encouraged to engage in voluntary discovery procedures regarding any matter, not privileged, which is relevant to the subject matter of the pending sanctions proceeding.

(b) *Limitations on discovery.* The administrative law judge shall place such limits upon the kind or amount of discovery to be had or the period of time during which discovery may be carried out as shall be consistent with the time limitations set forth in this Part.

(c) *Interrogatories and requests for admissions or production of documents.* A party may serve on any other party interrogatories, requests for admissions, or requests for production of documents for inspection and copying, and the party may then apply to the administrative law judge for such enforcement or protective order as that party deems warranted concerning such discovery. The party will serve a discovery request at least 20 days before the scheduled date of a hearing, if a hearing has been requested and

scheduled, unless the administrative law judge specifies a shorter time period. Copies of interrogatories, requests for admissions, and requests for production of documents and responses thereto will be served on all parties. Matters of fact or law of which admission is requested will be deemed admitted unless, within a period designated in the request (at least 10 days after the date of service of the request, or within such further time as the administrative law judge may allow), the party to whom the request is directed serves upon the requesting party a sworn statement either admitting or denying specifically the matters of which admission is requested or setting forth in detail the reasons why the party cannot truthfully either admit or deny such matters.

(d) *Depositions.* Upon application of a party and for good cause shown, the administrative law judge may order the taking of the testimony of any person who is a party, or under the control or authority of a party, by deposition and the production of specified documents or materials by the person at the deposition. The application shall state the purpose of the deposition and shall set forth the facts sought to be established through the deposition.

(e) *Supplementation of responses.* A party who has responded to a request for discovery with a response that was complete when made is under no duty to supplement the party's response to include information thereafter acquired, except as follows:

(1) A party is under a duty to seasonably supplement the party's response with respect to any question directly addressed to:

(i) The identity and location of persons having knowledge of discoverable matters; and

(ii) The identity of each person expected to be called as an expert witness at a hearing, the subject matter on which the witness is expected to testify, and the substance of the testimony.

(2) A party is under a duty to seasonably amend a prior response if the party obtains information upon the basis of which the party:

(i) Knows the response was incorrect when made; or

(ii) Knows that the response, though correct when made, is no longer true, and the circumstances are such that a failure to amend the response is in substance a knowing concealment.

(3) A duty to supplement responses may be imposed by order of the administrative law judge, agreement of the parties, or at any time prior to a hearing through new requests for supplementation of prior responses.

(f) *Enforcement.* The administrative law judge may order a party to answer designated questions, to produce specified documents or items, or to take any other action in response to a proper discovery request. If a party does not comply with such an order, the administrative law judge may make any determination or enter any order in the proceedings as the administrative law judge deems reasonable and appropriate. The administrative law judge may strike related charges or defenses in whole or in part, or may take particular facts relating to the discovery request to which the party failed or refused to respond as being established for purpose of the proceeding in accordance with the contentions of the party seeking discovery. In issuing a discovery order, the administrative law judge will consider the necessity to protect proprietary information and will not order the release of information in circumstances where it is reasonable to conclude that such release will lead to unauthorized dissemination of such information.

§ 356.21 Subpoenas.

(a) *Application for issuance of a subpoena.* An application for issuance of a subpoena requiring a person to appear and depose or testify at the taking of a deposition or at a hearing shall be made to the administrative law judge. An application for issuance of a subpoena requiring a person to appear and depose or testify and to produce specified documents, papers, books, or other physical exhibits at the taking of a deposition, at a prehearing conference, at a hearing, or under any other circumstances, shall be made in writing to the administrative law judge and shall specify the material to be produced as precisely as possible, showing the general relevancy of the material

and the reasonableness of the scope of the subpoena.

(b) *Use of subpoena for discovery.* Subpoenas may be used by any party for purposes of discovery or for obtaining documents, papers, books, or other physical exhibits for use in evidence, or for both purposes. When used for discovery purposes, a subpoena may require a person to produce and permit the inspection and copying of nonprivileged documents, papers, books, or other physical exhibits which constitute or contain evidence relevant to the subject matter involved and which are in the possession, custody, or control of such person.

(c) *Application for subpoenas for nonparty department records or personnel or for records or personnel of other Government agencies.* (1) An application for issuance of a subpoena requiring the production of nonparty documents, papers, books, physical exhibits, or other material in the records of the Department, or requiring the appearance of an official or employee of the Department, or requiring the production of records or personnel of other Government agencies shall specify as precisely as possible the material to be produced, the nature of the information to be disclosed, or the expected testimony of the official or employee, and shall contain a statement showing the general relevancy of the material, information, or testimony and the reasonableness of the scope of the application, together with a showing that such material, information, or testimony or their substantial equivalent could not be obtained without undue hardship by alternative means.

(2) Such applications shall be ruled upon by the administrative law judge. To the extent that the motion is granted, the administrative law judge shall provide such terms and conditions for the production of the material, the disclosure of the information, or the appearance of the official or employee as may appear necessary and appropriate for the protection of the public interest.

(3) No application for a subpoena for production of documents grounded upon the Freedom of Information Act (5 U.S.C. 552) shall be entertained by the administrative law judge.

(d) *Motion to limit or quash.* Any motion to limit or quash a subpoena shall be filed within 10 days after service thereof, or within such other time as the administrative law judge may allow.

(e) *Ex parte rulings on applications for subpoenas.* Applications for the issuance of subpoenas pursuant to this section may be made *ex parte*, and, if so made, such applications and rulings thereon shall remain *ex parte* unless otherwise ordered by the administrative law judge.

(f) *Role of the Under Secretary.* If a hearing has not been requested, the party seeking enforcement will ask the Under Secretary to appoint an administrative law judge to rule on applications for issuance of a subpoena under this section.

§356.22   Prehearing conference.

(a)(1) If an administrative hearing has been requested, the administrative law judge will direct the parties to attend a prehearing conference to consider:

(i) Simplification of issues;

(ii) Obtaining stipulations of fact and of documents to avoid unnecessary proof;

(iii) Settlement of the matter;

(iv) Discovery; and

(v) Such other matters as may expedite the disposition of the proceedings.

(2) Any relevant and significant stipulations or admissions will be incorporated into the initial decision.

(b) If a prehearing conference is impractical, the administrative law judge will direct the parties to correspond with each other or to confer by telephone or otherwise to achieve the purposes of such a conference.

§356.23   Hearing.

(a) *Scheduling of hearing.* The administrative law judge will schedule the hearing at a reasonable time, date, and place, which will be in Washington, DC, unless the administrative law judge determines otherwise based upon good cause shown, that another location would better serve the interests of justice. In setting the date, the administrative law judge will give due regard to the need for the parties adequately to prepare for the hearing and the importance of expeditiously resolving the matter.

(b) *Joinder or consolidation.* The administrative law judge may order joinder or consolidation if sanctions are proposed against more than one party or if violations of more than one protective order or disclosure undertaking are alleged if to do so would expedite processing of the cases and not adversely affect the interests of the parties.

(c) *Hearing procedures.* Hearings will be conducted in a fair and impartial manner by the administrative law judge, who may limit attendance at any hearing or portion thereof if necessary or advisable in order to protect proprietary information from improper disclosure. The rules of evidence prevailing in courts of law shall not apply, and all evidentiary material the administrative law judge determines to be relevant and material to the proceeding and not unduly repetitious may be received into evidence and given appropriate weight. The administrative law judge may make such orders and determinations regarding the admissibility of evidence, conduct of examination and cross-examination, and similar matters as are necessary or appropriate to ensure orderliness in the proceedings. The administrative law judge will ensure that a record of the hearing will be taken by reporter or by electronic recording, and will order such part of the record to be sealed as is necessary to protect proprietary information.

(d) *Rights of parties.* At a hearing each party shall have the right to:

(1) Introduce and examine witnesses and submit physical evidence;

(2) Confront and cross-examine adverse witnesses;

(3) Present oral argument; and

(4) Receive a transcript or recording of the proceedings, upon request, subject to the administrative law judge's orders regarding sealing the record.

(e) *Representation.* Each charged or affected party has a right to represent himself or herself or to retain private counsel for that purpose. The Chief Counsel will represent the Department, unless the General Counsel of the Department determines otherwise. The administrative law judge may disallow a representative if such representation constitutes a conflict of interest or is otherwise not in the interests of justice and may debar a representative for contumacious conduct relating to the proceedings.

(f) *Ex parte communications.* The parties and their representatives may not make any *ex parte* communications to the administrative law judge concerning the merits of the allegations or any matters at issue, except as provided in § 356.18(j) regarding emergency interim sanctions.

§ 356.24   Proceeding without a hearing.

If no party has requested a hearing, the Deputy Under Secretary, within 40 days after the date of service of a charging letter, will submit for inclusion into the record and provide each charged or affected party information supporting the allegations in the charging letter. Each charged or affected party has the right to file a written response to the information and supporting documentation within 30 days after the date of service of the information provided by the Deputy Under Secretary unless the Deputy Under Secretary alters the time period for good cause. The Deputy Under Secretary may allow the parties to submit further information and argument.

§ 356.25   Witnesses.

Witnesses summoned before the Department shall be paid the same fees and mileage that are paid witnesses in the courts of the United States.

§ 356.26   Initial decision.

(a) *Initial decision.* The administrative law judge, if a hearing was requested, or the Deputy Under Secretary will submit an initial decision to the APO Sanctions Board, providing copies to the parties. The administrative law judge or the Deputy Under Secretary will ordinarily issue the decision within 20 days of the conclusion of the hearing, if one was held, or within 15 days of the date of service of final written submissions. The initial decision will be based solely on evidence received into the record and the pleadings of the parties.

(b) *Findings and conclusions.* The initial decision will state findings and conclusions as to whether a person has violated a protective order or a disclosure undertaking; the basis for those findings and conclusions; and whether the sanctions proposed in the charging letter, or lesser included sanctions, should be imposed against the charged or affected party. The administrative law judge or the Deputy Under Secretary may impose sanctions only upon determining that the preponderance of the evidence supports a finding of violation of a protective order or a disclosure undertaking and that the sanctions are warranted against the charged or affected party.

(c) *Finality of decision.* If the APO Sanctions Board has not issued a decision on the matter within 60 days after issuance of the initial decision, the initial decision becomes the final decision of the Department.

§ 356.27   Final decision.

(a) *APO Sanctions Board.* Upon request of a party, the initial decision will be reviewed by the members of the APO Sanctions Board. The Board consists of the Under Secretary for International Trade, who shall serve as Chairperson, the Under Secretary for Economic Affairs, and the General Counsel.

(b) *Comments on initial decision.* Within 30 days after issuance of the initial decision, a party may submit written comments to the APO Sanctions Board on the initial decision, which the Board will consider when reviewing the initial decision. The parties have no right to an oral presentation, although the Board may allow oral argument in its discretion.

(c) *Final decision by the APO Sanctions Board.* Within 60 days but not sooner than 30 days after issuance of an initial decision, the APO Sanctions Board may issue a final decision which adopts the initial decision in its entirety; differs in whole or in part from the initial decision, including the imposition of lesser included sanctions; or remands the matter to the administrative law judge or the Deputy Under Secretary for further consideration. The only sanctions that the Board can impose are those sanctions proposed in the charging letter or lesser included sanctions.

(d) *Content's of final decision.* If the final decision of the APO Sanctions Board does not remand the matter and differs from the initial decision, it will state findings and conclusions which differ from the initial decision, if any, the basis for those findings and conclusions, and the sanctions which are to be imposed, to the extent they differ from the sanctions in the initial decision.

(e) *Public notice of sanctions.* If the final decision is that there has been a violation of a protective order or a disclosure undertaking and that sanctions are to be imposed, notice of the decision will be published in the FEDERAL REGISTER and forwarded to the United States section of the Secretariat. Such publication will be no sooner than 30 days after issuance of a final decision or after a motion to reconsider has been denied, if such a motion was filed. If the final decision is made in a proceeding based upon a request to charge by an authorized agency of an FTA country, the decision will be forwarded to the Secretariat of the involved FTA country for transmittal to the authorized agency of the FTA country for publication in the official publication or other appropriate action. The Deputy Under Secretary will also provide such information to the ethics panel or other disciplinary body of the appropriate bar associations or other professional associations whenever the Deputy Under Secretary subjects a charged or affected party to a sanction under § 356.12(a)(2) and to any Federal agency likely to have an interest in the matter and will cooperate in any disciplinary actions by any association or agency.

§ 356.28 Reconsideration.

Any party may file a motion for reconsideration with the APO Sanctions Board. The party must state with particularity the grounds for the motion, including any facts or points of law which the party claims the APO Sanctions Board has overlooked or misapplied. The party may file the motion within 30 days of the issuance of the final decision or the adoption of the initial decision as the final decision, except that if the motion is based on the discovery of new and material evidence which was not known, and could not reasonably have been discovered through due diligence prior to the close of the record, the party shall file the motion within 15 days of the discovery of the new and material evidence. The party shall provide a copy of the motion to all other parties. Opposing parties may file a response within 30 days of the date of service of the motion. The response shall be considered as part of the record. The parties have no right to an oral presentation on a motion for reconsideration, but the Board may permit oral argument at its discretion. If the motion to reconsider is granted, the Board will review the record and affirm, modify, or reverse the original decision or remand the matter for further consideration to an administrative law judge or the Deputy Under Secretary, as warranted.

§ 356.29 Confidentiality.

(a) All proceedings involving allegations of a violation of a protective order or a disclosure undertaking shall be kept confidential until such time as the Department makes a final decision under these regulations, which is no longer subject to reconsideration, imposing a sanction.

(b) The charged party or counsel for the charged party will be, to the extent possible, granted access to proprietary information in these proceedings, as necessary, under administrative protective order, consistent with the provisions of § 356.10.

§ 356.30 Sanctions for violations of a protective order for privileged information.

The provisions of this subpart shall apply to persons who are alleged to have violated a Protective Order for Privileged Information.

PART 358—SUPPLIES FOR USE IN EMERGENCY RELIEF WORK

Sec.
358.101 Scope.
358.102 Definitions.
358.103 Importation of supplies.
358.104 Report.

AUTHORITY: 19 U.S.C. 1318(a).

SOURCE: 71 FR 63234, Oct. 30, 2006, unless otherwise noted.

§ 358.101 Scope.

This part sets forth the procedures for importation of supplies for use in emergency relief work free of antidumping and countervailing duties, as authorized under section 318(a) of the Act.

§ 358.102 Definitions.

For purposes of this part:

Act means the Tariff Act of 1930, as amended.

CBP means the Bureau of Customs and Border Protection of the United States Department of Homeland Security.

Department means the United States Department of Commerce.

Order means an order issued by the Secretary under section 303, section 706, or section 736 of the Act.

Secretary means the Secretary of Commerce or a designee.

Supplies for use in emergency relief work means food, clothing, and medical, surgical, and other supplies for use in emergency relief work.

§ 358.103 Importation of supplies.

(a) Where the President, acting under section 318 of the Act, authorizes the Secretary to permit the importation of supplies for use in emergency relief work free of antidumping and countervailing duties, the Secretary shall consider requests for such importation under the following conditions:

(1) Before importation, a written request shall be submitted to the Secretary by the person in charge of sending the subject merchandise from the foreign country or by the person for whose account it will be brought into the United States. Three copies of the request should be submitted to the Secretary of Commerce, Attention: Enforcement and Compliance, Central Records Unit, Room 1870, U.S. Department of Commerce, 1401 Constitution Avenue, NW., Washington, DC 20230.

(2) The request shall state the Department antidumping and/or countervailing duty order case number, the producer of the merchandise, a detailed description of the merchandise, the current HTS number, the price in the United States, the quantity, the proposed date of entry, the proposed port of entry, the mode of transport, the person for whose account the merchandise will be brought into the United States, the destination, the use to be made of the merchandise at the designated destination, and any other information the person would like the Secretary to consider.

(b) If the Secretary determines to permit duty-free importation of particular merchandise for use in emergency relief work, the Secretary will notify the person who submitted the request, instruct CBP to allow entry of the merchandise identified in the request submitted under paragraph (a) without regard to antidumping and countervailing duties, and post notification of the determination on the Department's website.

(c) Any subject merchandise entered under paragraph (b) of this section must enter the United States normally within 60 days after the date on which the Secretary notifies the person who submitted the request or the merchandise will be subject to antidumping and/or countervailing duties, as applicable.

(d) Any subject merchandise entered under paragraph (b) of this section which is used in the United States other than for a purpose contemplated for it by section 318(a) of the Act may be subject to seizure or other penalty, including under section 592 of the Act.

(e) Any subject merchandise entered under paragraph (b) of this section is subject to the Department's reporting requirements in its conduct of an antidumping and/or countervailing duty administrative or new shipper review, as applicable.

(f) Any subject merchandise entered under paragraph (b) of this section will be excluded from:

(1) The calculation of assessment and cash deposit rates in an administrative or new shipper review under section 751(a) of the Act;

(2) "Commercial quantities" under 19 CFR 351.222; and

(3) The quantity allowed by, or revised price requirements established pursuant to, a suspension agreement under section 704 or section 734 of the Act, as applicable.

[71 FR 63234, Oct. 30, 2006, as amended at 78 FR 77354, Dec. 23, 2013]

§358.104 Report.

The Secretary will review and issue a report on the first five years of the operation of Part 358. The report will consider the impact of determinations to permit importation of particular merchandise for use in emergency relief work under this Part, on U.S. parties injured by dumped and/or subsidized imports.

PART 360—STEEL IMPORT MONITORING AND ANALYSIS SYSTEM

Sec.
360.101 Steel import licensing.
360.102 Online registration.
360.103 Automatic issuance of import licenses.
360.104 Steel import monitoring.
360.105 Duration of the steel import licensing requirement.
360.106 Fees.
360.107 Hours of operation.
360.108 Loss of electronic licensing privileges.

AUTHORITY: 13 U.S.C. 301(a) and 302.

SOURCE: 70 FR 12136, Mar. 11, 2005, unless otherwise noted.

§360.101 Steel import licensing.

(a) *In general.* (1) All imports of basic steel mill products are subject to the import licensing requirements. These products are listed in Annex II. Registered users will be able to obtain steel import licenses on the Steel Import Monitoring and Analysis (SIMA) System Web site. This Web site contains two sections related to import licensing—the online registration system and the automatic steel import license issuance system. Information gathered from these licenses will be aggregated and posted on the import monitoring section of the SIMA system Web site.

(2) A single license may cover multiple products as long as certain information on the license (*e.g.*, importer, exporter, manufacturer and country of origin) remains the same. However, separate licenses for steel entered under a single entry will be required if the information differs. As a result, a single Customs entry may require more than one steel import license. The applicable license(s) must cover the total quantity of steel entered and should cover the same information provided on the Customs entry summary.

(b) *Entries for consumption.* All entries for consumption of covered steel products, other than the exception for "informal entries" listed in paragraph (d) of this section, will require an import license prior to the filing of Customs entry summary documents. The license number(s) must be reported on the entry summary (Customs Form 7501) at the time of filing. There is no requirement to present physical copies of the license forms at the time of entry summary. However, copies must be maintained in accordance with Customs' normal requirements. Entry summaries submitted without the required license number(s) will be considered incomplete and will be subject to liquidated damages for violation of the bond condition requiring timely completion of entry.

(c) *Foreign Trade Zone entries.* All shipments of covered steel products into a foreign trade zones (FTZ), known as FTZ admissions, will require an import license prior to the filing of FTZ admission documents. The license number(s) must be reported on the application for FTZ admission and/or status designation (Customs form 214) at the time of filing. There is no requirement to present physical copies of the license forms at the time of FTZ admission; however, copies must be maintained in accordance with Customs' normal requirements. FTZ admission documents submitted without the required license number(s) will not be considered complete and will be subject to liquidated damages for violation of the bond condition requiring timely completion of admission. A further steel license will not be required for shipments from zones into the commerce of the United States.

(d) *Informal entries.* No import license shall be required on informal entries of covered steel products, such as merchandise valued at less than $2,000. This exemption applies to informal entries only, imports of steel valued at less than $2,000 that are part of a formal entry will require a license. For additional information, refer to 19 CFR 143.21 through 143.28.

(e) *Other non-consumption entries.* Import licenses are not required on temporary importation bond (TIB) entries, transportation and exportation (T&E) entries or entries into a bonded warehouse. Covered steel products withdrawn for consumption from a bonded warehouse will require a license at the entry summary.

§ 360.102   Online registration.

(a) *In general.* (1) Any importer, importing company, customs broker or importer's agent with a U.S. street address may register and obtain the user identification number necessary to log on to the automatic steel import license issuance system. Foreign companies may obtain a user identification number if they have a U.S. address through which they may be reached; P.O. boxes will not be accepted. A user identification number will be issued within two business days. Companies will be able to register online through the SIMA system Web site. However, should a company prefer to apply for a user identification number non-electronically, a phone/fax option will be available at Commerce during regular business hours.

(2) This user identification number will be required in order to log on to the steel import license issuance system. A single user identification number will be issued to an importer, customs broker or importer's agent. Operating units within the company (*e.g.*, individual branches, divisions or employees) will all use the same basic company user identification code but can supply suffixes to identify the branches. The steel import license issuance system will be designed to allow multiple users of a single identification number from different locations within the company to enter information simultaneously.

(b) *Information required to obtain a user identification number.* In order to obtain a user identification number, the importer, importing company, customs broker or importer's agent will be required to provide general information. This information will include: the filer company name, employer identification number (EIN) or Customs ID number (where no EIN is available), U.S. street address, phone number, contact information and e-mail address for both the company headquarters and any branch offices that will be applying for steel licenses. It is the responsibility of the applicant to keep the information up-to-date. This information will not be released by Commerce, except as required by U.S. law.

§ 360.103   Automatic issuance of import licenses.

(a) *In general.* Steel import licenses will be issued to registered importers, customs brokers or their agents through an automatic steel import licensing system. The licenses will be issued automatically after the completion of the form.

(b) *Customs entry number.* Filers are not required to report a Customs entry number to obtain an import license but are encouraged to do so if the Customs entry number is known at the time of filing for the license.

(c) *Information required to obtain an import license.* (1) The following information is required to be reported in order to obtain an import license (if using the automatic licensing system, some of this information will be provided automatically from information submitted as part of the registration process):

(i) Filer company name and address;

(ii) Filer contact name, phone number, fax number and email address;

(iii) Entry type (*i.e.*, Consumption, FTZ)

(iv) Importer name;

(v) Exporter name;

(vi) Manufacturer name (filer may state "unknown");

(vii) Country of origin;

(viii) Country of exportation;

(ix) Expected date of export;

(x) Expected date of import;

(xi) Expected port of entry;

(xii) Current HTS number (from Chapters 72 or 73);

(xiii) Quantity (in kilograms) and

(xiv) Customs value (U.S. $).

(2) Certain fields will be automatically filled out by the automatic license system based on information submitted by the filer (*e.g.*, product category, unit value). Filers should review these fields to help confirm the accuracy of the submitted data.

(3) Upon completion of the form, the importer, customs broker or the importer's agent will certify as to the accuracy and completeness of the information and submit the form electronically. After refreshing the page, the system will automatically issue a steel import license number. The refreshed form containing the submitted information and the newly issued license number will appear on the screen (the "license form"). Filers can print the license form themselves only at that time. For security purposes, users will not be able to retrieve licenses themselves from the license system at a later date for reprinting. If needed, copies of completed license forms can be requested from Commerce during normal business hours.

(d) *Duration of the steel import license.* The steel import license can be applied for up to 60 days prior to the expected date of importation and until the date of filing of the entry summary documents, or in the case of FTZ entries, the filing of Customs form 214. The steel import license is valid for 75 days; however, import licenses that were valid on the date of importation but expired prior to the filing of entry summary documents will be accepted.

(e) *Correcting submitted license information.* Users will need to correct licenses themselves if they determine that there was an error submitted. To access a previously issued license, a user must log on with his user identification code and identify the license number and the volume (in kilograms) for the first product shown on the license. The information on the license should match the information presented on the CF–7501 entry summary document as closely as possible; this includes the value and volume of the shipment, the expected date of importation, and the customs district of entry.

(f) *Low-value licenses.* There is one exception to the requirement for obtaining a unique license for each Customs entry. If the total value of the covered steel portion of an entry is less than $250, applicants may apply to Commerce for a low-value license that can be used in lieu of a single entry license for low-value entries.

§360.104 Steel import monitoring.

(a) Throughout the duration of the licensing requirement, Commerce will maintain an import monitoring system on the SIMA system Web site that will report certain aggregate information on imports of steel mill products obtained from the steel licenses. Aggregate data will be reported on a monthly basis by country of origin and steel mill product category and will include import quantity (metric tons), import Customs value (U.S. $), and average unit value ($/metric ton). The Web site will also contain certain aggregate data at the 6-digit Harmonized Tariff Schedule level and will also present a range of historical data for comparison purposes. Provision of this aggregate data on the Web site may be revisited should concerns arise over the possible release of proprietary data.

(b) Reported monthly import data will be refreshed each week with new data on licenses issued during the previous week. This data will also be adjusted periodically for cancelled or unused steel import licenses, as appropriate.

§360.105 Duration of the steel import licensing requirement.

The licensing program will be in effect through March 21, 2022, but may be extended upon review and notification in the FEDERAL REGISTER prior to this expiration date. Licenses will be required on all subject imports entered during this period, even if the entry summary documents are not filed until after the expiration of this program. The licenses will be valid for 10 business days after the expiration of this program to allow for the final filing of required Customs documentation.

[82 FR 1185, Jan. 5, 2017]

§360.106 Fees.

No fees will be charged for obtaining a user identification number, issuing a steel import license or accessing the steel import surge monitoring system.

§360.107 Hours of operation.

The automatic licensing system will generally be accessible 24 hours a day, 7 days a week but may be unavailable at selected times for server maintenance. If the system is unavailable for an extended period of time, parties will be able to obtain licenses from Commerce directly via fax during regular business hours. Should the system be inaccessible for an extended period of time, Commerce would advise Customs to consider this as part of mitigation on any liquidated damage claims that may be issued.

§ 360.108 Loss of electronic licensing privileges.

Should Commerce determine that a filer consistently files inaccurate licensing information or otherwise abuses the licensing system, Commerce may revoke its electronic licensing privileges without prior notice. The filer will then only be able to obtain a license directly from Commerce. Because of the additional time need to review such forms, Commerce may require up to 10 working days to process such forms. Delays in filing caused by the removal of a filer's electronic filing privilege will not be considered a mitigating factor by the U.S. Customs Service.

PARTS 361–399 [RESERVED]

CHAPTER IV—U.S. IMMIGRATION AND CUSTOMS ENFORCEMENT, DEPARTMENT OF HOMELAND SECURITY [RESERVED]

PARTS 400–599 [RESERVED]

FINDING AIDS

A list of CFR titles, subtitles, chapters, subchapters and parts and an alphabetical list of agencies publishing in the CFR are included in the CFR Index and Finding Aids volume to the Code of Federal Regulations which is published separately and revised annually.

Table of CFR Titles and Chapters
Alphabetical List of Agencies Appearing in the CFR
List of CFR Sections Affected

Table of CFR Titles and Chapters

(Revised as of April 1, 2018)

Title 1—General Provisions

I   Administrative Committee of the Federal Register (Parts 1—49)
II Office of the Federal Register (Parts 50—299)
III Administrative Conference of the United States (Parts 300—399)
IV Miscellaneous Agencies (Parts 400—599)
VI National Capital Planning Commission (Parts 600—699)

Title 2—Grants and Agreements

SUBTITLE A—OFFICE OF MANAGEMENT AND BUDGET GUIDANCE FOR GRANTS AND AGREEMENTS
I   Office of Management and Budget Governmentwide Guidance for Grants and Agreements (Parts 2—199)
II   Office of Management and Budget Guidance (Parts 200—299)
SUBTITLE B—FEDERAL AGENCY REGULATIONS FOR GRANTS AND AGREEMENTS
III Department of Health and Human Services (Parts 300—399)
IV   Department of Agriculture (Parts 400—499)
VI   Department of State (Parts 600—699)
VII Agency for International Development (Parts 700—799)
VIII Department of Veterans Affairs (Parts 800—899)
IX   Department of Energy (Parts 900—999)
X   Department of the Treasury (Parts 1000—1099)
XI   Department of Defense (Parts 1100—1199)
XII Department of Transportation (Parts 1200—1299)
XIII Department of Commerce (Parts 1300—1399)
XIV Department of the Interior (Parts 1400—1499)
XV   Environmental Protection Agency (Parts 1500—1599)
XVIII National Aeronautics and Space Administration (Parts 1800—1899)
XX   United States Nuclear Regulatory Commission (Parts 2000—2099)
XXII Corporation for National and Community Service (Parts 2200—2299)
XXIII Social Security Administration (Parts 2300—2399)
XXIV Department of Housing and Urban Development (Parts 2400—2499)
XXV National Science Foundation (Parts 2500—2599)
XXVI National Archives and Records Administration (Parts 2600—2699)

Title 2—Grants and Agreements—Continued

Chap.

XXVII   Small Business Administration (Parts 2700—2799)
XXVIII   Department of Justice (Parts 2800—2899)
XXIX   Department of Labor (Parts 2900—2999)
XXX   Department of Homeland Security (Parts 3000—3099)
XXXI   Institute of Museum and Library Services (Parts 3100—3199)
XXXII   National Endowment for the Arts (Parts 3200—3299)
XXXIII   National Endowment for the Humanities (Parts 3300—3399)
XXXIV   Department of Education (Parts 3400—3499)
XXXV   Export-Import Bank of the United States (Parts 3500—3599)
XXXVI   Office of National Drug Control Policy, Executive Office of the President (Parts 3600—3699)
XXXVII   Peace Corps (Parts 3700—3799)
LVIII   Election Assistance Commission (Parts 5800—5899)
LIX   Gulf Coast Ecosystem Restoration Council (Parts 5900—5999)

Title 3—The President

I   Executive Office of the President (Parts 100—199)

Title 4—Accounts

I   Government Accountability Office (Parts 1—199)

Title 5—Administrative Personnel

I   Office of Personnel Management (Parts 1—1199)
II   Merit Systems Protection Board (Parts 1200—1299)
III   Office of Management and Budget (Parts 1300—1399)
IV   Office of Personnel Management and Office of the Director of National Intelligence (Parts 1400—1499)
V   The International Organizations Employees Loyalty Board (Parts 1500—1599)
VI   Federal Retirement Thrift Investment Board (Parts 1600—1699)
VIII   Office of Special Counsel (Parts 1800—1899)
IX   Appalachian Regional Commission (Parts 1900—1999)
XI   Armed Forces Retirement Home (Parts 2100—2199)
XIV   Federal Labor Relations Authority, General Counsel of the Federal Labor Relations Authority and Federal Service Impasses Panel (Parts 2400—2499)
XVI   Office of Government Ethics (Parts 2600—2699)
XXI   Department of the Treasury (Parts 3100—3199)
XXII   Federal Deposit Insurance Corporation (Parts 3200—3299)
XXIII Department of Energy (Parts 3300—3399)
XXIV   Federal Energy Regulatory Commission (Parts 3400—3499)
XXV   Department of the Interior (Parts 3500—3599)
XXVI   Department of Defense (Parts 3600—3699)

XXVIII	Department of Justice (Parts 3800—3899)
XXIX	Federal Communications Commission (Parts 3900—3999)
XXX	Farm Credit System Insurance Corporation (Parts 4000—4099)
XXXI	Farm Credit Administration (Parts 4100—4199)
XXXIII	Overseas Private Investment Corporation (Parts 4300—4399)
XXXIV	Securities and Exchange Commission (Parts 4400—4499)
XXXV	Office of Personnel Management (Parts 4500—4599)
XXXVI	Department of Homeland Security (Parts 4600—4699)
XXXVII	Federal Election Commission (Parts 4700—4799)
XL	Interstate Commerce Commission (Parts 5000—5099)
XLI	Commodity Futures Trading Commission (Parts 5100—5199)
XLII	Department of Labor (Parts 5200—5299)
XLIII	National Science Foundation (Parts 5300—5399)
XLV	Department of Health and Human Services (Parts 5500—5599)
XLVI	Postal Rate Commission (Parts 5600—5699)
XLVII	Federal Trade Commission (Parts 5700—5799)
XLVIII	Nuclear Regulatory Commission (Parts 5800—5899)
XLIX	Federal Labor Relations Authority (Parts 5900—5999)
L	Department of Transportation (Parts 6000—6099)
LII	Export-Import Bank of the United States (Parts 6200—6299)
LIII	Department of Education (Parts 6300—6399)
LIV	Environmental Protection Agency (Parts 6400—6499)
LV	National Endowment for the Arts (Parts 6500—6599)
LVI	National Endowment for the Humanities (Parts 6600—6699)
LVII	General Services Administration (Parts 6700—6799)
LVIII	Board of Governors of the Federal Reserve System (Parts 6800—6899)
LIX	National Aeronautics and Space Administration (Parts 6900—6999)
LX	United States Postal Service (Parts 7000—7099)
LXI	National Labor Relations Board (Parts 7100—7199)
LXII	Equal Employment Opportunity Commission (Parts 7200—7299)
LXIII	Inter-American Foundation (Parts 7300—7399)
LXIV	Merit Systems Protection Board (Parts 7400—7499)
LXV	Department of Housing and Urban Development (Parts 7500—7599)
LXVI	National Archives and Records Administration (Parts 7600—7699)
LXVII	Institute of Museum and Library Services (Parts 7700—7799)
LXVIII	Commission on Civil Rights (Parts 7800—7899)
LXIX	Tennessee Valley Authority (Parts 7900—7999)
LXX	Court Services and Offender Supervision Agency for the District of Columbia (Parts 8000—8099)
LXXI	Consumer Product Safety Commission (Parts 8100—8199)
LXXIII	Department of Agriculture (Parts 8300—8399)

Title 5—Administrative Personnel—Continued

Chap.

LXXIV   Federal Mine Safety and Health Review Commission (Parts 8400—8499)

LXXVI   Federal Retirement Thrift Investment Board (Parts 8600—8699)

LXXVII   Office of Management and Budget (Parts 8700—8799)

LXXX   Federal Housing Finance Agency (Parts 9000—9099)

LXXXIII   Special Inspector General for Afghanistan Reconstruction (Parts 9300—9399)

LXXXIV   Bureau of Consumer Financial Protection (Parts 9400—9499)

LXXXVI   National Credit Union Administration (Parts 9600—9699)

XCVII   Department of Homeland Security Human Resources Management System (Department of Homeland Security—Office of Personnel Management) (Parts 9700—9799)

XCVIII   Council of the Inspectors General on Integrity and Efficiency (Parts 9800—9899)

XCIX   Military Compensation and Retirement Modernization Commission (Parts 9900—9999)

C   National Council on Disability (Parts 10000—10049)

Title 6—Domestic Security

I   Department of Homeland Security, Office of the Secretary (Parts 1—199)

X   Privacy and Civil Liberties Oversight Board (Parts 1000—1099)

Title 7—Agriculture

SUBTITLE A—OFFICE OF THE SECRETARY OF AGRICULTURE (PARTS 0—26)

SUBTITLE B—REGULATIONS OF THE DEPARTMENT OF AGRICULTURE

I   Agricultural Marketing Service (Standards, Inspections, Marketing Practices), Department of Agriculture (Parts 27—209)

II   Food and Nutrition Service, Department of Agriculture (Parts 210—299)

III   Animal and Plant Health Inspection Service, Department of Agriculture (Parts 300—399)

IV   Federal Crop Insurance Corporation, Department of Agriculture (Parts 400—499)

V   Agricultural Research Service, Department of Agriculture (Parts 500—599)

VI   Natural Resources Conservation Service, Department of Agriculture (Parts 600—699)

VII   Farm Service Agency, Department of Agriculture (Parts 700—799)

VIII   Grain Inspection, Packers and Stockyards Administration (Federal Grain Inspection Service), Department of Agriculture (Parts 800—899)

IX   Agricultural Marketing Service (Marketing Agreements and Orders; Fruits, Vegetables, Nuts), Department of Agriculture (Parts 900—999)

X   Agricultural Marketing Service (Marketing Agreements and Orders; Milk), Department of Agriculture (Parts 1000—1199)

XI   Agricultural Marketing Service (Marketing Agreements and Orders; Miscellaneous Commodities), Department of Agriculture (Parts 1200—1299)

XIV   Commodity Credit Corporation, Department of Agriculture (Parts 1400—1499)

XV   Foreign Agricultural Service, Department of Agriculture (Parts 1500—1599)

XVI   Rural Telephone Bank, Department of Agriculture (Parts 1600—1699)

XVII   Rural Utilities Service, Department of Agriculture (Parts 1700—1799)

XVIII   Rural Housing Service, Rural Business-Cooperative Service, Rural Utilities Service, and Farm Service Agency, Department of Agriculture (Parts 1800—2099)

XX   Local Television Loan Guarantee Board (Parts 2200—2299)

XXV   Office of Advocacy and Outreach, Department of Agriculture (Parts 2500—2599)

XXVI   Office of Inspector General, Department of Agriculture (Parts 2600—2699)

XXVII   Office of Information Resources Management, Department of Agriculture (Parts 2700—2799)

XXVIII   Office of Operations, Department of Agriculture (Parts 2800—2899)

XXIX   Office of Energy Policy and New Uses, Department of Agriculture (Parts 2900—2999)

XXX   Office of the Chief Financial Officer, Department of Agriculture (Parts 3000—3099)

XXXI   Office of Environmental Quality, Department of Agriculture (Parts 3100—3199)

XXXII   Office of Procurement and Property Management, Department of Agriculture (Parts 3200—3299)

XXXIII   Office of Transportation, Department of Agriculture (Parts 3300—3399)

XXXIV   National Institute of Food and Agriculture (Parts 3400—3499)

XXXV   Rural Housing Service, Department of Agriculture (Parts 3500—3599)

XXXVI   National Agricultural Statistics Service, Department of Agriculture (Parts 3600—3699)

XXXVII   Economic Research Service, Department of Agriculture (Parts 3700—3799)

XXXVIII   World Agricultural Outlook Board, Department of Agriculture (Parts 3800—3899)

XLI   [Reserved]

XLII   Rural Business-Cooperative Service and Rural Utilities Service, Department of Agriculture (Parts 4200—4299)

Title 8—Aliens and Nationality

Chap.

I   Department of Homeland Security (Immigration and Naturalization) (Parts 1—499)

V   Executive Office for Immigration Review, Department of Justice (Parts 1000—1399)

Title 9—Animals and Animal Products

I   Animal and Plant Health Inspection Service, Department of Agriculture (Parts 1—199)

II   Grain Inspection, Packers and Stockyards Administration (Packers and Stockyards Programs), Department of Agriculture (Parts 200—299)

III   Food Safety and Inspection Service, Department of Agriculture (Parts 300—599)

Title 10—Energy

I   Nuclear Regulatory Commission (Parts 0—199)

II   Department of Energy (Parts 200—699)

III   Department of Energy (Parts 700—999)

X   Department of Energy (General Provisions) (Parts 1000—1099)

XIII   Nuclear Waste Technical Review Board (Parts 1300—1399)

XVII   Defense Nuclear Facilities Safety Board (Parts 1700—1799)

XVIII   Northeast Interstate Low-Level Radioactive Waste Commission (Parts 1800—1899)

Title 11—Federal Elections

I   Federal Election Commission (Parts 1—9099)

II   Election Assistance Commission (Parts 9400—9499)

Title 12—Banks and Banking

I   Comptroller of the Currency, Department of the Treasury (Parts 1—199)

II   Federal Reserve System (Parts 200—299)

III   Federal Deposit Insurance Corporation (Parts 300—399)

IV   Export-Import Bank of the United States (Parts 400—499)

V   Office of Thrift Supervision, Department of the Treasury (Parts 500—599)

VI   Farm Credit Administration (Parts 600—699)

VII   National Credit Union Administration (Parts 700—799)

VIII   Federal Financing Bank (Parts 800—899)

IX   Federal Housing Finance Board (Parts 900—999)

X   Bureau of Consumer Financial Protection (Parts 1000—1099)

XI   Federal Financial Institutions Examination Council (Parts 1100—1199)

XII   Federal Housing Finance Agency (Parts 1200—1299)

Chap.

Title 12—Banks and Banking—Continued

XIII   Financial Stability Oversight Council (Parts 1300—1399)

XIV   Farm Credit System Insurance Corporation (Parts 1400—1499)

XV   Department of the Treasury (Parts 1500—1599)

XVI   Office of Financial Research (Parts 1600—1699)

XVII   Office of Federal Housing Enterprise Oversight, Department of Housing and Urban Development (Parts 1700—1799)

XVIII   Community Development Financial Institutions Fund, Department of the Treasury (Parts 1800—1899)

Title 13—Business Credit and Assistance

I   Small Business Administration (Parts 1—199)

III   Economic Development Administration, Department of Commerce (Parts 300—399)

IV   Emergency Steel Guarantee Loan Board (Parts 400—499)

V   Emergency Oil and Gas Guaranteed Loan Board (Parts 500—599)

Title 14—Aeronautics and Space

I   Federal Aviation Administration, Department of Transportation (Parts 1—199)

II   Office of the Secretary, Department of Transportation (Aviation Proceedings) (Parts 200—399)

III   Commercial Space Transportation, Federal Aviation Administration, Department of Transportation (Parts 400—1199)

V   National Aeronautics and Space Administration (Parts 1200—1299)

VI   Air Transportation System Stabilization (Parts 1300—1399)

Title 15—Commerce and Foreign Trade

SUBTITLE A—OFFICE OF THE SECRETARY OF COMMERCE (PARTS 0—29)

SUBTITLE B—REGULATIONS RELATING TO COMMERCE AND FOREIGN TRADE

I   Bureau of the Census, Department of Commerce (Parts 30—199)

II   National Institute of Standards and Technology, Department of Commerce (Parts 200—299)

III   International Trade Administration, Department of Commerce (Parts 300—399)

IV   Foreign-Trade Zones Board, Department of Commerce (Parts 400—499)

VII   Bureau of Industry and Security, Department of Commerce (Parts 700—799)

VIII   Bureau of Economic Analysis, Department of Commerce (Parts 800—899)

IX   National Oceanic and Atmospheric Administration, Department of Commerce (Parts 900—999)

Title 15—Commerce and Foreign Trade—Continued

Chap.

XI   National Technical Information Service, Department of Commerce (Parts 1100—1199)

XIII   East-West Foreign Trade Board (Parts 1300—1399)

XIV   Minority Business Development Agency (Parts 1400—1499)

SUBTITLE C—REGULATIONS RELATING TO FOREIGN TRADE AGREEMENTS

XX   Office of the United States Trade Representative (Parts 2000—2099)

SUBTITLE D—REGULATIONS RELATING TO TELECOMMUNICATIONS AND INFORMATION

XXIII   National Telecommunications and Information Administration, Department of Commerce (Parts 2300—2399) [Reserved]

Title 16—Commercial Practices

I   Federal Trade Commission (Parts 0—999)

II   Consumer Product Safety Commission (Parts 1000—1799)

Title 17—Commodity and Securities Exchanges

I   Commodity Futures Trading Commission (Parts 1—199)

II   Securities and Exchange Commission (Parts 200—399)

IV   Department of the Treasury (Parts 400—499)

Title 18—Conservation of Power and Water Resources

I   Federal Energy Regulatory Commission, Department of Energy (Parts 1—399)

III   Delaware River Basin Commission (Parts 400—499)

VI   Water Resources Council (Parts 700—799)

VIII   Susquehanna River Basin Commission (Parts 800—899)

XIII   Tennessee Valley Authority (Parts 1300—1399)

Title 19—Customs Duties

I   U.S. Customs and Border Protection, Department of Homeland Security; Department of the Treasury (Parts 0—199)

II   United States International Trade Commission (Parts 200—299)

III   International Trade Administration, Department of Commerce (Parts 300—399)

IV   U.S. Immigration and Customs Enforcement, Department of Homeland Security (Parts 400—599) [Reserved]

Title 20—Employees' Benefits

I   Office of Workers' Compensation Programs, Department of Labor (Parts 1—199)

II   Railroad Retirement Board (Parts 200—399)

Title 20—Employees' Benefits—Continued

Chap.

III Social Security Administration (Parts 400—499)

IV Employees' Compensation Appeals Board, Department of Labor (Parts 500—599)

V Employment and Training Administration, Department of Labor (Parts 600—699)

VI Office of Workers' Compensation Programs, Department of Labor (Parts 700—799)

VII Benefits Review Board, Department of Labor (Parts 800—899)

VIII Joint Board for the Enrollment of Actuaries (Parts 900—999)

IX Office of the Assistant Secretary for Veterans' Employment and Training Service, Department of Labor (Parts 1000—1099)

Title 21—Food and Drugs

I Food and Drug Administration, Department of Health and Human Services (Parts 1—1299)

II Drug Enforcement Administration, Department of Justice (Parts 1300—1399)

III Office of National Drug Control Policy (Parts 1400—1499)

Title 22—Foreign Relations

I Department of State (Parts 1—199)

II Agency for International Development (Parts 200—299)

III Peace Corps (Parts 300—399)

IV International Joint Commission, United States and Canada (Parts 400—499)

V Broadcasting Board of Governors (Parts 500—599)

VII Overseas Private Investment Corporation (Parts 700—799)

IX Foreign Service Grievance Board (Parts 900—999)

X Inter-American Foundation (Parts 1000—1099)

XI International Boundary and Water Commission, United States and Mexico, United States Section (Parts 1100—1199)

XII United States International Development Cooperation Agency (Parts 1200—1299)

XIII Millennium Challenge Corporation (Parts 1300—1399)

XIV Foreign Service Labor Relations Board; Federal Labor Relations Authority; General Counsel of the Federal Labor Relations Authority; and the Foreign Service Impasse Disputes Panel (Parts 1400—1499)

XV African Development Foundation (Parts 1500—1599)

XVI Japan-United States Friendship Commission (Parts 1600—1699)

XVII United States Institute of Peace (Parts 1700—1799)

Title 23—Highways

I Federal Highway Administration, Department of Transportation (Parts 1—999)

Title 23—Highways—Continued

II National Highway Traffic Safety Administration and Federal Highway Administration, Department of Transportation (Parts 1200—1299)

III National Highway Traffic Safety Administration, Department of Transportation (Parts 1300—1399)

Title 24—Housing and Urban Development

SUBTITLE A—OFFICE OF THE SECRETARY, DEPARTMENT OF HOUSING AND URBAN DEVELOPMENT (PARTS 0—99)

SUBTITLE B—REGULATIONS RELATING TO HOUSING AND URBAN DEVELOPMENT

I Office of Assistant Secretary for Equal Opportunity, Department of Housing and Urban Development (Parts 100—199)

II Office of Assistant Secretary for Housing-Federal Housing Commissioner, Department of Housing and Urban Development (Parts 200—299)

III Government National Mortgage Association, Department of Housing and Urban Development (Parts 300—399)

IV Office of Housing and Office of Multifamily Housing Assistance Restructuring, Department of Housing and Urban Development (Parts 400—499)

V Office of Assistant Secretary for Community Planning and Development, Department of Housing and Urban Development (Parts 500—599)

VI Office of Assistant Secretary for Community Planning and Development, Department of Housing and Urban Development (Parts 600—699) [Reserved]

VII Office of the Secretary, Department of Housing and Urban Development (Housing Assistance Programs and Public and Indian Housing Programs) (Parts 700—799)

VIII Office of the Assistant Secretary for Housing—Federal Housing Commissioner, Department of Housing and Urban Development (Section 8 Housing Assistance Programs, Section 202 Direct Loan Program, Section 202 Supportive Housing for the Elderly Program and Section 811 Supportive Housing for Persons With Disabilities Program) (Parts 800—899)

IX Office of Assistant Secretary for Public and Indian Housing, Department of Housing and Urban Development (Parts 900—1699)

X Office of Assistant Secretary for Housing—Federal Housing Commissioner, Department of Housing and Urban Development (Interstate Land Sales Registration Program) (Parts 1700—1799)

XII Office of Inspector General, Department of Housing and Urban Development (Parts 2000—2099)

XV Emergency Mortgage Insurance and Loan Programs, Department of Housing and Urban Development (Parts 2700—2799) [Reserved]

XX Office of Assistant Secretary for Housing—Federal Housing Commissioner, Department of Housing and Urban Development (Parts 3200—3899)

Title 24—Housing and Urban Development—Continued

Chap.

XXIV   Board of Directors of the HOPE for Homeowners Program (Parts 4000—4099) [Reserved]

XXV   Neighborhood Reinvestment Corporation (Parts 4100—4199)

Title 25—Indians

I   Bureau of Indian Affairs, Department of the Interior (Parts 1—299)

II   Indian Arts and Crafts Board, Department of the Interior (Parts 300—399)

III   National Indian Gaming Commission, Department of the Interior (Parts 500—599)

IV   Office of Navajo and Hopi Indian Relocation (Parts 700—899)

V   Bureau of Indian Affairs, Department of the Interior, and Indian Health Service, Department of Health and Human Services (Parts 900—999)

VI   Office of the Assistant Secretary, Indian Affairs, Department of the Interior (Parts 1000—1199)

VII   Office of the Special Trustee for American Indians, Department of the Interior (Parts 1200—1299)

Title 26—Internal Revenue

I   Internal Revenue Service, Department of the Treasury (Parts 1—End)

Title 27—Alcohol, Tobacco Products and Firearms

I   Alcohol and Tobacco Tax and Trade Bureau, Department of the Treasury (Parts 1—399)

II   Bureau of Alcohol, Tobacco, Firearms, and Explosives, Department of Justice (Parts 400—699)

Title 28—Judicial Administration

I   Department of Justice (Parts 0—299)

III   Federal Prison Industries, Inc., Department of Justice (Parts 300—399)

V   Bureau of Prisons, Department of Justice (Parts 500—599)

VI   Offices of Independent Counsel, Department of Justice (Parts 600—699)

VII   Office of Independent Counsel (Parts 700—799)

VIII   Court Services and Offender Supervision Agency for the District of Columbia (Parts 800—899)

IX   National Crime Prevention and Privacy Compact Council (Parts 900—999)

XI   Department of Justice and Department of State (Parts 1100—1199)

Title 29—Labor

Chap.

SUBTITLE A—OFFICE OF THE SECRETARY OF LABOR (PARTS 0—99)

SUBTITLE B—REGULATIONS RELATING TO LABOR

I   National Labor Relations Board (Parts 100—199)

II   Office of Labor-Management Standards, Department of Labor (Parts 200—299)

III   National Railroad Adjustment Board (Parts 300—399)

IV   Office of Labor-Management Standards, Department of Labor (Parts 400—499)

V   Wage and Hour Division, Department of Labor (Parts 500—899)

IX   Construction Industry Collective Bargaining Commission (Parts 900—999)

X   National Mediation Board (Parts 1200—1299)

XII   Federal Mediation and Conciliation Service (Parts 1400—1499)

XIV   Equal Employment Opportunity Commission (Parts 1600—1699)

XVII   Occupational Safety and Health Administration, Department of Labor (Parts 1900—1999)

XX   Occupational Safety and Health Review Commission (Parts 2200—2499)

XXV   Employee Benefits Security Administration, Department of Labor (Parts 2500—2599)

XXVII   Federal Mine Safety and Health Review Commission (Parts 2700—2799)

XL   Pension Benefit Guaranty Corporation (Parts 4000—4999)

Title 30—Mineral Resources

I   Mine Safety and Health Administration, Department of Labor (Parts 1—199)

II   Bureau of Safety and Environmental Enforcement, Department of the Interior (Parts 200—299)

IV   Geological Survey, Department of the Interior (Parts 400—499)

V   Bureau of Ocean Energy Management, Department of the Interior (Parts 500—599)

VII   Office of Surface Mining Reclamation and Enforcement, Department of the Interior (Parts 700—999)

XII   Office of Natural Resources Revenue, Department of the Interior (Parts 1200—1299)

Title 31—Money and Finance: Treasury

SUBTITLE A—OFFICE OF THE SECRETARY OF THE TREASURY (PARTS 0—50)

SUBTITLE B—REGULATIONS RELATING TO MONEY AND FINANCE

I   Monetary Offices, Department of the Treasury (Parts 51—199)

II   Fiscal Service, Department of the Treasury (Parts 200—399)

IV   Secret Service, Department of the Treasury (Parts 400—499)

V   Office of Foreign Assets Control, Department of the Treasury (Parts 500—599)

Title 31—Money and Finance: Treasury—Continued

Chap.

VI   Bureau of Engraving and Printing, Department of the Treasury (Parts 600—699)

VII   Federal Law Enforcement Training Center, Department of the Treasury (Parts 700—799)

VIII   Office of Investment Security, Department of the Treasury (Parts 800—899)

IX   Federal Claims Collection Standards (Department of the Treasury—Department of Justice) (Parts 900—999)

X   Financial Crimes Enforcement Network, Department of the Treasury (Parts 1000—1099)

Title 32—National Defense

SUBTITLE A—DEPARTMENT OF DEFENSE

I   Office of the Secretary of Defense (Parts 1—399)

V   Department of the Army (Parts 400—699)

VI   Department of the Navy (Parts 700—799)

VII   Department of the Air Force (Parts 800—1099)

SUBTITLE B—OTHER REGULATIONS RELATING TO NATIONAL DEFENSE

XII   Defense Logistics Agency (Parts 1200—1299)

XVI   Selective Service System (Parts 1600—1699)

XVII   Office of the Director of National Intelligence (Parts 1700—1799)

XVIII   National Counterintelligence Center (Parts 1800—1899)

XIX   Central Intelligence Agency (Parts 1900—1999)

XX   Information Security Oversight Office, National Archives and Records Administration (Parts 2000—2099)

XXI   National Security Council (Parts 2100—2199)

XXIV   Office of Science and Technology Policy (Parts 2400—2499)

XXVII   Office for Micronesian Status Negotiations (Parts 2700—2799)

XXVIII   Office of the Vice President of the United States (Parts 2800—2899)

Title 33—Navigation and Navigable Waters

I   Coast Guard, Department of Homeland Security (Parts 1—199)

II   Corps of Engineers, Department of the Army, Department of Defense (Parts 200—399)

IV   Saint Lawrence Seaway Development Corporation, Department of Transportation (Parts 400—499)

Title 34—Education

SUBTITLE A—OFFICE OF THE SECRETARY, DEPARTMENT OF EDUCATION (PARTS 1—99)

SUBTITLE B—REGULATIONS OF THE OFFICES OF THE DEPARTMENT OF EDUCATION

I   Office for Civil Rights, Department of Education (Parts 100—199)

Title 34—Education—Continued

Chap.

II   Office of Elementary and Secondary Education, Department of Education (Parts 200—299)

III Office of Special Education and Rehabilitative Services, Department of Education (Parts 300—399)

IV   Office of Career, Technical and Adult Education, Department of Education (Parts 400—499)

V   Office of Bilingual Education and Minority Languages Affairs, Department of Education (Parts 500—599) [Reserved]

VI   Office of Postsecondary Education, Department of Education (Parts 600—699)

VII Office of Educational Research and Improvement, Department of Education (Parts 700—799) [Reserved]

     SUBTITLE C—REGULATIONS RELATING TO EDUCATION

XI   (Parts 1100—1199) [Reserved]

XII National Council on Disability (Parts 1200—1299)

Title 35 [Reserved]

Title 36—Parks, Forests, and Public Property

I   National Park Service, Department of the Interior (Parts 1—199)

II   Forest Service, Department of Agriculture (Parts 200—299)

III   Corps of Engineers, Department of the Army (Parts 300—399)

IV   American Battle Monuments Commission (Parts 400—499)

V   Smithsonian Institution (Parts 500—599)

VI   [Reserved]

VII   Library of Congress (Parts 700—799)

VIII Advisory Council on Historic Preservation (Parts 800—899)

IX   Pennsylvania Avenue Development Corporation (Parts 900—999)

X   Presidio Trust (Parts 1000—1099)

XI   Architectural and Transportation Barriers Compliance Board (Parts 1100—1199)

XII   National Archives and Records Administration (Parts 1200—1299)

XV   Oklahoma City National Memorial Trust (Parts 1500—1599)

XVI   Morris K. Udall Scholarship and Excellence in National Environmental Policy Foundation (Parts 1600—1699)

Title 37—Patents, Trademarks, and Copyrights

I   United States Patent and Trademark Office, Department of Commerce (Parts 1—199)

II   U.S. Copyright Office, Library of Congress (Parts 200—299)

III Copyright Royalty Board, Library of Congress (Parts 300—399)

IV   National Institute of Standards and Technology, Department of Commerce (Parts 400—599)

Title 38—Pensions, Bonuses, and Veterans' Relief

Chap.

I   Department of Veterans Affairs (Parts 0—199)

II   Armed Forces Retirement Home (Parts 200—299)

Title 39—Postal Service

I   United States Postal Service (Parts 1—999)

III Postal Regulatory Commission (Parts 3000—3099)

Title 40—Protection of Environment

I   Environmental Protection Agency (Parts 1—1099)

IV   Environmental Protection Agency and Department of Justice (Parts 1400—1499)

V   Council on Environmental Quality (Parts 1500—1599)

VI   Chemical Safety and Hazard Investigation Board (Parts 1600—1699)

VII Environmental Protection Agency and Department of Defense; Uniform National Discharge Standards for Vessels of the Armed Forces (Parts 1700—1799)

VIII Gulf Coast Ecosystem Restoration Council (Parts 1800—1899)

Title 41—Public Contracts and Property Management

SUBTITLE A—FEDERAL PROCUREMENT REGULATIONS SYSTEM [NOTE]

SUBTITLE B—OTHER PROVISIONS RELATING TO PUBLIC CONTRACTS

50   Public Contracts, Department of Labor (Parts 50–1—50–999)

51   Committee for Purchase From People Who Are Blind or Severely Disabled (Parts 51–1—51–99)

60   Office of Federal Contract Compliance Programs, Equal Employment Opportunity, Department of Labor (Parts 60–1—60–999)

61   Office of the Assistant Secretary for Veterans' Employment and Training Service, Department of Labor (Parts 61–1—61–999)

62—100 [Reserved]

SUBTITLE C—FEDERAL PROPERTY MANAGEMENT REGULATIONS SYSTEM

101 Federal Property Management Regulations (Parts 101–1—101–99)

102 Federal Management Regulation (Parts 102–1—102–299)

103—104 [Reserved]

105 General Services Administration (Parts 105–1—105–999)

109 Department of Energy Property Management Regulations (Parts 109–1—109–99)

114 Department of the Interior (Parts 114–1—114–99)

115 Environmental Protection Agency (Parts 115–1—115–99)

128 Department of Justice (Parts 128–1—128–99)

129—200 [Reserved]

SUBTITLE D—OTHER PROVISIONS RELATING TO PROPERTY MANAGEMENT [RESERVED]

SUBTITLE E—FEDERAL INFORMATION RESOURCES MANAGEMENT REGULATIONS SYSTEM [RESERVED]

SUBTITLE F—FEDERAL TRAVEL REGULATION SYSTEM

300   General (Parts 300–1—300–99)

301   Temporary Duty (TDY) Travel Allowances (Parts 301–1—301–99)

302   Relocation Allowances (Parts 302–1—302–99)

303   Payment of Expenses Connected with the Death of Certain Employees (Part 303–1—303–99)

304   Payment of Travel Expenses from a Non-Federal Source (Parts 304–1—304–99)

Title 42—Public Health

I   Public Health Service, Department of Health and Human Services (Parts 1—199)

ii—III   [Reserved]

IV   Centers for Medicare & Medicaid Services, Department of Health and Human Services (Parts 400—699)

V   Office of Inspector General-Health Care, Department of Health and Human Services (Parts 1000—1099)

Title 43—Public Lands: Interior

SUBTITLE A—OFFICE OF THE SECRETARY OF THE INTERIOR (PARTS 1—199)

SUBTITLE B—REGULATIONS RELATING TO PUBLIC LANDS

I   Bureau of Reclamation, Department of the Interior (Parts 400—999)

II   Bureau of Land Management, Department of the Interior (Parts 1000—9999)

III   Utah Reclamation Mitigation and Conservation Commission (Parts 10000—10099)

Title 44—Emergency Management and Assistance

I   Federal Emergency Management Agency, Department of Homeland Security (Parts 0—399)

IV   Department of Commerce and Department of Transportation (Parts 400—499)

Title 45—Public Welfare

SUBTITLE A—DEPARTMENT OF HEALTH AND HUMAN SERVICES (PARTS 1—199)

SUBTITLE B—REGULATIONS RELATING TO PUBLIC WELFARE

II   Office of Family Assistance (Assistance Programs), Administration for Children and Families, Department of Health and Human Services (Parts 200—299)

Title 45—Public Welfare—Continued

Chap.

III   Office of Child Support Enforcement (Child Support Enforcement Program), Administration for Children and Families, Department of Health and Human Services (Parts 300—399)

IV   Office of Refugee Resettlement, Administration for Children and Families, Department of Health and Human Services (Parts 400—499)

V   Foreign Claims Settlement Commission of the United States, Department of Justice (Parts 500—599)

VI   National Science Foundation (Parts 600—699)

VII   Commission on Civil Rights (Parts 700—799)

VIII   Office of Personnel Management (Parts 800—899)

IX   Denali Commission (Parts 900—999)

X   Office of Community Services, Administration for Children and Families, Department of Health and Human Services (Parts 1000—1099)

XI   National Foundation on the Arts and the Humanities (Parts 1100—1199)

XII   Corporation for National and Community Service (Parts 1200—1299)

XIII   Administration for Children and Families, Department of Health and Human Services (Parts 1300—1399)

XVI   Legal Services Corporation (Parts 1600—1699)

XVII   National Commission on Libraries and Information Science (Parts 1700—1799)

XVIII   Harry S. Truman Scholarship Foundation (Parts 1800—1899)

XXI   Commission of Fine Arts (Parts 2100—2199)

XXIII   Arctic Research Commission (Parts 2300—2399)

XXIV   James Madison Memorial Fellowship Foundation (Parts 2400—2499)

XXV   Corporation for National and Community Service (Parts 2500—2599)

Title 46—Shipping

I   Coast Guard, Department of Homeland Security (Parts 1—199)

II   Maritime Administration, Department of Transportation (Parts 200—399)

III   Coast Guard (Great Lakes Pilotage), Department of Homeland Security (Parts 400—499)

IV   Federal Maritime Commission (Parts 500—599)

Title 47—Telecommunication

I   Federal Communications Commission (Parts 0—199)

II   Office of Science and Technology Policy and National Security Council (Parts 200—299)

III   National Telecommunications and Information Administration, Department of Commerce (Parts 300—399)

IV   National Telecommunications and Information Administration, Department of Commerce, and National Highway Traffic Safety Administration, Department of Transportation (Parts 400—499)

V   The First Responder Network Authority (Parts 500—599)

Title 48—Federal Acquisition Regulations System

1   Federal Acquisition Regulation (Parts 1—99)

2   Defense Acquisition Regulations System, Department of Defense (Parts 200—299)

3   Department of Health and Human Services (Parts 300—399)

4   Department of Agriculture (Parts 400—499)

5   General Services Administration (Parts 500—599)

6   Department of State (Parts 600—699)

7   Agency for International Development (Parts 700—799)

8   Department of Veterans Affairs (Parts 800—899)

9   Department of Energy (Parts 900—999)

10   Department of the Treasury (Parts 1000—1099)

12   Department of Transportation (Parts 1200—1299)

13   Department of Commerce (Parts 1300—1399)

14   Department of the Interior (Parts 1400—1499)

15   Environmental Protection Agency (Parts 1500—1599)

16   Office of Personnel Management, Federal Employees Health Benefits Acquisition Regulation (Parts 1600—1699)

17   Office of Personnel Management (Parts 1700—1799)

18   National Aeronautics and Space Administration (Parts 1800—1899)

19   Broadcasting Board of Governors (Parts 1900—1999)

20   Nuclear Regulatory Commission (Parts 2000—2099)

21   Office of Personnel Management, Federal Employees Group Life Insurance Federal Acquisition Regulation (Parts 2100—2199)

23   Social Security Administration (Parts 2300—2399)

24   Department of Housing and Urban Development (Parts 2400—2499)

25   National Science Foundation (Parts 2500—2599)

28   Department of Justice (Parts 2800—2899)

29   Department of Labor (Parts 2900—2999)

30   Department of Homeland Security, Homeland Security Acquisition Regulation (HSAR) (Parts 3000—3099)

34   Department of Education Acquisition Regulation (Parts 3400—3499)

51   Department of the Army Acquisition Regulations (Parts 5100—5199)

52   Department of the Navy Acquisition Regulations (Parts 5200—5299)

53   Department of the Air Force Federal Acquisition Regulation Supplement (Parts 5300—5399) [Reserved]

54 Defense Logistics Agency, Department of Defense (Parts 5400—5499)

57 African Development Foundation (Parts 5700—5799)

61 Civilian Board of Contract Appeals, General Services Administration (Parts 6100—6199)

99 Cost Accounting Standards Board, Office of Federal Procurement Policy, Office of Management and Budget (Parts 9900—9999)

Title 49—Transportation

SUBTITLE A—OFFICE OF THE SECRETARY OF TRANSPORTATION (PARTS 1—99)

SUBTITLE B—OTHER REGULATIONS RELATING TO TRANSPORTATION

I Pipeline and Hazardous Materials Safety Administration, Department of Transportation (Parts 100—199)

II Federal Railroad Administration, Department of Transportation (Parts 200—299)

III Federal Motor Carrier Safety Administration, Department of Transportation (Parts 300—399)

IV Coast Guard, Department of Homeland Security (Parts 400—499)

V National Highway Traffic Safety Administration, Department of Transportation (Parts 500—599)

VI Federal Transit Administration, Department of Transportation (Parts 600—699)

VII National Railroad Passenger Corporation (AMTRAK) (Parts 700—799)

VIII National Transportation Safety Board (Parts 800—999)

X Surface Transportation Board (Parts 1000—1399)

XI Research and Innovative Technology Administration, Department of Transportation (Parts 1400—1499) [Reserved]

XII Transportation Security Administration, Department of Homeland Security (Parts 1500—1699)

Title 50—Wildlife and Fisheries

I United States Fish and Wildlife Service, Department of the Interior (Parts 1—199)

II National Marine Fisheries Service, National Oceanic and Atmospheric Administration, Department of Commerce (Parts 200—299)

III International Fishing and Related Activities (Parts 300—399)

IV Joint Regulations (United States Fish and Wildlife Service, Department of the Interior and National Marine Fisheries Service, National Oceanic and Atmospheric Administration, Department of Commerce); Endangered Species Committee Regulations (Parts 400—499)

V Marine Mammal Commission (Parts 500—599)

VI   Fishery Conservation and Management, National Oceanic and Atmospheric Administration, Department of Commerce (Parts 600—699)

Alphabetical List of Agencies Appearing in the CFR

(Revised as of April 1, 2018)

Agency	CFR Title, Subtitle or Chapter
Administrative Committee of the Federal Register	1, I
Administrative Conference of the United States	1, III
Advisory Council on Historic Preservation	36, VIII
Advocacy and Outreach, Office of	7, XXV
Afghanistan Reconstruction, Special Inspector General for	5, LXXXIII
African Development Foundation	22, XV
Federal Acquisition Regulation	48, 57
Agency for International Development	2, VII; 22, II
Federal Acquisition Regulation	48, 7
Agricultural Marketing Service	7, I, IX, X, XI
Agricultural Research Service	7, V
Agriculture Department	2, IV; 5, LXXIII
Advocacy and Outreach, Office of	7, XXV
Agricultural Marketing Service	7, I, IX, X, XI
Agricultural Research Service	7, V
Animal and Plant Health Inspection Service	7, III; 9, I
Chief Financial Officer, Office of	7, XXX
Commodity Credit Corporation	7, XIV
Economic Research Service	7, XXXVII
Energy Policy and New Uses, Office of	2, IX; 7, XXIX
Environmental Quality, Office of	7, XXXI
Farm Service Agency	7, VII, XVIII
Federal Acquisition Regulation	48, 4
Federal Crop Insurance Corporation	7, IV
Food and Nutrition Service	7, II
Food Safety and Inspection Service	9, III
Foreign Agricultural Service	7, XV
Forest Service	36, II
Grain Inspection, Packers and Stockyards Administration	7, VIII; 9, II
Information Resources Management, Office of	7, XXVII
Inspector General, Office of	7, XXVI
National Agricultural Library	7, XLI
National Agricultural Statistics Service	7, XXXVI
National Institute of Food and Agriculture	7, XXXIV
Natural Resources Conservation Service	7, VI
Operations, Office of	7, XXVIII
Procurement and Property Management, Office of	7, XXXII
Rural Business-Cooperative Service	7, XVIII, XLII
Rural Development Administration	7, XLII
Rural Housing Service	7, XVIII, XXXV
Rural Telephone Bank	7, XVI
Rural Utilities Service	7, XVII, XVIII, XLII
Secretary of Agriculture, Office of	7, Subtitle A
Transportation, Office of	7, XXXIII
World Agricultural Outlook Board	7, XXXVIII
Air Force Department	32, VII
Federal Acquisition Regulation Supplement	48, 53
Air Transportation Stabilization Board	14, VI
Alcohol and Tobacco Tax and Trade Bureau	27, I
Alcohol, Tobacco, Firearms, and Explosives, Bureau of	27, II
AMTRAK	49, VII
American Battle Monuments Commission	36, IV
American Indians, Office of the Special Trustee	25, VII

Agency	CFR Title, Subtitle or Chapter
Animal and Plant Health Inspection Service	7, III; 9, I
Appalachian Regional Commission	5, IX
Architectural and Transportation Barriers Compliance Board	36, XI
Arctic Research Commission	45, XXIII
Armed Forces Retirement Home	5, XI
Army Department	32, V
Engineers, Corps of	33, II; 36, III
Federal Acquisition Regulation	48, 51
Bilingual Education and Minority Languages Affairs, Office of	34, V
Blind or Severely Disabled, Committee for Purchase from People Who Are	41, 51
Broadcasting Board of Governors	22, V
Federal Acquisition Regulation	48, 19
Career, Technical and Adult Education, Office of	34, IV
Census Bureau	15, I
Centers for Medicare & Medicaid Services	42, IV
Central Intelligence Agency	32, XIX
Chemical Safety and Hazardous Investigation Board	40, VI
Chief Financial Officer, Office of	7, XXX
Child Support Enforcement, Office of	45, III
Children and Families, Administration for	45, II, III, IV, X, XIII
Civil Rights, Commission on	5, LXVIII; 45, VII
Civil Rights, Office for	34, I
Council of the Inspectors General on Integrity and Efficiency	5, XCVIII
Court Services and Offender Supervision Agency for the District of Columbia	5, LXX
Coast Guard	33, I; 46, I; 49, IV
Coast Guard (Great Lakes Pilotage)	46, III
Commerce Department	2, XIII; 44, IV; 50, VI
Census Bureau	15, I
Economic Analysis, Bureau of	15, VIII
Economic Development Administration	13, III
Emergency Management and Assistance	44, IV
Federal Acquisition Regulation	48, 13
Foreign-Trade Zones Board	15, IV
Industry and Security, Bureau of	15, VII
International Trade Administration	15, III; 19, III
National Institute of Standards and Technology	15, II; 37, IV
National Marine Fisheries Service	50, II, IV
National Oceanic and Atmospheric Administration	15, IX; 50, II, III, IV, VI
National Technical Information Service	15, XI
National Telecommunications and Information Administration	15, XXIII; 47, III, IV
National Weather Service	15, IX
Patent and Trademark Office, United States	37, I
Secretary of Commerce, Office of	15, Subtitle A
Commercial Space Transportation	14, III
Commodity Credit Corporation	7, XIV
Commodity Futures Trading Commission	5, XLI; 17, I
Community Planning and Development, Office of Assistant Secretary for	24, V, VI
Community Services, Office of	45, X
Comptroller of the Currency	12, I
Construction Industry Collective Bargaining Commission	29, IX
Consumer Financial Protection Bureau	5, LXXXIV; 12, X
Consumer Product Safety Commission	5, LXXI; 16, II
Copyright Royalty Board	37, III
Corporation for National and Community Service	2, XXII; 45, XII, XXV
Cost Accounting Standards Board	48, 99
Council on Environmental Quality	40, V
Court Services and Offender Supervision Agency for the District of Columbia	5, LXX; 28, VIII
Customs and Border Protection	19, I
Defense Contract Audit Agency	32, I
Defense Department	2, XI; 5, XXVI; 32, Subtitle A; 40, VII
Advanced Research Projects Agency	32, I

Agency	CFR Title, Subtitle or Chapter
Air Force Department	32, VII
Army Department	32, V; 33, II; 36, III; 48, 51
Defense Acquisition Regulations System	48, 2
Defense Intelligence Agency	32, I
Defense Logistics Agency	32, I, XII; 48, 54
Engineers, Corps of	33, II; 36, III
National Imagery and Mapping Agency	32, I
Navy Department	32, VI; 48, 52
Secretary of Defense, Office of	2, XI; 32, I
Defense Contract Audit Agency	32, I
Defense Intelligence Agency	32, I
Defense Logistics Agency	32, XII; 48, 54
Defense Nuclear Facilities Safety Board	10, XVII
Delaware River Basin Commission	18, III
Denali Commission	45, IX
District of Columbia, Court Services and Offender Supervision Agency for the	5, LXX; 28, VIII
Drug Enforcement Administration	21, II
East-West Foreign Trade Board	15, XIII
Economic Analysis, Bureau of	15, VIII
Economic Development Administration	13, III
Economic Research Service	7, XXXVII
Education, Department of	2, XXXIV; 5, LIII
Bilingual Education and Minority Languages Affairs, Office of	34, V
Career, Technical and Adult Education, Office of	34, IV
Civil Rights, Office for	34, I
Educational Research and Improvement, Office of	34, VII
Elementary and Secondary Education, Office of	34, II
Federal Acquisition Regulation	48, 34
Postsecondary Education, Office of	34, VI
Secretary of Education, Office of	34, Subtitle A
Special Education and Rehabilitative Services, Office of	34, III
Career, Technical, and Adult Education, Office of	34, IV
Educational Research and Improvement, Office of	34, VII
Election Assistance Commission	2, LVIII; 11, II
Elementary and Secondary Education, Office of	34, II
Emergency Oil and Gas Guaranteed Loan Board	13, V
Emergency Steel Guarantee Loan Board	13, IV
Employee Benefits Security Administration	29, XXV
Employees' Compensation Appeals Board	20, IV
Employees Loyalty Board	5, V
Employment and Training Administration	20, V
Employment Standards Administration	20, VI
Endangered Species Committee	50, IV
Energy, Department of	2, IX; 5, XXIII; 10, II, III, X
Federal Acquisition Regulation	48, 9
Federal Energy Regulatory Commission	5, XXIV; 18, I
Property Management Regulations	41, 109
Energy, Office of	7, XXIX
Engineers, Corps of	33, II; 36, III
Engraving and Printing, Bureau of	31, VI
Environmental Protection Agency	2, XV; 5, LIV; 40, I, IV, VII
Federal Acquisition Regulation	48, 15
Property Management Regulations	41, 115
Environmental Quality, Office of	7, XXXI
Equal Employment Opportunity Commission	5, LXII; 29, XIV
Equal Opportunity, Office of Assistant Secretary for	24, I
Executive Office of the President	3, I
Environmental Quality, Council on	40, V
Management and Budget, Office of	2, Subtitle A; 5, III, LXXVII; 14, VI; 48, 99
National Drug Control Policy, Office of	2, XXXVI; 21, III
National Security Council	32, XXI; 47, 2

Agency	CFR Title, Subtitle or Chapter
Presidential Documents	3
Science and Technology Policy, Office of	32, XXIV; 47, II
Trade Representative, Office of the United States	15, XX
Export-Import Bank of the United States	2, XXXV; 5, LII; 12, IV
Family Assistance, Office of	45, II
Farm Credit Administration	5, XXXI; 12, VI
Farm Credit System Insurance Corporation	5, XXX; 12, XIV
Farm Service Agency	7, VII, XVIII
Federal Acquisition Regulation	48, 1
Federal Aviation Administration	14, I
Commercial Space Transportation	14, III
Federal Claims Collection Standards	31, IX
Federal Communications Commission	5, XXIX; 47, I
Federal Contract Compliance Programs, Office of	41, 60
Federal Crop Insurance Corporation	7, IV
Federal Deposit Insurance Corporation	5, XXII; 12, III
Federal Election Commission	5, XXXVII; 11, I
Federal Emergency Management Agency	44, I
Federal Employees Group Life Insurance Federal Acquisition Regulation	48, 21
Federal Employees Health Benefits Acquisition Regulation	48, 16
Federal Energy Regulatory Commission	5, XXIV; 18, I
Federal Financial Institutions Examination Council	12, XI
Federal Financing Bank	12, VIII
Federal Highway Administration	23, I, II
Federal Home Loan Mortgage Corporation	1, IV
Federal Housing Enterprise Oversight Office	12, XVII
Federal Housing Finance Agency	5, LXXX; 12, XII
Federal Housing Finance Board	12, IX
Federal Labor Relations Authority	5, XIV, XLIX; 22, XIV
Federal Law Enforcement Training Center	31, VII
Federal Management Regulation	41, 102
Federal Maritime Commission	46, IV
Federal Mediation and Conciliation Service	29, XII
Federal Mine Safety and Health Review Commission	5, LXXIV; 29, XXVII
Federal Motor Carrier Safety Administration	49, III
Federal Prison Industries, Inc.	28, III
Federal Procurement Policy Office	48, 99
Federal Property Management Regulations	41, 101
Federal Railroad Administration	49, II
Federal Register, Administrative Committee of	1, I
Federal Register, Office of	1, II
Federal Reserve System	12, II
Board of Governors	5, LVIII
Federal Retirement Thrift Investment Board	5, VI, LXXVI
Federal Service Impasses Panel	5, XIV
Federal Trade Commission	5, XLVII; 16, I
Federal Transit Administration	49, VI
Federal Travel Regulation System	41, Subtitle F
Financial Crimes Enforcement Network	31, X
Financial Research Office	12, XVI
Financial Stability Oversight Council	12, XIII
Fine Arts, Commission of	45, XXI
Fiscal Service	31, II
Fish and Wildlife Service, United States	50, I, IV
Food and Drug Administration	21, I
Food and Nutrition Service	7, II
Food Safety and Inspection Service	9, III
Foreign Agricultural Service	7, XV
Foreign Assets Control, Office of	31, V
Foreign Claims Settlement Commission of the United States	45, V
Foreign Service Grievance Board	22, IX
Foreign Service Impasse Disputes Panel	22, XIV
Foreign Service Labor Relations Board	22, XIV
Foreign-Trade Zones Board	15, IV
Forest Service	36, II
General Services Administration	5, LVII; 41, 105

Agency	CFR Title, Subtitle or Chapter
Contract Appeals, Board of	48, 61
Federal Acquisition Regulation	48, 5
Federal Management Regulation	41, 102
Federal Property Management Regulations	41, 101
Federal Travel Regulation System	41, Subtitle F
General	41, 300
Payment From a Non-Federal Source for Travel Expenses	41, 304
Payment of Expenses Connected With the Death of Certain Employees	41, 303
Relocation Allowances	41, 302
Temporary Duty (TDY) Travel Allowances	41, 301
Geological Survey	30, IV
Government Accountability Office	4, I
Government Ethics, Office of	5, XVI
Government National Mortgage Association	24, III
Grain Inspection, Packers and Stockyards Administration	7, VIII; 9, II
Gulf Coast Ecosystem Restoration Council	2, LIX; 40, VIII
Harry S. Truman Scholarship Foundation	45, XVIII
Health and Human Services, Department of	2, III; 5, XLV; 45, Subtitle A
Centers for Medicare & Medicaid Services	42, IV
Child Support Enforcement, Office of	45, III
Children and Families, Administration for	45, II, III, IV, X, XIII
Community Services, Office of	45, X
Family Assistance, Office of	45, II
Federal Acquisition Regulation	48, 3
Food and Drug Administration	21, I
Indian Health Service	25, V
Inspector General (Health Care), Office of	42, V
Public Health Service	42, I
Refugee Resettlement, Office of	45, IV
Homeland Security, Department of	2, XXX; 5, XXXVI; 6, I; 8, I
Coast Guard	33, I; 46, I; 49, IV
Coast Guard (Great Lakes Pilotage)	46, III
Customs and Border Protection	19, I
Federal Emergency Management Agency	44, I
Human Resources Management and Labor Relations Systems	5, XCVII
Immigration and Customs Enforcement Bureau	19, IV
Transportation Security Administration	49, XII
HOPE for Homeowners Program, Board of Directors of	24, XXIV
Housing and Urban Development, Department of	2, XXIV; 5, LXV; 24, Subtitle B
Community Planning and Development, Office of Assistant Secretary for	24, V, VI
Equal Opportunity, Office of Assistant Secretary for	24, I
Federal Acquisition Regulation	48, 24
Federal Housing Enterprise Oversight, Office of	12, XVII
Government National Mortgage Association	24, III
Housing—Federal Housing Commissioner, Office of Assistant Secretary for	24, II, VIII, X, XX
Housing, Office of, and Multifamily Housing Assistance Restructuring, Office of	24, IV
Inspector General, Office of	24, XII
Public and Indian Housing, Office of Assistant Secretary for	24, IX
Secretary, Office of	24, Subtitle A, VII
Housing—Federal Housing Commissioner, Office of Assistant Secretary for	24, II, VIII, X, XX
Housing, Office of, and Multifamily Housing Assistance Restructuring, Office of	24, IV
Immigration and Customs Enforcement Bureau	19, IV
Immigration Review, Executive Office for	8, V
Independent Counsel, Office of	28, VII
Independent Counsel, Offices of	28, VI
Indian Affairs, Bureau of	25, I, V
Indian Affairs, Office of the Assistant Secretary	25, VI

Agency	CFR Title, Subtitle or Chapter
Indian Arts and Crafts Board	25, II
Indian Health Service	25, V
Industry and Security, Bureau of	15, VII
Information Resources Management, Office of	7, XXVII
Information Security Oversight Office, National Archives and Records Administration	32, XX
Inspector General	
Agriculture Department	7, XXVI
Health and Human Services Department	42, V
Housing and Urban Development Department	24, XII, XV
Institute of Peace, United States	22, XVII
Inter-American Foundation	5, LXIII; 22, X
Interior Department	2, XIV
American Indians, Office of the Special Trustee	25, VII
Endangered Species Committee	50, IV
Federal Acquisition Regulation	48, 14
Federal Property Management Regulations System	41, 114
Fish and Wildlife Service, United States	50, I, IV
Geological Survey	30, IV
Indian Affairs, Bureau of	25, I, V
Indian Affairs, Office of the Assistant Secretary	25, VI
Indian Arts and Crafts Board	25, II
Land Management, Bureau of	43, II
National Indian Gaming Commission	25, III
National Park Service	36, I
Natural Resource Revenue, Office of	30, XII
Ocean Energy Management, Bureau of	30, V
Reclamation, Bureau of	43, I
Safety and Enforcement Bureau, Bureau of	30, II
Secretary of the Interior, Office of	2, XIV; 43, Subtitle A
Surface Mining Reclamation and Enforcement, Office of	30, VII
Internal Revenue Service	26, I
International Boundary and Water Commission, United States and Mexico, United States Section	22, XI
International Development, United States Agency for	22, II
Federal Acquisition Regulation	48, 7
International Development Cooperation Agency, United States	22, XII
International Joint Commission, United States and Canada	22, IV
International Organizations Employees Loyalty Board	5, V
International Trade Administration	15, III; 19, III
International Trade Commission, United States	19, II
Interstate Commerce Commission	5, XL
Investment Security, Office of	31, VIII
James Madison Memorial Fellowship Foundation	45, XXIV
Japan–United States Friendship Commission	22, XVI
Joint Board for the Enrollment of Actuaries	20, VIII
Justice Department	2, XXVIII; 5, XXVIII; 28, I, XI; 40, IV
Alcohol, Tobacco, Firearms, and Explosives, Bureau of	27, II
Drug Enforcement Administration	21, II
Federal Acquisition Regulation	48, 28
Federal Claims Collection Standards	31, IX
Federal Prison Industries, Inc.	28, III
Foreign Claims Settlement Commission of the United States	45, V
Immigration Review, Executive Office for	8, V
Independent Counsel, Offices of	28, VI
Prisons, Bureau of	28, V
Property Management Regulations	41, 128
Labor Department	2, XXIX; 5, XLII
Employee Benefits Security Administration	29, XXV
Employees' Compensation Appeals Board	20, IV
Employment and Training Administration	20, V
Employment Standards Administration	20, VI
Federal Acquisition Regulation	48, 29
Federal Contract Compliance Programs, Office of	41, 60

Agency	CFR Title, Subtitle or Chapter
Federal Procurement Regulations System	41, 50
Labor-Management Standards, Office of	29, II, IV
Mine Safety and Health Administration	30, I
Occupational Safety and Health Administration	29, XVII
Public Contracts	41, 50
Secretary of Labor, Office of	29, Subtitle A
Veterans' Employment and Training Service, Office of the Assistant Secretary for	41, 61; 20, IX
Wage and Hour Division	29, V
Workers' Compensation Programs, Office of	20, I, VII
Labor-Management Standards, Office of	29, II, IV
Land Management, Bureau of	43, II
Legal Services Corporation	45, XVI
Library of Congress	36, VII
Copyright Royalty Board	37, III
U.S. Copyright Office	37, II
Local Television Loan Guarantee Board	7, XX
Management and Budget, Office of	5, III, LXXVII; 14, VI; 48, 99
Marine Mammal Commission	50, V
Maritime Administration	46, II
Merit Systems Protection Board	5, II, LXIV
Micronesian Status Negotiations, Office for	32, XXVII
Military Compensation and Retirement Modernization Commission	5, XCIX
Millennium Challenge Corporation	22, XIII
Mine Safety and Health Administration	30, I
Minority Business Development Agency	15, XIV
Miscellaneous Agencies	1, IV
Monetary Offices	31, I
Morris K. Udall Scholarship and Excellence in National Environmental Policy Foundation	36, XVI
Museum and Library Services, Institute of	2, XXXI
National Aeronautics and Space Administration	2, XVIII; 5, LIX; 14, V
Federal Acquisition Regulation	48, 18
National Agricultural Library	7, XLI
National Agricultural Statistics Service	7, XXXVI
National and Community Service, Corporation for	2, XXII; 45, XII, XXV
National Archives and Records Administration	2, XXVI; 5, LXVI; 36, XII
Information Security Oversight Office	32, XX
National Capital Planning Commission	1, IV, VI
National Commission for Employment Policy	1, IV
National Commission on Libraries and Information Science	45, XVII
National Council on Disability	5, C; 34, XII
National Counterintelligence Center	32, XVIII
National Credit Union Administration	5, LXXXVI; 12, VII
National Crime Prevention and Privacy Compact Council	28, IX
National Drug Control Policy, Office of	2, XXXVI; 21, III
National Endowment for the Arts	2, XXXII
National Endowment for the Humanities	2, XXXIII
National Foundation on the Arts and the Humanities	45, XI
National Geospatial-Intelligence Agency	32, I
National Highway Traffic Safety Administration	23, II, III; 47, VI; 49, V
National Imagery and Mapping Agency	32, I
National Indian Gaming Commission	25, III
National Institute of Food and Agriculture	7, XXXIV
National Institute of Standards and Technology	15, II; 37, IV
National Intelligence, Office of Director of	5, IV; 32, XVII
National Labor Relations Board	5, LXI; 29, I
National Marine Fisheries Service	50, II, IV
National Mediation Board	29, X
National Oceanic and Atmospheric Administration	15, IX; 50, II, III, IV, VI
National Park Service	36, I
National Railroad Adjustment Board	29, III
National Railroad Passenger Corporation (AMTRAK)	49, VII
National Science Foundation	2, XXV; 5, XLIII; 45, VI

| | CFR Title, Subtitle or |
Agency	Chapter
Federal Acquisition Regulation	48, 25
National Security Council	32, XXI
National Security Council and Office of Science and Technology Policy	47, II
National Telecommunications and Information Administration	15, XXIII; 47, III, IV, V
National Transportation Safety Board	49, VIII
Natural Resources Conservation Service	7, VI
Natural Resource Revenue, Office of	30, XII
Navajo and Hopi Indian Relocation, Office of	25, IV
Navy Department	32, VI
Federal Acquisition Regulation	48, 52
Neighborhood Reinvestment Corporation	24, XXV
Northeast Interstate Low-Level Radioactive Waste Commission	10, XVIII
Nuclear Regulatory Commission	2, XX; 5, XLVIII; 10, I
Federal Acquisition Regulation	48, 20
Occupational Safety and Health Administration	29, XVII
Occupational Safety and Health Review Commission	29, XX
Ocean Energy Management, Bureau of	30, V
Oklahoma City National Memorial Trust	36, XV
Operations Office	7, XXVIII
Overseas Private Investment Corporation	5, XXXIII; 22, VII
Patent and Trademark Office, United States	37, I
Payment From a Non-Federal Source for Travel Expenses	41, 304
Payment of Expenses Connected With the Death of Certain Employees	41, 303
Peace Corps	2, XXXVII; 22, III
Pennsylvania Avenue Development Corporation	36, IX
Pension Benefit Guaranty Corporation	29, XL
Personnel Management, Office of	5, I, XXXV; 5, IV; 45, VIII
Human Resources Management and Labor Relations Systems, Department of Homeland Security	5, XCVII
Federal Acquisition Regulation	48, 17
Federal Employees Group Life Insurance Federal Acquisition Regulation	48, 21
Federal Employees Health Benefits Acquisition Regulation	48, 16
Pipeline and Hazardous Materials Safety Administration	49, I
Postal Regulatory Commission	5, XLVI; 39, III
Postal Service, United States	5, LX; 39, I
Postsecondary Education, Office of	34, VI
President's Commission on White House Fellowships	1, IV
Presidential Documents	3
Presidio Trust	36, X
Prisons, Bureau of	28, V
Privacy and Civil Liberties Oversight Board	6, X
Procurement and Property Management, Office of	7, XXXII
Public Contracts, Department of Labor	41, 50
Public and Indian Housing, Office of Assistant Secretary for	24, IX
Public Health Service	42, I
Railroad Retirement Board	20, II
Reclamation, Bureau of	43, I
Refugee Resettlement, Office of	45, IV
Relocation Allowances	41, 302
Research and Innovative Technology Administration	49, XI
Rural Business-Cooperative Service	7, XVIII, XLII
Rural Development Administration	7, XLII
Rural Housing Service	7, XVIII, XXXV
Rural Telephone Bank	7, XVI
Rural Utilities Service	7, XVII, XVIII, XLII
Safety and Environmental Enforcement, Bureau of	30, II
Saint Lawrence Seaway Development Corporation	33, IV
Science and Technology Policy, Office of	32, XXIV
Science and Technology Policy, Office of, and National Security Council	47, II
Secret Service	31, IV

386

Agency	CFR Title, Subtitle or Chapter
Securities and Exchange Commission	5, XXXIV; 17, II
Selective Service System	32, XVI
Small Business Administration	2, XXVII; 13, I
Smithsonian Institution	36, V
Social Security Administration	2, XXIII; 20, III; 48, 23
Soldiers' and Airmen's Home, United States	5, XI
Special Counsel, Office of	5, VIII
Special Education and Rehabilitative Services, Office of	34, III
State Department	2, VI; 22, I; 28, XI
Federal Acquisition Regulation	48, 6
Surface Mining Reclamation and Enforcement, Office of	30, VII
Surface Transportation Board	49, X
Susquehanna River Basin Commission	18, VIII
Tennessee Valley Authority	5, LXIX; 18, XIII
Thrift Supervision Office, Department of the Treasury	12, V
Trade Representative, United States, Office of	15, XX
Transportation, Department of	2, XII; 5, L
Commercial Space Transportation	14, III
Emergency Management and Assistance	44, IV
Federal Acquisition Regulation	48, 12
Federal Aviation Administration	14, I
Federal Highway Administration	23, I, II
Federal Motor Carrier Safety Administration	49, III
Federal Railroad Administration	49, II
Federal Transit Administration	49, VI
Maritime Administration	46, II
National Highway Traffic Safety Administration	23, II, III; 47, IV; 49, V
Pipeline and Hazardous Materials Safety Administration	49, I
Saint Lawrence Seaway Development Corporation	33, IV
Secretary of Transportation, Office of	14, II; 49, Subtitle A
Transportation Statistics Bureau	49, XI
Transportation, Office of	7, XXXIII
Transportation Security Administration	49, XII
Transportation Statistics Bureau	49, XI
Travel Allowances, Temporary Duty (TDY)	41, 301
Treasury Department	2, X;5, XXI; 12, XV; 17, IV; 31, IX
Alcohol and Tobacco Tax and Trade Bureau	27, I
Community Development Financial Institutions Fund	12, XVIII
Comptroller of the Currency	12, I
Customs and Border Protection	19, I
Engraving and Printing, Bureau of	31, VI
Federal Acquisition Regulation	48, 10
Federal Claims Collection Standards	31, IX
Federal Law Enforcement Training Center	31, VII
Financial Crimes Enforcement Network	31, X
Fiscal Service	31, II
Foreign Assets Control, Office of	31, V
Internal Revenue Service	26, I
Investment Security, Office of	31, VIII
Monetary Offices	31, I
Secret Service	31, IV
Secretary of the Treasury, Office of	31, Subtitle A
Thrift Supervision, Office of	12, V
Truman, Harry S. Scholarship Foundation	45, XVIII
United States and Canada, International Joint Commission	22, IV
United States and Mexico, International Boundary and Water Commission, United States Section	22, XI
U.S. Copyright Office	37, II
Utah Reclamation Mitigation and Conservation Commission	43, III
Veterans Affairs Department	2, VIII; 38, I
Federal Acquisition Regulation	48, 8
Veterans' Employment and Training Service, Office of the Assistant Secretary for	41, 61; 20, IX
Vice President of the United States, Office of	32, XXVIII
Wage and Hour Division	29, V
Water Resources Council	18, VI

Agency	CFR Title, Subtitle or Chapter
Workers' Compensation Programs, Office of	20, I, VII
World Agricultural Outlook Board	7, XXXVIII

List of CFR Sections Affected

All changes in this volume of the Code of Federal Regulations (CFR) that were made by documents published in the FEDERAL REGISTER since January 1, 2013 are enumerated in the following list. Entries indicate the nature of the changes effected. Page numbers refer to FEDERAL REGISTER pages. The user should consult the entries for chapters, parts and subparts as well as sections for revisions.

For changes to this volume of the CFR prior to this listing, consult the annual edition of the monthly List of CFR Sections Affected (LSA). The LSA is available at *www.fdsys.gov*. For changes to this volume of the CFR prior to 2001, see the "List of CFR Sections Affected, 1949–1963, 1964–1972, 1973–1985, and 1986–2000" published in 11 separate volumes. The "List of CFR Sections Affected 1986–2000" is available at *www.fdsys.gov*.

2013
19 CFR

78 FR Page

Chapter II

201.16 (a)(3) and (4) added; (c)(1) and (e) revised; (f) amended 23480
210.3 Amended 23480
210.4 (f)(3) revised 23480
210.5 (f) added...............................23480
210.6 Revised 23480
210.7 (a)(2) and (c) revised 23480
210.8 (b) introductory text, (c)(1) and (2) amended 23481
210.12 (a) introductory text, (6)(ii) and (11) revised; (a)(6)(i) introductory text amended; (a)(12) added..23481
210.13 (b) amended 23481
210.14 Heading revised; (a) and (b)(1) amended; (g) added...........23481
210.15 (a)(2) amended.....................23482
210.16 (b)(1) revised; (b)(3) redesignated as (b)(4); new (b)(3), (c)(1) heading and (2) heading added; (c)(2) amended 23482
210.17 Heading and (f) revised; (g) removed; (h) redesignated as new (g); new (h) added...............23482
210.21 (a)(1), (b)(1), (c) introductory text and (1)(ii) amended; (c)(3) revised; (c)(4) and (5) added......................................23482
210.27 (b) amended; (c) and (d) redesignated as (f) and (g); new (c), new (d) and (e) added............29623
210.28 (a) and (c) amended..............23483

19 CFR—Continued

78 FR Page

Chapter II—Continued
210.29 (a) amended 23484
210.34 (b) and (c) revised 23484
210.42 (a)(1)(i) and (c) revised 23484
210.43 (a)(1) and (b)(1) note amended; (b)(2) and (c) revised 23484
210.50 (a)(4) introductory text and (iii) amended; (d)(1)(i) and (ii) revised 23485
210.51 (a) revised 23485
210.54 Amended.............................23485
210.56 (a) amended.........................23485
210.58 Amended.............................23486
210.59 (b) introductory text and (c) revised 23486
210.60 Section designated as (a); new (a) and heading revised; (b) added.......................................23486
210.75 (b)(1) amended and (b)(3) revised......................................23486
210.76 (c) added.............................23486
210 Appendix A revised.................23486
    Appendix B added 23487

Chapter III
351 Nomenclature changes...........62418
351.102 (b)(21) revised 21254
351.301 Revised 21254
351.302 (c) revised 57795
351.303 (g) revised........................42691
351.313 Added 22777
351.408 (c)(1) revised 46804
354 Nomenclature changes...........62418
356 Nomenclature changes...........62418
358 Nomenclature changes...........77354

19 CFR—Continued

78 FR
Page

Chapter III—Continued
360.105 Revised 11092

2014

19 CFR

79 FR
Page

Chapter II
201.8 (d)(1) and (f) revised 35924
201.42—201.43 (Subpart F) Revised 46350
207.10 (a) revised 35924
207.11 (b)(2)(ii), (iii) and (v) revised 35924
207.15 Revised 35924
207.20 (b) revised 35925
207.23 Revised 35925
207.25 Revised 35925
207.28 Revised 35925
207.30 (b) revised 35925
207.45 (c) revised 35925
207.61 (e) revised 35925
207.62 (b)(2) revised 35925
207.65 Revised 35925
207.67 (a) revised 35926
207.68 (b) revised 35926

Chapter III
351 Policy statement 22371
351.303 Amended 69047

2015

19 CFR

80 FR
Page

Chapter II
201 Authority citation revised 39379
201.17 (a)(5) revised; (d) through (g) added 39379
201.18 (a) revised; (f) added 39379
201.19 (f) revised 39379
201.20 (j)(8) revised; (j)(9) and (10) added 39379
201.23 (e) revised 39380
201.34 (a)(3) revised 39380
206.2 Revised 39380
207.11 (b)(2)(v) revised 52618

19 CFR—Continued

80 FR
Page

Chapter II—Continued
208 Removed 39380
213—299 (Subchapter D) Established 39380
213 Transferred from Subchapter C to Subchapter D; authority citation revised 39380
213.2 (d) through (g) revised 39380
213.3 (a) revised 39380
213.6 Revised 39380

Chapter III
351 Policy statement 46793
351.103 (b) and (c) amended 36473
351.303 (b)(1) and (3) amended; (b)(2)(i) and (ii) revised 36473

2016

19 CFR

81 FR
Page

Chapter II
201.18 (b) and (f) revised 86576
201.20 (c)(5), (6) and (7) added 86577
220 Added; interim 67146

Chapter III
351 Policy statement 50617
351.102 (b)(38) revised; eff. 4-25-16 15645
351.401 (c) revised; eff. 4-25-16 15645

2017

19 CFR

82 FR
Page

Chapter II
201.32 (a) and (b) removed; (c) redesignated as new (a); new (a) amended; new (b) added 60865

Chapter III
360.105 Revised 1185

2018

(No regulations published from January 1, 2018, through April 1, 2018)

www.ingramcontent.com/pod-product-compliance
Lightning Source LLC
Chambersburg PA
CBHW061103220326
41599CB00024B/3899